D0041713

VOLUME 13 IN THE SERIES
Our Sustainable Future

Series Editors

Cornelia Flora
Iowa State University

Charles A. Francis
University of Nebraska–Lincoln

Paul Olson
University of Nebraska–Lincoln

John Opie

Ogallala

Water for a Dry Land

SECOND EDITION

University of Nebraska Press

Lincoln and London

⊗

Library of Congress Cataloging-in-Publication Data
Opie, John, 1934–
Ogallala : water for a dry land / John Opie.—2nd ed.
p.   cm.—(Our sustainable future; v. 13)
Includes bibliographical references and index.
ISBN 0-8032-8614-7 (pbk.: alk. paper)
1. Irrigation water—High Plains (U.S.)—History.
2. Ogallala Aquifer—History.   3. Irrigation—
High Plains (U.S.)—History.   4 Agriculture—High
Plains (U.S.)—History.   5. Agricultural ecology—
High Plains (U.S.)—History.   I. Title.   II. Series.
s616.U6 065 2000
333.91′3′0978—dc21
99-042161

. . .

*To Lora Jean (1934–1973) and
Christopher Charles (1957–1973)*

. . .

Contents

Illustrations

• • •

If we lived in a desert and our lives depended on a water supply that came out of a steel tube, we would inevitably watch that tube and talk about it understandingly. No citizen would need to be lectured about his duty toward its care and spurred to help if it were in danger. Teachers of civics in such a community might develop a sense of public responsibility, not only by describing the remote beginnings of the commonwealth, but also how that tube got built, how long it would last, how vital the intake might be if the rainfall on the forested mountains nearby ever changed in seasonal habit or amount. It would be a most unimaginative person, or a stupid one, who could not see the vital relation between the mountains, the forests, that tube and himself.—Isaiah Bowman, *"Headwaters Control and Use—Influence of Vegetation on Land-Water Relationships,"* Proceedings: Upstream Engineering Conference (Washington, D.C., 1937), pp. 76–95.

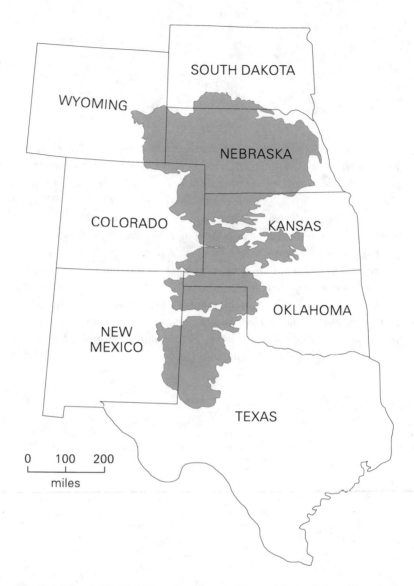

1. The High Plains and the Ogallala aquifer. The groundwater of the Ogallala aquifer underlies 174,000 square miles in eight states, but mostly in Texas, Oklahoma, Kansas, and Nebraska. This book gives special attention to the old Dust Bowl region of southwest Kansas and the Oklahoma-Texas Panhandle because this is the region under highest risk today because of heavy irrigation depletion of the aquifer.

. . .

Preface

A Quick Look at the Changes in This Edition

As many readers of the first edition of this book suspected, it was a work in progress. It still is. This book must reflect both continuity and flux of a region that depends heavily upon natural forces like soil and climate. Our story also must account for intensive and often capricious human disturbance of the plains and its groundwater. Since publication of the first edition in 1993 (actual research closed about mid-1991) several predictions unfortunately came true. These events are covered in the materials added to this edition (the update takes us through mid-1999). Chapter 8 in the first edition, on the drought of 1988, anticipated the severe multiyear drought cycle that did take hold in the mid-1990s. Folks in western Kansas saw no rain at all from October 1995 until April 1996. Wheat prices went through the roof, bringing over five dollars a bushel, but it made little difference to regional dryland farmers with little to sell.

On the other hand, the second half of Chapter 6, which focused on federal protection for family farmers in hard times, did not anticipate the turnabout in federal farm policies that will have enormous implications: the 1996 farm bill pulled apart the federal price supports, loan guarantees, and crop insurance that had been in place for fifty years. These supports are scheduled to be phased out over the seven years following passage of the bill. But this "Freedom to Farm" bill immediately released farmers to plant crops without restrictions. The result can be highly profitable as long as prices stay high, but if expected surpluses force commodity prices into the floor, less substantial farmers—usually the smaller, family-centered operations—will be in harm's way. By late 1998, prices collapsed again to around two dollars a bushel and seemed to remain locked at those low levels. Most irrigation farmers that I talked with in western Kansas in March 1996 and in eastern Colorado in February 1998, however, were pleased with the freedom to act on their own.

Another phenomenon caught most folks by surprise in the old Dust Bowl region of southwest Kansas and the Texas-Oklahoma Panhandle: industrial hog farms arrived from South Carolina, Missouri, and Iowa. These hog farms brought unexpected threats to local water quality by creating open ponds of liquid waste and by pumping more Ogallala water for meat production, as well as causing god-awful smells that effectively ended the country lifestyles of many local farmers. Some of this industrialization, described in a revised Chapter 4, was anticipated by the concentrated cattle feedlot operations run by local entrepreneurs like the Gigot family of the Kansas Sandhills, Steve Irsik east of Garden City, Kansas, and Hitch Enterprises in the heart of the Oklahoma Panhandle. The battle over hog factories may mark the end of a treasured rural culture on the plains.

Other parts of the book, notably sections on sustainability and on ecosystems in the Introduction and Chapter 9, underwent revision, clarification, and consolidation, while the history and theory in the second half of the appendix was completely rewritten.

Watering the Semiarid Plains

This book got its start in the upper atmosphere. My participation in a 1979 workshop on the human consequences of the greenhouse effect drew my attention to the old Dust Bowl region in the south-central High Plains.[1] This troubled farm country would be hit badly if global warming took hold in the twenty-first century. Always a land of little rain—averaging as little as twelve inches a year versus thirty inches in the midwestern Corn Belt—it repeatedly succumbed to seasons of extended drought. By the 1960s, however, mechanized irrigation from the underground water of the vast Ogallala aquifer turned the old Dust Bowl region into the breadbasket of the world. At least for a time.

This book is the story of how groundwater from the Ogallala aquifer revolutionized farming on the south-central Plains. Already, generations of settlers had been tantalized by a rich and deep soil in a flat treeless region, but they needed to find water. When homesteader John S. Gropp arrived about twenty miles northwest of Garden City, Kansas, in 1887, he rolled a large barrel of water three-quarters of a mile from a neighbor's well too many times before he hand-dug his own 220-foot well two years later.[2] The droughts that repeatedly broke farmers culminated in the Dust Bowl of the 1930s. In the 1960s, however, the use of groundwater for irrigation on a vast scale brought a remarkable security.

This book seeks to understand the effects, by the 1990s, of the rapid consumption and decline of Ogallala groundwater. How well have local farmers, water resource scientists, and government officials understood the Ogallala as a natural resource? Which actions were only wasteful and which were outright wrong? What actions can be taken, and are being taken, to sustain productive farming on the plains now that we know the Ogallala is not a limitless resource? The Ogallala problem is not unusual today. It is the kind of problem taken up worldwide under the concept of human and environmental sustainability—how to maintain a satisfying standard of living into the future. Indeed, the Ogallala problem is one of America's best case studies in that it will reveal how a modern technological society will or will not succeed in achieving sustainability.

Only two other books have appeared on the subject of the Ogallala aquifer and its impact on the High Plains. Most studies on western water problems focus on the more intense and more glamorous water wars in California and Arizona, while the Ogallala aquifer is relatively neglected. Donald E. Green's path-breaking *Land of the Underground Rain* (1973) devotes its attention to the aquifer under the Texas High Plains.[3] I am grateful for Green's invaluable regional history and technical detail, and I am also thankful for his review of this manuscript at its midpoint. Briefer but surprisingly detailed is Morton W. Bittinger and Elizabeth B. Green's 1980 *You Never Miss the Water Till. . . . (The Ogallala Story)*.[4] We compared notes about the Ogallala in Fort Collins, Colorado, early in the project.

Following extensive research and travel, many interviews, and several conference papers and articles, this book began to take shape. It takes the shape of an environmental history, which requires a broad scope and attention to sustainable development as well as coverage of important events over the last several decades. This updated edition will, I hope, make a valuable addition to the existing research.

I focus on one region that is at the center of extreme risk and repeated human responses to water, climate, and farming on the High Plains over the last 120 years. Southwest Kansas and the Oklahoma-Texas Panhandle, an area that runs from the Arkansas River on the north to the Canadian River in the Texas Panhandle, covers roughly 200 miles north-south and 150 miles east-west. This region presents three important phenomena that together offer a particularly apt case study for sustainable agriculture in America: (1) it was the heart of the 1930s Dust Bowl, America's greatest agricultural disaster; (2) it is at the center of intensive drawdown of irreplaceable Ogallala aquifer groundwater for irrigation; and (3) it is the hub of a highly profitable, vertically integrated agricultural industry, which includes cattle feedlots and beef processing plants, on a 250-mile radius from Garden City, Kansas, and which supplies up to 40 percent of the nation's dinner-table beef. By the mid-1990s, shiny metal sheds added hundreds of thousands of hogs, a change that is either a logical outcome of modern agribusiness or a troubling upheaval that threatens a precious plains lifestyle.

It should also be noted that three hundred miles to the north, Nebraska's lion's share of the Ogallala aquifer now makes up 67 percent of its entire groundwater.[5] This is the region north of the Platte River that underlies the Sandhills cattle-grazing region of western Nebraska. Already Sandhills inhabitants are fighting to prevent their water from being transferred to more parched regions. The more distant future belongs to the Ogallala in Nebraska, but that will require another book. This book gives its attention to the old Dust Bowl, a region that has been often wounded and often in need, and which is a vivid example of the historic trials of American agriculture.

For decades this particular heartland was tainted by failure so extreme that it drove away starving farmers, but it would come to symbolize America's conquest of drought. No other region displays as vividly the advantages and disadvantages of the High Plains. It is an unyielding and harsh land on which struggling farmers, now subsidized by costly government aid, produce surplus food. At the same time, the region has an advantage. Irrigation to help farmers and maintain production can last longer in the old Dust Bowl than in Colorado, Arizona, or California because there is less competition for groundwater from growing cities or industrial expansion.

A technological revolution after World War II enabled deep-well drilling, impeller pumps, low-cost engines, and low-cost fuels. By 1960, dryland farmers became irrigators, produced unprecedented surpluses (with yields as much as ten times greater than with dryland farming), and enjoyed prosperity. The Texas Plains were described, for example, as "the land of underground rain." But we must remember that Ogallala groundwater is a nonrenewable resource. The Ogallala cannot be restored because its original sources—winter runoff from the Rocky Mountains carried by braided streams to the plains—no longer replenish the aquifer. We must also remember that this enormous aquifer—it once contained three billion acrefeet—is not one of the original components of High Plains physiography or ecosystems. It is a separate geological entity. Ogallala groundwater is an imported resource used to support agriculture, much like federal prices supports. Yet, once it was reached, pumped, and then flooded or sprinkled onto crops, groundwater became integrated into plains farming. Irrigation did much to allow survival during the droughts of the 1950s and 1970s, and more recently, between 1988 and 1996.

After the Introduction sketches the problems that this book will address, Chapter 1 describes the central High Plains region as a physical resource, including the geological origins of the Ogallala aquifer as a nonrenewable resource, the surface features and soils, and the natural plants of the shortgrass prairie. Chapter 2 covers the long and painful and often self-defeating European attempts to settle the plains, America's "last frontier region." It includes a discussion of early quests for water and the short-lived plains version of the national Irrigation Crusade that took place in the early twentieth century. Chapter 3 centers on the region's history of dryland farming, federal interventions onto waterless "marginal lands," and the vulnerability of conventional settlement. Chapter 4 explores the remarkable irrigation revolution, from inadequate windmill technology in the early twentieth century to the deep wells, high-capacity pumps, and center-pivot sprinklers that industrialized the landscape in the 1960s. Chapter 5 compares the institutional attempts in Texas, Oklahoma, and Kansas to develop, manage, and conserve Ogallala groundwater on state and local levels. Chapter 6 describes one Kansas farm family's successful move into irrigation, their fragile future, and the implications of their story for independent family farming on the High Plains. Chapter 7 looks at the attempts to extend the use of Ogallala groundwater into the future and the movement toward sustainability. Chapter 8 discusses the effects upon water consumption during the severe drought of 1988 and the possible deeper threat of desertification during a long-term greenhouse effect climate change. A conclusion summarizes the book in the framework of sustainable development, and an appendix offers a final essay on the multifold attempts to learn the meaning of the plains.

A Brief Note on the Advantages of an Environmental Approach

While no book can be all-inclusive, this book probes topics that the traditional history book or policy study would consider irrelevant—those issues economists call "externalities." As an environmental history, it describes the geography, hydrology, and soils and plants of the region, and then connects these to human settlement, technology, and civilization. Environmental history reminds us, often painfully, that humanity, no matter how technologically sophisticated, is still embedded in nature.[6]

An environmental approach is advantageous because it enlarges our thinking and learning about the Ogallala aquifer and allows us to better understand why it is a troubled resource and why the people who use it prosper on the edge of failure. An environmental approach is openly reformist because it is based on the notion that if we only consider the human landscape—its politics, economics, institutions, and culture—our outlook will be badly flawed by a limited scope and an incomplete grasp of information.

These mistakes are made on a fundamental level. The economist and social critic, Kenneth Boulding, wrote, "All of nature's systems are closed loops, while economic activities are linear and assume inexhaustible resources."[7] As we explore the history of the Ogallala aquifer and the human actions that depleted it, it is important to recognize that such single-minded, market-driven linear habits have ignored environmental limits and encouraged runaway water waste, soil erosion, and exploitation of local farmers. We remain blind to the complex dynamics that hold a historic region together.

There is hope. When public policy is historically and ecologically informed it can *optimize* resource use rather than *maximize* its use to extinction and ultimate human deprivation. Technology can be redirected toward conserving resources, preventing pollution, restoring the environment, and sustaining the economy. Such actions can result in human prosperity at significantly lower environmental costs. Claude Lévi-Strauss described this redirection as "modesty, decency and discretion in the face of a world that preceded our species and that will survive it."[8]

In an environmental approach, the dynamics of human activity are extended to include the physical world filled not only with rocks and soils, water and air but also by living organisms that are born, flourish, and die on their own terms. The human history of the Ogallala gains new proportions when measured by a geological time scale of soil-building and drought cycles in addition to farmers' annual seasons in the field, thirty-year farmland mortgages, quarterly corporate profit-loss reports, and hourly shifts on the commodity markets. By thinking inclusively and making connections between human time and geological time, an environmental analysis can account more fully for the tight bond between human and environmental affairs than any single or linear factor can. Such a holistic approach examines the glue between humans and nature with equal attention to humans, nature, and the glue. It recognizes that the Ogallala is part of a multipath dynamic system that binds social, biological, and physical forces tightly together.

The transition to this comprehensive viewpoint is not easy. It can be difficult even to determine what is useful information; one person's cluttered noise is another person's healthy signal. Matching a theory with the crude realities of life can be a challenge. My approach here, which is discussed at greater length in the Appendix, emphasizes treatment of the Ogallala as a major element in a larger *nonlinear, self-organizing system*—the plains and its human inhabitants. This is a conceptual mouthful, but it allows us to see the connections between the technological, agricultural, environmental, and social forces that act both locally and distantly.[9]

The issue for the Ogallala region is to what extent human intervention (agriculture is always an intervention) upsets the self-regenerating capacities of the natural ecosystem. Will we cause enough damage to bring on environmental collapse of the region and subsequently make human survival there impossible? Can we identify ways in which human participation in the plains ecology can sustain itself? It is clear that both the environment and human agriculture are far more complex biological and social phenomena than is usually recognized by the marketplace and legislators. Most local farmers experience both complexities all too well.

From Nature's Ecosystem to Humanity's Infrastructure

The central High Plains was once a self-sustaining series of nested ecosystems that combined the forces of soil, grasses, grazing animals, occasional fire, climate, sunshine, and time. The original grasses were perennials, and they lived in a symbiotic balance with each other. Over the last 120 years, however, the native grasses have been replaced by tidy square miles of wheat, corn, and sorghums—the annual plants used in monoculture farming. Unlike the native grasses that were self-sustaining, these plants are domesticated and dependent upon constant human attention. By consuming the soil, and eventually the groundwater, of the plains, this European system of agriculture produced an abundance of food for people and their animals. By the early twentieth century, the region was called "the feedbag and breadbasket of the world." Europeans once described the plains as "empty and useless" territory that lay ready for consumption. It became a de facto colony that supplied raw materials to the rest of the nation. After settlement, the plains were chronically vulnerable.

Over the last hundred years, European settlement methods propelled the plains into ecological turmoil that induced heavy wind erosion of exposed soils during repeated cycles of drought. The result was catastrophic to both natural ecosystems and the human-driven agricultural infrastructure. The price was enormous. Badly disturbed environments became erratic and unsustainable. Large inputs produced meager results. Because of chronic ecosystem illness species were lost, grasses died, the soil blew away, crops and farms failed, children and the elderly became sick, people left. Recovery is unlikely because ecosystems are not fixed phenomena constant over long time periods; rather, they go through continuous changes based on the health of their biotic components. In the jargon of ecosystem science, they are stochastic and indeterminate. They are loose systems or weak wholes inherently vulnerable to external invasions and internal disruptions.

Can, and should, a natural environment be entirely replaced? The earlier ecosystem integrity of the plains can never be reestablished. The ecosystem that prospered before settlement was a complex and finely tuned interactive mechanism. European-style monoculture farming, with its links to world markets, government subsidies, and chemical fertilizers and pesticides, was differently complex and interactive. Will the natural ecosystem of the plains be transformed into a successful nature-resembling infrastructure (e.g., sustainable farmland), or will it become a degraded system on its way to ecosystem failure and infrastructure collapse. The latter scenario is becoming true on the High Plains.

•   •   •

The list of people who shared with me their experiences and their information to make the first version of this book possible is very long. The following is brief and undoubtedly incomplete. The names of Phil and Linda Tooms and Roger and Betty Trescott are fictitious, but the people they represent and the places in which those people live are real. Their need for privacy must be respected. Special appreciation goes to Esther Groves, reporter for the Liberal, Kansas, *Southwest Daily Times*, who wrote many articles about the Ogallala and led me to the good people of southwest Kansas and the Oklahoma-Texas Panhandle. I spent many hours with water management officials: Jeffrey K. Schmidt (and his knowledgeable secretary Joanne Hall), Gary Baker, Larry J. Kuder, Jerry L. Allen, and A. Wayne Wyatt in Kansas, Oklahoma, and Texas. They generously opened their doors, archives, and copying machines to me. I visited and talked and walked fields and saw the hardworking pumps and sprinklers with B. G. "Gene" Barby, Gayle Brown, Roland and Bonita Hoeme, Keith and Diane Allen, Paul and Patsy Boles, Ray Clark, and many others. Librarians and volunteers at the Finney County Historical Society and the Finney County Public Library, particularly in the invaluable collections in the latter's Kansas Room, were generous in their assistance. Special thanks goes to Edwin D. Gutentag, recently retired from the U.S. Geological Survey (USGS) in Denver. Ed was a USGS hydrologist in Garden City, Kansas, for two decades; he opened his personal files to me, located essential information, and even read parts of this manuscript for accuracy. Wayne Bossert of Northwest Kansas Groundwater Management District No. 4 corrected errors and gave good advice about the entire manuscript. I thank Michael "Micky" Glantz of the National Center of Atmospheric Research (NCAR) in Boulder for sharing his insights on the climate-agriculture-water interaction. Thanks also to campus colleagues who read the manuscript: Robert Lynch, Michal McMahon, John E. O'Connor, Eric Katz, and particularly Michael Black and Norbert Elliot, who waded through many parts two and three times. A near-final version was meticulously and thoughtfully analyzed by Patty Limerick of the University of Colorado. I received good advice from a reading by Deborah and Frank Popper of Rutgers University, and Donald Worster lavished generous attention and wise comments. Rose Scarano saved many a deadline with her emergency map pasting, captioning, and photocopying.

Following publication of the first edition of this book, I am grateful to the good people in Hayes, Colby, and Manhattan in Kansas; Kansas City in Missouri; Boulder and Sterling in Colorado; and San Antonio in Texas, for letting me try out raw versions and afterthoughts at their workshops and conferences. Special appreciation goes to hardworking and long-suffering Lori Triplett and her Great Plains Foundation for their efforts to create public forums on the Ogallala. Water management experts Wayne Bossert, A. Wayne

Wyatt, Steve Frost, and Curt Smith flooded me with new information. Kansas entrepreneurial farmer Steve Irsik and newspaper reporter Tim Unruh, of the Garden City *Telegram*, provided candid insights into current issues on the western Kansas Plains. Robert G. Bailey of the United States Forest Service in Ft. Collins, Colorado, shared his insights on ecosystem mapping. Craig Colton, geographer at West Texas State University in El Paso, and Paul Starrs, geographer at the University of Nevada–Reno, encouraged my venture into moral geography. Jim Sherow, historian at Kansas State University, his geography colleagues, David Kromm and Steven White, and Bill Riebsame, geographer at the University of Colorado, freely shared their insights. I enjoyed a blissful tour of hog confinement operations in Kansas and Oklahoma with geographer Chris Mayda, and John Fraser Hart and I traded outrageous ideas about industrial agriculture. Patient and loyal graduate students Mia Söderlund, Lise Fernanda Sedrez, and Keith Kloor reviewed large parts of this book for clarity and coherence. Also helpful in gaining a fresh perspective on a wearisome project were the many book reviewers of the first edition, who told me where I had done well and where I had missed the boat. My wife, Barbara, again exercised her prodigious patience, which again I tested.

Finally, my apologies to those important folks whose names I have inadvertently omitted. In thanking all the institutions and individuals that helped me make this book better, I must also say that any errors and inconsistencies that remain are my own responsibility.

Two remarkable outcomes of the first version of this book deserve special attention. It shared the George Perkins Marsh Award of the American Society for Environmental History as the most important book on environmental history for 1994. I am grateful for the honor.

Del Unruh, director of the University of Kansas Theater in Lawrence, took the daring step of writing a drama, ". . . To the Last Drop," which vividly chronicled the continuous struggle to find a satisfying life in Ogallala country. Del found a number of my stories about plains irrigators and environmental debates to his liking and incorporated them into his April 1996 production. As one audience member put it, "Unruh uniquely made a natural phenomenon—the Ogallala aquifer—one of the protagonists in a classic tragedy." In postproduction discussions we debated whether the next step would be a documentary or a musical.

· · ·

Earlier versions of parts of this book that have since been considerably revised have been published in or presented at the following:

"John Wesley Powell Was Right: Resizing the Ogallala High Plains," (paper presented at American Society for Environmental History conference, "Water Crises in Texas and the Southwest," Trinity University, San Antonio, Tex., May 25, 1998); to be published as "Resizing the High Plains," in *Fluid Arguments: Water in the American West*, ed. Mart Stewart (Tucson: University of Arizona Press, forthcoming).

"Moral Geography in Plains History," *Geographical Review* 88, no. 2 (April 1998) : 241–58.

"Pig Farming and the End of the High Plains: Agricultural Industrialization Faces Environmental Limits" (paper presented at the annual meeting of the American Association of Geographers, Boston, Mass., March 28, 1998).

"The High Plains as a 'Battered Region'—Moral Geography and Public Policy" (paper presented at the annual meeting of the American Association of Geographers, Ft. Worth, Tex., April 16, 1997).

"Does Its History Doom the Plains to Failure? Putting Chaos Theory to Work" (plenary address to the Great Plains Symposium, 1996, "Water and the Future of Kansas: The Ogallala Aquifer," Kansas State University and the Great Plains Foundation, Colby, Kans., March 5, 1996).

"The Ogallala Aquifer: Chaos in Natural Resource Development" (paper presented to the People, Prairies, and Plains Institute, Kansas State University, Manhattan, Kans., July 11, 1995).

"Is Sustainable Agriculture Possible in the Arid West? The Example of the Ogallala Aquifer" (paper presented at "Sustainable Use of the West's Water," a conference at the Natural Resources Law Center of the University of Colorado School of Law, Boulder, Colo., June 12, 1995).

"Future Prospects for Ogallala Sustainability" (paper presented at the Great Plains Symposium, 1995, "The Ogallala Aquifer," University of Missouri School of Law, Kansas City, Mo., March 2–3, 1995).

"Policy and Sustainability History" (paper presented at the Symposium on the Effects of A Zero Depletion Policy on the Ogallala Aquifer of the Great Plains, Ft. Hays State University, Hays, Kans., April 16, 1991).

"100 Years of Climate Risk Assessment on the High Plains: Which Farm Paradigm Does Irrigation Serve?" *Agricultural History* 63, no.2 (Spring 1989): 243–69.

"Water Runs Uphill to Money. But Will There Be Enough of Both to Keep the Desert Blooming?" *Orion Nature Quarterly* 7, no.1 (Winter 1988): 7–16.

"The Precarious Balance: Matching Market Dollars and Human Values in American Agriculture," *Environmental Professional* 10, no.1 (Spring 1988): 36–45.

"If John Wesley Were Alive Today . . . The Vagaries of Federal Water Management Policies in the Arid West, 1878 to the Present" in *Conference Proceedings: Water for the 21st Century, Will It Be There?, Center for Urban Water Studies* (Dallas: Southern Methodist University, 1985).

"U.S. Water Supplies: Scarcity amidst Plenty," *Britannica Yearbook of Science and the Future* (Chicago: Encyclopedia Britannica, 1982).

"What Will We Do When the Water Runs Out?" *Progressive Magazine* 45, no.7 (July 1981): 20–22.

"For a U.S. Water Policy," *New York Times,* December 30, 1980.

"America's Seventy-Year Mistake: Bad Weather in Good Country," *Seminar on Natural Resource Use and Environmental Policy* (Ames: Iowa State University, 1980).

"Research Opportunities in Retrospective Climate Impact Assessment: Case Study in Settlement and Farming on the Arid Great Plains, 1870–1940," *Final Report, Panel on Societal and Institutional Responses, AAAS-DOE Workshop on Environmental and Societal Consequences of a Possible CO_2-Induced Climate Change*, Carbon Dioxide Effects Research and Assessment Program, U.S. Department of Energy (Washington DC, 1980), 334–43.

Introduction: Learning to Think about the Ogallala

The goals of this book are to inform and persuade. It describes how an inestimable natural phenomenon—the Ogallala aquifer—came into being. The aquifer would not become a human resource until after World War II when farmers discovered it and learned to use it as a substitute for rainfall. This book chronicles over seventy years of repeated failures by the vaunted American farmer to overcome the harsh climate of the plains without the use of the aquifer. By 1960 new pumping technologies created a golden age of irrigation that has lasted into the present day, but as water levels decline this irrigation bonanza is disappearing for wheat, corn, and sorghum farmers on the south-central High Plains. Most irrigation farmers have already acknowledged a difficult future, but they have not necessarily solved the problem. This book offers both conventional and alternative ways of thinking about the connections that exist in the High Plains between groundwater, the kind of agriculture that can be produced in a difficult farming region, and the types of farming used.

Does Climate Still Matter?

Not many modern workplaces are directly affected by the weather. Protection from the vagaries of climate has long been one of the major objectives of human toolmaking and the industrial revolution. Jesse H. Ausubel writes, "Humans do not wait guilelessly to receive [a climate] impact, bear the loss, then respond with an adaptation. Rather they attempt to anticipate and fore-stall problems."[1] Modern technological society has learned to protect itself against cold and heat and rain and snow. Nevertheless, climate still influences construction, transportation, communications, fisheries, forestry, and tourism. Agriculture was, and still is, the most vulnerable to climate—rain, sun, wind, and temperature.[2] In the long run, climate, which is extremely fluid and fickle, is still the part of the environment that humans find the most difficult to control or modify.

In the lower United States this agricultural vulnerability was most severe on the central High Plains, a region that experiences a range of extreme climates but that is most often a parched land buffeted by dry heat, wind, and limited rainfall. These conditions, combined with the arrival of undertooled and undercapitalized frontier farmers in the nineteenth century, virtually guaranteed almost a century of repeatedly failed settlement. Not until the 1960s would these Dust Bowl conditions be mastered—for a time—by groundwater pumping and irrigation technologies that enabled highly productive farming in wheat, corn, alfalfa, and sorghums. Americans tried to introduce an environment in which they could survive and prosper. They appeared to solve the problems of the plains, and plains farmers entered the American middle-class mainstream. However, this fabricated environment cannot endure indefinitely. Usable groundwater will run out. Federal subsidies will decline. Alternatives involve new risks and uncertainties.

The history of the south-central High Plains can be understood as a series of crisis situations accelerated by repeated drought. As a result, the old Dust Bowl region became an inadvertent "experiment station" for crisis management on many levels, from local farmers to federal planners. Because of environmental conditions, when the south-central High Plains was settled as an agricultural region it went on permanent alert, experiencing crisis with no solution and no end. The problem of the plains will only be mitigated temporarily by today's dependency on Ogallala irrigation. Long-term environmental conditions, such as the reality of permanent drought with short-lived seasons of benevolent weather, have to be recognized. This requires the application of the new planetary history, which seeks a widened vision of the environment to include more than humans and human interests. Environment is the limiter after all.

The Place and Its Problem

In the 1880s large numbers of energetic and ambitious European farmers appeared on North America's unplowed High Plains. They began to accelerate the pace of nature's events and alter nature's intentions to suit their needs. One unfortunate result was the Dust Bowl of the 1930s, which occurred when fertile soil, no longer protected by native grasses, blew away. Later, with the adept use of technology, farmers learned to mine the underground water to overcome the lack of rain. This resource was consumed at a pace far beyond any known replacement. In a sense, a Faustian bargain was struck with the water, and today the other end of the bargain is coming due. In looking at this bargain, I suggest ways we can move beyond a Pyrrhic mastery of the plains toward an accommodative sustainable strategy.

The enormous Ogallala aquifer is groundwater trapped below 174,000 square miles of fertile but otherwise dry plains farmland. Unlike most of the world's water supplies, Ogallala groundwater is largely nonrenewable because its sources were cut off thousands of years ago. It is essentially "fossil water" that was generated ten thousand to twenty-five thousand years ago from the glacier-laden Rockies.[3] About ten thousand years ago the source-flow stopped, perhaps diverted by the Pecos and Rio Grande Rivers. However, more than three billion acre-feet (an acre-foot is a foot of water across one square acre, or 325,851 gallons) had been deposited under the plains. One misconception about the Ogallala aquifer (and about most groundwater) is that it stands in cavernous lakes or flows in thundering underground rivers. In reality, it trickles slowly, southeasterly, through sandy gravel beds, 500 to 1,000 feet a year, 2 to 3 feet a day. These vast water-saturated gravel beds, 50 to 300 feet below the surface, are 150 to 300 feet thick. About one billion acre-feet of Ogallala water were consumed by irrigation farmers between 1960 and 1990, mostly in southwest Kansas, the Oklahoma Panhandle, and west Texas. This is serious because groundwater is replaced only from the surface and mostly at less than one inch a year, while pumping is measured in

3

feet per year. Nothing can accelerate its flow, and artificial replacement remains impossible. Further, there are no natural alternatives in the region such as a major river that could be dammed or diverted. There is no equivalent to the Sacramento, Columbia, or Colorado Rivers on the High Plains. The flatness of the land prevented creation of large-scale dams by the Reclamation Service. And there is little rain.

Like angry mosquitoes on a vast forearm, over 150,000 pumps roar day and night during growing seasons on the plains. They feed water onto crops planted fencerow-to-fencerow on thousand-acre farms. Mountains of wheat and corn, when not shipped overseas or processed to make bread and breakfast cereal, are added to sorghums and alfalfa and dished out to herds of cattle lodged shoulder-to-shoulder in pens that cover hundreds of acres. Ultimately, these beeves are brained, served up to long rows of bone-sawing and meat-cutting dis-assembly lines, and packaged for supermarket meat counters. The world's largest beef processing plant is just west of Garden City, Kansas, in the heart of the old Dust Bowl.

The plains region has not always been so industrialized. Fifty years ago the loudest sound was not the noise of pump motors; it was the maddening wind of recurring dust storms. The laboring plains farmers and their families lived as close to the blowing soil and blistering sun as the original pioneers did 125 years earlier. Plains farmers seemed frozen in time because of the extreme climate conditions. It seemed they were doomed to a substandard, hardscrabble way of life. The soil was rich, but that mattered little when the spring and summer were rainless and scorching. Occasional seasons of rain merely fooled and teased. Mistakes were made and good people sacrificed their lives. It appeared that Americans were not invincible pioneers who would inevitably become prosperous farmers. Until the pumps and wells, engines and fuels, and know-how and cash took over, wherever the vast middle grassland received fewer than twenty inches of rain per year, farmers fared poorly.

The Ogallala is still one of the nation's great hidden treasures. It still contains over two billion acre-feet to support a region the size of three New York States, and probably only half of the water is accessible through known pumping technologies. Ogallala nonrenewability would not be significant for humans if Ogallala groundwater did not irrigate nearly seven million acres of old Dust Bowl land, turning it into high production grainfields. New pumping and irrigation technologies made this part of the High Plains one of the largest and most productive farmlands on the globe. It is rightly called the breadbasket of the world. However, over the next two decades irrigation coverage could fall to two million acres.[4]

Mechanized irrigation may offer only a half-century of prosperity for an otherwise harsh and hopeless region. The current pace of consumption does not allow another half-century. Instead, we may have at most one more generation of prosperity, maybe less if dire greenhouse desert predictions come true. Soon, the remaining water will be impossible to reach without prohibitively expensive deep pumps that consume costly fuels. This procedure would result in high-priced food—approximately twelve dollars for a pound of bread and sixty-nine dollars for a pound of beef in 1999 dollars—an unacceptable forecast in light of America's tradition of cheap food. Some critics say that irrigation's victory was temporary and deceptive. This book offers a framework by which to understand the Ogallala, its human implications, and possible future directions. Despite decades of trial and error and of government interventions, today both the Ogallala aquifer and plains farmers exist on the edge of extinction. There is no quick technological fix, and no one in the old Dust Bowl country seeks to return to the old hardscrabble ways. Even with a third of the total water consumed and only half of the rest usable, the presence of the Ogallala aquifer below the High Plains is still like having the waters of Lake Ontario nearby, ready to be tapped at will to flood the fields of corn, milo, wheat, and alfalfa.

Today pumps and wells and engines and fuels define the High Plains. Local irrigators in the 1980s were successful on a level that the wrung-out Dust Bowl farmers of the 1930s would have found astonishing. Kansans Phil and Linda Tooms, twenty or so crow-flying miles southwest of Sublette, switched from equipment sales and ranching in the early 1960s when they learned to irrigate. Phil still irrigates sixteen hundred acres, enjoys his history books in an air-conditioned suburban-style house, and serves on the board of a bank in Liberal.

A few miles away in the forlorn Kansas Sandhills, where even Dust Bowl farmers never settled, the entrepreneurial Gigot family, father and four sons, irrigate over fifty thousand acres of corn, wheat, and sorghums using about five hundred circling center-pivot irrigation sprinklers. Their operation is nicknamed the Gigot Empire. The family is worth tens of millions of dollars and is not loved by everyone in the neighborhood.

Similar in scale and impact is the Paul Hitch operation in Texas County, Oklahoma, where Hitch operates the nation's largest cattle feedlots and looks forward to a greater number of hog-confinement factories.

Betty and Roger Trescott, both in their eighties, live near the Hitch operation. After the pumps appeared in the early 1960s, their ability to flood their wheat fields allowed them to stay when dryland farming would not. Betty in particular is a firebrand who takes on anyone, including big oil companies and state water boards who want to take away Ogallala water from the farmers and force-feed it into rock formations to recover oil from an old oil field.

Another two hundred miles due south, across the narrow Oklahoma Panhandle into Texas and down to Lubbock, is A. Wayne Wyatt, who in his youth experienced painful farm losses before irrigation and who has lived through the entire history of widespread irrigation on the southern High (Staked) Plains. He manages the pathbreaking Texas Groundwater Management District No. 1, which opened its doors in 1952 to promote "controlled development" of Ogallala water, and which is gradually compelled to protect the remaining supply for "beneficial use" only. Similar districts appeared in western Kansas and eastern Colorado by the 1970s.

To allow only beneficial use has been extraordinarily difficult, and water "mining" has not been significantly reduced. Phil Tooms complains that his local Kansas Groundwater Management District No. 3 was belatedly organized only after almost half the available water had been consumed. Even the nearby Gigots, despite their ability to buy the newest irrigation technology, admit that their future contains less groundwater. The Trescotts are fighting to keep nonfarm interests from wasting water that morally and legally belongs to those growing wheat. Wyatt clearly understands he is fighting a long battle to keep water available for farmers. He also understands that, eventually, he will lose.

Why Is Irrigation so Attractive?

Irrigation on the High Plains is a very comforting technology. At the turn of a valve or the flip of a switch lucky farmers can flood fields, sprinkle crops, or drip water on vegetables no matter how dry the weather. The water is available on demand in defiance of the unpredictable climate of southwest Kansas or the Oklahoma and Texas Panhandles, where a fast-moving thundercloud might unleash a downpour in one area but only one mile away leave the neighbor's needy field dry. February might not give a farmer the last six inches of snow he needs to guarantee that his newly planted wheat field will be saturated with four feet of water. This is the traditional uncertainty that all farmers face not only on the plains but around the world wherever the rain is marginal and the local rivers run dry in summer.

Contemporary irrigation farmers on 1,280 acres in the old Dust Bowl country turn to a gushing steel umbilical, six to eight inches wide, plugging down two hundred and fifty feet to the once-glacier-fed freshwater of the Ogallala aquifer. At the top end, another finite resource, natural gas, fires up the four cylinders of a new International 605 engine, a Minneapolis-Moline engine, or a used Ford or Chevy v-8 engine. The engine's shaft, rotating at 1,200 rpm, runs to a reduction gearbox that shifts the torque from horizontal to vertical and powers a Johnson or Peerless impeller pump. The aquifer water rushes up the steel umbilical and into aluminum pipes at eight hundred to twelve hundred gallons per minute—the water ready to be soaked up by nearby fields overloaded with wheat, corn, or sorghums. At nine hundred thousand gallons laid on 130 acres of a 160-acre quarter section, corn requires the most water during a season. Wheat and sorghums need half that amount but alfalfa needs even more. A center-pivot sprinkler system, from drilling the well to watering the milo, cost a farmer in 1990 fifty thousand dollars to seventy thousand dollars per 160 acres depending on well depth and field needs. These prices are twice as much as those from 1976. Most irrigators need six to ten such systems to achieve efficiency. To pay for the equipment, irrigators need good wheat or sorghum prices, but in the late 1980s these were half of what they were in the 1970s. The borrowing power of farmers, based on land values, fell in the same period by about a quarter.[5]

7

It is too expensive for a new farmer to start up an entire irrigation operation despite the promised bounty. Almost all the farmers I interviewed spoke of the inability of a new generation of farmers to accumulate the capital needed to support large-scale irrigation. This is attenuated by the need to replace aging wells, pumps, motors, and sprinklers. Despite attempts at conservation, the future requires the kind of intensive water consumption demanded by an expanding High Plains beef industry, which needs six pounds of irrigated grain to produce one pound of feedlot beef. Cattle feedlots, which run tens of thousands of cattle through their pens every year, demand a minimum of eight to ten gallons of water per head per day. Newly introduced industrial hog operations are even more demanding of precious groundwater. Research shows that a one-hundred-pound hog produces 1.7 times as much waste as one human being and consumes thirty gallons of water per day, so that a hundred thousand hogs in a neighborhood—a smallish factory—would be the equivalent of introducing 170,000 people to a community to consume the water and use the sewers. Historically, meat consumption grows as living standards and social expectations rise; this is true globally. Higher meat consumption has been seen as a sign of better living standards. Third World peoples get their protein from beans, rice, and grains, but to them a higher standard of living includes meat in the dinner pot. Today the plains is locked into high water consumption to grow the wheat and water the beef, to grow the corn and water the hogs, and to process animal wastes.

Alternatives to irrigation are gloomy. From the viewpoint of a farmer, access to irrigation is the difference between keeping the wheat farm near Liberal, Kansas, or moving to a dismal trailer park next to the Chrysler minivan assembly plant in Illinois. When irrigation itself comes into doubt, the question is whether this agricultural heartland, upon which the nation and the world have learned to depend, can be sustained in any acceptable way.

The Plains Advantage
Irrigation on the High Plains has definite advantages over other irrigated regions in the United States and around the world. This region has already seen

sophisticated technological development and superior farm management since the grim Dust Bowl era. Whereas costs of new dams, reservoirs, canals, and distribution systems have been rising in Asia, Africa, and Latin America, irrigation on the High Plains does not face these large capital costs. High Plains irrigation is intensely localized and small-scale: it uses free-standing in-field pumps and sprinklers owned by individual farmers. In most of the world, including water bonanzas in California and Arizona, irrigation involves large publicly owned and debt-ridden systems of dams and diversion projects covering thousands of square miles. Tunnels and aqueducts move water hundreds of miles from source to farmer and high levels of waste that are created through evaporation cause major environmental degradation. In contrast, High Plains irrigators are free from distant technological breakdowns. They are independent of meddlesome collective decision making and complex water regulations. Restrictions on water consumption on the plains are relatively light, and decisions are local. Aside from initial equipment costs, maintenance, and the energy to fuel the pumps, water is free. Large-scale projects, however, must attach a price to water and depend upon heavy public subsidies to keep costs at a manageable level for intensive-use farming.

In its individualized framework, Ogallala water is directly translated into improved crop yields. On the plains, it is the farmer's point of view that prevails, not the engineer's infrastructure.[6] Large systems tend to deliver water on a fixed schedule; the local farmer can match water with the immediate needs of crops. Results are far superior on the plains compared to many other irrigation systems. This is the result of independent management decisions that can directly respond to local crop needs. This freedom is an unexpected benefit from what I have already established as the precarious limitation of water.

The absence of major cities on the central and southern plains is another advantage. Garden City, Kansas, Guymon, Oklahoma, and Lubbock, Texas, will never become Denver or Los Angeles or Phoenix. Farmers who cannot break even when their water costs scale up to seventy dollars an acre-foot cannot compete with cities who can afford from two thousand dollars to six thousand dollars an acre-foot, as is the case in Arizona. Farming is water intensive. The water a typical plains farmer needs for a year's wheat crop on 1,280 acres could serve twenty-four American families for a year. The metropolitan pressures that are driving out farmers in California and Arizona are unlikely to appear on the High Plains. Finally, although industrial use of water is six times more efficient than farming, the plains has the advantage of little heavy industry. Except for the threatening rise of wastewater from hog-confinement factories and the use of Ogallala water for oil field recovery, the plains is remarkably free of heavy water pollution.

The wild card in this poker game is global warming. The High Plains is inescapably threatened by the change in the world's chemical climate that follows great quantities of human-produced carbon dioxide, methane, and other substances being pumped into the upper atmosphere. According to global climate modeling, the U.S. High Plains is one of several regions around the world that is particularly vulnerable to intensive desertification if the predicted CO_2-induced greenhouse effect takes place. As global warming takes hold, greater threats of desertification to the plains will force heavier demands on already-stressed irrigation water. This climate shift would accelerate groundwater consumption to three times today's conservation rates and would thus seriously threaten most sustainability strategies. In 1989 Jim MacNeill wrote, "Global warming is a form of feedback from the earth's ecological system to the world's economic system. . . . A number of communities and regions have already crossed critical thresholds"[7] The greenhouse effect on the plains intensifies the region's greatest burden: drought and the constant threat of desertification.

The central High Plains are for many reasons strategically advantageous to continued irrigation farming. As cities spread in California and Arizona and consume water once allocated to farmers, the groundwater of the Ogallala aquifer will take on increased importance. When water scarcity leads to high prices in urban regions worldwide, the advantages of the nonurban, nonindustrial Ogallala region will become even more attractive. This should encourage more intensive water conservation that will, in turn, extend the lifespan of irrigation on the High Plains. The current spread of desertification elsewhere also makes the Ogallala more valuable. Where in 1989, the risk of desertification threatened an area containing one billion inhabitants, the United Nations Environment Programme (UNEP) now estimates that 60 percent of the 8.25 billion acres in arid or semiarid agricultural land worldwide is affected by desertification. More than a billion humans are threatened. While each year deserts grow by fifteen million acres, water use worldwide has doubled at least twice in the twentieth century and could double again before 2010. Eighty developing countries, in which 40 percent of the world's population live, are already experiencing strained water resources.[8]

Consuming a Nonrenewable Resource: Profligacy in Scarcity

In addition to the cash and credit subsidies they receive from the federal government, plains farmers have for generations received hidden environmental subsidies in "free" soil and water. Over time these forces have provided a false sense of security. Because it takes only fifteen dollars to pump an acre-foot of water using natural gas or thirty dollars using electricity, this free water has been profligately consumed. Conventional agriculture has treated natural resources, such as water and soil, as a common from which borrowing bears no economic costs. The goal of sustainable agriculture is to identify and track the real costs, both economic and environmental, of soil erosion, pesticide pollution, and aquifer depletion.

Pierre R. Crosson and Norman J. Rosenberg, of the Resources for the Future think tank, identify one of the forces that encourages this excessive use. They write that "markets are not well equipped to protect resources such as water . . . in which it is difficult to establish property rights."[9] Water laws, such as prior appropriation—"use it or lose it"—counter sustainable development. Instead of trying to change the laws, an imperfect first step is to include environmental costs in economic analysis. When private interests to a resource get too established, regulation of its use becomes difficult. Water is the globe's fugitive resource, always on the move, and thus it is hard to pin down to one place. Water is therefore treated as both private property (whoever owns the land has exclusive rights to the groundwater below) and common property (a free and inexhaustible resource belonging to the public). Since sustainable development, an alternative concept that is discussed in the last chapters of this book, seeks to integrate both environmental and economic factors in its broader analysis, it may be better at treating ownership and use of water than the original distinctions, which are clearly contradictory and unworkable.

The squandering of water has been encouraged by government subsidies that support widespread irrigation of surplus crops, particularly wheat. Subsidies intended to keep farmers from collapse continue to stimulate production even in the absence of demand.[10] These surplus crops, like obsolete military aircraft, are stockpiled at government expense. When farm subsidies began to cost governments in the United States and Europe over three hundred billion dollars a year, the 1985 U.S. farm bill tried to lower costs and surpluses by setting aside unplanted farmland as agricultural reserves. By inducing farmers to use excessive amounts of pesticides and fertilizers and to waste underground and surface waters in irrigation, subsidies also encourage "transitional unsustainability." It is clear that surplus food is being created at great hidden economic and human costs. Consumers, grain traders, or foreign buyers may pay less than half of real costs. The hidden environmental costs of lost water, soil, and abandoned or exploited farms are not easy to measure in dollars. These policies counter sustainable development.[11]

To the economic and environmental costs one must consider not only that surpluses have promoted expanding beef and hog industries that demand excessive amounts of water, but also that the independent family farm, which some argue should have died out with the horse-and-buggy, will continue to be protected. As long as farmers need subsidies and special credits to exist, they will remain the government clients they became in the 1930s. Most local plains family farmers depend upon free water to survive, and they would quickly go bankrupt if they had to pay the Corps of Engineers' estimated costs of three hundred dollars to eight hundred dollars an acre-foot for "new" water imported from the Mississippi. From the viewpoint of those who condemn the federal protection of family farmers, large corporate operations that can afford expensive equipment use water most efficiently. It is argued as well that the same independent family farmers who waste High Plains water also receive millions of taxpayer dollars to stay on the plains.[12] Supporters of family farms retort that their preservation is a sacred trust and that they ensure the survival of organic low-input farming.

Rewriting the Rulebook: Environment, Economics, and Agriculture

The debate over the plains is not agriculture versus environment. It is also not a simple choice between the survival of local farming and preservation of the remaining Ogallala supply. Instead, the debate can be understood by comparing the diverging interests of economics versus environment. But even this comparison does not generate a workable model for successful farming above the Ogallala. That must come from somewhere else.

An economics paradigm advocates high-yield commodity production that maximizes immediate profits as the most efficient application of plains farming. In this paradigm, soil and water are treated as part of the no-cost common that can keep plains farming profitable into the future. The economics paradigm assumes that the family farm is being rightly replaced by large-scale, deep-pocketed agribusiness.

A comprehensive agricultural paradigm is different from, and more complex and inclusive than, any solely economic or environmental approach.[13] Agriculture eludes definition. It builds on historic experience but belongs to no historic era, and it involves environment and economics, but it belongs to neither. Sustainable agriculture, in Stephane Castonguay's words, "is dependent upon the autonomy of the agricultural community to practice an agriculture that is environmentally sound."[14] Agriculture, as humanity's oldest intervention into nature, encompasses myriad geographic, technical, economic, social, cultural, and historical factors. One of the most elaborate elements of agriculture—the family farm—is discussed in Chapter 6. In Chapter 7 and in the concluding chapter, we look at the family farm, the future of irrigation from Ogallala groundwater, and continuous agriculture on the south-central High Plains to see how their destinies are intertwined.

Nevertheless, both economic and environmental paradigms have serious implications for agriculture. A common mistake today is to reduce agriculture to a subcategory of either environment or economics.[15] A better answer to the problem of irrigation on the plains may be through neither an environmental nor an economics approach. Instead, both can serve a larger agricultural community. New insights about agriculture can also be gleaned by using sustainability as a comprehensive model for successful modern agriculture.

After years of irrigating with Ogallala groundwater, irrigation on the plains is still in self-destruct mode, and the Ogallala aquifer is still a non-renewable resource. As such, our struggles with the Ogallala today can be understood as a representative microcosm of the difficult global search for sustainable agriculture.

1

. . .

The First Half-Billion Years

The soil is the one indestructible, immutable asset that the nation possesses. It is the one resource that cannot be exhausted, that cannot be used up.—position taken by the U.S. Bureau of Soils around 1900

Soil is a temporary interlude for rocks and minerals on their way to solution and to the sea.—soil scientist William A. Albrecht in 1956

Where did the Ogallala aquifer and its valuable landscape come from? All of it migrated from somewhere else, not only the plants and people. Hundreds of millions of years of geological restlessness created today's water-saturated underground beds of gravel and sand covered by layers of rock and fertile soil above and undergirded by rolling red rock below. The mighty geological time scale turns human history into an afterthought, for even the Ogallala aquifer lives for only a brief moment as plains soils race from the mountains to the ocean; today's dry landscape is a blink of the Maker's eye. The tall and short grasses of the plains ebb and flow like tides on a beach as they follow fickle shifts in rainfall patterns. Conventional farmers who force corn and alfalfa by draining the underground water supply are a mere interruption, like an itch that is quickly scratched. Other farmers, who see water, soil, and grasses as a collaborating ensemble they must join rather than overcome, will stay a while longer. The successful farmer listens to the nonhuman voices around him; as history has shown, this is not an easily learned skill.

15

For more than the last two thousand years of the current geological epoch, these forbidding and tiresome grasslands have covered fully one-third of the North American continent, its single most extensive terrain.[1] Some of the same wild grasses—bluestems, switchgrasses, gramas, cordgrasses—range across a thousand miles of middle America, from the southern edge of Lake Michigan to eastern Colorado, from West Texas far north into Canada. They differ in size and lushness, depending on moisture and temperature, and allow us to distinguish between the midwestern tallgrass prairie, the midland mixed-grass country, and the shortgrass High Plains. Since the 1870s, when John Wesley Powell called the High Plains a subhumid region, the description fits an environment where the rainfall is consistently less than that necessary for traditional eastern agriculture. Yearly rainfall is between twelve and twenty inches, compared to thirty to fourty inches east of the Mississippi. Effective rainfall can be much less because of evaporation from the extremes of wind and heat. A favorable factor, repeated by desperate boosters to the point of exaggeration, is that three-quarters of the rain comes during the growing season, April to September.[2]

The Trescotts' Place

Today Roger and Betty Trescott live on a two-thousand-acre Oklahoma Panhandle farm that is compact for a High Plains operation. It is divided into several wheat and alfalfa fields. Their ranch house is white, unpretentious, even small. They have no children and regret it. The yard immediately around the house is sparse and plain. Like most plains farmers, they do not have the familiar steep-roof red-painted barn of the East, but instead several large metal sheds where they keep their equipment and supplies. Inside the house, cleaning is simplified by use of heavy-duty plastic upholstery on some of the furniture. Everything is spotless. When they are out in the wheat fields, the Trescotts are some of the most traditional farmers described in this book because they practice flood irrigation.

The heart of the Trescott home is Roger's and Betty's shared office. He works on farm management while Betty cranks out reports and newsletters to alert fellow farmers and the public about major Ogallala water issues. Despite Roger's recent bout with back trouble, they both devote their attention to these public issues. He is tall, lean, expert, and bemused. Betty is a short ball of fire, blazing with energy, aggressively articulate, and meticulous in her research. Her reputation for presenting hammering testimony at Oklahoma legislative hearings on water abuse now precedes her in the Panhandle and the capital. One event that caught Betty's eye was a landmark December 1984 Oklahoma Supreme Court decision concerning the beneficial use of Panhandle groundwater: was it proper for Mobil Oil Company to draw large amounts of fresh Ogallala water, tens of billions of gallons, to force up the remaining oil in an old field (the process is called secondary recovery), or should Ogallala water, irreplaceable but admittedly existing in large amounts, be saved for the irrigation of crops, as Oklahoma law requires?[3]

Betty represented the Texas County (Oklahoma) Irrigation and Water Resources Association (TCIWRA). With her usual zeal and determination to persuade whoever would listen, she observed that "the late U. S. Senator Robert S. Kerr, Sr., is famous for his often repeated prediction that some day the price of a barrel of water will be higher than the price of a barrel of oil," and commented that "his prophecy is already come true. Right now, at our State Capitol Building and in the very building housing OWRB [Oklahoma Water Resources Board]—the State Department of Health Building—taxpayers are buying bottled water, imported from Arkansas at $33.60 a barrel, while the price of oil on the current (1985) market is $26.53." That would put the price of water at eighty cents a gallon, without doubt an unrealistically expensive example, but Betty Trescott's point was driven home.

Betty noted that Mobil Oil Company was licensed in 1984 by the Oklahoma Water Resources Board to pump fresh groundwater to recover thirty-five million barrels of oil. At a market value of twenty-eight dollars a barrel, $98 million worth of oil would require the use of $19.2 billion worth of water, priced at eighty cents a gallon, a one-to-twenty cost ratio. "In case anyone thinks it is an unfair comparison," said TCIWRA, "to use the cost of imported drinking water at 80 cents a gallon, we would be glad to substitute the value of the destroyed water at the cost of replacement—and then it would become obvious that 80 cents a gallon would be a great bargain."[4] When Ed

Gutentag, for many years the United States Geological Survey hydrologist in Garden City, Kansas, heard of Betty's claims, he first thought she was an environmental kook. He soon concluded, at the OWRB hearing, that "she was one of the few in the meeting room to grasp hydrology. Then I considered her a colleague."[5]

The controversy, of which more will be said in chapter 5, involved the four great geological resources—natural gas, water, oil, and soil—in the Dust Bowl region of the Oklahoma-Texas Panhandle and southwest Kansas. In Oklahoma, fuel from the Hugoton-Guymon field, the largest natural-gas field in the nation (and the second-largest in the world), is used to pump fresh Ogallala water, the largest and most exploited aquifer in the nation, not only for cropland irrigation, but also to recover oil from old fields. The soil of Texas County, rated high-quality Class III by the federal Soil Conservation Service, makes Ogallala water even more desirable to farmers, who in turn find themselves at odds with the oil companies.

The most relaxing spot on Roger's and Betty's land is reached after a brief drive (no one walks in Panhandle country) to their northernmost holding pond, which covers about an acre. The water is refreshing after the hot dusty fields. The pond is ringed by lush green trees, sweetened by the song of birds, and offers an oasis in the middle of the dry, raspy, flat landscape. The steady, noisy pounding of the nearby pump and engine is not an irritant but the symbol of their success as farmers. Roger moved to the Guymon, Oklahoma, vicinity in 1947 after learning to irrigate near Plainview, Texas. He drilled Texas County's fifth well down to the red-rock bottom of the aquifer at 300 feet. It cost him ten thousand dollars, a fortune in the late 1940s, but is now 50 feet deeper than it was when he started. He irrigates 1,720 acres of his 2,000-acre farm from several wells, but now with 30 percent less water than he used in the 1960s. In twenty years, furrow irrigation has lowered his overall pumping level from a depth of 190 feet to 240 feet. Within five years the Trescotts will run out of practical access to water when the pumping level descends 12 more feet; going deeper is too inefficient. They are also facing the crunch between low wheat prices and rising natural-gas costs. The Trescotts' irrigation system, as it floods each field to reach every plant, is also wasteful, losing more than 50 percent of its water to evaporation and runoff. The water is not easy to apply quickly to crops, but a shift to center-pivot irrigation, which has much less evaporation, would cost the Trescotts at least four hundred thousand dollars. If they were younger, perhaps they might have undertaken the transition.

Foundations

Roger's and Betty's farm is eighteen miles north by northwest of Guymon in Texas County, midway on the east-west axis of the Oklahoma panhandle. Their superior-quality soil and the pure groundwater beneath it are geological migrants; it took five thousand years for the Trescotts' soil to build up to its modern fertility before their land was homesteaded in 1911.[6] Underground, the water, now trickling ever so slowly, is ten thousand to twenty-five thousand years old, originally glacier runoff from the Rockies. Everything and everyone is an immigrant. The Trescotts arrived from west-central Texas in the 1940s. Previous farmers brought in dryland wheat, and before that the land supported semiarid grasses, such as buffalo grass. The most recent imports are corn and alfalfa, both demanding so much water that their natural western boundary lies in humid farm country more than three hundred miles to the east. Experts say, and farmers know, that traditional American farming should have halted a hundred miles to the east because there is not enough rain. But the combination of intrusive Europeans, plants and animals, soil and rock, and, above all, someplace else's water, gave rise to the farming that goes on in the Panhandle today. Remove just one of these immigrants and food production ends immediately.

The Trescott place once stood in a vast inland sea. Deep water covered the region for as much as fifty million years at a time. This geologic time span, begun half a billion years ago, is immeasurable on any human scale. The last great flooding took place sixty million years ago when the North American continent looked like a World War II life raft in the ocean, having dry sides but filled with shallow water in the middle and open at the north or south end or both ends. Today's Hudson Bay is the last large shallow remnant of this ancient sea; sixty million years ago it reached as far south as the Dakotas and even earlier as far as the Gulf of Mexico. Called the Rocky Mountain Trough, the inland sea was nearly one thousand miles wide and three thousand miles long. Each time it came, it laid down hundreds or thousands of feet of sediment. Over geologic time, the thick sediments surfaced many times when the seas withdrew, only to be eroded to slivers of nothing, just as the soils of the High Plains today are running to the Mississippi River and into the Gulf of Mexico. Geologic cycling is still in process: for twenty million years or so during the Jurassic Period (two hundred million years ago), the plains may have had a climate similar to that of modern times—dry and brisk—before slipping below the shallow sea again.

The first time Roger's and Betty's farm was under water may have been 580 million years ago (late Cambrian), when thousands of feet of limestone were layered on top of sandstone. After rising above sea level 400 million years ago (Devonian), virtually all of Oklahoma sank again 50 million years later to be rewarded with more thousands of feet of limestone and shale. Then, 275 million years ago (late Pennsylvanian), the land again rose above the waters, but within 25 million years Permian and Triassic seas buried the floor with one or two thousand feet of red sandstones and shales until less than 200 million years ago. The Oklahoma Panhandle and the rest of the region surfaced again before descending under a Jurassic and Cretaceous sea from 150 million to 65 million years ago. These tens of thousands of feet of level "layer-cake geology" marine deposits would have made Oklahoma one of the highest places on Earth were it not for thousands of millennia of erosion by water and dust-storm winds when the land stood above the seas. It is not clear when the region will slip below the waters again, but the record is promising.[7]

The picture changed dramatically about sixty million years ago (early Tertiary times) because of events two hundred miles to the west in the Rocky Mountains. Large amounts of water, active as rain, snow, and ice, have made the surface of Earth far busier than other planets in the solar system. It still is. On a celestial time scale, geologic changes took place at dizzying speed even in the seemingly placid Ogallala country. Activity of uplift and erosion at the Rockies would seem like a speeded-up movie. Rocky Mountain scenery would not be spectacular during the powerful Laramide orogeny (mountain-building period), when the ancestral Rockies first rose and expelled the seas seventy million Cretaceous years ago. The landscape was that of a high rolling country. In a moist and semitropical time, with an abundance of water, it was quickly worn down to a peneplain by the elements as rapidly as it rose. Nevertheless, valley floors still stood thousands of feet above sea level and mountain peaks a thousand feet higher. The continental backbone had appeared. This can still be seen in the upper levels of Rocky Mountain National Park, in the gentle curves that today's Trail Ridge Road (U.S. 36) traverses. The traveler on this highway also sees the sharper and steeper peaks and valleys carved out of the curves by the Pleistocene ice ages between five hundred thousand and ten thousand years ago. Today these mountains stand waist deep in their own tailings, like a candle burned halfway down into its own melting wax. The unthinkable tonnage of rocks and gravel and grit so speedily removed by the glaciers ended up as the surface of the High Plains, carried hundreds of miles by giant braided streams of which the Platte River is a younger and poorer sample.[8] These sediments covered the rolling hills of Roger Trescott's Permian red rock.

The Panhandle country was nudged upward by the same uplift of the Rocky Mountains. It also received a slight tilt of fifteen to twenty feet per mile eastward as the Gulf Coast area began its modern sinking. The Oklahoma Panhandle is midway along the gradual slope of debris running eastward from the Rocky Mountains. Topographic maps of the Trescotts' land show its highest point at 3,239 feet and never less than 3,150 feet. The Trescotts' surface terrain is not ocean-bed material like the red rock and limestone below but came from nonmarine outwash debris. In the last million Quarternary years, the Trescotts' land, from Permian red bedrock to surface soils, began to take on recognizable shape and quality. If Roger Trescott could take a colossal shovel and scrape off the most recent layers from his farm down to three hundred feet or so, he would stand on gently rolling redrock country that had been wearing down for millennia, just as all the other beds of rock, many long gone, had done before it. The oldest rocks under the debris were Permian red bedrock dating back to the watery deposits of broad, shallow, brackish seas 240 million years ago or more. Missing Triassic and Jurassic rocks signal tens of millions of years of rock removal until shallow seas encroached again a hundred million years later and lasted until about 96 million years ago. But the Trescott farm has no sign of the latter shallow seas as does Phil and Linda Tooms's Mesozoic place forty five miles to the north in Kansas. The Trescotts are Permian people.

Today's long-standing geological trend on the High Plains—steady wearing down of steadily rising mountains—became clear about five million years ago near the end of the Miocene times. The region's grassland would have been recognizable if we were crossing it today. Between five million and two million years ago, the climate again cycled cooler and drier in a global trend intensified by the rain shadow of the uplifting Rockies.[9]

The rocks, gravels, sands, soils, and water that arrived at Roger and Betty Trescott's future property were a hash of the Earth's entire multibillion-year geologic story. With the Ogallala rock and gravel came the water, or, more accurately, water was a major carrier of debris from the mountains. The flow eastward must have been spectacular in glacial times as it carried away the melting ice and snow with their gravelly burden. Airplane passengers today can still see the miles-wide flow pattern in the vast floodplains of the Platte River system. But the massive flow of water that had already created the Ogallala formation and kept it full was later—thousands of years ago—captured and diverted south by a recent geologic incident: the appearance of two rivers: the southward-flowing Rio Grande and Pecos.[10] What remains in the Ogallala formation is mostly fossil water drawn from the Rockies long ago. There is no massive and perpetual recharge (today it is a paltry inch-a-year trickle down) as was true for most of recent geological history.[11] The High Plains aquifer is like a flat, sandy beach where the tide has recently gone out; no new water comes in at the upper (western) end, yet it is naturally draining out the lower (eastern) end directly into streams and springs. Nevertheless, the scale of water originally held in the Ogallala formation is almost beyond reckoning: over three billion acre-feet (9.78 trillion gallons) under 174,000 square miles in gravel beds up to three hundred feet thick, moving east on an average of a foot a day.

22

All this geologic history tells us that the Panhandle country is a very changeable place. The top hundred feet or so of Roger and Betty Trescott's land also came from somewhere else. Some was rock and gravel from glacial times, but chewed up several times over by rivers as they moved it from place to place. Other parts came with the wind, either in vast moving dunes or simply blown there during several centuries of recurring dust bowls.

The Tooms Land

Forty-five miles north by northeast from the Trescott farm in Oklahoma is the three thousand-acre farm of Phil and Linda Tooms. They live in the northwest corner of Seward County, Kansas, on the western bank of the now-intermittent Cimarron River. When he drilled his first well in 1965, Phil Tooms reached his red bed at 465 feet. His share of the Ogallala wet gravels, as they filled in and leveled off the ancient hills and valleys, is about 250 feet thick. This is topped by about 215 feet of young mountain debris imported by water or wind during the Quaternary or Pleistocene ice age. Hence Tooms's farmstead stands at 2,750 feet above sea level, while his solid-rock red bed is at 2,285 feet.

The story of the Tooms's land is mostly similar to the Trescott account. It is made up of the scant remains of discontinuous seabed layers and leftover scraps of the Rocky Mountains, the rest still dribbling east toward the Mississippi and the Gulf of Mexico.[12] But about a mile south of Phil Tooms's house and farm and 2,400 feet underground, the Trescotts' 230-million-year-old Permian red seabed slips down northward at the rate of 15.4 feet per mile uncomfortably (layers of rock are missing) underneath an upper Jurasic–lower Cretaceous red bed that is a mere 135 million years old. Ninety-five million years of Triassic and Jurassic seabed has disappeared downhill and east into Oklahoma, Missouri, Louisiana, and underwater.

Phil Tooms is lucky when it comes to water in the Ogallala.[13] His land is smack-dab in the middle of a U–shaped rock structure thirty-seven miles southeast of the Bear Creek Fault and thirty-four miles west of the Crooked Creek–Fowler Fault. Over tens of thousands of years, a seventy-mile-wide stretch of rock running northeast to southwest was undermined by salt dissolution and collapsed into itself. Today the groundwater sits in a large seventy-mile-wide covered bathtub with the cover tilted southeast about 12.5 feet per mile. But the tub is not simply full of water; its bottom and lower sides are the red bedrock lying 465 feet deep on the Tooms farm, and it has been filled with 250 feet of unconsolidated silt, clay, sand, gravel, and caliche aquifer set down by Pliocene, Pleistocene, and Quarternary braided streams across an ancient floodplain before being covered by a lid of wind-blown modern soil.

Climate

When the emerging High Plains began their most recent rise above the inland sea, no great mountain barriers to the west shut off the flow of moisture-laden winds from the nearby intruding Pacific Ocean. The most fleeting migrant moving west to east across the plains was another fluid, in this case damp air. The water was picked up from the prehistoric Pacific shore only halfway as far west then as it is today: about where today's Colorado-Utah border is. Ten to five million years ago, when it was not under water, the vast American center from South Dakota to Texas was a moist, low-lying semi-tropical region with heavy vegetation, perhaps with valley forests and hilltop shrubs similar to today's neighborhoods around San Antonio, Texas, and Monterrey, Mexico.[14] The region is likely to become fecund again in the geologic future. In due time, the ancestral Rocky Mountains intervened to cut off rainfall to make the region as dry or drier than it is today. Today the High Plains stand under this rain shadow that forces clouds to give up their burden two hundred miles farther west than in earlier geologic time. The decade of rains in the 1880s that fooled so many aspiring settlers was not a promise of immediate change.

A worldwide cooling, begun a little more than a million years ago and still in process until a century ago, brought more arid and more contrasting climates than those of today. Dust storms raged across the plains as they had in every dry phase, becoming the major movers of today's rich loess soil. The landscape may have been as harsh as the modern drifting dunelands of Africa and Asia. The droughts and dust bowls that cycled in the recorded history of white explorers and settlers in the nineteenth and twentieth centuries

24

are but phases in a longer history. Scientists who contribute their days and nights to poring over prehistoric and historic tree rings, wide for wet times, narrow for dry, tell us that twenty-two-year cycles of dry and wet times can be discerned, seemingly associated with fairly regular sunspot incidents. Short term or long, the High Plains have not been a good place for man or animal for tens of thousands of years if the prehistoric records of animal de-population and the historic human depopulations are any indication. There were no permanent American Indian settlements in the Dust Bowl region. No doubt the immediate human future will see more droughts and blowing soils. The greenhouse effect, the human-induced warming caused by carbon dioxide released into the atmosphere from two hundred years of industrial coal burning, may quickly skew the data (see chapter 8). No doubt, on a geo-logical time scale, the wet climate will return, together with the rising inland seas, but today's thousand-year pattern points toward continued and increas-ing dryness.

Through all this the vast waters of the Ogallala aquifer waited under-ground, unknown and untapped, inexorably trickling eastward, surfacing occasionally in eastward-dipping riverbeds, then disappearing again, unre-plenished and hardly consumed.

Soil: Ecological Capital and Albrecht's Dilemma

The great modern naturalist Loren C. Eiseley said the greatest magic on this planet is the wonder of water. Together with Earth's other magnificent fluid, the atmosphere, water is valued because it is extremely interactive. It makes living things happen. On the High Plains, water's work is to make the good soil spring to life. In turn, soil is complex and dynamic, and, fortunately for us humans, it is extremely interactive with the plants that must feed upon it. Soil is potent, always in motion, as soil scientist William A. Albrecht stated so eloquently in the epigram at the beginning of this chapter, a vigorous and flowing medium ready to be used by wild grasses or set to the plow for wheat or sorghum. The irony of soil is its fluidity.[15] It is predestined to flow eventu-ally to rivers and the sea just as much as the rocks inevitably broke from mountains to become soil.

25

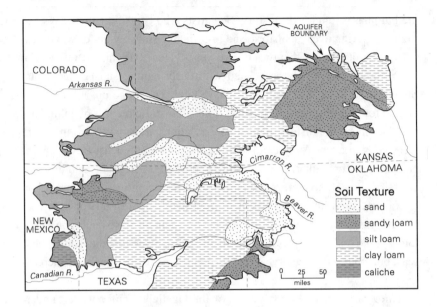

2. The soil types overlying the Ogallala aquifer of the central High Plains range mostly from sand to clay in southwest Kansas and the Oklahoma-Texas Panhandle. With irrigation, they proved to be some of the most productive in the nation. Redrawn from Richard R. Luckey, Edwin D. Gutentag, Frederick J. Deimes, and John B. Weeks, *Digital Simulation of Ground-Water Flow in the High Plains Aquifer in Parts of Colorado, Nebraska, New Mexico, Oklahoma, South Dakota, Texas, and Wyoming: Regional Aquifer-System Analysis,* USGS Professional Paper 1400-D (Washington, D.C.: Government Printing Office, 1986), 28.

What turns High Plains soil into good farmer's soil is a miraculous ecological balance between the right chemical salts and the presence of the right amount of water. Calcium, magnesium, potassium, sodium, and hydrogen, as well as nitrate and phosphate, in the top six to eighteen inches of the ground, mixed with the right amount of moisture, are necessary for the electrochemical exchanges between the roots of plants and ingredients in the soil. All the grains, every seed, and every morsel of the fruits and vegetables we consume depend on these exchanges. As a secondary result, we also can have meat to eat—beef, lamb, pork, chicken—because animals consume the plants, many inedible for humans. Animal and human survival depends on the ionization that makes the plants grow.

Root hairs, like the ones the weekend gardener sees in transplanting his tomatoes or her azalea, are enveloped in hydrogen carbonate. Hydrogen is a hyperactive element, and the solid nutrients, in the form of salts, are acquired by the plant in the hydrogen exchange between soil and root. The higher the concentration of chemical dynamics in the soil, the larger and better the crops. This is what makes Roger and Betty Trescott's soil into a world-class dirt—Richfield sandy loam—so prized that it commands the highest prices in Oklahoma's Texas County. The balance is delicate; if the soil lacks the nutrients or has too many salts or if moisture is too high or too low, plant growth is limited, as in the worn-out lands of Appalachia, or virtually nonexistent, as in Nevada's Great Basin.

An enduring soil has consistently offered each human civilization its long-term security, its ecological capital, which deserves to be reinvested rather than squandered. Good life-giving soil maintains a proper physio-chemical-electrical balance. The old phrase "salt of the earth" turns out to be remarkably appropriate.

In the broad sweep of human history, the closest approximation to an enduring artificial farm soil created by agricultural tillage is that now covering the great plain of western and northern Europe. Pioneering soil historian Edward Hyams called it "the perfect artificial soil."[16] It models the desirable combination of fertility and stability. In contrast to the insane devouring of North American soils over the last fifty years, European agricultural land advantageously emerged slowly from forest to farm over seven or eight thousand years. European society was largely an agrarian culture for most of its history and did not change until the last two hundred years. The heavy demands of rapid population growth, industrialization, and urbanization are recent happenings when measured by the millennia of a soil-making time scale. Elsewhere on the globe, the long-term results of grassland farming have not been good if the debilitation of China's wind-blown loess, the soil mining in India's history, and the shift from fertility to badlands across the Near East are representative. The quest for new virgin soils under the tropical forests of Brazil is a failure. Speaking of white European settlement on Oklahoma's soils, Hyams argued that in the United States fertility and stabil-

27

ity in the land were sacrificed to the American commitment to individual freedom (for example, private property) at all costs.[17] In Europe, by contrast, local geology, climate, technology, and social systems merged to create an ideal cultural balance which coddled the soil instead of the individual.

Unlike hydrogen, nitrogen is underactive. It does not easily combine with other elements for plants to absorb through their roots. Yet nitrogen is essential to every family of living things on earth. How is this riddle solved? How is nitrogen, which exists in the atmosphere, acquired by plants? The process is called nitrogen fixing.

Nitrogen fixing became even more mystifying when in 1837 a French chemist named Boussingault discovered that the soil of a field planted in clover, a legume, actually gained in nitrogen while a nearby wheat field showed no such gain. Somehow, it seemed, clover and other legumes took nitrogen from the air. Later in the century, in 1889, a Dutch scientist discovered that the strange nodules, called warts or galls, on the roots of legumes, such as beans, peas, and clover, were filled with millions of bacteria. The plants gave bacteria their energy through carbohydrates; the bacteria in turn captured nitrogen from the air and made it available to the plant. Once captured by the bacteria, the nitrogen took the form of nitrates, which plants captured chemically and converted into proteins. These proteins in turn were consumed by animals and humans. Usually one strain of bacteria to one plant did the job. It was a symbiotic relationship, since neither plant nor bacteria alone could achieve nitrogen fixation. Of the importance of nitrogen fixing, Peter Farb wrote in 1959: "Should some calamity overtake these bacteria, or a sudden change occur in the environment of the planet, that their numbers might be so seriously reduced . . . [the event would] collapse our superstructure of life, which is hinged to the nitrogen fixed by these microbes."[18]

Humanity's utter dependence upon the thin layer of rocky debris called soil is summed up in Albrecht's dilemma, so called after pioneering Missouri soil scientist William A. Albrecht. In order to feed himself, man intervenes in nature by plowing up virgin soil, planting crops which produce more useful food than would naturally grow on the land, but in the process he speeds up the depletion of nutrients from the soil with high levels of mineral solutions to feed his plants. The brief geologic moment of productive soil, "a temporary interlude for rocks and minerals on their way to solution and to the sea," is dangerously hastened by necessary human interference. On the High Plains, today's soil and wind erosion matches or surpasses the horrific Dust Bowl years.

A significant part of the soil above the Ogallala aquifer is windblown dust, or loess mantle, blown to the High Plains for the past million years from the crumbling rock of the Rocky Mountains by incessant strong winds. Dust storms are hardly a new phenomenon, nor are they entirely man made by poor land management. Over several thousand years, countless dust bowls of transitory loess deposited the incredibly rich clay soil so prized by nineteenth- and twentieth-century pioneers and immigrants. Today it commands premium farmland prices. Such soil has been named chernozem, a Russian word for black or dark brown earth (*chernyi* means a dark brown or black color), and by implication a rich and fertile substance. In contrast, forest soils, with their underlayer of gray, are called podzols, from the Russian *pod zola,* for ashes. Soil science got its start among observant peasants in Ukraine.

The American chernozem is the best in the world: early plains settlers who abandoned worn-out eastern forest farmland marveled that such soil still existed and that there was so much of it. Tradition told settlers that only forest soils were worthwhile. Hence tales of a new cornucopia of abundance captured from the plains soils reached incredulous ears; the notion that plains soil was unbeatable cannot be overestimated for its impact on American and world history. Even as early as 1673 explorer and missionary Louis Joliet exclaimed, "At first, when we were told of these treeless lands, I imagined that it was a country ravaged by fire, where the soil was so poor that it could produce nothing. But we have certainly observed the contrary; and no better soil can be found, either for corn, or for vines, or for any other fruit whatever. . . . Sometimes we saw grass . . . five or six feet high; hemp, which grows naturally here, reaches a height of eight feet. A settler would not there spend ten years in cutting down and burning the trees; on the very day of his arrival, he could put his plough into the ground."

Man cannot live by pulverized rocks alone. The soil that produces our food is more than an inanimate matrix of rocks and minerals; it is an organic living entity: bacteria, fungi, and microbes on one scale, insects, roots, the all-important earthworm, and such animals as the mole on a larger scale. A good little-bluestem acre on the arid Great Plains includes two and one-half tons of plant material in the first six inches of soil. The roots absorb the nitrates and other mineral compounds, absorb soil matter, and hold the plant in place. Farmers quickly learned not to cut their bluestem less than four inches above the surface, nor to allow their animals to graze it down excessively, or the underground sod would suffer, since the above-ground growth produced the sugars and starches the roots needed. The dense roots of quality bluestem withstand drought and can carry cattle through dry spells and winter. Prairie sod is a final synthesis of the entire plantscape; it is the great compromise between parent material, slope, climate, and previous plant life.

While many soils are created over a long time by the forces of climate and vegetation, in Texas County, Oklahoma, Roger and Betty Trescott's soil came during the Pleistocene as a thin mantle that combined silt and fine-textured sand (loess) brought by wind. It built up very gradually into virgin sod under native shortgrasses, taking much more time than in a moist climate. This mature soil is named Richfield sandy loam after its type area near Richfield in Morton County, Kansas.[19] It covers about 10 percent of Texas County, is listed among the most productive soils in the county, and commands premium prices on the local land market. A deep, dark, clayey soil, it is now about six inches thick and was less affected by Dust Bowl windstorms because of its medium texture. Sandier soils blew away faster and to greater depths. But almost eighty years of off-and-on cultivation has burned up a good deal of the fertility of the virgin sod.

It was easy to lose the advantage of virgin soil. When first plowed in the second decade of the twentieth century, virgin soil in Texas County sometimes yielded seventy-five bushels of wheat per acre, but by 1933, only twenty years later, 95 percent of the county's wheat land was abandoned under the pressures of soil depletion, drought, and depression. In 1961 it would average only eight bushels under typical dryland farming, but irrigation would revitalize production. When many of today's old-time irrigators began watering in 1961, wheat yields rose to 45 bushels per acre and grain sorghum yielded from 3,300 to 6,000 pounds per acre, depending on "common management" or "improved management."[20] Irrigation today also allows between 3.5 and 6 tons of alfalfa, which cannot be grown dryland.

Richfield sandy loam is Soil Conservation Service (scs) Class III soil, superior for a region with little rain and significant wind erosion. (Classes I and II are more productive, but because of climate conditions they do not exist in Texas County.) According to national scs standards, Class IIIs are "soils that have severe limitations that reduce the choice of plants, or that require special conservation practices, or both." Without irrigation, Richfield sandy loam can grow dryland wheat and, when the rains are good, sorghum. Central plains farmers, when they can pause to look and read, are told in their soil-survey manuals that

these soils need to be protected by a growing crop or a heavy stubble to help control wind erosion. . . . Use a cropping system that fits the moisture conditions. Fallow 1/4 to 1/3 of the field. . . . Wheat is likely to fail if it is sown in soil that is moist to a depth of less than 24 inches. Delay tilling fields that have been left fallow, until the danger of soil blowing has passed in spring. . . . Strip-cropping will help to reduce wind erosion, and the stubble will help conserve moisture by catching snow. Avoid excessive tillage and tillage that will leave the surface soil loose and powdery.[21]

Farmers are reminded that their use and management of the soil hinges on the realities of High Plains climate: low rainfall, strong winds, high temperatures in the summer, and low humidity. If the rains come late in spring, they are right for planting sorghum but too late to help wheat mature. Rains late in summer are good for planting wheat but too late to save a sorghum crop. In late winter and early spring, strong winds rip and tear at the soil and it must be protected. In summer, hot winds and low humidity bring high rates of evaporation.

Farmers also know that water is the key to successful farming. Immediately underneath the Panhandle topsoil is a dark grayish-brown compacted clay that is six to twenty inches thick. It advantageously stores large quantities of water. The 1961 edition of *Soil Survey of Texas County, Oklahoma* said few farmers "have access to an ample supply of [irrigation] water and have enough time and money to irrigate all of their land."[22] It added: "Farmers cannot control the weather, but they can adjust their farming methods to protect the soil from extremes of climate, to keep moisture in the soil" to depths at planting time between two and four feet. The 1961 techniques included crop residue (leaving crop debris on fields), stubble mulching, delayed fallow, strip-cropping, terracing, and contour farming. Farmers were warned that if there was not enough cover to protect the soil from wind and water erosion, emergency tilling, or roughening the surface with chisels, shovels, or listers, could provide quick protection, "but it does not provide long-term benefits. It dries the soil and breaks down its structure." Nothing was, or is, easy or clear cut on the plains.

There is the story of the plains farmer who, on being congratulated for a banner crop, grumbled, "Yes, but look what it did to the soil." He was all too aware that his equipment, interest on his outstanding loans, his house, barn, and outbuildings, his own living costs, and any crop profit for the year were paid out of his soil fertility and that it had limited capital. The fertile loess soil of the arid grassland, he knew, was originally so healthy as to continue almost indefinitely, but any farmer working the land every season spends a little more of this capital that is locked up in the thousands-year-old soil.

Albrecht's dilemma is at bottom an ethical paradox in both human and environmental terms. It is the conflict between the inevitability of soil destruction by farming and the imperative of soil construction to ensure continued food for a hungry world. At risk is the well-being of future generations.

When the newly arrived plains farmer hitched his newfangled lightweight John Deere polished-metal shear plow to his horses or oxen and sliced into the virgin sod to plant, cultivate, and harvest his corn or wheat, the soil took on a particularly granular body. If he was on quality land, the farmer judged its potential productivity when, in Albrecht's words, "he took a handful of soil, allowed it to run between his fingers, and said, 'This will be a good place to farm.'" The granular soil does not pack down but allows air and water to percolate through it; the microbes, bacteria, nitrogen, and carbon dioxide work more freely. Rainwater (and later irrigation water) does not run off immediately but filters into the soil, which in turn holds the all-important moisture. Even moderate drought can be endured by crops if water is stowed in porous soil.

Paradoxically, this mechanical shaping of granular soil, with all its physical and chemical benefits, also means that soil is vulnerable. Heavy rainfall pounds it into a gummy slush that quickly closes off further penetration of water. Additional water runs off, erodes the fertile surface soil, and carries it away. Both water and soil are lost in the breakdown of soil body. The effect includes chemical changes as well, since some salts—calcium and magnesium—encourage granulation, while hydrogen, sodium, potassium, and other salts encourage the goo. Farming the land, which increases the carbon dioxide and acidity levels, also encourages the making of goo rather than granules. The soil shifts from being physically stable to being unstable. Water does not seep in and stay; instead, it quickly erodes the soil. When soil loses its fine physique, it also loses the physical environment that allows the all-important chemical and mineral feeding of the plants that are grown in it.

Grasses

Little is left today of the lonely immensity that unnerved the first Europeans. High Plains space is still vast, but now it includes eye-catching markers: farm buildings and geometric fields; roads that run to a vanishing point in infinity; and the ubiquitous grain elevator in towns fourteen miles apart, because that was the round trip a farmer could make to town with a loaded wagon. The monotony that travelers see on the plains is in fact dispelled by the variety, colors, sizes, and shapes of the original tallgrass, midgrass, and shortgrass prairie.[23] The best time is early morning, although boots and jeans get soaked wading through the wet dew of the hip-high plants. Even the multiplicity of names, often for the same plant, provide a surprisingly diverse and pleasantly Middle American lexicography: ripgut grass, scarlet globe mallow, rubber rabbitbrush, blazing star, ironweed, puccoon, beardtongue, chickweed, blue grama, fescue, gumweed, red three-awn, spiderwort, phlox, prairie shoestring, big-leaf pussytoes, threadleaf sedge, silky sophora, fringed sagebrush, broom snakeweed, butterweed, coneflowers, buffalo grass, poverty catgrass, witchgrass, sand dropseed, Johnny-jump-ups, skeleton plant, muhly, switchgrass, lovegrass, pinweed, poppy mallow, sloughgrass, tumblegrass, violet wood sorrel, yellow tansy mustard, greenthread, big and little bluestem, porcupine grass, sideoats grama, purple lovegrass, false boneset, curlycup, gumweed, needle and thread, skullcap, and woolly loco.

The best time of year to enjoy the prairie is late July and early August, not the spring flowering. The weather is hot and dry and the stems and leaves of the grasses such as big bluestem, have lengthened and outgrown early flowering forbs or nongrass prairie plants (broad-leaved herbs, such as prairie cat's foot and wildflowers). Where it has not been farmed, the land is like an organic kaleidoscope, a veritable flower garden, as the wind blows and the weeks pass. There are multiple layers competing for space and sun, soil and water. Against a luxurious silver-green background, the summer-blooming plants—larkspur, roses, coneflowers—are met in midsummer by the first yellow and golds of the autumn-blooming forbs: ironweed, gentian, asters, sunflowers, goldenrod. The midcontinent grasslands are so vast that one could follow this process for a thousand miles from south to north, east to west, depending on altitude, geography, and season.

Geography and altitude, together with rainfall, also bring a progressive change between grasses in the humid eastern prairie and the dry Great Plains. Where rainfall is thirty-five inches a year or more, tall grasses, such as big bluestem and the hardy sloughgrass, dominate, while very arid plains are covered by blue grama and buffalo grass. The tallgrass prairie extends to a roughly north-south line a hundred miles beyond the western borders of Minnesota, Iowa, and Missouri, with a westward finger going across two-thirds of Nebraska. There is a mixed-prairie zone of both tall and short grasses until one hits the line of twenty inches of rain or less and an altitude of fifteen hundred feet or higher, roughly along the ninety-seventh meridian, cutting the Dakotas and Kansas into east-west halves and marking the Texas-Oklahoma Panhandle as dry country. It is convenient to keep in mind these three zones: eastern tallgrass prairie, a broadly transitional midgrass zone, and the western shortgrass plains.[24] It is not entirely rainfall that controls these differences today; it may be overgrazing in the west, first by buffalo and later cattle. The zones shift over the years as well, the tall grasses working west during heavy rains, as in the 1880s, or retreating during the big and little dust bowls of the 1930s and 1950s. Presumably, the drought of the summer of 1988 began to force the tall grasses to retreat before the advance of the western shortgrass.

Learning to Read the Open Landscape:
The Meaning of Grassland

Often the first response of pioneer farmers to open prairie country was to look for something better. They believed that only forest soil was fertile enough to farm. From a world history perspective, America's High Plains delineate a "frontier of cultivation" similar to geographical lines in Europe, Africa, and Asia that go back to the earliest archeological records of Western civilization. There is a boundary between land successfully used for growing crops and land best used for grazing and hunting. The question, according to geographer William E. Riebsame, and which is reinforced by the earlier views of A. H. Clark and Paul Sears, is whether the plains was a region capable of supporting "the human creation of socially nurturing landscapes"[25] or a region too fragile for the extensive farming that European settlers needed to survive. Plains farmers worked closer to the margin of survival and resource sustainability than pioneers in more inviting regions. In the words of botanist John T. Curtis: "The plant members of the mid-latitude grasslands for the most part were of no direct use to man. Their main value comes after they have been converted to high-protein foods (by grazing animals)."[26] Two reasons that explain why the vast midcontinent grasses persisted under harsh natural conditions are now clear: many plants were perennials, unlike farm crops, and many plants grew from the base rather than the tip, allowing them to withstand grazing first by buffalo and later by cattle.

However, the first farmers, and farmers ever since, wanted to do more than graze cattle. They attempted to force the land to support the high yields of monoculture wheat and corn. Curtis goes on to say that "Retrogression leads to decreased stability and to disorganization of the community pattern. The environmental changes accompanying the decline are in the direction of more xeric, lighter, and more variable conditions."[27] The price of disturbing environments is enormous. When ecosystems are frequently disrupted and stressed, they begin to exhibit signs of chronic ecosystem illness: they become chaotic and unpredictable. By considering the extent to which human intervention has upset the self-regenerating capacities of the natural ecosystem, we can try to identify ways in which human participation in plains ecology can sustain itself.

Early explorers and settlers who left the protective forest shelter and moved onto the American prairie rarely mentioned the ocean of tall grasses even though of the big bluestem, prairie sloughgrass, switchgrass, and wild rye of the eastern prairie stood taller than a man and reached unremittingly to the horizon. The U.S. Army expedition led by John C. Frémont in 1842 ignored the tall grasses. It was preoccupied with sightings of occasional trees and shrubs—oaks, elms, cottonwoods, hickory—that signaled watercourses. They were also markers of the more familiar and benevolent forest world.[28] When early settlers ventured onto the open country, their priorities were to find water, get away from the interminable wind, and get out of the hot sun. They looked over and beyond the grasses for clusters of trees in the distance.

Settlers who found themselves on the exposed land would find many uses for thick, tall clumps of sloughgrass.[29] Tall enough to hide horses, cows, and buffalo, it dominated the wetter bottomland along river courses and in swampy areas of the gently rolling tallgrass prairie. This hearty prairie cordgrass spread by seed and by underground rhizomes to form a classic prairie sod, which was impervious to fire and cold. Sloughgrass quickly acquired the name ripgut grass because the coarse, four-foot-long leaves had razor-sharp edges that could lacerate bare arms and hands. Plains region Indians used the tangled sloughgrass as thatching that they would cover with earth and European settlers used it to cover haystacks and corncribs. As winter approached, the immigrants burned sloughgrass as a poor fuel substitute. According to an 1884 account, "Large wisps of this are twisted, doubled, and tied by hand, being thus brought into compact and convenient form for putting into the stove. One or two of these twisted bunches are supplied every five or ten minutes, and they maintain a hot fire and [are] serviceable as that of wood or coal. The amount of hay thus used in a year for heating in an ordinary room is from eight to twelve tons. An hour's time is sufficient for twisting up a winter day's supply of this fuel."[30]

Sloughgrass also made good hay. Mowing it two or three times a year encouraged rapid new growth and protected soil from erosion. However, the stems and leaves were so tough and so often tangled that pitchforking a stack of it required substantial strength, and it had to be cut from the stack with a hay-saw.

Even more important to the first settlers who struggled to establish themselves on the treeless land were the big bluestem communities that blanketed the eastern prairie for thousands of miles. Bluestem grew in large soddy clumps, taking over the top two feet of soil with roots that spread a dozen feet into the ground. It was also called turkeyfoot because its stalks, up to eight feet tall, usually branched into three parts. Farmers, particularly in the Flint Hills of Kansas and the eastern half of Oklahoma, learned to read big bluestem as a sign of prime, well-drained prairie bottomland soil. For forage, pioneer livestock preferred big bluestem over other grasses, and fortunately, its quality and quantity were unequaled. This grass became overgrazed or plowed out over most of its original range until farmers learned that saving the lower six or eight inches during cutting ensured fast regrowth and good ground cover.

Between the massive stands of sloughgrass in the wet areas and the big bluestem in the dry areas stood the sod-making switchgrass, with its broad stalks branching out three to six feet high. Switchgrass tolerates severe winters and hot summer droughts. It provided nutritious food for livestock as either green forage or prairie hay. Similar to switchgrass is Canada wild rye, also known as nodding wild rye because its seed heads curve downward from the upward-pointing stems. Wild rye is also valuable for livestock as long as it is harvested early to avoid ergot infestation.

Moving onto the upland mixed-grass prairies of western Oklahoma, Kan-

37

sas, Nebraska, and South Dakota, one enters the region of the great cattle drives of the 1870s and 1880s that extended from southern Texas to the Abilene, Ft. Dodge, and Atkinson railheads. This semiarid rangeland was little bluestem country. Little bluestem was equal in nutrition, abundance, and staying power to the larger midwestern big bluestem. Its bunches had dense root systems, and the seed stalks, which waved like peacock feathers in the wind, grew two to five feet high. It grew well on sandy, shallow, and rocky soil as well as deep sod. The cattle trails, therefore, provided an opportunity to fatten up the herds on the rich prairie grasses that were not available in the southern rangeland. Before European intrusion, little bluestem may have been the most abundant grass in the American heartland, and it is still the most useful in the Flint Hills of Kansas and in Oklahoma. Today, cattle are shipped from the South and Southwest to graze on this superior little bluestem. Successful grazing requires stubble of four to six inches; without this growth little bluestem would be wiped out and less productive plants would take over. It can be harvested by combines, yielding three-quarters of a ton to two tons an acre, and it has been successfully seeded on large areas of once-farmed but abandoned plains land.

Little bluestem is joined by sideoats grama, whose name derives from the rows of oatlike seeds that hang on only one side of the long stem. Eighteen to thirty-six inches high with short roots, it provides high-quality nutrition for animals even on the uplands, ridges, and rocky fields. When a range is abused, sideoats grama will replace taller grasses unless it is grazed closer than two to three inches. Sideoats grama is so easily artificially seeded that it is almost fail-safe. It is good for conservation of eroded land and can be nitrogen-fertilized for better production. A companion grass is prairie (puff-sheath) dropseed, whose seeds are recessed into the stems. Only three to twelve inches high and with shallow roots, this dropseed prospers in dry, sandy soil unless it is forced out by taller, denser grasses. More nutritious and grown in small bunches is porcupine grass, or needlegrass. At two to four feet tall, it provides good grazing for cattle, although during the seeding season the sharp pointed seeds can stick in their mouths.

West of the ninety-eighth meridian in arid western Oklahoma, Kansas, and Texas, where the rainfall decreases from twenty inches to twelve inches a year, is home to the shortgrass prairie.[31] Even under drought conditions, when mixed grasses were driven eastward, buffalo grass and blue grama remained to feed first millions of buffalo and later beef cattle. Though it reproduces only by seed, blue grama, whose erect bunches reach only ten to twenty inches high, withstands extreme drought and alkaline soils and grows rapidly under favorable conditions. As the seed heads mature, they usually bend into a curve resembling a human eyebrow. Found with blue grama is buffalo grass, which spreads through seeds and strong surface runners. Its height—usually less than five inches tall—helps to protect it and the blue grama from being overgrazed. Because of its excellent ground cover, aggressive spread under use, wide climate adaptation, and relatively quick establishment, buffalo grass is ideally suited for erosion control on ranges and pasture lands where the soil does not contain too much sand.

From Grasses to Food

Scientists worldwide have identified more than two hundred thousand flowering plants, or angiosperms, which make up nearly two-thirds of all species of plants. Of these, the family Gramineae grasses dominate large areas of the earth: plains, prairies, steppes, savannas, pampas, and paramos. Overall, the natural grassland is estimated to have seven hundred genera containing as many as ten thousand species. Fossil grasses have been identified from the Tertiary period, 65 million years ago, and High Plains grasses date from the early Miocene period, 26 million years ago, to the Pliocene period of open, dry plains, 2.5 million years ago. Before the spread of human agriculture and domesticated grazing animals, at least 30 percent of the earth's land surface was once natural grassland. Much of this area has been put into cultivation in monoculture crops that do not mimic the original and successful ecosystems. The extensive and dense root systems of the natural grasses were instrumental in developing fertile soils and enabled some of the most productive future cropland in the world.

Cereal grains provided the foundation for the evolution of humanity's domestic animals and very likely, for humanity itself. By about 3,000 B.C. all of the major cereals had been brought under cultivation, and not a single new, major crop has been introduced since. Two hundred species of grasses can be called domesticated, and a dozen or so stand between us and starvation, with wheat highest on the list, rice or corn second, and sorghums high on the list.[32] They are concentrated foods that give high yields, are relatively easy to collect, travel well, and may be stored for long periods of time. One scholarly axiom posits that "no advanced civilization can develop without cereal culture." Technological and scientific improvements still work with the same basic germ plasm to grow stronger plants with higher levels of resistance to diseases, insects, and drought and that are easier to harvest.[33]

Prospective settlers on the open grassland quickly learned to read the grasses for the type and quality of land that would be good for agriculture. Large stretches of big bluestem meant superior, well-watered soil, while nodding or Canada wild rye succeeded best on medium-texture soils. Wild rye was called a decreaser; it signaled the rise of less valuable plants along with a possible decline in land and range quality. Among the middle grasses, the little bluestem was too widespread to provide information about what lay under it, but sideoats grama was an increaser, as it indicated that the soil under it had potential. To newly arrived settlers sideoats gramma suggested good land that could be bought cheap and built up through proper management. Prairie dropgrass told of dry, sandy soil of little use to the farmer unless it was irrigated and fertilized at high cost. Weedy June grass (Japanese brome, a foreigner or "exotic") signaled badly abused land in very poor condition—"don't buy it even if the price seems right!" Buffalo grass sent different messages depending on the environment. When found on middle or mixed-grass prairie land, it pointed out overgrazed but good land that still had farming potential. Dominant on the arid Great Plains, it showed good pasture lands that were not too sandy. Blue grama, the companion to buffalo grass, was often deceptive. It was an important increaser that could help mend abused or overgrazed land, but it also masked high-drought regions or alkaline soil because it can survive both.

Domesticated food grains have the same forms, soil needs, and climate demands as the native grasses; one only had to learn what matched what.[34] Only the species have changed, although the critical differences between perennial native grasses and annual domesticated grains that cause dramatic changes on the plains and threaten its sustainability are not always clearly understood. The tallgrass prairie that was once sloughgrass and big bluestem was readily handed over to their tall counterparts—corn and soft winter wheat. Mixed prairie of little bluestem and sideoats grama was transformed into fields of hard winter wheat and dryland grain sorghums. The shortgrass plains were turned into fields of hard winter wheat and some sorghums. Where the buffalo once roamed, soon cattle grazed on the blue grama and buffalo grass.

However, the exchange was far from equal. The original grasses, in all their variety, lived in a symbiotic balance even as plant domination ebbed and flowed. In spite of fire, climate fluctuations, animal grazing, and low-level Native American interference, the grassland would have continued indefinitely. The challenge to the European settlers who sought to reconstruct the grassland into a productive agricultural region was to devise another version of environmental health, including the capacity to produce a range of desirable surplus crops for markets, sustain a satisfying life for a growing human population, and have the staying power to endure the swings of a world economy. Whether these expectations could be fulfilled within the constraints of the arid environment, or whether both the environment and its people would be endangered is the ongoing dilemma being played out in the history of the Ogallala region.

The human need for wheat, corn, and grain sorghums that are processed into starches, oils, and proteins served to justify the difficult settlement of the plains by skilled farmers and still justifies the extraordinary effort to keep it in production. Early hunters on the plains required ten to fifteen square miles of land to feed themselves, but when cultivated the same area of land can feed five thousand people. The cereals grown in this region are rich with carbohydrates and protein. Cereals are significantly less expensive—as much as ten times cheaper—to produce than meats, if we consider the costs of land and water consumption. Of every ton of corn that Americans produce, 93 percent goes to feed a steer, hog, or chicken. Nevertheless, cereal grains form the primary foodstuffs for much of the world's poor.

Wheat, corn, and sorghums have been successfully mechanized and hybridized, and each has a major role in fueling the prosperity of a nation in which less than 2 percent of the population work are farmowners and in which one farmer has the capacity to feed six dozen others. This agricultural success story is so remarkable that it became a global model. Some argue that the success story became skewed when high yields resulted in huge surpluses and low prices, an end that works against the best interest of the family farm, to which productivity is not the solitary objective.

Wheat

Wheat can be grown in a wide range of climatic conditions. It is cultivated from the southernmost regions of South America to near the Arctic and thrives at elevations from sea level to over ten thousand feet. It adjusts to forty inches of rainfall in a growing season to ten inches. The remarkable flexibility of wheat allows for winter varieties to be planted in the fall and harvested in the spring, and for spring varieties to be planted in the spring and harvested in late summer. Most plains wheats are *Triticum vulgare (aestivum)*, a hard wheat used to produce flour for bread-making, and *Triticum durum*, a longer and narrower grain that provides the foundation for pastas. The hard red spring wheats are famous for possessing a high quantity of protein—12 to 15 percent—compared to the soft wheats of Britain, Europe, and Australia. The winter varieties often yield more bushels per acre, but such high-yield wheats often produce flour of poor baking quality.[35]

James C. Malin, historian, naturalist, and plains veteran, concludes that the excessive hardships encountered by settlers between the 1880s and the Dust Bowl era were partly the settlers' own doing because they could not adjust to an agricultural system without corn or soft wheat. Only belatedly and reluctantly did plains farmers turn to hard, or durum, wheats, after they were introduced to a specialized import, Ukrainian winter wheat, which prospered in a climate with limited water.[36] Wheat production was also revolutionized on the plains not only by John Deere's steel shear plow, the mechanized tractor, and chemicals, but also by harvesting. McCormick's mechanical reaper replaced the sickle, scythe, and cradle by mid-century. The modern combine harvester came into widespread use on the plains in the

1920s and 1930s. The self-propelled combine in 1940 cut the standing wheat grasses, threshed the grain from the straw and chaff, cleaned the grain, and discharged it into bags or grain reservoirs. The results were dramatic reductions in harvesting time and labor: in 1829 fourteen hours of labor were necessary to harvest one acre of wheat, but the modern combine harvests an acre in less than thirty minutes. Harvesting one bushel of wheat required three labor hours in 1829; today it takes five minutes. Wheat yields rose from 12.9 bushels (each weighing about sixty pounds, or twenty-seven kilograms) per acre in the mid-1930s to 32.7 bushels in the early 1970s.

Corn (Maize)

Water-hungry and cold-vulnerable corn is the least adaptable to the plains climate, while the most adaptable is either wheat or the sorghums. Corn, which is called maize in the rest of the world, is a larger grain than wheat and very different. It is planted not by broadcasting or spreading of seeds across the ground, but by planting individual grains, which is more labor-intensive. Corn scientist Paul Mangelsdorf wrote that "the maize plant was the bridge over which English civilization crept, tremblingly and uncertainly at first, then boldly and surely, to a foothold and a permanent occupation of America," first at Jamestown and Plymouth and eventually as the primary food of settlers who invaded the Midwest and West.[37] Swedish naturalist Peter Kalm was so impressed by the productivity of corn—principally by the high ratio between seeds harvested and seeds sown—that he called it "the lazy man's grain."[38] The problem was that corn, which needed water, would not grow easily west of the tallgrass prairie. This inability to grow corn and other accustomed crops prevented, at first, European settlement on the plains. Ironically, decades later, corn would be the crop of choice for the newly successful plains irrigators of the 1960s.

Margaret Visser, in her entertaining history of the American dinner table, describes how, with the exception of fresh fish, it is difficult to buy a product in a supermarket that has not been touched by corn.[39] White, odorless, tasteless, and easily molded, cornstarch is used in a long list of foods including baby foods, jams, yeast, baking powder, instant potato flakes, and dog food.

It colors soft drinks and tenderizes chewing gum. It coats paper products and is the neutral carrier for the active ingredients in headache tablets, tooth-paste, and cosmetics. Corn oil appears in cooking, mayonnaise, salad dress-ings, margarine, and MSG. Corn syrup is an almost universally listed ingre-dient in candy, ketchup, ice cream, processed meats, and wherever else shelf life needs to be long. Corn is also contained in automobile paint, gunpowder, insecticides, embalming fluid, hydraulic brake fluid, fireworks, and, of all things, agricultural poisons. Corn liquor helped shape American frontier history. Irvin S. Cobb wrote that corn whiskey "smells like gangrene start-ing in a mildewed silo, it tastes like the wrath to come, and when you absorb a deep swig of it you have all the sensations of having swallowed a lighted kerosene lamp. A sudden, violent jolt of it has been known to stop the vic-tim's watch, snap his suspenders, and crack his glass eye right across."[40] If we include the corn used to feed animals, Americans consume three pounds of corn per person per day. Still, maize is a badly balanced protein; it has led to pellagra, a deficiency disease caused by a shortage of the vitamin niacin.

Early in the twentieth century, hybridization changed corn from a wild grass to the "happy monster" of human genetic engineering. It became not only more productive and consistent, but more resistant to dwarf and streak viruses, ear worms, rootworms, and stalk borers. The ideal corn plant, ac-cording to Norman E. Borlaug, who won the 1970 Nobel Peace Prize for his controversial "green revolution," would be six feet tall, disease-proof, in-sect-proof, and drought-proof. Today corn rarely grows in the wild; the small number of hybrids instigated the onslaught of southern-corn-leaf blight that wiped out 15 percent of the nation's crop in 1970 at a cost of a bil-lion dollars. Scientist Walton Galinat concluded that unless genetic vari-ability is treasured and carefully preserved, "we and our mutually symbiotic food plants may vanish like the dodo."[41] By yield, hybrid corn became America's most important crop plant. By the 1980s seeds were bred to be productive and consistent, but also dependent on fertilizers, pesticides, and herbicides. After World War II, hybrids, which once accounted for 10 per-cent of farm-grown corn, began to dominate the corn belt from western Ohio to eastern Kansas and Nebraska. New hybrid-corn seed must be purchased each spring planting season, for the seeds saved from one year's crop lose much of the vigor and uniformity found in the original hybrids. The production of hybrid-corn seed has thus become big business in the United States. Since the 1930s, farmers have had to depend on outside sources for seed, a change that increased their economic connection to suppliers, bankers, markets, and government regulations.

Sorghum

Upon seeing a field of sorghum, uninitiated city dwellers, with no experience on a farm, may at first think it is another cornfield, but upon closer examination they would see that the leaves and stalks are quite different. The stalks are flower clusters of varying density, containing eight hundred to three thousand kernels. Grain sorghums of varieties like milo, kafir corn, Sudan grass, and millet probably originated in Africa. Its starchy seeds are edible and are consumed in porridge and flatbreads by people in Africa and India, and as sweet sorghum, edible oil, starch, dextrose, paste, and alcoholic beverages in the United States. Some sorghums are used to make hay, brooms, and brushes. Most sorghums in the United States are grown for animal fodder as feed grain or silage or on pastureland. Sorghums are high in carbohydrates, and they are an important source of protein and fats. Widely used on the plains because they are heat-resistant and drought-resistant, they also thrive in the subhumid climate of center-pivot irrigation.

Soybeans

Unlike wheat, corn, and the sorghums, which are cereals, soybeans (*Glycine max*) are legumes that function differently in the soil and as a food and that are used for widely diverse products. Plains farmers find soybeans appropriate because they are highly productive, offer high resistance to drought, and enjoy widespread markets. They prosper on nearly all types of soils found on the plains, from high, fertile, deep soils to sandy loams. Further, soybeans are exceptional rotation or alternative crops to cereals because they are nitrogen-fixing. Soybeans are becoming highly marketable because they provide proteins whose amino acids are more like animal proteins than vegetable

45

proteins. They are also a good source of thiamin and riboflavin. On the other hand, their carbohydrate content is low. Most soybean production in the United States is used for animal feed while elsewhere, as in Asia, they are consumed by humans. Americans consume soybeans in sweets, biscuits, infant foods, sausages, and mayonnaise and in nonfood products ranging from paint and paper to textiles and plastics. For many, they are a popular vegetable alternative to meat products. The United States along with Brazil and China are the leading producers of soybeans.

The Paradox of Farming: Sustaining the High Plains

Critics say that, in the long run, the transformation of the High Plains grassland into a bonanza of high-yield, chemically dependent, mechanized cropland is badly flawed, the result of poor information and misunderstandings about the ecology of the plains. The industrialized plains cannot endure without costly outside help. There is little connection, they say, between the conservation (sustainability) of unique plains resources, such as quality soil on flat land and bountiful groundwater, versus the pressures of commodity markets. The move from prairie diversity to monoculture fields stocked with wheat, milo, or corn—and narrowly specialized versions of each—has been made in ignorance, or disregard for, the first rule of ecology that diversity brings health while simplicity results in death. Soil, plants, climate, and other natural forces, alone and together, generate the complexity of ecological health. In Wes Jackson's words, "To maintain the 'ever-normal' granary, the agricultural human's pull historically has been toward the monoculture of annuals. Nature's pull is toward a polyculture of perennials."[42]

Regional organizations, such as the Kansas Rural Center, believe that the mistakes that led to the Dust Bowl will continue to destroy the plains as a resource and farming as a desirable lifestyle. Wes Jackson's Land Institute in Salina, Kansas, is working simultaneously to return parts of the High Plains to the original prairie landscape and to create a sustainable natural food-producing agriculture from perennial plants. This is a challenging program to combine plains ecosystem health with an innovative sustainable and productive agriculture. Agricultural plantings of corn, wheat, rye, and sorghums last only a season. If a tract of plains farmland is abandoned, within months the weakened prairie soil begins to drift and erode as was true in the Dust Bowl years. Today's monoculture inevitably means ecological destabilization. The plains grassland had its own rational stability—a health different from the health of high-yield profitable industrial farming. The objective of the Land Institute is to both build a diverse agriculture that can prosper on the plains as the native grassland once did and to serve human food needs. Jackson argued in 1980 that plains farming, like farming everywhere since the beginning of the Agricultural Revolution twelve thousand years ago, destroys more than it builds and that nowhere is this more vivid than on the plains.[43]

But first, for a century after the earliest European settlements in the 1870s, farmers on the plains would work their fields in traditional ways, would fail as drought hit and the soil blew away, would learn to irrigate with scarce water, and would be persuaded to load their declining fields with chemicals.

2

. . .

Finding the Water: Boom and Bust,
1870–1940

From the 98th meridian west to the Rocky Mountains there is a stretch
of country whose history is filled with more tragedy and whose future is pregnant
with greater promise than perhaps any other equal expanse of territory
within the confines of the Western Hemisphere.—
Farm historian A. M. Simons in 1906

Extensive areas of the Great Plains . . . must be classed as unsuited
to sustained cultivated crops, and should therefore never have been plowed.—
National Resources Planning Board, Public Works Administration,
United States Department of the Interior, 1936

If the Atlantic coastline of North America had been dry prairie instead of an
extended forest, settlement might never have taken place. Europeans might
have contented themselves with fishing its shores. Ingrained Old World
opinion told them that treeless open land could not be turned into fertile
farmland. The best poor man's country was hewed from forest: no trees, no
crop. After the eastern forest land had been cleared and settled and Americans again looked westward, they were not happy with what they saw. The
midcontinent grasslands seemed no more than a worthless rangeland in the
distant western backcountry.[1] The plains stood primarily as the obstacle—
America's empty quarter—for migrants headed for garden spots in Oregon
and California.

48

"A Forever Dangerous and Useless Place, Deserving Only to be Passed By"

The plains were bad news from the first. When Coronado began his surprisingly deep venture below the Rio Grande and tramped as far north and east as the wild Kansas country in 1540, he reported that the ocean of grass had "no more landmarks than as if we had been swallowed up in the sea . . . because there was not a stone, nor a bit of rising ground, nor a tree, nor a shrub, nor anything to go by."[2] The expedition had to navigate by sun and stars as if it were on the open ocean. Coronado had difficulty finding water, and he found neither gold nor clues to a passage to Cathay; instead he was forced to halt for roaming herds of massive buffalo as awesome as the land itself. Five soldiers on Zaldivar's 1598 expedition deserted in panic when they entered the endless plains; they were more willing to risk capture by Indians than penetrate the lonely land.

Historic doubts continued. About 1787, James Monroe set the stage when he flatly told Thomas Jefferson that the entire United States west of the Appalachians was no bargain: "A great part of the territory is miserably poor [and] consists of extensive plains which have not had from appearances, and will not have, a single bush upon them for ages. . . . The districts therefore within which these fall will perhaps never contain a sufficient number of inhabitants to entitle them to membership in the Confederacy."[3] Based on experience in Europe, the British Isles, and east of the Appalachians, the only land worth farming was that hewn from forests. No wonder Jefferson concluded that it would take a hundred generations before Americans would settle the continent to the western sea. (The actual total would be fewer than five generations.) The plains were too remote and inaccessible, devoid of the major rivers that had opened up so many other American regions. One early advantage of this geography was that no attacking army could sustain itself to invade the weak United States at its vulnerable backside. Even with major logistical support, a large-scale military force would disappear into the vastness. However, Jefferson, always the optimist, rushed in 1803 to accept Napoleon's offer to sell the 830,000-square-mile Louisiana Purchase wasteland at fifteen million dollars—three cents an acre.

The problem was that the American grassland could not be compared with any part of western Europe, while the Atlantic coast was forested like Europe. Like the distant steppes of central Asia, the American grassland might as well have been a moonscape to the first European visitors. The visible scene was a minimalist landscape of unbounded grasses, the flat surrounding horizon, and the infinite sky; any human presence shrank into nothingness. In 1810, Lt. Zebulon M. Pike shaped American opinion about the nation's new western territory when he reported that "a barren soil, parched and dried up for eight months in the year, presents neither moisture nor nutrition sufficient to nourish the timber. These vast plains of the western hemisphere, may become in time equally celebrated as the sandy deserts of Africa."[4] In 1821, Major Stephen H. Long reported his unhappy passage through the same Great American Desert; the land was unfit for cultivation and hence uninhabitable by pioneer farmers. Edwin James, a botanist with Long, spoke of a landscape of "of hopeless and irreclaimable sterility."[5] He wondered how animals survived. Unrequited forest man Washington Irving wrote in horror when he crossed the prairie in the 1830s that "there is something inexpressibly lonely in the solitude of the prairie . . . an immense extent of landscape without a sign of human existence . . . the consciousness of being far, far beyond the bonds of human habitation; we feel as if moving in the midst of a desert world."[6] The experience of marching for days, never emerging from formlessness and void, never seeing an end to emptiness, depressed other early travelers, such as Francis Parkman, and filled them with foreboding. Charles Dickens, already displeased with his American travels in 1840, took an instant dislike to the open country. "Looking toward the setting sun, there lay stretched before my view a vast expanse of what scarcely amounted to a scratch upon the great plank . . . a few birds wheeling here and there, with solitudes and silence reigning paramount around . . . oppressive in its barren monotony."[7] As late as 1856, Joseph Henry, the influential secretary of the new Smithsonian Institution, concluded that "the whole space to the west, between the 98th meridian and the Rocky Mountains, denominated the Great American Plains, is a barren waste . . . a country of comparatively little value to the agriculturalist."[8] After the Civil War the military commander of the plains region, Gen. William Tecumseh Sherman, reported that western settlement reached its workable limits at the ninety-ninth meridian. "There began the Great Plains 600 [*sic*] miles wide, fit only for nomadic tribes of Indians, Tartars, or buffaloes."[9] Today, for the 98 percent of Americans who do not live and work on a farm, the great grassy flatness covering the thousand miles between Chicago and Denver on Interstate 80 seems interminable, with few scenic or picturesque stops. Today's travelers still conclude that it is a mediocre and commonplace zone between the cosmopolitan East and the spectacular Rocky Mountains.

So much for the High Plains grasslands, a land of uninhabitable extremes. Pioneers understandably shrank from the sun-baked, waterless flatlands. The incessant wind too often fanned raging prairie fires, and the same wind brought nerve-wracking summers and fierce winters. Nor was there wood for fuel, buildings, or fences. Even on the midwestern tallgrass prairie it would take decades to dispel doubts before settlers edged nervously onto the benign Illinois and Iowa prairies. There they would discover the world's best, deepest, and easiest-to-work chernozem soils. But the waterless High Plains region was not the well-watered midwestern prairie. Far-reaching pioneers who dared to think of settling on the plains did find good soil under the blanket of grass, but only with water could it be put to work. Water became the plains obsession, and still is today.

As American expansion pressed across the Mississippi, adventurers, explorers, and settlers soon peered into that ominous landscape which was an affront to Manifest Destiny. Nevertheless, a few observant settlers soon deduced that the soil was unusually fertile, had no trees or rocks to clear before plowing, and was "nowhere too steep for the wagon or the plow." As early as 1811 the English botanist John Bradbury, deep in the Dakota plains, concluded: "It can be cultivated. . . . It will be one of the most beautiful countries in the world."[10] In a complete turnaround from Coronado, Pike, Long, Henry, and Sherman, a newly arrived plains wife could write: "We must pronounce this the most charming country our eyes have ever beheld. Beautiful rolling prairie, undulating like the waves of the sea, high limestone cliffs with immense bottom-lands, stretching into thousands of acres as rich

51

as it is possible for it to be, high tablelands, with a soil a number of feet in depth."[11] In 1831, Joshua Pilcher told Congress that anyone who saw the open grasslands as an impossible obstacle "must know little of the American people, who supposes they can be stopped by anything in the shape of . . . deserts."[12] A western booster agreed: "The skill and enterprise of American farmers will find the means of obtaining comfort and wealth in those regions, both of Kansas and Nebraska, which many are disposed to condemn as worthless."[13] Indiana senator G. S. Orth, member of an 1867 Republican junket onto the plains, announced that "our good 'Uncle Sam' has come here, and he brings with him science and civilization. He intends to plant permanently a part of his great family; for he is now founding empires."[14] A journalist asserted that the Great Plains offered "a garden three times the area of France."[15]

The midcontinent grassland was a novelty. To the aspiring young husband and wife of a farm family, rumors of a vast grassland, but under rainless skies, were not encouraging despite the national passion that Everyman deserved his God-given share of the virtually free land carved out of the public domain. The trick was to make a small amount of water go a long way, but wheat or corn for cash and survival needed more than a trickle. Irrigation was known to succeed in California, but where was the water in western Kansas? Year-round streams were rare and their banks were quickly captured by the first round of settlers, who claimed exclusive riparian rights.

The open country also required technological innovation and new farming practices. Back East, 20 or 40 or even 80 acres could be worked with hand tools, a plow, and horses, but not 320 acres in a half-section or 640 acres in the full section required to prosper on the plains. The new dryland farming required far bigger farms to field a decent crop, plus machinery to cultivate the bigger farm. A new farmer saw a treeless, arid, and desolate landscape. What features in the land would allow him to apply new skills and tools to guarantee his survival? He knew that he could plow the land and that it was extremely fertile. The potential for success seemed better with the appearance of John Deere's steel moldboard plow. Word spread that it "cut through the sod like a hot knife through butter." The new farmer could figure out how to get along without trees; the invention of ready-made wood-frame houses and barbed wire for fencing gave him a boost, and railroads would soon connect him with the East. The Indians had been subdued and pushed westward, and the 1862 Homestead Act offered (but often failed to deliver) free prime farmland to a settler committed to five years of toil and survival to prove up his property. A rush of new inventions offered him hope and may have made him overconfident by including windmills with the steel plow and barbed wire. Cyrus McCormick began selling a workmanlike mechanical reaper. It alone multiplied eightfold the land a farmer could harvest and seemed destined to guarantee success for dryland farming. Back East, the new roller process for milling wheat for bread encouraged larger plantings on more land, so the farmer's natural hesitancy was overcome by these technological advances. He had in his mind a successful picture to repeat: the bonanza farming of the Red River of the North bordering the Dakotas and Minnesota. Wheat, if not always water-hungry corn, could be grown profitably. In time, large-scale farming covered hundreds of acres instead of tens of acres. The new mechanized equipment seemed designed for flat, open country.

When Did the Frontier End and Successful Farming Begin?

One of America's premier geographers, Carl Ortwin Sauer, argued that the midcontinent grasslands were where the nation's frontier history really began.[16] In the eastern forests the first waves of white settlers deadened trees, cleared openings, and planted fields in ways little different from generations of European forebears. If frontier means an encounter with strange conditions requiring new responses, then the American frontier began not at the Atlantic coastline or the Appalachian Mountains, but at the prairie peninsula that edged onto today's Indiana-Illinois state line. The midland grasslands marked the starting point for a distinctively American history and American space.

High Plains historian Robert G. Athearn called the post–Civil War rush to the plains "the initiation of the final assault upon the American frontier. When the movement ended, a new nation stepped forth into the family of the world."[17] When does a frontier end? Not until 1912 did the Santa Fe Railroad

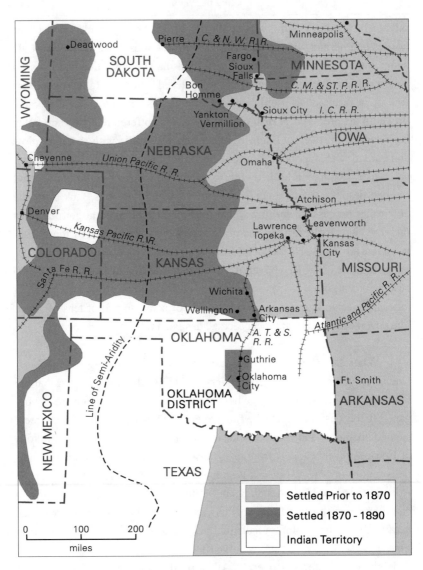

3. The farmer's frontier, 1870–90. Note the vertical twenty-inch rainfall "Line of Semi-Aridity" and early railroad expansion. Redrawn from Ray Allen Billington, *Westward Expansion: A History of the American Frontier*, 4th ed. (New York: Macmillan, 1974), 655, with permission of Macmillan.

intrude on the grasslands of southwest Kansas by building a branch line from Dodge City to Satanta along the old Dry Fork of the Santa Fe Trail. Before then, settlers bounced their wagons along the ruts of the centuries-old trail. There were no broad, smooth-flowing rivers like the Ohio or Mississippi to raft a farm family and its household goods, animals, and tools into the central High Plains. Roads and bridges (across dry washes) did not exist before 1912 in the sandy country on the north bank of the Cimarron River; wandering families simply rattled on cross-country. During the 1870s the Santa Fe had built its Pacific line along the Arkansas River thirty-five miles to the north, but that was a two-day roadless wagon ride away from farmsteads along the Cimarron. The Santa Fe was more intent on getting across the plains than on serving its cash-poor population and sparse resources. In 1888 the Rock Island reached the spot just north of the Oklahoma-Kansas border that would become Liberal, Kansas.

As for the Oklahoma Panhandle, in 1890 there was nothing in that no-man's-land except huge undeveloped ranches where buffalo and Indians recently roamed. The Denver and Fort Worth Railroad speculated by running tracks across northeast New Mexico into the Texas Panhandle. It found a limited seasonal business with the spread-out cattle ranchers, such as the Bates and Beals L-X cowboys, who set up temporary shop in the far southwest corner of Kansas (present-day Morton County) in 1877.[18] Not for fifty more years, in 1927, did the Santa Fe complete its line from Satanta across Grant and Stanton counties into adjoining Baca County in Colorado. Settlers then rushed in to capture still-cheap but now-accessible land; a railroad line meant they could get their wheat, corn, and alfalfa to market. Haskell County, the eastern terminus of the Santa Fe branch-line-off-the-branch-line, grew 93 percent in the 1920s. Next door to the west, Grant County boomed to nearly twice its 1920 population, and Stanton County on the Kansas-Colorado line in the late 1920s had fourteen people for every ten people earlier. Gradually the small towns north and south across Panhandle country were linked by a network of tracks. In 1930 the Rock Island connected Liberal with Amarillo, Texas. Not until the late 1920s and early 1930s would southwest Kansas and the Texas-Oklahoma Panhandle region over-come its frontierlike isolation.

If the frontier ended when railroads crisscrossed a region, then the Ogallala heartland had barely graduated from frontier status before the Depression and Dust Bowl devastated its towns and farms. If the frontier ended when the traces of civilization appeared—schools, churches, stores, law and order—then the region had moved from frontier to rural status decades earlier. If the frontier ended only when the geography had been domesticated, then the Ogallala heartland was still an untamed frontier region in the 1940s. If the frontier ended when local people could abandon a subsistence standard of living, then the central Great Plains had its first taste of prosperity in the 1950s, not so much from wheat or corn or alfalfa as from natural gas from the nation's greatest underground pool. Such industrial prosperity, however, also included the extreme swings of a boomtown economy. The frontier may have ended only when the farmer's tools matched his needs. Not until new irrigation technologies took hold in the 1960s would the previously undertooled local farmer substitute groundwater for rain to bypass environmental constraints. How temporary an environmental conquest this would be is still to be seen.

Regional historian James C. Malin offered an environmental test in the 1940s when he was one of the first to argue that the plains frontier ended only as settlers moved from primitive short-term exploitation to long-term conservation.[19] "The worst manifestations of soil blowing as related to agricultural operations occurred during the pioneering process," Malin wrote. "The country was new, the population was not settled-in on a firm and stabilized foundation in harmony with the new environment."[20] On these grounds the frontier has not yet ended in the region; in the long run, geography may never be conquered. Neither the tractors and mechanized harvesters of the 1920s nor the machinery for deep wells and full-field irrigation of the 1960s nor entrepreneurial motives behind both eras reflects a mature commitment to the conservation Malin sought. They are forms of continuous frontierlike exploitation. Whether the land-saving policies initiated by the 1985 Farm Security Act can bring major changes is still to be seen. On environmental grounds, the Ogallala heartland is still in the thrall of frontier conditions.

America's Seventy-Year Mistake: The Beginning

Waves of farm families filled with Jeffersonian idealism and Manifest Destiny moved onto the plains through the second half of the nineteenth century. To their surprise, they were often forced back by the lack of rain or groundwater, so they tried again. They learned that the myth of the desert was not entirely a myth. Like troops sacrificing themselves on the battlefield, fresh waves seemed always ready to step forward. New settlers learned painfully that less corn or wheat would grow on 160 acres in western Kansas than sprang forth on 40 acres in Illinois or Iowa, despite more hard labor and personal risk. The combination of drought and heat that struck in two succeeding summers, 1859 and 1860, forced hundreds to flee the territory. No soaking rain fell. Winter snows and their life-giving moisture were so light that for the first time in memory they did not hide the ground from view. A crop of less than five hundred bushels was harvested from 4,000 acres in Shawnee County as both winter and spring wheat failed. The settlers who remained survived only on charity coming from such distant points as Wisconsin and New York.[21]

The settlers who endured the grasshoppers in the summer of 1874 and the desperate winter of 1874–75 conceded the harsh limits of the plains. They reluctantly shifted from corn, the symbol of American prosperity, to wheat, strange new winter wheat instead of spring wheat. The hard red winter wheat, Turkey red, of new German-Russian Mennonite communities spread widely to become the new staff of life. American settlers also learned dryland farming techniques from the immigrant communities. Russian tillage methods, not those of the humid eastern United States, worked in the unfamiliar plains soil and climate, and Americans learned to let their fields lie fallow in alternate years to build up subsoil moisture from two years' rain, which in turn offered enough wetness to grow a single crop.

Congress tried to legislate an environmental fix to re-create a more familiar landscape: cover one-quarter of the region with forest to duplicate eastern farmland. The Timber Culture Act of 1873 promised to change the climate.

Whoever planted trees on 40 acres of his 160-acre quarter section and kept them growing for ten years received title to the entire 160 acres. This was so unlikely that the requirement was reduced to 27,000 trees on 10 acres with a 25 percent survival rate. Trees and climate change failed. In 1877, Congress tried again with the aptly named Desert Land Act, which discounted a full section of 640 acres to settlers who would water their land. Irrigation ditches were often no more than plowed furrows that ran uphill and downhill. Both acts produced more fraud and speculation than honest results. It also became abundantly clear that by restricting settlers to an inadequate 160 acres, the celebrated Homestead Act of 1862 failed to suit conditions beyond the ninety-seventh meridian. In early 1881 the Kansas legislature took an unusual step by assigning twenty-five thousand dollars, barely adequate even for that day, for immediate relief of farmers.

Despite these warnings, plains boosters reviled the renowned scientist and explorer John Wesley Powell as a doomsayer when he prefaced an 1878 government report with his view that realistically in the American West, including the High Plains, "the climate is so arid that agriculture is not successful."[22] Since "practically all values inhere in the water," the only land which the government ought responsibly to offer settlers was parcels where "the water could be distributed over them."[23] Using Utah as a dubious average, Powell concluded pessimistically that only 3 percent of the West could be so farmed. His argument was clear, direct, and precisely what potential settlers did not want to hear. It was possible to begin farming but impossible to succeed. Within five years everything would be lost. With dryland farming as a risky alternative, Powell urged a sixteenfold expansion of the homesteading quarter section to a minimum of two to four sections (1,280 to 2,560 acres, two to four square miles) to offer the best chance for success.[24] At the very least, he concluded, the day of the independent farm family that prospered on the famous quarter section was long gone and would never successfully settle the High Plains. Enemies drove Powell from his government post in the U.S. Geological Survey; he would receive more attention in the 1980s than in the 1880s.

Climate Anomaly: 1878–87

Then a miracle happened. In 1844, Josiah Gregg wrote that "the extreme cultivation of the earth might contribute to the multiplication of showers."[25] Now for a decade—approximately 1878–87—extraordinarily heavy rains fell on the High Plains country west of the ninety-seventh meridian from Texas to Canada. The rains encouraged frontier farmers to move into the region because they believed they could perpetuate the change from dry to moist weather. They could alter the forces of nature by the ordinary field practice of plowing the sod. "Rain follows the plow" became the popular slogan. These farmers, together with government agents, private boosters, and the American public at large, concluded that the weather had permanently changed and farming could begin in unlikely western places. The power of ordinary but Bunyanesque Americans to dictate favorable geographical change was not a strange claim in the age of Manifest Destiny. Mormon settlers happily reported that the level of the Great Salt Lake rose when they began irrigating and cultivating nearby land.[26]

The theory of increasing rainfall by plowing the land gained credence as a widespread scientific fact when it was endorsed by Joseph Henry of the Smithsonian Institution, the new American Association for the Advancement of Science (A A A S), and the most famous explorer-scientist of the day, F. V. Hayden, director of the U.S. Geological Surveys of the Territories. In 1880 Nebraska scientist Samuel Aughey concluded that, "after the soil is broken, a rain as it falls is absorbed by the soil like a huge sponge."[27] Then the soil evaporates a little moisture into the atmosphere each day, receiving it back at night as a heavy dew. Ironically, Washington's Government Printing Office was at the same time turning out hundreds of copies of John Wesley Powell's much-abused warning about the arid lands of the West. Powell's pessimism was countered by Aughey and real-estate promoter turned pseudo-scientist C. D. Wilber. They said that west of the 100th meridian the soil was fertile and rainfall was gradually increasing.[28]

Farmers and boosters in the western parts of Kansas and Nebraska were delighted with the new science. This was not intentionally bad science. In fact, it was not bad science for its day, but it was inadequate science to explain climate modification. In addition, it was widely believed that the spread of the railroads and telegraph lines also brought rains because the iron and steel rails and electric wires modified natural electrical cycles in an arid zone to induce the fall of moisture. Civil War veterans remembered that artillery fire, such as that at the Battle of Gettysburg, seemingly contributed to the deluge that followed. If Sherman would use more cannon to clear the plains of Indians, it might have the added benefit of bringing rain.

Boom and Bust: The Plains Experiment

The wonderful combination of more rainfall, better crops, cheap fertile land, and the beginning of an interlaced network of railroads was too good to resist. In 1878–79 the land office at Bloomington, which had jurisdiction in southwest Kansas, entered homesteads totaling more than 307,000 acres.[29] The spell of good rain encouraged a Chicago newsman to say in 1884 that "Kansas was considered a droughty state, but that day is past, and her reputation for sure crops is becoming widely known. . . . Land is cheap and a good home can be made to pay for itself in a few years."[30] Congregational minister Jeremiah Platt, visiting in the mid-1880s, concluded that "I am more and more convinced that there is a Great Western Kansas which, in fifteen or twenty years from now will be as rich and productive and valuable as is the eastern part of the state, making Kansas the greatest and grandest agricultural state in the union."[31] Modern agricultural historian Gilbert C. Fite wrote that new arrivals in western Kansas were undeterred when they rode past deserted claim shanties abandoned during the drought that occurred three or four years earlier. He quotes the *Larned* (Kansas) *Optic* claim that "the largest immigration ever known in the history of the state is now steadily flowing into southwestern Kansas" and the *Kinsley Graphic*, "Come on! There is still plenty of room, land is cheap here yet, and thousands of acres for sale." Edwards County was "literally spotted with new frame and board houses with here and there a sod house."[32] Unexpectedly fast settlement in western Kansas led to county-seat wars, including fatal gunplay over whether Hugoton or Woodsdale would be the Stevens County seat. Between 1885 and 1887, the population of the western third of Kansas rose 370 percent, from 38,000 to 139,000 people, just as the rains halted.

The boom ended more suddenly than it began, its collapse accelerated by disastrous blizzards in early 1886 in which 80 percent of all range cattle died. The decade of heavy rains ended unexpectedly, and drought returned in the late summer of 1887. In the successive summers of 1889 and 1890, farmers got only two and one half bushels of wheat an acre in the western counties and an even less-productive eight bushels of corn. Farmers in Grant County could not survive, much less prevail, when a dry summer gave them four bushels of corn or wheat per acre. One farmer reported that he had no wheat or rye at all from twenty-two acres, and his corn crop totaled less than a bushel.[33] Widespread crop failure was made worse because the previous boom times had encouraged many settlers into overexpansion and heavy debt. With disastrous overconfidence, settlers in western Kansas had put their first crops into feed corn instead of the seed corn that would have avoided outright starvation. Crops, boomtowns, and optimism withered, replaced by "the blues badly" and return to "relatives east, poorer, sadder, and much wiser." Western counties, such as Pawnee, began losing people who had come only two or three years before.

"Most all the people here that could leave have done so and what is here are too poor they cannot get away," said a Grant County inhabitant in late 1889.[34] Farm families holding some of the world's most fertile land were living, they said, on "Andersonville fare," remembering the notorious Civil War prison in the South. In early 1890, despite a mild winter, word went out that the state would have to supply seed corn (which a farm family ate only out of desperation) or see western Kansas abandoned. Most settlers were still too proud to accept direct relief, but Kansas farmers could accept seed corn. Drought took hold more severely in the summer of 1890 than it had in earlier years and spread from the Texas Panhandle to the Canadian border. Few people were ready to acknowledge that dry times were the norm rather than the exception, and most settlers (and bankers and businessmen) waited expectantly for the next rainy season and a return to "normal" weather. The rains returned in 1891 and 1892, but a combination of more drought and the Panic of 1893 once more created desperate conditions in western Kansas. This was followed in 1894 by one of the driest years on record (only eight to nine inches of rain) and a particularly heavy plague of grasshoppers.

Between 1890 and 1900, the number of farms in the twenty-four counties of western Kansas declined from 14,300 to 8,900. The entire decade of the 1890s brought only two years of good crops and five consecutive years of failure. By the mid-1890s, Hugoton's dozens of new houses emptied and its population stood at a mere 308 in 1915. Throughout the western counties people left behind only shuttered or windowless homes. Grass grew in front of rows of brick business districts as monuments to a fantasy that had no link with reality. In a colorful phrase, one observer complained about population claims of boomtowns in western Kansas: "Census returns prick the bladder of this inflation."[35]

The five years of homestead residency were soon called "the period of starvation." Plains historian Walter Prescott Webb wrote that "the government is willing to bet the homesteader one hundred and sixty acres of land that he'll starve to death on it in less than five years." A popular song told of "starvin' to death on my government claim." Passage of the Three-Year Homestead Act in 1912 admitted that the point of starvation was far short of five years: "Consequently it would be humane to shorten the required time of residence to three years."[36] By 1895, more than 184,000 people abandoned their farms and left Kansas.

The shadow of drought constantly hung over people of the plains as they entered the new century. Hence, Webb concluded, their existence focused on one element: "this primitive and elemental desire for rain."[37] The heavy rains had not persisted and would not return, but the myth of climate change did. For over seventy years, until the hammer blows of the 1930s, settlers were lured to the plains by the dream of more rain on the rich soil. First corn crops went dry, then sorghums and wheat, and finally the farmyard gardens so tenderly nourished by well water.

The fabled American homesteading dream broke down on the devil's anvil of the plains. By losing their capacity to be self-sustaining, starving farmers felt betrayed and, paradoxically, believed they had betrayed the American dream in their failure. Government agents had encouraged farmers to stay on the land despite the return of drought and economic pressures to abandon the land. Farmers themselves believed it was unpatriotic (and possibly even sinful) to desert their homesteads.

The unexpectedly harsh environment forced Americans to rethink their vaunted frontier settlement. First, it became clear that the plains were a permanent frontier because no one could bring more moisture to the land. Reclamation leader Frederick H. Newell of the USGS announced in the 1896 agriculture yearbook that the High Plains region was fated to succumb to periodic drought and periodic famine.[38] Second, hardships that farmers accepted because they were temporary and therefore conquerable were deep seated; permanent problems were inherent in dryland agriculture. In 1901, USGS official Willard D. Johnson called the rush to plains settlement an "experiment in agriculture on a vast scale . . . it nevertheless ended in total failure . . . [resulting in] a class of people broken in spirit as well as in fortune."[39] Third, the plains farmer was undercapitalized, undertooled, and underinformed to cope with the challenges he faced. Only a new type of credit economy and government cash, not to arrive until the New Deal, would bring a share of national prosperity to the plains. It also turned plains farmers forever into government clients.

Two failed frontiers marked the plains as a hard place. Webb writes of the short-lived but high-romance cattle kingdom of dryland ranchers before the farmers came.[40] Despite its well-financed British and German backing, it did not survive the winter of 1885–86. Nor could the cash-poor sodhouse farmers who followed—"nine children and eleven cents"—cope with the 1889–95 drought. Since large parts of the grassland remained in native sod, dust storms did not blow, but without rain the settlers concluded that "there is no god west of Salina."[41] The Great Plains, at first reviled as the Great American Desert, then celebrated as the Great American Garden, became a three-hundred-mile-wide, near-empty swath ranging from Canada to Texas. By the mid-1890s, the central plains had reverted to its virtually uninhabited prefrontier state. Even the Indians had never lived there except as hunters and nomads.

The First Struggle to Find Groundwater: Well Diggers

The first farmer to turn sod and look hopefully heavenward for rain in Finney County did so in 1878. Before the farmers arrived, there were ranchers, often Civil War veterans who parlayed the Homestead Act into significant spreads. But even hardy range cattle needed water, and the old Z6 or OX or XY Ranch staked itself out along the Arkansas River.[42] It took no genius to see that southwestern Kansas lacked enough rain. Springs and ponds and pothole-like playa lakes were rare. Despite this fatal flaw, adventuresome or desperate farmers were drawn to the treeless, fertile, and flat land so ready for the steel-tipped John Deere shear plow. Within a year, Finney County had 2,905 acres planted to crops. In an era when a farmer was mighty pleased to turn sod on four acres a day and plant seed on eight, this was energetic progress.[43] Getting to a reliable source of water quickly became a dire necessity.

In the early wet 1880s, new settlers in southwestern Kansas assured themselves they could farm successfully by drawing water from shallow wells, wet-weather draws, buffalo wallows, the rare spring, and, if they were lucky in choice of farm site, the Arkansas or Cimarron rivers. By the mid-1880s, the best access to water was already taken by earlier homesteaders and hopeful late arrivals were virtually doomed to failure, not by lack of skill, but by unlucky timing. Where there was a town well, a common sight on the open prairie was a horse-drawn wagon or even a box on skids bumping along loaded with water barrels covered with burlap. When homesteader John S. Gropp arrived in 1887, he had to settle on waterless land about twenty miles northwest of Garden City. For two years he rolled a large barrel of water three-fourths of a mile from a neighbor's well before he hand-dug his own well and had the hard luck not to find water for 220 feet.[44]

Nineteenth-century farmers knew that well digging was a nasty chore, but they did not anticipate the months-long hard labor to get one's own water on the plains. Back in the tallgrass prairie of Missouri, where many had come from, a family chore given to children was carrying buckets of water from the nearby stream or shallow well. A more convenient family well might occasionally descend twenty or thirty feet, lined with stone or brick or not finished at all. Water was brought up hand over hand in the two-bucket system using the familiar crossbeam and pulley. On the High Plains, not only was the water fifty or one hundred or more feet down, but settlers were dismayed by the layers of dense soil, sandy clay, and rocky conglomerate they had to dig through. Soon the part-time well driller appeared, often a neighboring farmer or town mechanic or an itinerant. He alone possessed the equipment to drill a six-inch hole which, if the homesteader was unlucky, went down more than two hundred feet. The six-inch hole would be sheathed in an iron casing, not only to prevent the collapse of the well, but also to offer a smoother journey for the unusual bucket, about four feet long but only three inches in diameter.[45]

Many farmers lucky enough to hit water under fifty feet might take on the major construction and engineering job of a well three or four feet wide. Water for a family and small garden patch meant a long spell of sweaty well digging on an open, sun-burnt and windy site. Hand-dug wells often went through a ten- or fifteen-foot stretch of sand that had to be laboriously curbed out with four-foot pieces of wood sawed and nailed into place. Hundreds of wells were dug by the homesteaders themselves, work that led to crippling accidents and deaths. As a local historian put it, "picture a digger down a hundred or two hundred feet watching an 80 or 100 pound bucket of dirt ascending to the top. . . . If the rope broke and dropped the load, he flattened himself against the wall as close as he could."[46] A falling hammer or shovel or piece of curbing, not to mention the collapse of a well wall, made him fearful of the slightest sound or movement. A dry well was not unusual, forcing the hard-pressed farmer to start all over again.

In a few rare cases, a good deep well lucky enough to tap the aquifer supported two hundred head of cattle, while typical wells barely furnished water for the sod house and a few barnyard animals. Very rarely, to the envy of all his fellows, a farmer might enjoy an artesian well, but most artesian wells were in the Dakotas. In hand-dug wells the water was lifted laboriously in the old-fashioned two-bucket system: one in the water when the full bucket was on top. It was an arduous and time-consuming task to lift the heavy bucketful of water by hand. At first, few farmers could afford the newfangled windmill, tower, and pump and were reluctant to throw hard-earned cash at an untested device. To keep up with the needs of ten or twenty cattle was probably impossible; watering an uneconomical twenty acres of wheat, much less water-needy corn, was unthinkable. No tinkerer, much less a manufacturer, had come up with a pump for the plains. In the first two decades of the twentieth century, however, the self-regulating factory-built windmill (see chapter 4) would water enough land, five to ten acres, to enable the homesteader to hold on when all others had to leave. But windmills did not feed the thirsty crops on a farmer's quarter section, much less a spread covering an entire square mile.

"Big Ditches" from the Arkansas River: The Garden City Experiment

Today, USGS survey maps show many intermittent streams in southwest Kansas. Local people call them wet-weather streams or dry draws. They can still be traced for twenty or fifty or even one hundred miles, sometimes with still-visible depressions where buffalo once pawed and wallowed to make a damp place deeper and wetter. Today the Arkansas River, once a full-flowing river from Colorado into Kansas, barely trickles when dust does not blow through its channels. One reason for today's barrenness is the declining water table as Ogallala water is drawn down. Another is that for decades upstream irrigators around Lamar, Colorado, have captured the river's water long before it reaches the state line. But at the turn of the century, the river flowed well through Garden City, Kansas; it got national attention, and the town's name seemed appropriate.[47]

For water to supply a growing population of irrigators, the Arkansas River got most early attention.[48] In the 1870s the river ran wide and deep; even in severe drought it flowed at least one to three feet deep and one hundred feet wide. After an upstream storm, it would rage through a channel four hundred feet wide. The biggest early problem was throwing a bridge that could span the channel. The river flow, fed from the Rocky Mountains, usually did not vary more than five feet between high and low water, although it did once go completely dry in the spring of 1883. Two Garden City farmers with irrigation-ditch experience, one from Colorado and the other from California, told stories of the wonders of irrigation projects that spread for miles along rivers in those states. They got more attention when drought hit again in 1879, the second year of settlement in Finney County. Farmers had barely turned the new sod before they looked around for water. Fear of no crops brought fresh interest in irrigation. The farmer with Colorado irrigation-ditch experience was apparently W. H. Armentrout; the California irrigator may have been George Finnup. They were joined by banker A. G. Landis from nearby Sterling. The three walked the banks of the Arkansas River and found, three miles west of Garden City, a place where an inexpensive earthen dam between an island in the river and the north shore would force water into an east-flowing ditch. In 1880, with money lent by Landis, Garden City's first irrigation canal was laboriously dug by local farmers; it was four miles long, eight feet wide, and two feet deep. Finnup reminisced in 1922: "We figured the expense to make the dam, cut the ditch to Garden City, and a few laterals would cost about seven or eight hundred dollars."[49] It eventually cost Armentrout two thousand dollars to divert water for one hundred acres. His ditch also served Squire Worrell, whose irrigated farm produced five crops of alfalfa in 1881 alone, a sharp contrast to his drought losses on the same land in 1879.[50] Successfully completed, the project worked so well that it was extended twice to run twenty miles northeast, well beyond Garden City.

The Garden City experiment received nationwide attention as part of the popular Irrigation Crusade that linked western prosperity to intensive irrigation.[51] In 1893, national irrigation spokesman William Smythe, applying his usual booster hyperbole, hailed Garden City as "the center and inspiration of irrigation development." Another ditch was dug between June 1880 and July 1881 by a group that called itself the Kansas Ditch Company. It was improved in 1882 to run more than thirty miles and extended again in 1901–1902 and renamed the Farmers Ditch by its new owners. As Garden City's fame spread, investors from as far away as Ohio financed the successful Southside Ditch on the south bank of the Arkansas River.

Garden City became an irrigation boomtown. Investors from Lawrence, Kansas, joined local speculator C. J. ("Buffalo") Jones to support the Great

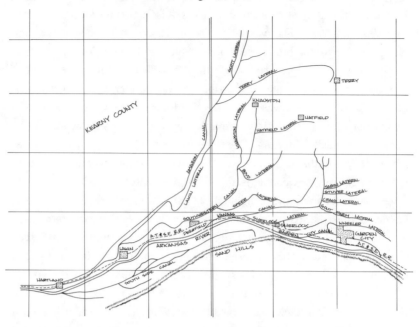

4. Garden City canals, ditches, and laterals tapping upstream Arkansas River water in 1892. These were the only large-scale community irrigation projects on the High Plains. But the Arkansas too often went dry early in the twentieth century, so the use of surface water alone proved inadequate for farming in the region. Twentieth-century groundwater irrigation would be on individual farms only. From the *Garden City Imprint,* May 7, 1892.

Eastern Canal, which spread a network of ditches and laterals 30 miles north of the Kansas Ditch. The Santa Fe Railroad promised funds, using income from its sale of railroad sections, but then it backed out and the canal was turned over to participating farmers in 1883.[52] By 1889 the Great Eastern, including its main laterals, extended 96 miles across the previously unsettled dry uplands north of Garden City at a cost exceeding one hundred thousand dollars; a year later the Great Eastern badly needed repair and served few farms.[53] Buffalo Jones also guided construction of the long-lived Amazon Ditch, which supplied farmers in Finney, Scott, and Kearny counties from 1890 into the 1960s. To build the Amazon Ditch forty-five-feet wide and nine feet deep, records show that the experienced construction team used a crew of fifteen men, thirty horses, two excavating graders, and several two-horse slips. They built the ditch and its farmstead laterals in less than two years for about one hundred thousand dollars. It eventually ran for 102 miles.[54]

This era of big ditches, totaling 336 miles of main canals to irrigate about 70,000 acres (far below Buffalo Jones's estimated 600,000 acres), encouraged a population explosion along the Arkansas River valley: from 10,000 residents in 1884 to 70,000 by 1888.[55] By 1882 a journalist could boast that the hardy farmers of Garden City had created

> a great newly-made garden [that] was laid out in beds of large size, each with a foot-high ridge around it, like the bottom crust of a pie. These are the dykes through which the water is let on the beds. Running the length of the fields parallel with the river was a ditch with swift-running water one or two feet deep; the water ran like a mill-race, and did not creep as in a canal, then there were lateral ditches crossing the fields, a ridge on each side preventing overflow. . . . I walked about over the little fields. The earth was soft like ashes. There is not a stone as big as a baby's foot for miles and miles. All sorts of vegetables had been planted; some grain was growing, and there was a field of the curious dark-green alfalfa, which sends its roots to water, six, eight, or ten feet, and can be cut four or five times a season.[56]

Fields were flooded two or three times a season. Field leveling involved horse-drawn scrapers made of wood and a length of railroad iron. Crop yields doubled and tripled with irrigation: up to seventy-five bushels of oats per acre, twenty-five bushels of wheat, and forty bushels of corn, as well as ten tons of alfalfa a year. Prosperity in southwest Kansas was linked entirely to water from the laterals and ditches off the river. In 1899, virtually all irrigation in southwest Kansas—95 percent of 200,000 acres—used Arkansas and Cimarron water. Irrigated farmland offered stability and hope for the future as nothing else ever did in the dry region. For a time, the population in and around Garden City took on boomtown proportions, growing from 1,315 in 1880 to 26,260 in 1890.

Despite old optimism about the return of heavier rainfall and new optimism about the success of water-conserving dryland farming, by 1889 most settlers in southwest Kansas admitted that irrigation was a necessity, not an optional improvement, for successful farming. Farmers who had settled the arid low hills north of Garden City, where the ditches could not run, were without a regular water supply. Beyond the irrigation ditches, only twelve families held out on the arid northern stretches of Finney County and only thirty families were spread out over the vast "north flats" of Kearny County. Foster Eskelund recorded that they supplemented their skimpy farm income by hiring out to work on ditches and by leasing their land to irrigation farmers who generally also invested in sizable herds of cattle.[57] The profitability of irrigation was clear. A newspaper correspondent wrote in September 1887: "There will be no more building canals and then waiting for the people to be converted. They are already converted by the strongest argument in the world—hot winds, protracted drought, and consequently almost total failure of crops."[58] But even the irrigators repeatedly compounded their own problems by having no interest in irrigation during a season of rains.

With the large Amazon Ditch, a new problem arose: there was not enough water in the Arkansas River to fill its main canal and laterals. Upstream Colorado irrigators were on the verge of diverting the entire flow of the Arkansas. As early as July 1888, the Garden City Ditch Company tried to protect irrigation by damming all but twelve feet of the river's remaining flow. In July 1890 the river went dry, and in 1893 rainfall declined to less than twelve inches for western Kansas; no water entered irrigation ditches until the last week in June, too late to save the burned-up crops.[59] The upstream irrigators in Colorado delivered the coup de grace in 1905 when about one hundred ditch systems serving over seven thousand farmers irrigated nearly half a million acres using Arkansas River water. USGS maps began to show the river as an intermittent stream when it entered Kansas. In 1907 a landmark U.S. Supreme Court decision, *Kansas* v. *Colorado,* established a concept of equity in economic terms but failed to deal with environmental and economic realities. Much later, in 1949, the Arkansas River Compact treated water solely as a commodity, but, despite local optimism, it had little effect on the future of irrigation in southwest Kansas.[60]

Farmers began to resist water contracts costing $500 over ten years and guaranteed by a first mortgage on the farmer's land.[61] New speculation in canal development was attracted by the promise that an irrigation system could be constructed for about fifty cents an acre, while the standard charge for existing irrigation stood at a dollar an acre a year. Irrigators complained that much of the new irrigable land lay "year after year in a state of nature producing nothing more valuable than weeds or buffalo grass" because it stood in the alternate sections of the Santa Fe land grant, too costly at $2.50 to $10.00 an acre.

Drought in Finney County, combined with a dry riverbed, meant that wheat production collapsed from an average high of twenty-five bushels per acre in 1889 to three bushels in 1895 and 1896. Corn fell from thirty bushels in 1889 to five bushels in 1893 and 1894. The 1890s brought investment from England, cooperative irrigation companies, and large landowners involved in sharecropping, "but even English capital could not raise crops in western Kansas in the 1890s."[62] Farmer irrigation associations acquired the bankrupt Kansas Ditch, the Garden City Ditch, and even the vaunted Amazon. When some rain reappeared in the mid-1890s, farmers aggressively planted wheat on 26,600 acres, compared to predrought planting of less than 1,000 acres. But profitable production on an intensive scale now depended on irrigation more than rainfall. Between 1895 and 1899, 10 percent of the remaining farmers hung on by reluctantly becoming dryland ranchers, shifting from grain crops to cattle. By the time another drought struck in 1900, planting collapsed to a low of 409 acres. No alternative dryland crops were known and the land was simply abandoned. As a result the population west of the 100th meridian in Kansas fell from 81,000 in 1889 to less than 50,000 in 1895, not to rebuild until the next century.[63] Wheat acreage would not rise above 26,000 acres again until 1908 during the so-called Agricultural Golden Age of high productivity and high prices. Homesteaders would not again risk their fortunes in the region until the palmier days of 1906–1907. It appeared that farming on the Kansas High Plains, despite the best new technologies and hardier wheat, would always remain a risky enterprise with low

Cost of Irrigation

Cost of irrigation under ditch, from 50 cents to $1.00 per acre per year.
Cost of irrigation from pump, as follows, according to lift:
RULE–"Eight cents per acre foot for every foot of lift."

Per acre foot we mean, sufficient water to cover an acre of ground to the depth of one foot, and you will not use to exceed, if your land is properly prepared, over from 3 to 5 inches per irrigation.

Table of Cost as Follows:

20 foot Lift	$1.60 per acre, foot	Per irrigation about	55 cents per acre
25 foot Lift	2.00 " " "	Per " "	66 " " "
30 foot Lift	2.40 " " "	Per " "	80 " " "
40 foot Lift	3.20 " " "	Per " "	$1.05 " " "
50 foot Lift	4.00 " " "	Per " "	1.35 " " "

Per acre foots we Cost of irrigation under ditch, from 50 cents to $1.00 per acre per year per acre foots. Cost of irrigation under ditch, from 50 cents to $1.00 per acre per year.

Crop Yields Under Irrigation Last Year

Wheat	30 to 63 bushels per acre	Corn	30 to 65 bushels per acre
Barley	35 to 65 " " "	Oats	40 to 90 " " "
Maize	40 to 60 " " "	Alfalfa	5 to 7 " " "
Irish Potatoes	200 to 300 " " "	Sweet Potatoes	200 to 400 " " "

These results will depend on the kind of farming and the amount of water used, yields varying as in all localities, the better the farming the more production.

Crop Yields Under Dry Farming Last Year

Wheat	15 to 35 bushels per acre	Corn	20 to 40 bushels per acre
Oats	20 to 35 " " "	Barley	15 to 35 " " "
Rye	15 to 30 " " "	Maize and Kaffir	15 to 35 " " "

These crops vary, as to the kind of farming and the amount of rainfall, and we are offering a large acreage of fine wheat lands, from which a single crop has more than paid for the land on which it grew.

ANNUAL RAINFALL AT GARDEN CITY, KANSAS, FOR THE PAST TEN YEARS.

Month	1920	1919	1918	1917	1916	1915	1914	1913	1912	1911
January	.20	.10	.70	.30	1.09	.45	.27	.15	.28	.00
February	.23	1.73	.75	.00	.00	2.54	.20	1.15	3.04	3.53
March	.21	1.45	2.48	.60	.60	.95	.13	.50	.98	.86
April	1.52	4.42	.92	3.52	2.50	2.98	1.73	1.05	2.36	.40
May	2.22	.98	2.67	3.60	.33	4.36	4.34	1.42	.67	2.91
June	3.79	1.14	1.88	2.48	3.56	2.28	2.54	3.28	4.16	1.46
July	3.45	3.19	4.01	2.23	.55	2.29	1.93	1.14	1.57	3.50
August	3.78	.54	.66	3.26	3.83	7.68	1.01	2.00	3.91	1.81
September	2.00	4.23	2.14	1.58	.87	2.61	.10	5.21	1.04	.22
October	2.10	1.23	4.44	.13	1.05	1.75	1.45	.23	.15	1.54
November	.69	1.28	.10	.30	.00	.12	.00	1.19	.29	.95
December	.33	.27	4.80	.16	.50	.13	.41	2.92	.05	1.66
Total	20.52	20.56	25.55	18.16	14.88	28.14	14.01	19.74	18.50	18.84

Average Rainfall 19.89 inches. For Past Ten Years.

The above table shows we have sufficient rainfall to supplement irrigation, which is a great advantage over the wholly arid irrigated sections, and yet we do not have enough rain to hinder farm operations and damage crops.

expectations. By 1949 less than 40 percent of southwest Kansas irrigation came from stream water; by 1966 it was less than 10 percent.

Discovery of the "Underflow" and Federal Reclamation

The canal companies tried to save themselves from the vagaries of river water by tapping into the "underflow." New settlers and old-timers alike took comfort in their belief in a vast underground body of "sheet water" that was constantly replenished, either from the Rocky Mountains or even the remote Arctic. Garden City residents, including a newspaper editor, went further by insisting that a cavernous underground river thundered along with more water than the Arkansas River had ever contained. It had the advantage that it was inexhaustible and would not go dry. The editor of a Texas Panhandle monthly, *The Earth,* wrote of "a water sheet . . . that is inexhaustible" and that could be "counted upon in all cases."[64] Did not artesian wells in the Dakotas already easily tap a strong underground flow? Yet there were no artesian wells in southwest Kansas and the Texas-Oklahoma Panhandle.

An unidentifiable Captain Livermore, with even more flimflam than most promoters, claimed that underflow water was glacier water from the Arctic, although how it traveled thousands of miles and then fanned out widely "is a matter to be worked out." But the water was so reliable that "the only power that could ever exhaust the Plains water supply would be an earthquake that would crack the flint bottom and give the water another channel."[65] The myth of a gigantic underground river underlying the Great Plains would not be abandoned easily. The Arctic theory remained a popular notion into the 1950s, the Ogallala's inexhaustibility into the 1960s—until irrigation-well levels began to decline noticeably. A historian of the Ogallala in Texas, Donald E. Green, observed that "the very massiveness of the

OPPOSITE: 5. The contents of the back page from a 1921 irrigation-land promotional brochure of the Garden City real-estate firm Charles I. Zirkle and Company vividly illustrates the contemporary boomer mentality. Zirkle made the best of marginal rainfall by claiming, "We have sufficient rainfall to supplement irrigation, which is a great advantage over the wholly arid irrigated sections, and yet we do not have enough rain to hinder farm operations and damage crops." From the Kansas Room files, courtesy of the Finney County Public Library, Garden City, Kansas.

Ogallala formation was partly to blame for the misconception. Early irrigators could pump a thousand gallons per minute from the extensive subsurface lake [*sic*] day after day without exhausting the supply."[66]

An 1891 United States Geological Survey investigation gave scientific credibility to popular belief in the underflow: it originated as runoff from the Rockies that flowed eastward, refreshed along the way by percolation from surface rain and snow.[67] In 1895 an official of the Kansas Geological Survey, Erasmus Haworth, reported: "The citizens throughout the tertiary areas of Kansas almost as one man have an unshaken faith that the waters precipitated along the eastern slope of the great Rocky Mountains very largely pass eastward and constitute at least an important proportion of the great body of water."[68] The idea was to tap the underflow by digging an irrigation ditch upstream to intersect the underflow and gravity-feed it into canals, laterals, and fields.[69] In 1889 the visiting U.S. Senate Committee on Irrigation and Reclamation of Arid Lands was urged to provide survey and experiment funds, which, if successful, would be augmented by an "abundance of private capital."

The search to identify the size of the underflow led the Kansas legislature in 1905 to order a Board of Irrigation technical survey in which twenty irrigation wells were to be drilled in several counties, using unoccupied school lands. Eastern Kansas interests ridiculed the attempt to find large groundwater supplies, but it was worth wasting thirty thousand dollars on a final, unsuccessful search, one said, to put the western "bow-wows" in their place.[70] Federal geologist W. D. Johnson visited Garden City in 1897 and encouraged capture of the underflow, although in his 1901 United States Geological Survey report he would conclude, as Powell had twenty-three years earlier, that "the absolute verdict must be that they [the High Plains in general] are non-irrigable . . . the only possible agricultural land of the High Plains belt lies within the valleys, where small patches here and there are irrigable." More confident was federal geologist Charles M. Slichter, who in 1904 took the trouble to drill several wells in a line across the river valley just west of Garden City. He concluded wrongly that the underflow moved eight feet every twenty-four hours, but he was on target when he claimed the flow was constant and that large amounts of water could be pumped if a cheap source of power could be found.[71]

In 1890 work began on an underflow channel at the head of the Great Eastern Canal. Costs were estimated at six thousand dollars but immediate benefits were set at twelve thousand dollars because the new water would enter the canal at more than nine hundred cubic feet a minute. However, the river flooded in the spring of 1891, destroyed the channel, and the experiment was not repeated. As late as 1902, newspaper editorials still urged construction of steam- or gasoline-powered pumping stations: "Cut the ditches loose from the river and install pumping plants."[72]

By the early twentieth century, only a trickle of Arkansas River water occasionally reached Garden City. Residents clamored for an experimental government-financed underflow-capture project, and as a result, one of the first projects of the new federal Reclamation Service was a series of pumps to capture thirty thousand acre-feet of water, half the estimated underflow of the Arkansas River. The Newlands Reclamation Act of 1902 released funds from the sale of public land to be applied to irrigation projects. The farmers who consumed the water were to repay construction costs to the federal government in a minimum of ten annual installments. Imitating the successful irrigation colonies of Utah's Mormons, California communities, and the well-known success at Greeley, Colorado, citizens organized the Water Users Association and enthusiastically oversubscribed the project, pledging more than twelve thousand acres in December 1905. Despite his belief in the reality of the underflow, Charles Slichter, now with the Reclamation Service, was convinced initially that no more than eighty-six hundred acres could be irrigated, although he later raised his estimate to twenty thousand. Slichter was soon to argue that the project would raise land values so much that it would be paid for easily by "those under the ditch."

Garden City's steam-powered electric station began transmitting power on April 1, 1908, to twenty-three pumps at one-thousand-foot intervals along a four-mile concrete conduit. Each pump, a No.10 vertical double upper-suction centrifugal device, was connected to nine or twelve wells fifteen inches in diameter and thirty to sixty feet deep in clay.[73] The year was the severest drought year in a decade and provided a good test of the project's effectiveness under dire conditions. In 1908, water drawn directly from the river irrigated 2,900 acres, while the new pumping plant covered 5,100 more. How much water actually reached the fields is not known, but engineers, farmers, and businessmen were disappointed in the coverage and stared in disbelief at the 75 percent that was lost to evaporation and seepage.

In August 1908, Secretary of the Interior James A. Garfield arrived to assess the results. He told the Water Users Association that "it is not right to charge the patrons for something they did not receive. . . . The patrons did not receive the water at the time when it was needed the worst."[74] On his return to Washington, however, he insisted on full payment of $3.50 per acre plus a building charge of $2.75 per acre for maintenance. Few farmers, with or without water, could afford $1,000 a year for ten years to service a 160-acre quarter section, and the association refused to pay. The next year, 1909, was a better one, with river water irrigating 9,400 acres and pumped water going to 6,500. This fell far short of the most conservative estimates; per acre costs shot up from $25 to $37.50 and finally exceeded $100. The government quit pumping in 1910 and sold out after World War I to the Garden City Company, which operated the system indifferently into the 1930s.

Arkansas River underflow had been misinterpreted; it would later be identified as part of the Ogallala aquifer, but it was not the answer to dry times and a dried-up surface river until new technology and new fuels became available. Charles Slichter repeated the common complaint about Kansas farmers, even those who became irrigators: they stubbornly stuck to large-scale wheat farming in the face of certain defeat while in the rest of the West small-scale irrigators were prospering. In 1908 he argued:

General agricultural crops grown in large tracts and farmed after customary methods for such crops will not pay a large return on the cost of pumping irrigation water. It is necessary to divide land into small holdings and to cultivate special crops such as melons, sweet potatoes, fruit or sugar beets in order to realize profitable results. In communities that have been accustomed to the cultivation of forage crops . . . it is probable that a complete revision of agricultural methods may be necessary. . . . It will be advantageous for the [Garden City] farmers to reduce the size of their farms.[75]

Slichter concluded in 1911 that "the plant itself is not a failure, but the people will not try to make it a success." In 1912 the new secretary of the interior, Walter L. Fisher, refused to intervene and blamed local intransigence: "The project at Garden City was taken up on the urgent request of the citizens of Kansas. . . . The works were built, were partly used, and any lack of success is due mainly to causes within the control of the persons who are now seeking relief."[76] Reclamation projects were booming in California and private entrepreneurs established irrigation communities, such as Greeley, Colorado, but the people of southwest Kansas rejected centralized and cooperative irrigation. The Garden City Water Users Association felt unjustly abused. It would gladly pay the $3.50 per acre per year if it got the promised two acre-feet of water per year. "But when the experiment showed conclusively that the plant was unable to deliver the promised water, what else could we do?" A state irrigation official wrote in 1913: "The big plant with its wasted $400,000 stands there idle, today, a monument to a theoretical dream."[77]

Industrial Crop Irrigation and Local Processing

Even before the rise and fall of Garden City's troubled federal reclamation colony, private industry saw an opportunity.[78] By 1900, sugar-beet companies in Colorado were operating successful irrigation-based processing plants and were looking to expand into western Kansas. Garden City businessmen organized the Cooperative Sugar Beet Growers' Association to join the American Sugar Beet Company of Rocky Ford, Colorado, in a five-hundred-acre experiment. Climate and soil conditions were excellent, but sugar beets required almost thirty-seven inches of rain a year compared to Garden City's nineteen-inch average rainfall. Similar conditions had been mastered by the irrigation colonies in Colorado and estimates suggested costs of eight dollars an acre to raise beets, with a practical minimum of five acres; the Kansas legislature chipped in a dollar a ton for "beets grown in Kansas and actually used for sugar manufacturing."[79] In 1901 almost three hundred acres planted in sugar beets produced 295,000 tons of beets. A processing plant in Holly, Colorado, bought more than 8,000 tons of Kansas sugar beets grown on almost seven hundred acres, and the state paid farmers a ten-thousand-dollar bounty. Business interests quickly moved into Garden City and quietly bought sixteen thousand acres, together with ownership of the Great Eastern, South Side, and Garden City ditches; thirty thousand dollars from businessmen soon sweetened the deal.

The $250,000 factory was large: a brick refinery 273 feet long, several office buildings, and 700 feet of beet sheds.[80] When in full operation in 1909, it could process eight hundred tons of sugar beets daily, consuming up to six million gallons of water in the process. The United States Sugar and Land Company established the United States Irrigating Company to clean, maintain, improve, and expand the irrigation canals it now owned. This included a 30,000-acre-foot reservoir named Lake McKinney, five miles by two and a half miles, created by an earthen dam several miles long. Fed by pumps and the intermittent Arkansas River, Lake McKinney kept sugar processing going during the severe drought of 1908. In addition, the company took full advantage of improved pumping technologies to establish a pumping plant of seventeen stations, nine wells, and a central gas-fired power plant. The entire operation was valued at $5.5 million, far beyond the $500,000 of the federal reclamation project. With $500,000 poured annually into the local economy, Finney County's population doubled between 1905 and 1907.

The sugar-beet operation, an early version of vertically integrated agribusiness, seemed to be the wave of the future on the High Plains wherever large quantities of groundwater could be found. By 1919 the company owned fifty-two thousand acres of sugar beets, ran its own Garden City Western Railway, processed waste beet pulp into cattle feed, operated an alfalfa mill, and supplied its own electric power to the sugar factory, irrigation pumps, and the public. But sugar beets require about the same heavy irrigation as corn, cultivation is labor intensive on small acreages, international markets are extremely competitive, and new processing technologies are costly. After struggling for many years, the beet factory closed in December 1955; the operation never expanded beyond its level in 1919, when it created almost four hundred seasonal jobs. By the 1960s the company operated primarily as a land-management business, leasing out almost twenty-three thousand acres, and was the largest absentee owner in Finney County. On its land, mostly north of the Arkansas River, groundwater depletion at 50 percent is the most serious in the county.[81]

Against the Kansas Grain: Frederick H. Newell's
Intensive Irrigation Farming

As early as 1894, C. H. Longstreth, director of the state horticultural society in eastern Kansas, stated the prejudice against farmers in southwest Kansas: "The irrigation question is simple. It means intense culture." Large-scale dryland farming, to which the western farmers were so unreasonably committed, would invariably fail in the face of extended drought. The task was to turn farmers into small-plot irrigators. The new nationwide Irrigation Crusade, strongest in California, announced that ten acres to a maximum of forty acres, well irrigated, was sufficient to support a family. Intensive farming meant raising onions, cabbage, sweet potatoes, tomatoes, grapes, cherries, and apples, with which a farmer had his hands full on twenty acres. Although there was not enough water to cover quarter sections, irrigation could serve small tracts. According to B. P. Walker, president of the Kansas Board of Irrigation in 1913, many farmers "have lived in western Kansas too long to be able to confine their labors to a small irrigated farm, since they have been accustomed all their lives to farming a [640-acre] section or more of land by dry-farming methods." In 1907, western Kansas farms averaged 800 acres, with 120 acres under regular cultivation. In the Arkansas River valley near Garden City, irrigators worked farms that averaged 160 acres, but even this was excessive to Irrigation Crusaders. They irrigated fields of alfalfa, sugar beets, and small grain crops like wheat, oats, and barley. They found that irrigation increased production by a third to a half, but they strongly opposed intensive farming.[82] Walker went so far as to urge that stubborn plains settlers be replaced with dedicated irrigators.[83]

Longstreth and Walker were the Kansas agents of the national Irrigation Crusade led by William E. Smythe, Frederick H. Newell, and Richard J. Hinton. Smythe was introduced to the virtues of irrigation at Kearney, Nebraska, in 1888. He took the lead at a statewide irrigation congress in Lincoln in 1891 and built the National Irrigation Movement, which later received the public blessing of President Theodore Roosevelt. When Smythe organized the Los Angeles Irrigation Congress of 1893, he was joined in the proceedings by Judge J. W. Gregory of Garden City, James S. Emery of Lawrence, and Joseph L. Bristow, the new editor of the *Irrigation Farmer* at Salina.

In 1894, Smythe returned to the plains to address an irrigation congress in Hutchinson, Kansas.[84] With his usual florid rhetoric, he called the new Garden City irrigation project the "beacon light for Kansas" and warned his audience, "You cannot afford to blunder. This is one of the times when blunder is worse than crime. You must not raise another crop of false hopes, a plant that has already been too prolific in Western Kansas." He repeated the new irrigation credo: "Wherever water can be had to irrigate forty acres of Western Kansas soil, every industrious family can win both a living and a competence." He told his audience that during the last forty years each Utah Mormon family on twenty irrigated acres had averaged $1,357.25 a year, or $482.25 over its cost of living. In Kansas a family of five that owned forty acres could support itself on twenty acres and net $500 a year from the other 20 acres. "Wherever a quarter section is now occupied by one family there ought next year to be at least four families, provided there is water for irrigation." Owners of quarter sections would profitably subdivide into twenty- to forty-acre parcels and use the proceeds to pay for a water supply.

> Remember that this is an entirely different sort of development from the old boom in town lots and wheat fields. All of that rested on a speculative basis. We are not planning a development that rests on self-sustenance first and then a wise surplus, which in ordinary years will bring us a reasonable profit. . . . It hurts me to ride through Western Kansas and see the desolate houses that serve as homes. We will change all this with irrigation. We will have little homes of pleasing architecture. We will surround them with pretty lawns, we will fringe them with trees and hedges, we will drape them with vines and deck them with roses, in a new Kansas dedicated to industrial independence.[85]

Smythe's overwrought prose gained credibility after Frederick H. Newell published his sober report, "Irrigation on the Great Plains," in the 1896 yearbook of the Department of Agriculture.[86] While Smythe was a journalist and promoter, Newell had credentials as chief hydrographer of the United States Geological Survey. But the message was the same: large dryland farmers foolishly waste the land and are doomed to failure; industrious smallholders on irrigated land are virtuous and will prosper.

Newell anticipated the debates of the 1930s and 1980s when he condemned the way the plains had been settled. Admittedly, during a rare good year a plains farm will bring "wonderful crops," but it will also encourage the useless plowing of thousands of acres. The "irregular and scanty rainfall" of the plains means that "total loss of crops and bitter disappointment inevitably follow, and the unfortunate settlers, if not driven from the country, alternate between short periods of prosperity and long intervals of depression."[87] These misled, inept, and intractable farmers have already damaged one-sixth of the nation's land when, properly irrigated and professionally tended, it could provide farmsteads "for millions more." Newell argued that the plains offer "boundless tracts of fertile soil" where, tragically, "the temptation to the settler is [still] to make his farm as wide reaching as the horizon, and to spread his efforts over hundreds of acres. The ever-recurring droughts stimulate him to try and till more land, in the hopes that he may recoup his losses in a fortunate year. He is in a certain sense a gambler, staking everything upon luck, and with the chances against him . . . it is almost impossible for him to see that his own hope of permanent success lies in limiting his operations to a comparatively few acres."[88] Newell acknowledged that plains farmers were stubborn and would rather emigrate than practice "un-American intensive farming."

Newell proposed that farmers abandon western Kansas and that, barring intensive irrigated farming, migration be cut off in order to return the region to pastureland. "Has the world not heard enough of droughts and crop losses, of famines and suffering, of abandoned farms and worthless Kansas mortgages? Why interpose to prevent the country from going back to its former conditions? It was, and can be, a magnificent grazing land."[89] He recommended government intervention, since the federal government was still the plains' largest landowner. Any attempt to irrigate a field on the scale of a quarter section is costly, unnecessary, wasteful, and deceptive. "The idea that any man on the boundless plains would concentrate his energies on 10 acres has seemed ridiculous. Yet this is what stern necessity is compelling the farmer to do, and is making him unlearn his old habits and methods, turning them over perhaps to grazing, and giving his main attention to the few acres almost within a stone's throw of his door."[90] This included abandonment of wheat or corn, which are too low in value for irrigated land and should be left to farmers in Illinois and Iowa.

Newell argued that intensive farming is high grade, diversified, and risk free. In a prophetic statement anticipating the technologies and practices of the 1960s, he concluded that plains farming depends upon individually controlled wells to tap groundwater supplies, since surface streams are uncommon and often intermittent. "It is often possible for the farmer to dig or drill the well himself, and he can purchase, sometimes on credit if necessary, the machinery, windmill, or pump for bringing the water to the surface."[91] In an open appeal to the crusty independent plains farmer, Newell argued that intensive farming thus preserved democratic freedom for the individual farmer, which he might have lost under a large irrigating colony. Newell then described state-of-the-art pumping and windmill technologies, believing that steam and gasoline power offered great promise in the future. He also emphasized skilled management techniques for the application of water and the cultivation of crops. Following these recommendations, any industrious farmer could begin to prosper on three to five acres. The Jeffersonian dream of the citizen farmer thus could still prevail in the arid West.

Newell's small-farms plan for the plains was resurrected during the Dust Bowl era. Agricultural extension agents in Meade, Grant, and Ford counties in western Kansas promoted live-at-home programs to encourage self-sufficiency when cash crops failed. Farmers were piously told to work harder toward diversification involving a combination of row crops for feed and grain; a mix of cattle, pigs, chickens, and turkeys; and gardening.[92] The Ford County agent preached that wheat had destroyed the region, that federal aid had failed, and that farmers loafed away three-quarters of their time because eight hundred acres of wheat needed only 411 hours a year. Farmers wryly observed that animals and gardens did not do well under Dust Bowl conditions.

Newell's Kansas reclamation crusade was reinforced by a colleague, Richard J. Hinton. Originally a newspaperman like Smythe, Hinton came to know the West as a government agent and writer for private industry, including the Southern Pacific Railroad. In 1886 he was commissioned by Congress to write *Irrigation in the United States,* perhaps the most important federal land study after Powell.[93] As Powell had done with Utah, Hinton gave special attention to California's ever-increasing water needs and the High Plains received secondary attention. But as Powell's influence declined, Hinton's rose. In 1889 he turned his attention to central plains farmers, in such destitute condition, he announced, that they would in the future be "the largest part of the population to be benefitted by irrigation."[94] Hinton followed Newell's lead and warned that existing large-scale dryland farming guaranteed an "element of [permanent] insecurity" as well as certain collapse in the face of endemic drought. The moral solution to plains poverty was still intensive low-acreage farming—"small detailed works" built through "neighborhood and individual exertion."

Despite his errors concerning the potential for artesian wells in southwest Kansas,[95] Hinton was right on target about plains groundwater. He concluded that the Arkansas River underflow did not exist but a very large, slow-moving, and "mysterious" aquifer did.[96] He supported USGS scientists in their conclusion that the aquifer was composed of slowly moving water that seeped eastward with little local recharge because of soil conditions and high evaporation rates.[97] Despite the conservation implications of this new information, Hinton proposed leaving groundwater to private development. A Walter Rusinek article on Hinton argues that "he appeared to advocate private control and pricing of water, a popular trend today dubbed 'privatization.'"[98] Rusinek concludes that in the long run Hinton did not advance plains irrigation with his privatization argument. "Inefficient pumps, low crop prices, expensive energy, and a government policy that favored surface works kept groundwater development too costly for wide use on the Great Plains until the 1950s. This . . . resulted in too little use during the severe drought of the 1930s and overuse in the post-war years."[99]

The High Plains Way: Decentralized Irrigation

With the ephemeral promise of California-style irrigation from the Arkansas River, wheat farmers around Garden City mortgaged themselves to buy hundreds and even thousands of acres in the dry open country, to dig costly irrigation ditches and peripheral canals, and to dream of abundant crops. Then, with the return of drought, coupled with upstream use in Colorado, the river ran empty on the "dazzling plain without timber and with little water." With communal failures like this, it is not difficult to explain why commitment to decentralized irrigation would become the High Plains way. The answer also may be the persistence of independent farmer values, each family living and working autonomously and determined to make or break in privacy. Neither the Garden City Sugar Company irrigation plan nor a major Reclamation Bureau project nor the cooperative or communitarian styles that succeeded elsewhere would become the irrigator's style in southwest Kansas. Farmers there also rejected Newell's criticism of large-scale irrigation; it insulted their plains know-how. The plains farm family was individualistic, settled on its own independent tract of land, and disinclined to share and divide responsibilities with a larger group, even a cooperative among neighbors. Personal success was measured by no machinery debts; all the land paid for; a ready supply of food and fuel, clothing, and a few conveniences; and deep loyalty to the perceived fundamental virtues of rural American thrift, hard work, and self-discipline. Cooperative ventures and centralized irrigation may have been extremely successful in California, but the plains farmer remained committed to ownership of his own total irrigation system, including wells, pumps, engines, ditches or piping, and all the costs and personal labor they involved.

In still another try, as crop prices rose, southwest Kansas farmers by 1909 had put down 684 pumps irrigating almost two thousand acres. In 1921 a Garden City farmland sales agent wrote this pitch: "Irrigation: Dollars for you where Water Means Wealth, in the Garden City district, America's Land of Promise, combined with Good Land, Rich Soil, Low Prices, and Reasonable Terms."[100] By 1924 the area had some twenty thousand acres "under pump" and eighty thousand "under ditch." Kansas Irrigation Commissioner George S. Knapp concluded after a 1,300-mile tour of the state that irrigation had reached its limits because since it was too costly outside the few river valleys in the west. Although Riverside, California, irrigators could pay for pumping from one hundred feet or more below ground because they could afford twenty dollars per acre on a two-thousand-dollar-orange grove yield, Knapp asked, "What crop could they raise in western Kansas which will make such a return as that?"[101] Irrigation, he said, was limited to pumping when the cost did not exceed 10 percent of the value of the crop and where the water table was not more than twenty feet below the surface so that it could be reached by windmill power. But Knapp also observed: "How do you suppose the farmers back there would like to throw a switch and save their corn crops this year at the cost of $1 an acre?"

The local farmer fought tenaciously to preserve his way of life. Sometimes he would plow up more ground for a bigger crop as prices fell; other times he would sell off cattle at a loss. The farm family had a stubborn pride that made it imperative to stay on the dried-out plains rather than face the gritty factories and boss-ruled politics of a distant industrial America. Dust Bowl historian Donald Worster noted that "the people of the [Arkansas] country were land- and machinery-rich . . . but in other respects they were closer to the sod-house era than to our own."[102] The frontier still held sway on the High Plains.

3

. . .

From Dryland to Dust Bowl:
Not a Good Place to Farm

On a small corner of the leeward side of a field, a particle of soil, broken loose by the wind, struck a cluster of soil particles like a cue ball striking the racked balls. The avalanching effect of soil erosion gathered force as it moved across the field. By the time the effects of one tiny wind-driven soil particle reached the opposite side of the field, a mighty force was assembled to assault the neighboring abandoned field. Soon a dirt storm was burning any living plant, while the soil around the plant's roots was joining the race across the stricken land.—Dust Bowl historian Paul Bonnifield

It is useless to single out any one set . . . the farmers, the bankers, the land speculators, the agricultural teacher or scientist—and blame one group or all of them for what has happened. We have all had a hand in it. . . . We wound our country and threaten its future by thoughtless actions which are . . . an inherited way of thinking—not thinking—about the land.—Secretary of Agriculture Henry A. Wallace in the 1930s

In his magisterial 1931 history of the Great Plains, Walter Prescott Webb concluded that the future of the region did not belong to irrigation. Neither Webb nor John Wesley Powell fifty years earlier anticipated the remarkable technological breakthroughs that gave plains farmers access to large amounts of Ogallala groundwater by the 1960s. Nor did they foresee the enormous capacity of the aquifer. Webb recognized that large-scale irrigation projects were under way in California and in irrigation communities like Greeley,

Colorado, but he correctly concluded that these did not suit the widely spaced independent farms of the plains. Individual plains farmers fended for themselves (and they often insisted on their independence at almost any price) in an environment rigidly limited by less than twenty inches of rain. More than half of the precious rain was evaporated by hot winds and bright sunshine. Fortunately, most rains came in the spring.

Under these conditions, despite the rash of failures, Webb urged dryland farming: "The conservation of soil moisture during dry weather by special methods of tillage."[1] It was not no-rain farming but low-rain farming in which certain soils, such as the common Dalhart sandy loam of the Texas-Oklahoma Panhandle, held some of the rainfall ready to be tapped. When a midwestern corn farmer showed up to try his luck on the plains, he turned the sod deep with a moldboard plow and tilled the fields smooth, but neighboring dryland farmers warned him that this hard work would only lead to soil blowing. The new settler learned to prepare the land by listing—"cutting the stubble with a double plow that split the slice"—and to leave untilled ridges as barriers against the wind. Always keeping the wind and moisture holding in mind, the farmer learned to plant his corn or wheat or sorghum in the shelter of the furrow. The rough fields offended the traditional sense of good farming and "critics regarded the trashy seedbed as careless farming," but it worked in the windy and droughty region.[2] Frequent harrowing and disking turned the soil and kept it moist. Besides drought-resistant crops, deep plowing, and frequent cultivation, farmers learned the critical importance of timing. A field had to be cultivated within a few hours after a rain to limit rapid evaporation in the low-humidity atmosphere. Using dry farming's careful management of resources, early twentieth-century farmers in southwest Kansas turned the corner toward prosperity without tapping the hidden and unknown waters of the Ogallala aquifer. Like so many solutions to the severe problems of the plains, it was a temporary victory.

"Successful dry farming also depended upon plant adaptation," Webb wrote. The first settlers experimented with Turkey red hard winter wheat, the sorghums, and kafir, the fodder crop "that never failed—that is, almost never."[3] The U.S. Department of Agriculture, although it cautiously played down dryland farming as the salvation of the plains, identified drought-resistant grains, particularly durum wheats for use in macaroni and spaghetti. The agency also encouraged mixed farming in wheat, sorghums, and millets so that farmers might not go down if one crop failed. Corn and alfalfa also were mentioned, but both were water-intensive crops and clearly needed irrigation; corn would return as a major crop only with the spread of modern irrigation. Alfalfa was new to plains farmers and they tried it only occasionally in a leftover field. Reminiscent of Irrigation Crusaders, bright-eyed dry-farming advocates also insisted that if the farmer found the right combination of trees, shrubs, grains, fruits, and vegetables, he could succeed on less than a quarter section. Pioneering agricultural scientist John D. Widtsoe claimed in 1911, one of American agriculture's most triumphant years, that the independent family farmer with four horses and basic equipment could live on 160 acres, even if he kept 80 acres in alternating summer fallow.[4]

For a time early in the century, dry farming would make the plains into "the last and best grain garden of the world." Wrote Webb: "[S]ettlers swung their plows into the [apparently] hopeless sagebrush lands, planted their wheat, waited, watched and prayed. To their amazement the seed sprouted and the young plants stood up bravely in the scorching sun and yielded a bountiful crop."[5] In 1910, in the middle of the pre–World War I boom time called the Golden Age of Agriculture, the central and southern plains had 11,422 farms averaging 520 acres each. Farm prosperity was so good and living standards so nearly matched the new urban wealth that 1909 to 1914 have been called the parity years ever since. In early 1918 a manager for the Texas Land and Development Company optimistically wrote that although Plainview, Texas, had only ten inches of rain, "a good wheat crop was produced and considerable feed was grown without irrigation."[6] During 1917 the company had easily sold seventy-five thousand dollars worth of unimproved land at twenty-five dollars an acre for dryland farming.

With the appearance in the decade before World War I of integrated mechanization—gasoline tractor, combine, and gasoline truck—dryland farming, never workable on a few acres, turned into farming on thousands of acres because the machines allowed rapid plowing and intensive cultivation. When machines and mechanical power became commonplace, they offered seemingly unlimited access to the flat, open grassland. Between 1910 and 1930, the man-hours needed to produce wheat fell by a third while land in wheat rose a third. A hundred years earlier it took fifty-eight hours to harvest an acre of wheat; by 1930, an efficient mechanized wheat operation on the plains could do the same in three hours.[7] When farmers believed they could get $2.50 for a bushel for wheat, they invested in high-priced land and expensive equipment.

In 1915 there were approximately 3,000 tractors in all of Kansas. Wartime demand and the appearance of the mass-produced and low-cost Fordson populated Kansas with more than 17,000 tractors by war's end. By 1930 there were more than 66,000 tractors, and despite the Great Depression the numbers exceeded 95,000 in 1940. According to a writer for *Harper's* in 1938, tractors like the International Harvester Farmall, the Fordson, the Case, and John Deere's two-cycle "poppin' johnny" changed the farmer from "a clod into an operator; from a dumb brute into a mechanic."[8] In 1926, farmers overcame the problem of tillage with Charlie Angell's one-way disk plow. Although it doubled or tripled the sod a farmer could break compared to the venerable moldboard plow, the one-way plow left behind a pulverized granular soil that would easily blow away.[9] Yet the organic material in a smooth, pulverized soil produced tremendous wheat crops. Forty-seven hundred combines in 1925 grew to more than 24,000 in 1930 and 42,800 in 1940. Harvesting, from on-field header to in-town market, declined from sixteen men to two, and the grain was handled only once or twice instead of five times. Efficiency in one area created bottlenecks elsewhere: the problem of hauling grain to market disappeared when the gasoline-engine truck replaced the team of horses. In 1920, Kansas farmers owned 3,900 trucks, which accelerated to 33,700 by 1930 and 42,600 by 1940.[10]

This triumph through mechanization put an entirely new cash pressure on the farmer. In earlier decades, equipment came from the local blacksmith when tools were not homemade. The majority of southern and central plains farmers in the 1920s still lived on their small quarter-section tracts of 160 acres; raised milk cows, pigs, and chickens; and generated a small cash crop from wheat, sorghum, or broomcorn. Donald Worster writes that during the 1920s, when more and more farmers wanted to buy a tractor, truck, and combine, they found they had to generate $4.00 an acre in new money to cover mechanization costs alone, equal to ten bushels of wheat at forty cents each. During the 1920s, when wheat averaged $1.03 a bushel and yields ranged from eight to eighteen bushels an acre, a farmer's mechanization costs were about 40 percent of his gross income, not to mention seed cost, hired labor, and land mortgage debt.[11] Few plains farmers would have their debts and loans paid off when wheat collapsed to twenty-five cents a bushel in the 1930s.

European famine after World War I encouraged vast new plantings that expanded plains plow-ups on more millions of acres. In Finney County, Kansas, 76,000 plowed acres in 1914 had grown to 122,000 by 1919.[12] In a 1986 essay, Donald Worster lays blame for plains failure upon "the Great Plow-up," which between 1914 and 1919 expanded plains wheatlands by 13.5 million acres, including 11 million acres of native grass; this allowed American farmers to enter world markets during World War I by shipping 330 million bushels overseas, a third of the nation's entire production and equivalent to the total annual wheat harvest during the Golden Age. Wrote Worster: "The war integrated the plains farmer more thoroughly than ever before into the national economy . . . [and] into an international market system. When the war was over, none of that integration loosened; on the contrary plains farmers in the 1920s found themselves more enmeshed than ever, as they competed fiercely with each other to pay off their loans and keep intact what they had achieved."[13] These bonds have never since loosened and mostly have become tighter. The promise of mechanized dry farming encouraged new settlement on the central and southern High Plains immediately after World War I. In southwest Kansas, 2 million wheat acres in 1925 became 3 million in 1930. Worster writes of a Texas wheat farmer, H. B. Urban, who in 1929, with one hired man, used his two International tractors to break 20 more acres each day.[14] In the last five years of the decade,

5.25 million acres were plowed up and wheat production rose 300 percent, bringing a severe glut by 1931.

The combination of mechanization debt, widespread plow-ups, and historically depressed wheat prices was terrible for plains wheat farmers; they collapsed under the fourfold hammer blows of wheat glut, prices that fell through the floor, and the arrival of both drought and depression. In his 1979 book *Dust Bowl: The Southern Plains in the 1930s,* Donald Worster argues that when the dryland plains farmers entered the world of modern industrial capitalism, it was not the salvation they expected. Instead, mechanization costs would accelerate the collapse of their independence and force them into bondage to market forces they could not control. Worster concludes that a widespread disregard of economic realities, plus public indifference to farmers, "was the work of a generation of aggressive entrepreneurs, imbued with the values and world view of American agricultural capitalism. They smelled an opportunity to create a profit on the Plains and . . . they started out to create that profit—to derive from the land both personal wealth and status. . . . they made the region say money instead of grass."[15] Worster says this is still the dominant policy toward plains farming today.

The tragedy of the plains lay in its contradictions. It had fertile land "in which a furrow can be plowed a hundred miles long." New plows, harvesters, and combines were designed specifically with the plains in mind. The region was inhabited by skilled, energetic, and eager people, but there was still not enough water to exploit the new technologies and bring lasting prosperity to hard-working farmers. Wrote Walter Prescott Webb: "This search for water has been the continuous and persistent movement that has gone on in the Great Plains country."[16] He wrote prophetically when he doubted that groundwater, whether from artesian wells or pumped by windmills or any other advanced technology, would turn the plains into a perpetual garden, since they "are paying out a store of water which has been long in accumulating."[17] He had no idea of the scale of Ogallala water storage, but he worried about rapid overconsumption: "Such utilization over a broad area would call for a re-supply 'beyond the possibilities of even the most humid climate.' . . . the ground water is an accumulation which has been made over long periods. It is a bank account of great size maintained at a given level by a balance of small deposits and small withdrawals annually."[18] But he thought the discussion was academic: "Throughout the region water lies below economical pumping depth for irrigation on any considerable scale."

Worster also concluded that mechanization and the speculative capitalist economy behind it pushed the plains ecology far beyond its limits and thus transformed an ordinary drought into the extraordinary Dust Bowl. These conditions further enfeebled the Jeffersonian farmer lifestyle that had been the American model since the earliest plains frontier settlement.[19] The answer, industrial capitalism, was worse, claimed Worster, than a harsh frontierlike life. Americans dedicated to farm life on the open plains began in the 1920s to abandon their frontier-outpost lives to become small businessmen. They went to the bank and borrowed money; crossed the street to use the money for a tractor, truck, and combine; rented another quarter section or two; and went into business to make money to pay back the bank.

Submarginal Land: A Bad Place to Farm

Considering past experience, some government officials concluded that farmers, even good farmers, had no reasonable justification to stay on the plains. Despite all other improvements, only access to water would bring survival, and there was not enough water. Local dryland farmers disagreed; they argued they could grow crops and prosper if prices were right. The 1930s would test both viewpoints and bring a confrontation.

In July 1931 dryland farmers in southwest Kansas harvested the biggest crop they had ever seen. Extensive fall rains and winter storms offered water-laden fields that farmers rushed to plant, cultivate, and harvest, but wheat had fallen to only twenty-five cents a bushel, one-tenth of its price at the end of World War I. In the middle of abundance, farmers were going broke. Then plains farmers experienced the second blow: a rainless August and September so severe they burned next season's feed crop. The dry spell continued into the winter. Reeling from this double stroke of misfortune, many farmers had abandoned their bare fields by the spring of 1932. March's strong winds built up into more than twenty dust storms that drifted blowing topsoil as

92

high as fencerows. The farmers who planted a spring crop averaged only five bushels per acre, although fortunate farmers near Hooker, Oklahoma, and Liberal, Kansas, surprised themselves with nearly thirty bushels.[20] There was no national grain surplus, yet prices hovered between thirty and thirty-six cents a bushel. More fields were left abandoned and more bare soil lay exposed.

In 1933, scientists at the Panhandle A & M Experiment Station at Goodwell, Oklahoma, recorded 70 days of severe dust storms in 1933. A neighbor ten miles away in Texhoma recorded 139 dusty days and 195 clear days from January through November 1933. With wry humor, farmers said they now "dusted" their seed into the soil. The wheat harvest would be the poorest of the entire Dirty Thirties. Whatever remained of alfalfa and wheat and milo went down to plagues of grasshoppers and rabbits. Farmers were soon stacking Russian thistle (young tumbleweed), bitter and laxative, to feed their cattle in the winter. Many were forced to sell their milk cows, losing the household's supplementary cream check. Farm families with nothing left in the fields or bank book ate rabbits; a rabbit drive in Kansas or Oklahoma might round up two thousand animals on a section or two of land. As a final blow, many farmers in the southern plains lost their gas leases when the oil and gas industry collapsed in the mounting Great Depression. Government relief programs would not start until 1934; that same year recorded the lowest level of rainfall during the entire 1930s drought. But hope for an end to bad times revived briefly when Goodwell, Oklahoma, recorded only 22 days of severe dirt blowing. This was smashed in 1935 with 53 days of dirt blowing at Goodwell, followed by 73 days in 1936 and 134 days in 1937, more than a third of the entire year.[21] Popular folk singer Woody Guthrie visited the area and reported that people were flocking to churches because it was the end of the world.[22]

The land drifted into desertlike dunes, the topsoil gone and hardpan exposed like a flayed skin laid open. The 1934 crop was good in Morton County, Kansas, but a total failure in neighboring Beaver County, Oklahoma. Wheat prices offered a morsel of hope when they finally crept up to seventy-five cents in July and ninety-four cents in August. But New Year's

Day 1935 opened with a severe dust storm, followed by repeated blowings in February and damaging winds of hurricane force in March. On the night of March 15 in Boise City in the western panhandle of Oklahoma, moviegoers could not manage the few blocks to their homes; a businessman returning home abandoned his car in town and spent the night in a hotel. Respiratory diseases, including "dust pneumonia," received attention in newspapers throughout the nation. The emotional strain of months and years of wind and blowing dirt led to suicides, beatings, and murders.[23] Few people who experienced it will forget the blackness and confusion of the apocalyptic dust storm of April 14, 1935, which darkened skies from Colorado to the East Coast and layered dirt on ships three hundred miles out in the Atlantic Ocean. It was fixed in American popular culture by Woody Guthrie's new song from Pampa, Texas: "So Long, It's Been Good to Know Ya."[24]

By the spring of 1932 vast acreages were abandoned to bare dirt. The swing was dramatic: in southwest Kansas's Hamilton County, 16,000 acres under wheat in 1929 rose to more than 103,000 in 1931 and then collapsed to 48,000 in 1932. In Morton County, it rose from 33,000 acres in 1929 to 113,000 in 1931 and fell to 59,000 in 1932. Seward County saw 139,000 acres in 1929, 170,000 acres in 1931, and 86,000 acres in 1932. Grant County went from 114,000 acres in 1929 to 196,000 in 1931 and down to 27,000 in 1932.[25]

If Dust Bowl farmers could not raise wheat, they believed they could temporarily return to cattle raising, since their land had once been ranchland. Unbeknownst to them, the detested "socialist" bureaucrats in Washington had plans to move now-hapless dryland farmers off submarginal land in Kansas and Oklahoma and replace them with cattle-grazing ranches spread widely across the plains. Ironically, fifty years later, in the 1970s and 1980s, both farmers and ranchers would be served by prosperous feedlots supplied by irrigated green fields of alfalfa and milo covering hundreds of acres in southwest Kansas and the Oklahoma-Texas Panhandle. Increased cattle grazing did help sustain Dust Bowl farmers until the beef market fell through the floor in 1933; lack of rain threatened the herds in 1934.[26] Any extended revival of ranching succumbed to drought: cattle could not wait for another year of bureaucratic delays before getting emergency feed. Ranchers had not helped themselves by habitually overstocking and overgrazing their over-burdened land. Several million acres of pastureland in the Dust Bowl region produced only 30 percent of the normal crop of grasses.

More water was the answer, but until the right technology could reach the deep-seated Ogallala groundwater, this need could be met only by more rain. Instead, federal relief came in the spring and summer of 1934. The New Deal would spend more than two billion dollars to keep the independent plains farmers on the land. Ranchers who took personal pride in their self-sufficiency now accepted federal loans to import cottonseed cake and al-falfa. Despite their fierce independence, stockmen in 1934 and 1935 gladly sold their cattle at rock-bottom prices as low as four dollars a head to an emergency government program, which then destroyed diseased or useless animals and distributed the remaining tough meat free to unemployed Americans.[27] Drought also brought the invasion of federal "locusts," who wanted to tell already-resentful ranchers how to improve pastureland, manage their scarce water better, and improve their herds.

The New Deal: Getting Good Farmers Off Waterless Submarginal Land

The question was raised in the 1890s, put to the test in the 1930s, and raised again in the 1950s. Could farming succeed on the central High Plains? Decent, hardworking farmers appeared to be sacrificing themselves repeatedly on land that lacked enough rain.

In a controversial 1979 book, Paul Bonnifield, trained historian and plains farmer, argued that in the 1930s the Roosevelt administration concluded that the settlement of the Dust Bowl had always been on submarginal land, that the region ought to be depopulated, farmers resettled elsewhere, and the land turned back to native grass.[28] Without extensive irrigation or some other significant improvement, the region did not offer practical habitation. Farmers damned the idea as "communist" intervention. A 1936 federal statement would hardly reassure them:

> Although crop failure, speculative expansion, absentee ownership, and depressed price levels were among the factors that precipitated the

relief situation . . . the frontier philosophy which assumed that the individual, if given complete freedom, will pursue an economic course that was to the best interests of society, led to the present dilemma of stranded communities, bankrupt farmers, and widespread unemployment.[29]

Nor was the problem of private ownership resolved. An enforced federal buyout from unwilling landowners was widely perceived as a direct attack on the inviolable constitutional right of private property. Any landowner, whether farmer or speculator, had no restrictions on what he did with his land; he could with impunity plow it to dust or let it wash down into the Gulf of Mexico. The new thrust toward conservation and land management heralded a revolutionary shift from this unfettered and historic laissez-faire philosophy.[30]

Decades earlier, Irrigation Crusaders Smythe, Newell, and Hinton had castigated plains farmers for foolish and inappropriate practices. In its 1936 report the new federal Great Plains Drought Area Committee blamed the extremes of the Dust Bowl on historic federal land policies that had encouraged settlement on submarginal land between 1880 and 1910. Dust Bowl hardships were made worse by misguided agricultural policy that had urged widespread and environmentally harmful plow-ups between 1910 and 1930. Plains farmers had been mistakenly lured onto the land and then wrongly urged to hang on. Echoing the sentiments of John Wesley Powell almost sixty years earlier, the 1936 report said: "The basic cause of the present Great Plains situation is our attempt to impose upon the region a system of agriculture to which the Plains are not adapted or to bring into a semi-arid region methods which are suitable, on the whole, only for a humid region."[31] In compensation "the federal government must do its full share in remedying the damage caused by [1] a mistaken homesteading policy [and 2] by the stimulation of war-time demands which led to over-cropping and overgrazing." These provoked "a system of agriculture which could not be both permanent and prosperous."[32]

As a result, the committee concluded that the Dust Bowl region had collapsed into seriously degraded environmental conditions far below its original frontier conditions; it was government's duty at the very least to return it to frontier status. Despite repeated attempts at settlement, the plains could never thrive as an agricultural heartland; instead, famine stalked settlers under the implacable dryness. At best the central Great Plains could serve as a grazing land to support a small number of hardy ranchers. The Great Plains Committee also admitted that the inhabitants, despite the double hammer blows of depression and Dust Bowl, "were in no mood to abandon their land. . . . They were willing to do all that was humanly possible to save it."[33]

As the committee saw it, the central plains were not terribly important to guarantee the nation's food base because the nation had a surplus of good farmland. The agricultural boom of the 1910s and 1920s involved a combination of expanded acreage and revolutionary advances in plant genetics, soil science, and mechanization. This technological revolution brought on a farmland glut. As early as 1923 a federal land-use management proposal, "The Utilization of Our Lands for Crops, Pasture, and Forest," had been developed by Lewis C. Gray in the USDA yearbook. With aggressive USDA backing, Gray urged the creation of clearly defined and specifically graded agricultural districts based on soil, climate, agricultural science, farm technologies, location near population centers, and even historical and cultural factors. Since the central Great Plains region lacked essential water and was beset by uncontrollable climate extremes, it failed to measure up to Gray's standards for good agriculture; hence the plains should cease to exist as a farming region. His plan would restrict new settlement, pull back from low-production hardship farming, and discourage further costly improvement of plains farmland. Instead the nation should put its resources into more improvement of the prosperous farming in the humid midwestern and eastern agricultural belts. In 1924 the Bureau of Agricultural Economics argued that there were "pathological farming areas" on the plains. This unfortunate label identified "diseased" areas that had been created by a combination of natural and human conditions.[34] At a 1931 conference on farmland use in Chicago, the keynote speaker reported that "the boomer days are over."[35]

Gray urged that submarginal lands be closed down entirely and allowed to revert to their natural state for future recreation, wildlife, or pasture. The people who mistakenly had been allowed to stake out submarginal land would be resettled on subsistence homesteads elsewhere. In many circles this USDA plan was considered progressive and humanitarian, based on the latest scientific land-use planning.[36] (This was also the era of Soviet collectivization, which was being watched with much interest throughout the world). Gray's plan failed to gain support in Congress, but the USDA continued to promote agricultural districting and resettlement as the Draconian answer to falling farm prices and failing farms. In its 1930 yearbook the agency argued that "much of the economic hardship suffered by farmers has been caused by too rapid expansion. . . . The eagerness of land-owning interests and selling agencies to induce farmers to occupy undeveloped areas, public encouragement to land settlement, and other influences have contributed to overrapid agricultural expansion."[37] Plains farmers had been devastated not only by the forces of nature, but also by private economic interests and political policies that were, it seemed, socially destructive and inappropriate for the plains. This statement stood in sharp contrast with aggressive land-sale promotion of the previous 150 years. With passage of the Taylor Grazing Act in 1934, a century and a half of selling off the public domain to promote on-site family farming came to an end. The act itself restricted most of the remaining public domain to grassland—80 million acres—and took it off the market. The government reversed the historic public sales by buying up devastated farmland to return it to grass.

In 1933 the incoming president, Franklin D. Roosevelt, strongly advocated agricultural districting and resettlement from submarginal lands. He followed up his controversial 1933 Agricultural Adjustment Act with appointment of a National Planning Board in the Public Works Administration of the Interior Department. The National Planning Board was packed with advocates for redistricting and resettlement. In 1934 it reported that "extensive areas of the Great Plains . . . must be classed as unsuited to sustained cultivated crops, and should therefore never have been plowed, but retained in grass for stock raising." Both the National Planning Board and the powerful Great Plains Committee damned the Homestead Act of 1862 for encouraging settlement on too-small 160-acre farms on submarginal land. The ghost of John Wesley Powell and his 1878 arid-lands report must have been hovering nearby.

The New Deal treated plains agriculture as a matured economy in decline,[38] yet there was regret over the apparent abandonment of the family farmer as a national symbol. Historian Donald Worster notes that federal officials, such as Rexford Tugwell and Lewis Gray, admitted that farming was an important cultural phenomenon, a major feature of the American Dream and Manifest Destiny, as well as an economic problem and that it deserved attention for its central role in the preservation of a national identity in troubled times. In a statement that would shape and color farm policy well into the 1980s, they said plains farming was "a valued way of life, not merely another 'industry.' "[39] Hence farmland policy was duty bound to seek to insulate the lifestyle of the independent farmer from the negative pressures of overproduction, commercialization, land destruction, and family poverty. Farm policy in the 1930s supported regional self-sufficiency and encouraged the remaining dryland farmers to graze cattle on locally grown sorghum silage. Fifty years later, in the 1970s and 1980s, the same region would be sustained in large part by large feedlots using locally grown silage. The difference was that the large amounts of silage would be grown under irrigation.

Lewis Gray's views were confirmed by an influential 1936 report, *The Future of the Great Plains*. The National Resources Board sought to eliminate "the numerous farm families now engaged in crude, self-sufficing systems of farming" unlikely to experience mechanization, afford costly irrigation, or accept other improvements. In angry reaction, Oklahoma soil scientist H. H. Finnell complained in a Boise City newspaper article in 1934 that "recent agitation for the abandonment of the plains on the grounds the land is submarginal or even marginal are [*sic*] not founded on any knowledge of the actual potentialities of our resources nor of the technic [*sic*] of utilization."[40] Finnell's answer was not abandonment, but appropriate dryland-farming techniques for a semiarid region. The USDA's 1935 yearbook complained that farm use was uncoordinated and that "wrong land uses" were still not put in check: "New uses had to be discovered for land withdrawn from production for export, submarginal farming had to be discouraged, and crop adjustment had to be coordinated with land utilization in general."[41] At first, desperate local farmers asked the federal government to declare an emergency, put the Dust Bowl under martial law, and create a "Dust Bowl Authority."[42] A local "Farm Practice Committee" naïvely fell into a federal trap when it argued for federal purchase of submarginal land and its return to grass. As land-retirement plans became reality, farmers soon balked at their loss of independence and property rights.

How was submarginal land to be identified before it could be bought, taken out of production, and restored? The problem of definition was not resolved. The word "submarginal" remained poorly understood by government agencies, the public, and the affected farmers: it was not measured by soil quality or water quantity, but by the more complex capacity of the farmer to sustain himself on his land. The federal answer was the intensive industrialization of agriculture, which left out the low-scale original settler, who did not have the cash, machinery, or know-how to industrialize. Submarginal came to mean the incapacity of historic farm practices to support large-scale mechanization, including irrigation technologies. If farmers had blindly rejected Smythe's and Newell's small-plot irrigated farming, they were not likely to support large-scale mechanized irrigation, but in the 1930s no one could agree whether technology was the cause of the Dust Bowl or its salvation or both.

A submarginal designation was very often arbitrarily determined by farm size. Sometimes the farm was too large: a 1937 on-site federal wind erosion survey concluded that most Kansas wheat and sorghum farms that ranged from 320 acres to over 640 acres could not be worked by financially strapped and undertooled farmers. Sometimes the farm was too small: 160 acres did not produce enough of a cash crop for a farmer to survive under conditions of drought and low prices. The National Resources Board offered opinions on social conditions and moral duty that angered plains farmers:

> The poor land areas are replete with social and economic maladjustments . . . they are literally the slums of the country. Incomes are low . . . credit is expensive, the people are often poorly housed and ill fed;

educational and cultural opportunities are meagre, while governmental services are either at a minimum or are provided at high expenses to both the community and the larger public. . . . [The government has the duty toward] the rehabilitation of the present occupants of the purchase areas now living a socially degraded existence as a result of their inadequate income, poor schools, and roads, and infrequent contacts with an outside civilization.[43]

Even farmer psychology came under scrutiny. Called colonists by the Great Plains Committee, Dust Bowl farmers were criticized for their lack of understanding of Great Plains land and climate and for their habitual application of unsuitable farming practices brought from the humid East. Their "rehabilitation" required revision of "deep-seated attitudes of mind."[44] The Great Plains Committee wrote that "erosion is . . . closely related to farm management and land-use practices. . . . The legislative program should encourage . . . modification of those land-use and cropping practices which are undesirable."[45]

Historian Paul Bonnifield concluded that the federal government had revived its old Indian-removal policies and now applied them to drought-stricken farmers.[46] Dust Bowl areas set aside for "permanent retirement" included parts of Meade County and the land south of the Cimarron River in Morton, Stevens, and Seward counties in Kansas, including the towns of Liberal, Hugoton, and Elkhart. In adjoining eastern Colorado, most of Baca, Prowers, and Bent counties joined the list. In May 1935, farmers were being offered a fire-sale price of $2.75 an acre to retire fifty thousand acres in Stevens County, but a timely rain, dramatic news of a natural-gas strike, a $10 million natural-gas pipeline construction project, and opportunities for on-farm gas leases left the Resettlement Administration empty handed. A 1935 census report noted that the average value per acre of land in Stevens County was $22.50 instead of the offered $2.75. In Morton County, where gas development was slower and farm conditions more desperate, land prices averaged $13.66 per acre, but a few farmers had already sold out to the administration for $3.00 to $5.00.[47] In late 1934 the National Resources Board received funds for the retirement of seventy-five million acres of unprofitable or waste land, and in April 1935 the Resettlement Administration was authorized to proceed (in 1937 the Farm Security Administration took over, and in 1938 the Soil Conservation Service). Seventy-five million acres of submarginal land on the plains, as well as in Appalachia and around the Great Lakes, was almost 8 percent of the nation's total agricultural land. Federal planners argued for government purchase of several million acres of privately owned farmland in the Dust Bowl region.

As for the farmers who insisted on remaining, they would be regulated on farm size, denied credit, and excluded from federal relief programs. They were to be left—abandoned—more on their own than the original settlers. Whether an advanced groundwater pumping technology that independent farmers could use, as described in the next chapter, would arrive soon enough was doubtful. It did the Dust Bowl–stricken small farmer no good when the Great Plains Committee urged "the enlargement of undersized operating units . . . through extension of credit under suitable restrictions." Only larger, wealthier operators with bank credit could expand their holdings. These "suitable restrictions" had been written into the Taylor Grazing Act.

By 1938 the new federal Kiowa Grasslands covered 91,173 acres. The project was made up of 4,133 abandoned acres, the rest purchased at four to eight dollars an acre of land under "serious misuse."[48] Cimarron National Grassland was created from 53,590 acres in Morton County, Kansas. In its attempt to restore the land, the federal government did not do much more than imitate the land-stabilization procedures used on private farms: listing and planting with forage sorghum and broomcorn and using winter rye instead of winter wheat.[49] When the program died in 1947, a national total of 11.3 million acres had been purchased, mostly on the plains, but far less than originally scheduled.

The first step toward federal reorganization of the nation's superior farmland was the creation of local soil conservation districts along geographical rather than political lines. There were precedents. As early as 1894 a Weather Bureau unit in the USDA had been assigned the mission of studying agricultural soils; it was to integrate "the relation of soils to climate and organic life."[50] In 1895 it became the Division of Soils in the Department of Agriculture and in 1901 gained the elevated name Bureau of Soils. With the Dust Bowl debates on soil erosion, marginal lands, and appropriate crops and land use for the plains, the Soil Erosion Service joined the Department of the Interior in 1933 and was shifted to the Department of Agriculture in 1935, where it became the Soil Conservation Service.[51] The SCS had the incredible luck to have for its first chief Hugh H. Bennett, "one of the few immortals of agricultural history." In a set opening talk as he preached the SCS gospel, Bennett said:

> [W]e tried to imitate nature as much as we could. We abided by the following basic physical facts, (1) land varies greatly from place to place, due to differences in soil, slope, climate and vegetative adaptability; (2) land must be treated according to its natural capability and its condition as the result of the way man has used it; (3) slope, soil, and climate largely determine what is suitable protection in all situations. . . . Above all . . . we tried to imitate nature.[52]

Bennett brought to the SCS a broad vision of public service, a deep allegiance to comprehensive soil conservation, and a dedication to the American farmer.

Nevertheless, farmers feared that the new SCS would spew forth restrictive regulations, for federal relief assistance often was available only to Dust Bowl counties that organized soil conservation districts. A 1937 editorial in the *Spearman* (Texas) *Reporter* dreaded government interference in the farmer's daily life. The Resettlement Administration, it said, would "plan gardens . . . determine what quantity and kinds of foods . . . supply the family's dietary needs; determine . . . foods . . . during the growing season and what foods . . . during the winter months; plan the family's clothing budget," and divide labor among household, kitchen, garden, and field work.[53] In 1937 the Resettlement Administration intensified these fears when it urged significant changes in Dust Bowl farming practices away from wheat to a combination of livestock and alternative crops. Farmers responded by voting down soil conservation districts. Eventually, new emphasis on local rule within the SCS made the districts palatable[54] and brought soil and water conservation districts to the High Plains. Few farmers could agree on a common course of action. Existing practices of overtillage pulverized the soil into more dust, and stubble burning reduced organic materials and soil building. Abandoned farms belonged to no one, yet an unattended farm blew severely.[55] Leaving the land alone was no solution.

Despite the move toward government-planned agriculture, federal help was not immediately forthcoming. The new and inexperienced Soil Conservation Service tried eastern water conservation practices, such as contour plowing. In its article on soil erosion, the 1934 USDA yearbook said nothing about wind erosion, although hundreds of dust storms had ravaged the plains, but when contour rows were in line with the wind, they often accelerated soil blowing.[56] Commonsense practices of listing, terracing, strip cropping, check dams, soil pitting, deep tilling, soil mulching, and summer fallow were intended to prevent water erosion and conserve moisture and had some effect on breaking the force of the wind. One of the first specific attempts to control wind erosion was made in Texas County, Oklahoma, by farmer Fred Hoeme, who invented the Hoeme Chisel, a cultivator that went as much as twelve inches into hard, dry soil below the dust, and it brought up large clods that broke the power of the wind and simultaneously created a listerlike trench to hold whatever rain might fall.[57] To use new conservation equipment often cost farmers much money and drove them deeper into debt to buy bigger and more powerful tractors with rubber-tired wheels. Even so, all attempts at water conservation and wind erosion control were bandaids without access to more water. Only sufficient water would shift Dust Bowl land from its submarginal status.

High Plains Boom and Survival During Repeated Dust Bowls

Nature and the market teased farmers at harvest time in 1935. Wheat prices went from seventy-nine cents in July to more than a dollar in August and to $1.21 in September, the best since 1929. But farmers who got 30 bushels in 1934 faced bare fields in 1935. There was the rare oasis of harvest: Beaver County's crop, which had failed in 1934, produced more than 148,000 bushels in 1935. In eighteen Dust Bowl counties, the 1936 harvest was about the same as 1935: less than a subsistence crop, but enough to allow the remaining farmers to hold on another year. Revived gas and oil leases helped. In 1937, harvests doubled in Texas County, Oklahoma, and the weather generally was less severe in the region. Prices dropped from $1.09 to eighty-eight cents per bushel between July and August, but it was enough to sustain farmers for another year. A grasshopper invasion in 1937 and 1938 seemed a final blow, to be followed by army worms; stretches of the Oklahoma Panhandle and eastern Colorado roads were slick with dead insects. Prices again collapsed in 1938 to less than sixty cents a bushel, but the worst was over in 1939.

Rain and war, a strange mixture of good and evil, revived plains life for the second time in the early 1940s. In 1942, even in places where five or six inches of topsoil had been lost, the central plains produced a record wheat harvest that surpassed the bumper crop of 1931. As a portent of the future, the record was set on a smaller acreage with more machines, better moisture management, and superior agricultural science. The 1942 crop record was topped in 1943 and again in 1944 as farmers patriotically set themselves to offer more food for a war-ravaged globe. The war ended in 1945, but postwar famine threatened hundreds of millions of victims and victors alike. Farmers doubled the 1939 yield, using only 2.5 million more acres on the central and southern plains.[58] Farm income rose 165 percent in the war years, 1939–45, while farm mortgage debt declined almost 20 percent. But, as Donald Worster noted, while production in the Texas Panhandle country rose $37,737,000 in value between 1935 and 1942, it cost taxpayers $43,327,000 in federal aid.[59]

The rules for survival on the plains, despite lessons taught by the great plow-ups from 1914 to 1929, were still being ignored. Between the mid-1930s and 1946, as much as 4,000,000 acres were replowed on the central and southern High Plains, 3,000,000 of which had previously been labeled unfit for cultivation, creating worse results than in the Dust Bowl era. Cheyenne County in eastern Colorado abutting the Kansas border, for example, had 512,000 farmed acres in 1935 and over 931,000 acres in 1945. Once again postwar bumper crops, high wheat prices, and soaring land prices encouraged farmers to capitalize on good times by reworking abandoned land.

By 1950, land that cost three or four dollars an acre in the 1930s sold for up to sixty dollars an acre, a sizable increase, even accounting for inflation. A new breed, the so-called suitcase farmers, who did not live on the land but directed hired laborers from a comfortable distance, were buying land in 5,000-acre parcels.[60] Corporations were formed specifically to plant profitable crops on parcels of 10,000 acres or more. It was not difficult in 1946 to make a million dollars, as one new corporation did on 28,000 acres in southeastern Colorado. Success was guaranteed by more and better machines, superior plant science, and field techniques that grew more on less water, aided by government money and advisers. For a while, industrial farming could be as profitable a money machine on the plains as anywhere else.

In Haskell County in 1947 it was difficult to argue with five million bushels of wheat that generated $3,333 per county inhabitant. After visiting the plains in 1947 a national magazine staffer wrote that "the voice of two-dollar wheat is far more persuasive than scientific facts on wind, rain, sun and soil."[61] Although he was impressed with the dramatic changes since the 1930s, he wondered about overconfidence in the newly industrialized farmers: they were "belligerently positive about their ability to take care of their land, no matter what happens." The new hope for the plains farmer in the postwar era was no longer self-preservation on a bone-dry landscape, but how to have a full share of the postwar boom.

The shift from simple land stewardship by the family farmer early in the century to exploitation for profit seemed irrepressible. Instead of conservation of the unique and limited resources of the plains, the answer seemed to be more cash for better equipment as farmers finally joined the rest of the United States in rushing toward a high-tech future. This was aided by agricultural exports. The Department of Agriculture repeatedly urged fencerow-to-fencerow plowing, and for the next forty years it would continue to press for high production. Postwar big-scale farming began to pull free from the constraints of government conservation so elaborately constructed in the 1930s—terraces, shelterbelts, soil-conservation-district rules—while hanging onto the safeguards of federal subsidies.[62] The conditions were right for the next step in heavy industrialization: pump large amounts of underground water for high-production irrigation. However, writing in a national magazine in 1947, Agriculture Secretary Clinton Anderson, who had experience on his own New Mexico farm, warned that "what we are doing in the western Great Plains today is nothing short of soil murder and financial suicide."[63] Better rains had also returned, averaging fourteen to seventeen inches in the 1940s, but when the hot dry winds came to eastern Colorado again in late 1948, not enough grass remained to anchor the soil.

Oklahoma soil scientist Howard Finnell had warned in 1947 that "we are heading into the same conditions that gave us the old Dust Bowl. The next Dust Bowl will be bigger and better. . . . We have been overrun by the plow-up. Soil conservation districts, organized by farmers to promote good land use, haven't had the backbone to stand up to the money pressure behind the plow-up." Kansas State College agronomist R. I. Throckmorton advised that ten million acres on the central and southern plains, including replowed marginal land, were again in harm's way.[64] Twenty years after the Great Dust Bowl, the rains once again failed in southwest Kansas and the Texas-Oklahoma Panhandle. A hot sun seared the landscape. Winds blew the topsoil away. As early as December 1948, the wheat land of southwestern Kansas received eastern Colorado soil blown its way and sent it flying eastward with its own load. Not since the 1930s did railroad crews have to halt their trains and shovel tracks clear. In mid-January in 1950 the topsoil was powder dry and as easily blown away as in the worst 1930s dust storms. At the end of March 1950 the lack of rain set all-time records. By mid-April, daytime darkness and zero visibility were again commonplace. As much as $275 million worth of wheat was lost.[65]

By early 1950 the wheat crop, devastated by lack of rain, could not hold the soil it was planted in. Land lay bare everywhere: new plowed land lost its grass cover, wheat fields failed, and intensive cattle raising meant overgrazed ranchlands. During the summer of 1950 the drought spread from Kansas and Colorado into the Oklahoma-Texas Panhandle, and farther south. In February 1952, winds that reached eighty miles an hour created a dust front to an altitude of twelve thousand feet; the soil drifted in dunes. By 1952 large tracts of land had lain open for three or four years. Colorado's

Baca County lost more than 70 percent of its 500,000 acres of wheat to the wind; 95 percent of the 250,000 wheat acres in Prowers County blew out or silted over. Hamilton County, Kansas, lost 95 percent of its wheat, worth $1.5 million. In early 1954, several inches of topsoil had been removed from the entire old Dust Bowl region, damaging about 11,700,000 acres.

In the first five months of 1954, only one inch of rain reached the ground. Garden City, Kansas, after the heaviest dust storm of the decade struck on February 19, 1954, next received a heavy load of snow, and townspeople waded through quagmires of mud on the streets and sidewalks. March 1954 was the worst month in several years of dust storms, with familiar results: wheat fields blown out, choking cattle, streetlights on at noon, stranded travelers. The agricultural experiment station at Garden City had recorded thirty more dust storms by June 30. Soil was blown off twice the acreage between 1954 to 1957 than had been lost from 1934 to 1937.

By the spring of 1955, dunes thirty feet high were not unusual. In one storm the dust cut a swath from Denver to El Paso and ran as far east as Wichita. The following spring of 1956 saw dust cover forty thousand square miles, resulting in closed roads and damaged hospital equipment. High abrasive winds scoured paint off license plates and smashed plate-glass windows. Normal rainfall, as farmers still hopefully called it, did not return until the spring of 1957, ten years after the first signs of drought in 1948.[66] Whether Dust Bowl conditions coincided with heavy sunspot activity or not, it became painfully evident that dry times and black blizzards would reappear in a predictable two-decade cycle.

There was less helpless inertia than in the 1930s. Unlike federal shakiness during the Depression, the postwar government was the richest in the nation's history and could generously aid farmers. It also helped that farmers still lived in boom times and were not already weakened by another long-term farmer depression, which in the 1920s had already broken agriculture's back by the time the Dirty Thirties rolled in. The Korean War of 1950–53 would hold farm prices at good levels. Without waiting for government aid, farmers in Morton County, Kansas, set their one-way disks for fourteen to twenty-four inches to conserve about five thousand acres. In 1955 a new technique called pitting offered better endangered-field conservation: disks on one-way plows were set off center. The rotating disks dug pits three or four feet long and several inches deep. These would catch and hold any rainwater and give native grasses—crested wheatgrass, bluestem, grama, and buffalo grass—a good start.

After delays the United States Department of Agriculture allocated $25 million in 1954 and 1955 for emergency tillage. Each farmer was now offered seventy-five cents an acre for listing, fifty cents for chiseling, and $1.25 for contour strip cropping to total no more than $1,500. In addition, farmers were paid for feed and hay. Federal aid programs, many set up in the 1930s, again came into play. The Dust Bowl–era Great Plains Drought Area Committee, for example, had identified policies to carry farmers through disaster, including foreclosure moratoriums, relief, and feed loans. The 1950s provided crop insurance, government supports (forward pricing), long-term loans with variable payments, grain and feed storage, short-crop alternatives, and sophisticated livestock marketing.[67] By August 1954 the Farmers Home Administration (FmHA) provided emergency loans for designated disaster areas covering thirty Kansas counties, thirty-seven Oklahoma counties, twenty-four Colorado counties, seventy-five Texas counties, and twenty-four in New Mexico.[68] To stave off bankruptcy, 3-percent loans could be used to purchase feed, seed, fertilizer, replacement stock and equipment, maintenance of buildings, and fence repair. These efforts kept the farmers solvent and on the land. Their creditors were told to stand by while they recovered.

The drought of the Filthy Fifties was frequently as severe as the one in the 1930s. Almost twenty-one million acres had been seriously damaged and remained vulnerable to more harm. Resettlement and reversion to grassland became unthinkable alternatives, leaving the search for more water as the only acceptable answer. Even after it rained in May 1955 and farmers could expect a good crop, sixteen million acres were still ready to blow.

The 1970s would see another severe drought, and a repeated cycle can be anticipated in the 1990s. In the drought year 1974, with rain seven inches below average, irrigators ran their pumps nearly twice as long as in the normal year 1973 and energy consumption rose 64 percent. Farmers recorded that their groundwater levels declined as much as three feet a year. These high figures continued until the return of normal rainfall in 1978.[69] An orbiting satellite scanning Earth in the late winter of 1977 clearly showed newly seeded West Texas farms blowing dust into Oklahoma as neighboring New Mexico grassland held steady.[70] But now geographer John Borchert could write, there is "a widespread belief that, though there will be future droughts, there need be no future dust bowl."[71]

Plains farming had transformed itself. Beginning in the 1950s, the historic family farm in many cases became a private, heavily capitalized and mechanized industrial operation. Today plains farmers resemble the nation's small businessmen more than their pioneer forebears.[72] Well-managed dryland farming could still offer the power to endure and prosper on the High Plains, it was believed. When fallowed ground was returned to production, it yielded twice as much wheat as unfallowed. Terracing improved wheat and sorghum yields. Worster wryly wrote: "Agronomists promised [the plains farmer] anew the tomorrow world of infinite abundance, when all the land would be contoured to the horizon, every drop of water captured and used, straight even rows of trees planted wherever they would grow—a landscape of engineering and efficiency."[73] Years earlier, scs conservationist Hugh Hammond Bennett had concluded that "farming will become an expert profession; the inexpert and inept will be forced off the land."[74]

The gospel of efficiency took over on the High Plains. By the late 1970s more than half the market value of Kansas's farm production came from those counties with more than twenty thousand irrigated acres.[75] Ogallala water was pumped onto the fields in a use-it-or-lose-it (prior appropriation) policy. By planting fencerow to fencerow at the highest efficiency, farmers could participate in the nation's ebullient postwar expansion. It was get big or get out. Farm size in Kansas doubled, irrigation acreage tripled, and the number of farms decreased more than half between 1940 and 1983, from 159,000 to 76,000. But whenever drought reappeared, it accelerated groundwater consumption to keep production up.

Disadvantages and Advantages of the Plains

The debate over marginal farming and resettlement is not over. Dust Bowl conditions marked the High Plains as an unusually harsh land where settlers and farmers would remain perpetually disadvantaged. It was the last major region frontiersmen settled. The history of repeated plains depopulation, including today's gradual outmigration, reveals inherent weaknesses in the land's capacity to support farmers and towns. Nor does this old Dust Bowl region appear to be essential to the survival of the United States as a prosperous and powerful society. Many irrigated crops, such as wheat, corn, sorghum, alfalfa, and the lesser grains, are surplus. Taxpayers are beginning to protest all-important federal subsidies. Why should American agriculture, no longer shaped by the family farm and now turned into big business, receive special privileges? The farmer is now the government's client, if not its ward. Most successful on the plains are large-scale, vertically integrated corporate operations; their commitment is less to the plains than the mining of its land and water for profit.

The question of removing grain farmers from submarginal plains land and returning the land to light grazing or empty grassland reappeared in a 1983 report compiled by the influential Office of Technology Assessment, an arm of Congress. In seeking to balance out the pros and cons of High Plains farming, the OTA is pessimistic about the future. The combination of food surpluses, low prices, depletion of groundwater, and reduced federal supports demonstrates inability to sustain current levels of agriculture and promises the possibility of another Dust Bowl.[76] The OTA recommends that Congress's limited agricultural appropriations be focused on "protecting and maintaining the long-term productivity of rain-fed agricultural resources" elsewhere at the price of limited commitment to irrigation or dryland farming on the plains:

> The problem of cultivating marginal or unsuited lands ("plow-out") has become particularly critical in the semiarid lands of the Great Plains . . . where the land is especially vulnerable to erosion. Some Federal agricultural programs encourage cultivation of fragile lands and thus contribute to resource degradation.[77]

One option OTA recommended to Congress was that it "withdraw those Federal programs that induce conversion of rangeland to uses not suited to that land and thus cause resource degradation that ultimately limits long-term productivity."[78] Unsuitable laws have already encouraged the conversion of rangeland, plow-ups, and extensive resource degradation, so, "Congress could withdraw Federal incentives that induce conversion of rangeland to cropland use where that use is not suitable for the resource . . . e.g., price supports, commodity loans, and disaster payments."[79]

The 1983 OTA report reviewed irrigation growth on the High Plains from 2,000,000 acres in 1944 to 13,000,000 acres in 1974. It noted that when the Ogallala aquifer is depleted under a farmer's land, he reverts to dryland farming (over 500,000 acres, mostly in Texas, between 1974 and 1979) and compensates by plowing up more rangeland (1,400,000 acres in Colorado and South Dakota between 1974 and 1983). OTA concluded that

> this trend has alarmed Federal and State Officials who fear that this land is too fragile for intensive cultivation and that the "Dust Bowl" days of the 1930s will return if irrigation water is in short supply or if a lengthy period of dry weather occurs.[80]

Limited ground cover, rainstorm runoff, and soil loss keep the land vulnerable for a repeat of the Dust Bowl. "If these areas are converted [to dryland farming] but later abandoned, how can they be rehabilitated and made productive again, and who should bear the costs of reclamation?"[81] The massive rescue provided by the New Deal in the 1930s (and recycled during the droughts of the 1950s and 1970s) should not be repeated. Irrigation transformed the High Plains, but as the aquifer runs dry, the landscape will shift to larger farm size, more nonsite ownership, changing land-use patterns, and more intensive integration of land values into global investment patterns. Food, land, and water on the plains will be transformed into costly commodities and on-site operations will be drastically unlike current plains farming. The OTA suggests that the changes will bring more, not less, degradation of land and water. According to this view, in the long run plains farming will be unsustainable, which, after all, is the definition of submarginal.

The most radical proposal was offered by land use planners Frank and Deborah Popper in late 1987.[82] Let us finally admit, they argued, that more than a century of repeated farm abandonments, dust bowls, costly government interventions, and environmental destruction has resulted in repeated failures. America's rural past, and technological civilization, has surrendered to environmental adversity in a wide swath of the Great Plains counties running from Texas to North Dakota. "Over the next generation, the Plains will, as a result of the largest, longest-running agricultural and environmental miscalculation in American history, become almost totally depopulated."[83] Federal resettlement programs in the 1930s were right on target. Depopulation should be aggressively encouraged to allow the plains to revert to their preagricultural condition. Frank Popper said this must include deprivatization to create an open and publicly owned Buffalo Commons, not only in the old Dust Bowl region, but selectively throughout the entire High Plains from Canada through Texas, almost one-sixth of the land area of the lower forty-eight states.

Despite stormy criticism from High Plains inhabitants, the Poppers seek to "recreate the 19th century. It will be the world's largest historic-preservation project, the ultimate national park," since Americans have failed to make much of the High Plains an economic or human success. "The brute fact is that in any plausible use, the bulk of Plains land is insufficiently competitive with land elsewhere. The only people who want it are already on it, and most are increasingly unable to make a living from it." Could a compromise be reached through partial nationalization if irrigation would be accepted as a land-conservation strategy for the rest? It requires only two irrigated acres to produce three acres' worth of dryland corn, sorghum, wheat, and cotton.[84] The answer, however, depends on today's heavy groundwater consumption and thus offers no long-term solution. The Poppers' critics, and they are many, might instead ask: Why not create federal relief zones like the proposed business enterprise zones?[85]

Frank Popper's proposal is too politically explosive to succeed. At the same time, it once again raises the question of Ogallala groundwater. If the surface land were set aside as a national preserve, would the stored water under marginal land be available for transfer elsewhere? If water under protected land was valued at five dollars an acre-foot and prime land next door could be irrigated at forty to fifty dollars an acre-foot, would a transfer benefit the region and the nation?[86] The debate about mining for minerals or drilling for oil under national parks might have ramifications that could be applied to Ogallala water. Reserved water rights, as they are protected in wilderness areas, could also apply.

But even the OTA admits that the High Plains, including the Dust Bowl region, has certain advantages that deserve attention.[87] Pioneering farmers spoke with pleasure of the wonderfully fertile soil and noted that the land was flat, rockless, and treeless. Any Missouri or Pennsylvania farmer who had struggled uphill and down behind his plow and horses, only to encounter innumerable tree stumps, found real satisfaction in plowing the plains. In addition, compared to the humid East, the plains environment was dry and therefore relatively disease-free for his crops. Low humidity meant many more cloud-free days. In more recent years, the High Plains have the advantage that they do not suffer from competition for water from booming cities as is the case in California and Arizona and Colorado. Industrial development is not the major problem (aside from water flooding for secondary oil recovery described in chapter 5) for the plains as elsewhere in the West. Thus the privatization and free-market debate does not currently include water ownership, rights, and pricing. As long as pumping is economically feasible, Ogallala water belongs to agriculture on the High Plains as nowhere else. Farmers can continue to produce crops in otherwise impossible areas, such as the Kansas Sandhills. They can experience higher yields than with dryland farming. Some other western water problems, including the long controversy over federal water subsidies and farmer paybacks, are not problems for the High Plains.

Concluding Note

Have the plains ever moved beyond their frontier exploitive status? Regional ecologist and historian James C. Malin argued that in the 1930s southwest Kansas and the Texas-Oklahoma Panhandle, much of it the last frontier not homesteaded until the early 1900s, were still in their pioneering or early exploitive stage, which had only been intensified by the tractor and mechanized harvester. True postfrontier mature settlement, he believed, should include conservation of land and water for long-term support of a successful rural agricultural society. The 1930s drought was a national tragedy because it overwhelmed the High Plains before maturity took hold, but in the future a well-conceived government assistance program and proper land management could, Malin believed, carry the region into its delayed agricultural prosperity. Plains historian Walter Prescott Webb, who wrote before Ogallala irrigation took hold and who advocated dryland farming, would cautiously agree. But geographer Carl Sauer believed that an ecological balance between successful farming and resource conservation would be possible only through the less mechanized and less capitalized world of small family farmers. Environmental historian Donald Worster concluded that the plains were rapidly becoming a helpless victim of capitalist exploitation.[88]

The plains during the 1930s were, as they always have been, a complicated and dynamic environment-human system. This chapter suggests many critical points of instability—dryness, soil blowing, low prices, low yields, farm-family weakness, poor or wrong information—where a small push anywhere had large consequences everywhere. The question today is not whether plains farming is in harm's way, but whether a small push—greenhouse-level drought or a fresh influx of federal credit to buy equipment and pesticides—will consume Ogallala water at an accelerating pace and bring the entire delicate agricultural house of cards crashing down.

4

. . .

From Windmills to Center Pivots, Feedlots, and Porkers

WE SELL RAIN!—1969 irrigation equipment advertisement

You can produce a lot more raising hogs than dryland wheat.—Paul Hitch, 1994

Windmills Were Not the Answer

The windmill is the familiar symbol of the independent plains farmer of the late nineteenth and early twentieth centuries. It appears in political cartoons, Dust Bowl photographs, and romantic farm films. Plains windmills failed to fulfill expectations because they could not water large fields.[1] A windmill could usually draw water from a maximum of thirty feet, so farmers were frustrated when they learned that good water lay directly underground, at as little as fifty tantalizing feet, yet they couldn't reach it. Windmill technology deserves credit because it provided an alternative to raising water bucket by bucket from hand-dug wells, but it could supply only the home and barnyard, or at the most, five acres of wheat or thirty head of cattle. The windmill would not become another major force in the technological revolution that Walter Prescott Webb said transformed the plains and raised farmers above survival levels. It would not join the ranks of Glidden's barbed wire, Deere's shear plow, McCormick's reaper, and Colt's revolver.[2] The need for the windmill was obvious. Webb said that plains farmers sought "a mechanical device that would raise water to the surface, one that would be economical in construction, inexpensive to operate, and capable of making slow but constant delivery."[3]

As early as 1872 the newfangled windmills and water tanks situated strategically along the Santa Fe and Union Pacific railroad tracks did not escape farmers' attention.[4] These were not the large, creaky windmills with massive wooden sails and revolving mill-houses that characterized the landscape of Holland or Spain. These were leaner wood and metal devices with spinning blades, twenty or thirty feet long, set on top of a simple platform. An old western Kansas saying had it that the trains ran only on days the wind blew. By the end of 1872, the Santa Fe ran through southwest Kansas. Each tank was on a ten-foot-high platform. The train crew would "jerk down" an iron spout to pour water into the steam locomotive's water jacket. Occasionally "jerk water towns" grew up around the windmill, tank, and maintenance crew, while smaller homemade windmills allowed cattle ranchers to fence their land into separate fields, each with its herd supplied by windmill and tank.

According to legend, as early as 1854 an old midwestern "pump doctor," John Burnham, weary of constant repairs, suggested to a young Connecticut mechanic, Daniel Halladay, that if a windmill could be made self-governing, it might well transform western farming. Halladay devised a windmill controlled by the centrifugal force of a weight; it turned itself into the wind and corrected its own speed. The response was astonishing. Halladay moved to Chicago to be closer to potential dryland markets. Quantity orders from railroads allowed the United States Wind Engine and Pump Company to dominate the new industry by 1862. By 1879, as the railroads spread across the plains and independent plains farmers became a significant market, sixty-nine manufacturers made more than one million dollars from windmills. Competitive shakeouts reduced the number of manufacturers to thirty-one by 1919, while sales reached nearly ten million dollars.[5] Important refinements in that period included reducing thirty-foot diameters to four to sixteen feet, with eight- or ten-foot windmills becoming standard. The introduction of curved steel blades led to higher efficiency, size reductions, and lower costs. And the wonder of the self-oiling mechanism delighted farmers who otherwise climbed the windmill in the midst of a blizzard or dust storm to lubricate the linkages. Manufacturing guidelines established by Fairbanks, Morse & Company, summarized the features that successfully sold windmills to farmers, townspeople, and railroads on the windy waterless plains:

1. Ability to be shipped knocked down and yet readily erected with simple tools by ordinary mechanics;

2. Interchangeability of parts;

3. Durability;

4. Minimum amount of material used, keeping down cost of material and transportation as well as erection;

5. Simple lubrication;

6. Self-governing, both as to staying in the wind and as to maintaining a uniform speed regardless of velocity of wind.[6]

The pumps under the spinning vanes ranged from five- to twelve-inch bore cylinders with a stroke of six to twelve inches. Farmers were told to use a pump cylinder that measured less in inches than the windmill diameter measured in feet: a twelve-foot windmill to serve a ten-inch pump. The well underneath the windmill and pump was usually a four- or five-foot-square pit excavated down to the water table, and it had to be relatively shallow.[7]

By 1895 farms around Garden City, Kansas, sported about 150 "wind-reservoir irrigation" operations. They typically included one or two windmills, a reservoir, and up to five acres under irrigation that were planted in vegetables and fruits for human consumption or alfalfa for animals. One Kansas official revived the Irrigation Crusade claim that a farm family could live well on five irrigated acres and become rich on twenty acres. Journalists visited Garden City, and articles in the *Review of Reviews* and the *Scientific American* gave the community a national reputation as America's center of windmill irrigation.[8] Still, one Kansas farmer complained that the windmills were overrated. The wind that was touted as so constant was, in fact, so irregular that the windmill ran only a third of the time—and even worse, he lost half his reservoir water through evaporation.[9]

Most farmers found windmills and pumps too costly to buy and instead built their own. Even local shop-made windmills were beyond the means of cashless farmers; the homemade mill took its place for a decade or more. One common home-built version was called the Jumbo:

> It is a simple home-made contrivance. Four posts are planted in the ground, then covered or boxed with boards. An axle with from four to eight spokes fastened to it, with paddles generally made of wood nailed on the end of the spokes like a steamboat's paddle wheel, is set on the box east and west to catch the prevailing south and north winds. A crank on one or both ends works the pump or pumps. The box shields the lower part of the wheel, while the top is fully exposed to the wind, and from its spinning round with a kind of comical merriment in a good south "prairie zephyr" it has probably [also] earned the name of "Go-Devil."[10]

The largest practical Jumbo that measured twenty-one feet in diameter and could, in theory, pump seven hundred gallons a minute at a fourteen-foot lift cost only $20 in scrap wood. In contrast, the average windmill kit sold by local manufacturers cost $75 for an eight-foot mill, $100 for a ten-foot mill, and $135 for a twelve-foot mill. By 1909, when costs declined, farmers could build their own reservoirs and install two twelve-foot windmills with ten-inch pumps for $330. Theoretically, one twelve-foot windmill could irrigate ten acres.

Casting theory aside, however, farmers learned that their $330 investment would, at best, water a total of eight acres.[11] Erwin H. Barbour, a contemporaneous observer, wrote of the delicate balance between failure and survival: "The mill may not net its owner over $100, but if the rest of the crop is a total failure, this is worth more than one hundred cents per dollar. [But] the mill may easily exceed the profits of the rest of the farm during exceptionally poor seasons."[12] The inherent pumping limits of windmill technology were quickly reached and did little to aid wheat farmers who owned 640-acre sections. An 1895 report by the Kansas Board of Irrigation Survey and Experiments was uncharacteristically pessimistic: the minimum survey tract of

6. A homemade jumbo windmill, ca. 1890s. Many farmers could not afford three hundred dollars for a factory-made windmill, so they often worked from rough sketches they made after looking at a neighbor's jumbo. Frequently a windmill was made from scrap wood lying around in the farmyard. Courtesy of the Nebraska Historical Society, W765.32.

forty acres (a quarter of a quarter section) required twenty-four windmills—a finding that meant that an average of less than two acres was being served by each eight-foot windmill.[13] One Scott County, Kansas, farmer, Fred Mahler, constructed a "windmill irrigation plant" in 1911 that was made up of a two-hundred-foot-wide, four-foot-deep circular reservoir supplied by ten ten-foot windmills to irrigate fifty acres of alfalfa. A neighboring farmer, E. E. Coffin, in 1912 put together a 210-foot-square reservoir five feet deep with water from six twelve-foot windmills, also for fifty acres of alfalfa.[14]

Neither farmer found it economical to expand their windmill irrigation operations further.

One Garden City venture in the early 1980s pushed windmill pumping to its limits. Local farmer C. H. Longstreth set up a fourteen-foot Halladay windmill that powered a quality eight-inch Gause pump that produced forty-four hundred barrels of water a day, enough to irrigate fifteen acres. A brief spell of rain in the mid-1890s revived hope and eroded local interest in costly and largely ineffective windmill irrigation. The Kansas Board of Irrigation Survey and Experiment lost most of its influence, Bristow's *Irrigation Farmer* shut down, and a plains newspaper wrote, "We have passed from the drought period and have entered an era of old time moisture supply. We will now stop talking about irrigation."[15] But by 1900, when drought returned, farmers again talked of the "underflow" and the "mysterious aquifer." Deep groundwater would be the next solution and would turn the plains into the "land of the underground rain." To successfully lift large quantities of groundwater to the parched fields was the challenge. Probably no more than a thousand acres were ever irrigated by windmills around Garden City, where, in 1905, a total of over forty-two thousand acres were irrigated from the old ditches and peripherals.[16] The ebullient irrigation promoter, William E. Smythe, unconvincingly wrote in his 1905 classic, *The Conquest of Arid America*, that Garden City windmills have "saved an enormous district from lapsing into a condition of semi-barbarism."[17] Smythe's Jeffersonian image of the happy and prosperous family farm on its ten or twenty irrigated acres would not take hold on the plains.

Yet Walter Prescott Webb wrote in 1931, at the end of the windmill era, that "these primitive windmills, crudely made of broken machinery, scrap iron, and bits of wood, were to the drought-stricken people like floating spars to the survivors of a wrecked ship . . . transforming the so-called Great American Desert into a land of homes." Still, windmills did not offer a new ship to continue the journey. Webb exaggerated the windmill's conquest of the plains when he concluded that "without it large areas would long have remained without habitation."[18] He did admit in his monumental history of the Great Plains that "the windmill mitigated the thirst of the Great Plains but did not assuage it. The search for water had to go on."[19] The answer to human permanence on the plains was elsewhere. Unlike the lure of the early rainy 1880s, windmill technology did not create a new rush of settlement. Curiously, Webb ignored technological developments that had existed since the turn of the twentieth century: (1) a pump capable of steadily drawing a large volume of water from a deep well, (2) that could be powered by a low-cost and suitable power plant, (3) fueled by low-cost energy, and (4) supported by known well-digging technologies.

Quest for Water on the Plains

It appeared that Zebulon Pike and Joseph Henry were right when they saw only the midcontinent as the Great American Desert. As long as four twelve-foot windmills were needed to water forty acres—southwest Kansas would not become prosperous. Scrambling pioneer farmers would have been incredulous at today's irrigated abundance. The notion that an acre of corn, which needs nine hundred thousand gallons of water during its growing season, could ever be a major crop on the High Plains seemed laughable when that notion was not the cause of a farmer's ruin.

In the first half of the twentieth century, when the irrigation ditches of the federal Reclamation Service transformed California, the plains stood on the verge of abandonment. In 1894 Joseph L. Bristow, who would become private secretary to the governor of Kansas and in 1895 help the state to establish a Board of Irrigation Survey and Experiment to test irrigation pumps, used his journal, *Irrigation Farmer*, to champion a Kansas irrigation revolution. Instead of relying on the dams, reservoirs, and centralized irrigation canals and ditches of the Reclamation Service, all inappropriate on the central plains, Bristow spoke for individual on-farm pumps. He wrote that a farmer who could pump his own water would be independent of the uncertainties of the irrigation ditch and the costs of the irrigation company, he would fit the Jeffersonian mold better than California farmers, and he could regulate the flow of water to his crops without dependence or intervention from the outside. Bristow added that the Kansas farmer need not worry about river, ditch, and peripheral levels and that he would not need to keep an eye out for the "ditch rider" nor worry about annual water rents. Enthusiasm for Bristow's ideas was dampened by cost: in South Dakota farmers painfully learned that their artesian wells, which required no windmills or pumps, still cost three thousand to five thousand dollars to drill and case each well.

In 1901 federal scientist Willard D. Johnson called plains farming since the 1880s "the agricultural experiment . . . in ignorance or disregard of the fairly abundant data, indicating desert conditions. . . . Though persisted in for several years with great determination, it nevertheless ended in total failure. Directly and indirectly the money loss involved was many millions of dollars . . . [and resulted in] a class of people broken in spirit as well as in fortune."[20] Walter Prescott Webb quotes farm historian A. M. Simons who, in 1906, wrote that the plains had a future "pregnant with greater promise than perhaps any other equal expense of territory" in the western hemisphere, but "whose history is filled with more tragedy" that left "a mass of human wreckage in the shape of broken fortunes, deserted farms, and ruined homes."[21] Irrigation advocate and engineer Frederick H. Newell wrote off the Great Plains in 1896 as a "region of periodical famine."[22] The rush of desperate farmers to windmills, despite their technological inadequacy, was a reaction of desperate men. As the 1880s boom proved misleading and disappointing, those who were able abandoned their farms and returned east or went west, and those who were condemned to stay turned to any device that might make water available. There is no more vivid example of an under-tooled, high-risk situation in American history.

Industrialization of the Plains: The Revolution Begins

There are usually three reasons why a new agricultural technology is adopted: an immediate crisis that threatens survival, the opportunity for better production, and the opportunity to reduce risks. Environmental philosopher Paul B. Thompson identifies agriculture as the heart of the "productionist paradigm."[23] Even when farmers regard themselves as stewards of the land, their work is organized around a fundamental transformation of plants and animals into food and fiber for human consumption. The food and fiber they create are intentionally created objects, not found objects as in hunting and fishing. Thompson sees three central ideologies behind farm productionism. First is the link between industriousness (hard work) and material well-being (high profits) that is always understood as virtuous. Second is the "doctrine of grace," by which productivity is a sign of God's favor and a key element by which farmers fulfill their designated role in America's Manifest Destiny to master a continental geography. In this light, the family farmer remains a venerable American hero even into the new millennium. Third is the myth of the garden, a tenaciously held belief by farmers, whose identities are directly connected to their ability to transform untamed nature into a tended garden. Thomas Jefferson and Hector St. John de Crèvecoeur described the archetypal American family farmer in the late eighteenth century, and the image has changed little as we move into the new millennium. Not only is the tended garden superior to wilderness on all counts, but the farmer inhabits this idealized middle ground—rural America—that prevails between wilderness and industrial society (another wilderness). The greatest new threat to the family farmer, according to Wes Jackson and Don Worster, is agribusiness, its own version of wilderness.[24]

THE FIRST NEW INGREDIENT: THE CENTRIFUGAL PUMP

In the 1890s the plains moved toward a new mechanical pumping technology. A version of the century-old English centrifugal pump was made much more efficient by a revolving metal impeller with diffusion vanes housed inside a cast-iron circular chamber with far tighter tolerances. Water was pulled into the center of the chamber where the impeller forced it against the outside walls where it then exited outward and upward through a discharge pipe. The pump could deliver several hundred gallons per minute, the quantity necessary for crop irrigation. Because it had no easily clogged valves, it was far easier to maintain. The primary drawback of the pump led to its ultimate failure: it had to be located no higher than twenty feet above water level. This meant that a wide pit had to be dug close to water level, and the pump was practicable only where groundwater levels were relatively shallow. At fifty feet to three hundred feet below the surface, the Ogallala remained mostly inaccessible.

In addition, the limits of existing power-transfer technologies, whether steam, internal combustion, or electric, created serious difficulties. Engines had to be on the surface for running and daily maintenance, and they had to be connected to the pump by a long leather belt and pulley that required constant adjustment, or, less successfully, by a long, carefully aligned vertical shaft that wore out its bearings with alarming regularity.[25] Farmers and mechanics complained that the leather belt, which tightened in winter and stretched in summer, broke or slipped and had to be repeatedly restitched. Replacing, lubricating, or adjusting the belt or shaft bearings was a dangerous job: the farmer descended into the well pit alongside a wildly spinning belt or shaft, and once down to the pump might have heavy overhead equipment come crashing down on him. One east Texas farmer wrote, "Imagine getting down into the pit to oil the pump with the mess of rope running at the velocity of the outside diameter of the 54" fly wheel with 6 or 8 fifty pound weights dancing on the tightener above your head. BAD DREAMS."[26]

By 1896 irrigators around Garden City, Kansas, used the new power and pumps to tap shallow water—less than ten feet underground—from the Arkansas River water table. This was a way to avoid the difficult and dangerous pits. Using steam power, a no.2 pump with a six-inch pipe delivered 245 gallons per minute. A larger no.3 pumped 625 gallons per minute, and at a meat processing plant in Hutchinson, Kansas, several no.6 pumps delivered 1,300 gallons per minute, a pace that equals today's pumping rates. Such pumps were already raising irrigation water in eastern Colorado, western Arizona, and the Sacramento Valley in California.[27] However, at a time when even a prosperous plains farmer generated only a few hundred dollars a year, and long before easy credit and federal subsidies, the centrifugal pumps were generally too expensive. The smaller no.2 pump that delivered between 150 and 250 gallons per minute cost $230 to $390, not including power plant or well-digging costs. Newell, who generally put the best opinion forward, admitted in 1902 that centrifugal pump irrigation costs were "considerably higher than the amount yearly paid for the maintenance of canals and ditches in the arid region, or the amount paid annually to a canal company for delivering water. It is rarely below $2 per acre irrigated, and

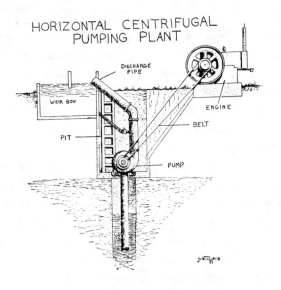

HORIZONTAL CENTRIFUGAL
PUMPING PLANT

DISCHARGE PIPE

WEIR BOX

ENGINE

BELT

PIT

PUMP

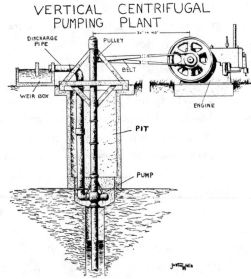

VERTICAL CENTRIFUGAL
PUMPING PLANT

DISCHARGE PIPE

PULLEY

BELT

WEIR BOX

ENGINE

PIT

PUMP

7. Late-nineteenth-century setups for a centrifugal pump. More efficient and reliable impeller pumps, together with the internal combustion engine, helped bring the first irrigation revolution to the plains. Reprinted by permission from Donald E. Green, *Land of the Underground Rain: Irrigation on the Texas High Plains, 1910–1970* (Austin: University of Texas Press, 1972), 44.

from this as a minimum, may rise to $5 or even $10 an acre."[28] Crops had to be far more profitable than current prices paid for wheat, sorghums, and corn. The need for a mechanically simple, inexpensive, and easily powered pitless pump was still not met.[29]

Aside from cost, few farmers, despite their jack-of-all-trades reputation, had enough mechanical know-how to take on the industrial technology of the pumping systems. It was one thing to straighten a bent bar on a mechanical reaper, but fiddling with a steam engine, gasoline motor, belts or shafts, or a pump was quite another. In the words of Hereford, Texas, farmer Roland Loyd, in 1914: "Worked about half of afternoon trying to start pumping outfit gave it up as bad job and cut weeds rest of afternoon. . . . Worked 'til 3:30 P.M. trying to start big engine. Then gave it up and went to town."[30] Before gearing became workable and inexpensive, the long leather belt that connected engine and pump demanded constant adjustment. If it was too loose it was inefficient; if it was too tight, it wore down pump shaft bearings. In the summer of 1914, Loyd cut the belt on June 29 when the temperature reached 103 degrees, sewed a piece in on July 21, and cut it again on both July 30 and August 1. These constant maintenance problems also kept farmers from irrigating at night. As a result, peak irrigation from a well only averaged about seventy-two acres in 1919, a remarkable amount compared to what was possible with windmills, but not enough for large-scale wheat farming.

Electric irrigation pumps existed but power lines from distant power stations did not. Only large enterprises, such as the United States Sugar and Land Company in Garden City, Kansas could generate their own electricity. Its 1909 plant used an oil-fired, four-hundred-horsepower engine to run a 350-kilowatt steam generator for electricity that was delivered to over fifteen miles of power line to fourteen pumps. Each pump could deliver 1,800 to 2,000 gallons per minute to irrigate thirty-five hundred acres.[31] If a central plains farmer in 1908 wanted to use electricity to run a five-inch centrifugal pump to raise about 450 gallons per minute from a water level of seventy-five feet, he would have to pay $3.94 per acre-foot, an unacceptable amount. Costs included the power line to his pump, expensive kilowatt-hour rates, and usually a surcharge per horsepower of the electric motor.[32]

THE SECOND NEW INGREDIENT: THE GASOLINE ENGINE

Steam engines that could run large pumps remained out of reach for low-income farmers. The eighty-horsepower steam engine that ran irrigation pumps for a prosperous farm near Mesa, Arizona, in 1900 demanded two trained engineers to service the engine and two firemen, who also cut wood for fuel. The daily running cost was $9.25. Irrigation engineer and advocate Elwood Mead estimated cost, with all expenses, to be $2.27 per acre-foot: "the expense of raising water by steam power is very great indeed . . . such water is too costly for constant use in ordinary farming operations."[33] A steam engine used near Holcomb, Kansas in 1904 could pump up to twenty-five hundred gallons per minute but it cost twelve thousand dollars, the equivalent of three years' gross income for a prosperous farmer.

Gasoline or oil engines were new, unreliable, and not generally available until after 1900. The late 1890s saw low compression, oil-burning Hornsby-Ackroyd-type engines of English design sold to pump irrigators in the Gulf Coast rice belt, in California and Arizona, and occasionally on the Great Plains. These were simple one- or two-cylinder "hot bulb" engines without spark plugs. They had large, heavy, cast-iron flywheels—up to four feet in diameter. The hot bulb protruded from the engine head, where it was heated with a torch. The heat was conducted into the cylinder head by a "spoon" or "lip" and ignited the oil while the flywheel was rotated by hand in small engines or by compressed air in larger engines. The engine then ran itself by reheating the hot bulb with each ignition. Even though the heavy crude oil used by these engines cost three to seven cents a gallon—less than a third the cost of gasoline in 1916[34]—the engine started with difficulty in cold weather, was inefficient, and usually cost nineteen hundred dollars to deliver and connect. But a large model generated a generous seventy horsepower.

Gasoline-burning internal combustion engines would become the power source of choice. In anticipation of the future, one Kansas farmer raised the rear of his car and ran a small centrifugal pump through a belt from his rear axle. In 1907 a twelve-horsepower gasoline engine, a no.6 centrifugal pump, and a well cost twelve hundred dollars, but its promise was its ability to irrigate one hundred acres.[35] The difference was dramatic when compared to the pumping capacity of a twelve-foot windmill. Larger ranchers and farmers quickly took advantage of the new technology. The King brothers north of Garden City operated five wells as deep as 150 feet to irrigate four hundred acres at a total cost of over three thousand dollars.[36] By 1912 over fifty gasoline pumps irrigated sixty-five hundred acres.

The combination of a centrifugal, or pitless, pump, rotary drilling rig, and internal combustion engine would become the future standard once efficiency and reliability increased and costs and servicing requirements decreased. In 1912 a Kansas State Board of Agriculture official wrote optimistically that "these large, deep wells, with the centrifugal pumps and powerful cheap oil-engines, are the means by which the underground waters will be utilized to irrigate the lands of this great territory."[37] Irrigation historian Donald E. Green describes this change in the High Plains as revolutionary as the Industrial Revolution that turned quiet rural countryside into an industrial landscape:

> Not only could one locate such a well easily by sight [a squat thirty-foot wooden tower], but the distinctive sound of the huge oil engine—some models weighed several tons—also identified it. Both four-cycle and two-cycle engines were used. . . . Both could be audibly identified by a slow, pulsating, unrhythmic pop-pop-pop. Some models were capable of blowing extraordinary blue smoke rings out their exhausts and high into the atmosphere. . . . A house was usually built over the pump, belt, and engine to protect the machinery from the weather, and the derrick jutted into the sky above one end of the house."[38]

Farmers, still in the age of the horse-drawn cultivator and wagon, were not adept enough at operating or repairing the new internal combustion engines to make pump maintenance anything less than a mystery. Lack of experience and poor information about water use did not help neophyte irrigators. Most farmers turned on their pumps only as a last resort when the plants were already withering. They know neither how much water would flood the fields or how to level the land for flood irrigation. Ditches were badly dug and choked with weeds such as Johnson grass. Many of the small number of these irrigators became disenchanted with the complexities of the new method. Four out of five buyers of irrigated farms from the Texas Land and Development Company could not continue their payments and lost their farms in less than a decade.[39] The irrigated wheat fields of the plains did not offer the rewards of the irrigated vegetable fields or fruit orchards of California. It was generally believed that the collective impact of high winds, extreme temperatures, threat of hail, and distance from markets limited farmers to wheat or alfalfa. Besides, "it may rain."

Irrigation equipment was by far the most sophisticated and costly farming item that the plains farmer might consider purchasing. Much of the profit for higher yields was simply plowed back into equipment. Green reports that in 1912 John H. Slaton paid $2,350 to dig a well and install a pitless pump and thirty-two-horsepower engine.[40] This was during a time when a prosperous farmer was pleased to have $500 ready cash for a year's worth of "improvements." Drilling and casing a twenty-six-inch well ranged from $4.00 to $5.25 per foot, which meant a cost of $500 to $600 for a 100- to 120-foot well. The Layne and Bowler pitless pump cost another $500. One thousand dollars might go to lumber and construction of the derrick, pump, engine shed, fuel tank, air compressor, and tanks. The new gasoline engines were expensive, especially since used auto engines from Fords, Dodges, and Chevrolets that are so commonplace today, were neither available nor reliable. The prices of twenty-five- to sixty-horsepower stationary oil-burning engines often put irrigation out of farmers' reach: the least costly, $1,000 to $1,600, were made by Charter, Van Sevrein, and Herr, and the most expensive, $1,800 to $2,500, were made by Primm and Bessemer. A turn-key well, ready to start, could easily sell for more than $6,000.

Using another measure, state agriculture economists concluded that cost per acre-foot of water, including depreciation, credit costs, fuel, and maintenance, ranged from $5 to $6.25. Many farmers who saw their future in irrigated alfalfa fields were told to expect to pay $12.50 to $15.60 for two and one-half acre-feet of water per acre, or over $1,000 for an eighty-acre tract. If the farmer harvested three tons per acre at $15 a ton, he would gross

$3,600, then deduct $1,000 for irrigation, $600 for harvesting and other costs for taxes and interest, depreciation on equipment, and seed and labor. These optimistic figures did not factor in the vagaries of weather or fluctuation of market prices. Most farmers on the plains in the 1910s and 1920s concluded that experimenting with industrialized high-technology irrigation was too great a risk.[41] Between June 1920 and December 1920 the price for wheat dropped from $2.58 to $1.43 per bushel, a change that effectively ended any remaining interest in high-priced irrigation. Plains farmers stayed with land-extensive dryland farming rather than attempt the capital-intensive, technology-intensive, and irrigation-intensive production.[42]

Compared to the halcyon days before World War I, a plains farmer in 1920 stood on the verge of a twenty-year depression. Farmland prices were 57 percent of their prewar value in 1921 and would collapse to 17 percent by 1928. By the spring of 1921, farmers' purchasing power went down to 63 percent of their prewar purchasing power even though the crop production was the same. The agricultural conundrum of the 1920s was not only low prices for farmland and farm products, but also overproduction. The national Irrigation Crusade abruptly ended. One irrigator on the Texas High Plains reported that his seventy-four-acre tract with one well provided a net profit of $196.53 after taxes and expenses in 1924, a figure that did not encourage the effort and cost of irrigation.[43] Not until New Deal AAA government subsidy checks were distributed in 1934 and 1935 was interest revived in farm mechanization. Even when it was, it was mainly channeled into trucks and tractors rather than wells, pumps, motors, and pipes.

In the late 1930s, federal policies first concentrated on better dryland farming through soil conservation rather than industrialization through irrigation. Despite the availability of efficient irrigation technology at reasonable cost, the Great Plains Committee concluded in 1936 that "Irrigation at best can cause only minor changes in the economic life of the Great Plains."[44] It identified only a few favorable areas with access to shallow underground water and generally discouraged federal funding. Additionally, they reported, irrigation would lead to greater overproduction of wheat, alfalfa, and grain sorghums. Unlike the extensive support given to dryland farming by the new Soil Conservation Service (SCS), no public agency, including the Reclamation Service, took an interest in plains irrigation. Donald E. Green concludes that only independent local entrepreneurs, such as banker Artemus "Artie" Baker of Lockney, Texas, in Floyd County, offered the credit that small farmers found unavailable elsewhere. Baker even arranged for shipments of steel well casings, Ford v-8 motors (a boxcar lot of fifty at $125 each), gear heads, pumps, and even professional well-drilling rigs and personnel.[45] In contrast to the Peerless Pump Company in Plainview, Texas, that required a five-hundred-dollar down payment for a two-thousand-dollar turn-key irrigation system, Baker required no down payment.

Despite the moves by federal agencies toward resettlement and labor-intensive soil conservation, some farmers began to believe that irrigation was a real alternative. The combined impact of the Depression and the Dust Bowl convinced farmers in Floyd and Swisher Counties in Texas that dry-land farming was unprofitable and that it would neither pay debts nor meet annual expenses. In their words, "when drouth and the depression had swept everything from us, we decided to give up dry farming and irrigate"; "I was 'flat broke' and ready to move when I installed a well on my place in May 1936"; with a well "you were sure of a crop; without a well you were sure of a failure."[46] Green suggests that a turning point was reached when "farmers began to think of irrigation as more than simply 'crop insurance' to be used during abnormally dry years." A Floyd County farmer said he finally realized that if he turned to irrigation only as "a last resort," he misused irrigation: "The average irrigation farmer watered with an eye on the sky for possible rainfall and usually waited until the last possible moment before he used his well. Consequently, his crops did not show sufficient margin of profit over that of the dry farmer." Instead, irrigation should be used "with an eye to producing capacity crops."[47] This view became the norm for irrigation across the High Plains. In time it would encourage overproduction and the heavy drawdown of the Ogallala aquifer.

In the late 1930s, new technologies, lower-cost equipment, and trouble-free pumps had trickled onto the plains. The individual elements of a high-capacity pumping system had been available in the 1920s, but the entire system would not come together until the 1940s. In the 1920s the size of the well needed for pitless bowl centrifugal pumps that could lift water from three hundred feet decreased to twelve inches or less. This improvement depended upon a great increase in pump revolutions from about 850 to 1,200 to 3,600 rpm and on advances in lubrication and bearings. The pump was in production by 1930 and put into use by municipal water systems, irrigators in the far West, and Gulf Coast rice growers. This deep well turbine pump in turn depended upon new engines that could outperform the 250 rpm of pre–World War I oil-burning internal combustion engines. By 1935 used, cheap automobile engines provided the necessary speed in the burgeoning irrigation country around Plainview, Texas. In Hale County, Texas, a farmer in 1938 could acquire a fancy Ford v-8 engine for $310 and a less powerful but equally workable Chevrolet engine for $235. Even then, the investment was considerable. The dangerous and inefficient engine belt that drove the pump was replaced by the right-angle geared pump head. It had been available since the teens but would not have worked with the slower engines. By making the gear on the engine shaft larger in diameter than the gear with which it meshed on the pump shaft, the pump could be made to rotate faster at lower and more efficient gasoline engine speeds. An 800-rpm engine could provide a pump speed up to 1,200 to 1,600 rpm.[48] Electric motors would have been better because of their flexibility, but they were expensive, as was electricity. The Rural Electrification Administration would help the plains farmers in the next two decades, but at this point power lines and poles to the pumps were still beyond most farmers' means.

"Rain when you want it" became the slogan for irrigation advocates. When rain failed to appear in the 1930s, interest in irrigation was predictably revived. In 1937 the first deep well outside Liberal, Kansas, brought a public celebration, including a parade sponsored by local merchants. "The parade then wound its way to the well, where hundreds of people and cars gathered to watch the spudding ceremony."[49] By the late 1930s, costs for drilling and casing the well, for the pump, gear head, motor, and housing, had fallen to a third of the costs in the 1910s and 1920s. A well as deep as 250 feet cost $650 for drilling and casing at $3.25 a foot. At $850, a pump was the most expensive item. The gear head, which dramatically increased efficiency and delighted farmers who hated the old belt, cost $270. A resourceful farmer was likely to recycle a motor from his junked auto. The shed for the entire unit would cost about $50 if it was not handmade from farmyard scrap. In total, a determined farmer could get into irrigation for under $2,000.[50] Compared to earlier operating expenses of about $6.00 per acre-foot, the 1938 irrigator could flood his field for $3.20 to $4.50 per acre-foot, including installed well and equipment, interest and depreciation, and fuel and maintenance. He still planted alfalfa, grain sorghums, and wheat, but a hundred acres in wheat might now net $1,200. From 1930 to 1936 near Plainview, Texas, the number of wells nearly doubled from 170, after declining since 1920, to 250. At the beginning of 1935, the region enjoyed 35,000 irrigated acres. By the end of 1936, there were 80,000 and by 1937, there were 1,150 wells.

Advances in technology would give the ordinary farmer access to irrigation, but it would be two more decades before it would be commonplace.[51] Two thousand dollars was usually beyond the reach of plains farmers. Even a small farmer who worked an entire 640-acre section would need four units, since one well and pump served only 160 acres at the most. Large operators had no trouble arranging credit based on their farm value and production. However, small farmers seeking to shift from dryland farming to irrigation did not have enough equity to take out a loan. What they needed were loans based on future production—a catch-22 situation.[52]

The Revolution Takes Hold: Irrigation Brings the Central Plains into the American Industrial Mainstream

After World War II, irrigation spread across the plains to help protect farming from another Dust Bowl. As long as struggling plains farmers could not afford irrigation and were thus without water, all other attempts to keep them on the land, including federal support since the 1930s, would be unable to solve the fundamental problem of the semiarid region. Only slowly did plains farmers comprehend the irrigation revolution. Instead of treating "water-on-demand" as a last resort and temporary safeguard against crop failure, irrigation offered them a regular and reliable means to guarantee in-

IRRIGATION LEGEND

NAME	Location	Date Drilled	G.P.M. Approx.	Depth	Size Pump	Type Engine	Static Draw Down	Fuel Used	Gravity Sprin'
Lee Larrabee	NW 16-34-33	1947-1948	1200		8"	LeRoi		Nat. Gas	288
R. A. Boles	SE 4-35-34	1950	1100	290	8"	MM 605	88'-90'	Nat. Gas	509
Jack Massoni	NE 12-33-33	1953	1000	140	8"	MM 605	8'	Nat. Gas	spr. 250
Harold Lower	NE 18-34-31	1947	1800	382	10"	Cat	184'-10'	Nat. Gas	240
Harold Lower	SW 9-31-32	1954	1800	385	10"	Cat	184'	Nat. Gas	316
R. Fields	SE 4-34-33	1948	1300	358	8"	LeRoi	170'-26'	Nat. Gas	480
Harold Stapleton	SE 6-31-32	1947	1800	387	8"	Cat.	177'-7'	Diesel	1127
Harold Stapleton	NW 6-31-32	1949	1300	387	8"	Cat	177'-7'	Nat. Gas	400
Loyd Marteney	NE 19-32-32	1949	750	308	6"	Waukesha	200'-7'	Nat. Gas	600
Loyd Marteney	NE 20-32-32								390
Dale Beard	NW 18-31-34	1951	900	375	8"	MM 605	180'-40'	Nat. Gas	211
Don Priefert	NE 10-34-33	1982	100	297	3"	Ford P-N	90'	Nat. Gas	20
C. C. Snyder	SE 17-34-33	1950	1200	336	8"	MM	205'-10'	Nat. Gas	480
Kenneth Metcalf	SW 7-34-33	1953	400	345	8"	Chrysler		Nat. Gas	130
C. J. Conover	S.W 6-31-33	1947	700	348	8"	MM 605	210' 50'	Nat. Gas	189
E. H. Good	SE 28-31-33	1950			10"	MM 1210		Nat. Gas	47'
Hitch Land & Cattle Co.	Sw 29-32-33	1950	1526	350	10"	LeRoi	190'-12'	Nat. Gas	442
Hitch Land & C. Co.	SE 22-32-34	1950	1500	800	10"	LeRoi	190'-15'	Nat. Gas	285
G. R. Downing	NB 18-32-34	1953			10"	Buda		Nat. Gas	294
Forrest Simpson	SE 4-31-33	1950	1500	400	8"	MM 1210	185'-12'	Nat. Gas	388
E. Boles	SE 10-32-34	1950	700	300	6"	IHC 450	205'-20'	Nat. Gas	202
Henry Hitch	Sw 14-32-34	1953			6"	Chrysler		Nat. Gas	
J. N. Hatcher	NE 18-32-33	1953	1800	400	10"	MM 1210	160'	Nat. Gas	320
Lambert Daley & Lam.	SW 16-32-33	1953	1800	397	10"	MM 1210	186'-20'	Nat. Gas	266
Edna Guthrie	NE 23-32-33	1953	1300	430	10"	MM 1210	185'-20'	Butane	318
Emery Ball	NE 16-31-33	1954	1000	370	8"	MM 605	190'-35'	Nat. Gas	160
Richardson & Cobb	NW 24-32-34	1954	1100	410	10"	Waukesha	160'-50'	Nat. Gas	550
Ted Lofland	N.W 11-35-34	1953	250	393	6"	220P Elec.	170'	Elec.	140
Fred Schmidt	Sw 5-31-32	1955	1800-2000	389	10"	Waukesha	150'-19'	Nat. Gas	150
David Schmidt	Sw 16-31-31	1954	1900	360	10"	Buda 1290	166'-34'	Nat. Gas	584
A. E. Cotton	N.10 6-31-33	1954	1800	352	10"	MM 1600		Nat. Gas	712
Frank Dufield	NW 14-32-32	1956	1300		8"	GMC V12		Nat. Gas	291
Keith Rosson	SW 29-31-31	1955	1950	418	10"	Buda	158'-48'	Nat. Gas	611
Dean Printz	NW 13-32-33	1955	2100	410	10"	Waukesha	185'-24'	Nat. Gas	480
M. Porter (J. Davis)	NE 23-31-32	1955			10"	Hudson		Nat. Gas	459
Jessie Thomas	NW 21-34-33	1955	1600	403	10"	LeRoi	170'	Nat. Gas	319
O. J. Wilkins Co	NW 30-32-31	1954	2000		10"	Cat.		Diesel Nat.	580
Hitch Land & Ca. Co	NW 30-32-31	1954	1396		8"	MM 800		Nat. Gas	609
Hitch Land & Ca. Co.	Sw 82-32-31	1954	1000		8"	MM 800		Nat. Gas	800
Henry Hitch	NE 21-32-34	1955			10"	2 Chrysler		Nat. Gas	253
F. H. Wellenberg	SE 20-31-31	1955		400	10"	Buda		Nat. Gas	158
Raymond Holt	SE 18-32-31	1955	1400	406	8"		225'-11'	Nat. Gas	153
John Grover	NW 18-35-34	1955	1000	353	8"	605 MM	90'-190	Nat. Gas	285
Lambert Daley & Lam.	N° 20-32-33	1955	1800	400	10"	Waukesha	185'-20	Nat. Gas	374
Joe Pittman	SW 17-32-33	1955	1800	300	10"	Buda	160'-40	Nat. Gas	593
Don Priefert	NW 10-34-33	1955	800-900	505	8"	MM 800	110'-200	Nat. Gas	193
Randall Bird	NW 2-31-33	1955	1500	360	10"	Gmc V12	180 -260	Nat. Gas	300
R. Pittman	SE 17-32-33	1955	2000	455	10"	Waukesha	179'-17	Nat. Gas	320
R. L. Dunlap	SE 16-34-32	1956	1300	230	8"		100'-100'	Nat. Gas	177
Ted Lofland	NW 18-35-34	1956	1300	321	8"	Waukesha	173'-17	Nat. Gas	310
C. C. Snyder	Sw 34-31-33	1956	2000	435	10"	970 Buda	100'-40	Nat. Gas	320
Waldo Wills	Sw 26-32-31	1956	1800	390	10"	2 Chrysler	179'-30'	Nat. Gas	497

8. Original tally sheet of the first modern irrigation wells in southwestern Kansas as recorded in the offices of the USDA Soil Conservation Service in Liberal, Kansas. Important historical data include the name of the pioneering irrigator, location of the pump, date drilled, flow in gallons per minute, depth to water, size of pipe, type of engine, and fuel type. Some of these wells are still in use, usually with deeper drilling and new pumps and well casings. Original file, USDA Soil Conservation Service Office, Liberal, Kansas.

135

creased production. A Texas experiment station study in 1948 reported that irrigators did not meet the potential of irrigation: they "seldom strive for maximum per-acre yields. They choose instead to spread water over the greatest possible acreage with the accent on increased total production rather than on the highest per-acre yield."[53] Soon, however, irrigation from the Ogallala aquifer would no longer simply be an emergency measure when all else failed.

Donald E. Green tells a representative success story that encouraged young war veterans to stay in plains farming:

> In Lamb County [Texas] a disabled World War II veteran owned 8 acres and rented 100 acres in 1945. By 1946 he had made a down payment on an 80-acre farm and borrowed money from a local bank to install an irrigation plant. With 70 acres in cotton in 1947 he produced 102 bales, enough to pay for the irrigation unit and the land. The veteran then made a down payment on another 115 acres, bought some new farm equipment, and drilled a well on his newly purchased land. By the end of 1948 he had 195 irrigated acres clear of debt.[54]

Irrigation began to have an impact on the Texas High Plains, where the number of irrigation wells rose from over 2,500 in 1941 to 4,300 in 1945. The little Dust Bowl lasted on the Texas Plains from 1947 through 1956, a longer drought than in the 1930s, but Texas farmers counteracted drought by drilling over 5,000 wells each year in 1953, 1955, and 1957. Compared to 8,400 wells in 1948, by 1957 there were more than 42,200 wells that irrigated 3.5 million acres.

By the 1950s the cost of a basic well and pumping system, about $4,000, had nearly doubled from 1938 prices. Drilling and casing a basic well cost approximately $1,300, the pump and gear head cost about $2,200, and a small automobile engine cost $500.[55] Equipment investment for irrigated land was two to three times more expensive than the initial investment for dryland farming. In the late 1950s, a 320-acre dryland farm carried about $6,600 in equipment, while a 320-acre irrigated farm carried $18,000 worth of equipment for five wells.[56]

9. Typical modern pumping systems in southwestern Kansas. *Top:* Centrifugal pump using a rebuilt v-8 automobile engine fueled by natural gas, serving water to an open ditch for flood irrigation. *Bottom:* One of Keith Allen's commercial large-scale pumps and natural-gas engines used to flood his alternative-crop fields. Photos taken in 1988 by the author.

The investment in the new irrigation technology fulfilled its promise by making farming much more predictable. Farmers pridefully believed, as they watched the throbbing engines and pumps and shiny pipes and gushing water, that they had at long last entered the modern machine age. Such a boomer psychology had not been seen among farmers since the turn of the century, when enthusiasm had been tied to the sweep of flat fertile land, good rain, and new tractors and combines designed for the plains. Following the despair of the 1930s, the irrigation boom gave the plains a second life. Irrigators were rewarded not only by two or three times the crop yield, but also with rapid increases in land values. Dust Bowl acreage in 1935 cost as little as $20 to $30 an acre, but by 1948, dryland farms were worth $50 to $125, while irrigated land sold for as high as $300 an acre, and no less than $150 an acre. To the south, in Lubbock, Texas, where irrigation had long prospered, farmland in the 1950s was valued at over $400 an acre.[57]

Irrigation wells began to appear gradually in southwestern Kansas, first in Finney County.[58] As in Texas, the little Dust Bowl of the 1950s pushed farmers further toward costly irrigation investment. By 1957 irrigation in neighboring Haskell County allowed farmers to produce twice as many bushels for four times the money from half the wheatland of 1936.[59] Bolstered by the reliability of Ogallala irrigation, and by the combination of fields of wheat, sorghums, and alfalfa that served cattle feedlots, farmers believed they had finally left the old frugal days behind. They were no longer frozen in time on a sodhouse frontier; it seemed that high-yield crop production was the direction of the future. After decades of bitter disappointing delays, farmers believed that the seemingly permanent plains frontier had been conquered, and America's Manifest Destiny was completed. Newly confident irrigators enthusiastically entered America's postwar consumer binge: the latest farm equipment, new kitchens and new cars, vacations to Florida and California, and teenagers playing organized high-school sports instead of toiling in the fields. One successful Haskell County farmer was proud that he and his family and their kitchen appliances and living room television, looked like the families and homes in *Life*, *Look*, and *Colliers*.

The three-legged stool of industrialized irrigation on the plains was cheap, fertile soil, plentiful, low-cost groundwater, and inexpensive fuel. By the mid-1970s, however, when less cash flowed into local communities, the intervention of government and markets would signal the loss of local autonomy, and farmers would start to complain about the decline of a valued rural society. However, in the 1950s, the transformation fulfilled the high expectations Americans had for modern plains agriculture. Yields were guaranteed regardless of a fickle climate, high production continued season after season, and technological prowess enabled more product with less labor.

Only the soil was part of the pre-European geography: both groundwater and fuel lay hidden far underground to be introduced by technological innovation. The postwar era of extraordinarily cheap fuels that lasted until the energy crisis of 1973 assured the widespread use of internal combustion engines. Gasoline sold for 11 1/2¢ a gallon in 1947 and would not rise above 35¢ a gallon until the early 1970s. There seemed to be little interest in shifting to the more flexible electric motors when the federal Rural Electrification Administration brought electricity to remote farmsteads in the southwestern Kansas and the Oklahoma-Texas Panhandle region after World War II. The typical cost to use an electric pumping motor for one hour was 49¢ in 1947, the cost of fuel to run a gasoline engine for one hour was 40¢ to 52¢, and the cost to fuel a butane-powered engine for one hour was 26¢ to 37¢. It was relatively easy to convert the widely used automobile engines to propane gas, and in 1947 natural gas from a farmer's own storage tank cost about 8¢ per gallon.

Moreover, irrigators could often depend upon free natural gas that they tapped from gas and oil wells on their own land. The existence of the world's second largest natural gas field—the Guymon-Hugoton under the Dust Bowl country—had been known since 1904. Its promise for irrigation energy was first promoted in 1927. A Plainview, Texas, dealer reported in 1949 that he sold liquefied petroleum (LP) gas to fuel more than 5,000 irrigation and tractor engines. By 1952 almost two-thirds of the 16,500 irrigation units on the Texas High Plains were powered by newly commercial LP butane or propane gas.[60] By 1958 more than two-thirds of Texas High Plains farmers had shifted to easily accessible natural gas, compared to only 3 percent prior to 1952. The cost of natural gas per acre-foot (including depreciation, interest, taxes, repairs, and other costs) was $5.15, compared to electricity at $6.58 per acre-foot, $7.53 per acre-foot for LP gas, and $8.70 per acre-foot for gasoline. Nevertheless, many farmers were too comfortable with their familiar gasoline engines to switch to natural gas.

INDUSTRIALIZING THE FARM: FACTORY WORK WITHOUT WALLS

In Texas County, Oklahoma, longtime irrigators Roger and Betty Trescott irrigate their fields with four pumps, and they reap the same crop yields as if they had invested in center-pivot units. But the modern flood and furrow irrigation they use demands more labor and consumes much more water than center-pivot irrigation. Flood irrigation can take up to two weeks to cover 150 acres, while center-pivot irrigation takes three to five days.

Simple flood irrigation once required farmers to dig out part of a ditch wall to channel water into field rows. Once the rows were thoroughly wet, they had to close the gap and then channel the water further down the field to the next set of rows. The rush of water would erode ditches and rows, and it took repetitious and muddy, backbreaking shoveling to repair breaks and overflows. More than 50 percent of the water in flood irrigation was lost to seepage and evaporation in open ditches between pump and field rows. Farmers used new, post–World War II materials including plastic, rubber, concrete and aluminum "gated" piping with outlets along its length, and durable, lightweight siphon tubes to carry and measure the water that traveled from ditches to field rows. This enclosed (closed conduit) system helped to conserve water for direct application to crops. A typical flood system began with a ten-, twelve-, or fifteen-inch concrete pipe laid three or four feet underground. It carried water from the pump to the field, where it would be connected to aluminum pipe at two-hundred-foot intervals. Installed concrete and aluminum pipe in 1949 cost $0.95 to $1.40 per foot, depending upon the diameter.[61] To encourage mechanization, which promised more efficient production, the USDA paid farmers approximately one-third the cost of installation of a closed conduit system. One important benefit of this system was that water under pressure could be delivered both to fields that were higher than the pump level and to fields in mildly rolling terrain. Mechanical land-leveling remained important, but it became less critical for successful irrigation of large tracts. By 1958 50 percent of the irrigated farms on the Texas High Plains had installed a closed conduit system.

Once committed to irrigation, plains farmers discovered that their work habits changed dramatically—farm work became "factory work without walls." Their physical labor was different, but it was not eased. They began to water night and day and also on Sundays, which in many farm communities had been zealously protected as a day of rest. Fabled American rural virtues, so enthusiastically protected even during the Dust Bowl years, would be reluctantly abandoned. Attracting their neighbors who trooped in to see stands of irrigated wheat, the new irrigators were called modern rainmakers who could place moisture where and when needed, guaranteeing abundant crops in spite of cloudless skies and torturing sun. They had less direct contact with soil and water and more with the mechanisms—pumps, gearboxes, motors, valves, and piping—of their watering systems. Farmers on the High Plains became familiar with terms like "make a set," "check the water," "change the water," "prewater," and "tailwater."[62] More convenient gated pipe still needed to be individually managed and adjusted in each plant row. Sometimes farmers discovered that they worked like unskilled factory laborers in the daily maintenance of leaky, grinding, and noisy machinery. Their work became both intensive—tied to the seasons—and extensive—year-round activity. Newell predicted as early as 1896 that the irrigation farmer would no longer worked like the traditional seasonal farmer.[63] Donald E. Green affirms Newell's prediction when he writes: "Labor began with preparing the soil in the winter. . . . Preparation included disking, chiseling, and applying fertilizer. Preplanting irrigation was required in the early spring if little moisture had accumulated during the winter. . . . [T]hrough the summer, farmers 'side-dressed' their crops with fertilizer and periodically sprayed insecticides on growing plants. Then in the fall winter wheat had to be planted . . . and combines gathered the grain sorghum crop."[64] Green continues: "Farmers often had to 'make a set' during

141

the late night or early morning. The spectacle of pickup trucks driving down country roads at 2:00 A.M., the bobbing of flashlights across distant fields, and the incessant distant roar of hundreds of irrigation engines became commonplace during what had once been the still of a plains summer night. As one reporter described the scene, '. . . big business is going on, and big engines are pumping.' . . . A spade and a pair of rubber boots in the back of a mud-splattered pickup truck marked the High Plains irrigator."[65]

Irrigation accelerated the mechanization of plains farming. It promoted the kind of intensive farming practiced in many regions across the United States instead of traditional extensive dryland farming. The inability of the soil and water to support the new demands would raise a new set of problems.

CENTER-PIVOT IRRIGATION EASES THE LOAD

Invented about 1950 by Colorado Plains farmer Frank Zybach, the center-pivot irrigator was, according to *Scientific American* in 1975, "the most significant mechanical innovation [worldwide] in agriculture since the replacement of draft animals by the tractor."[66] This "novel rotating machine," the writer continues, "enables the farmer to irrigate large tracts of land automatically." It caused a revolution because irrigation, although it had existed in various forms for ten thousand years, had always been synonymous with hard work and wasteful water consumption.

A typical center pivot on the plains is a thirteen-hundred-foot-long, six-inch pipe supported eight feet off the ground by a row of seven or more towers on large wheels. Sprinklers were attached at regular intervals, pointing up or down. One end of the pipe was set in the middle of a quarter section around which the pipe and wheeled towers circled. Water from the center flowed through the pipe and the pressure it caused at the end of the pipe actuated a mechanism—a "Trojan Bar"—that moved the outermost tower on a broad circular route. The rest of the towers, led by an alignment device, followed in line. As this center-pivot irrigation mechanism circled over a crop, farmers could apply water as needed. This circular pattern did not reach the corners of most quarter sections, which meant that between 120 and 132 acres were actually irrigated. Various "corner arms" could be attached to

10. Two examples of center-pivot irrigation in the 1980s, the top photo illustrating the original and less efficient high-level sprinklers that wasted water through wind and evaporation and the bottom photo showing a more efficient (up to 80 percent) drop sprinkler. Center-pivot irrigation also has the ability to water gently rolling country, as in the Kansas Sandhills, whereas flood irrigation required flat farmland that in some cases was laser-leveled by the scs. Photos supplied by Valmont Industries, Valley, Nebraska, and reprinted with permission.

143

cover an extra 19 to 45 acres—up to 96 percent of the field—or to water an irregular field. A center-pivot irrigator could track a complete circle in twelve hours, while applying about three-eighths of an inch of water in the traverse, but it was possible to slow the pace by adjusting the outermost tower. Typical irrigation scheduling called for one traverse every three to five days.

Center-pivot systems, which can apply water lightly and frequently, offered scheduled, man-made rains on demand, not laboriously made rivers of canals and ditches. Nebraska plant and water scientist William E. Splinter writes, "for the normally dry climate of the Great Plains the microclimate of a field being irrigated by a center-pivot system is quite similar to that of an oasis in a desert."[67] Grades of up to 30 percent could be covered, although at a rate higher than 10 percent, there was a threat of erosion and gullying. The center-pivot system could carry liquid fertilizer in its water and increase the ability of sandy soils to hold water-suspended nutrients. When high-capital, low-labor center-pivot irrigation brought a field to maximum production, it became necessary to use commercial fertilizers to replenish depleted soils. Sophisticated irrigation thus encouraged technological "soil mining." Traditionally, farmers protected their soil by rotating crops and using animal manure. However, the maximum-yield industrial farming does not encourage farmers to keep fallow fields or grow low cash value soil-building crops. As a result, beginning in the early 1950s, the ubiquitous high-pressure stationary or wheeled steel tanks containing anhydrous ammonia (the business in which the notorious Billy Sol Estes made his fortune in the 1950s) dotted the landscape. At more than 80 percent nitrogen, this chemical fertilizer in convenient gas form allowed farmers to rapidly replenish nitrogen in the soil after each harvest of grain sorghums or wheat. It seemed most efficient at first to put the liquid into the irrigation water between the pump and the field, but soon farmers used nozzles attached behind the plow points of chisel plows to apply it directly to the soil.

Center-pivot mechanization transformed plains irrigation into a high-technology industry. Farmers enjoyed the benefits of buried water-supply lines, electrically operated and computerized valves, low-pressure spray nozzles, and moisture sensors that were embedded in the soil. Scheduling involved strategic or critical-stage irrigation depending upon the crop, during tasseling and silking, head emergence, or pod and bean development. Irrigators who invested in the new systems went deeply into debt. In the late 1970s, corn peaked at $3.00 a bushel before collapsing to $1.25. As a result, land prices fell by almost half—from $920 to $500 an acre. Many Sandhill irrigators lost two-thirds of their borrowing power. Between 1971 and 1976, the high point of new installations, a complete sprinkler and well system ran $25,000. By the mid-1980s, a minimum-cost turn-key irrigation system on a quarter section cost $70,000, which meant that the per-acre cost was $437.50, about the same as it cost to buy an acre of land. It was not unusual to spend $200,000 for a state-of-the-art system, or $1,250 an acre, not including production costs in seed, equipment, fertilizer, insecticide, labor, and amortization. For comparison, if, per acre, 140 bushels of corn valued at $3.00 each are produced on 133 acres, the farmer grosses $420 an acre—less than the per-acre cost to install an irrigation system. Simultaneously, energy costs had soared. A typical center-pivot unit needed about fifty gallons of diesel fuel per acre per year to apply twenty-two inches of water. This was ten times the fuel necessary to raise and harvest a nonirrigated corn crop. Caught between their center-pivot systems and their bank loans, many irrigation farmers learned that living off crops alone was not enough, and they started asking how they could turn their crops into cash to pay debts as prices dropped.

THE GIGOT EMPIRE AND THE HIGH-YIELD PRODUCTION ETHIC

Today, in the heart of the old Dust Bowl country of southwest Kansas, Garden City farmer Clarence J. Gigot (starts like *jig* and ends like *spigot*) does not worry about drought like he did when he was a young man in the 1930s.[68] He now operates hundreds of "circles" of center-pivot irrigation sprinklers spread across the old agriculturally submarginal lands called the Sandhills. Each circle covers a 160-acre quarter section. The Gigot family—Clarence and his four strapping sons—bought over several years 2,800 acres of the sunburned and desolate Sandhills, much of it at a bargain-basement price of five dollars an acre. The USDA had designated the land submarginal to prevent attempts to do anything more than graze cattle on it, an activity that was limited to one steer per 160 acres. Other parts of this scrubland and dunes country at the corner where Kansas, Oklahoma, and Colorado meet had already been designated a federal grassland reserve during the Dust Bowl troubles. The U.S. government offered to resettle drought-broken farmers elsewhere.

While virtually everyone else abandoned their Sandhills farms, Gigot began to buy up the Finney County scrubland. At the time it must have appeared foolhardy, but Gigot now appears to have been incredibly shrewd. The family, which combined a frontier expansionist mentality with the tools of agribusiness, introduced center-pivot irrigation onto the bleached landscape. After hearing of a new irrigation device, Gigot and his sons, Dean and Terry, traveled over three hundred miles to Nebraska to see the center pivot in action. They bought one directly from the factory and installed it twelve miles southeast of Garden City. In the first year of center-pivot irrigation the quarter section yielded a remarkable 120 bushels of corn an acre.[69]

Today, Gigot's fields consistently yield two to three times the grain of his dryland-farming neighbors. In the 1960s they speculated on an additional twenty-two thousand acres in the Sandhills. Between 1972 and 1974 they applied for and drilled over one hundred wells, mostly in the Sandsage Prairie of the Sandhills. The Sandhills, notorious for its inability to hold water, was perfectly suited for center-pivot technology. Good loamy soil can hold two inches or more of water per foot of soil while sandy soil soaks up water quickly but holds less than one inch per foot.[70] Center-pivot irrigation offered several lighter sprinklings instead of a single heavy flood application. Crops otherwise entirely unsuited for the Sandhills could prosper: corn, alfalfa, sorghums, and wheat, even sugar beets and potatoes. In addition, center-pivot irrigation seemed destined to make Gigot prosper because it worked on both slightly hilly and flat terrain. Most of the Sandhills is made up of gently rolling terrain where ordinary flood irrigation would have been impossible.[71]

Others followed Gigot's lead, but he continues to dominate Sandhills irrigation. In 1965 11 center pivots watered 1,760 acres of Finney County's 150,000 acres of Sandsage Prairie. Nine years later, in 1974, there were 590 center pivots. Gigot's own center-pivot units peaked at more than 700 in the early 1980s.[72] In the 1970s Sandhills land prices soared from $25 an acre to $250 an acre, and irrigated center-pivot land commanded $1,200 to $1,500.

Gigot venturesomeness paid off handsomely. It is a conservative gamble: the Gigots work hard to make certain all the dice will roll their way before they place high-stakes bets. One of their most controversial gambles, and one of their most profitable, was the Water Depletion Allowance Case. When the Gigots purchased most of their irrigation land in the 1960s and 1970s, the price of land overlying the aquifer had already risen substantially, while groundwater supplies had begun to decline significantly. In a 1963 court case, *U.S.* v. *Shurbet,* a Texas farmer established his right to a water-depletion income-tax allowance for the decline in the aquifer that ran under his land, since it reduced the cash value of his land.[73] The Gigots went to court and in 1980 received a Justice Department ruling that they were entitled to the same deduction. They had asked for more than thirty thousand dollars in income tax refunds. As a result of the ruling in their favor, farmers across the Midwest and plains could save more than one billion dollars, and Kansas irrigators alone enjoyed tax relief totaling fifty million dollars a year. For a single quarter section of irrigated land, the annual depletion deduction would be twenty-four hundred dollars,[74] but farmers who were too far-sighted and acquired their land in the 1940s and 1950s before prices went up would receive no benefits.[75]

The confident Gigots could build their fortune on a naturally dry and dusty landscape because they had access to mechanized irrigation. Now they work over fifty thousand irrigated acres. They depend on computerized management to distribute fertilizers and pesticides on their fields and nutritional feed mix to the cattle in their feedlots. One Gigot manager observed that every effort is made to reduce labor, energy, and water costs and that each field is measured for the best balance between gallons of water per minute and bushels of corn or wheat per acre. Despite some retrenchment, the Gigots still operate more than five hundred circles, mostly under the family-owned Circle

Land and Cattle Company. The family's operations also include an equipment dealership (Gigot Irrigating), two massive feedlots (Gigot Feeders and Circle Feeders), Southwest Corn (the Gigot grain elevator company), Maxima Corporation (the Gigot fertilizer company), and Circle Research Corporation (the Gigot gasohol operation).

One of Gigot's sons, Dean, told a Wichita reporter who wrote of their achievement, "It's not raping [the land] to pump water. Water is something put there to use and I hope that I'm using it to the best of my ability."[76] To create a garden where once lay an abandoned landscape is premier stewardship. Dean told another interviewer, "Should we be using [the groundwater]? Damn right we should! The same doom sayers are claiming that the buffalo and the Indians should still be here. . . . The water is there for man to use, same as the soil, the trees and the oil. Use it with all the abilities that you have." The Gigots are reputed, by both friends and critics, to control "the most finely tuned irrigation management in western Kansas." Considering the dramatic contrasts in lifestyle might help to explain the Gigots' willingness to take high-stakes gambles, while their more cautious neighbors, like nearby farmers Phil and Linda Tooms, are not. The Gigots are more like cattlemen than farmers. A visitor to the offices of Gigot Feeders finds a world where the women are Texas-pretty and high-heel stylish, and where they are definitely secretaries, while the men all loom larger than life, striding around wearing boots, chaps, dusters, ten-gallon hats, and, yes, even handlebar mustaches as if they just came off the range (which many just did). If there is equality between men and women, as there is between Phil and Linda Tooms and between Roger and Betty Trescott, it is well-hidden in the Gigot Empire. The men hold the centers of power and authority while the women assist from the margins.

As for the future, the Gigots are businesslike realists. They expect to continue their technologically advanced water-conserving irrigation for a long time. Still, a Gigot Feeder manager did believe that declining Ogallala water levels would eventually shut everything down and return the region to submarginal scrubland. Dean Gigot also admitted that consumption had surpassed capacity: "We are overpopulated out here. My family's contention is stop the drilling, put in a five-year moratorium on new wells, and get a real good monitoring situation in place."[77] He did not acknowledge that his family drilled its wells before state regulations went into effect. They can continue to take as much water as they choose. Kansas groundwater official Gary Baker observed to a reporter that "the time will come when we'll be real sorry that the Sandsage Prairie [Sandhills] was ever developed. There's a tremendous amount of wind erosion already, especially on the irrigated prairie that you wouldn't otherwise be farming. Once you take away the natural vegetation cover on this land, there's no way to restore it. I sure don't want to live here when the aquifer goes dry, because this place is never gonna stop blowing. It's gonna be a new desert."[78] In the meantime, Gigot family assets currently exceed the thirteen million dollars reported in 1980.

Chasing after the Brass Ring: Cattle Kingdom Redux

Even in hard times, the Gigots discovered that they could cover their irrigation costs if they turned their operation into a vertically integrated cattle business. No outside middleman would skim off the profits. They would control the entire enterprise that began with flourishing crops on "free" soil, water, and sun and that climaxed with beef markets. Even after servicing the center-pivot irrigation systems, they continued to profit because they could make adjustments to buffer themselves when high costs invaded one or another of their operations. In the mid-1980s Gigot and his four sons conquered the plains to become the biggest corn producers in the nation. When corn was cheap they fed it to cattle in their feedlots and then benefited when cattle prices rose from twenty-nine dollars for one hundred pounds in mid-1973 to fifty dollars in July 1985 to seventy-eight dollars in May 1988.[79] However, because corn prices fluctuated and water levels were declining, the Gigots protected themselves in 1984 by switching a significant part of their production from risky water-intensive corn to more reliable wheat that could even be dry farmed. When a wheat glut brought federal restrictions, they planted grain sorghums, partly to feed their own livestock and partly to bypass restrictions on wheat production.[80] They also began to cultivate with a moisture-preserving no-till operation. With these strategies in place, if a grain

149

crop was no longer profitable on center-pivot land, they could successfully graze cattle on irrigated grasses. Dryland open-range beef production stood at twenty-seven pounds per acre, while cattle that consumed cool-season grasses under a center-pivot unit virtually guaranteed between seven hundred and nine hundred pounds of beef per acre.[81] Kenny Ochs, sales manager for Gigot Irrigation Company, summed up future survival on the old Dust Bowl High Plains: "As long as cattle make a profit, everyone profits." All the alternatives that allowed the Gigots to prosper—corn, wheat, sorghums, grass, and cattle—were tethered to water.

Beef production no longer means lone steers dotting the range. Instead, cattle are crowded onto grassless feedlots and fattened at high speed on concentrated feed, nutrients, growth hormones, and antibiotics set at scientifically designed mixes by computer. Ron Crocker, manager of Gigot Feeders, whose highway sign reads, "Custom Cattle Feeders. Open to the Public," proudly shows visitors the vast, open bins of thousands of tons of grain piled up like coal at a power plant and computerized feed mixes dumped into trucks from overhead hoppers. Much of the grain comes from the fifty thousand acres of Gigot irrigated fields that are operated as efficiently as the feedlots. Instead of the extensive family farming of the past, the Gigots practice intensive industrial farming with heavy soil conditioning and large-scale water consumption. In fact, an intensive-extensive combination dominates all levels of High Plains agriculture, from the spectacular amount of water that was once in the Ogallala, to the heavy pumping of water onto high-yield crops on thousand-acre farms, to the crowded cattle pens covering hundreds of acres. Ron Crocker openly asserts that when the Ogallala water is gone, the feed grains will go and everything else will shut down, including the feedlots.

Gigot Feeders services as many as twenty-five thousand cattle every week. Ten percent are Gigot owned, and the rest are on contract from ranches as far away as Missouri and Texas. The slaughterhouses and beef packers in the region consume ninety thousand head a week. According to a shiny, full-color brochure handed out to visitors, within a ninety-mile radius of the Gigot Feeders feedlots packinghouses have been established by Val

Agra, Excel, Hyplains Beef, National Beef, Swift, and Iowa Beef Processors (IBP). Thirty percent of America's livestock pass through packinghouses in Dodge City and Holcomb, Kansas. Four of every ten beeves in the United States is slaughtered within 250 miles of Garden City (from Pueblo, Colorado, to Wichita, Kansas). Neither Chicago, Cincinnati, nor Kansas City is the nation's meat packer, nor have they been for three decades. Rather than spending money to ship animals to central locations, the meat processing business moved to where the beef or pork was. The first local meat processors appeared in 1950 in the Garden City region, where corn, milo, wheat, and alfalfa grew, and the steers got fat in the first feedlots in the early 1950s.

The IBP plant in Holcomb, eight miles west of Garden City, was built in 1981. It is called the largest and most efficient beef processing operation in the world under one roof. Iowa Beef Processors, which became part of the Occidental Petroleum conglomerate in 1981, deserves a book to itself.[82] In the 1970s, when 35 percent of the nation's beef packing plants were going under, "Andy" Anderson of IBP created "boxed beef" and captured a quarter of the nation's beef business. Old-line meat packers—Swift, Wilson, Armour, Hormel, and Oscar Mayer—quickly lost their lead to boxed beef newcomers—IBP, Excel, and Conagra. Iowa Beef Processors's Holcomb plant never delivers the carcass to the supermarket butcher's door, as Swift and Armour had done. Instead, the meat arrives mostly bone-out and in manageable boxes. When beef carcasses were hung up to cure before delivery to retailers, a considerable amount of water weight was lost. However, with boxed beef the water is retained and each cut of meat weighs more. The Holcomb disassembly line does the heavy and difficult work before the boxes go out the door. The new plant immediately doubled IBP's capacity, and the company now claims an "annual kill capacity" of over one million head.

Visitors and reporters receive IBP's own shiny brochure, "The Cutting Edge." At the plant, streams of cattle are crowded up a long ramp. One reporter, officially unwelcome but posing as a tourist, made the rounds in the plant:

I enjoy eating meat, and I know that the cows must be killed. . . . A laborer clamps a chain around the hind leg of each steer and heifer. Another places a foot-long cylinder against each of their heads, and fires a steel rod into the skull. A huge chain sweeps down from an overhead trolley line. It swings the cattle upside down, and sends them clanging a couple of feet apart down a long chute. . . . And the disassembly process begins. Man and machine merge to separate the various parts in stages. The workers use electric knives. . . . No chaps or spurs necessary, just ear plugs, rubber boots, belly guards, and chain-mesh gloves. . . . Within fifteen minutes, 1,200 pounds of corn-fed steer have been reduced to tenderloins and rib eyes.[83]

People in and around Garden City expected to have the majority of the thirty-three hundred new jobs. But when the doors to the Holcomb plant were opened, the company admitted that "six out of seven workers who would leave jobs in the community to work at the plant would find the work too hard and distasteful and would quit."[84] Iowa Beef Processors has been cited by federal watchdog agency OSHA for "shocking and dismaying working conditions" in several of its plants. A study by the Kansas Rural Center concluded, "Meat packing is the second most dangerous industry after underground mining. Most workers stand on a production line and cut the same piece of meat with a knife all day long. . . . The most common physical complaint among workers is sore and cramped hands, due to gripping a knife all day in a 30–50 degree Fahrenheit environment. Workers often develop tendonitus, bursitus, arthritus [sic], muscle strain, or back strain, besides constant fatigue."[85] Iowa Beef Processors, known for its "tough labor policies," started to bring in immigrants—Cubans, Laotians, Vietnamese, and Mexicans, workers resented by local citizens. In 1982 IBP paid a base wage of $6.00 an hour, whereas an old-line packer like Wilson paid $10.50 an hour.[86]

At IBP 400 gallons of water are used to process one head of beef. The plant slaughters over 5,000 head of cattle per day, or 1.5 million head a year, which requires 600 million gallons of water pumped from the Ogallala.[87] If, as Ogallala supplies diminish, the rights to use water are sold at market prices—a practice both conservatives and conservationists recommend—it is unlikely that local irrigators or feedlot owners could compete with IBP for the water. But no one disagreed that the feed for the cattle shipped to the IBP plant would keep irrigation pumps running on the surrounding farms and that many people would receive a share of the profits in the chain that ran from the groundwater to the boxed steaks. It is clear that whoever controls IBP could control southwest Kansas. After IBP arrived, local feedlot owners wondered what had happened to their hard-earned prosperity once they realized that they would receive lower prices for their cattle, not higher.

Eight miles south and one and one-half miles southwest of the IBP plant in Holcomb, the Gigot family moved in a new direction. Dean Gigot expected approval in 1998 for his share of the concentrated and profitable business of hogs. His preliminary plans for new confined-hog buildings were typically grand: eighteen finishing units each capable of feeding 960 animals, four breeding units, and four nursery units, for a total of twenty-six shiny new sheds and several waste lagoons on a small corner of his land. Dean Gigot found himself in the middle of a controversy over potential pollution and its regulation. In March 1998 the Finney County board of zoning raised questions about authorization of his lagoon system, water rights for his hog operation, and impact on local water wells. His lawyer argued that Dean Gigot was not subject to county regulation because hog production was agriculture. Local opponents said they were blindsided. Farmer Bill Turrentine said, "It was all so quick and cut and dried." He also worried about the sandy soil in the area: "I sure hate to see them start down there. That's the best place in the world to contaminate everything," he noted, "That's pretty fragile geology."[88]

Steve Irsik: Spokesman for Family Agribusiness

Better known outside the plains than the Gigots, Steve Irsik is a savvy businessman in grain farming, cattle feedlots, and hog confinement. Wry, tough, generous, and seasoned, he is knowledgeable and articulate, and he appeals to diverse audiences, from readers of the *National Geographic* and *Christian Science Monitor* to television viewers. About the complexity and difficulties of plains farming, he wrote in January 1998:

The winter in the High Plains has been difficult if you are in the cattle business. We started the Fall off by having a horrible early winter blizzard in October—I lost no cattle located in the county but we did loose [*sic*] 1,000 head in our feedlots. I imagine the blizzard killed 50,000 in Eastern Colorado and Western Kansas with millions of pounds of beef lost due to shrink. In the country I know of individuals who lost $100,000 in dead cattle. Since the blizzard the majority of the days have been overcast and generally wet— this makes for wet & miserable cattle. When the animals are uncomfortable they do not gain as well thus our costs go up. In the past when this combination has occurred we experience increasing cattle prices—that did not happen this winter. So, we have the worst of all worlds, increasing costs with decreasing inventory and beef prices. Along with the weather you must add the currency & monetary problems in Asia (decreasing exports) plus record tonnage of competing meats (pork, turkey & chicken).[89]

Irsik has little patience with plains old-timers who want to preserve the economics and field practices of traditional wheat farming, nor does he see much value in organic, or alternative, farming. Traditional farming will continue to decline, he says, and continue to empty the plains of its farms, communities, and people. Organic, or alternative, farming remains unproven and faces too many technological and marketplace problems. True sustainability on the plains, he contends, is in value-added farming that makes the most of groundwater, soil, and grains.[90] Better end use should be the objective of plains farmers. Irsik became a premier example of vertical integration when he moved into the cattle feedlot business, supplied in large part by grains from his own fields. He moved cautiously into the industrial hog business after watching both local producers and multinational corporations enter the business profitably. Now several shiny, metal hog sheds dot the corners of his sections. He believed that the most efficient, sustainable, and profitable farming on the plains must have the features of agribusiness and that it should take advantage of contemporary technologies and management techniques to achieve factorylike output. Feed grains on the plains are inexpensive, and instead of selling low as a grain farmer it makes sense to use the grains for more profitable steers, dairy cows, pigs, and even chickens. In Irsik's view, more profit through industrialization would make local farmers secure and transform towns like Garden City into small but thriving metropolises.

Irsik's own feedlot business is the twelfth largest in the United States. His splendid ranch-style house, which sits in the midst of his own vast patchwork of irrigated fields and feedlots off state highway 50, east of Garden City, would sit well in a prosperous metropolitan suburb. An adjacent, timbered building contains his spacious office, the heart of Irsik Farms. He is optimistic about the future of the plains, especially expansion through corporate hog and dairy farming. Speaking to a newspaper reporter in 1994, he observed, "With people pressure in California and the Midwest, these industries need somewhere to go, and they are looking very seriously at the High Plains" because of the dry climate, excellent soils, available groundwater, and low human populations.[91]

Irsik is more optimistic about the future of groundwater consumption than most people who live and work above the Ogallala aquifer. He acknowledges that the groundwater will continue to decline but also sees highly efficient technologies, such as LEPA (low-energy precision application) irrigation, as a way to extend groundwater use for decades. The Ogallala will continue to be a premier resource for the region and a chief selling point to future agricultural industries. Steve Frost, director of Southwest Kansas Groundwater Management District, disagrees. He contends that too many irrigation farmers wait too long, installing water-saving systems only after pumping becomes too expensive. Nearly half the farmers of southwest Kansas still use wasteful flood irrigation that results in excessive saturation, evaporation, and end-of-field runoff. At the same time, Frost admits that "I don't see any reason to save the aquifer if saving it means devastating the economy."[92] Irsik's response is to get more farmers into more efficient irrigation and more profit from better end use of their grain.

The Transformation of Plains Farming into Industrial Food Production

THE PLAINS BECOME HOG HEAVEN

For most of the twentieth century, western Kansas and the Oklahoma Panhandle epitomized the ups and downs of a rural lifestyle based on growing wheat or corn for cash. Few people were rich and local communities experienced a gradual population decline. In the 1960s, the old dryland landscape became dotted first with center-pivot irrigators, with cattle feedlots by 1980, and with the metal sheds of hog buildings in the mid-1990s. To many local people, this movement into modern agribusiness was an intrusion upon their hard but satisfying agricultural society.

While hog production seemed to be a logical progression from irrigated fields and cattle feedlots, it did create a new agricultural geography. Following the lead of John Fraser Hart's important 1970 assessment of industrial agriculture, in 1997 geographer Owen Furuseth described the change as having created an imploded or collapsed landscape.[93] Instead of a sweeping landscape of wheat or sorghum that reaches to the horizon, hog production is concentrated on sites of ten to fifty acres. In such places, swine populations of as many as one hundred thousand animals are crowded into long rectangular sheds with concrete floors and tanks and with metal and plastic walls and roofs. These numbers stand in sharp contrast to the casual raising of a few hogs on a traditional farmyard. Large national and international corporations smelled profits and poured their capital into the confinement production system. Large amounts of low-cost waste are essential to the operations and their profitability. Fresh Ogallala groundwater is used to flush the confinement sheds clean of waste. The effluent is drained into the adjacent holding lagoons until the nitrogen-rich liquids are sprayed or applied through irrigation pipes onto cropland. Manure overloads threatened to pollute the fresh groundwater of the Ogallala aquifer. Land use became less agricultural and more industrial—the sheds were placed on the unwatered corners of center-pivot fields and the waste lagoons and adjacent fields became designated repositories for manure, compared by some critics to toxic chemical-waste dumps. Local inhabitants downwind of hog producers bitterly complained about the intense smells that caused respiratory problems. Critics doubted that hog production could still be classified as agricultural when the land itself played a diminished, highly specialized, and nontraditional role. Neil Hamilton, law professor at Drake University in Iowa, wrote, "Is the person who tends the corporate sow a 'farmer'? Of course not. . . . Industrialization boils down to lower cost, more uniform and more predictable food. There is no proof that farmers will be better off, land will be better treated or rural communities will be healthier."[94]

Seaboard Farms, Murphy Family Farms, or a similar corporation approached agricultural communities burdened by decades of a sparse and declining population and economic stagnation. As a means to turn their economies around, many county commissioners and state legislatures began to court outside industries, promising tax breaks, nonunion, low-cost labor, and environmental controls that were lightly enforced or nonexistent.[95] Oklahoma hog contractor Richard Alig told a reporter that "We are geared for a graze-out operation. . . . The bottom line is we make more on pounds of meat than on bushels of wheat."[96] Plains communities were attractive to corporations because they produced large surpluses of animal feeds and, in Ogallala country, enjoyed seemingly abundant groundwater. The central plains also had a low human population rate and a high evaporation rate that supposedly made smelly hog production more tolerable. It was a new consumption of a classic free common. The president of DeKalb Swine Breeders noted that on the plains manure lagoons can advantageously lose an average of fifty inches per year in evaporation and that what is not evaporated can be irrigated onto the extensive cropland units typical of the region. British-owned Pig Improvement Corporation (PIC) of Kentucky reported, "It is difficult to get a land base in Kentucky [for handling manure]. . . . Plus, Kentucky and Tennessee have lots of surface water and streams. . . . We can put together a more effective nutrient management program per head out here [in central Oklahoma] than in many other areas."[97]

Debates over the newly arrived hog sheds, with their waste and odors, pitted neighbors against each other. To nearby residents the sheds meant the sudden collapse of a cherished rural lifestyle that had been far less threatened (and perhaps assisted) by the center pivots and the feedlots. For local hog entrepreneurs, the confinement factories meant new economic opportunity and a highly desirable shift from historic uncertainties that have bedeviled agriculture. As hog production continues to grow exponentially on the High Plains from Wyoming to Texas, so do concerns among rural inhabitants and state legislators alike about a declining lifestyle and fears about environmental impacts.[98]

THE BUSINESS OF PIGS

Pound for pound, pigs are the most productive of the large farm animals. Americans ate more pork than beef in the past, especially on the frontier and in the rural countryside. The center of the pork industry was family farms in the tall-grass midwestern prairie across Ohio, Indiana, Illinois, Missouri, and Iowa. Corn, the region's archetypal crop, was the ideal food to fatten pigs. Where there was corn, there were pigs, and where there were pigs, there was corn. Iowa is said to have today three million people amid twenty-five million hogs, numbers nearly matched in Missouri. Industrial hog operations also became attractive to declining rural regions in the Old South of the Carolinas, on the High Plains of eastern Wyoming and Colorado, and across western Kansas and the Oklahoma-Texas Panhandle.

In 1994 the *Wall Street Journal* described pork production as having changed from being a "messy sideline for family farmers" to "techno-pork"—a profitable corporate investment that reflected high technology and high finance.[99] By 1994, for example, National Hog Farms had established a 27,000-acre spread along Colorado's South Platte River near Kersey, where 17,000 sows birth 320,000 pigs a year. One hundred and sixty-five employees earned an average salary of $15,000. It was described as "more like a factory than a farm. . . . Food arrives like clockwork. . . . 55 semi-trailer loads of corn and 14 truckloads of soybean are unloaded every week, [totaling] 3.4 million bushels of corn and 19,000 tons of soy a year. . . . The reproductive history of every sow is computerized. . . . Water flush-tanks wash away the accumulated manure every 12 hours,"[100] totaling 1.6 million gallons of waste every day, called "nutrients" by a company spokesman. One farm economist said, "There's no doubt what is driving this expansion. The average market price was $45 per hundredweight in 1993. With a $35 per hundredweight cost of production for the best producers, profits ran $25 per hog. Multiply that by one million hogs and you have $25 million profit."[101] By 1990 Americans were spending $26 billion annually on pork.

This was not the old barnyard farming. Large, specialized hog farms are like meat factories in which genetically bred animals spend their lifetimes in metal and concrete pens. They are fed by automatic devices that dispense scientifically balanced diets of protein concentrates, feeding supplements, and antibiotics. Production is three-tiered and often relies on separate operations in different locations. Sows are bred, gestated (114 days), and farrowed in one location. Two weeks after birth, the piglets are shipped to nurseries contracted with local farmers. After reaching about fifty pounds there, they are shipped to finishing sheds for four months to gain two hundred more pounds before slaughter. The master operation plans for Seaboard Corporation's Seaboard Farms surrounding Guymon in the Oklahoma Panhandle would total 6 genetic farms, 10 sow farms with 4,800 sows each, 14 nursery farms with a capacity of 9,600 piglets each, and 11 finishing farms of about 9,600 hogs each.

Critics insist that confinement sheds do not suit pigs, which are intelligent and active—they are able to travel thirty miles a day at a quick pace—and live in a highly social porcine community. Mega-hog producers are advised by L. R. Taylor in *National Hog Farmer* magazine to think of and treat the breeding sow as "a piece of machinery whose function is to pump out baby pigs like a sausage machine." *Hog Farm Management* magazine tells its readers: "Forget the pig as an animal. Test him just like any other machine in a factory. Schedule treatments like you would lubrication. Breeding season is a first step in an assembly line."[102] Journalist Mark Obmascik observed that "these plants make pigs like GM makes cars."[103]

Due to the threat of disease, confinement sheds are managed like an industrial "clean room," where employees and visitors scrub up and change into company coveralls. Inside the pig factories, the environmental hazards for workers are among the worst of any industrial operation, on or off farmland. The closed buildings contain combinations of noxious fumes: ammonia, hydrogen sulfide, phosphates, bacteria, feed dust, and decomposing fecal matter. A joint report by the American Lung Association and the University of Iowa asserted: "Animals have died and workers have become seriously ill in confinement buildings when hydrogen sulfide rises from agitated pits underneath." It added that "Several workers have died when entering a pit during or soon after the emptying process to repair pumping equipment. Persons attempting to rescue these workers have also died."[104]

At Seaboard Farms's new processing plant (once called a slaughterhouse or *abattoir*) in Guymon, Oklahoma, no hogs are held longer than twenty-four hours. They are restrained and stunned individually with electric probes placed behind their necks and then shackled to a clamp on a chained track. After a stab to the neck, their blood is drained. The bodies are dunked in hot water to dehair, and internal organs are removed. In a quick-chill room and freezer, the temperature of the carcasses is reduced to thirty-six degrees, which makes disassembly easier. A long line of workers, using lasers to control the size of the pieces, cut and trim the meat into thirty-pound boxes for the best cuts and two-thousand-pound "combos" for the rest. Fat and scraps go into the on-site rendering unit.[105] Seaboard Farms admitted that it may have to import workers willing to work under these conditions as IBP did in the 1980s for its boxed beef operation outside Garden City, Kansas.

THE UNEXPECTED PROBLEM: POLLUTION OF THE OGALLALA
After decades of local commitment to conservation had reduced aquifer decline by half, one danger from hog production was the renewal of heavy groundwater consumption. Seaboard Farms admitted that each of their 150 units consumes about 900,000 gallons of water a day, or 329 million gallons a year. The medium-sized pig factory run by National Hog Farms in eastern Colorado produces 350,000 pigs annually and requires nearly 2 million gallons of fresh water a day, much of which is used to flush manure from the sheds into holding lagoons before it is dumped onto adjoining land. Also a problem was year-round pumping as opposed to the seasonal pumping of irrigation farms that allows aquifer cone recovery.

An unexpected risk of hog farming was found to be the waste problem caused by a large population, a problem that had been previously unknown on the unindustrialized and little-populated plains. One land-grant university scientist described the pig as "that indefatigable and unsavory engine of pollution."[106] A 100-pound hog produces 1.7 times as much waste as one human being and consumes 30 gallons of water a day. A 10,000-hog, hog-finishing facility produces as much waste as a town the size of Garden City, and Seaboard Farms's operations in western Kansas, which total half a million hogs, consume the water and generate the waste equivalent to a city of 850,000 people. In comparison, the largest plains cities in the 1990 census were Lubbock, Texas, with 190,000 people, and Amarillo, with 160,000 people. Seaboard has the capacity to process as many as 4.5 million hogs on the central plains.

The threat of heavy pollution stems from large sewage and chemical pesticide storage and disposal basins that are common to industrial pork production. While some benignly call these basins "lagoons," critics call them "cesspools." A Norman, Oklahoma, engineer, Kathy Martin, argued that anaerobic (no oxygen required) lagoons were the least efficient at waste management, but that they were "the cheapest, low-maintenance and low-operating-cost treatment."[107] Vigorously debated are the flapper valves (check valves), which are aluminum disks intended to keep lagoon waste from backflowing into the freshwater well and thus directly polluting the aquifer. This could happen at the well at the confinement operation or during application from a center pivot's well.[108] Animal waste lagoons have been used since the 1950s but most were built for cattle feedlots. In contrast with the waste that collects in indoor hog confinement, cattle urine and feces dry on the lot, and the runoff collected is far less concentrated. Garden City reporter Tim Unruh interviewed Kansas State University agricultural engineer Pat Murphy and was told, "Cattle waste is managed through collection and disposal. Feedlots pump down their ponds once or twice a year and the manure is spread by trucks as a dry product. Pig waste disposal is in a liquid form often pumped through center-pivot operations."[109]

Contamination of the groundwater from leakage of the sewage lagoons posed a new problem for plains groundwater management. Overall, Seaboard Farms and Superior Farms filed for thirty pollution-control permits to allow production of 225,000 hogs annually. Despite industry opposition, researchers from Kansas State University conducted a study of workable lagoon liners, the aging of lagoons, and actual seepage rates of waste into the soil.[110] All lagoons, whether lined with clay or synthetics, are allowed to seep 1/4 inch per day, which would allow 91 1/4 inches per year. The industry admits that no technology exists that will not leak, but still, the goal is to minimize the risk. State legislation includes monitoring the wells and sensors, which are similar to devices placed under gasoline tanks at service stations, beneath lagoons to detect leakage.[111] One part of the debate is whether anaerobic activity would eliminate the biologically degradable manure and urine as it descends toward the aquifer.

In the best light, the nitrogen-rich manure spread onto cropland in these operations is similar to innovative multi–life cycle manufacturing that turns former waste into new products. Making the case for added value, Colorado hog contractor Leroy Phillips reported that he was able to increase cattle grazing from thirty head to sixty-eight head after spreading hog manure four times a year on less than 160 acres.[112] Seaboard sometimes sells back the land surrounding its facilities to farmers, and then provides those farmers with effluent from their hog farms as fertilizer for their wheat, corn, and milo crops. A Colorado water consultant says it's only a matter of time before National Hog Farms begins to contaminate groundwater with nitrates. "They have taken relatively poor land and are putting a very heavy load of waste on the ground," more than eight inches of hog waste per year on 2,800 acres, or 1,100 pounds of nitrogen per acre, a rate equivalent to a city of 250,000 people. "The groundwater is 30 feet down, so it will probably take five to 10 years before you see anything real bad. This will be a very expensive problem to solve."[113] As scale increases, the ecosystem's capacity to absorb pollution without serious damage is surpassed. Concentrations of waste from the lagoons may be dumped on the land in excess of the soil's ability to assimilate it. This results in uncontrolled runoff and the contamination of surface water and groundwater. Representing Seaboard, Jason M. Peters retorts that swine effluent is not a waste but that it improves crop production and that "This not only reduces the need for additional fertilizer elements but also provides organic matter and improves soil's physical and chemical properties."[114] Jarrod Stewart, of Cimarron County, Oklahoma, replied to Peters, saying, "In the end Cimarron County, its friendships, its culture, its land and its water will be flushed down stream to protect Seaboard's bottom line."[115] A rancher near Rolla, in Morton County, fears for the future of western Kansas: "If they're allowed to use this as a dump site, western Kansas will become one big cesspool with no water."[116]

WHEN SMELL IS NOT A TRIVIAL MATTER

Local citizens, often multigeneration plains farmers whose grandparents homesteaded the land, live in close proximity to tens of thousands of hogs crowded in containment buildings. They quickly learn of the collapse of their long-nurtured and cherished lifestyles, which included stepping out of their back doors into the fresh night air. Wanda and Ivan Smith, for example, who farmed 1,625 acres of wheat and corn just east of Guymon, were overpowered by the smells from the lagoons of Seaboard's three nearby hog barns. A reporter from the *Daily Oklahoman* visited them in April 1997 and wrote, "It's overpowering. It's nauseating. It burns your eyes and gets in your clothes."[117] Others complained that the smell was different than that of cattle and described it as like a litter box or like human waste. Researchers noted that "odor is subjective," but an activist responded, "When odor is so intense you can hardly breathe, it's not subjective."[118] An independent hog producer said, "I've been around hogs all my life and I've never been offended by the smell before but the odor we get from Murphy Farms [near Sheldon, Missouri] is overwhelming—no more opening up the windows at night, no more grilling out in the backyard, the kids can't play outside, friends and family don't want to visit. I just don't think it's right that somebody can come in and do that to you."[119]

Leon Chesin, waste management professor at the University of Nebraska, notes that from one building with one thousand hogs more than twenty-three tons of ammonia exit through the ventilation system per year.[120] If liquefied hog manure is applied by center pivot to a field in a five-miles-an-hour wind, neighbors less than a quarter of a mile away will smell the sharp, pungent ammonia in minutes. The Smiths, like many other homeowners near the lagoons of the containment operations, are frustrated by a 1993 Oklahoma law that exempted all state-licensed animal facilities—concentrated animal feeding operations—from nuisance laws that had been established to counteract "unreasonable interference with someone's use and enjoyment of their own property."[121] Animal facilities cannot be sued for odor or for destroying a neighbor's quality of life. Hog advocate Paul Hitch admitted, "Is it pleasant? No." But he added, "This is life in the country."[122]

Unable to apply nuisance or environmental laws, some property owners sought redress by arguing that their property values sank because no one would buy a house near a confinement operation.[123] Julia Howell of Hooker wrote to the *Guymon* (Okla.) *Daily Herald* in August 1995 castigating her neighbors for voting for the Seaboard packing plant: "My home's appraised value, where my husband was born and has farmed all his adult life, devaluated from six figures to zero immediately on just hearing hogs were coming only six blocks away, a multi-acre stinking, polluting cesspit full of hog manure, maggots and flies within yelling distance of where we farm and live. When a property is worth zero and can't be sold, then surely I won't have to pay taxes on said property, will I?"[124]

The federal Clean Air Act, which is enforced by the Environmental Protection Agency, does not apply to disagreeable smells, no matter how strong or pungent, and Oklahoma does not have regulations against odor unless the smell includes toxic chemicals. Doug Hamilton, biosystems engineer at Oklahoma State University, says the "hog stink" comes from dozens of compounds and volatile acids, some of which can be "extremely dangerous if you're in a confined space."[125] A Kansas environmental official admitted that if a lagoon is overloaded by sewage, the anaerobic bacteria die and the lagoon becomes stagnant. The resulting stench is terrible and causes respiratory problems and psychological disablement. Ironically, smells are intensified if the operation includes a digester, a device that uses bacteria to break up solids and reduce the polluting effects of wastewater. Odors can be carried by dust particles or spray (aerosol drift) from center pivots. Airborne threats include disease-bearing bacteria from aerated slurry and the breathing of poisonous hydrogen sulfide, but it hardly reaches a fifth of a dangerous concentration in the open air. Hamilton notes that people have died from working at hog facilities, but on the flat windy plains of the Oklahoma Panhandle, the levels are too low to be threatening.[126] Texas County landowner

Julia Howell, who, with her husband, Bob, owns a home three-quarters of a mile from an operation with forty-two thousand hogs, said, "I don't call them odors. They're toxic fumes."[127]

One corporate operator, Pig Improvement Corporation, said it tries to be a good neighbor. "The biggest challenge anybody will have when putting up a new livestock operation is location," said Dwain Bankson, an environmental operations manager for the company. "We try to find a location that's fairly isolated. . . . [W]hether it's a half mile from a neighbor or a quarter mile from a neighbor, we want to minimize the risk of their close proximity as much as possible. It's important to look at the wind direction and the speed for that particular area. . . . Once in a while somebody is going to smell us. We hope it's not a smell that lasts forever and forever and forever."[128] In western Kansas, a Seaboard official added, "We do what we can to reduce [the odor]. If somebody can come up with a magic potion to eliminate the odor problem we'd use it. But that magic potion just doesn't exist."[129] Seaboard Farms is experimenting with a yucca-plant extract that can be sprayed in lagoons or used in pig feed to cut ammonia output in half. Other strategies, including windbreaks of two or three rows of trees, can effectively reduce odor plumes.

HITCH ENTERPRISES

Paul Hitch of Guymon was frustrated enough with the antihog direction of public opinion and "mischief" by a governor's task force that in December 1997 he wrote the *Daily Oklahoman* about invasion of the rights of private property. He asserted, "You must let individual people use their own assets in whatever way they feel appropriate. If a farmer wants to use his land, his water, his money and his managerial ability to grow pigs, he should be allowed to do so without having to submit it to a vote of everyone in the county." He deplored trends that were "anti-business" and "anti-freedom."[130] The battle, local people said, was between individual freedom of choice or the pursuit of happiness (quality of life). To some citizens, freedom meant being able to stand on the porch and take a deep breath without gagging. To others, it meant the freedom to raise pigs. Hitch took a controversial step when he decided "to raise hogs on a grand scale" as he had done with cattle. He became the center of debate even more than the larger Seaboard Farms enterprises because "Hitch is one of us."[131] Some old friends and neighbors say "he sold us out,"[132] while others argue strongly that Hitch's hogs have done much to revive the Panhandle's economy. The general manager of Hitch's pork business, Mike Brandherm, said that the pork section of Hitch's company complements the company's earlier ventures: "What's really nice with the Hitch project is that, of course, they feed cattle, and we can apply the fertilizer from the pig farms onto the cropland and the grassland." He spoke in terms of vertical integration and product life-cycle: "Our plan is to graze cattle . . . next to the farms. It's really kind of symbiotic. They tie in very close together. We save on fertilizer costs and use very little land for the hog farm. The cattle operation benefits from that."[133]

Like the Gigots in southwest Kansas, the Hitch family is respected for being pioneering and innovative cattle ranchers, but they are also feared for their power. According to a newspaper report, "In the Oklahoma Panhandle, the Hitch name is akin to the Cartwrights of television lore," and Hitch is "the son, grandson and great-grandson of cattlemen."[134] Paul Hitch's great-grandfather, James K. Hitch, left Kansas and in 1884 arrived with a single herd of cattle onto the no-man's-land of the Panhandle, which, at that time, was a strangely autonomous region with no connection to any state or territory. James started a ranch along Coldwater Creek southeast of Guymon, which is now listed on the National Register of Historic Places. His son, Henry C. Hitch, built a ranching empire combined with large-scale wheat farming. Henry's son, Ladd Hitch, saw a future in the feedlot business. Paul, Ladd's son, built his father's operation into the largest cattle-feeding business in the United States. Three massive feedlots fatten about 130,000 head of cattle in the Panhandle country through Texas, Oklahoma, and Kansas.

When Paul Hitch first learned of Seaboard Farms's plan to expand hog production into Guymon and Texas Counties, he first worried about high feed-grain prices that would affect his cattle business. After considering "torpedoing" Seaboard, he provided "the Hitch seal of approval" that helped legitimize Seaboard's invasion of the Panhandle. One newspaper reporter, Danny M. Boyd, interviewed Hitch and wrote, "Cattle feeding is fiercely competitive, Hitch said, and farming is an up-and-down business, so he soon took a closer look at pork production and eventually built 28 hog barns on his land and rented them to Seaboard."[135] He was too optimistic in 1993, however, when he said that management of hog waste was going to be simpler than with cattle: "Cattle feeding is all outdoors. The hog production will be done in buildings. We do have some runoff containment problems that we have to deal with [with] cattle that are much greater than there are in hogs because it's outdoors."[136] By late 1997 Hitch Enterprises was one of the largest operations in the region. It farrowed fifteen thousand sows in twenty-eight buildings and produced as many as three hundred thousand pigs a year. Hitch owns sixteen well permits in Texas County. Groundwater use is a property right under Oklahoma law, and there are no limits to its use as long as the water is put to beneficial use (e.g., agriculture) and is neither being wasted nor polluted.[137]

As to odors, Hitch emphasized his decentralized operations. "Environmentally," he said, "we feel it's friendlier because we spread out the impact over a wider area. It lets us apply our fertilizer from our lagoons on more land, spread out over a greater area. It reduces the concentration of the odor to the surrounding areas." He added, "I will put up trees to diffuse the smell, I'll explore additives to the lagoons."[138] He also claimed that traditional flood or center-pivot irrigation uses thirty times as much water as concentrated animal agriculture in the Panhandle. It is value added, meaning that it offers more profits per unit of land and water, thus allowing less water consumption and better land conservation than crop farming alone. Not afraid of controversy, Hitch confronted a letter-writing campaign in the fall of 1997 to remove him as one of the five appointed members of the state Board of Agriculture, because, it was argued, he had a conflict of interest in supporting Seaboard's expansion and opposing stricter rules governing big hog farms. Hitch responded, "I think it is really inappropriate to say the guy that knows the most about what's going on should recuse himself from voting on the issue."[139] Others said Hitch was voting his pocketbook. One recent interviewer of Paul Hitch concluded, "He is a piece of work—the epitome of the American ideal of the rugged individualist, and an anomaly."[140]

Hitch's rapid expansion and the burgeoning of Seaboard operations led unhappy local farmers to form Safe Oklahoma Resources Development (SORD) to oppose groundwater depletion from the large hog farms, potential water pollution from waste lagoons, and offensive odors from waste ponds. Vancy Elliot of SORD, already enraged by smells from Seaboard barns several miles away, fired off an advertisement in the *Guymon Daily Herald* after she was notified that Hitch was building several hog units one and a quarter miles away on neighboring land. Elliot's ad, "Have Hitches Gone Hog Wild," led to retaliation. Hitch refused to buy feed grain grown on her land: "I just refused to buy their corn. I didn't put them out of business. I didn't harm them. They tried to harm me." Elliot responded, "Where do his property rights end and ours begin?" Other farmers who deal with Hitch got the message and refuse to comment about the hog barns, but one reflected, "I've always got a square deal from Paul."[141]

BATTLE LINES ARE DRAWN

Farmer protest reached unexpected vehemence against the hog corporations and their allies. In Colby, in northwest Kansas, Wayne Bossert, manager of Northwest Kansas Groundwater District No.4, read the political landscape, measured environmental impacts, and held direct meetings with representatives from the hog industry. He offered a set of guidelines that the industry said it could meet. Some of these were more rigorous or detailed than state guidelines. Lagoon designs were to allow no more than a tenth of an inch percolation per day and annual leakage measurement by lysimeter was to reach no more than twenty-five feet below a lagoon bottom. Lagoons with unacceptable levels were to be drained, relined with plastic, and monitored annually. Soil samples were to be taken in disposal fields at the seven-foot level with correction of wastewater disposal management plans if increased levels of pollution continue for three years or increase by 50 percent, and wastewater design was to include soil conditions and threats to freshwater supplies. Bossert said that no new hog production operations have opened in his district.[142]

Few observers could have predicted the widespread rejection of confined-hog operations by voters in Kansas. To the consternation of the mega-hog industry, only five of forty western Kansas counties, Finney, Lane, Meade, Ness, and Edwards, approved corporate swine facilities, while Cheyenne, Hodgeman, Kearney, Pawnee, Seward, Sheridan, Sherman, and Thomas Counties soundly defeated the proposed operations (other counties were undecided).[143] Hamilton County commissioners authorized hog facilities in 1994 but a public outcry over threats to local groundwater, air quality, soil, and land prices forced a vote in 1995, which went three-to-one against corporate swine operations.[144] Some citizens in Clay County feared the invasion of Seaboard and others after the commissioners allowed several local farmers to form a hog-farrowing corporation.[145] In April 1998, voters in Great Bend, in Barton County, who called the hog processing industry "a consuming, polluting, abrasive industry" ousted four city councilmen from office solely on the grounds that they supported Seaboard's plan for a plant.[146] But in April 1999, the same voters supported plans for a new Seaboard plant.[147] The battle lines continue to be drawn in the late 1990s. Hog corporations are poised for what could be dramatic growth in western Kansas beyond Seaboard's existing production plants. County commissioners find their decisions overturned by petitions; revotes are hotly contested. The Kansas Supreme Court ruled in January, 1998, that Murphy Family Farms could not build hog lots against local votes.

The state legislature in Topeka was directly drawn into the fray with a half dozen bills that would place a moratorium on new large-scale hog farms, give county officials control over the number and location of hog farms, rewrite the definitions of corporate and family farms, require financial bonds for future cleanup costs, and enact stricter environmental regulation of the industry.[148] Legislation would regulate separation distances between hog farms and homes. It would require soil testing, standards on lagoon liners, wells to monitor lagoon seepage, and facility closure plans. It offers tax credits to hog farmers who upgrade to protect groundwater and air. One legislator said that Kansas communities need a "way to control their destiny," and large log corporations represented "outside money, outside ownership," that takes away from Kansans' rural lifestyle.[149]

POLLUTION REMAINS A SERIOUS PROBLEM

Nineteen ninety-five was not a good year for pollution control at a number of hog factories around the nation. Critics made much of eight manure spills that polluted water resources in Missouri in the summer of 1995 and of complaints over severe pollution in hog-friendly Iowa.[150] A spill of 25 million gallons of waste from ten thousand hogs at a facility in North Carolina on June 28, 1995, made the national news. The largest such spill in North Carolina history, it polluted local rivers and streams, killed fish, and brought on algae blooms that threatened public health. Neighboring farmers described a rush of wastewater that rose to two feet over some fields. Blame for failure of the lagoon's earthen walls was laid upon heavy rains, mismanagement by facility operators, and lagoon design.[151] In late October 1995 at Seaboard's Hog Production Farm No.4 in Morton County, Kansas, the claylike, earthen liner of one of its newer sewage lagoons was damaged by wind. In an emergency measure, the lagoon's heavily polluted liquids were emptied into another lagoon a mile south by a temporary jury-rigged, above-ground pipeline using an irrigation-type pump (450 gallons per minute) instead of being spread onto farmland set aside for such disposal. Seaboard's problems grew when in early December 1995 the water blast caused by filling a lagoon eroded a ten-foot-wide crater and cut through the eighteen-inch-thick layer of compressed, silty soil. The Kansas Department of Health and Environment (KDHE) refused Seaboard's plan to build three hog farms at a nearby site called Feterita because the soil was too sandy and there was not enough farmland upon which to spread the hog sewage liquids.[152]

Seaboard was accused of health and pollution violations in 1996 and 1997, and then embarrassed by more problems in late 1997, when state agricultural officials discovered decomposing hogs spilling out of containers or dumped on the ground at thirty-five of its farms. Local residents near several of Seaboard's facilities had complained of dead hogs in front of their barns, of "waste fluids" leaking from rendering trucks transporting dead animals, "very strong dead animal odors" from its burial pits, and "large number of flies" around the pits. The state agricultural water quality director, Dan Parrish, said Seaboard's violations were the worst he had seen in his long career in the swine industry, with many "ripe and bloated" carcasses obviously many days old. Seaboard was fined $157,500 for thirty-five alleged violations of hog farm rules and settled in February 1998 for $88,200.[153] Simultaneously, the state agriculture department complimented Seaboard for "doing much better in its disposal of dead animals."

The stakes changed in March 1998 when the U.S. Environmental Protection Agency (EPA), using guidelines set by the Clean Water Act, addressed animal feeding operations (AFOs) and concentrated animal feeding operations (CAFOs) as significant threats to clean water.[154] Environmental Protection Agency administrator Carol Browner said this was the first federal attempt to regulate such an industry and that regulations would apply to approximately six thousand operations around the country. Permits that followed federal water-pollution guidelines would be required for farms with more than 1,000 cattle, 2,500 swine, or 100,000 laying chickens. She observed that waste from animal feeding operations in particular had become associated with threats to human health and the environment.[155] This included water bodies becoming saturated with nitrogen and phosphorus that induced the growth of oxygen-choking algae and even massive dead zones where fish and other aquatic life could no longer exist. Other states had passed hog farm control laws, notably the Carolinas, Missouri, and Iowa. Along with Kansas and Oklahoma, Colorado and Texas moved to issue permits and set strict standards for the operations.[156]

MOMENTUM IN THE OKLAHOMA PANHANDLE

Confrontation over economic development and lifestyle became polarized on the Oklahoma Panhandle in Texas and Beaver Counties. The debates focused on new threats of water and air pollution from hog-confinement factories. They renewed the controversy over how Ogallala groundwater was being consumed. Ladd Hitch, Paul's father, had enthusiastically invested in a twenty-seven-thousand-hog operation on a 160-acre site. He noted, "We have the climate, feedgrains, irrigation and aggressiveness on the part of the people" to attract new business. "I think the whole West will blossom with hog units."[157] Roy Ehly, veteran executive director of the Guymon Chamber of Commerce, noted that Guymon's boom "couldn't be happening if we didn't have the Ogallala Aquifer, a deep aquifer and good supply of water."[158] The president of SORD, Carla Smalts, of Keyes, said that the arrival of the corporate swine industry was certainly "a social, economic and environmental issue, and you can't separate them,"[159] but she wondered whether the industry was just a temporary "spike" for local economies. Rancher Kim Hobbs agreed, comparing the corporate swine boom to the short-lived expansion of the oil industry in the late 1970s: "When their money is gone, they will probably be gone, too, and we will still be here. We'll just turn the lagoon into a big stock pond."[160] Between 1991 and 1997, Oklahoma's hog population increased from about 200,000 to 1.3 million animals, a climb that led state attorney general Drew Edmondson to conclude, "we're exposed to a potential environmental disaster."[161] By the end of 1997, the number had grown to 1.7 million hogs. A permit request made by Seaboard Farms in December 1997 for a gigantic 259,000-swine farm on 8,000 acres (14 contiguous sections) in the Panhandle would raise the state's swine population well over 2 million animals.[162] Local groups complained that hog waste spread onto the land would end up in the water supply and in the Cimarron River.

Dominated by Seaboard Farms, Texas County became the leading hog producer in the state, but many battles were being fought in neighboring Beaver County, where new operations were pending. Longtime Beaver County farmer Elmwood Cook turned to hog production after concluding that few farmers can eke out a living on only wheat and cows. Cook spent start-up capital for feed, vehicles, and production equipment and on attorney fees for land deeds, loan agreements, and permits, including a bitterly fought water-use permit. He said he could market two thousand hogs a year to the newly expanded Seaboard Farms's Guymon slaughterhouse. Opponent Todd Lewis fears that hog farming sites—there are already three hundred hog barns within a six-mile radius of his house—will deplete Ogallala groundwater more rapidly than ever from areas where reserves are in short supply.[163] Groundwater pollution from lagoon seepage is also a threat. Elmwood Cook is a member of ProAg (Plains Residents' Organization for Ag Growth), while Lewis is a board member of SORD. Seaboard's hog division chief executive, Rick Hoffman, countered that Ogallala groundwater is well below the surface, which makes it difficult to contaminate, and that the abundant water can be profitably used in irrigation to produce corn to feed the pigs.[164]

The most intense conflict centered on an abandoned Swift packing plant outside Guymon in Texas County that Seaboard wanted to turn into a facility that would process over four million hogs a year. A Guymon community development study estimated that if the factory became active the town's population would double by the year 2000, from 7,803 people, the population in 1990, to almost 14,000, and that up to 1,400 new jobs would be created, a 35 percent increase. These changes would require expanded housing and schools, increased police, fire, and social services, new city water lines and water storage facilities, and two new water wells.[165] In December 1992, Seaboard began rebuilding and expanding the old packing plant to include stockyards, a kill area, a cold storage room, a cutting area, a shipping room, a rendering plant, and a laboratory. Texas County's unemployment rate dropped from 4.5 percent in 1991 to 2.8 percent in 1995. In 1993, before Seaboard's arrival, Texas County ad valorem taxes (real estate, personal property, public utility) were $5.6 million; in 1996, they were $7.8 million. Paul Hitch, who had a large contract with Seaboard, admitted, "I know we'll go through some growing pains in Guymon. But I'd rather go through growing pains than shrinking pains. We can look at a number of other little towns in the area and there is just not much left."[166]

Critics of the hog boom were dubious, citing the threats to water and air quality, which Guymon's community development study did not take into account. A separate January 1993 engineering report to the Guymon Utility Authority projected a daily industrial water demand at three million gallons or approximately nine acre-feet. "Assuming a 5 day week for a year, the consumption would equal 780 million gallons per year, or 2,394 acre-feet."[167] The report recommended that three new wells be connected to the Ogallala to increase pumping from 5,628 gallons per minute to 10,481 gallons per minute.

According to local activist Bonita Hoeme, "Prior to 1993 only four swine water allocation permits had occurred. Then, two months after the two-day hearing [by the Oklahoma Water Resources Board (OWRB) on February 17 and 18, 1993] over mega-hog operations, all restraint broke use. Almost immediately the swine applications poured in, fifty-four permits for one hundred and seventy wells, and swine allocation of 5,755 acre feet. I don't think the [pro-industry] OWRB has ever turned down an application."[168] As of October 7, 1995, Seaboard was permitted to draw 2,211 acre-feet annually from ninety-five wells for confinement operations in Texas County in addition to its requirements from the Guymon water utility for its processing factory. Concern was also raised about increased depletion of Ogallala groundwater from heavier irrigation that resulted from area farmers growing corn and milo to sell as feed to Seaboard.[169] Hoeme noted that Ogallala water use peaked in the early 1980s because since then local farmers had invested in better technology, learned more efficient irrigation management, and practiced conservation. She wrote: "Collectively, irrigation farmers have invested millions of dollars in sprinklers, tail water return pits, underground pipes, to *save* water and have come a long way—they thought they were making sustainability more possible—they didn't know it would be given to the hogs."[170] As Hoeme testified to an April 1995 OWRB meeting in Oklahoma City, "We didn't know we were saving it to give to a bunch of hogs. We thought we were saving it for future generations. We will be out of water and we will be polluted. If you can't help us, where else can we go?"[171] She wondered how the OWRB justified its actions in light of its own policies on beneficial use of water for agriculture and antidegradation of natural resources and the environment.

Other farmers agreed with Bonita Hoeme. Carla Smalts, who lives between Guymon and Keyes, learned that Seaboard wanted to drill about forty wells on the three-thousand-acre ranch next to hers. How could this be allowed, she asked in a lawsuit, after she voluntarily stopped irrigating thirteen years ago and did not have sufficient household water? VaLois Ramon of Goodwell spoke out against the "tremendous amount of waste" that would be created by a mega-hog farm and possible nitrate contamination of the Ogallala and surface water sources. Hooker's Julia Howell reported that

"Every water permit granted by the Water Resources Board for hog houses allows for total depletion of our water. One acre-foot is generally considered enough for a family of four for a year. Figure out how many years we will be robbed of at this rate. Even irrigators won't do this. The Panhandle is their home and they hope to be here the rest of their lives."[172]

In April 1997 the Oklahoma Board of Agriculture, which always prided itself on promoting agricultural production, began to police the burgeoning corporate hog industry by passing licensing rules, setting distance limits, holding public hearings for discontented neighbors, and requiring documentation about waste management on hog farms.[173] A hog farm regulation bill was passed in June that required presite inspection to identify acceptable animal waste disposal plans in new construction. The bill prohibited the disposal of liquid waste within three hundred feet of an existing drinking well. It required prior notices and public hearings for neighboring property owners. The new regulations did not take effect until September 1, 1997, and the intervening months brought a licensing rush in which more than two hundred corporate hog farm businesses in the Panhandle were grandfathered to sidestep the more stringent rules.[174] In July 1997, the OWRB, also historically prodevelopment, began to require licensing for groundwater consumption by confined animal feeding operations. The licensing included plans for pollution prevention, animal waste management, and engineering of waste lagoons.[175] By March 1998, Governor Frank Keating signed a statewide moratorium on future hog farms with more than five thousand swine. This action prevented the processing of applications for 720,000 more hogs in the state. The state was primarily concerned with better regulation of lagoon leakage into groundwater and soil testing for excessive phosphorus.[176]

The controversy continued to split communities and pit friends against each other when in April 1998 the Oklahoma legislature began to explore laws that would keep pig manure farther than three hundred feet from a water well.[177] At issue was the use of center-pivot irrigation systems to capture hog waste from lagoons, mix the waste with water, and spread it onto the land. Critics said contract farmers would be put out of business because the three hundred-foot-prohibition reduced the amount of land on which they could spread effluent. They reminded the public and legislators that farmers have always spread animal manure on their fields and that using nutrient recycling instead of chemical applications is an important element of sustainable agriculture. Supporters of the legislation claimed the distance should be five hundred feet in sandy areas because waste easily permeates sandy soil and can quickly end up in a shallow groundwater supply.[178]

IN PRAISE OF PIGS, OR, WHAT, FINALLY, IS WRONG WITH HOGS? The plains region is straddling independence and industrialization. A 1992 University of Missouri study calculated that for every five million dollars in swine contracts, up to forty-five new industrial jobs would be created. But they also reported the loss of up to 135 independent farmers. Critics of mega-hog operations saw low wages in the containment and packing plants, with about a quarter of the jobs offering between twenty thousand and forty-five thousand dollars a year and three-quarters paying below the poverty level, at around sixteen thousand dollars a year. In Missouri, working conditions induced an annual turnover rate of 100 percent. A Minnesota hog farmer concluded that independent farmers had a better overall impact upon local communities: "Rather than having one corporation in the community supplying 15 to 20 jobs in its feedlot, you have 100 farmers each making an extra $17,000 a year. So you have more families in the community attending churches, sending kids to school, buying groceries," who are long-standing, permanent local citizens rather than transient low-wage workers.

Large-scale animal production of hogs and cattle that began after the successful development of industrial management and confinement technology is little more than a decade old. Raising domestic animals on the plains in small numbers did not substantially modify either the native ecologies or the methods of grain farming. But the numbers of animals increased from a few dozen to thousands, concentrated in less than a quarter section of 160 acres. When the fields are overloaded, manure used to produce feed crops becomes animal waste to be impounded and disposed of elsewhere, not returned to the fields. A historic nutrient cycle is broken in which nitrogen-rich animal waste becomes an industrial pollution problem. Such fertilizer-cum-waste is debated as an acceptable risk as in any factory operation. The identifiable and widely praised rural lifestyle also comes under threat as the land is informally divided between uninhabitable no-man's-lands near hog operations and mini-metropolitan regions around small, bustling plains cities. Plains society has historically given commercial activity less of a role than in other parts of the United States in order to protect the lifestyle attached to traditional High Plains wheat farming.

Hog-confinement operations are a logical outcome of America's productionist agriculture that stressed highest possible yields by the fewest possible workers. Agriculture in its productionist mode is the deliberate transformation of materials from a less-valued state (raw materials like wheat or corn) to a more-valued state (hog parts in supermarket-ready boxes). There is little doubt that, while hogs require large amounts of water, chemicals, and animal feed and they pollute the air, land, and water, their introduction is value added, with more dollars generated by hog production than wheat production from the same precious natural resources. The total efficiency of hog farming is high when measured solely in dollars gained. Thus the attitude toward hog production depends upon priorities and whose ox is being gored (or whose pig being stuck). One priority is to see more output from natural resources. An alternative priority, to decrease the consumption of resources like water and soil through better management yet produce grain with high yields, is to rid the plains of hogs. Higher output usually means the reduction of pollution and waste materials, but with hog farming, waste and pollution increase substantially. Another priority, to protect the ecology of large tracts of the plains, might promote a thoroughly industrial agriculture concentrated on relatively small sites. This method emphasizes the efficiency of intensive farming, but it is not necessarily an agriculture that preserves the existing human community.

DEAD ZONES ON THE PLAINS: INDUSTRIAL AGRICULTURE FORCES NEW MAPPING

If operations like hog confinement are here to stay, what can we do? State and federal regulations are effectively creating hog zones that circle up to

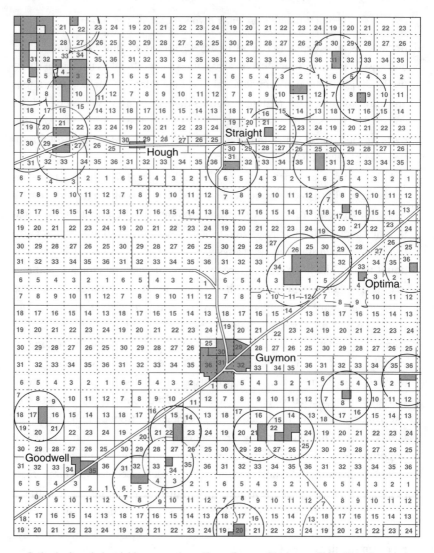

11. Setbacks from industrial hog operations, Texas County, Oklahoma. If a radius of one and one-half miles is drawn around industrial hog operations, each circle or set of overlapping circles creates a zone that is legally and socially "uninhabitable" due to strong odors, manure-covered fields, and polluted groundwater. Circles drawn by the author on a Seaboard Farms map showing a detail of its industrial operations near Guymon, Oklahoma, about 1995.

178

four miles around the sheds and lagoons (and perhaps related manure-spreading fields). These are not habitable by people and are built away from towns, parks, and natural preserves. Should there also be hog-free zones around population centers and where farmers and ranchers live? Should the creation of every large industrial hog operation also foster open nonindustrial land? Thus hogs and people could coexist as neighbors, although uneasily.

In mid-1998 legislation on hog pollution in the plains states of Texas, Oklahoma, Kansas, and Colorado indeed restructured the region. Instead of following the geometry of sections and counties, the legislation laid out the land in terms of groundwater-well spacing and the distance of hog-confinement lagoons from residences and communities. For example, Kansas Substitute House Bill No.2950 requires setbacks up to five thousand feet between a residence and a hog-confinement operation to create large buffers, or dead zones, around hog-confinement operations, where human habitation and commercial or recreational activities would not be desirable. Where liquid waste is applied to cropland, which is customary, it could be sprayed no closer than three hundred feet from a water well (even the owner's well) and one thousand feet from a habitable structure.[179] At present no mapping describes the extent of such dead zones.

In Oklahoma new mapping is required that identifies the impact of buffers between hog-confinement sheds and their adjacent lagoons and waste treatment fields that might depopulate entire areas. Figure 11 shows how mapping can portray the impact of legally defined setbacks from dwellings, drinking water, and nonfarm activities. Local residents are urging a buffer of two to three miles between habitable structures and hog-confinement operations because of odors and air pollution; the current regulated distance is between a quarter-mile or three-quarters of a mile. Waste lagoons cannot be closer than three hundred feet from a water well, and wells must be spaced a quarter-mile apart. Well-spacing regulations are being fought by hog producers, who need concentrated and large-scale water supplies twenty-four hours a day.[180] Of special interest, although it is not currently addressed, is the identification of the threat and direction of migrating underground water pollution plumes, under regulation by the EPA and the Clean Water Act. The Clean Air Act does not cover odors except when they contain harmful substances such as hydrogen chloride. However, local inhabitants would find the mapping of so-called odor pollution plumes important, based on intensity, wind direction, and distance.

Concluding on Chickens

The Gigot family in southwestern Kansas shrewdly looked at the farmers' share of consumer prices. Economists would call their decisions a matter of adding value to a basic crop, a difference that is similar to selling finished lumber to Japan instead of raw logs. Some comparative 1988 supermarket-shopping figures support Gigot manager Ochs's argument that beef was a better way to go than selling wheat.[181] A farmer's share of a five-pound bag of all-purpose wheat flour, retailing at $1.02, is $0.27, or 26 percent. In contrast, of a pound of choice beef that costs the shopper $2.42, the producer earns $1.38, or 57 percent. By comparison, the producer receives 12 percent of the cost of potatoes and 7 percent of the cost of a loaf of white bread. Milk depends upon subsidies in many states, but corporate dairy farmers from California made their move into southwest Kansas in the early 1990s because of cheaper feed, land, and general operation conditions.[182] A farmer might do better with a combination of eggs—62 percent of retail cost—and chicken—50 percent. Alternative-crop advocate Keith Allen, near Sublette, Kansas, is looking into poultry for the High Plains. Seaboard Farms also raises chickens in other states, so when its critics fought only hogs they saw only half the problem. A chicken processing plant that Arkansas-based Western Product Recovery Group is considering building in Dodge City could process daily up to fifty thousand two-year-old hens recycled from egg-laying companies.[183] According to one account, "The chickens would be made into a product fit for human consumption [*sic*] and marketed mostly in Eastern Asia. . . . Leftover parts—beaks and feathers—would be ground into livestock pellets."[184] While the corporate litany was the same— the plant would produce one hundred new jobs—city manager John Deardoff saw problems with the amount of water required by the plant, 250,000 gallons per day year-round, and the limitations of Dodge City's water and sewage systems. He was particularly concerned about the high organic nitrate load in the wastewater that the plant would generate. The company plans included buying existing wells in the area and seeking state permission to dig more wells on their site. Oklahoma's governor, Frank Keating, noted that phosphorus-laden poultry waste is even more of a threat to water supplies than hog waste.[185] In Rice County, Kansas, the nation's largest egg producing company, Cal-Maine Foods, will double the state's chicken population by 1999, with almost two million chickens on a forty-acre site. In a classic example of the major shifts in agricultural land use introduced by the new industrial agriculture, it also purchased 850 acres designed solely to apply the 150 daily tons of manure,[186] a lot comparable to a parking lot in relation to a shopping mall.

On the High Plains, the switch from wheat and corn to cattle and hogs as the source of profit has meant a deliberate move into modern factory production. The effects are still being felt in the disappearance of independent farmers who once had heroic status. The shift was meant to keep the High Plains prosperous and populated, but whether this strategy will succeed is not clear. The commitment was certainly to meat over grains. About half the corn crop never leaves the farm but is used as food for livestock. Overall, 80 percent of the grain produced in the United States is fed to animals, much of it to cattle for fattening.[187] Still, the vaunted efficiency is not there. Despite improved breeding and feeding practices, beef still ranks as the most expensive meat in terms of the cost of feeding the animals. As the most productive of food per unit of the larger domestic animals, pigs do somewhat better, but they are engines of intense pollution.

5

. . .

A Tale of Five
Water Conservation Districts

Farmers typically refuse to treat water as a regular economic good, like fertilizer, for
example. It is, they say, a special product and should be removed from ordinary mar-
ket transactions so that farmers can control conflict, maintain popular influence and
control, and realize equity and social justice.—Arthur Maass and Raymond L.
Anderson in a 1980 study

The current paradox of High Plains irrigation is how to have one's cake while
gulping it down. Plains farmers are as dependent upon irrigation as cigarette
smokers are upon nicotine. They cannot break the habit without paying a
heavy price. Corn and alfalfa cannot survive without their thirty-inch seasonal fix, and each head of cattle in a feedlot demands a minimum of eight
gallons a day and often up to fifteen gallons. As water levels decline, there
will be a ripple effect on so-called externalities.[1] Suppliers of irrigation
equipment will shut down. Bankers will be forced to foreclose on worthless
land. Scarcity of grains, if not replaced by sources off the plains, will inflate
consumer prices of bread and beef. American foreign policy would suffer
because the United States would lack the grain surpluses to influence other
nations. The availability of water on demand since the late 1950s has created
a sense of security that masks the enormity of the historic struggle to grow
abundant crops under Dust Bowl conditions.

The addiction to a disappearing resource has not helped the transition
from exploitation to conservation of Ogallala groundwater to go smoothly.

The idea of conservation goes against the conventional stream of American consumerism, and plains irrigators during the 1960s, 1970s, and 1980s were celebrating their belated participation in its benefits. For generations Americans saw only visions of limitless resources across an unpeopled continent. Many European visitors were amazed at American wastefulness as compared to their own stewardship in crowded countries. The post–World War II industrialized nation soaked up resources faster than ever. Only in the last decade have plains irrigators noticed that Ogallala water levels were beginning to drop as much as three feet each year. Even those state agencies specifically appointed to protect the water joined the boom.

Despite conservation actions, the first objective of the five agencies described in this chapter is the profitable consumption of groundwater. The oldest agency, dating from 1951, is the regional Texas High Plains Underground Water Conservation District No.1. It is followed by the statewide Oklahoma Water Resources Board that originated in 1972, the Western Kansas Groundwater Management District No.1, also from 1972, the Southwest Kansas Groundwater Management District No.3, from 1976, and the Northwest Kansas Groundwater Management District No.4, from 1977. On the High Plains, "groundwater management" means "economic development." Today, even with local control of water consumption by irrigators and water districts, agriculture consumes far more water than is being replaced in the aquifer. This varies widely across Ogallala country, but the overall effect is still continuous decline.

As a result, modern Cassandras still speak ill of plains prospects. In 1984, California law professor Frank J. Trelease wrote: "Only two states [New Mexico and Colorado] on the fringes of the [Ogallala] aquiver have recognized that irrigation use of this water is a mining process, and that when the water is exhausted (or fallen too deeply) the overlying farmland must revert from irrigated crops back to dryland wheat or cattle grazing."[2] Earlier, in 1977, a federal General Accounting Office report described dangerously high "ground water overdrafting" levels on the Texas High Plains that would predictably make irrigation fall from almost 8 million acres in 1975 to 2.2 million in 2020, leading to "significant social and economic dislocations. . . . A return to dryland farming could substantially reduce the income of the farmers in the area [whose] per capita income was less than the national average and was projected to decline over time."[3] Despite their common hostility toward the radical plans of Frank and Deborah Popper, all the farmers interviewed for this book acknowledged that the end of widespread irrigation is inevitable.

Still, the High Plains have a distinct advantage over other water-needy parts of the country. Agriculture is by far the highest consumer, taking 90 percent of plains water. The old Dust Bowl region of the High Plains—southwest Kansas and the Texas-Oklahoma Panhandle—has no major metropolitan cities to compete for water. Lubbock and Amarillo in Texas, Guymon in Oklahoma, Liberal and Garden City in Kansas are unlikely to become new Denvers, Phoenixes, or Tucsons. Elsewhere in the West, the uncontrolled growth of cities brought on water wars (depicted in the movie *Chinatown*) in California, Arizona, New Mexico, and Colorado. Outside the plains, western water, historically applied to farm fields, is being shifted more and more to crowded populations that can pay a thousandfold more for it than farmers. Sixty-two miles north of Denver, for example, water supplied by the Big Thompson project is being transferred from "underutilized" farm use at forty dollars an acre-foot to urban use at more than twelve hundred dollars an acre-foot.[4]

For a long time irrigators were tranquilized by the size of the resource. The three billion acre-feet of water in the gravel beds of the Ogallala, which allowed hundreds of thousands of gallons to be pumped daily from individual wells, made Ogallala water seem inexhaustible. Or irrigators, like early settlers of the Texas High Plains, continued to believe that it was an inexhaustible resource, a massive fast-flowing subterranean river instead of irreplaceable water trickling slowly through gravel beds.[5] The original myth told of a grand underground river that swept down from the snowfields of the Rocky Mountains as far away as Canada. An outlandish Captain Livermore, who told stories of subterranean rivers from the Arctic, found his way into reminiscences of old-timers in the Texas Panhandle. Don H. Biggers, who began irrigating land in Lubbock County in 1911, remembered that the water moved across the bottom of his pit well at a mile an hour. "Livermore was right. It was not melted snow from distant mountains, but glacier water from the Arctic, thousands of miles away. How it gets to the Plains and then spreads out is a matter to be worked out."[6] Ironically, the most ambitious construction project proposed in the 1970s was the multibillion-dollar North American Water and Power Alliance, which was to bring water from northwest Canada to the plains through vast sluices shaped from the valleys of the Rockies.

Popular belief in the inexhaustible resource lasted into the 1950s; geologists and hydrologists, however, had been drawing less-sanguine conclusions since the 1910s. Contrary to that state's usual optimism, the first accurate analyses came from Texas. In 1938 the senior hydrologist of the U.S. Geological Survey, Walter N. White, warned at a Texas groundwater conservation meeting that "practically everywhere that large supplies of water can be obtained from wells the popular belief has developed that the water is inexhaustible. This belief in many parts of the United States has led to disastrous over-development."[7] At the time White gave his warning, early versions of efficient and powerful pumps already had begun to lower water levels on the Texas High Plains. In 1939 the Texas Board of Water Engineers reported that "there has been a general decline in the water table in the principal pumping districts of the High Plains during the last few years." In Deaf Smith County, water levels began to drop more than a foot a year, and in 1949 the board warned of exhaustion "within 5 to 10 years."[8] Accelerated by the stresses of the Little Dust Bowl of the 1950s, groundwater levels in the irrigated Texas High Plains averaged a decline of forty-three feet (and as much as one hundred feet in parts of Hale, Lubbock, and Floyd counties) in the twenty-two years between 1937 and 1959, well before the heavier demands of center-pivot irrigation systems were felt. The measure of water inexhaustibility depended not on the water itself, but on the speed and scale of the technology that could consume it.

High consumption was also encouraged by conflict over property rights and freedom of action. The problem of prior appropriation is not nearly as intense on the High Plains as in California or Arizona. The earliest irrigators, who got the best rights to use water, tended to overappropriate and overuse,[9] but the same general philosophy, use it or lose it, pervaded western irrigation everywhere. Overlapping drawdown cones between wells too close to each other made aggressive irrigators rush to flood their fields with groundwater before falling levels gave them dry wells. More cautious irrigators complained that aquifer levels were declining far too rapidly because of unnecessary consumption of too much water by others, sometimes for unneeded crops. A good supply of groundwater under a farmer's land not only assured him of on-demand water for crops, but doubled and tripled his property value and thus his borrowing power.

Usually the first legal step to regulate Ogallala groundwater was to restrict it to agriculture. Groundwater has been a public resource owned by each state since the federal government separated water from land in the Desert Land Act of 1877 and turned water over to the western states. All three states in this study adopted the guidelines "reasonable beneficial use" and by it meant agricultural use. This was not only for economic survival, but because water dedicated to farming was regarded as an essential social good.[10] That is, its free use kept the independent farmer on the land, the productivity of irrigation guaranteed food surpluses, and thus it kept the nation strong and independent. Private use of this public resource was conditional; the irrigator could not waste the water he could rightfully take under his land by either nonagricultural or excessive use. Furthermore, the preambles of all the High Plains water agencies state that groundwater must be dedicated to farmland production. This is an unquestioned moral good. According to a 1936–37 Oklahoma Supreme Court decision, water use in the state must be controlled by "beneficial use" and "greatest need" for "agricultural stability."[11]

The second step is more efficient management of agricultural watering. Reasonable beneficial use is difficult to establish. Wasteful practices, declining water levels, questions of ownership, preservation of the farm economy, and, not least, fear of heavy-handed government intervention encouraged the creation of self-governing groundwater conservation districts on the High Plains.[12]

From the beginning, the High Plains water management agencies combined economic development and democratic participation. However, as

Ogallala depletion becomes more extensive, these same interests are providing the means to create long-term water conservation programs. Further, to a remarkable degree, the combination of development, conservation, and localism are consistent with recent global philosophies of sustainable development.[13] Conservation policymakers can keep long-term economic needs in mind even as they bring a shift away from raw economic exploitation for higher profits. The transition is helped by the fact that most High Plains farmers agree that their golden age of intensive irrigation, approximately between 1960 and 1990, is history. The water economy of the High Plains (except for the water-rich Sandhills of western Nebraska) is moving from its exploratory-expansionist phase to its mature conservation phase.[14] Peak heavy use may have been recorded between 1978 and 1983 when irrigated land reached a high point of seventeen million acres, then declined to sixteen million acres in 1990.[15] During the past few decades, the very success of heavy irrigation from the Ogallala aquifer forced decisions to protect the flow from accelerated decline and the unacceptable phasing out of irrigation. Local populist management may be the way to shift from today's destructive development to a transitional conservation management leading to sustainability.

Texas High Plains Underground Water Conservation District No. 1

Unlike their Kansas counterparts two decades later, Texas High Plains irrigators in the 1940s lobbied vigorously against state legislation to regulate groundwater. If the Ogallala failed, farmers were convinced that there were stronger and deeper aquifers to make up deficits, and that new technologies, yet to come, would guarantee high recharge levels.[16] Plains farmers are determinedly independent, and Texas irrigators were unsurpassed in their prideful self-assurance.

The issue headed over the rights of private property. In 1947 the *Southwestern Crop and Stock* journal editorialized: "It is unsound to advocate to a farmer that he curtail pumping when with top market prices he can pay for his irrigation installation in the first year of its operation."[17] A November 1948 editorial pronounced that "West Texans can consider the water their own—to use or waste as they please."[18] But in 1949, Texas set a precedent

187

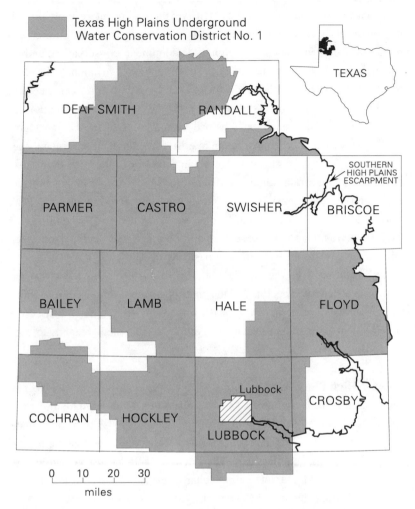

TEXAS

DEAF SMITH

RANDALL

SOUTHERN
HIGH PLAINS
ESCARPMENT

PARMER

CASTRO

SWISHER

BRISCOE

BAILEY

LAMB

HALE

FLOYD

Lubbock

CROSBY

COCHRAN

HOCKLEY

LUBBOCK

0   10   20   30
miles

12. Outline of the first groundwater management district in the Ogallala aquifer region, Texas High Plains Underground Water Conservation District No. 1, with headquarters in Lubbock. Original boundaries were established by local vote in September 1952 and expanded to their current version in May 1967 and April 1969. Farmers in Swisher, Briscoe, and most of Hale counties refused to join. Redrawn from cover map, "Estimating Soil Moisture by Feel and Appearance," *Water Management Notice*, Texas High Plains Underground Water Conservation District No. 1, Lubbock, Texas, September 1985.

188

by legislating the first underground water-conservation districts on the High Plains. Its bedrock goal was to ensure the continued profitable industrialization of a depressed region. District No. 1 would be headquartered at Lubbock, where depletion was the worst. It would issue drilling permits, control well spacing, regulate water consumption, develop workable recharge (to refill the aquifer), and prevent water waste. Most important to the success of these measures, which appeared so radical, the groundwater district itself would be governed by a board of local irrigators. Individual landowners would continue to have exclusive rights to their water, but it would be managed water.

Virtually no one accepted the notion that the irrigator should give up his personal right to underground water. One Hockley County irrigator represented public opinion when he told the local newspaper, "I favor no control, but if we must have it, let it be local." Management by a state board was out of the question; federal control was unthinkable. Yet virtually everyone agreed with a 1950 editorial of the *Tulia Herald* of Swisher County: "If there is not some regulation of water pumpage there is a real danger—note the fall of the water table this year—of this country having to exist on dry farming and range economy." As the debate heated up, the *Amarillo Sunday News-Globe*, in a special report on May 28, 1950, quoted a farmer as saying, "What's caused this underground water crisis . . . Abuse of our natural resources, that's what caused it. . . . It's those who want to squeeze every last drop of wealth from the land every year." But another said he was "somewhat puzzled about all this excitement over the wells going dry. . . . My well has been going good since 1936, and it's still going strong." Another reflected the dominant mood: "All the water under my land belongs to me. No government, no association, nobody can tell me how to use it. I've never wasted any water in my life. I couldn't afford it. . . . I don't intend to live in a country full of Hitlerism laws."

In a regional vote on September 29, 1951, two entire counties—Lubbock and Parmer—and parts of eleven other counties—Lynn, Lamb, Hockley, Deaf Smith, Floyd, Castro, Bailey, Armstrong, Randall, Potter, and Cochran—voted to form Texas's first groundwater management district. Significantly, three of the most intensively irrigated counties, Hale, Swisher, and Crosby, refused to join. (In May 1967 parts of Hale County did join, followed in April 1969 by parts of Crosby County.) Ultimately, an area of 8,149 square miles, or 5,215,600 acres, would be served by the new district. Texas High Plains Underground Water Conservation District No. 1 opened for business in April 1952 and on February 1, 1953, set forth its first regulations covering all full-scale irrigation wells (pumping 100,000 gallons per day or more). Compliance was voluntary. In the meantime, land under pump expanded from 650,000 irrigated acres in 1946 to 2,700,000 irrigated acres in 1954.[19]

The district regulations did not provide immediate relief. Between 1951 and 1958, the average water level fell twenty-eight more feet. In 1954, at least six farmers who started irrigating in 1953 were back into dryland farming. The general manager of the district concluded that "our conservation program is about twenty-five years or more too late." In June 1950 the *Tulia Herald* had asked, "Which is better, a super abundance for a few years and then nothing or reasonable abundance for many years?" In 1954 the district's regulations on new wells set minimum distances from existing wells: four-inch pumps were 200 yards, five-inch 250 yards, six-inch 300 yards, and eight-inch 400 yards. Old wells could not be replaced with larger ones without a permit.[20]

Most important, a unit of government was created to follow environmental lines. It made physical geology primary, in this case the thick underground layer of water-filled gravel and sand. Although political and economic boundaries were not eliminated (three counties overlying the aquifer voted against joining the district), nevertheless the intent of the district was to cross man-made borders to establish a management program suited to a natural resource. All in all, formation of District No. 1 was a remarkable political step to identify and manage an environmental entity. It had been anticipated only by the creation of soil conservation districts by the Soil Conservation Service in the 1930s. The idea of districts along nature's lines was surprising in light of the long tradition of the extremely rigid geometric patterning of the land—sections and quarter sections—by the historic federal land survey and sale since 1785.[21]

Wayne Wyatt has been manager and groundwater hydrologist of District No. 1 for many years, and over the last thirty-five he has seen the best of times and the worst of times as farmer, irrigator, and district manager. "I began my farming career when I was in high school. In the early fifties we were in the most severe drought we had ever seen. Our production was virtually zero. I bought cows for $400 and sold them for $175 after buying alfalfa and feeding them for two years."[22] A family friend staked him to an education at Texas Tech University, where he studied agriculture and ended up in hydrology. He also struggled with bare-bones farming on rented land with his brother, who was two years older. Only years later did he discover that the loans they received for tractors and combines were secretly cosigned by his landlord to help the two young men. In the 1950s, he remembers, "there was no federal support, no deficiency payments, nothing. I was living off mother and dad, living at home. Dad survived but he was a pretty tough gent. I didn't survive."

Out of his own youthful experience, Wyatt agrees with Phil Tooms in Kansas and Roger Trescott in Oklahoma that a young farmer today is even less likely to succeed in the still-harsh Dust Bowl country without friendly cash aid. Wayne Wyatt concludes that the older generation stood their ground for the sake of the farm lifestyle more than for the promise of financial success: "Well, let's squeeze this back to my dad. He's 78 years old now. He was good as a farmer. He didn't worry about making money or not. He made a damn good crop he could be proud of. Finally he got old enough that his energy level was not adequate. He'd still love to go out there today. He's out at my place today, working outside."

Thirty years later, in the 1980s, even with federal supports, the picture is worse because of heavy debts for land and equipment. Said Wyatt: "Ten years ago you could have a crop failure and in two years be out. You could manage to pay off your debt and be back into an opportunity for profits. [Today] you really got to have four out of five good years. Now if you have crop failure or something, it takes you ten years to recover." Despite the recognized virtues of irrigation, farming remains a high-risk, undependable activity. The High Plains region is still one of the toughest places to farm in the United States. Wyatt observed that "climatic conditions, hail storms, personal management skill, and plain old circumstances—a single isolated bad misjudgment—would get people into a hell of a mess." Despite all the improvements, the 1980s were more troublesome to farmers than the 1970s, and no farmer who was interviewed for this book believed that the 1990s promised better days. The next century could be worse.[23]

Love of farming even in thin times, and loyalty to harvesting "a damn good crop" despite dry land and scarce water, make Wayne Wyatt's job at District No. 1 satisfying. Seated in his pleasant air-conditioned office in an unpretentious one-story building on a shady side street near downtown Lubbock, Wyatt does not seek to turn the world upside down solely to protect Ogallala water and save the small farmer. As is true in Oklahoma, where the matter went to the state supreme court, major oil companies in Texas also tap vast amounts of groundwater for secondary and tertiary oil recovery. But Wyatt plays down the impact. "Of the total water used, the oil companies take on the order of 2 to 3 percent or less in a particular county, like ours. So we really don't find any sufficient problem with it. It isn't that big of a deal. Even local people can't seem to get concerned about it. Most of the time the way the oil company does business, they buy the ground, they buy the ground water, and they've got a right to use it. They have to get the permits for the wells just like any irrigator and we issue the permits. As long as they don't infringe on the rights of the adjoining landowners, and we don't see any major pollution occurring, we don't interfere. Haven't for years."

While sidestepping the trading-water-for-oil-recovery controversy, the district tries to reassure farmers of their private property rights. A brochure distributed by the district quotes a March 1956 editorial by Allan White in the district's newsletter, *The Cross Section*, to promise suspicious farmers that Hitlerism is not on the way: "The Water District was not created to do away with the rights of the individual but rather . . . to maintain those . . . rights and . . . provide for orderly development and wise use of our own water." The brochure also claims that "the powers that can be exercised by districts under this law supplant and exceed the ground-water regulatory powers of any other unit of government, either State or Federal."[24] Popular representation also is evident in the district's structure: a five-member board of directors supported by five-member committees from each of the fifteen counties, "a grassroots network of 80 elected officials." According to the brochure, when the district was formed by popular vote in September 1952, financing for it was established by a maximum tax of fifty cents per hundred dollars of county and state valuation. In 1952 the district's net tax revenue was $42,189.31 based on five cents per hundred dollars per acre. In 1973, on the same nickel rate, the district netted $283,453.40, a sevenfold gain in twenty years. In 1984 the actual rate was seven and a quarter mills per hundred dollars of valuation, still a small percentage of the allowable maximum.

The state legislation, Underground Water Districts Act of 1949, provided that districts "make and enforce Funds to provide for conserving, preserving, protection, recharging, and preventing waste of the underground water."[25] From the first it was clear that the mission of a district was not groundwater preservation but its most efficient use, even if that is also its greatest use. This included detailed geological and hydrological surveys "for development, production and use of the water" as well as to "determine limitations which should be made on withdrawing underground water." Recharge is a major agenda, but with little practical progress. The district is also the administrative center for well permits, drillers' logs, and record keeping on drilling, spacing, and production of wells.[26] To this Wayne Wyatt added that the district disseminates scientific data and reports on new technologies to encourage water efficiency and guarantee continued prosperity for regional irrigators.

The line drawn between Ogallala water conservation and Ogallala water development may be a difference of style more than substance. In 1975 the district distributed a policy paper by Frank A. Rayner, who emphasized (Rayner's italics) that

> *there must be groundwater development before there can be groundwater management—groundwater management is groundwater development.* Groundwater management is not prohibiting groundwater development; it is finding equitable means for making reasonable use of groundwater supplies. . . . *Groundwater management is prohibit-*

ing the vested interests of the few from thwarting the best interests of the many.[27]

In this populist-cum-entrepreneur mode, Rayner opposed closing any groundwater basin to further development or additional well drilling. He fervently argued that such control and regulation hobbles the study of existing water supplies and closes exploration for "new and deeper groundwater supplies by severing the profit incentive expected from the drilling and developing of new and deeper water wells. . . . the ultimate solution of local problems primarily rests with the local unit of government." Rayner concluded:

> What is groundwater management? The individual extracting water from a well constitutes groundwater management—whether his use of the groundwater is for a beneficial or wasteful purpose. . . . Since most wells are privately owned, groundwater management is the management of private properties, and the resultant management of individuals—a people management problem.[28]

Despite the attempt to bring the boundaries of the district into convergence with the boundaries of the aquifer, Rayner noted that the creation of the district in 1951 had little to do with environmental protection. Instead, it meant the protection of farmers' groundwater as valuable private property. He was convinced that the pressures of the 1950s drought threatened direct state and federal intervention. As a result, the district's own irrigators had to take control of their own destinies.[29] He argued (the italics are his):

> Under the present private ownership of groundwater—the landowner owns all groundwater tarrying beneath his land—there are absolutely no legal constraints preventing . . . local governments from acquiring and developing groundwater, *if* they purchase it from the landowner. However . . . if groundwater was the property of the State, and if the State would issue a groundwater permit to some local authority, it could develop the landowners' groundwater without the present purchase cost. . . . [At issue is] the all American profit motive.[30]

By 1978, only three years after Rayner's policy paper for the district, the

Texas Supreme Court moved to prevent groundwater waste: withdrawing groundwater could be "negligent" and "willfully wasteful."[31] By 1982 the district's newsletter, *The Cross Section*, reported that wasteful open ditches were a thing of the past. It reported water savings through tailwater recapture, dropped sprinkler heads on center-pivot systems to reduce evaporation loss, control of well spacing, and cost-in-water tax-depletion allowances.[32]

Based on the premise, according to Wayne Wyatt, that "we're going to run out of money [to pay for pumping] before we run out of water," the district provides detailed hydrological atlases for each of its fifteen counties. "If you have 100 feet of saturated thickness, you ought to get 1,000 gallons per minute. If you go down to 50 feet of saturated thickness, you might be able to get 200 gallons per minute. You would have to drill additional wells to maintain" center-pivot irrigation equipment. "Say you're drawn bone dry down to 25 feet. You can figure out well yield is only 50 gallons and 50 gallons would probably not be economical. At that point the irrigator would say no, I'm through irrigating." Since at least 50 percent of land value depends on the capacity to irrigate, the results would be devastating. Wyatt concludes that the high point was reached in 1983, when top-quality irrigated land sold for eight hundred dollars an acre, and prices have fallen 15 to 20 percent since then. Dryland farming is no alternative when it comes to land values.

The district devotes a great deal of attention to irrigation efficiency (water use and cost related to crop prices) to keep the water running, particularly in view of pumping costs that are likely to increase four to ten times. A major goal is to ensure that future crops can be irrigated even when pumping rates drop below fifty gallons per minute. This includes new low-pressure overhead sprinklers, soil moisture monitoring, irrigation scheduling, tailwater and other water reuse systems, recharge through small rainwater-storage lakes called playas, furrow dikes (rediscovered from 1930s conservation practices), low- or no-tillage practices (also practiced since the earliest dryland farming days), and the science of crop water consumption. As elsewhere, when the mature irrigation phase is reached, the trend is away from historic overpumping and toward minimum-water-use conservation.

Even while Ogallala waters showed important declines in District No. 1, irrigators still had mixed feelings about extensive water management because "when you start talking about a man's water, you get into real trouble." According to a 1975 survey, seven of every ten irrigators supported the way the district was doing its job, although one farmer reflected the minority view when he said, "All I want is to be left alone. If I can't make it on my own I'll go out of the farming business. This is the way it ought to be with everything. Survival of the fittest." But most agreed with the irrigator who supported local regulation "because I fear large corporate farming operations . . . that can drill too many wells . . . and would get all the water."[33]

Wayne Wyatt concludes that High Plains irrigation is still flourishing in its own golden age, which began after World War II and will extend into the 1990s. After that irrigation will begin a gradual but inevitable decline. At that time, Ogallala water will become scarce enough and costly enough that even the best irrigators, now defined as the most water-efficient irrigators, will have to reduce the acres they water. They will be ready, since they have been practicing more efficient sprinkling since gas costs began to climb during the energy crisis of the mid-1970s. But attached to this accomplishment were the high technological costs and capital debts of an industrial enterprise. Virtually all farmers interviewed for this book said success or failure depend less on hands-on farming skills and more on the solid knack for business management described in the next chapter.

The Oklahoma Difference: TCIWRA versus OWRB

America's legal system encourages vast open spaces for profitable maneuvering by individuals and corporations. Despite the recent growth of regulations concerning natural resources, strict water management still constitutes a sketchy web rather than an all-inclusive net.

This sievelike regulatory process is nowhere more evident than in the interaction among three natural resources in the Oklahoma Panhandle. Fuel from the Hugoton-Guymon field is used to pump fresh Ogallala water, the largest and most exploited aquifer in the nation, to recover oil from old oil fields. This process is the result of technological prowess, the profit motive, old-boy politics, and the fastest possible consumption of irreplaceable natural resources.

On December 20, 1984, after fifty-two months of costly litigation, the Oklahoma Supreme Court found against the Oklahoma Water Resources Board. The O W R B had granted a temporary permit that allowed a New York-based company, Mobil Oil Corporation, to pump fresh Ogallala groundwater into an old oil field, the Morrow, to push out some of the remaining oil. The most prominent member of the O W R B is Robert S. Kerr, Jr., of Kerr-McGee Oil. The *Oklahoma Observer* editorialized in its January 10, 1986, issue that "the Oklahoma Water Resources Board has always been a cruel hoax, poorly administered, universally condemned by those who cherish Oklahoma's environment, under constant attack from a handful of rapacious oil operators." It also took a shot at Kerr: "Bob Kerr's father was Mr. Water in Oklahoma. . . . [He] would weep if he could see the crassness of his namesake today."[34]

Secondary or tertiary oil recovery involves the injection of water under pressure into an oil-bearing formation; the oil is pushed by the water toward an existing well. But since oil and water do not normally mix, the water soon bypasses the oil, which in turn is trapped. To overcome this problem, a slug of chemical surfactant (similar to a modern household detergent) is injected, which allows the oil to mix with the passing water and continue on to the well. The surfactants frequently are chemicals—at best carbon dioxide and alcohols but often phenols—that are toxic to plants, livestock, and humans even at very low concentrations. Commonly used polymers, such as polyacrylamide, and aluminum solutions permanently contaminate the water and threaten to contaminate formations through which they pass. The concentration of chemicals in the water is fifteen thousand times greater than the federal Environmental Protection Agency water-quality limit for drinking water.[35]

The process is called waterflood. It was opposed by the Texas County Irrigation and Water Resources Association, a citizens group made up of irrigators dependent on the Ogallala aquifer in the Oklahoma Panhandle. Unlike Texas and Kansas, Oklahoma has no water conservation districts; instead, the Oklahoma Water Resources Board administers a statewide master plan. On paper the plan is exemplary and is intended to favor agriculture, but without local districts, citizen-interest groups have come to play a key role. The

13. Ownership of land and wells in Texas County, Oklahoma. Section of a privately published county map of Texas County, Oklahoma. According to local farmers and irrigation district officials in the old Dust Bowl region, the most informative maps are these county maps identifying the locations of oil and gas wells and, particularly, the ownership of sections, half sections, quarter sections, and quarter quarter sections. Ownership includes the right to pump water. Mobil Oil and Cities Service are two of the largest landowners in the excerpt shown above. Map reprinted by permission of Kansas Blue Print Company, Inc., Wichita, Kansas.

198

association insisted the waterflood illegally wasted fresh water when saltwater could be pumped from another, deeper aquifer. The association deftly turned the problem into an environmental and moral debate as well as a legal action and an economic quarrel. Quoting the legislation that created the board, including a unambiguous statement about the beneficial use of water for agriculture, the association condemned the permit. It was wasteful of irreplaceable water, caused permanent harm to the environment, was not cost-effective in the long term, and served no beneficial interest except, inappropriately, Mobil's short-term profits.

The temporary permit spanned twenty years, through 1998. Critics were suspicious because the company began its fresh-water use for oil recovery in 1965 with no permit or hearings about waste, pollution, or beneficial use. By 1979 it had consumed almost 25,000 acre-feet, or more than 8 billion gallons. The company began by leasing water rights to 3,442 acres overlying the aquifer. In its temporary permit it sought to take each year an average of 6,375 acre-feet of fresh groundwater and pump it into the oil field. In Texas County alone, Mobil's project soon covered 24,540 acres with ninety-six injection wells. The final result is a thirty-three-year waterflood that began in 1965 and is to end in 1998, consuming more than 24 billion gallons of water to force up 46 million gallons of leftover oil, a ratio of 520 gallons of water consumed on site to produce a gallon of oil.[36]

The association demanded review of the board's ruling because, it argued, Mobil's freshly pumped water, to be effective, had to be blended with chemicals to move the oil. Such used water could not be returned to the natural hydrological cycle. It was "polluted and lost permanently," not available for human, animal, or plant consumption. Mobil Oil countered that its use was beneficial under Oklahoma water law. Mobil merely borrowed the water from the state, used it in the oil field, then pumped it down into storage in a deep shelf of porous rock, the Glorieta formation. The confrontation was between the oil company, which put no cash value on the water because it concluded that technology would eventually find a way to clean the used water of additives and oil residues, and irrigator groups, who claimed the water was "limited, valuable and irreplaceable." Mobil engineer R. A. Irwin argued in 1985 that "there is no waste because it is reused and reused and re-used. It will [eventually] be recycled seven to ten times."[37] Mobil attorney Gary Davis pointed out at a December 3, 1985, meeting of the Oklahoma Water Resources Board that if Mobil's use of fresh water was waste by pollution, other beneficial uses were, too. "Irrigation water is lost down ditches, to evaporation, and to the Gulf of Mexico; but the water used in the Mobil process would remain in Oklahoma for future consumption."[38]

The association opposed three specific practices allowed by Mobil Oil's permit. The first was to take fresh Ogallala water from five hundred feet and pump it down six thousand feet into the Morrow gas and oil formation, where it was "permanently removed from nature's water cycle." Saltwater from the Glorieta aquifer at nine hundred feet was available to Mobil, costing the company $0.52 cents more per barrel, reducing profit from $12.03 to $11.51 per barrel. The company would save about $24 million over a thirty-three-year period. Second, the water was moved too many times through the Ogallala, raising the risk of pollution from leaking pipes. The water would be raised from the Ogallala to the surface, then pumped down through it to the oil field, then the used water would be returned to the surface and pumped down again to storage in the Glorieta, a total of four risky operations. Third, there was the risk of "fracking," in which Ogallala water could be lost or polluted by geological cracks or crevices that caused mingling of fresh, salt, and polluted water, particularly with the changing pressures of forced injections.

The momentum was in Mobil Oil's favor. Legislation in 1972 emphasized "reasonable" and "beneficial" groundwater use regardless of heavy depletion. In a 1977 case, *Texas County Irrigation* v. *Cities Service Oil Co.*,[39] the Oklahoma Supreme Court had "stamped its imprimatur on the use of fresh groundwater in secondary oil recovery." This was called the Texas County Doctrine. But in its 1984 turnaround decision, the Oklahoma Supreme Court quoted critically from the 1972 law: "Waste of water means any act permitting or causing the pollution of fresh water or the use of such water in an inefficient manner or any manner that is not beneficial."[40] The court used a definition of pollution—turning fresh water into waste water—from a 1981 law:

Pollution means contamination or other alteration of the physical, chemical or biological properties of any natural waters of the State or such discharge of any liquid, gaseous, or solid substance into any waters of the State as will or is likely to create a nuisance or render such waters harmful or detrimental or injurious to public health, safety, or welfare, or to domestic, commercial industrial, agricultural, recreational, or other legitimate beneficial uses, or to livestock, wild animals, birds, fish, or other aquatic life.[41]

Contamination would occur as the fresh water was used in the oil field; discharge would take place as the used water was removed and stored in the Glorieta saltwater aquifer at six thousand feet.

The court then chided the OWRB: "Mere recitation that the Board finds that waste will not occur is insufficient. A finding of no waste must be supported by evidence in the record." It then noted that the evidence "establishes undisputively that the tertiary [waterflood] process proposed by Mobil is one in which [contaminating] detergent additives and polymers will be mixed with the fresh water to reduce the water's surface tension so that more oil can be recovered from the formation." Not only had Mobil tried to ignore the effects of the additives, it had not yet explained how the contaminated water would be disposed of, only "somehow." Nor had Mobil submitted documentation required by the OWRB's own regulations concerning alternative use of saltwater, total project costs, the expected amount of recovered oil or gas, and why fresh water was desired. Instead, Mobil merely stated the costs of oil recovery as compared with irrigation of certain crops.

The court ordered the board to reexamine Mobil's request in light of its own rules. Justice Evonne Kauger added her concurring opinion:

I am still concerned with the responsibility we share to prevent the unbridled consumption of fresh groundwater and to exercise both the will and the wisdom to conserve the good earth, with the certain knowledge that unless we act, the Ogallala aquifer probably will be exhausted by the year 2020. We cannot wait until tomorrow to worry about this problem. It must be faced today, before the last acre-foot of

water is sucked from the breast of the Ogallala, and the Panhandle becomes a desolate desert—a stark and silent monument to our un-
willingness responsibly to function, and a place where the price of water exceeds the price of oil. . . . I can think of no commodity which
affects and concerns the citizens of this state more than fresh groundwater.

She concluded that "the issuance of the temporary permit [to Mobil Oil] was
an invalid exercise of jurisdiction by the Oklahoma Water Resources Board"
because it had failed to follow its own fact-finding procedures. In fact, she
noted, at the time, January 8, 1980, that the board granted Mobil's temporary
permit, it had not yet established its own rules concerning the use of fresh
water for oil recovery. It seemed curious, she said, that this was done almost
three months later, on March 31, 1980. She then concluded:

Because no rules had been adopted by the Board, it had no authority to
conduct a hearing, to take evidence, to make findings of fact, or to issue temporary permits to mine fresh groundwater for use in tertiary oil
recovery. The issuance of the permit is void, invalid, and of no effect.

In a paraphrase of the board's own rules and regulations, Justice Kauger also
concluded that "reasonable diligence and reasonable intelligence militate
against the use of fresh groundwater in enhanced oil recovery operations."
The board had encouraged wasteful consumption of fresh groundwater by
giving Mobile a twenty-year deadline to consumer a water resource at "not
less than two acre-feet" per year. "The 'pie' is being divided without a determination of the size of the pie—yet everyone is consuming the pie," she
said. She remembered that Mobil was seeking 51,211 acre-feet, or approximately sixteen billion gallons, of water. "If Mobil uses the amount of water
it has the *right* to use under the terms of the temporary permit . . . Mobil can
fill a family-size swimming pool every minute; it can fill an Olympic-size
swimming pool every twenty-three minutes." Keeping the larger picture in
mind, Kauger wrote: "While other states implement programs to conserve,
protect from pollution, and guard with zeal the diminishing fresh water sup-

plies, Oklahoma has initiated a program which by its very nature encourages complete consumption of its fresh groundwater within a twenty year span. . . . it is not a reasonable exercise of reasonable intelligence and reasonable diligence to sanction a process which causes a loss of unestimated billions of gallons of fresh groundwater. . . . The Dust Bowl was not a mirage." The justice observed that it was problematic enough that irrigation, a well-defined beneficial use, had already dropped the water table one hundred feet in forty years. If the same water source also was applied to enhanced recovery of oil, "no one can predict a twenty-year life-span. . . . The alarming facts are: one flood project by one company will use 16 billion gallons of fresh water; Mobile is not the only oil producer to use, or to desire to use the water; nor is the field to be flooded Mobil's only oil field or the only oil field which will be developed; nor is Oklahoma the only oil producing state that overlies the aquifer."

Nine days after the supreme court decision was issued, a flurry of pro-Mobil activity energized the Oklahoma legislature. Identical legislative bills, Senate Bill 282 and House Hill 1447, created a new state water policy that would no longer require fresh-water use-permit applicants to demonstrate that "waste will not occur."[42]

The Texas County Irrigation and Water Resources Association complained that "this legislation, if enacted, completely repeals and annuls the decision of the Supreme Court. It legalizes waste by pollution and waste by depletion under the guise of 'beneficial use.'" Texas County irrigator Bob Fowler said at a hastily convened hearing that the actions of the Oklahoma Water Resources Board, "the authorized agency to protect and conserve all of the waters of Oklahoma," is instead like "putting Dracula in charge of the Blood Bank."[43] Neighbor Roger Trescott testified that "unless the legislators can name the various tertiary methodologies, identify the chemicals that are allowed to be injected, understand the concentrations of toxicity that can be in the produced water, the potentially serious disposal problem . . . then they should not blindly rubber stamp this dangerous legislation." The TCIWRA attorney, Tom Dalton of Tulsa, reported that "the proposed law *falsely assumes* [his italics] that if groundwater has a 'beneficial' use, waste

203

will not occur through pollution or depletion." State Sen. Tim Leonard opposed the bill because, unlike the supreme court decision, it tried to yoke together the concepts of beneficial and nonwasteful use, which were not identical concepts.

The association complained that the legislation would allow an oil producer to use a thousand barrels of fresh water to produce one barrel of oil and claim that it was a beneficial use of water. Was not fresh water wasted if saltwater could be used instead? Was not fresh water wasted by commingling with harmful chemicals? Would not water be wasted if after two or three decades of pumping, still 80 to 90 percent of the oil remained in the ground?[44] Gerald Hofferber of the association said, "Even in the use of fresh water for the highest and nobles purposes—sustaining life, cleanliness and health, it is possible under certain circumstances to waste it. . . . the same would be [even] true for agricultural purposes. If agriculture is actually polluting, then we too need to clean up our act, because no one has the right to waste our groundwater." But once the legislation removes the safeguard requiring that waste will not occur, it is easy to argue for any number of beneficial uses.

The association noted that Publication 25 of the Oklahoma Water Resources Board had already stated that fresh water should never be used for secondary recovery because it is lost forever. Said attorney Dalton: "This [new] legislation adopts as state policy the notion that you can contaminate and pollute water while using it, and not be required to clean it up. Under no other condition have you ever [before] been able to take and pollute water and leave it dirty for others to use." Another anti-Mobil argument was that the water polluted by the oil-recovery process was then stored in the Glorieta aquifer, an underground formation that Mobil had not purchased or leased. Virgil Higgins of the association wrote in 1975 that "this is not salt water disposal—it is really [polluted] salt water storage."[45] Irrigator Betty Trescott noted that free storage already existed with natural gas. Farmers make contracts with energy companies to pump natural gas from under their ground. The contracts are often "dedicated to perpetuity," or until the gas company wants the gas. "It's like having big gas tanks under ground. We store [the gas] for them, absolutely free," she said.

In October 1985 the Oklahoma Water Resources Board, pressured by the objections of the Texas County Irrigation and Water Resources Association, Save Our Water, Inc., and other groups, ordered an in-house report. The document stunned the board by recommending that Mobil Oil be refused the right to pump water from under the land it owned or leased. The report, compiled by OWRB staff, did accept Mobil's claim that the intended use of the groundwater "is a beneficial use,"[46] but it insisted that Mobil's use was waste by pollution and hence could not be permitted by state law. Mobil's argument took a desperate turn. "Virtually all uses of water, including irrigation and municipal uses, alter to some degree, the physical, chemical, or biological properties of ground water." Hence, argued Mobil, such a narrow reading of the law could prevent anyone from using the water, even the most efficient and virtuous irrigators, because any use of the water would modify the water. On this basis the board could not grant groundwater permits to anyone, yet Oklahoma water law promoted a "policy of utilization." The company claimed that the water left after a thirty-three-year recovery process would be "available in situ for withdrawal and use for further enhanced recovery use [and it] could be withdrawn, treated and used for all beneficial uses." The oil company defended its actions on the grounds that it is theoretically possible to find a technological fix to decontaminate or to reuse contaminated water. In contrast, the report given to OWRB concluded that "there is only a possibility that the water could be used for a beneficial use at some future time, without more [treatment, and] constitutes a loss of the water for beneficial use and therefore is waste by pollution."[47]

In an extraordinary strategy, Robert S. Kerr, Jr., moved that the board adopt only certain portions of the report, which, TCIWRA said, were "favorable to oil companies." The OWRB voted for Kerr's motion and Mobil, instead of a flat rejection based on the report, received another temporary permit to use 25,660 acre-feet of fresh Ogallala water in Texas County between 1985 and 2007.

The combination of a state agency and a powerful corporation were hard to beat. Like Texans, Oklahoma Panhandle irrigators worried about government interference. Now corporate America rifled their cash drawers as well.

TCIWRA President Norman Steinle of Hooker wondered: "It is difficult to understand why five of the nine [OWRB members] considered themselves such instant experts as to reverse their own staff's recommendation at a [monthly meeting], lasting a few hours."[48] The association argued: "Someone should do an energy audit on this scheme. . . . no colony in darkest Africa has ever been more exploited than the Oklahoma Panhandle. Our natural gas is 'dedicated' to the industrial northeast. Our surface water is dedicated to Oklahoma City. And with passage of S.282 our valuable Ogallala groundwater will be dedicated to oil companies." Mobil wrote gas-lease holders who were receiving royalties from Mobil in a campaign to support Mobil's controversial application, but when these owners, many of them also irrigators, learned that fresh water would be depleted and polluted, they supported the denial instead. One owner who would receive royalties from the tertiary recovery, Allan Fischer of Hooker, Oklahoma, said, "I would prefer to go broke today farming and have fresh water for my children in the future."[49] TCIWRA worked to raise funds to file an appeal and urged area people to buy back the eight billion gallons of water Mobil sought to consume. Mobil Oil is continuing to use Texas County fresh water for tertiary recovery despite the 1984 Oklahoma Supreme Court decision. The matter is in litigation. There has been no cease-and-desist order.

A David against Goliath is Gene Barby, who operates a thirteen-thousand-acre family ranch on the eastern edge of the Oklahoma Panhandle. He is also a thirty-year veteran petroleum geologist with his own oil business. Barby has been president of the water-advocacy organization Save Our Water, Inc., and spokesman for the Oklahoma Cattlemen's Association. He complains that, with no permit, Mobil Oil had, since 1965, already consumed 8.1 billion gallons of fresh Ogallala water. Gene Barby testified:

> The reason is nothing more than greed for corporate profits. It costs more to lift a barrel of brine water from 2700 feet than it costs to lift a barrel of fresh water from 500 feet. Lifting costs using brine water is 61 cents per barrel whereas lifting costs for fresh water is 11 cents per barrel. This amounts to less than 2 percent of the projected net income for the field, calculated over a 20 year life.[50]

Significantly, Mobil profit is tied much more closely to world oil prices. Barby observed that between 1961, when Mobil purchased the oil field, and 1985, the company made an eightfold profit as oil prices escalated from $3.30 a barrel to $27.50. He then reported on his own operation, in which he used saltwater from four thousand feet even when abundant shallow fresh water was available: "Yes, it was more expensive to lift this brine water, but the operators were independent oil men who were concerned with the environment." Later he observed that Mobil's claim "moves us miles backwards in conservation. It is a revolutionary concept that will cause disaster for our children and grandchildren." He was particularly agitated over the Mobil Oil statement that the use of fresh water for irrigation constituted a waste. "Who has ever suggested that using fresh water to grow crops is a waste?" he asked. Mobil Oil is looking into carbonates from Colorado.

The Case of Kansas

Kansas irrigators now face the water scarcities that Lubbock farmers experienced two decades earlier. Garden City hydrologist Andy Erhart tried to make water conservation acceptable to farmers facing higher costs. Protection of Ogallala water would protect agriculture, the farm family, and irreplaceable resources. As early as 1957 in an article written for a special edition of the *Pratt Daily Tribune*, he set down the basic priorities by which he still operates. A well-planned and well-managed irrigation system needs to (1) increase the efficient use of available water supplies, (2) reduce labor requirements, (3) prevent excessive erosion, and (4) permit maximum production.[51] Southwest Kansas Groundwater Management District No.3 was created in 1976 out of such thinking.

The district is legally dedicated to management and conservation (controlled use) of the groundwater under its jurisdiction. Its management of the Ogallala is widely accepted as the primary means for economic stability in the district. Its 1976 birth was a local initiative—the will of the people is repeatedly affirmed in the documentation—to build democratic bridges between individual freedom and community power. When the district was being planned, a citizens group, the Southwest Kansas Irrigation Association, held a series of town meetings in the fall of 1973 "to sense the will of the people" concerning the formation of a groundwater management district. A

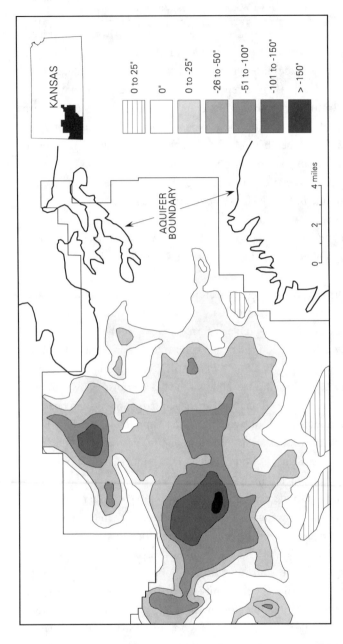

KANSAS

0 to 25"

0"

0 to -25"

-26 to -50"

-51 to -100"

-101 to -150"

> -150"

AQUIFER
BOUNDARY

0   2   4 miles

14. The region covered by the Southwest Kansas Groundwater Management District No. 3, showing water-level changes between 1940 and 1980. Redrawn from the May 1, 1986, "Revised Management Program III: Rules and Regulations, and Policies and Standards," Southwest Kansas Groundwater Management District No. 3, Garden City, Kansas.

steering committee came out of the meetings to identify and organize a district that included all of eight counties and parts of five others in southwest Kansas. After state approval, Southwest Kansas Groundwater Management District No. 3 was organized in February 1976 by a large five-to-one majority (1,155 in favor, 230 opposed, an 83 percent majority) of the voters. The district exists as a localized corporation managed by a local board of thirteen directors serving staggered three-year-terms, with four officers named by the board.

The case of F. Arthur Stone put Kansas water management to an early test. In December 1979, Stone, a Finney County irrigator southwest of Garden City, applied for permits to drill seven wells. In February 1980 his application on two of them was denied because they exceeded the area depletion rate. Stone drilled the two wells anyway. The driller he hired from across the border in Colorado remained silent; he needed the work. But in May 1980, to no one's surprise, Southwest Kansas Groundwater Management District No. 3 got wind of the wells, and in June the chief engineer of the Kansas Division of Water Resources ordered Stone to stop pumping water from the two wells. Stone and the engineer found themselves in an angry personal confrontation on Stone's land and the case went to court. Stone's attorneys argued that Kansas water laws were unconstitutional invasions, takings, and deprivations of private property. State attorneys argued that the regulations were a valid exercise of the police powers of the state to manage groundwater for public benefit. In 1981 the state supreme court upheld the state, and the district began prosecution of Stone on thirty-seven counts. Stone responded by moving, according to district bylaws, to disband the district, or at least to replace existing board members with his own candidates at the annual election. He failed to both attempts, but the Stone case signaled more litigation and conflict over the equitable distribution of water as Ogallala groundwater becomes more scarce.[52]

There is still confusion about who controls the water. Well into the 1940s, Kansans could claim three different water rights. Riparian rights involved ownership of land bordering a stream or natural lake, with equal claims by all owners to the infinitely adjustable reasonable-use policy. Absolute ownership based on traditional common law is the law of capture, or however much one can pump regardless of consequences to the water table or the neighbor's well. Prior appropriation is also known as "first in time, first in right" ownership. No matter how much water, or how little, or how much the supply has changed, the first user can still claim his entire original supply, even if later users run out. This was still beneficial and reasonable use. But one had always to consume his full allotment or forfeit his right: use it or lose it.[53]

For Kansans, the matter of who owned the water came home when in 1944 the Kansas Supreme Court struck down state laws based on the widely supported appropriation theory.[54] With surprising speed, the state legislature passed the 1945 Water Appropriation Act. It "solved" the problem by apparently taking no sides. It declared water a public resource which belonged to all the people of the state. Water was severed from land ownership; the state then took control of the water by controlling the allocation process. The effect of the law was to act according to prior-appropriation principles and continued support of the philosophy that "unused water is waste water."[55] It was said that only by undercutting riparian rights and common law for the sake of prior appropriation could Kansas water be profitably developed. Kansas water-law specialist Earl B. Shurtz wrote in 1967: "Unused water could not wisely be held in perpetuity for a common law owner who may never have use for it, without resulting in underdevelopment, permitting the water to flow out of the state and on toward the ocean, as an economic waste and loss of a valuable natural resource."[56] But according to state planners in 1982, if full use was made of appropriated rights each year, as the law still encourages, then western Kansas would run dry in twenty-five years.[57] The case of F. Arthur Stone demonstrated the classic confrontation between private rights and public interest that has characterized much of American resource history.

The district's 1986 *Management Programs* published the updated rules, regulations, policies, and standards of the district. It set a grass-roots-democracy tone by opening with an 1878 statement by John Wesley Powell:

> The people in organized bodies can be trusted. . . . residents should
> have the right to make their own regulations . . . the entire arid region

[should] be organized into natural hydrographic districts, each one to be a commonwealth within itself . . . the plan is to establish local self-government by hydrographic basins.[58]

District No. 3 was organized to implement a recognized need to manage and conserve the groundwater supplies of the district. The appropriation of groundwater in Kansas, including specifications and regulations, had been institutionalized in the Kansas Groundwater Management District Act of 1972, which added local groundwater-management districts to the 1945 Kansas Division of Water Resources. The district has policies that control irrigation-well permits and spacing to promote water conservation and efficient water use. The intent is to prevent economic deterioration (for example, a return to dryland farming) and stabilize agriculture. Nevertheless about 18 percent of all the district's groundwater reserves had been consumed by 1990, and in some places it was more than 50 percent. Since 1978 a district also can designate some of its territory to be an "Intensive Groundwater Use Control Area," where levels are declining dramatically, where waste or deterioration exists, or where the "rate of withdrawal equals or exceeds the recharge rate."[59] The last includes almost all of southwest Kansas, and by 1984 four areas already had received the ominous IGUCA designation. In extreme cases, all new water development can be halted in such an area, and existing withdrawal levels face reduction. The IGUCA allows for many different and creative alternatives for enhanced management. Local people complain that such controls are an illegal taking of individual property rights, and the issue may be thrashed out in the courts. District No. 3 planned to close down 80 to 90 percent of its district to new development in 1991. It has become clear that Ogallala groundwater depletion was, and still is, inevitable, but it can be carefully managed over several decades to limit harm to irrigators and the larger economy they support.

District planning also admits to a water table that is declining one to five feet each year, but at a decreasing rate with better management and an increasing rate during drought years like 1988. The district emphasizes conservation and efficient use of groundwater, including the use of crops requiring less water, irrigation scheduling, water-saving tillage and cropping practices, water metering, recharge methods, and tailwater reuse. About 20 percent of water is lost by tailwater runoff or deep percolation, which amounts to about 400,000 acre-feet. A complicated formula was established to limit aquifer depletion in district areas where pumping exceeded the planned depletion rate. The formula now covers most of the district[60] and attempts to limit depletion to not more than 40 percent during a twenty-five-year period. By 1977 in Finney County, six out of ten applications for new wells were denied; by May 1987, nearly 90 percent of new well applications were being denied as contrary to depletion-policy guidelines.

The data gathered by the Soil Conservation Service in Haskell County described some recovery under district management but still pointed toward long-term Ogallala water decline. Harold Stapleton's well No.5 at the county's northern border,[61] just east of U.S. 83 between Liberal and Sublette, descended to water 194 feet deep in 1966, 240 feet in 1984, and 237 feet in 1986. Jack Dufield's well No.6 at the eastern border went from 172 feet in 1971 to 212 feet in 1984 and back slightly to 204 feet in 1986. Henry Guttridge's well No.7, at the western border of the county went down to 129 feet in 1970, 169 feet in 1980, and rose to 144 feet in 1986. Once, in 1979, when measurements were taken while the pump was running, Guttridge was in a cone down to 227 feet before he got to his water. One acre of irrigated corn in western Kansas uses at least 9 million gallons of water during a dry year. Another of Jack Dufield's wells in Seward County went down in 1977 to 211 feet to reach water, a drop of more than 18 feet since 1966 and more than 31 feet since 1940.

The district covers more than 5.7 million acres of prime farmland largely in Class I, II, and III soils (the Trescotts' Oklahoma soil was a better grade of Class III), most of which can be irrigated with modern equipment and techniques. Irrigation is identified as the essential instrument "to stabilize and increase crop production" in this predominantly agricultural region. In 1975, about fifteen years after new pumping technologies were readily available, approximately 1.6 million acres were irrigated from about 7,800 large-capacity wells providing 100 to 3,000 gallons per minute. Nine years later, in

1984, at the peak of irrigation, over 1.8 million acres were irrigated from 9,800 wells. In 1975, about 3 million acre-feet of water was consumed and about 3.5 million acre-feet was used in 1984. In the mid-1980s, approximately 75 percent of irrigation was gravity flood and 25 percent by sprinklers, primarily center pivot, but this ratio is being quickly reversed with the rapid spread of more efficient sprinklers. Haskell County, for example, was 79 percent irrigated in 1984 (295,000 of 371,200 acres), using 1,048 wells pumping more than 564,000 acre-feet. Finney County was 41 percent irrigated with 1,662 wells producing more than 506,000 acre-feet irrigating 270,000 acres of a total 662,880. Haskell County, almost three-quarters irrigated, was the twenty-first most-productive county in the nation with $344 million and Finney County was thirty-eighth with $225 million. In sum, of six western Kansas counties in 1982, 963,000 acres were irrigated, or almost 30 percent of the total, with one-third under center-pivot sprinklers and two-thirds under gravity irrigation (mostly gated pipe and some ditch).[62]

According to its statement of purpose, District No. 3 is not interested in keeping the water locked in its beds of sand and gravel; its mission is "to provide the greatest total social and economic benefits . . . for the longest period of time."[63] After the state law was passed in 1972 but before local district controls went into effect in 1976, the rush to drill new irrigation wells brought significant declines in groundwater levels, down fourteen feet in Grant County by 1974 and nine feet in Finney County by 1976. The Gigot family's Circle Land and Cattle Company alone drilled over one hundred wells between 1972 and 1974.[64] Only higher energy costs, not conservation principles, prevented a continued rapid slide. Irrigation still consumes up to ten times the recharge, even without a rash of new wells. But if higher market prices covered energy costs, all-out pumping would resume.

No one doubts that the future of southwest Kansas is closely tied to heavy use of water for intensive irrigation. A quarter section of irrigated corn may demand three acre-feet of water in a particularly dry season. Further expansion of groundwater pumping is not mentioned much, economic lasting power (sustainable development) a lot. Some irrigators, such as the Gigots, are moving out of corn, but alfalfa or sugar beets need even more water, so they must turn to less-profitable wheat or milo or an alternative crop yet to find a market. The water, doled out in far smaller quantities, is there to sustain a workable way of life for farmers in southwest Kansas, but the High Plains Ogallala Aquifer Regional Study of 1982 predicted that at present consumption rates, by the year 2020 three-quarters of Kansas's current High Plains irrigated land will be back in dryland acreage.[65]

Kansas District No. 3 goes to a lot of trouble to minimize waste. Waste of water is defined as:

(1) Groundwater that has been diverted or withdrawn from a source of supply, and is not used, managed or reapplied to a beneficial use.

(2) Any act or omission causing the unreasonable deterioration of the quality of water.

(3) Groundwater which an irrigator permits to escape and drain.

(4) Groundwater applied to an authorized beneficial use in excess of the needs for such use.[66]

A public advocacy group, the Kansas Rural Center, does not believe the issue of waste or beneficial use is simple. Mary Fund of the center writes:

The term "beneficial," though, is still rather ambiguous, since what is beneficial to one person may still be seen as wasteful by someone else. For example, lawn watering to the city dweller is an important use of water—beneficial to lifestyles, self esteem, and aesthetics, but open to question by some in arid regions, or during drought. In the same vein, irrigating corn with irreplaceable fossil water when we have record harvests and the price is below the cost of production, is also open to question by some people. Therefore, we suggest that in addition to minimizing waste, conservation also implies recognition of "appropriate use"— the use of water that fits the particular situation, climate, and supply.[67]

Other water-management-district regulations cover tailwater control and waste, well-spacing requirements, measuring devices, and aquifer depletion, limited to no more than 40 percent in twenty-five years within a two-mile radius (8,042 acres) of a proposed well. Violators lose their right to pump water following a formal complaint and thirty-day notice until they comply with the regulations of the district.

Once a well is drilled, there are not yet any rules or regulations to control the scale of pumping. Farmers north of the Arkansas River are atop groundwater that is already 50 percent depleted, and the remaining 50 percent is not all accessible or of good quality. One farmer told Mary Fund of the Kansas Rural Center that his water was being pumped out from underneath him, but hydrologists doubt any declines except from the nearest well.[68] Ogallala water naturally moves five hundred to one thousand feet a year from northwest to southeast. Fund raises the unexamined question of fair distribution of the remaining water. There were complaints of injustice when Master Land Company of Oklahoma applied for sixteen wells in 1981. At the public hearing sponsored by the district, a farmer argued: "It seems that the bigger and more powerful the corporation or individual is, the more influence they have in obtaining well permits." The district approved fifteen of the sixteen wells, and the general manager of the Master Land Company noted that "water rights are administered on a fair and equal basis, regardless of the size of the company."[69]

As a followup, the Kansas legislature in 1986 passed a law that obligates "an applicant for a permit to appropriate water to adopt and implement conservation plans and practices." These included improved water-use efficiency (higher yields for the same water or the same yields with less water). Together with an analysis of traditional flood irrigation and newer sprinkler and trickle alternatives, conservation methods could include water metering, irrigation scheduling, tailwater recovery, land shaping and leveling, and better information about soil characteristics, climate conditions, topography, and crop requirements. The objective was to make better use of Ogallala water through more efficient equipment and better management. Goals were set at 5 percent better performance. The Soil Conservation Service cooperated with the publication of a Kansas irrigation guide that offered data on irrigation needs, based on an 80 percent chance of rain, for western Kansas crops.[70] Under these conditions, wheat needed an acre-foot, sorghum fourteen inches, corn sixteen inches, and alfalfa more than two acre-feet. Simultaneously, the Kansas State Board of

Agriculture, through its Division of Water Resources, announced the requirement of conservation plans for "all new applications to appropriate water for beneficial use" beginning January 1, 1989. The plans were in the name of the public interest, and had to be technologically and economically feasible, curtail waste of water, serve reasonable needs of the water user, and "be limited to practices of water use efficiency."[71]

Zero-Depletion Irrigation in Northwest Kansas District No.4: Betting the Farm

Wayne Bossert is a tall, lean man. He is intelligent and savvy. His western Kansas twang and his love for the people of Colby belie his New Jersey origins. Trained as a hydrologist, he has been the executive director of the Northwest Kansas Groundwater Management District No.4 since it opened its doors after a public referendum in 1977. In 1990 the district took a step beyond those taken by other Ogallala groundwater-management plans: it set a zero-depletion goal to be reached within ten years. This got the attention of local irrigators, who felt they had been poleaxed. Bossert's logic was simple. He saw that, despite sophisticated water-management strategies, groundwater levels continued to decline.[72] Bossert told a newspaper reporter that "the declining levels meant zero depletion anyway, so why not opt to reach the same goal earlier while retaining an acceptable quantity of water for future management options."[73] Kansas agricultural economist Orlan Buller agreed, "The question is not if, but when and how fast are the adjustments within the region going to happen."[74] Bossert noted that the district's thirty-six hundred wells were consuming water at a scale that lowered the district's water levels an average of two feet a year. Considering the vast amount of water for which the district was responsible, this decline was unacceptable. Worst-case wells had declined as much as fifty-nine feet between 1966 and 1990.[75] He courageously (though some said it was foolhardy) redirected the concept of efficiency away from cost benefit of crop yield and toward less water consumption. Farmers might not have accepted Bossert's assertion that under the new district philosophy, "any operator who increases efficiency will not have the option of putting the same water on added acres for increased production. He or she will have to sustain the current acreage and production and simply pump less water."[76] If water levels reach zero sooner rather than later, Bossert wondered how farmers would pay off the expensive equipment they invested in to irrigate more efficiently. He wrote that "This scenario simply continues the 'overcapitalization' cycle which has caused much of the decline problem in the first place."[77] Bossert's plans were moved forward when the state of Kansas placed a moratorium on such acreage additions beginning February 1993.[78] The results would be measurable in neither dollars nor in immediate benefit to irrigation farmers in his district. Instead, he persuaded his district board to give their highest priority to protection of aquifer levels in order to perpetuate indefinitely irrigation-based personal security for regional farmers.

The district's approaching deadline could not be met, Bossert asserted, by the traditional methods of education and demonstration: "The board's aggressive posture comes from their belief that early conservation is significantly more valuable than late conservation."[79] Hence the board sought aggressive upgrades in water-use efficiency through positive incentives, disincentives, regulations, and "any other method." It justified its preemptive management policy to reach 85 percent minimum efficiency within five years because farmers were consumers of a state-designated public resource for their profit. Direct action included a year-long moratorium on water rights development that began in February 1990. By June 1990 the district required "safe yield" for all future groundwater development. By September 1990 the district board recommended that a cap be put on the amount of water that could be withdrawn, a decision that jump-started the move toward zero depletion. For most areas, withdrawals would be restricted to two-tenths of 1 percent for every foot of water remaining in the ground. A complex mathematical formula determined that if a specially designated management area had an average remaining saturated thickness of 60 feet, it would experience 3 feet of additional decline before regulation began. A zone with 125 feet of water would get 11.7 feet of additional decline before regulation took effect. By May 1991 the district board agreed to establish zero depletion (ZD), defined as a stabilized water table.

The district experienced great difficulty in matching its draconian goal with the immediate needs of local farmers who irrigated for their survival. In areas where heavy depletions were common practice, farmers were allowed to take more water to protect their economic well-being. In 1992 a tough-minded compromise was reached that permitted ten more years of decline, sacrificing 22 percent of Ogallala groundwater to protect the remaining 78 percent.[80] If it weren't made, Bossert admitted, "some of these [farmers] would hit it [zero depletion] in three years," well before they could make adjustments in equipment and management practices, such as drip irrigation.[81] Flood irrigation has an efficiency rate of 50 percent or less, while well-managed drip irrigation can reach 90 percent, with different varieties of center pivot in between. Raising irrigation efficiency from 70 percent to 90 percent would extend the life of the aquifer by 20 percent, save irrigators $7 million, but cost about $210 million, a figure that could be justified only over the long term.[82]

Can water consumption be limited only to what is needed by highly efficient irrigation systems, as the state of Kansas decreed in a nearby region (Walnut Valley/Cheyenne Bottoms) with a water supply problem? In 1991 Bossert's board set water-efficiency standards for typical crops at rates some farmers might have seen as marginal: 1.24 acre-feet per acre (acft/ac) for corn (instead of almost three acre-feet consumed by some other plains irrigators), 0.98 acft/ac for milo; 0.99 acft/ac for soybeans, and 0.59 acft/ac for wheat. The results were impressive. Bossert reported that in 1994, when total irrigation water use in Groundwater Management District No.4 was 396,396 acre-feet, only 9,131 acre-feet were consumed in excess of actual crop requirements, a mere 1.03 percent of all water pumped for irrigation.[83] Bossert insisted that his primary agenda was to treat the difference (880,833 acre-feet were appropriated for agriculture, down from 1,053,297 acre-feet in 1980) as a future asset and not as surplus water that could be applied to additional acres for more profit. In support of this, the statewide Kansas Water Authority is considering water banking, which involves deposits of water rights that can be held and reallocated according to local needs.[84]

Bossert acknowledged that other significant issues arose out of the new policy: Can water rights be set aside without losing them? Can so-called irrigation efficiency credits be traded on an open market, like industrial pollution rights? Can efficiency upgrading be mandated if it requires costly equipment? One ambiguous approach was to have any water-scarce region designated by the state as an Intensive Groundwater Use Control Area (IGUCA), but since this strategy surrendered most decision making to the state water office it was not well received by the local district members. One innovation was to divide the district into groundwater units (management areas, or MAS): hydrological basins based on natural ecosystem, well-density areas based on agricultural infrastructure, together with existing legal townships. This holistic approach would allow consistency in evaluating water rights, water use, conservation practices, and climate conditions to understand water declines and protect remaining groundwater resources.[85] The greatest immediate challenge to the district's plans was a vote against the attachment of water meters, which were already mandated for new or refurbished wells, to all wells. Accurate water-level data were essential to the success of the plan since data from an unusually wet year might suggest that efficiency gains were not important.

According to the *Colby* (Kans.) *Free Press*, "Though this [zero depletion] may not mean an end to irrigation, it does herald an end to an age where unrestricted usage endangered the future of water in this portion of the state."[86] In 1990 the water in storage under the district's land was approximately 40.5 million acre-feet. By the time the goal was to be fulfilled, 31.6 million acre-feet would be left. The newspaper article writer hoped "that the ensuring regulation does not crumble the regions [*sic*] economic structure." As a buffer, the district's plan allotted current irrigators ten years of unrestricted pumping rights to help them to make the transition into highly efficient farming, both irrigated and nonirrigated. For Bossert, saving the water for future generations took precedence over short-term profits. As he wrote, "An ability to save one's allocation for future use or sale does not promote the 'race to the well' scenario that would be a significant negative factor in all other programs that are driven by a 'systems' or 'trigger' approach. Additionally, once each right is quantified, the owner immediately realizes the finality of his or her non-sustainable rights. This will undoubtedly result in significant personal conservation decisions."[87] He noted that the district's goal was to "solve the decline problem with as little economic and social disruption as possible," but definitely to solve the problem.

The plan by District No.4 involved major policy changes that redistributed costs and benefits among irrigators, businesses, taxpayers, and consumers by placing protection of the aquifer above historic economic, social, and political goals. The district's long term goal is also to protect economic stability for irrigators who want to stay irrigators in the future. Nonirrigated agriculture is less desirable because its success varies greatly from year to year depending upon rainfall and climate. Moreover, the average value of crop production in northwest Kansas between 1985 and 1989 was forty-three dollars higher for an irrigated acre than for a nonirrigated acre.[88]

As a last resort, Bossert recommended to the Kansas Department of Commerce that the region move "toward a replacement economy of some kind to compensate for the lost agricultural economy."[89] This implied that even if alternative agriculture were introduced, it was unlikely to continue without extensive irrigation. "An ag [sic] approach," he continued, "might be to promote price supports for less water-intensive crops within the federal farm program," meaning less corn and more grain sorghums, wheat, beans, or sunflowers that use less water. A non-ag approach might be to make the Ogallala into a perpetual water supply to attract lower water-use industries that could afford high water prices. Bossert nevertheless sought to preserve an agricultural economy for northwest Kansas. He advocated a creative, multifaceted, four-pronged program to keep farmers on the land: high efficiency irrigation, active weather modification (e.g., cloud seeding) to increase rainfall by 9 percent (thus reducing pumping by 6 percent) and prevent costly hailstorms, incentives (e.g., subsidies) to plant less water-intensive crops, and flexibility in the trading of water rights.

How to Save Ogallala Water: Squeeze More Rain from the Sky
In April 1998, a dozen or so wheat farmers in Cheyenne County in western Kansas expectantly watched rain-heavy clouds roll in from the west. They

knew from experience that when these large dark clouds passed over their fields sometimes it rained on their land and sometimes it didn't. But in the rain-short country, every storm was worth watching, and the spring of 1998 was already droughty. As the farmers inspected the clouds, they also saw the movement of several single-engine light planes around the lower part of the clouds and a twin-engine craft near the top of the storm. Such aircraft, they concluded, were part of a cloud-seeding project sponsored by several groundwater management districts in western Kansas and eastern Colorado. During four April storms these Cheyenne County wheat farmers watched the planes spread their silver iodide and watched the storms pass with nary a drop on their fields. At the next public meeting of the Western Kansas Groundwater Management District No.4, in Colby on May 7, 1998, these farmers stood up, angry, and complained they weren't getting their "fair share" of rainfall. They said that after the planes flew around the clouds the clouds disappeared instead of dumping rain on their fields. Cloud seeding was meant to both stimulate rainfall and suppress hail; the only difference is that more seeding agent is used for hail suppression than for rain stimulation. To the farmers, their experience was proof that cloud seeding had to stop—"We'll take the hail to get the rain"—or they would go out of business.

Wayne Bossert and Curtis D. Smith, program director of the Western Kansas Weather Modification Program (WKWMP) in Lakin, took the complaints very seriously.[90] After all, drought during the growing season is no laughing matter. Bossert and Smith had repeatedly heard the same complaints over the twenty-four-year history of the program. However, Smith's weekly newsletter, which described flights of his aircraft, reported no missions during April.[91] Bossert told the farmers at the meeting that the connection between the flight of the seeding planes and lack of rain was scientifically incorrect. Smith supported Bossert in his program's weekly newsletter. Smith did not make light of the plight many seemed to be experiencing, but he wrote that "the ultimate cause of any apparent lack of rainfall is due to nature itself, pure and simple." Northwest Kansas was on the eastern edge of a larger Colorado region that was going through a long-term drought. Smith continued with a specific example to document his argument, "In 1996 our total annual seeding agent output [spread into storm clouds] was roughly twice what it had been on average for all previous years. If seeding to suppress hail really does suppress rainfall, then why didn't Western and Southwestern Kansas turn into a desert in 1996 when 85% of all seeding flights were flown to suppress hail and another 10% were combined hail suppression/rainfall stimulation flights?"[92] He noted that within his seeding district, 1996 produced a fourteen-county rainfall average of 65 percent above normal instead of drought. Smith wryly noted, "Unfortunately, the real problem is that human emotion is getting in the way of reason and common sense again." A Kansas State University report about the 1997 seeding stated, "there is currently little evidence available to support the Robbing Peter to pay Paul hypothesis that seeding to increase rain in one area will deprive some other area of its normal rainfall."[93]

The Cheyenne County wheat farmers certainly followed their own logic when they looked at four storms, saw circling airplanes, and then felt no rain. Smith noted that the county's drought was on the same level as other areas of Kansas in which no cloud seeding was being done. In fact, parts of the county had higher than average levels of moisture. It is the nature of rainfall, he observed, "that it tends to be widely variable over large areas of the country." Smith turned to Dr. Brad Smull, a Cheyenne County landowner and a distinguished storm meteorologist, who was with the National Severe Storms Laboratory in Norman, Oklahoma. Smull found no evidence that cloud seeding caused any decrease in rainfall and was doubtful about any significant impact from cloud seeding.[94] He thought it was still too experimental and would rather spend funds elsewhere.

Bossert said he continually fielded complaints about cloud seeding and had even been accused of personally altering the data: "We never indicated that rain augmentation would prevent drought. In fact we continually stressed that during drought years was the worst possible time to conduct the efforts—it simply does not work when no rain was going to fall anyway!"[95] The WKWMP knew that cloud seeding did not make rain, but that it was an attempt to increase the amount that reached the ground during a rainstorm. Similarly, cloud seeding would not end a heavily damaging hailstorm, but it was an attempt to reduce the amount of hail that reached the ground. Over the program's twenty-four-year history, its data showed important reduction in hailstorm effect; storm insurance premiums, paid by virtually every farmer as an important safeguard, had actually gone down significantly. (In 1998 storm insurance in Gray County, which had a twenty-four-year-history of seeding, was two and one-half times cheaper than Sheridan County, which had only seeded for two years. In 1960 their insurance rates were nearly identical.) Ironically, the data history was inconclusive on the creation of more rain, and Ogallala groundwater continued to add its water to the fields during the growing season.

The 1998 season for the WKWMP began operating on a round-the-clock basis from April 22 to September 21.[96] For the first time, it included three eastern Colorado demonstration areas in addition to all or part of twenty-two western Kansas counties. It used two radar sites for storm detection at Lakin and Colby, widely dispersed airports at Dodge City, Johnson, Syracuse, Scott City, Goodland, and St. Francis, and nine aircraft, all single-engine Piper Comanches except for one twin-engine Piper Navajo based in Dodge City for upper-cloud seeding. The radar and planes would serve a target area of 16,309 square miles (10,438 million acres) that covered almost 20 percent of the state of Kansas and a small eastern edge of Colorado. The program began in 1975 as a high priority at the Western Kansas Groundwater Management District No. 1, where it was known first as the Muddy Land Program.[97] Designed to operate during the period when crops were planted, grown, and harvested, its primary goal was to increase area rainfall and secondarily to decrease crop-damaging hail.

Besides the Cheyenne County farmers, the WKWMP had other noisy critics throughout its target area, who claimed that even if the program did no actual harm, neither did it do any good and that it was a waste of hundreds of thousands of dollars. Bossert, after more than a decade of advocacy, had only brought his District No. 4 into the program in 1997. Smith, pointing to significantly cheaper wheat and corn insurance rates for the long-term seeded regions, asked, "What else could have so dramatically lowered these rates within the seeding target area alone?" He noted that in unseeded eastern Colorado, the insurance companies were making payments of 102 percent of their premiums between 1985 and 1997, while in the weather modification target area, the payout was only 54 percent of premiums. To critics of the methodology and its cost, he retorted, "If you subscribe to the belief that God made the sky and it should be left alone, then you should also believe that he made the soil, and each of us, and these items should be left alone as well."[98]

During the 1990s, three twin-engine Cessnas repeatedly spread silver iodide over 9.8 million acres in thirteen counties of the Texas Panhandle region and in two counties in northeastern New Mexico. Administered by (Texas) High Plains Underground Water Conservation District No. 1 and operating from airports in Amarillo and Lubbock, the planes operate by finding likely cloud formations from a radar in Littleton, Colorado. Each flight path is mapped, including the latitude and longitude coordinates of each silver iodide flare dropped. During 1997, for example, eighty-six missions were flown between May 30 and September 30, with 1,514 flares dropped into developing thunderstorms. If it does rain, rainwater samples are collected from at least six area rain-gauge sites to check for the presence of silver iodide,[99] which accumulates in soil and surface water at barely detectable levels. District manager A. Wayne Wyatt, with assistant manager Ken Carver, wrote in 1997 that if cloud seeding added one inch more rainfall during a growing season, farmers could expect per-acre increased income of $18.40 for corn, $10.45 for grain sorghums, and $20.50 for wheat. This income compares favorably to per-acre cloud-seeding costs of $0.05 to $0.08. Across the district, cloud seeding could increase farming profits by $81 million. Wyatt and Carver also noted that a similar precipitation enhancement program in southeastern Colorado between 1971 and 1990 brought two to four more inches of rain than normal during the years that planes seeded the clouds.[100] Not only did increased precipitation reduce the demand for water from the Ogallala aquifer, but higher humidity resulted in lower evapotranspiration rates.

Conclusion

All five organizations, the Texas High Plains Underground Water Conservation District No. 1, the statewide Oklahoma Water Resources Board, and the regional Kansas Groundwater Management District Nos. 1, 3, and 4, have a common mission—even if it is not always well-served—to provide the means to continue indefinitely the use of Ogallala water for agriculture. The Texas and Kansas districts are committed to controlling water withdrawals through allocation and metering, to careful well spacing, to a continued shift from flood to center-pivot irrigation, to strong support of conservation technologies such as LEPA, to scientific monitoring of climate and plant evapotranspiration, to water replacement through cloud seeding and recharge (which is admittedly minimal), and to intensive management of water application according to soil and crop needs. The problem with their commitments is that they do not keep in mind that the Ogallala is an environmental resource that is mostly nonrenewable and that is being used up very quickly. None of the agencies confront the fact that pumping water for irrigation is a mining operation as much as coal, gold, or oil. U.S. Geological Survey hydrologist John Bredehoeft stated this problem clearly when he wrote, *"To the extent that we are mining groundwater, we are running out of water."* [101]

However, according to agricultural policy analyst Earl O. Heady, focusing on ways to protect the Ogallala from water mining ignores other national and international problems, including population growth, a potential scarcity of food supplies, and extended drought. He believes that these should overshadow declining Ogallala levels. Unlike more pessimistic analysts, Heady believes that the advent of new efficient technologies, despite lower water levels, will continue to support current food production, and probably surpass it. [102] According to this view, the Ogallala can be sacrificed. Heady does admit, however, that the surplus conditions of the 1960s, when sixty million acres were held out of production, are not likely to return in the future, which adds pressure to mine water to irrigate farmland. After all, an irrigated cornfield produces 115 bushels an acre, compared to 89 bushels on an eastern humidland farm, and 48 bushels on a dryland field. [103] "I am optimistic about our ability," he writes, despite declining water levels, "to continue growth in agricultural productivity and food production." Heady argues for a bullish future at least as productive as the past based on "our ability to recreate conditions of the past," [104] instead of an alternative future.

To others, Heady is perpetuating a Maginot line mentality. Societies everywhere have the propensity to prepare for a repeat of their last crisis, as the French did before World War II when they made the Maginot line a splendid defense for a repeat of World War I. The continued heavy consumption of irreplaceable Ogallala water, no matter how judiciously regulated by state or regional agencies, will make the future of the High Plains different from the past.

6

. . .

Making Irrigation Work for a Family Farm: Phil and Linda Tooms on the Moscow Road

And he gave it for his opinion, that whoever could make two ears of corn, or two blades of grass, to grow upon a spot of ground where only one grew before, would deserve better of mankind, and do more essential service to his country, than the whole race of politicians put together.—Jonathan Swift, 1726

Irrigation is one of humanity's most important innovations. The great cities and cultures of the ancient Near East, of India and China, and of Mexico and Peru depended upon the development of this sophisticated technological complex of lifts and pumps, canals and laterals, workforces and schedules that had to be sensitive to land, water, and climate. On the High Plains today, on a less grand scale, mechanized and powered irrigation assures an abundance of food in a difficult, even hostile, environment, and to many it keeps secure a modern version of the independent farming lifestyle that Americans cherish.

To survive as irrigation farmers, Phil and Linda Tooms of southwest Kansas need more land, water, capital, equipment, and management skill than suits the traditional image of the family farm. Yet they do not practice agribusiness. The Toomses represent mechanized large-field farming defined by skill in using soil and water, environmental sensitivity to the nurturing of their land, family ownership, a sense of belonging to a specific place, and loyalty to rural values. They stand midway between the industrial Gigot family and the more traditional Oklahoma Trescotts. The Toomses are not

participants in the small but growing organic-sustainability farming represented by the Land Institute; they feel it is naively idealistic about hard labor,
per-acre yields, and markets. Instead, the Toomses seek to be the best mainstream, or conventional, farmers they can be, a choice they believe will lead
to long-term success. Because they live in semiarid country, the irrigation
practices of the Toomses, probably more than any other factor, will determine whether they can perpetuate and even enhance a satisfying and productive farm life. Their experience can be seen as a quest for sustainable
agricultural development that emphasizes environmental management, site-
specific activity, local decision making, and moderate prosperity.

Phil and Linda Tooms live about a half mile north of the graded-dirt Mos-
cow Road and five miles west of the main road, U.S. Route 83, which runs
between Sublette to the north and Liberal to the south. Their spacious and
comfortable ranch house is tree-shaded and the green front lawn overlooks
gently rolling, buff-colored fields and grassland. Their backyard contains a
shaded, stone patio with wrought-iron furniture and a garden protected from
the plains sun and wind by bushes and trees, while beyond the garden the
view opens to the flat, dusty plains landscape. The wind blows and the song-
birds sing in the oasis that the Toomses began to build in 1954, starting with a
small cabin—"a little old dinky building unchanged since 1912." The old
frame is now encased in their modern suburban-style home that holds the
amenities of middle-class consumer society: a color television and a VCR in
a comfortable family living room, a kitchen with convenient appliances, and
an attached three-car garage. The home office, with its computer, is the center of farm management operations. Unlike many suburban homes, however, the Toomses' house contains hundreds of books that are for reading,
not for show. Phil Tooms is a history enthusiast who sometimes speaks to local groups about southwestern Kansas history.

On the west side of the house are the buildings of a modern working farm.
Instead of a barn there are large, plain metal sheds for tractors, field implements, trucks, and storage. Here, Phil exercises his jack-of-all-trades know-
how. The yard does not have the eastern humidlands smell of straw, manure,
and animals. Instead, it smells of oiled gears from the melange of aluminum

machinery housings, painted steel implements, engines of all sorts, and a red gas tank on struts. The farmyard, buildings, and equipment are all strangely silent; despite the machinery this is not a factory. The machinery is taken elsewhere, onto the fields, to do its work. This farmyard is a parking lot and repair shop more than the center of a constant flurry of activity, as it might be in Pennsylvania or Illinois. Yet nowhere is it clearer that irrigation farming depends upon a vast diversity of large, powered equipment and the skills to use them.

Most of the Toomses' land is west of the Cimarron River. The most striking landmark on their farm is a shiny natural-gas pipeline that surfaces on their land, crosses over the river on its own metal bridge, and then snakes underground on the other side, which is still the Toomses' land. The Cimarron River is wide and shallow like most streams in this flat country. With dead cottonwood trees along its edges and scrub bushes in the streambed, it looks like it has been dry for a long time. Phil, Linda, and their two grown children remember when the river flowed year-round and even flooded. But as Ogallala aquifer levels declined, the river's surface water seeped underground. Phil Tooms is convinced that upstream irrigation in Colorado captured much of the river's supply. Because the riverbed cannot provide water for crops or cattle, they must irrigate from deep groundwater or farm dryland. The natural-gas pipeline, as well as gas wells and a small oil well, with its praying mantis-like rig, provides a steady and substantial income. The loss of either gas or Ogallala water would bankrupt the Toomses.

In his sixties, Phil Tooms is a large, husky man, linebacker-sized like many plains farmers, at ease working with his equipment, and comfortable on High Plains farmland. A confident director of the People's Bank in Liberal and a member of the local businessmen's club, Phil Tooms would be considered a successful businessman anywhere. A local boy, son of a used-farm-implement salesman, he saw his future not in farming but in cattle, which he believed better suited the semiarid region. He did not start out to irrigate, but after he began to grow feed for his cattle he irrigated eighty acres in 1956 for a better yield, and one thing led to another until he got out of cattle and into irrigation farming.[1]

Four generations of family history did not encourage a future in plains farming. Thomas Tooms, a Civil War veteran, had adventuresome sons who, in 1887, preceded the railroad into southwestern Kansas. They were lured by a deceptive but short season of heavy rains that seemed to promise a better climate, and by cheap land. However, when the rains ended, the family, including Phil's father, "didn't know how to handle their dry land." Like many failed plains farmers he moved to California for a short time in the 1920s when "there was no government help and you either made it or you left the country." Back in Kansas in time for the 1930s crises, the family survived by trading used farm equipment. Remembering this history made the Tooms family dubious about direct hands-on plains farming.

Nevertheless, Phil and Linda Tooms moved from town to a piece of ranch land in the mid-1950s. September through late May of their first year was rainless. "We were just desperate to have some sure sort of grain" for cattle feed. Linda observed that they turned to irrigation farming because it offered exceptional security compared to the uncertainty of dryland farming or ranching. In this seemingly simple choice, they dramatically changed the direction of their lives. They moved away from familiar farm and field practices and toward the promise of newfangled irrigation, a form of industrial farming. They applied their untested skills to running costly machinery—pumps, engines, gearboxes, pipes, and sprinklers—set permanently on the fields. They found themselves thrown into the novel demands of daily irrigation practices and had to learn how to finance and manage their operation as if it were a small industrial factory.

Linda remembered their initial fascination with irrigated water. It was both an agricultural triumph and a symbolic victory over the plains. "This is a semiarid area, you know. Every time it does rain you try to hold on to all that moisture to sustain the crop the next year. With average rainfall twenty bushels of wheat [per acre] is a good deal. You live in that sort of [semiarid] environment and then . . . you can actually have [irrigation] water when you want to put it down the rows. Your crops flourish and it is just like gardening in the desert and making it blossom." Irrigation water was more than insurance, however, it was at the center of the new venture to which they had committed their lives. "That small, littlest good" of irrigation on eighty acres was so rewarding that "we put down another well and we gradually got to be bigger and bigger in irrigation."

Linda also concluded that even though many farmers were too ready to jump into irrigation as the cure for all the region's woes, it was not a magic bullet:

> Too many people state they can put water on any kind of ground, spend the same amount on fertilizer, and think they're going to get the same yield per acre as they would on class A or 1A ground. They'll spend the same amount of money per acre as the man that's going to get, say, 175 or 200 bushels of corn. You can go out here on a piece of poor ground and try to spend the same amount on it, fertilizers and insecticides, and you're going to be lucky to get 100 bushels and you'll go into a hole. If you are a real poor farmer, it'll cost you just as much to raise a poor crop if you don't get it done right.

The technological innovation called irrigation does not guarantee success. Amidst the complex of land, water, capital, equipment, and management, it was still good management and an indefinable love of farming that held the key to success. In the farmer's world nothing is guaranteed.

Phil and Linda now irrigate over eighteen hundred acres of wheat and alfalfa, with some milo and a little corn. Their first well was drilled in 1950. At 300 feet deep, it reached sufficient water. Phil did not start large-scale pumping until 1956 when he spent fifty-six hundred dollars for a Peerless pump and a 413 International industrial engine to start flood irrigation. In 1956, fifty-six hundred dollars was considerably more than the cost of a Cadillac or a small farmhouse, and it could buy three tractors. This first well, a moderate six inches in diameter, still produces its original seven hundred gallons per minute. Since then the pumping level has dropped 37 feet. In 1964, to irrigate another field, Phil drilled a second well to 486 feet and put in another Peerless pump and a 605 International engine for a total of sixteen thousand dollars. He also spent fourteen thousand dollars for an early Valley no.1260 center-pivot sprinkler. In 1964 thirty thousand dollars would buy a three-bedroom suburban house, a Ferrari, or basic equipment to set up a young farmer. With these commitments between 1956 and 1964, Phil Tooms broke with his past and risked his future to large-scale flood and center-pivot irrigation. The last of his seven wells went into service in 1975. At that point he could not turn back; if he failed he would only go bankrupt and have to leave farming entirely. In the early 1990s, such a turn-key irrigation system would cost at least seventy thousand dollars per 160-acre quarter section and could cost as much as two hundred thousand dollars. The Toomses' 1964 well is already sanded in from 465 to 360 feet, and they had an eighteen-thousand-dollar repair bill on that well in 1986. Between 1981 and 1986 alone, they discovered that the per-foot cost of drilling a new well had gone up from thirty-five to fifty dollars.

Phil Tooms is not a pure irrigator; few people in the region are. His nonirrigated land amounts to 640 acres of dryland wheat and over 3,500 acres of dryland grass, on which he contracts with a local feedyard to graze cattle in the summer, 8 acres per head. The remaining 900 acres is in summer fallow. He estimates that most of his soils are Dalhart, with some Ulysses and Richfield. Dryland farming alone is not much of an alternative. Linda wondered, "Sometimes I think it would be interesting to figure out how much profit you made in the good year on dryland [farming] compared with the profit you made on a good year with a wonderful yield in irrigation and just see where the margin is." But she also noted that if everyone practiced only dryland farming, "we would probably not have this surplus [to feed the world]. When you can produce three times [dryland yield] under irrigation you can see how you are producing more than is otherwise possible." Plains farmers take tremendous pride in their high productivity.

Phil Tooms concluded that he would not have had the financial resources to start irrigating in the 1980s. In agreement with other plains farmers and conservation district officials, Phil believes that extensive irrigation from the Ogallala is under severe pressure. While some water will always remain, the combined problems of high equipment costs, pumping from deeper levels, and increasing energy costs cannot be overcome at the low grain prices that have prevailed for several decades. The high-consumption irrigation era that opened in the 1960s ended, many farmers believed, in the 1990s. Linda said that their early 1960s success in irrigation meant "needing bigger machinery and more machinery and more help and it's just a vicious thing where we need to borrow more money to, you know, keep us going. Every well you put down you don't realize it at the time because at that point the prices were good."

Linda, who spoke like a corporate manager, said that in the 1980s the only people who were successful were those who owned "their own land paid for already. You either have to inherit it or marry it and then you've got to be a tremendous manager after you get it"; "or," she added, "have oil or gas [wells]. Our salvation has been that we have oil and gas." At one point Phil remembered Kansas State ("K State") data that showed farmers required eighty-five to ninety bushels of milo per acre to break even. Linda retorted, "To break even, you've got to get it over that. What if you get hailed out? You still got that crop, and your [crop] insurance [only] gets your seed back to you." Phil remembered that in 1974 he had eight hundred head of cattle that he sold for less than they cost and lost $100,000 cash. "Well, you lose that kind of money and it takes years to recover. One might have to triple one's net income to start paying back the debt." Phil and Linda figure they operate about $350,000 worth of equipment to work their land and that it costs them $250,000 a year to run the farm. Annual income is generated from a mixture of crop sales, cattle grazing, natural-gas leases, and outside business.

They talk like industrial managers but both Phil and Linda love the rural independence of a farmer's lifestyle, and they would not switch to another vocation. Irrigation brought them a successful farm life on the plains with a standard of living comparable to metropolitan prosperity. This balance is the point behind the idea of rural-urban parity established according to 1910–14 standards. Successful irrigation results in immeasurable satisfactions. "We're living in a wonderful age," said Linda, "when you can produce all this food. And there's so much emotion tied to the land. It is a love relationship." But when Wes Jackson, Wendell Berry, or Robert Rodale and organic farming were brought up, Linda sniffed, "Who wants to live that way? We wouldn't be satisfied to live like my mother grew up. You couldn't afford a car. You couldn't afford what's considered normal living in this day and age." She disapproves of those who criticize farmers for overusing the air conditioning in their tractors. "The person saying that works in an air-conditioned office. If he would come out and just spend an hour on a tractor, he would realize that we want [air conditioning] in our work life too. I'm an American citizen and I have these rights too. You can't go back and buy a 1960-style tractor."

Phil Tooms estimated that by the early 1990s, start-up costs for a successful irrigation farm would come to $1.5 million for land and equipment, and that the amount of land necessary for successful family farming would be at least forty-five hundred acres owned and twenty-five hundred leased. Even as a successful irrigator, Phil concluded that his best years were 1968, 1969, 1974, and 1978, with far less profitability since then. In addition, he observed that irrigation equipment, once thought good for thirty years, requires replacement within ten years. Speaking of his 1956 well, Tooms said, "I don't know how long steel set there in the ground with the pressure of sand and the aquifer pushing in on it, the corrosion, the rust, when is that steel going to give up? Collapse. When that well collapses, I am not spending fifty dollars a foot to drill a new well because it will not pay off. I'm not going to do it."

While irrigation gave Phil his start, he sustains himself with gas leases, banking, and land deals. He believes that 60 percent of the usable water in the Ogallala aquifer was consumed before tough regulations were set in place in 1976 with the formation of the Kansas Groundwater Management District No. 3.[2] Between 1977 and 1987, even after strict controls, the water level in his 1950 well descended 21 feet, from 199 to 220 feet. Costs for natural gas that rose from $0.29 per hundred cubic feet in 1986 to $0.52 in 1987 to $1.40 in 1988 may end his irrigation practice before the water runs out. Phil and other plains farmers are using progressive improvements in water efficiency to maximize their capacity to pump Ogallala water. Phil first switched from flood irrigation to center-pivot sprinklers, then to low pressure, and then to drop sprinklers closer to the ground. His future, he said, includes surge valves and tailwater recovery in order to save water and cut energy costs.

Phil Tooms, like A. Wayne Wyatt of Texas Conservation District No. 1 and irrigator Gene Barby in Oklahoma, wonders where the young farmers will be coming from when he and his generation retire. His son is a lawyer in New York City. His daughter and her husband wonder about their future on the plains. "This young guy's fuel costs, his machinery costs, his labor costs are going to be worse, and yet his commodity price is no better." Tooms suggests that while many good irrigators around him are not going to survive the decline of Ogallala water, they should try dryland farming. A well-managed and efficient dryland farming operation could still prevail on two to four times his irrigated land. "People have confidence in the farmer around here. The farmer will keep trying and a lot of them don't know anything else. The farmers are different than any union like the teamsters or steel workers union. Farmers are very independent." He said,

> The little guy who has five or six quarters of ground and maybe four or five or six irrigation wells and he's not making it. I think what people resent is that they see this big corporation over here with fifty or two hundred or three hundred or four hundred wells and getting large government payments. You get a load of this bitterness toward the government, too. I think some of these big corporations received two million dollars from the PIK program. The little guy looks at that and he says that's too much to give one guy. I think we'll see high food prices if the big corporations take control. Corporations can afford to hang on to their wheat and wait for higher prices. Then the price of bread would get maybe to two dollars a loaf. If that happens someday, in twenty years, then we're going to look back to these days and say, "Hey, why didn't we help these little farms out so that they can stand in."

Phil Tooms wondered whether the small farmers are naively optimistic, or whether there are other reasons to farm than for profits alone. Commitment to farming as a way of life is difficult to shake off. "It just boggles the mind. If you owned a chain of stores like Walmart, you follow the law of supply and demand. They're not going to buy a bunch of stuff and let it set; they're buying stuff they can turn over quickly. The farmer absolutely doesn't use that same mentality." Farming is the nation's economic anomaly: it does not fit into the usual market rules. Phil sees an entire way of life at stake. "Only one entity in the world can help the farmer," he said, "and that is the U.S. government. [But] I still think that people in our government feel that we could do with half the [three million] farmers in the United States." This is a prophecy that came true in the late 1990s.

Tooms laid the blame for overproduction and the resulting high irrigation consumption on wrongheaded federal policy:

> A lot of grass that was plowed up out there should never have been plowed up. There was a time when Butz [Earl Butz, former agriculture secretary] was saying we'll never be able to keep up with the world, the population will continue to grow, and we must plant fencerow to fencerow. That's when a lot of farmers got into trouble because they said, "Well, if that's the case, let's get out here and buy some of this land." Dear God, the land prices started going up and they just kept buying it, and started buying bigger machinery, for three or four years. In Iowa a lot of this land that is selling today for eighteen hundred or two thousand dollars [an acre] someone bought it for four thousand dollars an acre. They invested a lot in machinery. They went broke.

Nothing is more basic to the American agricultural tradition than land-ownership. High Plains land prices are directly linked to available water; farmland with a good supply of Ogallala water brings high market prices. As director of People's Bank, Phil Tooms watches over the good and bad fortunes of local land. Like other plains farmers, Phil believes ownership of good farmland is fundamental to his entire identity as a farmer, both personally and professionally. High-quality topsoil should be the first measure of good land and whether the tract is dryland or irrigated should be the second measure. But the picture has gotten complicated. As the water gets depleted and irrigation costs go up, Phil noted, "irrigated land has probably taken the biggest punch" from local banks that are anticipating tougher times in the near future:

Our appraisal officer this year [1987] took off 25 percent to 30 percent valuation on irrigated land in our trust department. Land that was selling for $1,200 an acre a few years ago now brings $650. It costs so much to produce an irrigated crop. When a fellow comes in to borrow money, he's got to fill out a cash flow form to tell how much fertilizer, how much herbicide, how much insecticide, how much his payments are on his land, how high his repair is on his well or sprinkler, how high his taxes are, how much return he's going to make. His cash flow form tells how much he's going to need to operate that year. He needs to project. "Well, I'm going to raise 110 bushels of milo and the price of milo this year is only going to be $1.70 a bushel compared with $2.25 in the past two or three years." So he is going to get a lot less for his return and is it going to float? The banker looks at this and says, you can't do it, there's no way.

Tooms is not vertically integrated with his own feedlots as is the nearby Gigot family. Instead, he sells his alfalfa to the local Alfalfa, Inc., feedlots in Sublette, Kansas, his milo to Supreme Feeders in Liberal, Kansas, and his wheat to Cargill and to Collingworth. In the area, three meat packing plants process almost one hundred thousand head of cattle weekly. Phil noted that a lot of cattle consume a lot of alfalfa and that "it would be impossible to produce the beef without irrigation because with dryland farming we couldn't guarantee the grains that it takes." Tooms also remembered that he had been told that Americans were foolish to be so inefficient with grain when so much of the world's population is starving. It takes six pounds of grain to grow a pound of beef. Linda wondered, though, "who would you get to eat six pounds of grain?" Locally, all sorts of jobs were tied to irrigation. Feedlots locked in high levels of irrigation.

Linda knew that irrigation is essential to the economic well-being of the region, but she was also sensitive to overproduction. Irrigation farmers in southwest Kansas have joined farmers in the Dakotas and western Canada to produce more grain than can be exported or consumed domestically. The end results are large surpluses and low prices. "We became expert producers," but "here there's just a few crops that we can really raise successfully: alfalfa, milo, corn, and wheat." Linda remembered that when they built their first well in 1956 farm experts from Kansas State University came and stressed "push, push, push for more yields." That is when they irrigated their first eighty acres.

The Family Farm: Its Contract with America

The family farm has long been cherished as the place where the patriotic virtues of rugged individualism, industriousness, and personal self-sufficiency are practiced best. These virtues, which still define America's identity, were earned by working the land on the frontier and in rural society. So said Crèvecoeur, Jefferson, Frederick Jackson Turner, and puffed-up congressmen trying to squeeze a few more dollars into their districts. But agricultural productivity above all else is the motto of corporate farming, and this puts the family farm at risk. While concerns are raised over the negative environmental effects of agriculture such as blowing soil, waste water, and nonpoint chemical pollution, farming continues to be a major source of image, metaphor, and myth about the intimate bond between humanity and the wider natural world. Agriculture extracts resources from the natural world, but it is rarely castigated as are mining and logging. Americans are nostalgic about raising and eating their own food as a communion with nature's larger whole. Aldo Leopold received attention by writing that if people did not own and work farms they would face a separation from nature. They would forget that milk does not come from a plastic container, peas do not come from a freezer, and meat does not come from a shrink-wrapped box.

Any examination of the family farm in the late twentieth century runs into incredible complexity, but a few useful generalizations can be made. The idea of the Jeffersonian yeoman farmer that has shaped both reality and myth about American agriculture included on-site ownership, family labor, agrarian values, land stewardship, and generational continuity. In 1986 the philosopher Paul B. Thompson identified the core features of the yeoman farmer: household members own the land, perform the labor, control the capital, and make the important economic decisions.[3] Agricultural economist Willard W. Cochrane called the family farm a "single enterprise farm firm."[4] He remembered that historic frontier farmers hunted game and collected wild foods from the place they plowed and harvested and asserted that more important than income off the farm were ownership of land and lifestyle. The goal of a 1979 conference in Nebraska was to establish the identifying marks of a successful contemporary family farm:

Owner-operation, in which the rights and responsibilities of ownership are vested in an individual who works the farm for a living;

Independence, with financing from within its own resources using family labor and management to build the sweat equity and cash flow;

Economic dispersion, in which large numbers of efficient sized farms operate with equal access to competitive markets;

Family centered, in which the family lives its life in harmony with its workplace, the responsibilities shared by all family members;

Commercially diversified, as to commodities produced as an economic precaution to reduce price risks and maximize the use of farm resources to produce production inputs internally;

Innovation and adoption of technology, to reduce family labor or make it more efficient.[5]

The conclusive definition was, "the family farm carries with it a commitment to certain values which include conservation, frugality, responsibility, honesty, dignity in work, belief in community, caring for future generations, neighborliness, and self-reliance."

In the modern American economy, family farming can also be defined, or set apart, as a unique enterprise.[6] It intertwines like no other enterprise the labor force, the role of women, the unusual involvement of children, ownership, capitalization, management, and location. One rural sociologist wrote,

Farm family members work together with varying degrees of solidarity, seeking to reach the common goal of a profitable farming operation. . . . Farm families that lost their farm also lost the major basis of their interaction. . . . Farm families are also unique because of their demand for family labor in terms of career planning for farm children. . . . When the family farm is foreclosed and this option is gone, the young adolescents often have a great sense of anger and betrayal. Not only is the present destroyed, but their sense of future as well. . . . The very agrarian values that built farm families and kept them in farming make it difficult to restructure their lives.[7]

Overall, the American family farm has persisted for more than 100 years on the plains (and more than 200 years nationally) as a decentralized cottage industry in an increasingly industrialized world. American society committed itself to private and independent farm ownership in early colonial times and institutionalized it in the Land Survey Ordinance of 1785, which would not be significantly modified for the next 150 years.[8] Few questions were raised about the essential weaknesses inherent in the on-site, family-operated farm. It is difficult for individual farmers to calculate risk and build their own safety net when climate, land, and prices are uncertain. The expectations of modern farmers have been frozen by legislation and farm policies linked to the parity years of 1911–14. Irrigation's golden years, roughly 1960 to 1990, a small bump of prosperity in a risky frontier zone, may have been as misleading as the parity years. Small farmers are prone to be wrapped up in their own mythology, unable to cope with the inherent limits of independent farming on the plains, and disengaged from the trends of contemporary society.

As irrigation brought prosperity to the High Plains, smaller farmers were pushed out of the way because it was assumed that only industrial farmers could afford and manage extensive field watering. This seemed to be the result of the "hectic 1970s."[9] Cochrane called it "cannibalism."[10] Compared to 1950, half the number of High Plains farmers worked the same amount land in 1980, while the regional economy grew. Phil Tooms and other local farmers came close to the truth when they expected the number to be halved again by the year 2000. No one, especially not politically sensitive congressmen and USDA officials, openly advocates abandonment of the family farm. The 1998 USDA report by the National Commission on Small Farms titled *A Time to Act* repeats the praise of the small farmer.[11] Phil Tooms, the Trescotts, and even the Gigots claim their personal identity stems from family farming. But fewer and fewer operations still thriving on the High Plains fit the mold. There are many historical parallels. The shift from family farms to large-scale, centralized agribusiness operations can be compared to the demise of ma-and-pa neighborhood grocery stores after World War II as supermarkets became commonplace. Similarly, the early American iron industry at first depended upon locally produced iron "pigs" before it moved toward centralized and vertically integrated factory mills. A similar vertical integration, based on mining the land and water, can be seen today at cattle feedlots and hog-confinement operations in the old Dust Bowl.

Some phenomena never find a steady state. The plains farm system may be one of them. It exists in a state of irregularity, jumps and starts, and unexpected swings away from center. This is called aperiodicity and it is why American farm policy may be a doomed policy. It seeks to steady agriculture's historic oscillations, but American farming on the High Plains never will evolve into a steady state. Instead, it will follow its own nonlinear rationale. James Gleick's reminder that "nonlinearity means that the act of playing the game has a way of changing the rules"[12] means that farm policy can never catch up with either the game or its rules. The fault lies not only with government policy. When plains farming is accepted as aperiodic and nonlinear it becomes clear why the small farmer became a long-term government client.

A harsh climate continues to dominate plains life more than either farm policy, the independent farmer, or, it appears, large-scale irrigation. Despite the brilliant technological feat that High Plains irrigation is, the severity of drought plains farmers experienced may be far surpassed in the future. Some climate forecasters wonder whether the drought year of 1988, discussed in Chapter 8, was the forerunner of the next dry spell scheduled for the 1990s, which did take hold as predicted. The 1990s drought could be the first real taste of the dire greenhouse effect resulting from the accumulation of carbon dioxide in the upper atmosphere due to the burning of fossil fuels.[13] A gradual rise in world temperatures over the last several decades may now be taking its toll. "CO_2 doubling" of two to three degrees Celsius would mean

Sahel-like or Great Basin-like desertification of the central High Plains. Global computer modeling—the "General Circulation Model" or GCM—indicates that some parts of the world will become warmer and dryer and that others will become cooler. The modeling places the Gigot, Tooms, and Trescott farms at the center of an utterly waterless and barren wasteland. During the first decades of Ogallala groundwater consumption, downdraft under irrigated farms averaged two feet a year, but with energetic management irrigators reduced this to one foot a year. The drought year frightened them when their crops soaked up a three-foot aquifer decline. With their water running out, not even the Gigots could make the desert bloom.

Regardless of other forces, it was abundantly clear by 1980 that the federal government's interest was in high productivity and that government policy targeted corporate agriculture differently than the family farm. Despite claims to the opposite, the 1985, 1990, and 1996 farm bills reflected the same bias. This reality was admitted in *A Time to Act*.[14] A forceful, poignant, and populist plea to save the family farm, it admits that government policies and practices have discriminated for decades against small-farm operators.[15] The report deliberately picks up where Jimmy Carter's Secretary of Agriculture Bob Bergland left off nearly two decades earlier in *A Time to Choose*. Bergland warned that existing policies and programs "reinforce or accelerate the trends towards ever-larger farming operations, [where] the result will be a few large farms controlling food production in only a few years."[16] The situation by 1998 was not encouraging; according to *A Time to Act*, there were three hundred thousand fewer farmers than in 1979. They were receiving 13 percent less of every consumer dollar spent on food. Four firms controlled over 80 percent of the beef market. While 94 percent of America's farms were still small farms in 1998, they received only 41 percent of all farm receipts. Out of the nation's two million farms, 122,810 farms—all large—received the majority of farm receipts.[17]

The report made the future look gloomy for small farmers, who were identified as those with less than $250,000 gross receipts annually (with a net cash income of $23,159). Small farmers, per the report, had little or no control over setting the price for the crops since prices were set not by the marketplace but by a oligopsonistic consortia of large agribusiness operations. To compete, farmers had to invest in new, highly efficient agricultural technologies that demanded new higher levels of capital. Further, most small farmers were marginalized because they produced undifferentiated raw commodities such as corn or wheat, which served the most profitable segment of food production: the companies that processed, packaged, and marketed food. Between 1910 and 1990 the share of the total agricultural economy received by farmers dropped from 21 percent to 5 percent.[18] The urgency of change was accelerated by the passage of the 1996 farm bill that eliminated federal support on many levels.

The report nevertheless insisted that "small farms have been the foundation of our Nation," once more invoking Jefferson. It referred to "our nation's historical commitment to small farms."[19] It noted that small farms have their own unique systems of management, skill, and ingenuity; that they fuel local economies and energize rural communities; that they hold up traditional values of self-employment and ownership of land; and that they maintain a widely praised way of life. The report implied, but did not specify, that small farmers might persevere primarily through niche agriculture based on low capital investment, intensive labor and management, and high-value crop and livestock production. They could attract a segment of consumer economy that was interested in identity-preserved grains, organic grains, free-range chickens, natural beef, and food-grade corn. Such niche, or specialty farming, could include direct marketing of organic foods to consumers outside the industrialized food stream such as new-generation cooperatives, local farmer's markets, subscription farming, and farm-to-chef avenues.[20]

A Time to Act added that small farms deserved preservation for their "public value" as alternatives to agribusiness. This included an efficiency rate that was equivalent or better than larger commercial operations, as well as superior biological diversity and ecological resilience.[21] Large farms had unreported hidden costs such as the loss of market competition, risk to food security, heavy consumption of fossil fuels and industrial chemicals, and the environmental consequences of animal confinement production. In addition, small farms contributed more than farm production to American society:

> Small farms embody a diversity of ownership, cropping systems, landscapes, biological organization, culture, and traditions. Since the majority of farmland is managed by a large number of small farm operators, the responsible management of soil, water, and wildlife encompassed by these farms produces significant environmental benefits. Decentralized land ownership produces more equitable economic opportunity for people in rural communities, and offers self-employment and business management opportunities. Farms, particularly family farms, can be nurturing places for children to grow up and acquire the values of responsibility and hard work.[22]

The commission pulled on national heartstrings when it reported at its first hearing that "the greatest thing that agriculture furnished this country is not food or fiber, but a set of children with a work ethic and a good set of values."[23] Where small farms declined, the local community deteriorated. To support this assessment, it quoted University of California anthropologist Dean MacCannell: "We have found depressed median family incomes, high levels of poverty, low education levels, social and economic inequality between ethnic groups, etc. . . . associated with land and capital concentration in agriculture. . . . Communities have a few wealthy elites, a majority of poor laborers, and virtually no middle class [which] has a serious negative effect on both the quality and quantity of social and commercial service, public education, local governments, etc."[24] The commission's recommendations emphasized the need to support a new generation of beginning farmers,[25] but in large part it only recommended more of the same attention from existing federal agencies. Implementation is doubtful. The report noted that "At present, USDA does not emphasize the needs of small farms in its strategic plan."[26]

In terms of agricultural sustainable development, the family farm may persist as the best local on-site choice, despite its many serious defects and apparent obsolescence. It alone embraces a complex variety of agricultural, environmental, economic, social, and cultural values. This variety makes it durable because its priorities are multiple. Above all, the family farm does not give sole allegiance to short-term profits that contradict sustainability. It is more likely to accept the initial sacrifices required for a shift to low-input organic agriculture. If short-term profits had been its primary interest, the family farm would have disappeared long ago.

Becoming Loyal to the Family Farm

Whose interests does consumption of the Ogallala serve? What does American agricultural policy protect? After working through volumes of data and reels of computer tape in 1980, the USDA identified 575,000 primary farmers. Primary farms were classified in terms of efficient production, strategic crops, gross sales, large size, and superior geographical location. The 1980 USDA report concluded that "these farms will most likely influence the effectiveness of the commodity programs as now structured, and they will be the largest beneficiaries of the program benefits."[27] What should not have been surprising was that the USDA's primary farmer in 1980 was not necessarily the historic family farmer, but still the level of public surprise was considerable. Where and when had the priorities changed, and why, and how?

The USDA based its strategy on a specific national goal to determine what farm type would assure low consumer prices and adequate production levels for domestic and global needs today and into the future. This strategy has been agricultural policy for most of the twentieth century, and it has been an informal strategy for most of the nation's history. The primary farms listed were those operations that produced almost 80 percent of the nation's food and fiber although they made up less than 20 percent of all farms.[28] There is a tendency to lose sight of the individual farmer as one considers worldwide markets, the chemical industry, agribusiness interests, and even environmental protection, all of which tend to make the local producer invisible.

The USDA also targeted a more select group of 115,000 farms that produced almost three-quarters of all the nation's strategic foods: wheat, corn, and soybeans. These 115,000 farms could produce enough to fulfill the nation's basic grain needs, support overseas exports, and still maintain a surplus. Geographically, we were told that wheat farmers do best in Kansas and North Dakota on 1,500 acres with gross sales of $105,000 (1980 dollars). Primary corn or soybean farmers fare best in Illinois and Iowa on 640 acres grossing $145,000. Totally discounted by the USDA report were rural farm residences—44 percent of all farm households—with sales of less than $5,000 and small farms—34 percent of all farms—grossing $5,000 to $40,000. Lack of federal support for nonprimary farms made them more vulnerable to other forces. On the High Plains, vulnerability means a higher level of climate-dependence as farmers become unable to pay the increasing costs of irrigation.

More recent studies outside the USDA include a 1992 congressional OTA review that confirmed the shift of primary farm production into the hands of a progressively smaller number of operators. Almost half (47 percent) of America's billion acres of farmland is held by 4 percent of landowners. Sixty percent of the net cash farm income is earned by only 7 percent of the nation's two million farms. By the year 2000, OTA estimated, about fifty thousand of the largest farms in the United States will account for 75 percent of agricultural production. The USDA admitted in 1992 that federal benefits remained disproportionately distributed to a few wealthy producers, mostly industrial operations: 68 percent of government farm payments went to the wealthiest 19 percent of agricultural producers.[29] In contrast, small farms that earned less than one hundred thousand dollars in annual sales, and that made up 82 percent of the two million farms in America, received 31 percent of government payments.

In an apparent turnaround from the 1980 USDA analysis, the 1990 farm bill, the Food, Agriculture, Conservation and Trade Act (FACTA), specifically recognized the economic importance and human value of family farming as a means to achieve sustainable agriculture. The goals of the bill were to include support for owner-operated small- and moderate-sized farms and to "build on the entrepreneurial skills, self-employment tradition, and the [existing] resource base of rural communities." However, when the details for sustainability were spelled out, the conventional agenda reappeared: large surpluses from industrial agriculture based on costly technology. The real objective of the 1990 farm bill was to lock in American agriculture as a servant to "competitiveness of food production within the global economy." "Sustainability" was folded into "competitiveness" to the extent that only agribusiness provided acceptable levels of scale and efficiency. Critics of the actual outcomes of the 1990 farm bill concluded that the family farmers would again be excluded from federal recognition.[30]

High Plains Family Farmer as Government Client

Despite the romance, it is historically clear that family farmers were neither heroic nor independent on the High Plains. Instead, they dug deeply into three resources to help them survive for limited periods of time. Abundant land was the first free good. Mining the land provided a way to stay alive and enjoy a false prosperity until it eroded and blew away in the 1930s, with even worse damage in the 1950s and 1970s. As land costs rose, Ogallala water became the farmers' next free good, as it still is. They prospered (still too rarely and infrequently) because they could exploit abundant, inexpensive water. The appearance of commercial agriculture—agribusiness—only intensified exploitation of land and water. The third good, society, mitigated individual farmer risk. Farmers depended on social mechanisms, particularly credit institutions, market prices, railroad policies, and government planning, to minimize adverse climate effects. During the drought and depression of the 1890s, state agencies in the Dakotas and Nebraska provided welfare relief, albeit reluctantly, and the U.S. Army was ordered to make surplus supplies available to destitute farmers. Federal legislation such as the Timber Culture Act, the Desert Land Act, and the Reclamation Act, while they created tempting opportunities for speculators, were also attempts to reduce farmer risk.[31] But there was little talk of alternative social institutions that could minimize unexpected climate changes. In contrast, German immigrants who held onto their traditions of the extended multifamily community,[32] where support went deeper and longer, were far more effective in keeping people on the land in hard times than the American single-family homesteaders.[33]

In the 1930s the New Deal continued to buffer risk on the High Plains when it singled out the independent, on-site family farmer for protection. A sequence of farm bills beginning with the Depression-era Agricultural Adjustment Act of 1933 that was reinforced by legislation in 1938 and 1949 were efforts to protect farmers from damaging climate changes and market downturns. If farmers agreed to restrict how much they grew of a specified set of crops, they were assured of a subsidy when crop prices were low. As a result, farmers would presumably receive sufficient annual income to survive while limiting crop surpluses. What had been an emergency crop-subsidy program turned into a long-standing government policy upon which farmers learned to depend. Farm crop prices did have an aperiodic, or boom-and-bust, history, and farm program payments were society's way of acknowledging that farming is a risky but essential business. Such federal intervention successfully supported farmers through the little Dust Bowls of the 1950s and 1970s and thus prevented the hardships of the 1930s. In this sense, the moral geography was highly successful. Government subsidies saved the rural economics of the plains during the farm recession of 1987, when they were 74 percent of Nebraska's net farm income. Even in a more prosperous 1993, subsidies made up 39 percent of the state's net farm income. Economist Barry Flinchbaugh of Kansas State University noted that between 1989 and 1992 government payments made up 52 percent of the net income of farms in his state that had up to $34,000 net yearly income. He worried, "Take away the government payments and they have about $17,000 to live on. Take away their income from off-farm jobs and they're living in poverty."[34] Government policies set not only prices but also loan rates. Moreover, the government provided money to offset farmers' losses when natural disaster struck, such as droughts, hailstorms, unseasonable frosts.[35]

Over the last fifty years as the government attempted to buffer farmers from natural disasters like the Dust Bowl and human mistakes like the Depression, it turned independent farmers into dependent clients. On-site American family farmers have been the recipient of special privilege that involves large sums of federal money and discreet policies to protect them from natural disasters and market forces. So insulated throughout history, we might see farmers as excessively vulnerable workmen artificially isolated from harsh reality instead of the free and spirited yeoman widely admired in congressional rhetoric, newspaper editorials, and the public eye. The yeoman figure was not to be allowed to wither away. Having created its clients, the federal government was obligated to protect them as federal wards. Agriculture became, in agricultural economist Wesley F. Peterson's words, "the industry which, on the surface, seems to come closest to the perfectly competitive model [of capitalism] (many firms, undifferentiated products, etc.), [yet] is the one where government intervention is the most extensive."[36]

Federal protection from the risks of drought eventually introduced a range of new risks more familiar to corporate industry. Family farmers became dependent upon expensive equipment, chemical pesticides, and high energy consumption, all of which led to debt. They shifted from labor-intensive to capital-intensive farming. Whether intentionally or not, federal commodity and credit policies drove virtually all farmers, large and small, into the patterns of high water-consumption industrialized farming.[37] Hidden costs can rise when the need for expensive conservation irrigation equipment transforms "free" water into debt-producing water. The burden shifts from the vulnerable natural resource to the vulnerable farmer. An irrigator in Swisher County, Texas, said "it was 1976 when we bit the bullet and decided to go dryland. From 1976 to 1980 I accumulated a quarter of a million dollars in debt. . . . Every time I went to the bank, I had lost more money. . . . You might have one really good year followed by three or four bad ones"—exactly the risk that irrigators worked to avoid. The farmers around Sublette, Kansas, concluded they can pump until early in the next century and then restart dryland farming. The Oklahoma *Comprehensive Water Plan* of 1980 concluded that farmers who return to dryland farming at only one-third the wheat or milo production of their irrigated farms will experience failure.[38] Still uncertain was whether existing conservation practices, described in the next chapter, accomplished more than covering up a problem. The old assets, fertile land and individual skills, are now masked or even diminished by external inputs like farm chemicals. Alternative farming advocates like Robert Rodale concluded that high capitalization and debt may do less to protect the family farm from erratic rain and soil depletion than do certain biological approaches.[39]

In this light, as long as the individual farmer practices "conventional" rather than "sustainable" farming, he or she is part of the problem rather than part of the solution. A New York state farmer spoke for other farmers when he wrote,

> I don't know a farmer who enjoys using chemicals, but faced with a mortgage payment and a crop-threatening pest, the choice is inescapable, and you spray. . . . [E]vidence seems clear that [agricultural chemicals] don't yield safer, healthier food. Farmers know this: They're not being paid enough to produce safe, healthy, life-sustaining foods, nor to be good stewards of the Earth. Society asks them to do this for free, for altruistic reasons. . . . We must ask ourselves, what is the real cost of putting a meal on America's table? . . . [T]he bottom line of our cheap food system . . . isn't on the supermarket tape. We need to factor in the decline of soil fertility, erosion, and related problems, food safety, polluted groundwater, the health troubles of farmers and farm workers, tax money used in commodity payments, and the destruction of our family farms and rural communities.[40]

This special status of agriculture in the United States, says ecologist Richard Lowrance, "will mean that the public will hold agriculture, as an industry, to higher standards of environmental quality and safety than other industries."[41] Fee Busby, writing from the perspective of the think tank, the Winrock International Institute for Agricultural Development, calls environmental protection the end of Manifest Destiny.[42] The public sees agriculture as a special interest group rather than as a source of traditional values.[43] Rarely has any ecological element, or maintenance of a sustainable physical environment, been considered. Nevertheless, in the words of Richard Duesterhaus, "the consumer has come to expect food that is plentiful, nutritious, and free from contaminants and-or other ingredients that may cause short- or long-duration health hazards."[44] Such expectations from consumers cannot be escaped. Economic expectations are reflected in higher quality production at lowest possible costs, environmental demands as resource conservation and pollution avoidance, and social needs in terms of revived rural communities and the well-being of farm families.[45]

Discounting the Family Farm: Federal Farm Acts of the 1990s

The 1996 Federal Agricultural Improvement and Reform Act brought a fundamental change in federal farm policy that dated back six decades. It appeared to accelerate the takeover of industrial farming on the plains and across the nation by removing hard-times federal protection. Instead, market prices would determine what crops were grown. This was particularly attractive at a time when grain prices were at their highest since the early 1970s and still soaring. A few pessimists complained that markets are notoriously fickle and often react strongly to uncertainties like climate impacts, wars, and economic moods. Nicknamed the "Freedom to Farm Act," the 1996 farm bill immediately ended production curbs on the primary plains crops of wheat, corn, and feed grains. Gradually, over seven years, it would eliminate crop price supports to allow marketplace forces to take control. The act assumed that all-out production is good. It eliminated set-aside programs designed to control surpluses. A cosponsor of the bill, Republican senator Richard Lugar of Indiana, said, "we will begin to trust the market for the first time in a long while."[46] A spokesman for the food giant Conagra urged support because in his view the legislation allowed farmers to respond directly to international markets opened by new trade agreements (General Agreement on Tariffs and Trade [GATT] and North American Free Trade Agreement [NAFTA]) "by being able to plant what they want and essentially as much as they want."[47] The proindustry American Farm Bureau Federation added, "Farmers will have greater flexibility to produce for the market."[48]

For medium and small farmers, the 1996 farm bill was a "bill of uncertainty" that favored short-term benefits over seven years and played down the threat of "long-term economic pain for independent family farms and for other rural communities."[49] The government would also end its catastrophe insurance, leaving farmers to negotiate with private insurers. Illinois corn and soybean farmer Mark Chenoweth said that the legislation gambled the future of agriculture in America. He questioned whether farmers could exist without Depression-era subsidies and survive in a free market when they had failed in the past. "The short-term will be friendly," with $36.5 billion set aside for transition payments, but the "long term could be bearish."[50] He noted that subsidies were designed to keep farmers on the land despite un-predictable changes in weather, production, and overseas demand. Wheat farmer Henry Vinduska of Mynard, Nebraska, noted that subsidies and defi-ciency payments "helped stabilize low market years," and added that farm-ing does not regulate itself very well: "Too many people would get carried away and surpluses would build up, and we'd be in a lot of trouble again with low crop prices." He concluded, "the bigger [farms] are, the better they do. I'm afraid there may not be a place for small farmers."[51] The National Farmers Union angrily complained that the "Freedom to Farm Act" sold out American farm families to the special interests of agribusiness. It said that the dangerous trend of concentration of agriculture in the hands of a few cor-porations would only accelerate. Still, most plains farmers interviewed by this author were pleased to choose their own crops.

Family farm advocate Dan Nagengast of the Kansas Rural Institute noted that farmers could not respond to price changes immediately because they have a built-in delay that would be fatal in many cases: "If the wheat crop proves as disastrous as it now [March 1996] looks, prices will rise even higher. No farmer can respond because it will take another cropping cycle to get to the next wheat crop. Then, will everyone respond and the resulting glut send prices tumbling? I've always suspected that there is something fishy about waving the 'market' around as the response to all social ills. Farmers need a year to respond. Grain traders do it in the flick of a computer key."[52] He added:

I question whether the US can afford to throw away farmers for a brit-tle system of expert oriented, monocropping, based on satellite tech-nology and totally dependent on imported oil both for production and shipping. . . . [A]gricultural concentration will continue and many farmers will be forced to forget farming or become agricultural indus-trialists [resulting in] increased wealth for the already wealthy, more rapid disappearance of topsoil, clean water, rural communities, and [loss of] a flexible food system that once could respond to war, satel-lites on the blink and limited fuel supplies. . . . We need an economy that offers productive, satisfying work to millions of people rather than great wealth to a fortunate few in the near future.[53]

America's Moral Geography (1933–96): Why Make the Plains a Special Case?

The High Plains of the continental heartland offered major environmental challenges to successful human habitation. Native Americans had used large parts of the plains as either transitory hunting grounds or a no-man's-land between tribes. Settlers and promoters looked at the geography of the plains and could not see it for what it was: a thin-skinned and vulnerable ecosystem. Europeans described the plains as "empty and useless" territory that lay barren, ready for consumption. Environmental systems in other parts of America's large and diverse geography such as the eastern coastline, the prairie midwest, California, and even the South had the resilience to support European expectations. Europeans treated these regions like plentiful sources of raw materials upon which to build a comfortable material civilization. They demanded well-watered soils and plentiful timber, underground minerals, and hydrocarbons, and they expected the same from the plains.

European settlers misconceived the High Plains region. To them it was strange and distant and may as well have been Chad or Nepal. The plains became a de facto colony that supplied raw materials to the rest of the nation. Internal sustainability was lost to the consumer mainstream. Charles Ginzburg writes, "Somebody's financial gains can be related, more or less directly, to the distress of distant human beings [and ecosystems], thrown into poverty, starvation, and even death."[54] Americans learned at the price of great cost and suffering of humanity's power to entirely undermine the survival of entire regions. The High Plains ecosystem would never recover. As a result, human poverty persisted for decades and generations. The plight of High Plains agriculturalists during the devastating Dust Bowl resulted in a national crusade and instigated the development of federal farm aid programs. After the Dust Bowl, Americans began compassionately legislating money, and now they have done so for over sixty years. We can describe this process as a *moral geography* that swallowed up billions of dollars in a comprehensive program of federal subsidies, price supports, low-cost loans, crop insurance, and agricultural extension training. Environmental protection included shelter belts, contour plowing, soil banking, conservation reserves, and training in soil and water management. These costly activities seemed like the right thing to do; they sustained virtuous farm families living in a difficult place.

Frontierlike conditions persist on the plains. Its human populations have not gained independence from the need for continuous waves of settlers, intensive use of soil to the point of erosion, consumption of previously hidden groundwater, and large distributions of federal cash and incentives. In other words, it contains people put at chronic high risk. Hardworking inhabitants are sacrificed to distant markets. Despite decades of difficult and costly human effort, their farms and towns remain artificially constructed entities that are perpetually vulnerable to collapse. The willingness of the federal government to continuously shore up the plains from total collapse suggests an extraordinary public sense of responsibility (or guilt) toward the region.[55] New federal agencies, like the Soil Conservation Service of the U.S. Department of Agriculture, were given the mission of changing severe erosion in the Dust Bowl region to soil conservation. The objective was to create a working habitat that would protect the existing social pattern and local family farming at almost any cost.

Joan C. Tronto, a philosopher of geography, wrote, "For a society to be judged as a morally admirable society, it must, among other things, adequately provide for care of its members and its territory."[56] Moral geography is not the same as environmental ethics, which seeks normative or final rules. Moral geography is deliberately conditional, not normative. A conditional approach means a responsive approach to a contemporary state of affairs in a specific geographical region. It does not mean relativistic or fickle, which is the way government policy sometimes appears. Moral geography can be both a process and a condition, a state of mind and a physical reality defined by time and place. A moral geography is both an ethical choice made about a particular people and place and an internal logic that belongs to a particular people and place. The application of moral geography takes hold when government policy identifies a geographical landscape and its inhabitants as being in need and deliberately responds to save that region.

Agricultural analyst Don Paarlberg wrote that the individual farmer has a privileged position in American society. He or she is exempt from labor laws that regulate child labor, working conditions, and minimum wage. He or she receives preferred transportation rates. The farmer's major asset is public goodwill, but Paarlberg wonders if this is dwindling rapidly.[57] Kenneth A. Cook suggested that the American public entered into a social contract with plains farmers that recognized the enormous cost farmers bore to turn the plains into the American breadbasket. Taxpayers were willing to share the human burden of agricultural production because they viewed the family farm as a place where American values were upheld. The public recognized that with the environmental limits of the plains farmers would likely continue to need assistance from the government. Agricultural economist John E. Ikerd cautions that "Many farmers feel special responsibilities to society . . . for providing food, clothing, and shelter for the people. . . . [In return] society has given special consideration and concessions to farmers reflecting these critical relationships. . . . [F]armers [have] a set of values that cannot be captured in the dollar-and-cent language of most economic analyses. . . . But farmers cannot live on appreciation from society."[58]

One question addressed by a moral geography is highly problematic: what is an authentic response to a particular region and what is inauthentic? As Americans, we have historically designated some places as good, such as Yosemite, and other places as evil, such as Love Canal. A nuclear power plant is good to some people and evil to others. Even though on the plains in the 1990s crops were mostly surpluses, its population declined, and its landscape remained unspectacular, the region remained tied to America's revered frontier and its people to virtuous family farming. Authentic or not, the plains is the location of strongly felt entitlements. Americans laid a great burden of Manifest Destiny and economic prosperity upon the plains. What if the High Plains did not carry this moral load? Should it revert to the Poppers' Buffalo Commons empty grassland? Should it be available for factory farms of cattle, hogs, and chickens that would make it interchangeable with North Carolina, Missouri, and Iowa? Can the story of the plains have a different outcome than what it is now—a charity case—based on an internal logic defined by a unique local culture and distinctive environment? The primary question raised by white European ventures onto the High Plains is whether an invaded natural system would become a successful nature-resembling ecosystem (e.g., sustainable farmland), a transformed ecosystem (a function of the larger industrial/metropolitan infrastructure), or a degraded system that virtually guarantees failure in the foreseeable future.

In the second half of the twentieth century when the plains fell away from the forefront of American attention, it became a region beyond the frontier's edge. By the mid-twentieth century, American social space stopped at the boundaries of suburbia, and any unique features beyond suburbia became irrelevant. Agricultural and rural America now stand on the other side, as if they were in an alien wilderness beyond historic norms and rules. Competing visions of plains farmers took hold. One beholds plains farmers resting comfortably with acreage in dryland wheat farming, an equivalent amount in irrigated grains, and some cattle on grassland. Another vision beholds the local farmer as an aggressive and successful businessperson-entrepreneur who competes against national corporations by using his or her own wheat, milo, and corn to feed cattle in lots and pigs in shiny sheds. One vision evokes comfortable middle-class aspirations, while the other is closer to the jet set. The hog industry saw the plains as one of several interchangeable regions with similar features: a weak and vulnerable economy and a low population that was unlikely to challenge the environmental impacts of hog production. Despite a limited water supply, the plains had the advantage of a dry climate that would reduce odors. To old-timers the industrial interchangeability of hog production trivializes the plains and encourages indifference toward unique landscapes and human diversity. Corporate hog production, with its smells and pollution, intruded upon the plains because the plains region was "off the map" and outside society. Moral geography was replaced by moral indifference so that the issue involved not the difference between good and evil places but places to which society was largely indifferent and whose misuse did not evoke concern. To paraphrase a statement by a cowboy who spoke about the Pecos River, "There is no justice west of suburbia."

7
. . .

The Future of Plains Irrigation:
A New Gospel of Efficiency

The Eleventh Commandment— Thou shalt inherit the Holy Earth as a faithful stew-
ard, conserving its resources and productivity from generation to generation. Thou
shalt safeguard the fields from soil erosion, thy living waters from drying up, that thy
descendants may have abundance forever.—W. C. Lowdermilk, assistant chief,
Soil Conservation Service, 1956

If the efficiency of an irrigation system is increased by 5 percent from 55 to 60 on a
160-acre field of corn, . . . [and] assuming the pumping head was 250 feet and diesel
fuel was $1.25 per gallon, the monetary savings would amount to $1,244 per year.—
Kansas Water Facts Sheet, Soil Conservation Service, U.S. Department of Agriculture, mid-1980s

Success Measured by the Acre-Foot Conserved

For more than three decades plains irrigators have been persuaded to plow
fields and water plants "fencerow to fencerow" to feed the world and keep
domestic prices low. Between 1940 and 1980, agricultural production doubled and then tripled through a combination of mechanization and agricultural science that was unimaginable earlier in the century. These innovations kept plains irrigators in business producing high yields to compensate
for declines in crop prices. But these remarkable advances were rarely intended to save water. Instead, they encouraged frontierlike exploitation of a

257

free resource, water. It would be the last free resource to support farming on the difficult plains. According to conventional thinking, the mission of the agricultural enterprise has always been to make the natural environment more pliable for a select few cash crops. This production ethic deliberately seeks the highest possible yields on a short-term basis, with little regard to how extensively it soaks up minerals and organics from the soil or irreplaceable freshwater from the Ogallala. From another angle, the same soil and water were liberally consumed to keep the vulnerable family farm in place. Today, as production costs go up and supplies of soil and water go down, more farmers are shifting their thinking from changing the environment to changing the crops. Which produces more dollar-value per gallon pumped, they ask, wheat or corn, cattle or grains, hogs or cattle?

Difficult choices cannot be postponed forever. Heavy irrigation helps to guarantee profitable high yields, while water conservation will stretch out the crop-saving groundwater. Even efficient consumption is still heavy consumption. Based on complicated equations, if a plains irrigator in southwest Kansas or the Texas-Oklahoma Panhandle plants corn on one fifth of his land and applies 2.5 acre-feet of water, his well levels are likely to decline three feet per year. If the same farmer plants less-demanding (.75 to 1 acre-feet) wheat but on 40 percent of his land (to maintain the same profit), his well levels would decline a bit more.[1] Farmers are now learning to measure yields, and successful farming, not by the acre or by market price but by the cost of an acre-foot of groundwater. Using new groundwater conservation methods, if a plains farmer could survive on less than a one-foot decline, he would see it as a major accomplishment.

High Plains farming is being forced to move away from exploitation of the land and water. In contrast to their history of profligacy and wastefulness of bountiful groundwater, contemporary High Plains irrigators who began large-scale pumping in the 1960s are now interested in water conservation. This involves better management of individual irrigated fields and more effective regional groundwater management districts. For example, plains irrigators were among the first to use the Conservation Reserve Program of the 1985 farm bill to take their marginal fields out of production. Original irrigators A. Wayne Wyatt, Paul Hitch, Steve Irsik, the Gigots, and the real people behind the pseudonyms Tooms and Trescott have come face-to-face with water scarcity in their lifetimes.

From Short-Term Development to Long-Term Sustainability: What Are the Chances for Change?

Pessimists say that we cannot sustain irrigation's golden age indefinitely. Secured by an abundance of inexpensive water that assured high yields, plains farmers were protected from the impact of low prices while they gave American consumers cheap food and while their surpluses served world markets. This secured a worthwhile trade-off between lowered water levels for more food (and national prosperity). Today, in contrast, increasingly scarce water levels alone prevent any return to the golden age of irrigation. We are confronted by the threat of Ogallala consumption doubling or tripling because of a blitzkrieg combination of less efficient, aging equipment, the end of federally supported land set-asides, eroding soil, high-consumption agribusiness, and the warning of the next drought (possibly intensified by global warming). In the old Dust Bowl region we have seen that virtually all local irrigators see a future with far less water. Acceptance of this reality and appropriate responses to it have been central themes of this book. Very few irrigators believe that they can successfully revert to dryland farming; to them the High Plains has a future only in widespread irrigation. Virtually all of the irrigators interviewed for this book do not take seriously the Land Institute's experiments in alternative farming with perennial grains. They conclude that it cannot sustain commercial farming on the plains. As Linda Tooms told me, alternative crop farming presently offers insufficient yields, poor markets, and a return to poor working conditions. Yet a method of alternative sustainable farming may be able to keep farmers on the plains longer while also dramatically reducing environmental damage, reviving a popular, rural way of life, and conserving water for future generations.

Optimists seek to reverse the trend toward scarcity by using new techniques that conserve water and guarantee high yields. Optimists believe that plains farmers, and the world, have only begun to explore the capabilities of increased agricultural production with decreased use of Ogallala water. Most importantly, optimists say farmers are still using, and wasting, far more water than they need to keep profits and yields at satisfactory levels. The real answer, they say, is better water management.[2] Without radical changes, on-farm efficiency rose from 53 percent in 1975 to 59 percent in 1982, and it continues to rise as more irrigators shift to improved center-pivot and drip-trickle methods. Older flood and furrow irrigation is, conservatively, 15 percent to 20 percent less efficient.[3] By the mid-1990s, using so-called LEPA technology that included dragging waterlogged "socks" through crops at ground level, 95 percent efficiency has been reached. The combination of better management and new technologies offers plains irrigators the capacity to cover three sections instead of two sections with the same amount of water and still grow wheat and sorghums. Today's irrigators who are committed to efficiency have surpassed the productivity of dryland farmers by three to four times. All in all, a combination of strategies—planting drought-tolerant crops, using surge systems for furrow irrigation or converting to sprinkler systems, managing irrigation scheduling, reusing tailwater, and implementing special tillage procedures—have already increased groundwater efficiency. Between 1974 and 1984 water consumption in the region covered by the Texas Groundwater Management District No. 1 fell from 8.13 to 5.24 million acre-feet while production remained essentially stable.[4]

If water conservation becomes the rigorous discipline of the plains, irrigation can be stretched out to keep the High Plains in its historic agriculture for a while longer.[5] Plains irrigators are learning to stretch out their farming careers by recognizing a broad integrated approach that, according to policy analyst David R. Cressman, "strikes a balance between the [economic] goals of high crop yields and [environmental] protection of the land's productive capacity. . . . [Protection of the land involves] nondegradation or, preferably, enhancement of the elements and processes in the biosphere that support plant growth."[6] By using less water for more productivity, High Plains irrigators have probably extended their current prosperity from ten, twenty, or even thirty years, but in the long term this is not much time, and it certainly does not promise sustainability.

The mood in the old Dust Bowl region is cautious. The goal is to preserve past achievements and conserve resources to keep the future stable if not buoyant. No one has devised an alternative comparable to the current irrigation strategy based on expensive equipment, skilled management, and cheap petroleum energy. The efforts directed toward water management are prodigious. Words like *phreatophytes, albedo,* and *evapotranspiration* come into play. Each issue of the Texas District No. 1 newsletter, the *Cross Section,* offers readers information about the latest engineering and genetic developments. There is a sense of urgency.

New Conservation Technologies for the Irrigators' Farms

Based on this author's numerous on-site interviews and a 1985 High Plains survey by Kansas State University geographers David E. Kromm and Stephen E. White, it is clear that local farmers, seeing their well levels decline, are acting ahead of public thinking and policymakers who want to extend Ogallala groundwater supplies.[7] The two leading concepts are *mitigation* and *efficiency,* when once the bywords were development and production. Conserving water at the pump head is front-end mitigation; higher grain yield (profitability) per unit of water is a move away from waste toward efficiency.[8]

PLANT SCIENCE

The shift from changing the environment to changing the crops includes biotechnological modifications: the manipulation of physiological mechanisms that influence the uptake, use, and loss of water by plants, defined as their water stress or drought tolerance.[9] A yet-ambiguous technological fix through genetic engineering could conceivably stretch irrigation much further into the future. For most of the twentieth century, crop gains from plant breeding averaged 1 to 3 percent each year for High Plains corn, wheat, and sorghums. Between 1970 and 1990, the proportion of harvestable wheat increased from 35 to 50 percent.[10] However, beginning in the 1970s, incremental technological changes did not bring the same levels of improved yields and higher per-acre profits. The 1980s saw only marginal gains. During the 1970s and 1980s, wheat and corn production remained constant after decades of doubling and tripling.[11] It was as if High Plains soils were fully

261

exploited and crops fully developed no matter how much water was dumped onto them. The last possible grain or kernel had seemingly been pushed out of wheat and corn and milo. It was thought that without some dramatic improvement the future involved a less adaptable farm economy with fewer buffers. The old buffers—soil, water, appropriate crops, and efficient equipment, and even government cash and credit, appeared to be used up.

Nevertheless, the technological-fix mentality remains generally unchanged among many plains irrigators, particularly in anticipation of discoveries in genetic engineering. In this view biotechnology offers a wish list, says agricultural scientist Earl O. Heady, of dramatic breakthroughs, including "increasing crop adaptation to stress conditions; . . . hybrid wheat; increased protein content of corn; breaking the yield barrier of soybeans; improving photosynthetic efficiency of plants; developing nitrogen fixation by nonleguminous plants; . . . improved efficiency of those that now fix nitrogen in the soil; . . . improving the efficiency of nutrient uptake of plants."[12] The genetic potential of corn is said to be nine hundred bushels per acre.

The balance sheet for irrigation plant technology now includes agronomic water-use efficiency (WUE). Water-use efficiency compares the amount of crop or forage produced—the amount of harvestable or economic biomass—with the amount of water consumed by evapotranspiration.[13] Research includes tissue-culture work with protoplast fusion and recombinant DNA technologies to reduce stresses of salinity, drought, flooding ion toxicities, nutrient deficiencies, temperature extremes, and photosynthetic efficiency. Classic plant breeding such as hand-pollination is not being ignored. In all cases, there are important trade-offs. According to a 1980 study on plant adaptation, "Breeding lines [e.g., specific plants] that use water efficiently in a dry environment may not do as well as other lines under more favorable water conditions. This is because tradeoffs exist regarding plant responses in different environments. Therefore selecting plants for wide adaptability may be selecting for mediocrity."[14]

Plants have biological clocks: it takes a total of one thousand degrees Fahrenheit over a number of days for a corn plant to shift from germination to being able to form a tassel.[15] Tasseling is the most vulnerable time for corn, and irrigation is critical. Data on light intensity, air temperature, length of day, and soil-moisture levels allow precise information to be gathered about corn such as covered leaf area, carbohydrate production, dry-matter weight, and grain yield.[16] A lysimeter measures the water being evaporated from the soil or transpired through the plant leaves from sun and wind. Such devices improve crop-watering versatility and conservation efficiency. Plants have stress days: with a device called a contact auxanometer, which measures the diameter of a plant's stem, a change in growth rate can be detected within five minutes. It was discovered that since corn grows about 20 percent per day in its early stages, lack of water at specific times created stresses that can cause irreversible damage to the future of the crop. A crop like sorghum is not as easily stressed. Computer modeling of the interaction between plant-growth patterns and water application led to better irrigation scheduling that conserved Ogallala water.

Some attempts to reduce water needs are unusual. In this era of lean diets, after processing beef a lot of tallow is left in the plants around Garden City, Amarillo, and Lubbock. Beef fat is abundant, cheap, and undesirable—unless it is used as an antitranspirant. Crops under irrigation lose a significant amount of water through transpiration from their leaves into the atmosphere. A Texas Agricultural Experiment Station research team, with not a vegetarian among them, mixed the dense waxy tallow with water at several levels to test for phytotoxicity, or the tendency of plant leaves to burn, wilt, and die when a fatty substance is sprayed upon them. The most successful concentration was 2 percent beef fat to water. The first test on a potato crop yielded an increase of more than five hundred dollars per acre compared to untreated plants because the sprayed potatoes were of higher quality. Current work is on higher concentrations of tallow to water "so farmers won't have to carry around so much water."[17]

Reflectants and *albedo* are two words that mean the same thing: the more a plant can bounce back the sun's light and heat, the less water it will lose to the atmosphere. One problem of coating plants to prevent water loss is that photosynthesis can also be reduced, but with soybeans at least, neither photosynthesis nor yield were reduced. Net photosynthesis in sorghums was reduced by almost a quarter, but the total yield actually increased. Artificial coatings worked best in regions of high temperature and high humidity and less well in the High Plains low humidity climate. Yet such albedo treatment could extend, it is argued, the western range of soybeans into the dryer zone.[18]

The widespread drought of 1988 and 1989 called attention to unusual research in the water needs of plants. For more than four years, USDA scientists have known that drought-stricken plants emit high-pitched noises as their cell structures break down.[19] These sounds are normally too high-pitched for humans to hear, but special electronic gear can listen to the screams for water. Under normal conditions, water and the nutrients it carries flow from the soil into the plant under tension into a plant's water tubes. But if there is not enough water in the soil the tension builds and the tubes break and collapse, making ultrasonic noises. By using these sounds as signals of water deprivation, irrigation farmers could determine precisely when to release water into the fields or start the center-pivot irrigator. In addition, sound measurement of this plant-stress could point to new plant varieties that are better equipped to move water and nutrients from the soil into roots and leaves. It is fortunate that the sounds of the tension fractures, 100 kilohertz, are too high for normal human hearing, which goes up to 20 kilohertz, or fields across the High Plains would be noisy indeed. U.S. Department of Agriculture scientists also studied whether insects that cause damage are attracted by the noise of the stricken and vulnerable plants.

BETTER INFORMATION

Equally sophisticated as technology that listens to plants is the use of electronic meters to measure soil moisture in the fields when and where crops grow. Four basic soil types hold water differently. There are also three categories of soil water: plant available water, which is self-explanatory, gravity water, which descends below roots, and molecular water, which is too strongly bound to soil particles to be released to plants. Moisture blocks and resistance meters identify how much "plant available water" can be applied. A soil-moisture block looks like a small soldering iron. It contains a parallel pair of stainless steel electrodes attached to wires, and it is cast into a small gypsum block—hence the name "electrical-resistance gypsum blocks." As any high school chemistry or physics student knows, electrical resistance between the electrodes indicates soil moisture. The blocks are buried vertically at one-foot intervals to a depth of four feet, with the wires exposed at the surface and staked for easy identification. Resistance is measured with a resistance meter and is directly read as soil moisture. The blocks and wires are destroyed at tillage time, but the entire inexpensive device has to be replaced annually because the gypsum deteriorates.

Other devices to measure soil moisture are tensiometers, which measure soil-water suction, or the force of attraction of the soil for water. A water-filled tube with a porous top and vacuum gauge, it looks like a shiny cattle prod.[20] More state-of-the-art is the neutron moisture meter, which is costly but reliable and accurate. It uses a radioactive source and electronics to meter for moisture. Composed of a gauge and probe, when lowered into the soil it emits radioactive fast neutrons (6,000 miles per second) that collide with hydrogen atoms in water in the soil. As they lose energy, the speed of the neutrons decreases to about 1.7 miles per second and the neutrons become slow. The probe becomes surrounded by a cloud of slow neutrons. The denser the cloud, the more water is in the soil, and it is this density that is measured by the above-ground detector and gauge. The neutron moisture meter is a health hazard that demands special storage, transportation, and handling and a license from the state department of health. It is accurate only at eight inches or more below the surface, since too many fast neutrons escape through the soil surface at shallower levels. For installation, permanent aluminum tubes, virtually transparent to neutrons, are buried below plow depth and covered with soil that is removed to make annual measurements. Unfortunately, metering can be skewed if the soil contains boron, cadmium, or iron or forms of soil hydrogen in humus, calcium carbonate, and gypsum.[21]

Rediscovering Traditional Practices for Water Conservation

Far less unusual but also more subjective is the time-tested "feel and appearance" method to estimate soil moisture. The farmer goes to his field with a soil auger or sharpshooter spade, digs three sets of four-foot holes to find an average, grabs a handful of soil from each, squeezes it in his hand, and tests it by appearance and texture. According to twelve photographs in a full-color brochure offered by the Texas High Plains Underground Water Conservation District No. 1, at one extreme is sandy clay loam that is powdery-dry and easily crumbled. This indicates 0 to 25 percent available moisture. At the other extreme is silty clay loam soil that "forms a soft, sticky, plastic (pliable) ball, easily ribbons out between thumb and forefinger, slicks readily." This indicates 75 to 100 percent available moisture.[22] By following a feel and appearance chart and knowing his soil type, a farmer can decide when and where to irrigate. "As a good rule of thumb, the irrigator should begin irrigating before the soil moisture level in the upper two feet of the root zone profile falls below 50 percent available moisture. . . . Soil moisture in the three- and four-foot levels could be compared to a savings account."[23]

Other methods range across the variables of the inexact science called irrigation efficiency. These include analysis of the different ways soil structure holds and transmits moisture and nutrients to plants, the different abilities among plants to acquire water from the soil, the differences in plant responses to drought stress, and different water needs of plants during the growing season. Highest transpiration and crop yields take place when the soil is kept consistently moist. "Plant transpiration is a mandatory cost."[24] The so-called harvest index includes the fraction of each individual plant that is of the most economic value to the farmer. The goal is to develop plants that produce more grain with less vegetation and plants that are less sensitive to brief periods of water stress. To these matters of soil chemistry and plant genetics are added the traditional mechanics of water conservation such as avoiding waste by controlling runoff at the end of the field, correcting tendencies to overwater, and meeting problems of evaporation, seepage, and soil erosion.

Improving on Flood Irrigation and the Center Pivot

Waste is still significant across the plains, and it is particularly evident in flood (furrow) irrigation. In one season, the old, open, unlined ditches in fine, sandy loam soil typically lost five thousand gallons of water per foot of ditch, or over twenty-one acre-feet from one-quarter mile of open ditch. The lost water could have irrigated sixty-five additional acres with a 4-inch application. By late 1989, in the Texas District No. 1, these ditches were being replaced by more than ten thousand miles of underground pipeline. With the new pipeline in place, labor costs were cut more than half, fuel efficiency doubled, and water consumption was cut by a quarter.[25] In another case, typically 20 percent of the water flooding onto a field can run off as tailwater because the farmer tries to make certain his entire field gets watered. Groundwater management districts made tailwater recycling pits a high priority. In Kansas, over twelve hundred new pits were constructed between 1978 and 1982. Another control is surge irrigation, in which special pumps cycle the flow of water by spurts and delays into furrows in order to spread the moisture in a uniform application, while avoiding waste by seepage into the ground. Texas High Plains irrigator Melvin Bentzen was told by the SCS that he needed only 3.5 inches of water to fill his soil to field capacity, but he was using 8 inches. Using a surge valve in 1982, he doubled his earlier irrigation area on 4.9 inches of water, a 15 percent increase in water-use efficiency that paid for his surge valve.[26] Laser-beam land-leveling, which reduces water costs by allowing more uniform water distribution thus eliminating dry or waterlogged spots, is a public service provided by the SCS, since equipment costs run from twenty-one thousand to fifty thousand dollars.[27] The simple act of leveling a field to a slope of 0.5 percent allows a farmer 10 percent better water-application efficiency than before leveling.[28]

Center-pivot irrigation is the proven technology that serves both development and conservation. When farmers convert from furrow irrigation to center pivot, they find they pump 20 percent less water with little difference in yields. When center-pivot irrigation first came into use, as much as 50 percent of the irrigation water was lost on hot, dry, windy days. Because the sprinklers sprayed upward and were high above the soil surface, evaporation could not be controlled. However, in recent systems sprinkler heads point downward and are positioned lower. These are called partial dropline or full dropline center-pivot sprinkler systems. Their spray covers less area but offers better control. Center pivots with partial droplines can reach 80 percent efficiency, with only 20 percent water loss because they are inherently more flexible in applying smaller amounts of water for crop and seasonal difference. Early sprinklers demanded high pressure because their circling motion was water-driven. Newer sprinklers have electric drives, and water pressure has been reduced four- to tenfold. The new Low-Energy Precision Application (LEPA) takes the use of drop tubes further, allowing efficient and uniform irrigation at less than ten pounds pressure.[29] Less pressure means that irrigators can continue to sprinkle even as their pumping declines.

Alternatives to the popular center pivots, such as trickle or drip micro-irrigation, offer 90 percent efficiency, but they are very expensive, management-intensive, and better suited to vegetables and fruits rather than large grain fields.[30] In an August 1984 interview, James Mitchell, on a 317-acre farm near Lubbock, Texas, turned to drip irrigation devices that measure out drops of water at the base of each plant. The technology was expensive, but it saved water and energy. "You can almost spoon-feed a crop with them. With those old sprinklers, on a windy day you could feel the mist a quarter of a mile away. The amount of water [and pumping costs] they wasted was just tremendous."[31] Mitchell also uses surge pumps that provide water between rows of crops in timed pulses. Wasteful runoff is avoided by machine-made furrow dikes, small mounds of dirt every few feet along irrigation rows. As a result, Mitchell's well-water levels remained nearly constant for several years.

MANAGEMENT STRATEGIES

State groundwater districts, the SCS, and farmers seek better management practices.[32] Wasteful irrigation includes full irrigation, which meant turning on the pumps and letting them run until the farmer judged that the field was saturated. Much of the water escaped below the root zone, but fields were kept constantly wet during the growing season, and the farmer felt comfortable about the safety of his crop whether rain came or not. Open ditches lose up to 30 percent per one thousand feet, meaning that an irrigator who needed to add four inches of water per acre to the plant root zone would need to pump six inches of water per acre to get the required four inches. It is still not unusual to find that half the water pumped from the Ogallala is lost through evaporation and deep percolation.[33]

A better practice, called irrigation scheduling, brought more savings but also more complexity for local farmers, who had to learn when to apply water, in what quantity, and when to shut off the pumps. One farmer reported that with scheduling, he needed only two-thirds the water on a field 50 percent larger than on a nearby unscheduled field.[34] Generally, proper timing and the application of sufficient water can increase yields 10 to 30 percent at critical stages of crop growth such as tasseling and silking, head emergence, or pod and bean development.[35] Still, most farmers still feel most confident with full (and excessive) irrigation.

For further savings, farmers can turn to limited irrigation, which provides water only at critical crop stages and pushes plants to their limits of stress and tolerance.[36] This requires relatively drought-resistant, deep-rooted, or dense-rooted crops as well as crop rotations to rotate growth periods of different crops on a single farm. A further refinement combines limited irrigation with dryland farming: the upper half of a field is fully irrigated, the middle quarter uses furrow/tailwater runoff, and the lower quarter uses natural rainfall together with any remaining runoff. With this management strategy, sorghum yields rose a third on the same amount of water. Other management strategies include alternate furrow irrigation, skip-row planting, and staggered planting dates. Both scheduling and limited irrigation indicate that farmers have been overwatering their crops for the past three decades.[37] Now the managerial ability of farmers and their willingness to change their work habits provide better results.

As water becomes more scarce, farmers are being told to sacrifice perhaps 10 percent of a field based on the argument that they will save more than they will lose because of the saved costs of energy, capital, labor, and maintenance. One such underirrigated wheat field—using so-called deficit irrigation—lost a quarter less water through evapotranspiration yet received the same net income.[38] With the saved water, farmers are told they can irrigate additional land, or in a time of scarcer water, continue to irrigate. Soil Conservation Services guidelines suggest that a field provides roughly the same net income when it is only seven-eighths irrigated.

Other management skills involve practical on-site engineering, or mechanical land treatment, which means conserving land by building tailwater recovery pits and erosion dams, terracing sloping land, and controlling for other erosion, seepage, and runoff. Runoff farming puts crops in widely spaced rows at the base of contour strips that have been treated chemically or mechanically to increase runoff. Runoff farming works well on abandoned irrigated land otherwise prone to dust and tumbleweeds.[39] Other mechanical land treatment shapes furrows by pitting, land imprinting, terracing, and the contour furrowing of the 1930s as well as the still-older deep plowing or ripping.

Conservation tillage is new, controversial, and popular.[40] Kansas leads the nation in this stubble mulch or no-till farming, in which much of the previous crop's residue is left on the field during the planting and growing season. Not only is water erosion remarkably reduced and moisture better held, evaporation can be reduced by 30 percent. Bypassing traditional cultivation also allows savings in fuel costs and labor hours, but there are new costs in weed control and pesticides. In addition, farmers who identify good farming with tidy farming have difficulty with the debris-filled fields of no-till. Clean fields look best but may not be saving water.

The objective of conservation—to use less water—also serves the profit-margin objective—to keep the farm successful—if successful crop yield is measured not only by net income, but also by acre-foot consumption of water. According to one model, if irrigation costs double it means a 20 percent reduction in net farm income, which, in turn, forces closure of low-income farms and encourages large-scale consolidation and movement toward vertical agribusiness.[41] Equally troublesome is that if higher irrigation costs push farmers into new, higher value crops, the changes can require more water, more risk, new machinery, more labor, more sophisticated management, and several years of heavy investment before the first returns. These sacrifices cause most farmers to stay with familiar field crops.

The Privatization of Water: Make the Irrigator Pay His Own Way

Today, although the long-term effects of declining aquifer levels are accepted, the water is not given a dollar value. Most consumers of High Plains groundwater still treat it as a free good, available to the first taker at no cost for the water itself.[42] It takes only fifteen dollars to pump an acre-foot using natural gas and thirty dollars using electricity. Hence this free water has been generously consumed on profligate levels. Waters laws, such as prior appropriation (use it or lose it) also counter sustainability. Pierre R. Crosson and Norman J. Rosenberg of the think tank Resources for the Future write that "markets are not well equipped to protect resources such as water . . . in which it is difficult to establish property rights."[43] An imperfect first step is not to try to change agriculture, but to broaden economic analysis to include environmental costs. One controversial solution, more applicable elsewhere in the West than on the plains, is privatization of water, remembering that in Kansas, Oklahoma, and Texas groundwater is by law a state-controlled public resource.[44] The economic, political, and societal climate of the 1980 has encouraged such efforts.

There is an old irrigationist maxim: "Water flows uphill to money." The privatization argument is that the nation's farmers are wasteful and extravagant with their water consumption because it costs so little. They also have first right to waste it—the policy of prior appropriation. True conservation, it is argued, would take place when water is separated from land ownership and allowed to float on an open market: "Water will start reflecting its true price."[45] On the High Plains there is little competition for Ogallala water from new cities, as in Arizona, although Mobil Oil's use of water for oil recovery is not the only such case in Oklahoma or elsewhere.

The objective of privatization is to measure a water resource entirely according to its price on current markets.[46] In California, Arizona, and central Colorado, for example, water from federal reclamation projects that sells to farmers for ten dollars an acre-foot could be marketed to a growing retirement city for more than one thousand dollars per acre-foot. Regions with extra water—not being currently consumed—could sell and ship it elsewhere. This is the argument behind shipping water from the Great Lakes to the plains or from the water-rich Sand Hills of western Nebraska to parched regions elsewhere on the plains. In August 1984 the San Diego (California) County Water Authority paid ten thousand dollars for the option to buy Yampa (Colorado) River water from the local water conservation district.

271

The option fell through, but San Diego would have picked up the water out of the Colorado River through southern California's system of canals.

Privatization creates enormous pressures to abandon the long history of water's nonmarket function based on a water ethic. As early as 1937 the Oklahoma Supreme Court decided water use must be controlled by beneficial use and greatest need for the sake of agricultural stability set by safe annual yield. In the American West, water costs have been set extremely low to support the farmer, in perpetuity a low-cost, high-consumption consumer. In turn, the farmer's privilege is based on the externality that he sells his crops well below real water cost (particularly if all factors, including an ecological deflator, are included) to guarantee traditionally low food prices for the consumer.[47]

The ability of farmers to pay high prices for water as required by privatization is yet to be demonstrated. Under ideal conditions they can be much more efficient, from less than 40 percent for flood irrigation to more than 75 percent with scheduled sprinkling. Drip irrigation offers as much as 90 percent efficiency, but an underground version being tested on the plains costs at least $15,000 per forty acres. California and Arizona farmers admit that their federally subsidized $5 to $10 an acre-foot is relatively inexpensive water and that they can tolerate new $17 rates, but they would have to shut down at the $55 predicted for 1994. As perennially low-cost users, farmers have little flexibility to absorb higher water prices. A peak agricultural use price of approximately $70 an acre-foot (in 1977 dollars) is often compared to urban pricing as high as $2,500 per acre-foot. The U.S. Army Corps of Engineers claims farmers could afford $120 an acre-foot, yet its own calculations for a major High Plains water-importing project from the Mississippi and Missouri rivers range from $320 to $880 per acre-foot.[48]

Farmers' headroom to absorb high water prices is constrained by food prices acceptable to the American consumer and world markets. When water levels eventually drop below economical pumping levels, one estimate is that grain prices for feed or food would rise 10 percent annually and meat prices 20 percent annually.[49] Would the public pay ten dollars (1977 dollars) for a loaf of bread or forty dollars for a pound of steak to allow the farmer to buy irrigation water at competitive water prices? Cheap water has always buffered other farming costs to keep food prices low. This is water's historic "duty" throughout the nation. No wonder plains farmers have zealously guarded their individual access to water under their land with their own wells, pumps, and irrigation systems.

This argument for water conservation and management on the basis of the efficiency of market prices has been rejected by those who insist that other, different, forces also affect natural resources. Policy analyst Mark Sagoff, for example, believes that the measurement of resources by the marketplace alone—who is willing to pay the most—ignores the historic and powerful American tradition of public interest. Efficiency is not the only guiding force; Americans do not put a dollar value on the Bill of Rights or protecting wilderness or even the 1985 farm bill's aid to private farmers. Americans, Sagoff and others argue, see themselves not only as private consumers but also as members of a larger community that supports environmental protection and public welfare aside from cost-benefit analysis.[50] According to this antiprivatization, antimarketplace argument, the ethical duty of water as a low-cost free good for farmers is not an externality or secondary matter but a direct social or cultural priority reflected in public policy. Water may run uphill to money, but it also flows steadily and strongly toward the national interest. Sagoff concludes that although public policy (government) is expected to stay neutral toward individual freedoms, it is also expected to serve a national good (protecting natural resources, such as air and water) for the sake of the nation's well-being. State water laws and groundwater management districts are based on the protection of the public interest. The Stone case in Kansas and the Mobil Oil case in Oklahoma are examples of the privatization debate.

Individual farmers and local conservation boards cannot include the true cost of water in their economic balance sheets without immediately reporting devastating losses. As a result, the free-goods equation is being reversed; groundwater irrigation can be sustained only by increasing the costs of capital (energy costs), equipment (drip irrigation), and management skills (labor). By using more efficient equipment and better management, Texas High Plains farmers reduced their average water use by half (from 1.38 acre-feet per acre in 1977 to 0.68 in 1990) while crop yields rose, a net increase in efficiency.[51] But other forces control the irrigator's future; actual declines of water levels are still inevitable, which means that proportionally higher pumping costs will take a bigger bite out of low farm income. In the 1960s, natural gas cost $6.07 to lift an acre-foot of water 250 feet; by the 1980s the new gas cost was as high as $36.49 per-acre foot. Electricity cost seven times more than it did in the 1960s, as did liquefied petroleum gas, or LPG, while diesel fuel was three to five times more.[52] These rising expenses can be balanced temporarily with successful waste reduction and a better ratio between water use and crop yield. Hence, according to today's equation, conservation of water does not make the farmer's pockets jingle with extra cash.

Importing Outside Water

Why not bring more water to the plains instead of devising costly ways to conserve water? The historical record is not good. Nineteenth-century frontier farmers believed in the myth that rain follows the plow. They chased the unusual rains of 1878–86, and as a result they failed, starved, and lost their farms. Dependence on surface water in the Arkansas River as it ran past Garden City, Kansas, proved wrong, and the underflow proved confusing. In the twentieth century, cloud seeding is more scientific but its potential is unclear.[53] Nor have attempts at artificial recharge to rebuild the aquifer brought any significant change in the rate at which the water is running out. Texas District No. 1 is experimenting with air injection, which, like water-infusion secondary recovery in old oil fields, would seek out leftover unpumped water. Where the Ogallala sand and gravel waters have a clay lid, air pressure conceivably could drive water up and out through wells at the cost of fifty dollars per acre-foot. At present, this is too costly.[54] This capillary water (so called because it is held by surface tension on sand and gravel) may be as much as 25 percent of the total; the Texas High Plains might have 840 million acre-feet of capillary water that would otherwise be unreachable. Other water-recovery plans, such as the use of surfactants, heat, vibration, and osmosis, were rejected as costing three thousand dollars an acre-foot or more.

Several projects have been proposed to import outside water from abundant sources, such as the Canadian Rockies or the Great Lakes. The border which divides the plains and the Rockies between Canada and the United States is a political line, not an environmental or geographical border. Vast quantities of surface water in Canada, mostly stored in year-round glaciers and snowfields, together with torrential high-mountain rivers renewed each snowy winter, could meet and surpass all conceivable agricultural needs on the central and southern plains.

This tantalizing resource, a thousand miles distant and in the hands of another albeit friendly nation, tempts the American predilection toward large-scale technological solutions. The first such plan came surprisingly early: Eli Newsom, speaking in 1896 before the newly formed Nebraska State Irrigation Association, outlined an irrigation plan which was ambitious but not outlandish. Everyone knows, he said, of the vast and inexhaustible supply of underground water topped by the Great Plains. This underflow was a massive body of water from the Rocky Mountains, or perhaps from the Arctic, that could instead be channeled to huge underground reservoirs controlled by lateral tunnels. Fed by gravity, discharge tunnels would direct the water to centralized surface outlets from which large agricultural regions could be irrigated. Newsom, a former immigration booster for the Santa Fe Railroad, concluded that the lack of pumping technology could thus be effectively overcome: "Today we find the pump too limited and too expensive, too uncertain and troublesome, to practically serve the increased demand of the practical irrigator. . . . *Throw the old pump away* and substitute nature's forces. Gravity . . . like charity, never faileth."[55] Newsom believed he would become "the Elias Howe of the Irrigation Methods," but he did not have a George Washington Goethals to engineer the project or the backing of a Theodore Roosevelt for the venture; if his geology had not been so wrong, his plan might have been as technologically feasible and as demanding as the Panama Canal.

Seventy years later, two plans stayed within the nation's political borders. The 1968 Texas Water Plan sought to divert 5.8 million acre-feet a year to the water-starved southern High Plains from the abundant supplies of the lower

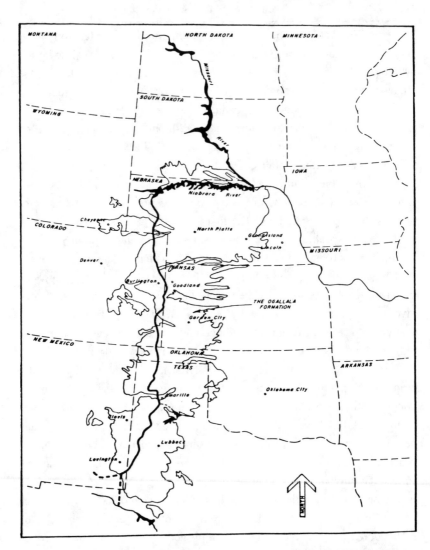

15. The 1967 Beck plan for rerouting Ogallala water. It was presented by R. W. Beck and Associates, consulting engineers, and sought to transfer water internally across the High Plains, most notably by reversing the flow of the Niobrara River in northern Nebraska. But the plan encountered major deterrents, particularly rising energy costs, environmental-impact statements, upper Missouri River navigation problems, political questions, and, above all, construction costs. From Morton W. Bittinger and Elizabeth B. Green, *You Never Miss the Water Till . . . (The Ogallala Story)* (Littleton, Colo.: Water Resources Publications, 1980), 95, with permission of Resource Consultants, Inc.

Mississippi River by means of fourteen hundred miles of canals and seventy-one pumping stations. Construction was scheduled for 1977 through 1985, but rising energy costs—more than fifty billion kilowatt-hours of electricity would be needed each year to pump and raise the water—ended this dream.[56] More ambitious was R. W. Beck's 1967 plan to divert water from the upper reaches of the Missouri River in the Dakotas by reversing the course of the Niobrara River in northern Nebraska.[57] Between 9 and 15 million acre-feet would be lifted upstream to the head of a large canal in western Nebraska and the water would be channelized to flow by gravity south into the parched central and southern High Plains. Once again the plan foundered on rising energy costs and environmental impacts, as well as concern for commercial transportation on the lower Missouri.

The 1975 Rocky Mountain plan of consulting engineer William G. Dunn would take water from Canadian mountain rivers—the Peace, Athabasca, Smoky, and Mackenzie—and from upper tributaries of the Columbia River, and run it through Alberta rivers and the upper Yellowstone, Missouri, and Snake rivers. In 1977 the cost of the project, including hydroelectric facilities, was estimated between forty and fifty billion dollars. Several large reservoirs in Montana would hold nearly one hundred million acre-feet of water and distribute twelve to twenty-five million acre-feet a year through 5,850 miles of aqueducts onto the plains.[58] Similar was U.S Bureau of Reclamation engineer Lewis G. Smith's plan to tap Mackenzie River water rather than the Yukon River.[59] Water intended for the High Plains would be stored in a massive reservoir at seven thousand feet in the Centennial Valley of southwestern Montana. In 1968 cost estimates were twelve billion dollars for delivery of forty million acre-feet annually.

The most remarkable plan appeared in the 1960s: the North American Water and Power Alliance (NAWAPA) project to import "excess" water from western Canada not only to the central and southern plains but to other chronically parched regions of the United States. Another project of engineering consultants, the massive plan was attractive to a citizenry that also supported a successful multibillion dollar National Aeronautics and Space Administration moon-landing program, nationwide Great Society bureaucracies, and assurances of both guns and butter during the Vietnam War.

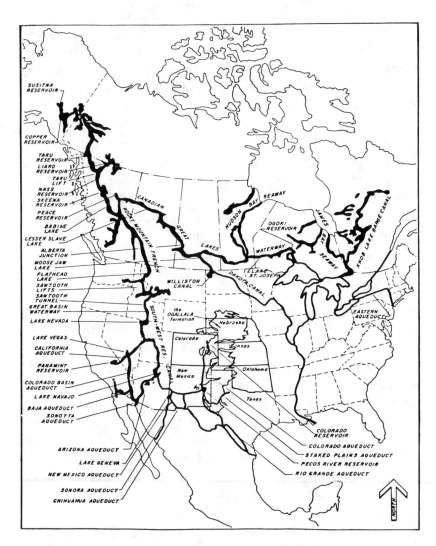

16. The 1965 NAWAPA water-transfer plan. The most ambitious water-import plan was the North American Water and Power Alliance proposal from a California-based international consulting engineering firm, the Ralph M. Parsons Company, to bring water across the entire continent from Canada into the United States and down to Mexico. NAWAPA ran into grave environmental, political, diplomatic, and economic problems. Costs doubled and tripled from the original estimate of one hundred billion dollars in 1964. From Bittinger and Green, *You Never Miss the Water*, 98, with permission of Resource Consultants, Inc.

Senator Frank Church of Idaho expressed the opinion of many regional advocates: "We must not be deterred by its size. To perform the task before us, we may well need a program as far-sighted as was the Louisiana Purchase."[60] Under the plan, 158 million acre-feet of water would be diverted south each year from water-rich western Canada (estimated to provide 633 million acre-feet to rivers that flow to the oceans) primarily through canals in the reconstructed valleys of the Rocky Mountains (the Rocky Mountain Trench, combining the upper reaches of the Peace, Fraser, Columbia, and Kootenay river valleys). This is the equivalent, said Colorado water resource expert Morton W. Bittinger, of 125 percent of the annual flow of the Mississippi River at St. Louis. At least 80 million acre-feet (the rest going to Canada and Mexico) would go to the western United States, including the High Plains, by way of new aqueducts: the Colorado and the Staked Plains. Opponents were dismayed by the environmental, economic, and political problems. Estimated costs rose from $100 billion in 1964 to $200 billion in 1977 to $300 billion in 1982, roughly equivalent in each case to the annual defense budget of the United States but presumably spread over thirty years. The pressures of drought in the early 1970s encouraged support, but the energy crisis and rising fuel costs after 1973 dampened interest.

These spectacular plans ran aground on rising energy costs, growing environmental concern, and changing public sentiment toward large reclamation projects. All of them beggared the three-billion-dollar Central Arizona Project, which was belatedly completed in 1990 despite high costs, delays, and protests. USDA water policy official Herman Bouwer observed that when "water runs uphill to money . . . [it] does not bode well for agriculture, which traditionally is accustomed to inexpensive water for irrigation."[61] He noted that all large water transfer schemes involve capital costs of several thousand dollars per acre-foot per year. An existing project like the Central Arizona Project is costing $2,000 per acre-foot per year, discounted by subsidies that give farmers $52 per acre-foot; the California Aqueduct runs about $100 per acre-foot. Bouwer argued instead for better conservation of existing water.

A changing national mood, weary of costly pork-barrel projects and sus-

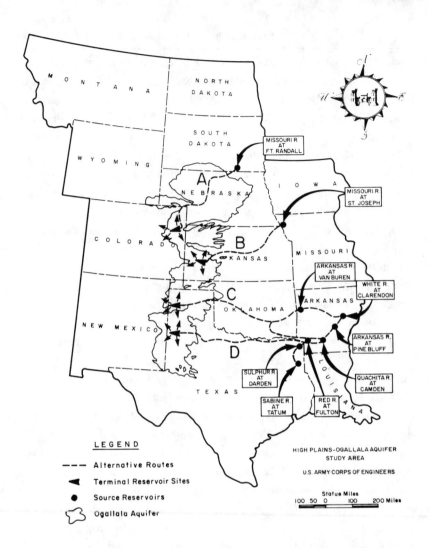

17. Interstate water-transfer route alternatives from the 1982 U.S. Army Corps of Engineers plan. A primary mission of the *Six-States High Plains–Ogallala Aquifer Regional Resources Study*, written in 1982 by three consulting firms for the U.S. Department of Commerce and the High Plains Study Council, was to identify new sources of water to replace the depleted Ogallala Aquifer. The map identifies potential alternate routes of supply from the Mississippi River. Serious difficulties included financing, environmental effects, politics, and the cost to High Plains irrigators. From *Summary Report: Six-State High Plains–Ogallala Aquifer Regional Resources Study* (Austin, Tex.: High Plains Associates, 1982), 71.

picious of a ballooning federal deficit, did not prohibit the six-million-dollar 1982 Six-State High Plains Ogallala Aquifer Regional Resource Study ordered by Congress and sublet by the United States Department of Commerce to private consultants. It was not the first federal water study, of course, but it was the first to pay significant attention to the long-ignored Ogallala. In 1950, President Truman's Water Resources Policy Commission barely recognized the High Plains when it considered groundwater in only ten pages of a two-thousand page report.[62] In 1955 President Eisenhower's Advisory Committee on Water Resources briefly reported that regulation and management of groundwater belonged to the states; acknowledging wastefully high consumption, it recommended further study.[63] This was followed in 1959 by a Senate committee that held twenty-five public hearings (none on the High Plains) and barely mentioned Ogallala aquifer draindown. Much more ambitious was the 1968 National Water Commission, which conducted a five-year, five-million-dollar study but gave only 5 pages to groundwater mining on the High Plains in its 537-page report. The commission admitted that major consumption problems had national implications but concluded that groundwater management belonged to the states and local agencies.

A background paper for the 1968 commission forecast that the federal government could be called upon for "costly rescue projects" when water levels ran low in critical regions. The author proposed legislation to encourage conservation. Such a costly rescue was used as a threat in 1977 when President Carter's secretary of the interior, Cecil Andrus, noted that "groundwater overdraft situations [based on] unwise resource practice" could bring unpopular federal interventions. The states, Andrus argued, need "to bring laws, rules, and institutions governing water into the 20th century [or] the Federal government will . . . step in and another area of state prerogatives will be lost."[64]

A Carter task force concluded in 1978 that federal farm supports "may be contributing directly to shortages of underground water reserves." An editorial in the *Southwest Kansas Irrigator* (Ulysses) quickly headlined: "Carter Task Force Fears Farming May Be Too Profitable."[65] A 1979 Carter task force recommended: reduce federal actions contributing to groundwater depletion, provide federal remedies for groundwater depletion, and work with the states to develop consistent groundwater management programs. A March 1979 editorial in the Texas High Plains Underground Water Conservation District No. 1 newsletter, *The Cross Section*, quickly retorted that "the National Water Policy with respect to groundwater appears to be tied to some mystique of conservation, translated to mean 'cut back,' 'control pumping,' 'regulate.'"[66]

It was in this suspicious climate, based on apprehension over Ogallala water losses and fears of heavy-handed federal intervention, that the Department of Commerce study started. It also began in an era that feared for American and world food supplies based on a widespread belief that most of the nation's and the world's agricultural lands were already under full production.[67] An outside water resource to relieve depletion (and avoid a return to less-productive dryland farming) on the High Plains seemed to be an appropriate response to the perceived crisis (which faded away in the 1980s). Water-policy analyst Morton W. Bittinger concluded in 1980 that "if a large importation project is going to be tackled, it is time to get started." The time required even to design and construct a NAWAPA or Smith project could be 10 or 20 years (akin to the construction history of a typical U.S. nuclear power plant). Adding in the time required to solve the financial, political, social, and environmental problems could mean 30 to 50 years before delivery of water.[68]

The six-million-dollar High Plains Study (as it was commonly called) began in 1978 and was published in 1982 under contract from the Department of Commerce to the consulting firms of Camp Dresser; McKee, Black and Veatch; and Arthur D. Little. It was the first to set High Plains agriculture (and Ogallala groundwater) into a broader economic and political framework. The congressional legislation creating the High Plains Study (Public Law 94–587, Section 193) stated: "In order to assure an adequate supply of food to the Nation, and to promote economic vitality of the High Plains Region, the Secretary of Commerce . . . is authorized and directed to study the depletion of the natural resources of those regions . . . presently utilizing the declining water resources of the Ogallala aquifer, and to develop plans, to increase water supplies in the area and report thereon to Congress."[69] Using 1974 data, it reported that on the High Plains 1 percent of the nation's people living on 6 percent of the nation's land area produced over 15 percent of the nation's wheat, corn, sorghum, and (in Texas) cotton and 38 percent of its livestock. It identified 150,000 irrigation wells that served 14.3 million acres in 1980, compared to 3.5 million acres in 1950. Another 18.3 million acres were in dryland farming and another 18 million acres in dryland grazing and fallow land. It estimated that Ogallala groundwater totaled 3.05 billion acre-feet in 1974, 77 percent of it in Nebraska. Eight percent was in Kansas, 2 percent in Oklahoma, and 9 percent in Texas. This water was being consumed at the rate of 22.14 million acre-feet annually despite better efficiency that had reduced per-acre water use 30 percent, from 2 acre-feet to 1.4 acre feet. The water optimistically concluded that about 23 percent of the existing aquifer water would not be consumed until 2020, but the remaining water would be largely inaccessible or too costly to pump.

The study seemed predisposed, with little supporting evidence, to portray the agricultural future of the High Plains in the most favorable terms possible, including the creation of 350,000 new jobs by 2020 on top of the 1,000,000 jobs of 1977.[70] The study asserted that the High Plains deserved priority attention over other regions. It had "large quantities of flat, productive agricultural land which is amenable to mechanized production of fiber, grain, and livestock commodities of significant importance in national and international markets. The area has deposits of oil and gas, which are finite in quantity, and deposits of ground water which receive . . . very little recharge in the southern parts of the Region."[71] The report noted that rainfall is inadequate in both quantity and seasonal reliability "to realize the potential productive capacity of the area's land resources." Acceptable levels of food production depend on irrigation; without irrigation it would fall to a third or quarter that of irrigated yields. Considerably more than half of the southwest Kansas and Oklahoma-Texas Panhandle water would be consumed, the rest of lower quality and less accessible at deeper levels.[72] Yet the study predicted that by 2020 an additional 3,800,000 acres would come under irrigation in the region served by the aquifer. Contrarily, it stated that "even with the most effective water conservation program possible, over five million acres currently irrigated will be returned to dryland production or native vegetation by the year 2020 because of declining water supplies.''

The study is flawed. Its basic division between northern Ogallala and southern Ogallala at the Kansas-Oklahoma line does not make geohydrological, agricultural, or economic sense. A 1977 USGS Ogallala study plan was more appropriate:

> The High Plains is divided into four roughly equal segments by the valleys of the major rivers that cross the High Plains from the Rocky Mountains. The streams that divide the Ogallala Formation into major segments are the Platte and the South Platte Rivers, the Arkansas River, and the Canadian River. These rivers flow through valleys 1 to 10 miles wide. The Platte and Arkansas Rivers are incised 100 to 300 feet below the High Plains. In contrast, the Canadian River has incised its valley nearly 1,000 feet. These major streams act as lines along which natural discharge from the Ogallala aquifer occurs.[73]

The report is widely optimistic about increased irrigation potential, future grain yields, energy alternatives, agribusiness fixes, and outside water sources, among other factors. Corn production is projected to double between 1977 and 2020; instead, corn is declining as a major crop on the High Plains because of its heavy water demands. In Kansas alone, wheat production is projected nearly double between 1977 and 2020.[74] Donald Worster has also observed that the study concluded that a return to dryland farming would be supported by significantly higher commodity prices on world markets. ''Yet,'' Worster states, ''the bushel price of wheat *today* (1991) is no higher than it was in the 1950s!''[75] The study also favors large-scale expansion of vertically integrated cattle-feedlot operations; these are extremely sensitive to water supplies. The study pays little attention to a still-declining number of farms or to the inevitable rise in the cost of irrigation retrofitting and the burdensome debt left over from the more prosperous 1970s.[76]

The study makes an innovative contribution by recognizing the connections linking High Plains water resources to commodity prices, energy costs, interest rates, inflation rates, and export markets. "A collapse in the export market would have a more significant effect on the economy of the High Plains Region more likely variations from the projected levels of energy price, agricultural productivity, or domestic economic growth." Its recommendations cover four major interacting forces affecting food production on the High Plains: water resources, market forces, production technology, and societal institutions. Particular attention is given to which forces are prone to change, which forces can be reasonably managed, and which forces are beyond reasonable control. Emphasis is placed on the "production enterprise management" of agribusiness, including the supply of capital, technological fixes, and the role of regulatory agencies.[77] The study also recognizes the all-important connections with local oil and gas production and feedlot and meat-processing operations.

Predisposed to the continued growth of High Plains agriculture along its current high-yield, high-water-consumption pattern, the study breaks no new ground in the answers it offers.[78] It supports current thinking that irrigation will continue into the known future as the only workable substitute for the water-poor High Plains climate. The plan identifies four basic methods to achieve the goals ordered by Congress: improving irrigation efficiency, restricting groundwater use, increasing the region's water supply, and establishing a broader economic base for the region.[79] "For the near term, it appears that a major commitment to water conservation should be made, since many desirable results of water conservation can be realized relatively quickly and at relatively low cost. Both public and private activities are needed." The study gives considerable attention to voluntary or mandatory conservation methods, most of which are already providing significant improvements in water-use efficiency. The study warned that continued high Ogallala water withdrawals "could result in economic failure of irrigation in the near future, with devastating results to the region." It also stated that "regulation of ground water withdrawal is a state responsibility."[80]

The most controversial recommendation of the High Plains Study supported future imports of water from outside the region. While the study ignores the grandiose N A W A P A plan, it does explore the feasibility of importing water in four possible ways from the Missouri or Mississippi rivers. But the study acknowledged that water costs would be prohibitively high. If farmers can ill afford $70 to $120 per acre-foot in 1977 dollars, then the transfer costs of Route B (from the lower Missouri at Saint Joseph to west-central Kansas) from $226 per acre-foot to $569 per acre-foot and of Route C (from the Mississippi River in Arkansas to the Texas High Plains) make outside-water costs prohibitive. These costs do not include distributing water to individual farms from the pipeline terminals. A 1978 Bureau of Reclamation study for Oklahoma estimated that recovery of construction costs (capital costs) alone to move water from the Mississippi directly to individual farms (farm headgates) would require a total of $2,150 per acre supplied.[81] The study does not include expensive subsidies (as in existing reclamation projects west of the Rockies) or substantially higher consumer food prices as a means to pay for imported water. Construction time was estimated optimistically at ten to fifteen years. Its final recommendations in December 1982 were not optimistic: "It was not possible to conclude that major multistate conveyance systems will be financially feasible in the foreseeable future; importation costs would be quite high in relation to ability of water users to pay for imported water."[82]

New Dryland Farming: Better Than Abandoning the Land

Caught in an iron triangle between declining Ogallala water levels, low commodity prices, and rising costs, a few plains irrigators have already become plains dryland farmers. Forced into retreat they felt defeat, but it is not the dryland farming their grandfathers knew. It is a more sophisticated, more complex enterprise using new methods combined with hard labor and the intuitive experience of mature farmers.[83] Nevertheless, the dryland farmer reverts back from dependable irrigation to luck with the weather: the right rain at the right time. If the prospects are not favorable, no crop is planted and the field is left fallow for better water conditions. One newer dryland management practice is flexible cropping, in which a crop is planted only if carefully measured stored soil water and expected rainfall promise a satisfactory yield.[84] Winter wheat, for example, is difficult for flexible cropping because it is planted in the fall before most water is accumulated. Dryland farming is daunting, but the alternative may be abandonment of the plains.

New dryland farming can also involve altering the microclimate conditions of growing plants. Microclimate technology is often simply a modern way of describing the windbreaks and shelterbelts successfully advocated and installed in the late 1930s. Cold winds in spring and fall can physically damage plants, while freezing damages plant tissues. Arid winds put plants under severe moisture stress that brings wilting, desiccation, and poor production. The same winds erode the soil and sandblast young plants. Postwar fencerow-to-fencerow planting brought down the successful tree windbreaks planted in the 1930s. Since then, farmers have begrudged field space to windbreaks. Shelterbelts also interfered with the mechanical operation of large center-pivot sprinkling systems.[85] Successful in-field windbreak experiments have included double rows of corn sheltering irrigated sugar beets or, with irrigated sorghum, ryegrass.[86]

Most new dryland farmers do practice some limited irrigation. As plains farmers move away from water-sensitive crops, such as corn and soybeans, and toward more sorghums and wheat, crop rotation can involve the cycle of irrigation-fallow-dryland. One management practice is the above-mentioned limited irrigation-dryland system, in which the upper half of a field is fully irrigated, the next one-quarter is a tailwater-runoff section using runoff from the fully irrigated section, and the lower quarter is managed as a dryland section dependent on rainfall only for its water. On the Texas High Plains this system offers high water-use efficiency compared to full or conventional irrigation.[87]

One proven practice rubs the good farmer wrong; he takes pride in his weed-free and stubble-free clean fields, the historic sign of his industry and virtue. Conservation tillage, also mentioned earlier, uses crop residues as soil cover; whatever is not worth harvesting is not cleaned away but left on the fields. This no-till or low-till farming leaves the field surface rough, holds water in place, reduces evaporation, controls wind and water erosion, and increases organic matter in the soil. The goal is to capture rainfall and hold it in storage in the soil;[88] in addition, soil erosion is reduced—cut to one-third in Nebraska tests. Energy costs and the work put into cultivation also go down. Results are enviable. In dryland wheat, conventional tillage in the 1930s and 1940s yielded no more than seventeen bushels per acre while stubble mulch and minimum tillage in the 1960s and 1970s produced over thirty-two bushels an acre, and there are predictions with improved no-till yielding forty bushels per acre. Sorghums rose 50 percent from 2,190 pounds per acre to 3,150 pounds.[89]

No-till production has its costs. No-till wheat yields change enormously from year to year, depending on annual rainfall. Yields are much higher in good years and much lower in bad years than conventionally tilled and irrigated wheat. It is also harder to seed crops into heavy stubble, with 10 to 30 percent less production than on conventional fields. Most controversial is the abundance of weeds and insects and the harboring of potential plant disease in crop residues. This paradoxically demands heavy herbicide and pesticide application on low-till or no-till fields, which Wes Jackson vividly has called "chemotherapy on the land."[90] His view is reinforced by agricultural scientist David Pimentel, who notes that insects' ability to develop resistance to every new pesticide has meant an actual rise in crop losses because of the risks of monoculture. If farmers cut their use of chemical pesticides in half and rotated their crops with biological pest control, food prices would rise less than 1 percent.[91] Intensive use of herbicides not only raises costs significantly but in too many cases makes fine-textured soils under chemical fallow (weed control with herbicides) too hard to seed.[92] Unsolved problems include uneven seed germination, low soil temperature in spring, and environmental pollution by the heavy use of chemicals. Nevertheless, no-till is one of the few regional substitutes when the water disappears.

Arguments against dryland farming may still be persuasive. According to a cautious 1982 federal study, if the high point of irrigation was the late 1970s and early 1980s, the gradual transition to dryland farming since then could reduce gross farm income to half the irrigated levels.[93] Part of a decline is also psychological, since family farms and small towns, still admired as the bearers of basic American values but sensitive to agricultural decline, would be first to weaken and disappear. A region's institutions and communities can only go so far in adapting to water scarcity.[94] Rural communities would experience the ripple effect of weakness in farming. Banks would quickly be affected by defaults by farm borrowers. Lack of credit for less-efficient or more highly leveraged farms would force them to cease operations. Support businesses, from equipment suppliers to the local Wal-Mart discount store to doctors and lawyers to filling stations and local newspapers, would lose their "critical mass" for successful operation.[95] Without competition, prices go up before the lone remaining business shuts down. Schools, government, churches, and services weaken and roads and bridges and utilities suffer. Younger community leaders leave farm and town, and for the older leaders, malaise and defeatism often defeat efforts at stabilization or recovery. Farmer know-how, including the subtle and arcane skills of successfully planting, cultivating, and harvesting 640 acres of High Plains crops, can disappear forever when it skips a farm-family generation. First the satisfaction of a skill is lost, then a career, and finally work as meaning for life. Texas sociologists Albert and Ruth Schaffer conclude: "If a drought should persist for several years, many farm communities will cease to exist."[96]

Alternative Crops: Keith Allen's Experiment

With the threat of failure, whether from declining groundwater, dryland farming, or the swath of social effects, the farmers' search for high-value alternative crops may accelerate. Wheat and sorghums have never been truly adapted to extended dryness and prosper best under irrigation, while corn and alfalfa have always been unlikely crops for the High Plains. Those scientists and farmers who work under the conventional wisdom of highest possible productivity search for new plants, mostly native to arid regions in the United States and Mexico, that can be adapted to environmental stress and provide a marketable product. In 1978 the National Science Foundation identified fifty-four such potential crops.[97]

One farmer who is trying alternative crops lives in Haskell County, Kansas, where farmers are reputed to be more risk taking and innovative and less committed to a single piece of worn-down land on short water rations.[98] Keith Allen is in his early thirties, of medium height, has a wiry build, and

sports a sandy mustache. Like every farmer in the area, he wears the ubiquitous adjustable cloth cap with a slogan or seed or implement company name
in front above the bill. The cap is worn indoors and out, sitting or standing or
riding. He farms seventeen miles north of Sublette.[99] Meeting with him for a
double-cheeseburger lunch in the town's Pheasant Inn (it also offers a small
salad bar), Allen gives a double impression: the idealistic farmer-irrigator
who sees a bountiful future in profitable alternative crops and the wary entre-
preneur who is already a product-testing consultant to feed companies to
guarantee that he gets in on the ground floor of any new food-production developments in the region. His fields are test acreages for alternative crops.
He rents his farmland, but his father and uncle own considerable acreages
and he hopes to follow in their stead.

The difference is that Keith Allen has a degree in agronomy from Kansas
State University and has chosen to specialize in alternative crops. He is still
rare, but not alone. Kansans already have advocacy in alternative crops at
the nationally known Land Institute, led by Wes Jackson, and the Kansas
Rural Center, a broad-based public-interest group. Keith Allen himself established the aggressive High Plains Growers Association. As energy costs
to pump the Ogallala went higher, he concluded that he needed to generate
three times the cash per acre compared to the region's conventional crops.
If natural gas rose to $1.70, he would shift from water-intensive corn to milo.
If it went up to $2.80, he would use half the water for a limited milo crop. If
natural gas went up to $10.00, he would have to abandon existing production
and turn to alternative crops, such as canola (rapeseed), provided that a market had developed.

Other alternative crops are guar, which is similar to soybeans but produces a resin, and sunflowers, which can yield 80 percent more in Kansas
than in the better-known sunflower region of North Dakota. But Gary Baker
of District No. 3 in Garden City observed that farmers would need to get
twenty cents a pound for sunflowers instead of today's ten to twelve cents.
Nevertheless, Jeff Schmidt of the Soil Conservation Service in Liberal noted
that while in 1987 there were only four hundred acres of sunflowers in his region, this doubled in 1988 and he was bullish about the future.[100] As for new,

improved versions of existing crops, wheat can yield more valuable gluten, and grain sorghums (milo) are more profitable as a source of ethanol. In the past southwest Kansas farmers also have raised sugar beets (around heavily irrigated Garden City), highly profitable popcorn, and even watermelons and tomatoes. Baker also wondered about the introduction of beans—pinto, lima, great northern—but Schmidt noted that a drip irrigation installation for vegetables costs fifteen thousand dollars for 40 acres. Keith Allen and others have not yet felt the pressure to turn to gopher weed, kenaf, or Jerusalem artichokes, which require little or no irrigation water. With efficient and intensive drip irrigation for a variety of vegetables, he has concluded that farmer cooperatives can succeed where individual farmers could not, either on extensive dryland farming or with costly irrigation. There are successful historic precedents among cooperatives in Colorado and Nebraska.

As water costs rise and water supplies become scarcer, there will be more Keith Allens, not only among the adventuresome farmers of Haskell County but throughout the old Dust Bowl region. They cannot change the water and land, nor do they have the power to raise grain prices. The future of generous government supports is in doubt, so their options are limited. One answer is several new field crops that are less water intensive, but the right crop must include a combination of successful production, the creation of a marketing infrastructure, and willing consumers. On the farm, alternative crops would demand reeducation for weed, insect, and disease control, appropriate tillage, fertilizer and irrigation practices, use of pesticides, and new investment in equipment. New management would require new understanding of yield levels, per-acre net returns, and marketing to buyers and processors.[101]

High Plains farmers have historically produced food for humans or animals. They speak of their positive service to society: feeding the nation and the world. But this may be disrupted when they feel compelled to grow nonfood crops as the only means of survival. Guayule is a native perennial plant of the southwest United States and north-central Mexico; it produces rubber and does it best when less than twenty-five inches of water is applied. An advantage for the plains climate is that guayule prospers in a wide temperature range up to 120 degrees Fahrenheit, but a major disadvantage lies in its fail-

ure and death at the freezing temperatures that also hit the plains. As is true
with most new plants, processing operations and commercial guayule production do not exist. Another connection with rubber is in the annual plant
crambe, which produces plant oil with a high erucic acid content; it can be
used for rubber additives. Crambe is a cool-season crop requiring significant
irrigation, but profit per acre could be much higher than it is for today's High
Plains crops. Today's harvesting technologies, however, still damage mature seeds and the rubber-additive market is very competitive. The combination of guayule and crambe might see a tire factory outside Garden City instead of IBP.

Slightly better known is jojoba, a perennial shrub from the same region. It
produces oilseeds about the size of an olive with 50 percent oil by weight. It
requires as little as five inches of water a year for survival, but irrigation allows faster growth with bigger plants. Again, jojoba is not a food; the oil can
go into detergents and is the only known source of unsaturated liquid wax
other than sperm-whale oil. The same commercial-production questions remain. Only vertically integrated operations are likely to succeed, linking
growing crops through seed-crushing facilities to marketing. If plains
farmers find it necessary to grow an alternative food, the seeds of buffalo
gourd yield a protein oil similar to corn oil, and the meal product can be used
as an animal feed. It is another perennial plant, in this case a spreading fruit
vine from the North American West needing only twelve inches of rain.
Year-round cattle forage—sainfoin, a perennial legume; alfalfa; and some
wheat grasses—is being investigated by Texas researchers.[102]

Wes Jackson's Land Institute at Salina

The introduction of perennials instead of annuals has attracted the interest of
the innovative Land Institute at Salina; it has experimental test fields for alternative crops. One is leymus, a ubiquitous temperate-zone grain-produc-
ing grass long known by gathering peoples since the Vikings, American Indians, and Russians. Once used for roof thatch and basket making, it can be
woven into mats and natural rope; it is also a forage crop and can be harvested for hay or silage. Historically, leymus also served as human food in

Central Asia in times of drought when conventional crops withered and died. It has received more attention recently because its protein content rivals that of red beans and its fatty-acid percentage surpasses all other seed grains, including amaranth, wheat, high-protein corn, rice, and oats. In fields its perennialism reduces erosion and cultivation efforts, and it works in a polycultural system. On a Land Institute field, it yielded over eight hundred pounds per acre, about half of a wheat yield on the same plot.[103]

The institute is also experimenting with native prairie vegetation, such as the common animal forage eastern gama grass, which produces the same per-acre yield as did early corn five thousand years ago. The primary goal of the institute is "to develop an agroecosystem that reflects more the attributes of climax prairie than do conventional agricultural systems based on annual grain crops"[104] in order to identify crops for sustainable agriculture. "Our work flows from a philosophical basis that regards nature, that is the patterns and processes within the native prairie ecosystem, as the most appropriate standard for sustainable agriculture on the Great Plains."[105] In the drought summer of 1988, institute researchers discovered that while the drought reduced seed yields on most of its monoculture plots, yields of eastern gama grass and leymus rose on polyculture plots. In a mission statement for the institute, West Jackson and Marty Bender wrote: "We believe that the best agriculture for any region is the one that mimics the region's natural ecosystems. . . . our goal is . . . to create prairielike grain fields." Jackson wrote elsewhere that "the agricultural human's pull historically has been toward the monoculture of annuals. Nature's pull is toward a polyculture of perennials."[106] According to Jackson, perennials offer less soil loss, reduced energy needs compared to monoculture cultivation, and less pesticide and fertilizer dependency, and they would reverse the decline of genetic diversity.[107] Not the least, perennial agriculture, because it draws on existing plains plants, would require little or no irrigation, thus achieving the ideal Ogallala groundwater zero-depletion goal.

The Land Institute is taking a broad-based look at grain sorghums, the current standby of both irrigators and feedlot suppliers, long harvested as an annual monoculture. Sorghums are among the world's staples, along with maize, wheat, barley, and rice. Researchers at the institute note that the sorghums are taxonomically related (the same tribe, *Andropogoneae*, of the grass family, *Gramineae*) to two plains grasses, big bluestem, a major Kansas tallgrass, and eastern gama grass. Of African origin, sorghums did not appear in the United States until 1857. By the 1960s, with the advent of irrigation, Kansas became the center of the "milo belt" as production multiplied tenfold. It is grown almost exclusively as a feed-grain crop, second only to corn in importance. New hybrid grains, true yellow milos, are more digestible with higher nutrition than before. The vegetative biomass (the plant aside from its grain) is fed to livestock as forage, silage, green chop, and hay. In India and Central America, sorghums are human food in breads and tortillas and are not converted into meat. Africans make the grain into a porridge, including a sorghum couscous.

On the plains, sorghums are attractive because their root systems are more efficient in extracting soil water than corn and they require less water for growth than corn, barley, or wheat. Hence they have better drought tolerance. Maize requires weekly irrigation and heavy pesticide application. A sorghum field needs as few as three irrigations per growing season and attracts fewer pests. Land Institute researchers also see sorghum as a natural herbicide, since it prevents the spread of certain grasses and broadleaf weeds. A hybrid of milo, sudan grass, and sordan grass is also apparently a soil desalinator and can play a role in soil reclamation while simultaneously serving as livestock food.[108] Among several experiments, Land Institute researchers chose so-called long-season sorghums (entire growing season) to intercrop with early maturing millet and tropical maize and with late-season cowpeas and certain beans. Total yield is 50 percent better than sole cropping. Grain sorghum is perennial in its native tropical and subtropical environments but cannot survive temperate winters. The institute's goal is to develop a winter-hardy perennial grain sorghum by cross-cultivating it with Johnsongrass, a winter-hardy perennial sorghum better known as a particularly distasteful weed. If it is successful, Ogallala farmers in the old Dust Bowl would have a familiar crop and commodity that would need planting only two or three times a decade. The institute notes, however, that seed companies might be loath to market it. In addition, sorghum prices are a sixth less than corn, and livestock is supposed to do better on corn than milo. A long-term, integrated, whole-system approach to sorghum will have to take more into account than prices and animal feed. A positive outcome to the Land Institute's research, however, would help to fulfill its long-term goal of making perennial polyculture the agricultural wave of the future on the High Plains. This would assist the farmer by reducing his costs and his labor and help the regional environment by reducing water consumption and limiting chemical use.

Other crops mentioned are mung beans, kochia, fourwing saltbrush, pearl millet, amaranth, and guar, some of which are ancient low-yield crops associated with the agricultural revolution in the Middle East ten thousand years ago. Alternatives to new high-value crops include the use of known field crops with improved yields, decreased costs, and new technologies and new management.

Conclusion

This review of current groundwater conservation also needs to consider strategies examined in previous chapters. Wayne Bossert's zero-depletion response to water loss runs up against current irrigation needs, but it recognizes that saved water keeps future generations on the plains. Bossert joined the pioneering efforts of the weather modification program by Kansas District No. 1 in Scott City, together with A. Wayne Wyatt's Texas District No. 1, in order to reduce groundwater consumption by inducing more rain. Wyatt is also exploring aquifer recharge. Another direction is suggested by value-added animal confinement operations in cattle or hogs that seek maximum profit from each gallon of water. Incentives to solve the plains water problem come from plains conditions: Ogallala groundwater is likely to stay dedicated to food production. The plains will probably not find itself embroiled, like the Southwest, over water for heavy industry or metropolitan sprawl.

It is widely acknowledged that access to sufficient water for high-yield production is limited and will gradually change High Plains farming. In 1970, farmers around Sublette, Kansas, concluded they had three hundred years of water left in the aquifer. By 1980 their estimate had fallen to seventy years and by 1990 to less than thirty years. Using current techniques, local irrigators once said, they would be happy to last until the end of the century. More than half of the usable water was gone and levels continued to drop as much as 2 feet a year.[109] In a 1976 study of Ogallala supplies in Parmer County, Texas, midway along the New Mexico border, a well that had a saturated thickness of 110 feet (storing 15 acre-feet and allowing pumping rates of 1,000 gpm) in 1974 would by 1984 be down to 52-foot saturated thickness (storing 7.5 acre-feet and allowing 500 gpm) and in 1994 to an unpumpable 37 feet (storing 5 acre-feet and allowing 300 gpm).[110]

Answers to declining water supplies are also sought in more profitable alternative crops like canola (rapeseed), sunflowers, and popcorn, in more efficient technologies like drip irrigation, in better management techniques like irrigation scheduling, and in water-holding techniques like no-till farming. Other answers include horizontal drilling and the use of vertical turbines, greater well and pumping efficiency, reduction of center-pivot pressures by half, improved on-farm conveyance systems and tailwater recovery, and alternative furrow irrigation, as well as better know-how on plant growth and water stress. Efficiency can rise dramatically under ideal conditions, from the miserable 45 percent in furrow irrigation to 75 percent with scheduled sprinkling from groundwater. Drip irrigation that goes directly to the roots of plants offers 90 percent efficiency. However, extremely high equipment costs skew these advantages. The end of extensive irrigation for intensive farming may also mean the end of family farming on the High Plains.

The arid climate of the High Plains may have the direct impact its inhabitants have not felt for sixty years. With yields three times higher and with unprecedented capital investment, the stakes are far higher now than in the 1930s. Because intensive agriculture is vulnerable to changes in its environmental base, not only would grain production be ended by desertification, but today's all-important cattle feedlot operations would be halted by sun, wind, and temperature extremes. Frontier conditions on the High Plains can still control our future. As water levels decline, High Plains agriculture will be subject to unpredictable interruptions from its old enemy, climate.

Farm economist Willard W. Cochrane sees a pattern in climate and our reaction to it. The period 1930–37 was a period of uncertainty and instability until the technological payoff that began in 1937 and continued for an extraordinary fifty years. Cochrane contends that as long as government intervention continues it prevents the return to the chaos of the 1930s, but, he warns, the last fifty years of abundance cannot be repeated.[111] Additionally, the last fifty years saw new technologies that increased the power of large-scale industrial farming and simultaneously caused the weakening of the smaller family operation that did not have access to the latest technological fix. The problem is that such fixes are often isolated and narrow solutions that can produce unintended social and environmental disruption. The family farmer is driven away and the soil and water become depleted. Many of the individual responses to declining groundwater described here are under attack because they only support prevailing bad habits or ignore their possible impacts. Treating water in isolation from larger chronic problems creates solutions that are piecemeal, disengaged from a long-term, workable plan. Critics from the Land Institute in Kansas and from Nebraska's Center for Rural Affairs say that a preoccupation with technological and managerial fixes will fail since the root of the problem is in the existing plains farm system, irrigated or not, because it is not sustainable.

8

. . .

The Move toward a Drier World:
The Summer of 1988

The great drought of 1988 was most severe on the northern plains in the Dakotas and Montana; it was less severe in the old Dust Bowl heartland of southwest Kansas and the Oklahoma-Texas Panhandle. As the summer progressed, however, the awful combination of sun, wind, and lack of rain once again began to hammer the Dust Bowl, the region best prepared to protect itself from lack of rain. Not only had lessons been learned the hard way from the 1930s, but farmers, suppliers, bankers, and extension agents had been tested by the droughts of the 1950s and 1970s.[1] Most important, the south-central High Plains enjoyed their climate substitute: heavy irrigation from large groundwater supplies. The waters were receding, but no doubt they could carry farmers through one more time. The next time around, however, would the new threat of a man-induced global warming—the CO_2 or greenhouse effect—overwhelm the substitute? On the plains a newsman called the spring of 1988 "this eerie spring—a spring without thunder, a spring without rain. . . . some rangeland barely turned green this spring. . . . Many fields of spring wheat, pathetically trying to head out on plants only four inches high, would be almost too short to harvest." The lack of rain had a finality about it: "Rain—even in torrents, even tomorrow—would come too late."[2]

Once more it is clear that the plains cannot be understood in isolation. The jet stream, Earth's high-altitude climate maker, spent the spring and summer of 1988 flowing off course far to the north, responding to below-average ocean surface temperatures along the equator in the Pacific.[3] As a result, a vast stretch of the United States, from Montana through Georgia and most of the East, suffered through record stretches of ninety-degree-plus temperatures. Forty-five days and nights of pounding heat were contrasted with Noah's flood of forty days and forty nights. Francis Bretherton of the National Center for Atmospheric Research (NCAR) in Boulder, Colo., frightened people when in October 1987, well before the drought, he spoke prophetically to *Time* magazine of the greenhouse-effect consequences of a doubled atmospheric concentration of CO_2: "Suppose it's August in New York City. The temperature is 95 degrees; the humidity is 95%. The heat wave started on July 4 and will continue through Labor Day," a span of fifty-five days.[4] In reality, the 1988 New York heat wave lasted forty-four continuous days, started well before July 4, with the temperature and humidity in the nineties, and continued through August 18.

On the plains, the first to be hard hit were ranchers; their cattle demanded daily water and access to grazing. Nineteen eighty-eight was already their second or third year of drought. As early as the middle of May, Texas ranchers were burning thorns off prickly-pear cactus with gas torches. In Minnesota a Soil Conservation Service official said, "There are drifts of dirt like snowdrifts in the ditches and lots of dirt in the air and lots of dirt in the houses." In a modern twist, a farmer near Minton, South Dakota, pulled out his snowblower. "It worked. I created a mini-dust storm blowing the soil back onto my wheat field."[5] Farmers used the 1930s term "black blizzards" to describe murky conditions that reached from the old bonanza country of the Red River Valley of the North in the eastern Dakotas down into eastern Colorado and the Texas Panhandle. In the Southeast, an Atlanta water bureau official summed up farmers' feelings nationally: "There's a double drought, a drought of reality and a drought of anticipation." This reflected the fears of plains farmers while they waited uneasily to see if 1988 was the beginning of the next Dust Bowl, expected by the early 1990s.[6] LaVerne G. Ausman, longtime Wisconsin farmer and USDA official in charge of the federal response to the drought, spoke of the sense of impotence and despair brought on by day after day of no rain. "There isn't anything more disheartening. You're totally helpless. You just watch your crops wither away."[7]

By mid-August the U.S. Department of Agriculture made front-page news when it predicted a 37 percent plunge in the nation's corn crop, a 23 percent drop in soybeans, a 13 percent drop in wheat, and a 31 percent overall drop in all grains. In early August, President Reagan belatedly signed a $3.9 billion disaster-relief bill, the costliest ever: "This bill isn't as good as rain, but it will tide you [farmers] over until normal [*sic*] weather" returns. The president's comments mimicked the old hope for better weather that farmers had laid to rest in the 1930s. Said a plains insurance agent: "Farmers aren't buying anything but crop insurance." A *New York Times* editorial on August 26, 1988, proposed that crop insurance be required of any farmer who benefited from federal income supports. In Draconian language, it concluded, "Perhaps the only way to persuade individual farmers to take charge of their fate will be to deny them special relief the next time disaster strikes." The editorial may have signaled exasperation with federal farm support during endlessly cycling crises and the end of the nation's loyalty to the myth of the independent farmer. Ultimately, this drought consumed twenty billion dollars of disaster-relief for nine million acres of farmland.[8]

Some people profited from the drought. At the Chicago Board of Trade, where much of the nation's supply of wheat, corn, and soybeans is traded in the volatile futures market, the volume of trading soared to 170 percent of normal as big grain users, food-processing companies, tried to lock in prices from grain-elevator operators. At the beginning of May, wheat futures hovered around $3.30 a bushel and reached $4.20 in early July. Corn stood at $2.30 in early May and neared $3.60 in early July. One market journalist claimed that "bullish traders . . . gleefully detail the damage that the drought has already wrought. . . . one would think that the entire corn crop will consist of nothing but cocktail party-size baby ears. . . . Predictably, the price action has been galvanic."[9] Another bullish soybean trader said, with more passion than sense, that "it will never rain again in your or my lifetime. Climatic changes are in the process of transforming Illinois and

Iowa into the Gobi Desert. . . . since we're repeating the weather conditions of the Dust Bowl years, it stands to reason that the corn crop is doomed to come in with yields 65% or so of normal like it did in 1936."[10]

Some midwestern and plains farmers, having already speculated and lost on the right climate for their stunted fields, decided they could survive only by gambling a second time on the futures markets. Critics called it a highly volatile "de facto insurance policy on at least a portion of their crops to lock in prices before the harvest."[11] Prices soared in June, but scattered midwestern showers in July caused prices to collapse to their daily permitted limits. Wheat highs of $4.20 in early July were down to $3.70 by the end of the month, while corn futures fell from $3.60 to $2.75.[12] Shortages of durum wheat for pasta, corn oil for margarine, soybeans for mayonnaise, soybean meal for chickens, and feed corn for cattle pushed consumer prices up 5 to 7 percent, the highest rise since 1980. A fifteen-ounce box of Cheerios that cost $1.98 in October 1987 sold for $2.14 in June 1988.[13] A one-pound loaf of white bread rose 10 percent between April 1987 and June 1988. A 6 percent increase in food prices would cost a typical American family of four more than $300.00 a year. Nevertheless, food costs still accounted for only 17 percent of the American consumer's pocketbook, less than half that of Europeans. Despite the swings, it was clear that consumer food prices would not soar because low consumer prices are one of the USDA's sacred tenets.

With drought damage in Canada, China, and the United States, the globe had only a fifty-four-day supply of stockpiled grain, down from eighty-nine days earlier in 1988 and below the sixty-day global minimum set by the United Nations Food and Agriculture Organization.[14] It was the lowest figure since the food crisis of 1972 and 1973, when wheat prices doubled and corn prices tripled. The drought laid waste Canada's farm belt and ravaged China's central and southern grain belts.[15] In this fourth drought since 1980, Canada's prairie grain crop fell to about thirty-three million tons, down a third from 1987 levels. "We've had people up here who've walked away from their crops." In China, 65 million acres of grain from 196 million acres of farmland had been hit by a heat wave and two-thirds of the country's peanut and soybean crops were lost for the year. Chinese meteorologists believed the drought to be global, the result of an increase in sunspot activity or the greenhouse effect. There were fears that if the United States, which produces a fifth of the world's grain, abandoned export subsidies because of short supplies, it would bring more famine to poorer nations. Two and a half billion dollars had been spent in the Export Enhancement Program to encourage foreign nations to buy American wheat, and build their need for it, at twenty-five dollars to thirty-three dollars a ton less than in the United States. In December 1987 the Soviet Union's dependence was ensured when it bought wheat for forty-two dollars a metric ton less than the domestic going price in the United States, a subsidy of more than a dollar a bushel.[16]

The green revolution had been widely expected to overcome global food scarcity by the early 1960s. Historic importing nations, such as India, China, Brazil, and Mexico, became major exporters.[17] But if a worldwide drought hit for several consecutive years, the United Nations Food and Agriculture Organization in Rome concluded that it would collapse food surpluses and threaten widespread hunger on a global basis; the green revolution was running out of steam. A USDA report in early August noted that the 1988 American grain harvest was the smallest since 1970 and even smaller than the Soviet harvest. Lester Brown of the environmentally oriented Worldwatch Institute argued that even if the fifty-four million fallow acres in the United States were put back into production, the cumulative effects of loss of farmland to erosion and development, depletion of water for irrigation, and higher costs for farm equipment globally meant less agricultural resiliency. Between 1965 and 1983, for example, India more than tripled its wheat harvest but has hardly raised its output since.[18] Virtually everyone agreed that another global drought year in 1989 would be catastrophic.

Ghost of the Dust Bowl

The drought that drove half a million people off the land in the 1930s would not be repeated in the 1980s.[19] As many as sixty-four million acres of land had been abandoned fifty years earlier, compared to only fourteen million acres in 1988. The dry spell was severe, even more severe for some plains farmers than it was in the 1930s, but when a young farmer could raise three times more wheat per acre than his father or grandfather, or five times more corn, he had a greater capacity to recover in the next wetter season. Hence his borrowing power was better and could tide him over. In 1984, following the bad drought of 1983, harvests had nearly doubled. Farmers also were protected by government subsidies and drought relief born out of the sufferings of the 1930s. After the 1930s experience, over fourteen million acres on the High Plains—grassland, fallow land, conservation reserve—had been set aside as unsuited for farming. In the 1980s, at considerable taxpayer cost (but willingly offered to support the family farmer), government agencies prevented wild swings in prices, supplies, and production.[20] Up to two years' worth of wheat and corn prudently could be set aside to stabilize supplies and prices.

Not the least, better farming skills meant that the 1988 winter wheat crop came through virtually unscathed compared to the minuscule wheat harvests of the 1930s. Genetically superior seed varieties were available now, together with better fertilizer and pesticide know-how. Following the creation of the USDA's Soil Conservation Service in the 1930s and the widespread creation of soil conservation districts throughout the High Plains, farmers learned to contour and terrace the land, practice minimum tillage, plant grain in strips, and graze cattle more carefully. A combination of higher wheat prices (because of the drought), standard subsidies, emergency drought relief (from the federal government), and crop insurance (farmer good sense) pulled farmers through.

Soil erosion was severe in 1988 and dust storms caused heavy environmental damage. Plains farmers lost a year's crops and permanently damaged their land. A North Dakota state conservationist observed, "Landowners aren't only concerned about losing their crops this year; they're also concerned about losing their soil, because that's their livelihood." Damage was measured by a formula: an acre that lost about fifteen tons of topsoil, or three times what the land can regenerate in a year, was a damaged acre that could receive federal attention. In such a case, nutrient loss—nitrogen, phosphates, potassium—runs $576 per inch of topsoil. Kansas State University researchers say that wheat yields drop 5.3 percent for every inch of topsoil lost to erosion, with corn declining more and grain sorghum a bit less.[21] In 1988, 1.5 million Kansas acres were vulnerable, 200,000 in the Oklahoma Panhandle, and 3.8 million in West Texas, or four times normal.[22] Across the entire plains, almost 12 million acres were damaged by erosion and 19.5 million acres lacked cover and were at risk, ready to blow.

Drought in the 1980s and the 1990s would have a more global effect than in the 1930s because of the intensive high-yield farming that now prevails on the plains. Together with irrigation, the combination of superior genetic strains, intensive use of fertilizers and pesticides, and better on-farm management transformed American agriculture in the 1970s and 1980s. But widely predicted claims of future yields of five times as much corn per acre and three times as much wheat as fifty years earlier actually resulted only from precisely defined conditions rarely experienced in the field. Farmers had unrealistically fine-tuned their crops to match ideal climate patterns instead of a generalized drought. The high yields of modern industrial farming, with its reliance upon a small number of basic plains crops—wheat, milo, alfalfa, and corn—matched to specific chemicals and irrigation methods, would be extremely vulnerable to both drought and limited irrigation. The discovery and application of underused but more adaptable crops could take a decade. If the greenhouse effect took hold tomorrow or a no-rain climate anomaly appeared in the 1990s (the opposite of the decade of extraordinary rain from 1876 to 1885), a spell of hotter, drier conditions would find farmers once again vulnerable to any extreme.[23] Climate still mattered.

Amaranth is a heat- and drought-tolerant grain, but Keith Allen north of Sublette, Kansas, had learned that alternative crops require public acceptance and markets before they become profitable. The Land Institute is exploring means to improve the cattle forage characteristics of naturally occurring plants, such as Illinois bundleflower and leymus. The institute also urges a move away from today's industrialized monoculture, no matter how productive, to the more flexible diversity field (polyculture) planting, which would mix grain crops with legumes, sunflowers, and perennial grasses. In this way farmers could mimic the historic prairie, which survived under all weather conditions, but it is unlikely that this alternative would offer the high-yield productivity on which the agricultural economy depends. Plant physiologists are also pushing to determine why plants fail at times of extreme stress, such as heat or drought. Can proteins be inserted to protect crops? Such research for alternative or sustainable agriculture, long a stepchild in the nation's federally financed research and development programs, has grown little since 1980.[24]

Unlike traders in the Chicago pit, who profited handsomely, and unlike America's consumers, whose pocketbooks were not rifled, drought-stricken farmers took the brunt of the collapse. Reduction of wheat storage from a two-year supply to a one-year supply and of soybeans from a year to six months drove commodity prices to their highest prices in a decade at a time when plains farmers had little to sell. Farmers had looked forward to the beginnings of a recovery from a six-year-long debt-ridden agricultural recession; it had already forced the largest number of farm and bank failures since the 1930s. One in every six farmers in one Minnesota county had fallen behind on his debt payments. Commodity prices stayed high, but the ability of farmers to cover the inevitable lean years by taking advantage of a fat year or two slipped away with the drought. Echoing his predecessors of the mid-1930s, a farmer said: "High prices don't help if you go into town with an empty truck."

In 1988 farming was once more between a rock and a hard place. An eighty-eight-year-old Montana rancher who had weathered the 1930s told a reporter: "Back then, things cost less and everybody had a little money to get by. That's all you needed was a little income. Our expenses today are 10 times higher, maybe 20 times higher. So even if you make a little money, you're still going to be short. You can't pay for the equipment. This drought is going to put a lot of ranches out of business."[25] By June 1988 land prices, upon which loan equity is often based, stopped climbing and started slipping. As the drought continued into early 1989, a Kansan from Hays wrote the *Wall Street Journal* that "our little patch of wheat is dead. The evergreen shelter belt is more brown than green. The creek is barely running and most of the migrating water fowl are bypassing our country because the ponds are dry. The weather that scares the birds and animals has us worried too. But that's nothing new to Kansans. . . . [Your statement that] 'the name Kansas became a byword for the impossible and ridiculous' doesn't bother Kansans more. . . . Wall Street looks to a lot of us to be a hell of a lot less predictable than Kansas weather. . . . while Kansas weather may be ridiculous, Kansans are sublime."[26]

The Case for Irrigation . . . and Its Limits

One well-established regional alternative was to ignore the drought. Whoever irrigated his land could still proceed as if the drought of 1988 had never come. Larris Hollis, a hands-on Wisconsin farmer with over three hundred acres in corn and hay and also a Milwaukee stockbroker who watched farm production trends, observed in June that the driest Wisconsin spring in a century meant that his crops came nowhere near their moisture requirements. By contrast, he noted, the irrigated High Plains were "in pretty decent shape" no matter the absence of rain.[27] Established High Plains irrigators could be envied for their ability to ignore the drought. They could schedule irrigation and not wait for rain. If, for a field of corn, more water was needed to support day 40 through day 50 of the growth cycle, when the plants begin to grow substantially, then so be it at the flick of a pump switch. But without irrigation, said Hollis, "what we need is several days of nice gentle rain . . . a good soaking" of the kind that center-pivot irrigation provides by flipping a switch on the normally rainless Kansas Sandhills of the Gigot family. "[Irrigators] can pick and choose."[28]

Because of 1988's delayed rains, farmers' irrigation engines worked harder than before pumping water; by May they had recorded approximately 50 percent more pumping time. Gary Baker, manager of Southwest Kansas Groundwater Management District No. 3, noted that farmers around Garden City had planted 10 percent more corn (wheat was a swing crop for them) in 1988 than in 1987. In the drought, their rate of groundwater declined almost 3 feet in 1988 alone compared to a twenty-year average of 1.8 feet. This was all the more disappointing because in recent years irrigators using conservation methods had reduced their annual decline to a foot or less.[29] Like an evil portent, dust storms swirled through all of Kansas west of Wichita. scs official Jeff Schmidt went out to check on crops damaged by sand and static electricity. He called for emergency tillage as serious soil erosion hit fields emptied of their crops.[30]

Throughout the United States during the 1980s, over 270,000 farmers—more than 11 percent of all U.S. farmers—abandoned their fields. Most High Plains farmers, now heavily insulated by irrigation, efficient machinery, sophisticated plant science, and federal prices and credit supports, survived the drought of 1988. As commodity prices were kept high and grain surpluses hit their lowest levels in a decade, farmland prices began to rise by the fall of 1988. Hugoton, Kansas, grain farmer James Kramer concluded that "we could see two or three years of a relatively stable farm economy, if the weather is fairly normal."[31] In Hugoton's Seward County, where pick-and-choose irrigators were plentiful, the 1982 National Resources Inventory recorded, probably at the peak of plains irrigation, that 113,600 of the county's 263,800 cropland acres were irrigated. In Finney County, 244,400 acres, almost 30 percent of the farmland, were irrigated from 2,267 wells, largely with sprinklers. In Haskell County it was 263,900 acres, more than 71 percent, from 988 wells and 90 percent sprinkled.[32]

On the central and southern High Plains, any long-term drought, such as from global warming from the greenhouse effect, would reduce crop acreage as much as 25 percent.[33] Some of farmers worst fears materialized as drought continued into 1989 on the central High Plains, with little snow in the winter and belated rains in the spring.[34] In February, farmers around Liberal, Kansas, did their regular tests of soil moisture. Instead of the four-foot moisture depth needed to plant their milo, they found two feet. Instead of forty-eight inches needed to plant their wheat, they found thirty inches of moisture. At Hays in the middle of Kansas it was reported that gravediggers were not hitting moisture at six feet. Those who planted wheat in the hope of fall rain and winter snow (neither appeared) were compelled to destroy their crops because yields were so low it was too costly to harvest. Furthermore, the crop had been unprotected by snow and left exposed to sandblasting winter winds. The result was winter kill of 20 percent of the crop, and by May the USDA projected total loss on fourteen million of fifty-five million acres planted in the fall. With no leaves, young wheat plants must start all over again from the top of their root systems, but, farmer Larry Kern near Salina said, "the wheat's just not rooting down . . . to the subsoil because there's no moisture down there for it to get."

A year earlier, in the spring of 1988, the winter wheat crop had ripened before it was hit by intense drought in May and June, but in the spring of 1989 little rain or snow meant no ripening. In March the wheat plants were a shriveled brown instead of greening up. Since bare land might blow, the Soil Conservation Service recommended "ghost crops" (no profit) of wheat for ground cover.[35] U.S. wheat stockpiles fell close to a seventeen-year low, only a third of the previous year's mark. Kansas farmers abandoned a fifth of their winter wheat acreage, and the fields that were harvested dropped by 10 bushels an acre. Kansas, the biggest wheat-producing state with one-quarter of the nation's output and a third of its hard red winter wheat, faced the worst harvest in thirty-two years, with its one-billion-dollar crop down more than a third. Heavy rains, up to seventeen inches, made up for deficits from late April to mid-June, but it was too late for wheat, although just right for another try at milo.

In late December 1989, after six more months of drought, Kansas farmers once again worried about lost wheat crops and more severe damage from erosion. Little rain had fallen since September in wheat-growing regions, and lack of snow cover in southwest Kansas and the Oklahoma-Texas Panhandle region, together with double-digit below-zero temperatures, meant failure. In 1989 a central Kansas winter wheat farmer harvested only seven bushels an acre instead of his usual thirty-five, his net worth down to twelve thousand dollars after paying off the interest and part of the principal on last year's operating loan. A Kansas crop specialist worried: "Many farmers had operating loans last year that they couldn't repay because of crop failures. Now they are facing the threat of two in a row. . . . we're looking at a rising number of distressed farms."[36]

Thinking the Unthinkable: The Greenhouse Effect

The High Plains drought of 1988 reflected global climate events that signaled the impact of human influence as well as nature's capricious shifts. Not since

1936 had a dry April and May been followed by an even drier June and July, as took place in 1988. According to the standard measure, the Palmer Drought Index, the 1988 drought was the fourth worst on record based on its impact on cropland; the top three worst years were 1934, 1936, and 1954.[37] Average global temperatures in the 1980s were the highest measured since 1869, the year that reliable records were first kept. Within a twelve-year period, seven years—1980, 1981, 1983, 1987, 1988, 1990, and 1991—had been the warmest on record, and the rest of the 1990s have kept up the warming pace. Temperatures have been rising gradually and steadily for the last hundred years, but the sharp rise detected in the 1980s may be, according to some scientists, the beginning of much sharper increases to come over the next two decades. In 1998, the New York metropolitan area saw no snow in February for the first time since 1869. Since the nineteenth century, global temperatures rose nearly 0.5 degrees Celsius, which is 28 percent of the warming (1.8 degrees Celsius) expected by the year 2030.[38] Federal climate program director Alan Hecht was joined by geologist Dewey M. McLean of Virginia Polytechnic University in concluding that the recent warming is probably not part of a natural trend since the earth is now at the later stages of a period between ice ages, which means that the temperatures should be growing cooler with an approaching ice age.[39] Climate scientist Michael Oppenheimer of the Environmental Defense Fund noted that the world is already one degree Fahrenheit warmer than a century ago and that "within the lives of our grandchildren, it could become a blistering 8 degrees hotter. . . . [R]emember that small temperature changes can remake the face of the earth: The planet was [only] 8 degrees cooler during the glacial age."[40] "We may be moving through an entire geological epoch in a single century," an unacceptable pace, said John S. Hoffman of the global atmosphere program at EPA.[41] Stanford climatologist Stephen H. Schneider, formerly of the National Center for Atmospheric Research (NCAR), reminded *Science* readers that the planet Venus, with its dense CO_2 atmosphere and temperatures of 700 Kelvin, and frigid Mars, with a thin CO_2 atmosphere, are both examples of "runaway greenhouse."[42]

The cause could be a full-scale global greenhouse effect, evidence that industrial carbon dioxide, methane, nitrous oxide, and other gases are trapping heat in the atmosphere.[43] Signs of global warming can be seen in warming global temperature patterns, increased atmospheric water vapor, rising sea-surface temperature, and dramatic seasonal fluctuations.[44] Some greenhouse effect is natural; the earth would be frozen and lifeless without it. However, if rising man-made greenhouse gas emissions remain unrestrained and if the climate is highly sensitive to a worst-case scenario, temperatures could rise at 0.8 degrees Celsius each decade—sixteen times faster than the average rate of warming over the past one hundred years. As it is, the world's oceans soak up heat and chemicals (half the carbon dioxide humans produce) and do much to slow increasing temperatures. What may temporarily protect our children and grandchildren from unbearable heat may be the world's oceans, which have a heat-absorbing capacity more than forty times that of the atmosphere.

Ironically, over geologic time the plains region contributed to global cooling. In the last sixty-seven million years, the grasses increased the breakdown of soil minerals. When the vast inland seas covered the region, the resulting potassium, calcium, and magnesium ions were captured by marine organisms, which together with carbon dioxide (CO_2) formed the carbonate skeletons that made up layers of limestone. This systematic removal of carbon dioxide may have contributed to the overall global cooling during the Tertiary period.[45] Despite the best international efforts, including agreements like those reached at Kyoto in 1997, few experts conclude that carbon dioxide emissions will be reduced in the next several decades. Indeed, emissions are expected to rise by 10 percent above 1990 levels by 2010. On the plains (as elsewhere), this means that vigorous adaptation to anticipated new conditions deserves highest priority.[46]

Geochemist Wallace Broecker at the Lamont-Doherty Geological Observatory wondered whether the unusual temperature rise in the 1980s might "provoke the [earth's climate] system into another mode of operation," or as *Science* put it, "one not at all to the liking of humans and other living things."[47] Human societies are remarkably resilient to climate changes that reach known extremes, but other than distant ice-age data, we do not have any experience with the temperature swings of a CO_2 doubling.[48] Oppenheimer noted that the new warmer world would be a place with no stability—only change.[49] Climate is notoriously variable and can even have regular patterns of change such as El Niño or twenty-year drought patterns. But a climate extreme is a significant shift from the normal state, and it can have disastrous impacts on human welfare.[50]

Climate is one of the globe's most turbulent and unpredictable phenomena. Schneider, looking over NCAR's computers that model tomorrow's trends based on yesterday's data, concluded that any prediction more than six hours into the future is like sorcery.[51] Schneider would probably agree with research meteorologist Edward Lorenz who said, "We might have trouble forecasting the temperature of [a cup of hot coffee] one minute in advance, but we should have little difficulty in forecasting it an hour ahead."[52] Nonlinear systems, despite their short-term uncertainty, shape themselves toward identifiable long-term outcomes.

Uncertainty makes all planners, policymakers, scientists, and politicians uneasy. The *New York Times* editorialized on January 27, 1989, that "Climatologists will argue for many years whether the greenhouse warming has started. But there's every reason to take action immediately, and not wait until that debate is concluded. Once warming begins, its momentum will continue—even if gas emissions could be stopped immediately—for the three decades or so that it takes to heat the oceans. At that point the planet will again be in equilibrium, but at a much higher temperature than that of the initial warming signal." Schneider, writing in *Science*, concluded, "whether the uncertainties are large enough to suggest delaying policy responses is not a scientific question per se, but a value judgment."[53] It is a matter of decision making with imperfect information. Decisions are not in the hands of scientists but those of politicians.

When considering the impact of the greenhouse effect on the Dust Bowl, Schneider warns, "What is new is the potential irreversibility of the changes that are now taking place."[54] Swedish scientist Bert Bolin stressed the severity and universality of the subject: "Climatic problems will be part of people's lives over the next century."[55] Americans have great difficulty thinking and acting in a framework longer than four-year presidential terms and annual corporate reports. Thinking about climate in this case must span more than eighteen thousand years (since the last ice age) or twenty-five thousand years (the supposed age of the Ogallala aquifer). As University of Chicago atmospheric scientist V. Ramanathan noted, "by the time we know our theory is correct, it will be too late to stop the heating that has already occurred."[56] Ramanathan labeled the current warming a test of the greenhouse effect by "an inadvertent global experiment" that has reached "the crucial stage of verification."[57]

By late 1995, whatever doubts remained about human influence upon the global climate were dispelled by simultaneous and joint reports of international scientific studies made by teams in California, Colorado, the United Kingdom, and Germany.[58] Climatologist Tom Wigley concluded, "We can claim, with a high statistical confidence, to have identified an anthropogenic signal in the observed temperature change,"[59] although some of his colleagues are concerned about reliability problems in long-term studies that last a half-century or more. In all the recent studies changes pointed toward a global warming, but how much and how soon was open to debate. Predictions ranged from 0.5 to 3.0 degrees Celsius by 2050 and between 1.8 and 3.6 degrees by 2100 if no action to reduce emissions of greenhouse gases is taken. Whatever the scope of possibilities, long-range warming data showed upward movement that made 1995 almost a full 1.0 degree Celsius warmer than 1910.[60] The trend continued into the late 1990s. Gradual warming, scientists feared, could set off wide disruptions of human societies by causing a rise in ocean levels and contrary trends of greater desertification and heavier rains depending upon region. According to one newsletter account, "Deserts are expected to expand, and the heartlands of continents to become drier. . . . In summer, water would evaporate faster, drying the soil."[61] However, the High Plains, according to one computer model, might be free of dramatic change, but it will be dryer and warmer. Other related studies attempted to identify warming-and-cooling cycles in the overall upward trend, reviving a sometimes dismissed idea of twenty-two-year drought patterns driven by solar activity.[62]

Depending upon small changes, any climate can have varying natural behaviors or outcomes. Like most climatologists watching for greenhouse trends, Schneider is concerned that "a kick from outside," meaning human-induced industrial gases, could force climate to shift its patterns from the unusual slight temperature fluctuations of the last hundred years to oscillating extremes in the twenty-first century. By altering temperature and precipitation patterns, greenhouse gas-induced climate change may create new climate conditions that in many regions would be considered extreme.[63] The oscillations could become a steady pattern of irregular wide swings that would send humanity (and the rest of life on the globe) into a new existence. The problems presented by climate extremes would rapidly exhaust the known means to solve them. A single year's heat wave, as in the summer of 1988, made commodity prices first skyrocket and then wildly fluctuate. It tied up shipping in shrunken rivers, decimated the world's food reserves, brought record smog levels to cities, terminated any last remaining hope for helpless populations in Africa's Sahel, intensified long-term water wars, and profoundly affected humanity's psychological security. Few farmers can cope with extremes that might unexpectedly shorten growing seasons.

With far greater extremes in regional climates, the spread of a Sahel-like desert onto the High Plains or the equivalent of a Bangladesh monsoon in Chicago twenty years from now would have devastating effects on population shifts, food resources, and the nation's well-being.[64] While a U.S. Weather Service official played down the permanent impact of 1988 ("This is a tough summer well within the normal range of variability"), the normally cautious James E. Hansen, a NASA research scientist, "shook up a lot of people" when he told a worried Senate subcommittee in June that he was 99 percent certain of a permanent human-induced greenhouse warming.[65] If this were so, the measures devised over the last fifty years to protect farmers against drought such as irrigation, crop insurance, or emergency measures like the multibillion dollar federal drought bill of August 1988, would be like pitching money into a black hole.

Plains Agriculture in a Warmer World

Most agricultural impact studies are based on the results of general circulation models (GCMs) that indicate that rising levels of greenhouse gases are likely to increase the average global surface temperature by 1.5–4.5 degrees Celsius over the next one hundred years.[66] The great food belt of middle America would likely move north into central Canada and become less productive because of poorer soils and a much shorter growing season. Despite its recognized coarseness, the global climate modeling done by NASA and NOAA almost invariably placed the central and southern High Plains in harm's way if a CO_2 doubling took place, with hot, dry, cloudless weather. The High Plains would experience a perpetual Dust Bowl far more severe than anything it experienced in the 1930s.[67] Soil moisture levels would drop 40 to 50 percent, levels that Gary Baker in Garden City, Kansas, reported as destroying wheat crops in the spring of 1989. Multiple studies correlated by Schneider indicated that the old Dust Bowl region (Arkansas-White-Red River basin) is the fourth most vulnerable to greenhouse impacts in the nation (after the Great Basin, Missouri Basin, and the state of California) because of extreme water consumption, extreme climate variability, and groundwater loss.[68] While the greenhouse effect would not be uniform across the globe, the United States would have specific "winners" and "losers," and the old Dust Bowl region is always listed as a "loser." The projected climate change would amplify extreme weather events such as hot spells and storms.[69]

Agricultural geographer Linda O. Mearns, in a low-moisture study in Goodland, Kansas, learned that at its current normal climate, the plains region is marginal for wheat production, which makes farming highly vulnerable to the intensity and timing of climate changes.[70] Another NCAR report described the plains as an extreme continental grassland system that during the droughts of the 1930s and 1950s went through important changes in plant production systems and modifications in land surface characteristics.[71] Grasslands exist within rather narrow climatic zones, and relatively small climate changes could lead to large modifications. The grasslands have become increasingly sensitive to distress because of unsustainable land-use practices. No historian of the plains, and no long-term farmer, would have been surprised by the report's conclusion that farming remained very much a "stretch" on the marginal plains and that land-abandonment was a likely outcome. Further global warming that would reduce rain and increase temperature could lead to the substitution of the existing grasslands by "desertlike ecosystems"—a woody canopy cover such as juniper trees instead of perennial grasses.[72] Today the threat to the High Plains is desertification that Michael H. Glantz, climate and social impact analyst at NCAR, calls "a self-accelerating process" that "feed[s] on itself, and as it advances, rehabilitation costs rise exponentially."[73] Glantz observed that when physical pressures resulting from highly mechanized technologies to force high-food yields become intensified by drought, desertification, which is always damaging to humans and the environment, can result. He quotes the 1977 United Nations Nairobi Conference on Desertification:

> The deterioration of productive ecosystems is an obvious and serious threat to human progress. In general, the quest for ever greater productivity has intensified exploitation and has carried disturbance by man into less productive and more fragile lands. Overexploitation gives rise to degradation of vegetation, soil and water, the three elements which serve as the natural foundation for human existence. In exceptionally fragile ecosystems, such as those on the desert margins, the loss of biological productivity through the degradation of plant, animal, soil and water resources can easily become irreversible, and permanently reduce their capacity to support human life.[74]

The difference between the High Plains and Africa's Sahel exists only by degree. A journalist gloomily concluded, "The return of a Great American Desert would threaten agriculture worth $32 billion, farm assets estimated at $197 billion, wildlife, water supplies and transportation. Dust storms—which proved dense enough to suffocate cattle during the bone-dry 1930s—would clog ducts as far away as the east coast—Geologists say living among active dunes would be nearly impossible."[75]

The Great Moving Dunes of the Plains

Modern humans live in a period called the Holocene in which the climate has been relatively stable and serene. According to recent analysis by paleoclimatologists (scientists who study ancient and long-term weather) the last century and a half has been deceptively tranquil, even considering perturbations like the Dust Bowl. Apparently, the Dust Bowl would have turned into a major geologic incident if the drought had lasted.[76] This is particularly true of the dunes, or sandhills, that cover much of western and central Nebraska (home to the largest dune field in the Western hemisphere) and that stand along the Arkansas River in Kansas and in small parts of Oklahoma and west Texas. Such sandhills are covered by a thin layer of grasses and look like low hills. During a drought, heat and dryness kill most vegetation, leaving bare sand, which is blown into Saharalike dunes. Early explorers who labeled the High Plains "the Great American Desert" were not exaggerating. A 1796 account of the Nebraska Sand Hills described a great desert of drifting sand, without trees, soil, rock, water or animals of any kind. One early-nineteenth-century drought lasted long enough to make Zebulon Pike, in 1810, see a region he compared with "the sandy deserts of Africa." Plains spokespeople Marty Strange and Elizabeth Ann R. Bird of the Center for Rural Affairs concluded in 1992 that the dunes in the Nebraska Sand Hills could reactivate under dryer and warmer conditions, break up the scanty vegetation and thin layer of topsoil overlying them, and blow away with the prevailing northwest winds.[77] Farming in the area, such as that of the Gigot operation in the Kansas Sandhills, accelerates this process of desertification. A desert is created when the wind blows enough sand to bury roads and farmhouses. The dunes were on the verge of becoming active when the drought ended in 1936.

If the greenhouse effect makes the High Plains both drier and warmer long enough to touch off Saharalike conditions, the next several drought cycles bear watching. (Elsewhere, as in the Mississippi Valley, climate change would initiate five-hundred-year floods.) The actual changes can be instigated by relatively modest changes in the global patterns of atmospheric circulation, as indicated by the widespread effects of El Niño. The last 150 years, a time frame that acts as the foundation for our definitions of "normal" weather, was unusually placid. Yet, paleoclimatologist Jonathan D. Overpeck concluded that the Holocene period has experienced climatic swings "large enough to dwarf changes seen in the instrumentally based climate record of the last 150 years." The shifting dunes begin to go into their Sahara mode after three or four years of drought. "If you superimpose [the greenhouse effect] on one of the warm, dry periods we know has recurred repeatedly in the last 1,000 years or more," concluded USGS geologist Daniel Muhs, "you're looking at an enormous impact on the landscape."

Climate Complexity and Limited Human Response

Farmers made quick adjustments to climate extremes such as seasonal drought. But when a drought hits a marginal region like the plains, it can mushroom into a climatic disaster. This is especially true as more high-value agriculture becomes a fixture of the plains. There is no doubt that in the future humanity will become more dependent upon the plains for its food supplies. How is society increasing the vulnerability of people and the environment to climate impacts? Are the plains at greater risk to extreme events? Is the level of risk even higher because the plains depends upon a narrow spectrum of agricultural technologies and is affected by market forces beyond its control? Will the demand for food production on the plains rise because of a dangerous combination of global warming and population growth? In the words of Roger A. Pielke, Jr., at NCAR, even when the "frequency and magnitude of climate events remain constant . . . societal impacts (in terms of economic and other measures) increase because more people and property have put themselves (or been placed) in harm's way."[78] Pielke argues that current social and economic patterns will indeed continue to intensify regional vulnerability.

Increased concentrations of CO_2 are not all bad. When plants absorb more carbon they grow bigger and more quickly, and this could boost crop productivity. The predicted doubling of CO_2 might increase photosynthesis rates. These increases would improve yields of so-called C3 plants such as wheat and soybeans, but C4 plants such as maize, sorghum, and many pasture and forage grasses are already efficient and would not be as dramatically affected. These advances would be compromised, however, by a warmer and dryer climate that would reduce soil moisture and increase evaporation rates

317

(5 percent for each one degree Celsius rise in average annual temperature). These would interfere with germination and other key stages in crop-life cycles. As farmers know, an extended dry spell when crops are flowering can be more detrimental than a drought just before harvest. Overall, increased summer dryness, intensified and more frequent droughts and heat waves by 2030 on the High Plains, could reduce yields by 10 to 30 percent. During the extended drought of 1988, corn yields dropped by 40 percent. For the first time since 1930, American grain consumption exceeded production.

Human response would include abandoning dryland farming and changing graze animals—shifting from cattle to goats, for example. Cattle on the southern and central plains would begin to weigh less because of reduced digestibility of forage and the direct impact of higher temperatures on their physiological conditions. Improvements in animal breeding and other management practices could compensate in part for the changed climate conditions.[79]

Hansen argues that while natural forces bring on droughts and other climate changes, the greenhouse effect acts on these natural forces to make such weather extremes even more likely.[80] Irrigation was an exceptionally successful response to Dust Bowl conditions, but how long can it support the High Plains under the pressure of both CO_2 doubling and aquifer depletion? Dryland crop yields could drop by 18 percent and irrigation yields could see reductions of up to 21 percent. In compensation, using the example of Texas alone, thirty thousand more acres would have to be irrigated.[81] Water resources would become even more vulnerable than they are now. All versions of predicted climate change for the High Plains show reduced precipitation and therefore higher levels of groundwater consumption.[82] The high-efficiency water management practices meant to stretch out water supplies will inevitably meet with water depletion. Even with a higher efficiency, a spring 1989 Texas water resources study reported a 5 to 25 percent increase in groundwater consumption during the 1988–89 season to raise identical crops.[83] The greenhouse effect combined with the already-existing water depletion problem will undoubtedly force some to respond, out of desperation and panic, to abandon the region, as was recommended and legislated in the

1930s. There are no dramatic or new solutions such as the irrigation technologies that transformed the 1930s Dust Bowl into a 1960s garden. Despite the recommendations of the 1982 Department of Commerce and Corps of Engineers reports, using water importation as described in the previous chapter is unlikely.

We can learn from history. From the Dust Bowl experience of the 1930s Americans have learned how to reduce the impact of climate change. The equally severe droughts of the 1950s and 1970s and the most recent intermittent dry spell from 1988 to 1993 did not produce the earlier desperation.[84] These repeated responses to climate extremes have worked to reduce America's vulnerability to long-term climate change. Unlike other vulnerable regions in the world such as Ethiopia, Somalia, or Sudan, plains farmers are not landless, poor, isolated, or burdened with armed conflict. They enjoy good trade connections and a solid economic infrastructure.

The need for good management is immediate. Our time frame does not allow ecosystems to adapt naturally to climate change. Ecosystem adjustment is measured in several decades, but climate changes can affect nutrient cycling and plant production in as short a time as between one and five years, while human responses can take ten or more years.[85]

Society must ensure that our food production is not threatened and can continue in a sustainable manner. The better and more specifically we can predict future climate impacts, the better we can adapt. But on the grounds that we may never be able to accurately predict regional or local climate impacts, management decisions may have to work with worst-case scenarios.[86]

Plains farmers, individually and in collaboration with local groundwater management districts, have developed effective hazard management to respond to climate variations. As we saw in previous chapters, they showed successful crisis containment. Their strategies for coping with climate extremes such as droughts will provide important guidelines for adapting to long-term climate change.[87] Today's needs can inform the expected problems of tomorrow.

9

. . .

A Final Look:
Pumping the Ogallala Is a One-Time Experiment

If my land has cried out against me,
and its furrows have wept together;
if I have eaten its yield without payment,
and caused the death of its owners;
let thorns grow instead of wheat,
and foul weeds instead of barley.
—Job 31:38–40

The Ideological Burden Carried by the Plains

The High Plains region is rarely seen in its own light. Instead, through magical spectacles we perceived the region in terms of a variety of predetermined expectations. Geographers have sometimes described such an ideological load as a "thick" cultural context.[1] Such a geography can be richly referential and culturally resonant, regardless of its physical realities. In the case of the plains, the thick context changes over time, reflecting shifting understandings of plains agriculture as well as swings in Americans' sense of responsibility to others. Peirce Lewis and Grady Clay remind us that the geography of the United States mirrors the values of American society. There are no secrets in the landscape; it is our most blatant autobiography, warts and all.[2]

On the plains, confusion set in because of different visions by farmers, government agencies, bankers, and the public. Historian Donald E. Worster concludes that this confusion helped induce the Dust Bowl disaster. One per-

320

son's signal was another person's noise. What are the plains? There are at least six ideas, none mutually exclusive:

Is it a geographical zone of tantalizingly good soil but with an impossibly dry climate?

Is it the historical completion of Manifest Destiny, including American exceptionalism, triumphalism, and giantism?

Is it a highly productive source of commodities ("the breadbasket and feedbag of the world"), controlled by world markets?

Is it a growing pile of debts owed to the bank? Did credit control farmers and corporations?

Is it the basis for a cherished and valuable lifestyle based on the image of the Jeffersonian yeoman farmer?

Is it what the mega-hog industry would have us believe, another North Carolina, Missouri, or Iowa—a region interchangeable with other rural regions?

Which of these frameworks is most authentic? Do they all belong to a plains identity? Some geographers, like Stephen Birdsall and Yi-Fu Tuan, describe this as the world of "variable regard."[3] Are there self-validating (i.e., authentic) features of a landscape and its people that require a specific response? The question raised by reformers, even those who see the plains from a variety of perspectives, such as Wes Jackson, Worster, and the people at the Kansas Rural Center, is that an authentic geography offers equity through self-reliance, ensures a participatory society, encourages recognition of diversity, and is committed to the protection of local conditions.[4] The plains can also be defined in terms of bioregions, internal carrying capacity, and a sustainable economy.[5] Douglas Coffman advises, "Far from signifying failure, easing our death-grip on the dry plains will greatly enhance the natural productivity of the landscape, thus improving long-range prospects for social and economic renewal. . . . Nature must be the chief architect."[6]

Bending the Rules on the High Plains

The story of plains agriculture seems to contain more catastrophe than victory. What long-term forces can still bring on painful and life-threatening collapse?[7] The climate is more likely to become worse than better. Is the High Plains a region of perpetual risk, or have there always been successful corrective measures? Did irrigation bend the rules? On the Kansas Sandhills, how was one man, Clarence Gigot, able to make a garden out of another man's desert? If climate instability—a capricious force—was the historic norm for life on a farm in Haskell County, what stability allowed its people to persist?[8] What are the future conditions that would promise success or threaten failure?[9]

America's early plains farmers lived under conditions of extremely high risk. In today's lingo, they were undertooled, underinformed, and undercapitalized. A single incident of a broken axletree or smashed kneecap, bad seedcorn or a rainless June, could put them out of business. This vulnerability alone tells us how frontier settlement differed from more stable situations.[10] Humidland responses to a fixed dryland climate—planting trees, growing corn—had already failed. When, in the early 1880s, frontier farmers encountered unexpectedly heavy rains the promise appeared to have come true. They concluded that a permanent climate change had taken place that would open a new region for farming. In arriving at this conclusion, they committed three errors.

First, they failed to appreciate the gap between the agricultural know-how they brought with them and the great scale by which environmental conditions could threaten their survival. Earlier successful settlements from the East Coast onto the unexpectedly fertile treeless midwestern prairie of Illinois and Iowa had encouraged them to believe that their farming skills and technical resources gave them the power to conquer any geography. No matter how extraordinary the conditions were, they optimistically believed that their resources were superior. To this must also be added their conviction that they were on the vanguard of an irreversible and irresistible Manifest Destiny. Considering their limited resources and parochial know-how, the problem was that they did not have the ability or backup resources to respond flexibly to surprises. They took the unusually severe conditions too lightly, responded too rigidly, and were thus mastered by the High Plains elements for seventy years.

Second, frontier farmers could not distinguish between signal and noise; that is, they did not separate useful information—the long history of a permanently arid region—from misleading and useless information—heavy rains that they did not realize would be temporary. This limitation was attenuated by their agricultural success in the humid East, government and railroad boosterism, and the inherent limits of single-family, self-sufficient subsistence farming. The chaotic swings that characterized human history in Ogallala country were often useless noise since scientists, policymakers, and farmers ignored them to look for steady patterns that would ensure continued monoculture. Chaos theory (e.g., nonlinear, self-organizing systems theory) questions whether the orderly, linear systems are the aberrations, while the irregular oscillations tell the true story.[11]

Third, we need to consider secondary and tertiary impacts—the so-called ripple effect. American farm policy is not the engine that runs our agriculture; it is a subset of a much larger economic system. In the United States today the engine is usually the marketplace, which does not account satisfactorily for social and environmental externalities. Gleick writes, "It would be like looking at the universe through a red filter—you see what is happening at that particular wavelength of light, but you miss everything happening at the wavelengths of other colors, not to mention that vast range of activity at parts of the spectrum corresponding to infrared radiation or radio waves."[12] The problem, when seen in environmental terms, is that farm problems are solved with a too-narrow source—only a red filter—of acceptable information. The result is often unacceptable: for example, escalating insecticides to greater levels of toxicity or encouraging farmers to overcome low grain prices by consuming "free" water to irrigate increasingly larger acreage. While they seek to stabilize farming, such actions may force the system into more extreme oscillations.

Would a water crisis trigger a collapse elsewhere in the system? Does drought or groundwater depletion affect farming by resulting in less access to credit and mortgage money because the local farmer becomes a higher risk? Pressures on the autonomous on-site farm family would multiply, causing increased conflict and possible breakup. Can a single aspect such as depleted soil, an empty well, a drought, or an increase in costs deprive farmers of their livelihood? Can farmers successfully respond to one or two critical changes without modifying the entire farming culture? Today, would a dramatic rise in energy costs alone, as high as a not-unlikely ten dollars per one hundred cubic feet of natural gas, bring irrigation pumping to a sudden halt in southwest Kansas? That the Ogallala aquifer is being depleted, for example, already has a wide impact on farm size, ownership, land-use patterns, land values, and outside private and public investment. When public decisions combine farming with economics and environment, it is like comparing oranges with apples with peaches. Flawed societal decisions can amplify climate reversals as well as disperse them.

The Comforts of Irrigation

The transformation brought by irrigation cannot be overemphasized. It offered a long-sought and forceful climate substitute. The lack of water was such a severe problem that there were repeated attempts to declare the region submarginal and redundant, off-limits to further attempts at farming. Much of the land, like the Sandhills of southwestern Kansas, seemed more suited to light cattle grazing than wheat production. But after World War II, the irrigated land produced famously high yields at an environmental price to be paid in some indefinite future. By the 1950s and 1960s, water was being pumped from each of hundreds of wells at the rate of a thousand cubic feet per minute to water quarter sections of wheat, alfalfa, grain sorghums, and even corn. Irrigation on the High Plains was not merely a response to climate; it became its replacement. When plains farmers irrigate, it means that they do not have to wait for the ever-elusive rain.

Irrigation became as indispensable as the land and sunshine. At first farmers tapped the groundwater only as a last resort when the rains failed, and often they applied the water when it was too late. By the 1960s, however, irrigation was integrated into farming as the single most important action to guarantee high yields. Flooding or sprinkling the fields on a regular basis joined wide use of fertilizers and pesticides in the new industrialized farming. Farmers could schedule irrigation into cropping plans by starting a pump. The noisy motors, running day and night, changed farming from pastoral and seasonal to machine-dominated.[13] Cutting off the water meant shutting down the farm. The alternative, dryland farming, became a dubious last resort.

Top yields that matched corn or sorghum production in Iowa, Illinois, and California were made possible by irrigation, a change that had an overwhelming effect on plains farming.[14] As late as the 1950s, much of America's commercial farming relied on large tracts of cheap land. While more humid regions would use new technologies to raise their yields, until Ogallala irrigation took hold, High Plains agriculture seemed destined to remain a big-acreage, low-yield region. In 1950 the Ogallala had irrigated 3.5 million acres of farmland; in the 1990s it irrigates 16 million acres. In the 1990s the plains seemed capable of matching grain production with any other part of the nation.

The irony of Ogallala irrigation is that while it has done so much to prevent perennial disaster from drought it has created new risks and expenses. Its need for heavy equipment investments, integration into outside markets, and dependence upon government support all transformed a highly valued farming lifestyle into an industrial operation. Boomlike development started a rush to consume soil and water and a demand for costly equipment and new fertilizers and pesticides. Profit-centered production has undermined customary rural lifestyles and shortened the life span of water and land. Phil and Linda Tooms expect their irrigation operation to retrench in the next decade; they are not encouraging their children to stay in farming. Technological and management skills will be worthless unless an answer is found for declining water levels. The Gigots will undoubtedly squeeze the last drop of water onto their sorghum fields before moving their full operation into cattle processing. Paul Hitch, in the central Oklahoma Panhandle, and Steve Irsik, east of Garden City, Kansas, find answers in reliable and value-added cattle and hog production. A. Wayne Wyatt, at the Texas District No. 1 in Lubbock, is optimistically looking into high-pressure groundwater recharge, but with little success thus far. In Oklahoma, Betty and Roger Trescott have retired from their farm, with no one to succeed them in their irrigation operation. This is the case with many of the original 1960s irrigators; there are far fewer farmers and irrigators in the next generation.

The One-Time Experiment

By the time we know whether today's monoculture irrigation farmers can survive with less groundwater, it may be too late to save enough water to keep them on the land. Reasons to tap the aquifer abound. American farmers suffered and failed during the Dust Bowl because they didn't have the technology to reach the groundwater. The New Deal committed the federal government and society to drastic steps that would keep farmers on the plains despite insufficient water. Post–World War II irrigation technologies have protected farmers from the harshness of drought from the 1950s through much of the 1990s. Irrigation helped create today's highly productive and profitable industrial farming on the plains. Without massive infusions of groundwater, high-production industrial agriculture on the High Plains is an untested hypothesis, and alternative agriculture has not been applied on any significant scale. Pumping the Ogallala remains an unrepeatable and irreversible experiment in continuous depletion.

Better use of Ogallala water would protect the social fabric of the plains from environmental collapse and resulting economic failure, but suddenly shutting down the pumps would tear the social fabric. The long-term goal for agriculture is sustainability. Like most environmental perspectives, sustainability tends to be cautious and conservative. Where conventional profit-based farming promotes transitional instability because of its singular loyalty to maximum profits on the short term, sustainability offers a more inclusive picture of economic performance.

Ogallala Irrigation: Its Different Masters

For almost forty years, the irrigated High Plains have provided surplus food for a needy world, aided in overcoming the trade deficit with grain exports, benefited both the independent family farmer and agribusiness, and sustained historically low American food prices. But can the Ogallala waters serve all these masters? Despite crosscurrents and overlapping evident in

326

USDA definitions, public opinion, farm bloc interests, and ecological goals, there are several distinguishable models of agricultural productivity and sustainability. Unpacking these approaches can help to understand how the farm lobby, special interest groups, and federal planners each seek to influence Ogallala pumping and allows us to better identify what answers, if any, each offers to declining water supplies.

Conventional Agriculture and Transitional Instability

In brief, conventional agriculture is how American farming has dedicated itself over time to the highest possible productivity using industrial equipment, heavy agrichemical inputs, risky monoculture, and few soil-building crops.[15] This massive industrialization is attractive because it has produced remarkable yields. On the plains, the strategy of maximum consumption of resources required the acceptance of soil erosion and water and energy exploitation to produce a large surplus of a narrow range of commodities.[16] Americans praised this production ethic because it also served nonproduction goals. Since high-technology labor efficiency dramatically reduced the number of working farmers while protecting high yields, more labor could be applied to nonfarm occupations to support increasing demands of a consumer society. This approach has been institutionalized over the last century, particularly since the 1930s, by costly farm-support policies whose original goals were to support on-site family farmers, build commercial markets, and preserve low food expenses for nonfarmers. This original version of conventional agriculture was never purely practiced: market monopolies have been sustained by the railroads, which became major agricultural landholders in the nineteenth century, and then by large-scale agribusiness in the twentieth century. Traditional farmers have not been served well by this conventional agriculture model. Crop prices fell and stayed low, while costs of machinery, land, chemical inputs, and interest rates rose.

Conventional agriculture only remotely includes social forces, and it does not take into account most environmental constraints. The hidden ecological cost of lost water, spent soil, and bankrupt farmers is not easy to measure in dollars. Conventional agriculture is environmentally blind and slips too easily into a subset of economics. Most farmers find they must adapt to economic efficiency as measured by the marketplace. This is now rigorously institutionalized in the farm bill of 1996. The function of the marketplace is to transfer resources, goods, and services to those who are willing to pay the most for them; this reflects, say neoclassical economists, their value to society. Conventional farmers are held in the grip of market forces and government price supports that tend to accelerate the consumption of irreplaceable soil and water—hence the water wars of California and the decline of farming in water-poor states like Arizona and New Mexico. The threatened small farmer and the threatened environment will fail if it is measured in market terms alone.

THE ENVIRONMENTAL WORLDVIEW: ITS AGRICULTURAL DIMENSIONS

Environmental debates today tend to encompass the problems of industrial pollution, urban blight, population growth, wilderness protection, and global climate warming. Agriculture's large-scale land and water consumption is also receiving long-overdue attention.[17] Agriculture consumes over 80 percent of the nation's freshwater supply and probably half is wasted. One objective of sustainable development is to track soil and water consumption as real environmental costs, compared to the historic treatment of natural resources as a free commons. It is clear that vast food surpluses are being created at great environmental costs not passed on to the consumer, grain trader, or foreign buyer. In this view, high-chemical-use monoculture creates disturbingly exploitive consumption of soil and water that will throw farmland into shock. This view also holds that there are large regions of marginal land on the plains that should never have been farmed and that should now be retired.[18] An argument of this viewpoint is that Congress should "decouple" support payments from the usual commodity programs and "recouple" them to environmental recovery.[19] In this way, agriculture's environmental externalities such as soil and water could be internalized. Minnesota Senator Rudy Boschwitz wrote, "Congress must restructure the nation's farm policy, placing conservation at the core—not just as the

328

periphery."[20] Environmentalists insist that more attention be given to impacts beyond the fenceline and beneath the soil whose real costs to society are currently unrecognized.[21]

This thinking is based on a far broader environmental worldview—biocentrism—that concludes that humanity is best understood as being enclosed within nature. This turns on its head the historic western view wherein land, water, and energy serve market value alone. The balancing act is between environmental degradation and a healthy farm society and a clean, safe, natural environment and profitable agriculture. Can more wheat, corn, and milo (and alternative crops) be produced using less water, chemicals, soil, fuel, and capital? The early years of the twenty-first century are likely to become a time of radical reconfiguration for plains farming in the old Dust Bowl region. At present, maximum economic yield (MEY), which urges highest fencerow-to-fencerow production, is still the controlling viewpoint. The pace at which Ogallala water is consumed could even rise. A shift from MEY to MSY (maximum sustainable yield) would conserve Ogallala water for another generation, or indefinitely, but it might not make enough net profit to keep today's farmers on their land.[22]

Field studies made between 1974 and 1978 by William Lockeretz showed little difference between organic and conventional Corn Belt farms, a finding that demonstrated that sustainable agriculture need not be less profitable than conventional agriculture.[23] The farms using alternative methods had lower yields but this was offset by lower costs for fertilizer and pesticides. Even when increased labor costs were included, there was still little difference. In a drier region, organically farmed soils offer the advantage of greater water-holding capacity than conventionally farmed soils. Low-input sustainable agriculture might, in fact, have the advantage on the plains because conventional agriculture requires so many external supports.[24]

Several different versions of the conventional approach are largely indifferent to sustainability interests, while others are responsive to sustainable development:

Food Security. This appears to be the dominant viewpoint in American agriculture today. Fostered in the 1970s and 1980s by the U.S. Department of

Agriculture, but hardly limited to it, this viewpoint emphasizes expansion of agriculture to serve rapidly expanding global food needs. Its claimed social good is to minimize human misery by establishing high food-surplus levels. It seeks to prove the Malthusian formula wrong.[25] Americans take pride in their ability to offer their fellow citizens and the world large surpluses that act as buffers against flood, drought, and other catastrophes that have in the past caused widespread poverty and famine. Conservation and protection of the resource base, including land and water, are downplayed and excluded from cost-efficiency calculations. The centerpiece of the 1996 farm bill is emphasis upon neoclassical concepts of production and efficiency and supply and demand, which are believed to serve the general good. This viewpoint also contends that scientific discoveries and technological fixes will consistently compensate for current and future environmental problems. It is an approach that ignores negative impacts on the labor force and agricultural society. It serves nonagricultural or external interests, including U.S. foreign policy (i.e., GATT, NAFTA, and relations with Eastern Europe and Russia, Japan, China, India, and Africa), the balance of payments (U.S. food exports substantially reduce the deficit), and low U.S. food prices (a sacred tenet of the USDA and Congress). This food security approach is used to justify the fastest possible expansion of cropland through intensive use of irrigation, chemical fertilizers, mechanized equipment, and energy consumption. In it, farming is seen as another form of industrialization.

Sustainability. This position emerged in recent years primarily as a critique of the food security approach. It concludes that the goals of high-yield production are the source of needless soil depletion, pollution, and disruption of natural and human resources. These encourage transitional unsustainability by inducing farmers to use excessive amounts of pesticides and fertilizers and to waste underground and surface waters in irrigation.[26] Sustainability gives priority to: (1) preservation and improvement of fertile soils, (2) maintenance and expansion of supplies of clean water, and (3) protection and regeneration of a satisfying quality of life for the workforce. Admittedly, the food security approach can be applauded for its attention to the elimination of starvation. This is virtuous. Nevertheless, its scope is too narrow, separates agriculture from other human and natural forces, and, says Paul B. Thompson, isolates humanity "from the feedback mechanisms that inform us when we are increasing our vulnerability to a breakdown in the environmental system that supports agricultural practices."[27] The emphasis in sustainability is placed on the on-site balance between agriculture and nature, or, as in Congressman George Brown's words, the use of "stable, self-maintaining ecological systems [of farming] tailored to suit local variations in knowledge, climate, soils, and biological diversity." Critics of the sustainability approach argue that its production levels would not match global population growth.

Variations on the two primary agricultural paradigms are

1. *Profit-motive or marketplace:* detaches itself entirely from agricultural values and treats food production primarily as a business operation in which success is measured by quarterly and annual profits.

2. *Organic farming/Jeffersonian yeoman:* gives primary attention to farming as a way of life producing both the best citizens (civic virtue) and sufficient crops.[28]

3. *Third World:* inappropriate to American agriculture but stands as a global generic model by which other types are measured. It centers upon small family, tribal, or community operations that have limited access to equipment, fertilizers, and pesticides and that suffer from low productivity, intensive hand-labor, and heavy environmental degradation despite their goal to achieve a self-sustainable rural society.

None of these approaches is neutral in its effects upon the wider society, and each has specific social, technological, and economic repercussions.[29] None of these approaches are free from nonagricultural forces. The food security model tends toward corporate agribusiness, with rapid momentum now virtually guaranteed by the 1996 farm bill. It leads to fewer and larger farms, more mechanization, greater need for entrepreneurial skills, more farm specialization (monoculture), higher debt, more external inputs from government, science, and industry (subsidies, machinery, chemicals, skills), and greater environmental costs such as soil erosion and chemical pollution. It forces the collapse of traditional rural economics and the termination of the family farm lifestyle. The stewardship model receives favorable attention because of the historic American reformist or populist critique of corporate power, the growing public dedication to environmental protection, and the surprisingly durable American myth of the independent family farm. The related organic farming model offers an alternative lifestyle based upon self-reliance and long-term farmland preservation.

The profit-motive view can be criticized for ignoring issues unique to farming, while the organic farming view is criticized for low production and antiquarianism. Strident opposition to organic farming has mellowed with a wider public acceptance of it as a valid balance of conservation and production and with the sustainability guidelines first included in the 1990 farm bill. In September 1989 the National Academy of Sciences reported that farmers who apply little or no chemicals to crops can be as productive as those who use pesticides and synthetic fertilizers. The academy recommended changing congressional and USDA farm policies that discourage farmers from trying natural techniques and encourage the overuse of agricultural chemicals, including costly and toxic herbicides, pesticides, and artificial fertilizers. The academy urged "Well-managed alternative farms [that] use less synthetic chemical fertilizers, pesticides and antibiotics without necessarily decreasing, and, in some cases, increasing per-acre crop yields" and "Wider adoption of proven alternative systems [that] would result in ever greater economic benefits to farmers and environmental gains for the nation."[30] At least 5 percent of the nation's 2.1 million farmers, said the academy, have adopted such techniques.

Irrigation from the Ogallala: An American Venture in Sustainable Development?

More and more, today's attempts to lengthen the time that local farmers can tap the Ogallala are comparable to attempts around the world to stretch the use of limited resources.[31] At worst, if Ogallala water becomes inaccessible over the next ten to twenty years, the region will become unmanageable and will revert to a deserted wasteland. At best, by rethinking the Ogallala and reworking High Plains agriculture, we could create a model for sustainable development.

The concept of sustainable development gained currency in the 1980s. It seeks to balance basic human needs with the protection of scarce resources. It is commonly defined as "development that meets the needs of the present without compromising the ability of future generations to meet their own needs."[32] Currently, the effort is to make certain that (1) environmental costs and environmental protection are included in economic growth and (2) technological innovation is appropriate to human and environmental needs on a regional and local basis. One debate that centers around sustainable development is whether the concept is self-contradictory, an oxymoron, because economic growth uses up natural resources. The term "sustainability" has often been used in place of sustainable development. There is also a close connection with "appropriate technology," a concept first given credence in 1943 by E. F. Schmacher and that emphasizes smallness of scale, decentralization, low capitalization, labor intensity, environmental sustainability, and restoration of meaning and dignity to the workplace. It raised serious doubts about the durability of industry (large-scale, capital and chemical intensive, resource depleting, and high consumption) as merely "business as usual." Sustainability's emphasis on the maintenance of essential ecological processes received fresh momentum with the publication in 1987 of *Our Common Future* by the World Commission on Environment and Development.[33] This attempt at linking environment and development into one overall agenda included declarations at the largest-ever international environmental gathering in Rio de Janeiro, the 1993 UN Conference on Environment and Development.

Growing world food needs and shrinking and depleted soils and water supplies worldwide make sustainable agriculture perhaps the most challenging aspect of sustainable development. The American Society of Agronomy said, "Sustainable agriculture is one that, over the long-term, enhances environmental quality and the resources base on which agriculture depends, provides for basic human food and fiber needs, is economically viable, and enhances the quality of life for farmers and society as a whole."[34] It is both a tall order and a sharp turn away from industrial farming that measures success by short-term profits. Whereas sustainable development urges ecosystem-based farming,[35] most farmers are locked into an economic and technological system that rewards waste, pollution, and inefficiency.

According to this exploitive industrial approach, we can successfully consume the soil and water of a specific ecosystem as long as we compensate for the loss by increasing man-made replacements such as machinery, chemicals, and financial support. This justifies a wide range of responses toward the plains, from federal price supports to industrial cattle and hog production. Thinking of a man-made infrastructure as a workable substitute for a natural ecosystem is the basis for a no-holds-barred approach that pours all available resources into an agricultural problem: artificial fertilizers and pesticides, genetically engineered high-yield crops, heavy irrigation, heavy-duty equipment, and large-scale capitalization. Attention is devoted to profit-making components (well-watered, chemically fertilized, and pesticide-protected fields of high-yield monoculture crops) that create a bizarre and unsustainable giantism, while other parts (family farm, soil quality, water supply) are played down and languish. The entire system thus becomes vulnerable to collapse.[36]

The flaws of such "productionism" recently received attention in the USDA's 1998 report, *A Time to Act*. The report suggested that America's family farms could become models of sustainable agriculture by lowering their capital investment, more intensively relying on management and labor, and using farming practices that made the most of local ecosystem conditions. In short, they advocated turning weaknesses into strengths. "Sustainable farming systems provide small farms a means to develop efficient, biologically based systems that rely less on purchased inputs and yield greater returns to a farmer's ingenuity and management skills."[37] Often strapped for cash, small farmers should make the most of on-farm resources and focus on family and community rather than the highest possible profits. Farmers were urged to consider local topography, climate, pest populations, and soil characteristics, thus selecting species and varieties that are well-suited to the conditions on their farms. Soil and water management, for example, would avoid soil and water mining and enhance and protect their quantity and quality as an integrated part of the production process.

The Last Great Federal Bailout: Sustainability Plans
of the 1980s and 1990s

After decades of debate over the nature of farmland protection, ecologically based conservation appeared in the 1985, 1990, and 1996 farm bills.[38] The 1985 farm bill, significantly labeled the Food Security Act—and particularly its Conservation Reserve Program (CRP)—added environmental protection and resource conservation policies to traditional production-oriented and market-based farm commodity programs, including support for Low-Input Sustainable Agriculture (LISA). The 1990 FACTA (Food, Agriculture, Conservation and Trade Act) committed the nation to supporting a link between environmental protection and family farming to international competitiveness. But the new connection has turned out to be a difficult shotgun wedding since it forces contradictory worldviews—forcibly linked by cross compliance—into bed together. Best management practices (BMPs) can be at odds: an environmental protection BMP is not likely to be identical with an agricultural productivity BMP.[39] As two congressional researchers wrote in 1989, "A farm manager views pollution and how to control it from the perspective of farm productivity; the environmentalist views the problem and its control from the perspective of environmental quality."[40] Farmers received contradictory, and hence self-defeating, messages from the government. Minnesota Senator Rudy Boschwitz noted, "When farmers are required to reduce the number of acres they have in production, they usually compensate by farming the rest of their land more intensively, using additional fertilizers, herbicides, and insecticides. Year after year, acreage limitations have failed to achieve intended reductions in total production of program crops."[41]

Low-Input Sustainable Agriculture was a new name for an old idea—profitable conservation farming—that became a small part ($3.9 million) of federal farm policy with the passage of the 1985 farm bill.[42] Donald Worster

335

has written that the soil conservation program that began in 1935 as part of the New Deal expressed a new social and environmental ethic that is now coming into its own: "each generation was to leave the earth in as good shape as it had found it, or in even better shape."[43] An expanded L I S A ($40 million) became S A R E (Sustainable Agriculture Research and Education Program) in the 1990 F A C T A. Both are belated acknowledgments that soil and water mining are fatal to both farmers and farmland and that the trouble is accelerated by expensive equipment and chemicals.[44] Low-Input Sustainable Agriculture and S A R E evolved mainly as a reaction to the failure of modern industrial agriculture to protect the environment and to the economic failure that continues to bedevil most independent farmers who practice conventional agriculture. Even the staid and generally intransigent U S D A admitted that L I S A's appearance is "a criticism of capital-intensive, chemical-intensive monoculture."[45] Nevertheless, the tendency of the 1990 farm bill was to define sustainability in ways that favored large-scale industrial farming and defeated support for the self-employed family farmer. The problem of local survival was not being addressed.

Low-Input Sustainable Agriculture nevertheless reflected interest in the recovery of a more inclusive definition of American farming: "to provide an abundance of food and fiber in a way that is harmless to humans and the environment and sustainable for generations to come."[46] Organic farming advocate Robert Rodale concluded that L I S A reflected the belated appearance of the powerful American conservation tradition that goes back to Gifford Pinchot, Hugh Hammond Bennett, and the Progressive Era.[47] Of L I S A, U S D A official Neill Schaller says that "we are talking about an even bolder union—a marriage of agricultural productivity and profitability, resource conservation and environmental protection, and the enhancement of health and safety."[48] The farm bills of 1985 and 1990 did have a positive environmental impact. Between 1982 and 1992, sheet and rill erosion on U.S. cropland declined from 4.1 tons per acre to 3.1 tons per acre. Crop residue management practices, which reduce soil erosion and air pollution and can improve water quality, were used on 99.3 million acres in 1994, whereas they were used on only 71.7 million acres in 1989. The 1996 farm bill, however, defined agricultural success through its direct relationship to the marketplace.[49]

Still, groundwater mining was largely ignored in the farm bills of the 1980s and 1990s. In the 1980s, most environmental action by government toward farmland protected highly erodible land and reduced chemical pollution. A 1989 study of CRP activity in Colorado's Baca County, which lies over the Ogallala at the Kansas border, does not consider groundwater.[50] The county had the greatest number of acres (266,851) in the nation enrolled in CRP, yet the effects upon groundwater management were not addressed. Thus, while High Plains soil erosion received attention, the overdraft of Ogallala water remained an invisible issue in the farm bills. One revision that was recommended for CRP would have encouraged the retirement, in the 1990s, of twenty million or more irrigated acres because the groundwater beneath them was dropping rapidly.[51] In this case CRP would have added groundwater depletion to soil erosion as an environmental standard of measure.[52] Despite evidence to the contrary, CRP and LISA farm policy still assumes that plains irrigators will successfully turn to dryland farming when they can no longer pump water.[53] The question is not theoretical, since about 13.8 million of the 39.1 million irrigated western acres are in groundwater decline areas, notably in Kansas, Oklahoma, and Texas. Even though drought is a repeated phenomenon with dramatic impacts, federal policy planners still treat it as an anomaly.

The Sustainability Ethic: Doing the Right Thing

This book is not a morality tale or a tragic history that seeks to tar capitalists and consumers and whitewash conservationists and organic farmers. Embracing the good is interwoven throughout this book on the Ogallala. But what is the good? The conflicting economic, agricultural, and environmental viewpoints compared here involve difficult ethical compromises and moral decisions that affect the lives of everyone in the United States. Social policy reflects not just individual self-interest but public values we choose collectively. Philosopher and policy analyst Mark Sagoff writes of "important shared values" to which the American public has historically sacrificed

337

prices and efficiency.[54] Americans have long contended that the role of government is not to merely correct market errors but to reflect a sense of national well-being. Throughout American history, so-called benevolent issues such as the antislavery movement, women's rights, the Marshall Plan, open immigration, urban welfare, and environmental protection have been claimed to represent widely held national values not accurately reflected in self-interest, market efficiency, and profits. Americans are willing to support policies not tied to the profit motive; Americans agreed to support family farms because of the cultural value placed on them. Public debate concerning High Plains agriculture consistently seeks to guarantee that the public good can be accomplished despite conditions of risk and uncertainty.

In 1896 the ethically laden phrase "duty of water" was used by Frederick H. Newell, chief hydrologist of the U.S. Geological Survey, to describe the physical application of water to a field. Newell added that the duty of water involved "the relation between the quantity of water and the area which can be irrigated. . . . It depends upon the climate, the amount of rainfall, the variations of temperature, the character of the soil and subsoil, the methods of cultivation, the kinds of crops, and perhaps more than all upon the skill of the irrigator."[55] Newell aggressively advocated small-scale irrigation as a virtuous and efficient activity that served the entire nation. In California, he proposed, farm families could prosper on as little as five acres. In otherwise barren regions that covered one-eighth of the American West, including large parts of Kansas, Oklahoma, and Texas, irrigation promised bountiful crops that encouraged farmers to settle. It stabilized farm life and avoided "bitter disappointment" for "unfortunate settlers," who, in Newell's realistic assessment, "if not driven from the country, alternate between short periods of prosperity and long intervals of depression."[56] In addition, the alternative—dryland farming—worked against the American "gospel of efficiency" because it consumed vast acreage with low production. The proper application of water was also, according to Newell, "a businesslike investment" in the Progressive Era. As a result, the duty of water included the capacity to grow healthy productive plants, uplift farmers who irrigated, and serve the virtue of economic prosperity.

An ethical dimension is also part of the modern environmental movement. Pioneering ecologist Eugene P. Odum would agree with Worster's argument that environmental analysis is "born out of a moral purpose."[57] Odum finds that comprehensive environmental science offers society something of greater value than traditional reductionist science: "There is much to be said for a procedure that combines a few carefully selected systems-level properties that monitor the performance of the whole, with selected 'red flag' components such as [water,] a game species or a toxic substance that, in themselves, have direct importance to the general public."[58]

In this context, water should be prioritized and treated differently than other agricultural resources like equipment or pesticides because it is the essential ingredient for farming in dryland regions. Just as Odum finds energy a useful common denominator between man and nature, water for food can become the meeting point—the focus for a holistic strategy—between an ethical imperative (saving the farmer) and resources conservation (saving the water). If water is given value outside the economic marketplace and environmental reserve, the debate over the ethical duty of water could be addressed in legislation and regulation. The mission of the United States has long been to create a good society with well-being for all its inhabitants, not merely an indifferent government.[59] Ethical questions—doing good things— go far beyond prices, markets, and efficiency.

Shifting into Socially and Environmentally Sustainable Agriculture

While making broad-based connections between economics, agriculture, and environment is akin to ancient priests reading entrails to divine the future, these connections can suggest the importance of an inclusive agroecological model. Today's conventional farming, now dominated by short-term, in-and-out agribusiness, cannot continue indefinitely. Mary Fund, of the Kansas Rural Center, wrote in March 1996 that "sustainable agriculture is a goal, not a fixed technology. It is an ever changing approach to farming that changes as the body of knowledge grows about eco-systems and agriculture."[60] More recently, attention has been given not only to environment and economics but also to the societal context of resource management and development. Canadians D. Scott Slocombe and Caroline Van Bers, for example, are shifting their attention: "We should be thinking in terms of sustainable societies, not sustainable development."[61] They argue that a sustainable society is attentive to personal rights, family stability, and health and safety in addition to productivity and a respect for nature. Strategies to build a farmer-oriented Socially and Environmentally Sustainable Agriculture (SESA) would include:

1. Support long-term economic viability for small to moderate-sized farms such as the family farm to ensure social, economic, and environmental diversity necessary for agricultural and ecosystem stability.

2. Make farming attractive and achieve farm resiliency (e.g., reduce the escape to cities) by supporting self-employment, training for hands-on management, minimizing farm debt, improving farm safety, and encouraging low-input self-sufficiency.

3. Support rural communities that provide the working social framework of goods and services to encourage society beyond cities and suburbia.

4. Promote good environmental stewardship based on locally appropriate knowledge by looking at long-term environmental integrity together with long-term productivity and conserving soil and water, reducing dependence upon capital-intensive equipment and chemicals, creating new crops and markets, promoting individualized on-site response to local climate and geography, and encouraging diversity of crops.

5. Make farming meaningful by encouraging its support through citizen participation and government support. Because of its fundamental role in human affairs, farming should be seen as an essential and central enterprise for the well-being of civilization.

6. Move from corporate capitalism toward participatory democracy by constructing an economic picture wider than the agribusiness marketplace to encourage widespread responsible ownership of productive resources by those who work on farms.[62]

The outcomes of SESA would be sufficient production of human food and fiber, protection (rather than abuse) of the resource base, economic viability of on-site farming, and supportive (instead of exploitive) national and international farm policies. Much of this book has been dedicated to understanding Ogallala groundwater as part of a larger agricultural system whose existence is played out on the High Plains. In most instances today, the larger conventional agricultural system, which is heavily committed to agribusiness and the external marketplace forces of an exploitive world economy, has been extremely abusive of plains water, soil, and people. Socially and Environmentally Sustainable Agriculture describes a better system that has come to be known variously as sustainable, alternative, regenerative, low-input, and agro-ecological.

Turning the Plains into a Geography of Hope

Andrew H. Clark, Paul B. Sears, and, most recently, geographer William E. Riebsame have asked if the plains region was too fragile to support "the human creation of socially nurturing landscapes."[63] David M. Smith, a philosopher of geography, seeks a "geography of everyday moralities which 'glue' together the assumptions and arguments of particular peoples in particular places." He contends that justice and sustainability are "grounded in the lived experience of particular people in time and place as well as in the abstractions of philosophical debate."[64] Riebsame concludes that "after a century of settlement and transformation, the Great Plains still spark controversy over the proper human use of semiarid grasslands."[65]

In the halls of Congress, when a farm bill is being debated, it is hard to argue against the productivity of the settled plains, despite the price paid in both depletion of water and soil and repeated punishment of its people. The region's reputation as the breadbasket and feedbag of the world is a moral geography that dominates recent thinking reflected in the farm bills of the last fifty years. Today, industrial farming plays a major role in the ability of each American farmer to feed eight dozen other people, compared to four others when the nation began. It is remarkable that less than 2 percent of Americans work on farms, compared to 30 or 40 percent of the population in many nations around the world. This success story—perhaps the most important in all of modern history—does much to define American prosperity overall.

Kenneth A. Cook, of the Center for Resource Economics, called for "a new social contract between farmers and society." He said that, "For its part, society will have to recognize the enormous cost farmers already bear to conserve natural resources and protect the environment. Taxpayers will have to be willing to share more of that burden—probably a great deal more—as external costs of agricultural production becomes internalized."[66] Why should Americans at a distance from the plains worry about the deepening problems of the plains, its people, and its soil and water? "We accept," says Smith, "the universality of certain grand moral sentiments or values" such as human equality and social justice. They are the core of American morality described by Sagoff and Smith.[67]

Final Note

Most environmental history originally gave its primary attention to understanding the wilderness. But unlike agriculture, wilderness is said to function without human activity and does not inform humanity except as a contrast. Environmental historians have devoted their attention to industrial and urban waste and pollution, where the remains of nature are hard to find in the fumes and the concrete. Here humanity is dominant and dangerously isolated. It is impossible to measure human value—or any value—against itself.

Agriculture explores humanity's most profound and opportunistic link with nature. Humans have now enjoyed ten thousand years of subdued soil and domesticated plants and animals, but we have also used nature in a surprisingly narrow vein that industrial agriculture narrows still further. Farming remains our most rudimentary and profound form of environmental management. When compared to the diversity of nature's species, the variety of crops and animals we farm seems a thin sliver indeed. Yet farming is probably the only place left where humans continuously and directly experience the nonhuman world. Farmland is a once-natural place that was entered, cut back, and rearranged into a domesticated landscape. Despite mechanization and chemicals, agriculture is still our most intimate "living tether" to the natural world. The physical setting, natural or modified, is still the primary agent controlling agricultural success. Agriculture is the least prone of all fundamental human activities to be permanently transformed—truly domesticated—into an environment of artifacts—the clusters of things that people have made. Even a genetically altered ear of corn is closer to the soil than a steel bar is to iron ore. Farmers, though distanced from nature by reconfigured soil, reshaped plants, and chemical additives, must still deal with the basic stuff of their physical surroundings: climate, soil, organic matter, and water.

The High Plains environment was, and is, easily harmed. Farming on the High Plains has created dangerous dependencies on scarce resources and fragile processes. The Ogallala aquifer could have lain forever like a sleeping behemoth in a bed of gravel and sand under solid rock, but human intervention captured its water to turn a desert into a garden. Although environmental history can be complex, the logic of this book has been simple: without irrigation, the region encompassing southwest Kansas and the Oklahoma-Texas Panhandle would have remained a hostile and unproductive frontier environment. It still experiences hot windy summers and harsh winters. Water is not easily acquired. Even today, dryland farming remains high-risk farming about which the best local producers have serious doubts. The label, "Dust Bowl," is apt. Still, the region became one of the most productive farming regions in the world. This dramatic turnabout depended on extraordinary technological innovations in irrigation and the overall industrialization of agriculture. As groundwater levels decline, workable alternatives for sustainable development are being explored that would have less effect on the Ogallala aquifer and that would still serve human needs. The inescapable droughts and repeated depopulations, together with the accelerated overconsumption of Ogallala groundwater, continue to make the region so vulnerable that farming prevails only with heavy government support. The livelihood of hundreds of thousands of people depends upon this flimsy infrastructure.

The Ogallala belongs to humanity because we are a globally dominant species whose needs spin a perhaps illusory web of mastery. The whole world depends upon the Ogallala. Its wheat goes, in large part, to Russia,

China, and Africa's Sahel. Its pork ends up in Japanese and American super-markets. Its beef goes everywhere. As a result, the clear, fresh waters of the Ogallala are being unnaturally gulped up at ten times their pace of replacement. Over the next fifty years, when the world's food needs multiply five or ten times, the Ogallala waters, fulfilling Adam Smith's eighteenth-century prediction, will become as precious as diamonds.

• • •

Appendix: Puzzling Out the Plains

The early struggle of settlers on the High Plains led not to comfortable settlement but only to more struggle. Unlike successful earlier settlement across Appalachia and through the Midwest, the vaunted yeoman farmer seemed unable to conquer this drought-prone region. Instead, farmers went through decades of hardship. The problem attracted a galaxy of scientists, geographers, sociologists, and historians, who sought to comprehend the tough region. The cry for water in a dry place like the Dust Bowl region must be more than background noise for historians; rather, it is the first and essential signal to come out of the cosmic roar. What happened to Manifest Destiny when Americans, like marathon runners, "hit the wall" of drought on the High Plains? The lack of water put farmer-settlers at perpetual risk. The struggle on the plains should have forced revision of the settlement myth forged from the midwestern and eastern frontiers. The successive failures to turn the High Plains into another cornucopia revealed that the American dream had limits.

The Social Construction of the Plains

Cosmologists—people who study the universe—face a conundrum that also applies to the plains, its water, and its farms. Physical theory of the cosmos suggests that the expanding universe should have been uniformly smooth after the big bang. Instead, for still-unknown reasons, the universe became lumpy, fortunately for us, having clumped into galaxies, stars, planets, plants, pigs, and people.

Raw information about the plains is equally difficult to interpret. Numerous historians and theorists argue that information has no order until we impose patterns on it. The French anthropologist Claude Lévi-Strauss assayed that "a truly total history would confront [us] with chaos . . . a truly total history would cancel itself out."[1] Thus the historian, geographer, or some other observer must create a mental picture that binds together events that would otherwise spin off into space. The event, which can be something like the poor spring wheat harvest of 1996 and its local, national, and global implications, is like the physicist's quark—real but gone in a flash—and yet it is part of a complex continuous process. The philosopher Paul Ricoeur carries us further when he says an event is not a brief episode but a "variable of the plot."[2] Ricoeur concluded that historical explanation makes pattern out of unthinkable chaos; it makes the "intelligible spring from the accidental, the universal from the singular, the necessary or the probable from the episodic." Making patterns allows the accidental—one thing after another—to become meaningful sequence—one thing because of another. The social theorist Max Weber wrestled with historical cause-and-effect and concluded, "The number and type of causes which have influenced any given event are always infinite and there is nothing in the things themselves to set some of them apart as alone meriting attention. . . . Order is brought into this chaos only on the condition that in every case only a *part* of concrete reality is interesting and *significant* to us, because only it is related to the *cultural values* with which we approach reality."[3] By dint of the questions we ask, we are delighted when we find clumps in the smoothness.

Raw facts about the plains make no sense until those facts are assembled into patterns dictated by our interests. We see the plains as an incomprehensible black box that we pry open by identifying and organizing its natural and human components, a process that includes many variables:

water	farmers	prices and commmodity markets
soil	crops	government intervention
climate	technology	public values
grasses	banking	

By concretizing our information around these reference points, we find signals in the noise. Our goal is to make intelligible chaotic phenomena and uncover the relationship among them. For example: How do local crop needs shape groundwater consumption? Will groundwater stop being a free good and be given a price? Why is there so much resistance to higher water efficiency in hog production? Whatever the plains scenario, the Ogallala aquifer, originally not part of the grassland or farming, is a dominate feature of the plains.

Conventional History: Frontier Triumphalism

We have already seen in Chapter 1 how military expeditions in the early nineteenth century reported the plains as the Great American Desert. This made the first settlements in the 1870s all the more extraordinary. Yet, they were seen as the inexorable fulfillment of the nation's Manifest Destiny. A rare decade of heavy rains in the late 1870s and early 1880s was cheered as a climate improvement that demonstrated that God and destiny were on America's side. This enthusiastic optimism was reinforced by railroad promotions, small-town boosterism, and the promise of agricultural productivity that would match or surpass the remarkable abundance of the prairie Midwest.

Such optimism reflected the American belief in national triumphalism. A tantalizing concept, triumphalism shows up in most American history textbooks. Broadly speaking, it was based on the premise that human history, until the last three hundred years of a three-million-year past, had been dominated by unspeakable scarcity. European immigrants remembered long histories of the food, tools, and shelter that made them painfully vulnerable to plagues, starving times, and bitter winters. In general, scarcity and suffering were alleviated by the Industrial Revolution of the nineteenth century. Mass production turned Americans into consumers of material goods and raised their living standards to such high levels that Roman emperors would have been envious. The tenets of triumphalism are hypnotizing: the power of science and technology is unlimited, nature can be tamed to serve humanity, material progress is inevitable, and enlightened humans like Americans represent the pinnacle of all creation. This transformation was understood to depend on large food surpluses produced by durable Jeffersonian yeoman farmers who efficiently used abundant virgin soils. Triumphalism encouraged environmental imperialism: we can twist nature any way we wish and turn the world into our artifacts. Whether during the bonanza years of the early twentieth century, the irrigation revolution, or industrial agriculture, plains farming was lauded as the best example of America's ability to overcome adversity to turn a desert into a garden.

FREDERICK JACKSON TURNER'S FRONTIER THESIS

Frederick Jackson Turner, Wisconsin historian, gave a popular shape to America's passionate westering. His 1893 frontier thesis, which never took the plains experience into account, enthusiastically claimed that a truly American character was forged from the frontier struggle in the Old West along the Appalachian frontier.[4] He wrote, "What the Mediterranean Sea was to the Greeks, breaking the bond of custom, offering new experiences, calling out new institutions and activities, that, and more, the ever retreating frontier has been to the United States directly, and to the nations of Europe more remotely."[5] The frontier line between free land and settled land had expanded westward for three hundred years. Americans sat, as if at a parade, and watched the frontier recede. As we watched, we saw the traders, the steamships, the railroads. From the early seventeenth century to the close of the nineteenth century, civilization pushed forward. To Turner, American expansion into its "empty" western regions provided the stimulus for a unique national character. "The wilderness masters the colonist." It was both a *place*, the zone of free land beyond the western edge of settlement, and a *process*, in which old habits fell to the pragmatic needs of wilderness survival. But plains settlement belied the advance, since farmers spent a hundred years under frontier conditions until the federal government bailed them out in a decidedly unfree manner. Failure on the High Plains undermined Turner's argument.

Ray Allen Billington, the leading heir of Turner's frontier thesis, argued for the existence of a unique frontier environment, both social and physical, that endowed the pioneers with traits that were particularly American: self-made, independent, dynamic, and freedom-loving.[6] Billington's approach was particularly relevant to the plains because in it the farmer was the forgotten man of frontier expansionism in the West. "If the trappers and the drovers had their way, there would have been no frontier"; they sought to protect raw nature and "hold civilization back, to protect the beaver streams from intruders, to guard the grasslands from the plow" in order to protect their occupations. It was "the farmers [who] were the true harbingers of advancing civilization. Not until the forests fell before their axes, their plows broke the prairie sod, and their barbed-wire fences crisscrossed the plains would the West be won."[7] Billington concluded that in the three decades after 1870, the years of premier settlement of the High Plains, more land was settled and placed under cultivation by farmers than in all the prior history of the continent: 430 million acres were settled and 225 million acres were put to the plow or grazed. "This was the greatest movement of peoples that the world had known to that day," and it marked the triumph of America.

WALTER PRESCOTT WEBB AND THE "GREAT FRONTIER"
Native Texan, teacher, and writer, Walter Prescott Webb hated the plains but loved them more. He virtually created for Americans the great "presence" of western space and time when he published *The Great Plains* in 1931. Webb, who wrote before technology tapped the Ogallala, agreed with John Wesley Powell that insufficient water would perpetually limit settlement on the plains and that those who attempted settlement would always find life a trial. He believed that vaunted American technological prowess had found its master. Webb also took care to note that plains conditions were improperly benchmarked by a wetter East: "It has been customary to speak of the rainfall in the West as deficient. The term is relative, coined or adopted by a people from a wetter region. Had the Great Plains been taken over by a people from a desert, another term, expressing the opposite meaning, would no doubt have been applied. The Spaniards, for example, said less about the aridity of this region than the Anglo-Americans."[8] Webb wrote before the 1930s Dust Bowl, but he could have foretold its impact. He did not anticipate the irrigation revolution of the 1960s and 1970s, but he did insist that the

High Plains climate would necessarily exert environmental limits over human well-being.

Webb highlighted climate factors usually ignored by historians. He wrote, "The distinguishing climatic characteristic of the Great Plains environment from the ninety-eight meridian to the Pacific slope is a deficiency in the most essential climatic element—water. . . . This deficiency . . . conditions plant life, animal life, and human life and institutions. In this deficiency is found the key to what may be called the plains civilization. It is the feature that makes the whole aspect of life west of the ninety-eight meridian such a contrast to life east of that line."[9] Webb was among the first to acknowledge the problems of the plains: unfriendly and unconquerable climate extremes characterized by insufficient rain, intense heat and cold, and the steady, strong, maddening wind. He quoted a 1925 U.S. climate report that wind velocities on the plains averaged fourteen or fifteen miles an hour in the Panhandle country, "winds which are ocean-like in character, as vast stretches of the plains are themselves ocean-like in their monotony and in their unbroken sweep to the far-away horizon."[10] The impact of plains wind, Webb concluded, "offers an alluring study for the student of social institutions and for the psychologist."[11] Intensified by blistering heat and extreme dryness, the "furness blasts" from June through September invite economic disaster: "Over ten million bushels of corn were destroyed in Kansas in one season. It is not uncommon for fine fields of dark-green corn to be destroyed in two days." Winter norther winds and blizzards (the "grizzly of the plains") are equally devastating. Webb told the story of an eastern visitor who asked a cowboy, "Does the wind blow this way here all the time?" "No, Mister. It'll maybe blow this way for a week or ten days, and then it'll take a change and blow like hell for a while."[12]

In a lesser-known and more philosophical work, *The Great Frontier* (1952), Webb anticipated the limits to growth debate of the early 1970s. He wrote that "the passing of free land should be registered by the passing of cheap food," and that the end of the four hundred year-European expansion boom will also signal the decline of rampant capitalism.[13] "In the Age of the Frontier western European society lived on the returns from its capital; today the capital is being consumed."[14] Webb extended Turner's question to ask: what will the United States, and the world, be like without its four hundred years of frontier expansionism? Webb was unusual among historians of his day in that he was concerned with environmental problems that would not be acknowledged until in the 1970s and 1980s: "we always deal with man in an environment, and we believe that the two are reciprocal factors which complement and adjust themselves to each other."[15]

GILBERT C. FITE AND THE FARMER'S FRONTIER

Oklahoma professor Gilbert C. Fite, born in the Midwest and educated in South Dakota and Missouri, invoked the frontier thesis but put the farmer in the foreground.[16] "The West," he wrote, "experienced a number of frontiers, but it was the farmers who furnished most of the population."[17] He admitted to "certain Jeffersonian prejudices about rural America" because "more than any other group," farmers "were mainly responsible for finally bringing the frontier to [a successful] end."[18] Fite gave special attention to the High Plains because farmers experienced it as the zone of greatest challenge, compared to the relative ease of settlement in Oregon and California. The plains were the final test of America's frontier fortitude and the completion of Manifest Destiny. In Fite's view, the winter blizzards and summer droughts were typical frontier challenges to be conquered. As declared by an eastern businessman in the 1860s, once the plains had been plowed, "here the forests too will come." At man's bidding, "every product of the earth that ministers to human contentment will come,"[19] in true fulfillment of the frontier's promise. Fite acknowledged that the plains were boom and bust but that each new boom time, which was inevitable, carried farmers into higher rural prosperity. Fite also admitted that small groups of farmers abandoned their rugged individualism when drought forced them on the public dole, at first distributed by army relief and state agencies.[20] But the majority battled on as autonomous laborers. Despite these rare qualifications, Fite kept the frontier story intact by describing farmer pluck and luck and by maintaining the idea that on the plains there was sufficient rain to enable farmers to master their environment and move toward a successful rural society that marked the end

351

of the frontier. A rural society centered on small towns, surrounded by prosperous family farms, was at the heart of a benevolent American prosperity.

The Reformist Tradition

The problem with American triumphalism is that it has generally discounted environmental problems such as resource depletion, toxic-waste dumps, unhealthy cities, and lack of wilderness protection. The same triumphalism largely ignored the farmer's reconfigured soil, reshaped plants, and chemical additives. Out of American triumphalism emerged a form of giantism. The nature of capital creates a false notion of an infinitely expanding environment. In the 1960s and 1970s, the Ogallala was treated as if it would forever water an increasing number of fields. Despite declining water levels, shrinking numbers of family farms, and persistently low crop prices, triumphalism maximized grain production and blinded Americans to the need to optimize Ogallala pumping to save water, revive local farmers, and limit the impact of prices. Instead, most economists and government planners (and even most farmers) think that the money economy will maintain expansive Ogallala farming. As long as only marketplace rules are applied there will be no way to prevent resources such as water from reckless consumption and no way to prevent the family farm from slipping away.

PROGRESSIVE AND NEW DEAL REFORM

We saw in Chapter 2 the rise of the William E. Smythe's Irrigation Crusade during the Progressive Era that lauded government planning and scientific efficiency. To Smythe and others, extensive plains farming on large acreage was wasteful, old-fashioned, geographically inappropriate, and doomed to failure. In contrast, as a model these reformers looked to five- to ten-acre California-style intensive irrigation farms that would overcome the deficits of plains geography and climate.

As the low prices and "plow-ups" of grassland of the 1920s accelerated into the Dust Bowl disaster of the 1930s, federal reformers looked to drastic alternatives. In 1934 the Land Committee of the National Resources Board published a comprehensive review of the nation's natural resources.[21] With a strongly reformist mandate, the committee asserted the primacy of public interest over private property rights and thus contradicted the tradition of transferring public lands into private hands. Heedless and unplanned land exploitation must be replaced by land-use planning that served the general welfare. Uncontrolled private landholding has induced the abuse of the nation's soil and threatened to "destroy the physical foundations of national welfare."[22] The board held that soil exhaustion could not be overcome by better equipment and highly productive hybrid crops. The committee was pessimistic and predicted indefinitely declining yields. Seeking major land reform, it proposed several major steps. It recommended immediate action to reduce soil erosion, which it believed was one of agriculture's most acute problems. This led to the formation of the Soil Conservation Service in 1936. It advised that wrongheaded settlement by ill-equipped farmers on impoverished land be prevented, forcibly if necessary. It noted that plains farmers had long lived in the rural equivalent of slums because farm family incomes were so low and were not capable of rising as long as the land was of such poor quality. Yet farmers continued to drain the soil of its fertility. As much as seventy-five million acres nationwide needed to be taken out of production. At the same time, the 1934 Taylor Grazing Act withdrew the remaining public land from homesteading. The Land Committee took its most drastic step by urging farm families to resettle, as we saw in Chapter 3. Overall, about six million acres were removed from farming on the plains. Post–World War II land-reform projects such as the water-transfer proposals of the Department of Commerce's 1982 *Six-State High Plains-Ogallala Aquifer Regional Resources Study*, the promising but politically ill-fated *National Agricultural Lands Study* of 1980, and the hopeful 1998 USDA report *A Time to Act* never came to fruition.

PAUL B. SEARS: LEARNING TO READ THE PLAINS

Stormily received when it was first published in 1935, *Deserts on the March*, by biologist-turned-historian Paul B. Sears, turned upside down the popular textbook version of America's benevolent westward expansion.[23] While Webb emphasized harsh environmental conditions, Sears blasted destructive human exploitation that severely damaged a fragile and difficult environment. According to Sears, the settlers' blind push on the plains was a reckless invasion of a delicately balanced climax environment of soil, water, plants, animals, and climate. As a result, they did violent harm to this balance (and consequently to themselves). When settlement reached the High Plains, the nation's vaunted combination of mechanical invention, exuberant vitality, and unparalleled speed destroyed the opportunity to turn the plains into a region of sustainable agriculture. This intensified the drought and dust storms that drove half a million people away in the 1930s.[24]

Sears reintroduced a global perspective proposed by George Perkins Marsh seventy years earlier. Hadn't China and India and Greece and Rome, brought about their own downfall by overexploiting the land? Weren't all civilizations built on the borrowed capital of diminishing soil fertility?[25] On the plains, modern profit-oriented, high-production, mechanized agribusiness mined the soil at unexpected and unacceptable speed. This had disastrous impacts, largely because of the refusal to acknowledge the limits the region's climate places upon intensive farming. Using the emergent science of ecology, Sears emphasized the fragile balance between soil and humus and water and climate, which, if weakened, could make a region uninhabitable. "It is not too far off to say that when life enters new territory, environment dictates the terms."[26] The native grasses on the plains are durable but the single-crop farming that replaced them is not. Overplowing and overgrazing made the excellent plains soil vulnerable to wind and water erosion.

DONALD E. WORSTER: CAPITALISM MADE PLAINS FAILURE CHRONIC

Other statements of reform focus on whether the Dust Bowl experience revealed a chronic agricultural failure on the plains and was not a single terrible moment. Kansas-bred historian Donald E. Worster found that the combination of aggressive human intervention and an unexpectedly vulnerable environment guaranteed trouble for both the European invaders and the High Plains environment. In his 1979 *Dust Bowl: The Southern Plains in the 1930s*, Worster argues that the 1930s Dust Bowl became a disaster raised to catastrophic proportions by human error, which exacerbated the worst drought cycle in 360 years.[27] Worster moves beyond strict historical analysis to offer a cautionary and reformist statement.[28] High Plains troubles resulted not only from a misunderstood climate but from mechanized, single-crop, exploitive farming that was a form of exploitive capitalism rather than anything remotely self-sustaining.[29] The results will not be easy to overcome even with the best resources and intentions. Unlike historic Chinese deforestation or Mediterranean soil destruction, "the Dust bowl took only fifty years to accomplish. It cannot be blamed on illiteracy or overpopulation or social disorder. It came about because the [capitalist] culture was operating in precisely the way it was supposed to. . . . the inevitable outcome of a culture that deliberately, self-consciously, set itself that task of dominating and exploiting the land for all it was worth."[30] When a fragile environment was invaded by such narrow-minded settlers, the result was "tragic, revealing, and paradigmatic" for American civilization. Can a humane society really be founded on "a highly mechanized system of cropping plants and animals, making the earth a vast food factory, controlled by a very small number of multinational corporations"?[31] Worster concluded that the Dust Bowl tragedy, and society's responses to it, was a judgment on the quality of the twentieth century.

FRANK AND DEBORAH POPPER: EMPTYING THE PLAINS

Frank and Deborah Popper, regional planners from New Jersey, stirred up plains farmers when, in 1987, they made a county-by-county population study that showed persistent decline over a significant part of the region from the Dakotas to Texas.[32] They concluded that large parts of the plains have consistently proved resistant to stable settlement. In their view, portions of the region's agricultural and energy economies are now in near-depression. Soil erosion is high. The Ogallala's water table is dropping. Many plains counties and towns enjoyed their highest populations before 1930, some before 1920, and others have been declining steadily since 1890. The reason, say the Poppers, is economic and environmental miscalculation in areas where permanent settlement should never have been allowed. The hardships and out-migration of the Dust Bowl were only the worst example of a continuous process. Today, the process is making the plains nearly uninhabitable on environmental or agricultural grounds: "In the 1990 census the majority of plains counties in all ten plains states lost population. The losses seem likely to continue. The depopulating areas constitute the reemergent frontier of the Plains."[33]

The Poppers proposed a radical solution that became the flash point for vehement defenses by plains boosters. The Poppers called for a "Buffalo Commons," which would be a new regional economy centered not on agriculture but on land preservation. It would cover about a quarter of the plains land area, primarily in nine rural counties that contain only 6 percent of the plains's population. "The fences will come down, shortgrass will be replanted, and native species like buffalo, elk, antelope, deer and their predators will be restored."[34] Included would be an integrated buffalo–Native American culture. The Buffalo Commons, concluded the Poppers, offers a way to attain a self-sufficiency and stability never before available to European settlers, but that may have been true for earlier Native American inhabitants. It would amount to the nation's most advanced experiment in replacing extraction of soil and water with preservation.

Natural Resources Analyses

THE NEBRASKA GEOGRAPHERS: LAWSON AND BLOUET

It became clear that triumphal frontier history woefully failed to explain the High Plains, its settlement, and its farming. Instead, the complex plains phenomena demanded an approach that joined together environment and people. Cultural geographer Merlin Lawson and his colleague Brian W. Blouet put together a conference in 1973 that sought to examine myths and realities that shaped plains history. The results were published in 1975 as *Images of the Plains: The Role of Human Nature in Settlement*.[35] This collection of essays focused on explorer and settler visions of the plains geography, including real and imagined climatic hazards. The essays emphasized the lasting influence of original impressions, such as the plains as the Great American Desert, and how such views controlled behavioral responses of settlers often regardless of real conditions. Drought was almost pathologically denied despite its effects of hardship, starvation, and out-migration. At the other extreme, the imaginative promise of the plains as a potential garden that would mirror eastern abundance caused settlers to feel guilty if they failed to grow plentiful crops. Both sides of the desert-garden paradigm were nonfunctional and destructive.

Blouet was joined by historian Frederick C. Luebke in 1979 to publish *The Great Plains: Environment and Culture*, the findings of a conference of historians and geographers in 1977.[36] The team argued that the natural environment is more than a stage or setting; instead, it is a dynamic relationship that connects humans and nature. High Plains communities, for example, are strongly driven to standardization by American business practices, while the physical geography of the plains affects functions, numbers, and spacing of towns in different ways than in the East or Midwest. Plains conditions also requires larger farms, more technology, fewer people, and fewer supporting institutions. Did these conditions allow sustainability or hold the plains in a colonial status? Were plains institutions less resilient than elsewhere and therefore more prone to rapid decline?

In 1981 Lawson and colleague Maurice E. Baker published another set of essays, *The Great Plains: Perspectives and Prospects*, out of a 1979 conference at the Center for Great Plains Studies in Lincoln, Nebraska.[37] Their essayists combined social science and natural resource analysis. They admitted that the High Plains has not been an easy place in which to live. Successful analysis of the risks of the plains must be based, they said, upon the study of natural resources that have been modified by human action together with regional social, political, and economic institutions that have been shaped by geographical conditions. In this light, past policies can be satisfactorily understood and a foundation can be created for future decision making. (This attentiveness to future planning is a typical rationale for plains studies.) What, realistically, are the available resources on the plains? How can policymakers anticipate future conditions? The studies emphasized the need to move away from notions of continuous economic development based on markets and private enterprise as well as the need to recognize that conditions on the plains have limited agricultural use in the past and will continue to do so.

Water for Irrigation

Groundwater issues, particularly the importance of the Ogallala aquifer for successful farming on the semiarid south-central High Plains, have been largely defined by a geologist, two historians, and two geographers.

ED GUTENTAG: GEOLOGICAL SCIENCE DEFINES OGALALLA DECLINE

Much of the information about the discovery, use, and fate of the Ogallala aquifer is based on sketchy and anecdotal records. U.S. Geological Survey geologist Edwin D. Gutentag changed the shape of information about High Plains groundwater by conducting a systematic hydrological survey of the aquifer zone from northern Kansas through the Oklahoma Panhandle and into Texas.[38] From the 1960s to the 1980s he served in the USGS office in Garden City, Kansas. There he led a team of USGS scientists to establish a database that definitively mapped the decline of the Ogallala aquifer during the critical first two decades of irrigation. Gutentag and his team combined maps of irrigated cropland with measurements of water pumped from a small sample of irrigation wells, from which they developed estimates of water use for all irrigated areas. This mapping, which definitively connected irrigated cropland and groundwater withdrawals, was intended to provide water managers with a means to evaluate the effects of various management strategies on the aquifer. Eventually Gutentag's team applied data from four technologies: Earth observation by satellite, digital-image processing, geohydrologic techniques for spatial analysis, and automated digital cartography. Gutentag's data, and the work of his successors, became the foundation for continued record-keeping and mapping by the three state-supported groundwater management districts in western Kansas.

DONALD E. GREEN

In 1973, in *Land of the Underground Rain*, Texas historian Donald E. Green produced the first comprehensive history of one of the Ogallala's primary irrigation regions, the Texas Staked Plains.[39] While it is not exactly an environmental history, Green's pioneering study integrates hydrology, irrigation technology, agriculture, politics, and economics in a history that covers nineteenth-century hard times, the few periods of sufficient rain and high prices, the difficult Dust Bowl years, and the transformation of the southern High Plains due to drilling, pumping, and irrigation technologies. Green took the first steps to identify the problem region, its environmental challenges, and a series of historical responses, not all successful.

THE KANSAS GEOGRAPHERS: KROMM, WHITE, AND PLAINS REDUX

Just as Gutentag established physical data to understand the function of Ogallala groundwater, Kansas geographers David E. Kromm and Stephen E. White broke new ground with a rigorous survey of how High Plains residents saw the troubled irrigation economy of the region. In 1984 they sampled a cross section of households totaling 956 persons in fourteen counties of six High Plains states.[40] The results verified the authors' general perception that the primary irrigation issues on the plains were a complex and interactive mix of economics, technology, and farming. Irrigators gave high priority to low crop prices, high fuel and equipment costs, the continued depletion of groundwater, the need for better groundwater regulation, and irrigation management. The positive impact of irrigation upon plains farming was reflected by the perception that low rainfall was no longer the greatest fear among the farmers. A long list of depletion controls was topped by better irrigation efficiency and the clear identification of problem zones.

Kromm and White quickly found themselves involved in policy questions of groundwater management. A 1992 survey that followed up on their 1984 work revealed that most irrigators favored vigorous but local control as the best means for sustainable management of the aquifer.[41] Few interviewees in any of their surveys doubted that Ogallala groundwater levels were declining, a problem they recognized as affecting their future economic well-being. Most irrigators had put hard cash into waste-saving technologies and were aggressive water-conservation managers. But they complained about the maze of bureaucracy and regulation demanded by federal, state, and regional groundwater-management districts.

In another approach, White raised serious doubts about the widely reported depopulation of the Ogallala region and the collapse of its agriculture society. He discovered significant population growth in numerous counties. In a direct response to the Poppers' proposal for the removal of people and the creation of a grasslands preserve, White concluded that his data demonstrated that "Population has actually increased slightly for the entire region between 1960 and 1990 but has become more concentrated. The findings challenge the feasibility of applying the buffalo commons approach to the Ogallala region."[42] Both Kromm and White concluded that their data justified belief in the social resilience of the High Plains.

JIM SHEROW: ENVIRONMENTAL HISTORY OF A REGIONAL WATERSHED

Kansas historian James Earl Sherow, in his 1990 study, *Watering the Valley: Development along the High Plains Arkansas River, 1870–1950*,[43] offers more than a study of water or agricultural development; he uses a watershed to shape a new form of regional history. Sherow treats the High Plains Arkansas River Valley, from the river's origin near Leadville, Colorado, to its movement outside the High Plains at Dodge City, Kansas, as his primary geographical unit instead of towns, counties, and states. His water-based metaphor for agricultural development is organic: "What makes a particular organism adaptable or maladaptable depends on its own nature. It is possible to explore how well irrigation companies filled their niches by examining the factors that led to their creation and molded their operations."[44] Using the tools of history, geology, engineering, law, politics, economics, and agriculture, Sherow describes the creation of an agricultural system in the river valley that was dependent upon water, its control, and its management. He also uncovers the unending and inevitable discord created when inhabitants of the valley do not have enough water because of monoculture farming, private enterprise, and external economic forces. Despite engineering expertise, he concludes that "the 'conquest' of nature always remained incomplete. Indeed, people in the Arkansas River Valley worked in a dialectical relationship with nature,"[45] which they largely did not understand.

The Controlling Power of Climate

A number of studies, primarily by geographers and agricultural scientists, have been based on the premise that the largest variable for agricultural success on the High Plains is climate, especially recurrent drought.

NORMAN J. ROSENBERG: BUILDING STRATEGIES FOR FUTURE RESPONSES TO DROUGHT

Studies in the 1970s led by Norman J. Rosenberg, when he was agricultural meteorologist at the University of Nebraska, were among the first to recognize in scientific terms—quantification and analysis—that drought was a characteristic feature of the High Plains not a random happening.[46] He suggested that it does not need to be a dramatic event. Rosenberg and his group of researchers learned that even small negative deviations in precipitation—virtually nonevents—will push a region into drought. One of their goals was the development of long-range climate forecasting. Rosenberg confirmed that weather conditions in the mid-1970s were in a drought cycle like those in the 1890s, the 1930s, and the 1950s. He and his team identified a history of clear links between drought and agricultural productivity and the decline of rural society. They analyzed the role of improved response to drought enabled by technological and energy-intensive agricultural systems and the improved reaction-time by government. They also looked at potential defenses against drought such as weather modification, expanded irrigation, and agricultural management techniques. Out of these different features of drought impact and response, Rosenberg sought to build an integrated framework to forecast future drought and to improve society's capacity to mitigate them by advance preparation as well as direct response.

MARTYN J. BOWDEN: SETTLER IMAGES OF THE PLAINS

The historical geographer Martyn J. Bowden assumed that drought is the primary controlling factor determining successful settlement and long-term prosperity on the plains. Because of the refusal to acknowledge chronic drought by farmers and the public, the actual damage is more severe. Because there are recurrent fears that the Dust Bowl could be repeated, Bowden sorted through the mythology to collect climate data and identify the real occurrence of drought on the High Plains.[47] Bowden concluded that American perceptions of the High Plains repeatedly shifts between the plains as the Great American Desert and the Great American Garden.[48] The myth of the desert reflected early nineteenth century antipathy by a "forest-society" toward grassland settlement that was reinforced by drought and depopulation in the 1890s and 1930s. The garden image included false conclusions about rainfall, soil quality, heat, wind, cold, and the capacity of the region to grow corn, since corn symbolized agricultural prosperity. Bowden noted the historic irony that the myth of the garden coincided with data on unusually heavy rains in the 1860s (said to be the result of wartime cannon fire) and again in the early 1880s (ostensibly the result of rain following the plow).

The question was how to find the right signals in all the noise. Bowden and his colleague Richard A. Warrick integrated dendroclimatological (tree ring) and sunspot cycles, tracked down nineteenth-century climate data that had been gathered, for example, by army fort medical doctors on the plains, and made inferences from data on wheat-yield declines, population migration, farm transfers, and federal relief programs. This data reinforced the historic memory of climate impact on society. Bowden and Warrick arrived at two conclusions. First, a "lessening" hypothesis suggests that technology and societal infrastructure can reduce the impact of climate change, as demonstrated in the minimized effects of the drought of the 1970s compared to the 1930s. Second, this protection creates a "partially closed livelihood system" in which local farmers become less self-sufficient and more dependent on the external supports of world markets, federal aid, and new machinery. They become less able to fend for themselves in a crisis: e.g., debts cannot be paid off. The larger society feels a ripple effect more than when local farmers alone bore the brunt of hardship. The systems of supports diminish the self-sufficiency and independence of the family farmer, and thus erases his historic identity. By identifying "pathways of drought impact" through regional,

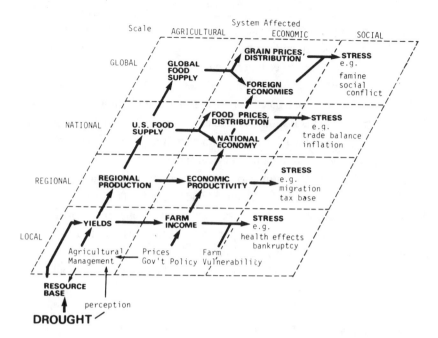

Scale
System Affected
AGRICULTURAL   ECONOMIC   SOCIAL

GLOBAL

**GLOBAL
FOOD
SUPPLY**

**GRAIN PRICES,
DISTRIBUTION**

**FOREIGN
ECONOMIES**

STRESS
e.g.

famine
social
conflict

NATIONAL

**U.S. FOOD
SUPPLY**

**FOOD PRICES,
DISTRIBUTION**

**NATIONAL
ECONOMY**

STRESS
e.g.
trade balance
inflation

REGIONAL

**REGIONAL
PRODUCTION**

**ECONOMIC
PRODUCTIVITY**

STRESS
e.g.
migration
tax base

LOCAL

YIELDS

**FARM
INCOME**

STRESS
e.g.
health effects
bankruptcy

Agricultural   Prices   Farm
Management   Gov't Policy Vulnerability

**RESOURCE
BASE**

perception

DROUGHT

18. Drought impact pathways. This diagram identifies the widespread and complex effects of High Plains drought as its impact spreads regionally, nationally, and internationally, and influences farmers and communities, consumer prices, and international trade, even causing a global threat of famine. From Richard A. Warrick and Martyn J. Bowden, "The Changing Impacts of Droughts in the Great Plains," in Merlin P. Lawson and Maurice E. Baker, eds., *The Great Plains: Perspectives and Prospects* (Lincoln: University of Nebraska Press, 1981), 113.

national, and global society, Bowden and Warrick provided a systems-analysis structure that clarifies the vivid man-environment interaction described by Webb, Malin, Worster and others. They argued that environmental problems like drought (and presumably global warming), when identified soon enough, can be affected by public policy and planning for the future.

MICKY GLANTZ AND THE CONTEXT OF GLOBAL DESERTIFICATION
Michael H. Glantz, social scientist at the National Center for Atmospheric Research (NCAR) in Boulder, Colorado, was among the first to explore the web of links between the natural forces of drought and agriculture in semi-

arid regions. He explored the likely convergence between global warming as measured by carbon dioxide in the atmosphere and the rate of Ogallala consumption.[49] Glantz observed that radically different and geographically distant natural phenomena often interacted closely and shaped each other. He also identified the interconnections between agricultural trends, global marketplace forces, social institutions, and changing environmental conditions.

Glantz positioned the High Plains within the framework of desertification trends around the world, both in historical and modern terms. He concluded that desertification will continue to expand and bring human hardship around the world, of which the High Plains is one example. The challenge in all cases, he believed, was to bring to bear aggressive management of arid and semiarid agriculture in order to support local populations, avert hardship and starvation, and prevent out-migrations. He described the Ogallala region as one human-environment experiment that might be a worldwide resource for management strategies.

The Environmentalist Window onto the Plains

Historical confusion about the true nature of the High Plains centered on the nature of its droughts, whether traditional American dirt farming could prevail, and whether alternative actions could make up for the plains deficits. These alternatives included irrigation from groundwater and federal price supports. A scientific base began emerging in the late nineteenth century that offered a better integrated view of the High Plains as a distinctive ecosystem with well-defined climate conditions.

FREDERICK E. CLEMENTS

Biologist Frederic E. Clements, a Nebraska native, studied the native plains grasses, and his conclusions did much to invent American environmental science. Donald E. Worster's important 1977 study, revised in 1994, *Nature's Economy: The Roots of Ecology*,[50] cites Clements's emphasis on the inevitable, delicate, and nervous interplay between plains ecology and its settlement: ''From Clements' plant studies emerged a coherent and elaborate system of ecological theory that was not only preeminently influential in the new science, but also had important things to say about the pioneers' relation to the American grassland."[51]

Clements emphasized that a natural landscape was less "an aimless wandering to and fro" in some kind of a meaningless chaos, but "a steady flow toward stability that can be exactly plotted by the scientist" into the ecological "climax." In the long run, the intertwined variables of heat and cold, rainfall, and wind are the forces that control soil dynamics and vegetation shifts. Clements's climax condition "is a unified mechanism in which the whole is greater than a sum of its parts and hence it constitutes a new kind of organic being with novel properties."[52] If on the plains "only one kind of [natural] community deserves to be called the mature stage," then human intervention, which diverts this mechanism to its own purpose, brings on a fatal chaos. What does human invasion tear apart, and can anything satisfactory be built in its place? In Clements's words, "There is good and even conclusive evidence . . . that the prairie climax has been in existence for several millions of years at least."[53] According to Clements, writes Worster, "it was not possible to have both a climax state of vegetation and a highly developed human culture on the same territory. . . . [T]he pioneers and homesteaders unwittingly prepared the soil for a social and ecological disaster: the Dust Bowl of the 1930s."[54] Americans could not comprehend the full extent of the opportunities and pitfalls of their westward expansion until ecology and history had been wedded.

JAMES C. MALIN

Kansas-born and -bred James C. Malin wedded climate and history to build a holistic ecological approach toward grassland settlement.[55] Writing in the 1940s and 1950s, Malin took issue with Clements's "permanent climax" view that the plains had been irremediably harmed, instead sharing University of Chicago plant ecologist Henry Chandler Cowles's conviction that the grassland was an open ecological system undergoing continuous change. Malin identified cycles of drought and erosion long before human arrival on the plains: "Man's turning over of the sod with the plow is only a more complete process of cultivation of the soil that took place continuously in nature." The Dust Bowl, nevertheless, was surely intensified by pioneer settlers who still farmed in an early "exploitive stage" as the drought struck.[56] While settlement changed the land, it was not the pillage so often portrayed in popular denunciations of European settlement. Instead, the climate is perpetually in flux, the soil and vegetation in constant turmoil.

Successful plains settlement by people accustomed to forest culture should have involved the slow adaptation of human technologies and institutions to new conditions, not the fastest-possible soil mining and water exploitation. In this light, Malin was unaware of similar work by the French *Annales* historians Marc Bloch and Fernand Braudel.[57] Malin's synthesizing approach remained largely unknown except to a small group of loyal students at the University of Kansas, who knew his privately published typescripts, one of which was his 1947 *Grasslands of North America*. Malin went further than his predecessors, and virtually all who wrote later, in building a unified picture that covered the geological underground, surface topography, climate, soil dynamics, plants, animals, and impacts of insects and fire. In this way he was able to identify human opportunities and pitfalls as the plains were settled. The grasslands, Malin believed, were so unlike earlier American settlement experiences that they tested American innovation and ingenuity. "New skills acquired by man create new natural resources and new opportunities. The process is indeterminate."[58]

CARL ORTWIN SAUER

Geographer Carl Ortwin Sauer did equal justice to the web of physical environmental conditions and their role upon human settlement, but he was far less optimistic than Malin about the potential for farming the plains. Humans can quickly and irreparably damage the natural productivity of the plains, he believed, and as a result harm themselves.[59]

Born in Missouri and raised in the Black Forest country of Germany, Sauer studied geography at the University of Chicago and there came under the influence of Cowles. Sauer's extremely influential 1925 paper, "The Morphology of Landscape," broke with the environmental determinism of his day. The earth was the scene on which the activity of man unfolds itself, a living whole composed of a series of moving points on a variety of moving

366

lines. Sauer saw too clearly civilization's power to exploit nature to be a determinist; instead he actively promoted "the humane use of the earth."

Like so many plains interpreters, Sauer sought to find a workable balance between the vicissitudes of grassland conditions and the virtuous industry of "homefolks," but he was bearish about the future.[60] In the tradition of George Perkins Marsh and Aldo Leopold, he elaborated a land ethic. In a 1956 essay, "The Education of a Geographer,"[61] he insisted on reverence for land as humanity's living tether, in part to compensate for historic exploitation. Further, Sauer did much to organize the landmark 1955 conference "Man's Role in Changing the Face of the Earth," in which High Plains studies played an important role.[62]

Sauer used the early settlement of American grasslands as an example of conspicuous consumption by human invaders. The actions of settlers on the High Plains frontier, when they broke the prairie sod, burned off the grasses, and aggressively worked to adapt to local conditions, gave Sauer insights about initial human response to environmental challenges. This historic event, when the forest-society unexpectedly encountered the flat, open, fertile midwestern prairie, was a particularly vivid human-environment encounter.

Sauer emphasized the power of settlers' "psycho-milieu," their preconceived picture of "barrens," whether they were in Kentucky, the Midwest, or the plains. He argued that the emotion-laden set of mental expectations was as powerful a force as the physical reality.[63] A specific and identifiable geography is out there, a combination of landforms, climate, and vegetation. However, humans highlight certain features and ignore others, based on their cultural baggage. In sharp contrast to Turner, Billington, and Webb, Sauer understood the cultural baggage carried to the frontier as the ultimate shaping force of settlement. No wonder plains settlers held out so long in hope of rain and in vain struggled to force their eastern humidland farm ways on the drylands.

Sauer looked nostalgically to a plains "golden age" in the early 1900s, when farming was less destructive because it did not have consumption-oriented technology. This era suggested to him that harmony could be achieved between a sustainable environment and the satisfaction of human

367

needs, if humans could control their greediness. Sauer believed that the past experiences of rural settlement offered guidelines for a balance between capacity of land and requirements of modern society.

"MAN'S ROLE IN CHANGING THE FACE OF THE EARTH"

The High Plains had a preeminent role in global environmental studies during the 1955 international symposium "Man's Role in Changing the Face of the Earth," held at Princeton; its proceedings were published under the same title in 1956. The participants openly sought to promote a newly identified ecological approach by advocating a stock-taking of human knowledge "by synthesis, transcending the limits of present disciplines or branches of science."[64] The publication saw its roots in the work of George Perkins Marsh ninety years earlier and anticipated Rachel Carson's pathbreaking *Silent Spring* by six years. The ability of humanity to alter the organic and inorganic world became an ethical issue. Settlement and agricultural exploitation of the High Plains were treated as examples of imprudence that demonstrated the need for caution. Several presenters shaped their disciplines and influenced the interpretation of plains ecosystems, its agricultural infrastructure, and especially water resources in irrigation. Notable were Karl A. Wittfogel's classic "The Hydraulic Civilizations," Malin's "The Grassland of North America: Its Occupance and the Challenge of Continuous Reappraisals," John T. Curtis's "The Modification of Mid-Latitude Grasslands and Forests by Man," and Andrew H. Clark's "The Impact of Exotic Invasion on the Remaining New World Mid-Latitude Grasslands." These articles, by combining geology, hydrology, soil and plant science, climate, and agricultural invasion, created the framework for plains environmental studies that held for the rest of the century.

WILLIAM E. RIEBSAME

The views of 1956 were reinforced in 1990 by the publication of *The Earth as Transformed by Human Action: Global and Regional Changes in the Biosphere over the Past 300 Years*, the outcome of a symposium at Clark University in 1987.[65] Again, the High Plains were highlighted as a zone in environmental turmoil. Geographer William E. Riebsame put the plains in global perspective as one of the world's frontiers of cultivation, a boundary region that exists perpetually at the meeting point between environmental zones. Human intervention had distinctive features, in this case Manifest Destiny, quick, cheap land acquisition of public lands by private interests, and capital-intensive, mechanized farming that accelerated resource consumption. The chief results were high-yield wheat production that by 1910 made the region "the breadbasket of the world" and by 1930 induced a devastating drought and depression. Undesirable changes that continued into the 1990s included soil depletion and soil transformation, depletion of Ogallala groundwater, and the collapse of the American family farm. In his review of the current tension between catastrophist and adaptionist interpretations of plains future, Riebsame was cautiously optimistic: resource-protection tactics are effective, regional resources are in good shape, agricultural land use has persisted, although small towns and a rural lifestyle are still in decline.[66] Despite the need for sustainability, Riebsame sees the continuation of a long-standing bias toward growth and development as the framework for future plains planning.

Elsewhere, Riebsame raises questions about the ability of plains society to respond to the worsening climate threatened by global warming. Is plains agriculture fundamentally adaptable, "able to change form and function markedly under new conditions," or is it resilient, "likely to attempt to maintain 'normal' operations via disaster relief and other social maintenance schemes in future droughts."[67] He asks how much social change Americans can tolerate once disaster strikes: "Americans arguably will tolerate only a limited increase in the rate of outright Great Plains farm failure, personal loss, and out-migration. Nor will they abide a recurrent of the 'Dust Bowl' disaster, but will flood the plains with support for relief and recovery . . . [but] people will not easily acquiesce to a centrally-coordinated retrenchment."[68] The question is how large, or small, is the pool of options available in the face of environmental change.

Focus on Plains Farming as a Lifestyle

We saw in Chapter 6 the ongoing struggle to identify the family farm and save it for the sake of a lifestyle. All farming was once organic, sustainable, and family-based; if it weren't, the inhabitants of America might still be hunters and gatherers. The modern farm lifestyle movement in America that rebelled against what it saw as the flawed activity toward humans and nature that characterized industrial agribusiness included Louis Bromfield in Ohio in the 1930s and Robert Rodale in eastern Pennsylvania after World War II. On the plains, Wes Jackson took up the cause when he created the Kansas Land Institute. This was followed by the Kansas Rural Center in the eastern part of the state and more recently by farmer-philosopher Fred Kirschenmann in central North Dakota. What drives these reformers is the fear that today's conventional factory farming, in Jesse Ausubel's words, is too "brittle" in the face of climate change.[69] Truly sustainable modern farming, as was true with ancient farming, can creatively perpetuate itself only when it is primarily grounded in complexity, variety, and openness rather than narrowly predetermined monoculture and marketplaces. Philosopher Morris Berman concluded, "If you fight the ecology of a system, you lose—especially when you 'win.' "[70] The problem is that an ecosystem, or holistic, approach, unlike industrial production, consumerism, or even stewardship, is not part of a recognizable American reform movement or tradition. It remains an alternative movement that would require important reconsiderations of American agriculture, marketplace economics, social institutions, and even cultural values. It works against society's marketplace-oriented work ethic in that it neither produces the cheapest possible food nor uses the fewest farmers. Wes Jackson's restorative agriculture demands a national restructuring well beyond stewardship or sustainability.

WES JACKSON AND THE LAND INSTITUTE

Wes Jackson's Land Institute in Salina, Kansas, is working simultaneously to return parts of the High Plains to their original prairie landscape and to create a sustainable, natural food-producing agriculture from perennial plants. This is a challenging program to combine plains ecosystem health with an innovative sustainable and productive agriculture. One institute researcher describes the original conditions of the plains as a foundation for human sustainability as well: "The prairie ecosystem existed as a complex web of interdependent relationships among plant, animal, and microbial species. Critical nutrients were garnered, retained, and recycled efficiently by the prairie's biota. Generations of prairie grasses, thriving during the moist springs and hot summers, then drying in autumn and winter, accumulated thick mulches of leaves and stems that gave rise to deep dark soils. These rich prairie soils have made the highly productive Great Plains granary possible."[71]

The Land Institute is primarily a research and educational institution that advocates by example rather than political action. A threefold agenda focuses on learning how the prairie ecology functions, breeding plants to develop perennial grain crops, and developing polyculture cropping systems. Hence the Land Institute says,

> The agriculture we envision, modeled on the prairie, would be composed of herbaceous perennial seed crops grown in mixtures. These mixtures will take advantage of differences among species in growth period, nutrient use, and water requirements. We will incorporate into the design of perennial polycultures various principles of ecosystem function discovered in studies of the prairie ecosystem. Thus we will address nutrient cycling, ecological succession, long-term stability of yield, and biological management of insects, diseases, and weed within agro ecosystems. The herbaceous perennials we are developing for polyculture, eastern grama grass, wild rye, and Illinois bundle-flower, have either been derived from native prairie or are analogous to species occurring in native prairie.[72]

Ecologist Stuart Pimm warned that the Kansas Land Institute faced daunting problems when it tried to recover pre–European settlement environmental conditions: "Order comes out of chaos in a very simple, profound and topological way. The problem is how we can get order quickly, because we are not in the business of creating prairies over a million years."[73] That the work of the Land Institute is to find a method of sustainability by returning the land to what it was before European invasion means that, in their strategy, groundwater from the Ogallala would not be needed.

KANSAS RURAL CENTER

The Kansas Rural Center has a similar agenda to Jackson's operation—sustainable agriculture, rural life, and the long-term health of the land—but it is an advocacy and farmer-support organization rather than a research center. It is a private, grassroots operation that believes that sustainable farming provides a desirable lifestyle. It has vigorously criticized recent industrial pork operations in western Kansas just as it raised questions about large-scale cattle feedlots and long-term depletion of Ogallala groundwater. It has published several studies on groundwater consumption and suggested policies that stress low-consumption crops and techniques.[74] The center observed that current trends toward industrial mega-farming can only destroy the natural resources such as soil, water, and good farming habits that support agriculture. Agribusiness, it believes, undermines the satisfactions of rural and farming life and exports the wealth of the land outside the region. The center emphasizes the importance of rigorous application of water law, water regulation, and water policy as a means to shape conservation of the Ogallala. When factory hog farming threatened western Kansas, it encouraged county voters to reject the operations and protect farm lifestyle and groundwater quality.

The center provides reports that encourage sustainable farming such as profitable diversified crop rotation, reduction of nonpoint agricultural pollution, livestock grazing based on pasture rotation, organic versions of traditional crops, and farm co-ops. The center's heartland network of regional workshops and telephone conferences connects family farmers who find themselves alone and isolated when testing innovative practices that lead to sustainability.

Both the Kansas Land Institute and the Kansas Rural Center expect continued depletion of the Ogallala aquifer, but the strategies of industrialization and sustainability that they advocate could not be more different. Mary Fund, director of the Clean Water Farms Project of the Kansas Rural Center wrote, "farmers shouldn't have to choose between polluting and economic solvency. There are other options. The key to protecting water quality is in changing the way we farm," including conversion from confinement feeding, with its heavy water flushing, to pasture pig production.[75] She claimed that nonpoint source pollution can also be reduced by converting cropland to grassland, limiting access to streams, and turning to legume-based crop rotation in place of chemical fertilizers and pesticides.

FREDERICK KIRSCHENMANN

North Dakota farmer Frederick Kirschenmann, who is also an academically trained philosopher, says society is faced with choosing between an industrial agriculture or an agriculture based on nature.[76] He observed that "A farm is not a factory—it is an organism made up of numerous suborganisms, each alive and interdependent, each affected in numerous, complex ways" by outside forces—money, chemicals, technology, market prices—that are invariably disruptive. "A cow is not a production unit but a biological organism."[77] The factory-type farm that considers fields and animals "production units," said Kirschenmann, and where economic performance is based on year-end bottom line is quickly becoming so dominant that there may be no return. True, the more complex a technical system is, the better it can insulate farmers from cycles of drought; however, this can bring increased vulnerability to catastrophe. Components from old settlement patterns can recombine in unforeseen ways, pushed by radical economic forces (Worster's capitalism), to produce an agricultural zone (the old Dust Bowl) that is neither economically nor ecologically sustainable.[78]

The ecology-based farm treats itself like a complex interrelated organism that has biological limits and where economic performance is, in Kirschenmann's words, "judged by the long-term health and achievement of the total organism within a larger bioregion." He is concerned that we have limited time in which to put this organic model into effect because of three common fallacies. The fallacy of misplaced concreteness says, for example, that soil is measured by its maximum yield instead of its organic health. The fallacy of reductionism involves, for example, the "economic threshold" for insecticide application rather than the destruction of beneficial insects and natural predators. The fallacy of unlimited growth ignores the reality, according to Williams E. Reeds, who Kirschenmann quotes, that "a dependent part cannot grow indefinitely within a limited whole."[79]

Edging toward a Comprehensive Agricultural Worldview

Agriculture is a complex system almost beyond comprehension. It is uniquely dependent upon both a functional natural ecosystem and an efficient human infrastructure. Agriculture is sociology, politics, economics, history, and ethics together with a combination and recombination of geology, hydrology, plant and soil science, and climate. The result is, in the words of systems scientist D. Scott Slocombe, a dynamic "sociobiophysical" system.[80] The classic three dimensions in the physical world—longitude, latitude, altitude—need to be integrated with the additional dimensions of time (duration), energy (dynamic change), shape or form (metabolism), and multifold human interventions. This would create a hybrid procedure between hard and soft science and assure attention to the multidimensional aspects of groundwater use in the old Dust Bowl. Pioneer ecologist Eugene P. Odum complains that "today we have only half a science of man." He urges large-system corrective links between ecology and economics, ecology and political science, and ecology and social benefits: "A human being, for example, is not only a hierarchical system composed of organs, cells, enzyme systems, and genes as subsystems, but is also a component of supraindividual hierarchical systems such as populations, cultural systems, and ecosystems. . . . It is in the properties of the large-scale, integrated systems that hold solutions to most of the long-range problems of society."[81]

The initial ecology of the High Plains—climate, soil, grasses, water—combine to make a physical reality that will not entirely disappear under a social, economic, and technological blanket—the agricultural infrastructure. Soil is still soil, water is still water, and climate is uncontrollable. Nature always interrupts the farmer's best-sown plans.

Still Bound to Place, Space, and Time

The essential quality of farming is its physical location at a given point in time. This translates to commitment to a particular piece of land, such as Roger and Betty Trescott's flood-irrigation farm in central Oklahoma or Steve Irsik's Kansas cattle feedlots. These site-centered needs raise doubts about the workability of decentered, or placeless, abstractions such as a national farm policy or the strategies of a multinational corporation. Researchers at the Kansas Rural Center prove the point of this unworkability in the example of a 1976 agribusiness failure that caused profound problems in Edwards County in southwest Kansas.[82] The First National Investment Company bought 9,664 acres of sandy pasture land and acquired rights to put down forty-eight wells for irrigation. But as an absentee, or nonfarm, investor, the company was more heavily committed elsewhere. Despite exclusive access to water on its property, it let the newly plowed sandy soil, vulnerable to wind erosion, blow away as its farm managers lackadaisically came and went. In 1982 over three thousand acres were foreclosed and fell into the hands of the Connecticut General Life Insurance Company. Fortunately, the land is now under local management and is used to grow low-value alfalfa and grasses. In the process, though, various local businesses, including the county co-op, were saddled with unpaid bills and contracts. There is high risk in corporate speculation not only for the corporation, but also for smaller, unprotected local businesses. When the marketplace is the only measure for action on the High Plains, the local farm picture becomes distorted, and severe damage occurs rapidly.

Agriculture is local everywhere in the world; it succeeds or fails depending on the ability of a tract of land to produce a crop.[83] The United States has treated the particularity of farmland in contradictory ways. On the one hand, the Land Survey Ordinance of 1785 sold specific tracts into private hands, and subsequent acts such as the Homestead Act of 1862 intensified the specificity by requiring farmers to live on the land. On the other hand, the 1785 act spread the geometric grid as a smooth pattern across a landscape that was lumpy with hills, streams, valleys, arid lands, and wetlands.[84] Geographer Yi-Fu Tuan wrote from the point of view of localism, "a place is not only a fact to be explained . . . [I]t is also a reality to be clarified and understood from the perspectives of the people who have given it meaning."[85] Geographer Doreen Massey writes, "Local uniqueness matters. . . . Spatial differentiation, geographical variety, is not just an outcome: it is integral to the reproduction of society and its dominant social relations. . . . [by] recognizing and appreciating the importance of the specific and the unique."[86] Thus we find that only through the on-site activities of the Toomses, the Trescotts, the Gigots, Paul Hitch, Steve Irsik, and the Allens can the environmental issues come to life.

Site-specific farming is not like any other industry. The forces that shape crops respond directly to different magnitudes of water, wind, and sunshine. Even markets, technologies, government policies, and national eating habits ultimately focus on a single tract of farmland. Early pioneers of sustainable agriculture like William Albrecht, Aldo Leopold, and Robert Rodale attempted to formulate an ecologically benign approach to agriculture that stressed the long-term health of a unique tract of land. To plow, plant, cultivate, and harvest a quarter section in western Kansas was not a business but a way of life small in scale, relatively simple, resource-conserving, and environmentally nonviolent. In this view, industrial farming, because of its centralized decisions, and applying a mechanical model, sacrifices the integrity of a specific tract of land.[87]

This focus on place is not simply an academic exercise; folks like the Hoemes battle the invasion of mega-hog operations because they realize that such factory operations trivialize the uniqueness of their lives and the particularity of the plains. They refused to see the plains as interchangeable with North Carolina, Missouri, or Iowa. The angry people around the hog operations at Guymon instinctively knew their lives were being torn apart. They saw their home region collapsing into a formless and generic landscape measured by corporate profits. They understood that modern industry has the ability to rapidly transform a specific landscape anywhere so that it becomes a "nowhere" indistinguishable from anywhere else, a transformation that geographer David Harvey called indelible and irreversible.[88] When agriculture is thus generalized—and made applicable anywhere—it becomes a subset of economics or policy that cares not about qualities of a specific piece of wheatland or irrigation farm.

In the jargon of academic geography, an individual piece of land thus treated becomes decentered, a statistic that loses much of its power to enhance local well-being and quality of life. This is what happens when a region is broken into its component parts like the cheap land and free water that encouraged the hog factories in Oklahoma and Colorado. Geographer J. Nicholas Entrikin describes why the plains were attractive to hog entrepreneurs: "the search for profits encourages the pursuit of technical innovation or locational advantage. The latter is gained through movement to areas of relatively inexpensive land rents, labor costs, etc., which helps to reduce the cost of production and thus increase the competitive advantage of the firm and eventually increase profits." Entrikin adds, "Capitalism . . . erodes differences based on variations in the natural environment and on the historical experiences of a group, differences that contribute to the specificity of places."[89] The great American philosopher Josiah Royce, whom Entrikin quotes, concluded, "local traditions, the reverent memory of the pioneers, the formation of local customs, the development of community loyalty" teach the all-important lesson "that in the formation of a loyal local consciousness, in a wise provincialism, lies the way toward social salvation" and the secure foundation for American democracy.[90]

Ultimately, the irrigation farmer's decisions are local.[91] What crop should he plant in a forty-acre quarter of a quarter section? The decision between which tractors, plows, spreaders, and harvesters to use depend upon the piece of land, its crops, and the resources and skills of the farmer who plows in the shadow of his own home. When should the farmer fertilize and how should he exercise weed control? How will the crops and soil respond to the application of nitrogen? Nitrogen fertilizer, which is costly and energy-intensive, is affected by local factors like tillage, irrigation, crop rotation, level of residual soil nitrate nitrogen, the yield goals of the farmer, and the level of threatened pollution. The farmer's detailed planning of irrigation scheduling is applied to a single center pivot over 130 acres in a quarter section. Effective use of groundwater to irrigate a piece of farmland depends upon a specific pumping rate, the benefits and limitations of a sprinkler system, chemical inputs, the rate of evaporation in the flood, soil, and plants, the water scheduling needs of corn versus alfalfa, the personal management ability of the individual farmer, and, not the least, the weather.

Natural resources stewardship, and an environmental ethic, also begins at home, where on-site farmers wrestle with soil erosion and wasted water.

377

Decision Model for a Grain Farmer

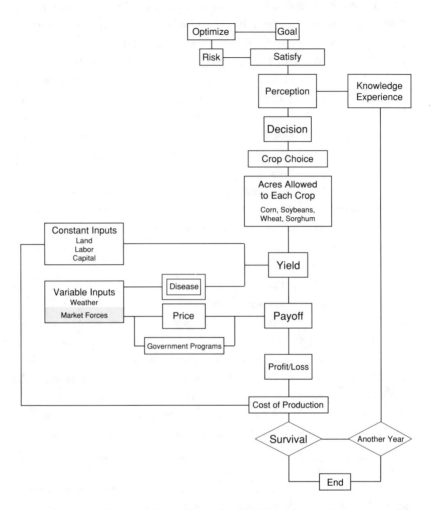

19. A decision model for a grain farmer. The modern High Plains farmer who is a commercial grain producer works like a corporate manager as much as a hands-on farmer. This diagram outlines the complex factors that such a farmer must keep in mind to be successful. Some High Plains farmers have computerized their activities, following this model. Redrawn from Kent McGregor, "Effect of Climate Change on Cropping Structure of Shawnee County, Kansas: A Bayesian Model," *Agricultural History* 63, no.2 (Spring 1989): 206, with permission of the Agricultural History Society.

Guidance for sustainability can be found in the application of scientific principles of ecosystems and biodiversity. Irrigation farming, like all farming, involves continuous interaction with the basic physical and organic mechanisms on a specific piece of land: the biochemical, genetic, and molecular mechanisms of what happens when plants take up water, the mechanisms of plant responses to environmental signals, the intrusion of chemical fertilizers, herbicides, and pesticides, the complex yet fundamental mechanisms underlying photosynthesis and regulation of the plant life cycle, and the molecular and cellular mechanisms of disease. The farmer integrates these into the local ecosystem structure and its constantly changing dynamic functions. In Ogallala country, as this book shows, all the agricultural models are inevitably local. They must be applied to groundwater pumped at individual farms.

What Can We Learn from an Ecological Approach?

The science attached to this book is ecology. Attention has also been given here to geology and hydrology, soil chemistry and plant science, physical geography and climatology. Our particular interest has been the interactions between the physical environment of landscape, soil and water, the organisms that spring from them, and the human and animal consumption of those organisms as resources for subsistence and profit.

Ideally, ecosystems are richly diverse, nonlinear, self-sustaining dynamic entities. That is, according to the very qualities that define ecosystems, they experience continuous changes (perturbations) in their baseline conditions, they live by complex feedback loops of energy flow, nutrient (nitrogen and phosphorus) cycling, materials exchange, and information, and they prosper through multiple processes, changes in magnitude over time, and cumulative effects. Ogallala groundwater under the central High Plains became a prominent part of plains agriculture, which is itself a version of a nonlinear, self-organizing system—the plains ecosystem.[92] Odum writes, "One first delimits an area, a system, or a problem as a sort of 'black box.' Then, energy, material, and organism inputs and outputs, and major functional processes [primarily grain production, for example] of the system as a whole are examined. Following this principle, one then examines those components

379

and processes [populations, internal cycles and feedbacks, and food webs] that are operationally significant by observing, modeling, or perturbing the system."[93]

This is not easy thinking. A nonlinear approach opens a range of new questions about nature and poses a new set of problems to solve. In his 1987 study of chaos theory, James Gleick could have been thinking about plains ecology and its agricultural infrastructure when he wrote: "Tiny differences in input could quickly become overwhelming differences in output. . . . Errors and uncertainties multiply, cascading upward through a chain of turbulent features" that are both unpredictable and certain. The well-being of an ecosystem depends on its initial conditions. "In science as well as in life, it is well known that a chain of events can have a point of crisis that could magnify small changes. . . . [C]haos meant that such points were everywhere."[94]

Botanist John T. Curtis reported about the plains that

> Man's actions in this [grassland] community almost entirely result in a decrease in its organization and complexity and an increase in the local entropy of the system. His activity in reducing the number of major communities, climax or otherwise, and in blurring the lines of demarcation between them by increasing the range of many of their components likewise reduces the nonrandomness of his surroundings. Man, as judged by his record to date, seems bent on asserting the universal validity of the second law of thermodynamics, on abetting the running-down of his portion of the universe.[95]

The physical transformation of the plains by human intervention, because the plains were vulnerable to such intervention, should have forced adaptation into substitute lifestyles and lowered economic goals. Farmer-settlers should have altered their expectations of prosperity once they began to confront the aridity of the plains. Instead, the lauded Jeffersonian yeoman farmer struggled valiantly in a region where he was doomed to failure. Americans found it difficult to admit that homesteading, sodbusting, and monoculture farming were mistakes. If the engine begins running too fast, it will burn out, and some of the parts will destruct before the others. Environmental systems have adjustment mechanisms, of which information is one; Odum writes, "These thermodynamically nonequilibrium systems require strong inflows of high quality energy [e.g., information] and a means [policy] of dissipating disorder if they are to survive, evolve, and improve."[96]

One of the major hazards of the Ogallala as an agricultural phenomenon is the incompleteness, or indeterminacy, of its future. If an ecosystem/infrastructure is to avoid harmful distortion because of the introduction of large unpredictable inputs from outside—such as large amounts of free capital and revolutionary technology—the system must have a means of dissipating the input. A small-scale fluctuation, declining wheat prices worldwide, for example, can be amplified by nonlinear dynamics and result in a macro impact such as local depopulation. This dominant uncertainty should be obvious, but often it is not: open systems always exchange material with their surroundings. Openness allows the spontaneous creation of new dynamic elements, or, in human terms, a "surprise." For example, in the late 1970s, when land prices were high, interest rates were low, and international food demand was high, farmers prospered. But few anticipated the crisis of the late 1980s and its multiple causes that fed on each other in a systems interaction: high value of the dollar, high interest rates, the decline of inflation, the worldwide commodity glut, and the international debt crisis, all of which combined to drive down grain prices, which, in turn, decreased farmland prices and farmers' borrowing equity. These variables shifted again in the mid-1990s. Unfortunately, most High Plains farmers still seek a single solution, "Give us a better price, and we will not have a farm problem."[97] Until the Dust Bowl, most Americans believed the optimistic credo that nature was strong enough to resist destruction by human agencies. Now we see that this was mistaken.

We need to be reminded that Ogallala groundwater does not have intrinsic value and that it was originally not part of the plains ecosystem. It became important only with the discovery of irrigation technologies. In this light, the Ogallala aquifer is neutral—it can serve family farms or corporate hog operations or it can be wasted. But to sustain it to support long-term farming and human occupation of the High Plains, the Ogallala must be accepted as a fundamental social good of widespread public interest. It can be protected only if such protection serves "good" objectives. The philosopher Paul B. Thompson, drawing on the views of William Aiken, E. F. Schmacher, Wendell Berry, and Aldo Leopold, described a multipath ethic in agriculture that would help to sustain it as a self-regulating system. From this perspective, the values attached to "economic goals need to be moderated by values that state clearly our society's dependence upon natural systems."[98] Agriculture, seen through this analysis, does have a moral purpose beyond the economic goals of production and efficiency. Odum's attention to ethics is as central as his attention to energy's dominant role in ecosystems: "Going beyond reduction to [ecological] holism is now mandated if science and society are to mesh for mutual benefit."[99]

. . .

Notes

Preface

1 Panel on Societal and Institutional Responses, Workshop on Consequences of a Possible CO_2-Induced Climate Change, American Association for the Advancement of Science/U.S. Department of Energy, Annapolis, Md., May 1979.

2 *History of Kearny County Kansas* (Garden City: Kearny County Historical Society, 1964), 364–65.

3 Donald E. Green, *Land of the Underground Rain: Irrigation on the Texas High Plains, 1910–1970* (Austin: University of Texas Press, 1973).

4 Morton W. Bittinger and Elizabeth B. Green, *You Never Miss the Water Till. . . . (The Ogallala Story)* (Littleton, Colo.: Water Resources Publications, 1980). Despite its brevity (116 pages), this study is exceptionally detailed, accurate, and useful.

5 "The segment north of the Platte and South Platte Rivers is unlike the other three segments. A large part of this northern segment is the Sand Hills of Nebraska, where a thick section of windblown sand overlies the Ogallala Formation. The permeable nature of the Sand Hills permits rapid infiltration of precipitation. It has been estimated that as much as 25 percent of the precipitation is recharged to the water table. As a result, there is little or no surface runoff, the water table is near the land surface, and streams draining the Sand Hills are fed by ground water" (John B. Weeks, "Proposed Plan of Study for the High Plains Regional Aquifer-System Analysis," U.S. Department of the Interior [USDI], Water Re-

sources Division, working paper for February 2–3, 1978, staff meeting, U.S. Geological Survey, [Denver]) 6.

6 This is one of the major tenets of the modern environmental movement and an essential aspect of environmental science. One of the earliest public affirmations was sprinkled throughout Rachel Carson, *Silent Spring* (Boston: Houghton Mifflin, 1963). A more recent scientific position is reflected in the standard textbook by G. Tyler Miller, *Sustaining the Earth*, 3rd ed. (Belmont, Calif.: Wadsworth Publishing, 1998), 17–68. Also see the discussion in John Opie, *Nature's Nation: An Environmental History of the United States* (Ft. Worth, Tex.: Harcourt Brace College Publishers, 1998), 1–7.

7 Quoted in William D. Ruckelshaus, "Toward a Sustainable World," *Scientific American* 261, no.3 (September 1989): 169.

8 Interview, 1972, in Morris Berman, *The Reenchantment of the World* (Ithaca: Cornell University Press, 1981), 235.

9 Analysis according to nonlinear, self-organizing systems theory offers "a framework for addressing the complex, interdisciplinary problems of 'managing' and understanding the natural and human environments and particularly the interface between the two" (Berman, *Reenchantment*, 257). Examples are Erich Jantsch, *The Self-Organizing Universe* (New York: Pergamon Press, 1980); G. Nicolis and I. Prigogine, *Self-Organization in Non-Equilibrium Systems* (New York: John Wiley, 1977); D. N. Parkes and N. J. Thrift, *Times, Spaces, and Places: A Chronogeographic Perspective* (New York: John Wiley, 1980); H. Ulrich and G. J. B. Probst, eds., *Self-Organization and Management of Social Systems* (Berlin: Springer Verlag, 1984); Eugene P. Odum, "Input Management of Production Systems," *Science*, January 13, 1989, 177–81. For a less technical popular discussion, see Berman, *Reenchantment*, and James Gleick, *Chaos: Making of a New Science* (New York: Penguin Books, 1987).

Introduction

1 Jesse H. Ausubel, "Does Climate Still Matter?" *Nature* 350 (April 25, 1991): 649–52, and a response to Ausubel's article by Nick Sundt, "Proof Negative," *Nature* 352 (July 18, 1991), 187.

2 Glantz, head of the Environmental and Societal Impacts Group, National Center for Atmospheric Research, interview by author, Boulder, Colo., May 25, 1988. See H. H. Lamb, *Climate History and the Modern World* (London: Metheun, 1982); Reid A. Bryson and Thomas J. Murray, *Climates of Hunger: Mankind*

and the World's Changing Weather (Madison: University of Wisconsin Press, 1977); Fernand Braudel, *Civilization and Capitalism, 15th-18th Century*, vol. 1, *The Structures of Everyday Life: The Limits of the Possible* (New York: Harper and Row, 1981); and William Woodruff, *Impact of Western Man on the Global Economy, 1650–1960* (New York: St. Martin's Press, 1964).

3 See Edwin D. Gutentag, David H. Lobmeyer, and Steven E. Slagle, *Geohydrology of Southwestern Kansas*, Kansas Geological Survey Irrigation Series 7 (Lawrence, Kans.: University of Kansas, 1981), and Gutentag et al., *Geohydrology of the High Plains Aquifer in Parts of Colorado, Kansas, Nebraska, New Mexico, Oklahoma, South Dakota, Texas, and Wyoming (High Plains RASA Project)*, U.S. Geological Survey professional paper 1400-B (Washington, 1984).

4 Data studies and predictions of this sort are gathered from many sources. See, for example, William F. Hughes and Wyatee L. Harman, *Projected Economic Life of Water Resources, Subdivision Number 1, High Plains Underground Water Reservoir*, technical monograph no. 6, Texas Agricultural Experiment Station (College Station: Texas A&M University, 1969); Oklahoma Water Resources Board, *Appraisal of the Water and Related Land Resources of Oklahoma*, publication no. 44, region 12, (Oklahoma City: Oklahoma Water Resources Board, 1973); Gail P. Thelin, Frederick J. Heimes, and James R. Wray, *Irrigated Cropland: The High Plains, 1980*, plate 1, professional paper 1400-C, U.S. Geological Survey (Washington, 1987); and High Plains Study Council, *A Summary of Results of the Ogallala Aquifer Regional Study, with Recommendations to the Secretary of Commerce and Congress*, Economic Development Administration, U.S. Department of Commerce (Washington, December 13, 1982).

5 Interview by author May 5, 1988, with Andy Erhart, agricultural advisor, and Al Rauhut, sales manager, of Henkle Drilling and Supply Company, Garden City, Kansas. Information confirmed in May 6, 1988, interviews with Kenny Ochs of the Gigot Irrigation Company, Garden City, and with Jeff Schmidt of the USDA Soil Conservation Service office in Garden City.

6 Sandra Postel, *Water for Agriculture: Facing the Limits*, World Watch Paper 93 (Washington: The Worldwatch Institute: 1989), 12, 40.

7 Jim MacNeill, "Strategies for Sustainable Economic Development," *Scientific American* 261, no. 3 (September 1989): 156.

8 Ibid., 157.

9 Pierre R. Crosson and Norman J. Rosenberg, "Strategies for Agriculture," *Scientific American* 261, no.3 (September 1989): 128.

10 World Commission on Environmental and Development, *Our Common Future* (New York: Oxford University Press, 1987), 122–23.

11 MacNeill, "Strategies for Sustainable Economic Development," 158–59, 163–64.

12 World Commission on Environmental and Development, *Our Common Future*, 125.

13 See William Lockeretz, "Major Issues Confronting Sustainable Agriculture," in *Sustainable Agriculture in Temperate Zones*, ed. Charles A. Francis et al. (New York: John Wiley, 1990), 423–38.

14 Stephanie Castonguay, "The Technological Function of the Environment in a Sustainable Agriculture" (paper presented at "The Environment and the Mechanized World," a conference of the American Society for Environmental History, University of Houston, Tex., February 28–March 3, 1991).

15 I regrettably fell into this common trap in two recent articles, "100 Years of Climate Risk Assessment on the High Plains: Which Farm Paradigm Does Irrigation Serve?" *Agricultural History* 63, no.2 (Spring 1989): 243–69 and "The Precarious Balance: Matching Market Dollars and Human Values in American Agriculture," *The Environmental Professional* 10, no.1 (Spring 1988): 36–45.

Chapter 1

1 See the overall viewpoint of John A. Harrington, Jr., and Jay R. Harmen, "Climate and Vegetation in Central North America: Natural Patterns and Human Alterations," *Great Plains Quarterly* 11 (Spring 1991): 103–12.

2 See the classic report by Willard D. Johnson, "The High Plains and Their Utilization," *Twenty-First Annual Report of the United States Geological Survey* (Washington: Government Printing Office, 1901), 4:657–59, and the analysis in Conner Sorensen, "A History of Irrigation in the Arkansas River Valley in Western Kansas, 1880–1910" (M.A. thesis, Wichita State University, 1965), 8–10.

3 *Oklahoma Comprehensive Water Plan* (Oklahoma City: Oklahoma Water Resources Board Publication 94, 1980), 22–25.

4 "Oil, Gas Applications," *Oklahoma Oil Reporter, Weekly Edition* 4, no.20 (20 May 1985): F-5.

5 Correspondence from Edwin D. Gutentag of the USGS, Denver Federal Center, January 1989.

6 Curtis Marbut, "Soils of the Great Plains," *Annals of the Association of American Geographers*, 13 (March 1923): 41–66.

7 See the summary in *Appraisal of the Water and Related Land Resources of Oklahoma: Region Twelve* (Oklahoma City: Oklahoma Water Resources Board, 1973), 19–27.

8 Nevin M. Fenneman, *Physiography of Western United States* (New York: McGraw-Hill Book Company, 1931), 11–12.

9 See R. F. Diffendal, Jr., "Plate Tectonics, Space, Geologic Time, and the Great Plains" *Great Plains Quarterly* 11 (Spring 1991): 83–102.

10 Edwin G. Gutentag et al., *Geohydrology of the High Plains Aquifer in Parts of Colorado, Kansas, Nebraska, New Mexico, Oklahoma, South Dakota, Texas, and Wyoming. (High Plains RASA Project)* U.S. Geological Survey Professional Paper 1400-B (Washington, 1984), table 7, 33.

11 Wayne Bossert of Kansas District No.4 considers the inch-a-year recharge generous: "Our data indicates closer to .5 inches/year natural recharge." Correspondence, January 19, 1991.

12 Bruce F. Latta, *Geology and Ground-Water Resources of Finney and Gray Counties, Kansas: Bulletin 55 of the State Geological Survey of Kansas* (Lawrence: University of Kansas Publications, August 1944), 19–23, and O. St. John. "Notes on the Geology of Southwest Kansas," *Fifth Biennial Report of the Kansas State Board of Agriculture* (1885–1886), 135.

13 Southwest Kansas geology and hydrology have been served well. See Latta, *Geology and Ground-Water Resources of Finney and Gray Counties, Kansas,* 46–119; Thad G. McLaughlin, *Geology and Ground-Water Resources of Grant, Haskell, and Stevens Counties, Kansas: Bulletin 61 of the State Geological Survey of Kansas* (Lawrence: University of Kansas Publications, July 1946), 37–86; V. C. Fishel and Betty J. Mason, *Ground-Water Levels in Observation Wells in Kansas, 1965: Bulletin 125 of the State Geological Survey of Kansas* (Lawrence: State Geological Survey of Kansas, June 1957; Margaret E. Broeker and John D. Winslow, *Ground-Water Levels in Observation Wells in Kansas, 1965: Bulletin 184, State Geological Survey of Kansas* (Lawrence: University of Kansas Publications, August 1966), 16–17, 26–27; Barbara J. Dague, *January 1987 Water Levels, and Data Related to Water-Level Changes, Western and South-*

Central Kansas (Lawrence: U.S. Geological Survey Open-File Report 87–241, 1987), 21–23, 55–56, 120–22.

14 See Gutentag, *Geohydrology*, 12–13; R. T. Coupland, "The Effects of Fluctuations in Weather Upon the Grasslands of the Great Plains," *Botanical Review* 24 (1958): 274–317; J. R. Borchert, "The Climate of the Central North American Grassland," *Annals of the Association of American Geographers* 40 (1950): 1–39; D. D. Collins, "Macroclimate and the Grassland System," in R. L. Dix, ed., *The Grassland Ecosystem: A Preliminary Synthesis* (Fort Collins, Colo.: Range Science Department Science Series, No.2, 1969), 29–39.

15 William A. Albrecht, "Physical, Chemical, and Biochemical Changes in the Soil Community," in William L. Thomas, Jr., ed., *Man's Role in Changing the Face of the Earth* (Chicago: University of Chicago Press, 1956), 648–49.

16 Edward Hyams, *Soil and Civilization* (New York: Harper Colophon Books, 1976; reprinted from the original 1952 edition), 230–72.

17 Hyams, *Soil and Civilization*, 138–50.

18 Peter Farb, *Living Earth* (New York: Harper and Row, 1959, 103; see also Firman E. Bear, *Earth: The Stuff of Life*, 2d ed. (Norman: University of Oklahoma Press, 1990).

19 The basic soil handbook used by farmers and the local offices of state and federal agencies is, in Texas County, by Hadley C. Meinders, Maurice Mitchell, Edward S. Grover, and Jimmie W. Frie, *Soil Survey of Texas County, Oklahoma* (Washington: SCS, USDA, and Oklahoma Agricultural Experiment Station, 1961, 1984). Most of the following information is based on this handbook, which offers a general survey of soil science, soil maps, and aerial photographs. A farmer is readily able to identify the soil types on his land and plant and irrigate accordingly. For Kansas, see George N. Coffey and Thomas D. Rice, "Reconnaissance Soil Survey of Western Kansas," *Field Operations of the Bureau of Soils* (Washington: USDA, 1910); James L. Burgess and George N. Coffey, "Soil Survey of the Garden City Area," *Field Operations of the Bureau of Soils* (Washington: USDA, 1904), *Soil Survey of Finney County, Kansas* (Washington: SCS, USDA, 1965).

20 Meinders et al., *Soil Survey of Texas County, Oklahoma*, 26–27.

21 Ibid., 19.

22 Ibid., 23. See also 27–33.

23 Perhaps the only book published in Bartlesville, Oklahoma, by Phillips Petroleum Company, appeared in 1963 with the unlikely title (for an oil company's publication) *Pasture and Range Plants*. Phillips fertilizer salesmen gave them

as premiums to their clients, but the well-researched book, unique in content, has acquired a nationwide life of it's own. It is a treasure trove of colored drawings and descriptions of seventy-seven varieties of grasses, forty-four kinds of legumes, fifty-five forbs, three woody plants, and three miscellaneous plants. The last six—Texas buckeye, common chokecherry, Gambel oak, ergot, common horsetail, and arrowgrass—are listed because they are poisonous, as are twenty-three of the forbs and five of the legumes. None of the grasses is listed as poisonous. The book's grasses, legumes, and forbs are not exhaustive, but W. F. Martin, Phillips chairman and chief executive officer, said he hoped the book would "prove a worthwhile, lasting contribution to the nation's health, growth, and prosperity." See also W. Rydberg, *Flora of the Prairies and Plains of Central North America* (New York: New York Botanical Garden, 1932); Great Plains Flora Association, T. M. Barkley, ed., *Atlas of the Flora of the Great Plains* (Lawrence: University Press of Kansas, 1977); Great Plains Flora Association, introduction by T. M. Barkley, *Flora of the Great Plains* (Lawrence: University Press of Kansas, 1986).

24 See Harrington and Harman, "Climate and Vegetation in Central North America: Natural Patterns and Human Alterations," 103–12.

25 William E. Riebsame, "The United States Great Plains," in *The Earth as Transformed by Human Action; Global and Regional Changes in the Biosphere over the Past 300 Years*, ed. B. L. Turner II (New York: Cambridge University Press, 1990), 561.

26 John T. Curtis, "The Modification of Mid-latitude Grasslands and Forests by Man," in *Man's Role in Changing the Face of the Earth*, ed. William L. Thomas (Chicago: University of Chicago Press, 1956), 729. Also see, in the same collection, Andrew H. Clark, "The Impact of Exotic Invasion of the Remaining New World Mid-latitude Grasslands," 737–62.

27 Curtis, "Modification of Mid-latitude Grasslands," 734.

28 J. C. Frémont, *Report of the exploring expedition to the Rocky Mountains in the year 1842, and to Oregon and California in the years 1843–1844*, 28th Cong., 2nd sess., H. Doc. 166. Also see the discussion of early perceptions in David F. Costello, *The Prairie World* (New York: Thomas Y. Crowell, 1969), 5–10.

29 John Madson, *Where the Sky Began: Land of the Tallgrass Prairie* (Boston: Houghton Mifflin, 1982), 9–10. Also see F. Gerhard, *Illinois as It Is* (Chicago: Keen and Lee, 1857), n.p.

30 Quoted in Costello, *The Prairie World*, 40.

31 See J. E. Weaver and F. W. Albertson, *Grasslands of the Great Plains: Their Nature and Use* (Lincoln, Nebr.: Johnsen Publishing, 1956); J. E. Weaver, *North American Prairie* (Lincoln, Nebr.: Johnsen Publishing, 1954); N. French, ed., *Perspectives in Grassland Ecology* (New York: Springer Verlag Ecological Studies 32, 1979), 135–55; and T. R. Vale, *Plants and People: Vegetation Change in North America* (Washington: Association of American Geographers, 1982).

32 See Charles B. Heiser, Jr., *Seeds to Civilization: The Story of Food*, new ed. (Cambridge: Harvard University Press, 1990), 61, e.g.

33 See U.S. Department of Agriculture, *Grass: Yearbook of Agriculture for 1948* (Washington, 1948), and A. S. Hitchcock, *Manual of the Grasses of the United States*, miscellaneous publication 200, USDA, 2nd ed., revised by Agnes Chase (1951).

34 Still unmatched is H. L. Shantz, *Natural Vegetation as an Indicator of the Capabilities of Lands for Crop Production in the Great Plains Area*, bulletin 201, USDA Bureau of Plant Industry (Washington, 1911).

35 Heiser, *Seeds to Civilization*, 67.

36 James C. Malin, "The Grasslands of North America: Its Occupance and the Challenge of Continuous Reappraisals," in *Man's Role*, ed. Thomas, 359–60.

37 Quoted in E. J. Kahn, Jr.'s entertaining and informative article, "Corn," *New Yorker*, June 18, 1984, 72.

38 Ibid.

39 Margaret Visser, *Much Depends on Dinner: The Extraordinary History and Mythology, Allure and Obsessions, Perils and Taboos of an Ordinary Meal* (New York: Macmillan-Collier, 1986), 23–24.

40 Quoted in Kahn, "Corn," 53–54.

41 Ibid., 88.

42 Wes Jackson, *New Roots for Agriculture* (San Francisco: Friends of the Earth, 1980), 114.

43 This is the dominant thesis in Jackson, *New Roots for Agriculture*, 2–3 and passim.

Chapter 2

1 John C. Hudson, "Who was 'Forest Man?' Sources of Migration to the Plains," *Great Plains Quarterly* 6, no. 2 (Spring 1986): 69–83.

2 George P. Hammond and Agapito Rey, *Narratives of the Colorado Expedition* (Albuquerque: University of New Mexico, 1940), 2:186ff. For early European images of the Great Plains as a barren zone, see Waldo R. Wedel, "Some Early

Euro-American Perceptions of the Great Plains and Their Influence on Anthro-pological Thinking," in Brian W. Blouet and Merlin P. Lawson, eds., *Images of the Plains: The Role of Human Nature in Settlement* (Lincoln: University of Nebraska Press, 1975), 13–20; David M. Emmons, "The Influence of Ideology on Changing Environmental Images," in Blouet and Lawson, *Images of the Plains*, 125–36; John Kirtland Wright, "Terra incognitae: The place of the imagination in geography," *Annals of the Association of American Geographers* 37 (1947): 1–5; and the broader studies by W. Eugene Hollon, *The Great American Desert, Then and Now* (New York: Oxford University Press, 1966), esp. 9–20 and 33–52, and the classic statement of Walter Prescott Webb, *The Great Plains* (Boston: Ginn and Company, 1931), esp. 94–114, 141–59, and 486–89.

3 Quoted in Carl Ortwin Sauer, "Conditions of Pioneer Life in the Upper Illinois Valley," in John Leighly, ed., *Land and Life: A Selection from the Writings of Carl Ortwin Sauer* (Berkeley: University of California Press, 1967), 12; see also Martyn J. Bowden, "The Great American Desert and the American Frontier, 1800–1882: Popular Images of the Plains," in T. K. Mareven, ed., *Anonymous Americans: Explorations in Nineteenth Century Social History* (Englewood Cliffs, N.J.: Prentice-Hall, 1971), 48–79.

4 Quoted in John L. Allen, "Exploration and the Creation of Geographical Im-ages of the Great Plains. Comments on the Role of Subjectivity," in Blouet and Lawson, *Images of the Plains*, 3–12.

5 Quoted in Robert G. Athearn, *High Country Empire: The High Plains and Rockies* (Lincoln: University of Nebraska Press, 1962), 19; W. Eugene Hollon's *The Great American Desert, Then and Now,* remains the most comprehensive study of the concept.

6 Washington Irving, *A Tour of the Prairies* (Norman: University of Oklahoma Press, 1956 reprint).

7 Quoted in John Madson, *Where the Sky Began: Land of the Tallgrass Prairie* (Boston: Houghton Mifflin, 1982), 17; see also John F. Davis, "Constructing the British View of the Great Plains," in Blouet and Lawson, *Images of the Plains*, 181–85.

8 Quoted in Wedel, "Some Early Euro-American Percepts of the Great Plains and Their Influence on Anthropological Thinking," 15.

9 Quoted in Athearn, *High Country Empire*, 57.

10 Quoted in Bradbury's traveling companion, Henry M. Brackenridge, *Travels in the Interior of America* (Cleveland: Arthur H. Clark Co., 1904 reprint of 1819 original), 267.

11 Quoted in Athearn, *High Country Empire*, 59.

12 Joshua Pilcher, *Remarks to the U.S. Senate* (Washington: S. Ex. Doc. 39, 21st Cong., 2d sess., 1831), 19.

13 Quoted in Athearn, *High Country Empire*, 60.

14 "Speech of Senator G. S. Orth of Indiana," in *Proceedings of Meeting of Excursionists—1867—Fort Harker, Kansas* (Saint Louis, Mo.: S. Levison, 1967), 49.

15 See David M. Emmons, "The Influence of Ideology on Changing Environmental Images. The Case of Six Gazetteers," in Blouet and Lawson, *Images of the Plains*, 125–36.

16 Carl O. Sauer, "Homestead and Community on the Middle Border," *Landscape* 12, no. 1 (1962): 3–7.

17 Athearn, *High Country Empire*, 183–84.

18 See Paul Bonnifield, *The Dust Bowl: Men, Dirt, and Depression* (Albuquerque: University of New Mexico Press, 1979), 15, 27–29.

19 Much of Malin's work was privately published in limited editions or appeared in regional journals. Of the literature still in print, see the excellent collection of Malin's writings in Robert P. Swierenga, ed., *History and Ecology: Studies of the Grassland* (Lincoln: University of Nebraska Press, 1984); see also the important discussion by Donald Worster in "The Dirty Thirties: A Study in Agricultural Capitalism," *Great Plains Quarterly* 6 (Spring 1986): 107–10.

20 James C. Malin, "Dust Storms: Part Three, 1881–1890," *Kansas Historical Quarterly* 14 (November 1946): 391–413.

21 See Kenneth S. Davis, *Kansas: A History* (New York: W. W. Norton and Company, 1976, 1984), 74, 121–22.

22 John Wesley Powell, *Report on the Lands of the Arid Region of the United States*, reprint edition (Boston: Harvard Common Press, 1983; originally published 1879), 1; see also Wallace Stegner, *Beyond the Hundredth Meridian: John Wesley Powell and the Second Opening of the West* (Boston: Houghton Mifflin, 1953).

23 Powell, *Lands of the Arid Region*, 38–39.

24 Ibid., 37–38.

25 Quoted in Paul Horgan, *Josiah Gregg and His Vision of the Early West* (New York: Farrar, Straus & Giroux, 1979), 48.

26 This was the thesis about "increase of streams" and "rise of Great Salt Lake" and "theory of human agencies" by Grove Karl Gilbert in the chapter that was inserted in Powell's arid-lands book to counter Powell's pessimistic conclusions. G. K. Gilbert, "Water Supply," in Powell, *Lands of the Arid Region*, 57–77.

27 Samuel Aughey and C. D. Wilbur, *Agriculture Beyond the 100th Meridian* (Lincoln, Nebr.: n.p., 1880).

28 See the discussion of the different viewpoints in Gilbert C. Fite, *The Farmer's Frontier, 1865–1900* (New York: Holt, Rinehart and Winston, 1966), 114.

29 See David W. Craft, "A History of the Garden City, Kansas, Land Office, 1883–1894" (M.A. thesis, University of Kansas, 1981[?]).

30 Quoted in Fite, *The Farmer's Frontier*, 117.

31 Quoted in Athearn, *High Country Empire*, 191.

32 Quoted in Fite, *The Farmer's Frontier*, 117, 118.

33 Craft, "A History of the Garden City Land Office," 31.

34 Quoted in Fite, *The Farmer's Frontier*, 127.

35 Quoted in Athearn, *High Country Empire*, 196.

36 Webb, *The Great Plains*, 423–27, 431.

37 Ibid., 375.

38 Frederick H. Newell, "Irrigation on the Great Plains," *Yearbook of the United States Department of Agriculture 1896* (Washington: USDA, 1897), 168–69.

39 Willard D. Johnson, "The High Plains and Their Utilization," *Twenty-First Annual Report of the United States Geological Survey* (Washington: Government Printing Office, 1901), 4:681.

40 Webb's classic narrative is "The Cattle Kingdom" in *The Great Plains*, 205–69; compare with Athearn, *High Country Empire*, 127–51, Hollon, *The Great American Desert*, 120–40, and Robert G. Athearn, *The Mythic West in Twentieth-Century America* (Lawrence: University Press of Kansas, 1986), 25–37.

41 Quoted in Athearn, *High Country Empire*, 227; see also 207–26.

42 See the folksy but informative essays by old-time Kearny County resident Foster Eskelund in *History of Kearny County Kansas* (Garden City: Kearny County Historical Society, 1964), 363–67.

43 See another local biographical history by Leola Howard Blanchard, *Conquest of Southwest Kansas* (Wichita: n.p., 1931), 151–52.

44 Reported in Eskelund, 364–65.

45 See Webb, *The Great Plains*, 334–35.

46 Eskelund, 365.

47 See James Earl Sherow, *Watering the Valley: Development along the High Plains Arkansas River, 1870–1950* (Lawrence: University Press of Kansas, 1990), esp. 3–9, 79–119.

48 Charles S. Slichter, "The Underflow in Arkansas Valley in Western Kansas," *Water Supply and Irrigation Paper No.153* (Washington: USGS, 1906), and Erasmus Haworth, "Physiography of Western Kansas," *University Geological Survey of Kansas* (1897), 2:12–13.

49 Quoted in Blanchard, *Conquest of Southwest Kansas*, 87; see also 1883 and 1889 correspondence and files in the Kansas Room of the Finney County Library in Garden City.

50 Sherow, *Watering the Valley*, 83–84.

51 See the detailed study in Conner Sorensen, "A History of Irrigation in the Arkansas River Valley in Western Kansas, 1880–1910" (M.A. thesis, Wichita State University, 1965).

52 See correspondence by irrigation-ditch pioneer James Craig quoted in Blanchard, *Conquest of Southwest Kansas*, 89–94.

53 Sherow, *Watering the Valley*, 84–86.

54 See Eskelund, 358–60.

55 See Sorensen, "A History of Irrigation," 37–41.

56 Quoted in ibid., 43.

57 Eskelund, 356.

58 Quoted in Sorensen, "A History of Irrigation," 60.

59 *Climatic Summary of the United States: From the Establishment of Stations to 1830, Section 40-Western Kansas* (Washington: Government Printing Office, 1930), 11–18.

60 Sherow, *Watering the Valley*, 6–7, 101–19.

61 See Sorensen, "A History of Irrigation," 22–27.

62 Ibid., 66.

63 From 81,279 in 1889 to 49,850 in 1895, according to Gerald Aistrup, "An Investigation of the Relationship Between Climatic Conditions & Population Changes in Western Kansas, 1865–1900," (M.A. thesis, Fort Hays Kansas State Teachers College, 1956), 4, 41 and 55.

64 *The Earth* (April 1904), 3.

65 Quoted in Donald E. Green, *Land of the Underground Rain: Irrigation on the Texas High Plains, 1910–1970* (Austin: University of Texas Press, 1973), 166.

66 Ibid., 168.

67 See Richard J. Hinton, *Irrigation in the United States*, S. Misc. Doc. 15, 49th Cong., 2d sess., 1887, Serial No. 2450, 42, and *Irrigation: The Final Report of the Artesian and Underflow Investigation and of the Irrigation Inquiry*, S. Ex. Doc. 41, 52d Cong., 1st sess., 1892, Serial No. 2899, 303. In 1970, USGS hydrologist Charles N. Gould rejected the Rockies theory in *The Geology and Water Resources of the Western Portion of the Panhandle of Texas*, United States Geological Survey Water Supply and Irrigation Paper No. 191, 40.

68 Erasmus Haworth, "The Geology of Underground Water in Western Kansas," *Report of the Kansas Board of Irrigation Survey and Experiment* (1895–96), 44.

69 Sorensen, "A History of Irrigation," 103.

70 Ibid., 152–53.

71 See the discussion in Sorensen, "A History of Irrigation," 107–8, and in Sherow, *Watering the Valley*, 91–94.

72 Quoted in Sorensen, "A History of Irrigation," 114–15.

73 Specifications of the project are reported by Andy Erhart, "Early Kansas Irrigation," *Irrigation Age* (February 1969): 20-CN1–4.

74 See Sorensen, "A History of Irrigation," 119–20.

75 Quoted in ibid., 123.

76 Quoted in ibid., 123.

77 See ibid., 123–24.

78 Sherow, *Watering the Valley*, 88–91.

79 Sorensen, "A History of Irrigation," 129.

80 Ibid., 132–33.

81 Mary Fund and Elise Watkins Clement, *Distribution of Land and Water Ownership in Southwest Kansas* (Whiting: Kansas Rural Center, 1982), 38–39.

82 Sorensen, "A History of Irrigation," 179.

83 Ibid., 177.

84 See Lawrence B. Lee, "William Ellsworth Smythe and the Irrigation Movement: A Reconsideration," *Pacific Historical Review* 41 (Spring 1972): 289–311.

85 *Proceedings, Second Annual Convention, Kansas Irrigation Association,*

Hutchinson, November 23 and 24, 1894 (Hutchinson: News Publishing Company, 1894), 34–38.

86 Washington: Government Printing Office, 1897, 167–96.

87 Newell, "Irrigation on the Great Plains," 167.

88 Ibid., 169–70.

89 Ibid., 170.

90 Ibid., 173.

91 Ibid.

92 Pamela Riney-Kehrberg, "From the Horse's Mouth: Dust Bowl Farmers and Their Solutions to the Problem of Aridity," paper presented at the Symposium on Agriculture and the Environment, USDA and Agricultural History Society, June 19–22, 1991, Washington, D.C., 2–3.

93 Hinton, *Irrigation in the United States.*

94 Quoted in Walter Rusinek, "Western Reclamation's Forgotten Forces: Richard J. Hinton and Groundwater Development," *Agricultural History* 61, no.3 (Summer 1987): 23.

95 See Sorensen, "A History of Irrigation," 109.

96 Richard J. Hinton, "A Report on the Irrigation and Cultivation of the Soil Thereby," *Irrigation: The Final Report of the Artesian and Underflow Investigation of the Irrigation Inquiry*, S. Ex. Doc. 41, 52d Cong., 1st sess., Serial No.2899, 10.

97 See the discussion in Rusinek, "Western Reclamation's Forgotten Forces," 28–31.

98 Ibid., 34.

99 Ibid., 35.

100 Charles I. Zirkle and Company promotional brochure, Kansas Room, Finney County Library, Garden City.

101 Quoted in Vernon E. Bundy, "Kansas Irrigation is Successful as Local Proposition," *Topeka Daily Capital*, August 10, 1924; see also "Irrigation is a Big Success in Arkansas Valley," *Topeka Daily Capital*, December 20, 1925.

102 Donald Worster, *Dust Bowl: The Southern Plains in the 1930s* (New York: Oxford University Press, 1979), 129.

Chapter 3

1 Walter Prescott Webb, *The Great Plains* (Boston: Ginn and Company, 1931), 366–67.

2 Mary M. W. Hargreaves, "The Dry-Farming Movement in Retrospect," in Thomas R. Wessel, ed., *Agriculture in the Great Plains, 1876–1936* (Washington: Agriculture History Society, 1977), 152.

3 James C. Malin, *Winter Wheat in the Golden Belt of Kansas: A Study in Adaptation to Subhumid Geographical Environment* (Lawrence: University Press of Kansas, 1944), 187, and "The Adaptation of the Agricultural System to Sub-Humid Environment," *Agricultural History* 10, no.2 (July 1936): 131.

4 John J. Widtsoe, *Dry-Farming: A System of Agriculture for Countries under a Low Rainfall* (New York: Macmillan Company, 1911), 301.

5 Webb, *The Great Plains*, 366ff.; see also pp.348ff. and Robert G. Athearn, *High Country Empire: The High Plains and Rockies* (Lincoln: University of Nebraska Press, 1960), 259–62. Webb depended on William McDonald, *Dry-Farming: Its Principles and Practice* (New York: Century Company, 1910), and Widtsoe, *Dry-Farming*. For a more recent analysis, see Hargreaves, "The Dry-Farming Movement in Retrospect," 149–65; "Land-Use Planning in Response to Drought—The Experience of the Thirties, *Agricultural History* 50, no.3 (October 1976); and *Dry Farming in the Northern Great Plains, 1900–1925,* Harvard Economic Studies 101 (Cambridge: Harvard University Press, 1957).

6 Quoted in Donald E. Green, *Land of the Underground Rain: Irrigation on the Texas High Plains, 1910–1970* (Austin: University of Texas Press, 1973), 103.

7 "Changes in Technology and Labor Requirements in Crop Production: Wheat and Oats" (Washington: WPA National Research Project A-10, 1939); R. S. Kifer, B. H. Hurt, and Albert Thornbrough, "The Influence of Technical Progress on Agricultural Production," *Farmers in a Changing World: 1940 Yearbook of Agriculture* (Washington: USDA, 1940), 509–32; Wayne Rasmussen, "The Impact of Technological Change on American Agriculture, 1862–1962," *Journal of Economic History* 22 (December 1962): 578–91.

8 Morrow May quoted in Donald Worster, *Dust Bowl: The Southern Plains in the 1930s* (New York: Oxford University Press, 1979), 91; and see Robert C. Williams, *Fordson, Farmall, and Poppin' Johnny: A History of the Farm Tractor and Its Impact on America* (Urbana: University of Illinois Press, 1987).

9 Worster, *Dust Bowl*, 94.

10 Paul Bonnifield, *The Dust Bowl: Men, Dirt, and Depression* (Albuquerque: University of New Mexico Press, 1979), 47–50.

11 Worster, *Dust Bowl*, 92.

397

12 See A. B. Genung, "Agriculture in the World War Period," *Farmers in a Changing World: 1940 Yearbook of Agriculture*, and Lloyd Jorgenson, "Agricultural Expansion into the Semiarid Lands of the West North Central States during the First World War," *Agricultural History* 23, no. 1 (January 1949): 30–40; see also Gilbert Fite, "Plains Farming: A Century of Change," *Agricultural History* 51, no. 1 (January 1977): 254, and James H. Shideler, *Farm Crisis, 1919–1923* (Berkeley: University of California Press, 1957).

13 Donald Worster, "The Dirty Thirties: A Study in Agricultural Capitalism," *Great Plains Quarterly* 6 (Spring 1986): 109, 111–13; see also Vance Johnson, *Heaven's Tableland: The Dust Bowl Story* (New York: Farrar, Straus and Company, 1947).

14 Worster, "The Dirty Thirties," 112.

15 Ibid.

16 Webb, *The Great Plains*, 319 and passim.

17 Ibid., 328.

18 Ibid., 330–31.

19 Worster, *Dust Bowl*, 6–7, 44–45, 48, 56–59, 94–97 and passim. The long-term quest to hold to the Jeffersonian ideal is a major thesis in John Opie, *The Law of the Land: 200 Years of American Farmland Policy* (Lincoln: University of Nebraska Press, 1987).

20 Bonnifield, *The Dust Bowl*, 64.

21 See ibid., 70–72.

22 1940 Interview with Woody Guthrie by Alan Lomax, *Woody Guthrie Library of Congress Recordings* (New York: Elektra Records E K I 271/272, n.d.).

23 See Bonnifield, *The Dust Bowl*, 74–75.

24 Woody Guthrie, *Dust Bowl Ballads* (New York: R C A Victor L P V-502, 1964 reissue of April 26, 1940, recording).

25 See the statistics in Bonnifield, *The Dust Bowl*, 58–59.

26 See ibid, 123–26.

27 Robert Lambert, "The Drought Cattle Purchase, 1934–35: Problems and Complaints," *Agricultural History* 45 (April 1971): 85–93, and see the discussion in Worster, *The Dust Bowl*, 110–17.

28 This is the argument developed in the second half of Bonnifield's *The Dust Bowl*, 91 and passim; see also the critique of Bonnifield in Harry C. McDean, "Dust Bowl Historiography," *Great Plains Quarterly* 6 (Spring 1986): 120–21.

29 Quoted in Bonnifield, *The Dust Bowl*, 117.

30 The treatment of farmland as unrestricted private property is analyzed in Opie, *Law of the Land*, esp. chaps. 2 and 11. Bonnifield claimed that the economic collapse of the Great Depression—bank closings, unemployment, bankruptcies and equipment forfeitures, bare land and empty towns, the decline of implement sales and land values—did not overwhelm the Dust Bowl region as profoundly as it did the rest of the nation. He argued that "the region had two frontier settlement and development patterns occurring simultaneously" that were mistakenly identified as part of the national failure in the 1930s (Bonnifield, *The Dust Bowl*, 97–105). One, the discovery of the world's second-largest reservoir of natural gas, the Hugoton-Guymon field, brought on the speedy capitalization and industrialization of the region and large reductions in dependence on difficult farming conditions; large numbers of people began to prosper from natural-gas production. Second, the mechanization of farming, with the rapid infusion of tractors, combines, trucks, specialized plows, and other field equipment made agricultural production more efficient, reduced labor needs, and offered production security even in dry times. Large-scale mechanized dryland farming, not small-plot irrigation, would offer plains farmers long-term stability. According to Bonnifield, these technological advances limited the effects of the Great Depression. The region was already well into its own readjustment, admittedly a difficult one, of its work force. A population decline, increased mechanization, and farm consolidations were expected and were merely accelerated by the 1930s drought. Bonnifield concludes that "the region did not plunge into the depression until nearly two years after it struck the East." He admitted that "southwestern Kansas [would] suffer the largest reverses of the eighteen dust bowl counties. Nevertheless, during the twenty-four-month period [of 1937–1938], southwestern Kansas had only six months when business conditions were below the national average." Bonnifield, *The Dust Bowl*, 105.

31 Quoted in Richard Lowitt, *The New Deal and the West* (Bloomington: Indiana University Press, 1984), 42–46, 55–63.

32 *Report of the Great Plains Drought Area Committee* (Washington: Government Printing Office, 1936), 4.

33 *The Future of the Great Plains: Report of the Great Plains Committee to the House of Representatives* (Washington: H. Doc. 144, 75th Cong., 1st sess., 1937).

34 See the discussion in Harry C. McDean, "Dust Bowl Historiography," *Great Plains Quarterly* 6 (Spring 1986): 123.

35 Quoted in Worster, *The Dust Bowl*, 184.

36 See Albert Z. Guttenberg, "The Land Utilization Movement of the 1920s," *Agricultural History* 50 (July 1976): 477–90.

37 *Yearbook of Agriculture 1930* (Washington: USDA, 1930), 36.

38 See Worster, *The Dust Bowl*, 184–97; for federal responses, see also Mary W. M. Hargreaves, "Land-Use Planning in Response to Drought: The Experience of the Thirties," *Agricultural History* 50 (October 1976): 561–82, and Theodore Saloutos, "The New Deal and Farm Policy in the Great Plains," *Agricultural History* 43 (July 1979): 345–55.

39 Worster, *The Dust Bowl*, 188.

40 Quoted in Bonnifield, *The Dust Bowl*, 114.

41 *Yearbook of Agriculture 1935* (Washington: USDA, 1935), 46.

42 Pamela Riney-Kehrberg, "From the Horse's Mouth: Dust Bowl Farmers and Their Solutions to the Problem of Aridity," paper presented at the Symposium on Agriculture and the Environment, USDA and Agricultural History Society, Washington, June 19–22, 1991, 7–12.

43 *The Future of the Great Plains*, 175, 182.

44 Ibid., 63.

45 Ibid., 105.

46 Bonnifield, *The Dust Bowl*, 107–9.

47 See Bonnifield, *The Dust Bowl*, 148–49. Relocation itself seemed deceptive. In one case the government placed farmers on inadequate 30- to 60-acre subsistence homesteads at Los Lunas, New Mexico. Resettled farm families were compelled to support themselves by nonfarm employment, and the resettlement farms themselves were on submarginal land according to the government's own test. In the New Mexico case, no water rights for irrigation were included, which left the relocated farmers helpless. The government seemed intent in getting farmers off the land and into the general labor force. The resettlement of Cimarron County, Oklahoma, farmers onto undeveloped mesquite land in southwest Texas led to complaints that the farmers were being coerced into bare-bones homesteading under worse conditions than the old frontier days. Nor would they gain title until they purchased the land they themselves were developing for twenty to thirty-five dollars an acre. Bonnifield concludes that

"the Resettlement Administration was simply a real estate developer who operated at an advantage and kept control of vital aspects of the farm operation."

48 See R. Douglas Hurt, "The National Grasslands: Origin and Development in the Dust Bowl," in Douglas Helms and Susan L. Flader, eds., *The History of Soil and Water Conservation* (Washington: Agricultural History Society, 1985), 144–57, and Hurt's "Federal Land Reclamation in the Dust Bowl, *Great Plains Quarterly* 6 (Spring 1986): 94–106.

49 Bonnifield, *The Dust Bowl*, 173–84.

50 *Report of the Secretary of Agriculture 1894* (Washington, 1895), 22.

51 Wayne D. Rasmussen, *History of Soil Conservation: Institutions and Incentives* (Washington: USDA, 1981), 7.

52 Quoted in Wes Jackson, *New Roots for Agriculture* (San Francisco: Friends of the Earth, 1980), 55.

53 *Spearman* (Tex.) *Reporter*, April 22, 1937.

54 *Farmers in a Changing World: Yearbook of Agriculture 1940*, 413–14.

55 This subject is given particular attention in Pamela Riney-Kehrberg, "From the Horse's Mouth: Dust Bowl Farmers and Their Solutions to the Problem of Aridity."

56 *Report of the Great Plains Drought Area Committee*, 5.

57 See Bonnifield, *The Dust Bowl*, 156

58 See the analysis in Vance Johnson, *Heaven's Tableland: The Dust Bowl Story* (New York: Farrar, Straus and Company, 1947), 274–75.

59 Worster, *The Dust Bowl*, 223; see also Murray R. Benedict, *Farm Policies of the United States, 1790–1950: A Study of Their Origins and Development* (New York: Octagon Books, 1966), 449–90.

60 See Leslie Hewes, *The Suitcase Farming Frontier: A Study in the Historical Geography of the Central High Plains* (Lincoln: University of Nebraska Press, 1973).

61 John Bird, "The Great Plains Hit the Jackpot," *Saturday Evening Post* (August 30, 1947: 16, 90.

62 Worster, *The Dust Bowl*, 225.

63 *Country Gentleman* 117 (September 1947): 85.

64 Quoted in Worster, *The Dust Bowl*, 226.

65 See R. Douglas Hurt, *The Dust Bowl: An Agricultural and Social History* (Chicago: Nelson-Hall, 1981), 141.

66 Hurt, *The Dust Bowl* 140–44.

67 See Philip J. Thair, *Meeting the Impact of Crop-Yield Risks in Great Plains Farming*, NDAES Bulletin 392 (Fargo, N.D., 1954), and Great Plains Council, *Research Conference on Risk and Uncertainty in Agriculture* (Proceedings, Bozeman, Montana, August 10–15, 1953), NDAES Bulletin 400 (Fargo, N.D., 1955).

68 Hurt, *The Dust Bowl*, 151–52.

69 Lloyd E. Dunlap, Edwin D. Gutentag, and James G. Thomas, "Use of Ground Water During Drought Conditions in West-Central Kansas," report prepared for USGS) 1979 spring meeting, Garden City, Kansas.

70 Edwin Kessler et al., "Duststorms from the U.S. High Plains in Late Winter 1977: Search for Cause and Implications," *Proceedings of the Oklahoma Academy of Science* 58 (1978): 116–28.

71 John Borchert, "The Dust Bowl in the 1970s," *Annals of the Association of American Geographers* 61 (March 1971): 13.

72 *Another Revolution in U.S. Farming?* (Washington: Agricultural Economic Report No.441, ESCS, USDA, 1979), 42–75.

73 Worster, *The Dust Bowl*, 223–24.

74 Quoted in ibid., 225.

75 Mary Rule, *Water in Kansas: A Primer* (Whiting: Kansas Rural Center, 1984), 7.

76 Office of Technology Assessment, *Water-Related Technologies for Sustainable Agriculture in U.S. Arid/Semiarid Lands* (Washington: U.S. Congress, Office of Technology Assessment, OTA-F-212, October 1983), 41–43; see also William Franklin Langrone, "The Great Plains," in *Another Revolution in U.S. Farming?*, 335–61.

77 OTA, *Water-Related Technologies*, 24.

78 Ibid.; see also 343–44.

79 Ibid., 343–44.

80 Ibid., 35, 165.

81 Ibid., 42.

82 Personal interview and correspondence with Deborah Epstein Popper and Frank J. Popper in August 1990; see also "The Fate of the Plains," in Ed Marston, ed., *Reopening the Western Frontier* (Washington: Island Press, 1989), 98–113; "Saving the Plains: The Bison Gambit," *Washington Post*, August 6, 1989; and "The Strange Case of the Contemporary American Frontier," *Yale Review* (Fall 1986): 101–21.

83 Quoted in Andrew Cassel, "Grasslands plan urged for Plains," *Philadelphia Inquirer*, June 19, 1989, 2a.

84 See the discussion by James W. O'Leary in Ernest A. Engelbert and Ann Foley Scheuring, eds., *Water Scarcity: Impacts on Western Agriculture* (Berkeley: University of California Press, 1984), 175–77.

85 See the discussion by Estevan T. Flores in Engelbert and Scheuring, *Water Scarcity*, 327.

86 See the discussion by Charles V. Moore in ibid., see also pp.122 and 277.

87 OTA, *Water-Related Technologies*, 3, 5.

88 See the extended discussion of these different positions in the Appendix, "Puzzling Out the Plains."

Chapter 4

1 See T. Lindsay Baker, "Irrigating with Windmills on the Great Plains," *Great Plains Quarterly* 9 (Fall 1989): 216–30; Volta Torrey, "Catching the Western winds: Windmills through the years," *American West* 20, no.2 (March–April 1983): 45–51; and the detailed study by Anne M. Marvin, "The Fertile Domain: Irrigation as Adaptation in the Garden City, Kansas Area, 1880–1910," (Ph.D. diss., University of Kansas, 1975).

2 See Walter Prescott Webb's final summation in Chapter 8, "The Frontier as a Modifier of Institutions," in *The Great Frontier* (Austin: University of Texas Press, 1951–52), 239–79.

3 Walter Prescott Webb, *The Great Plains* (Boston: Ginn, 1931), 336. Also see Frederick H. Newell, *Irrigation in the United States* (New York: Thomas Y. Crowell, 1902).

4 See Kenneth D. McCall, "Growth of Irrigation in Scott County, Kansas," *Report of the Kansas State Board of Agriculture* 63, no.262 (August 1944): 10–12.

5 See Webb, *Great Plains*, 337.

6 Letter from Fairbanks, Morse & Company to Walter Prescott Webb, July 15, 1927, *Great Plains*, 340.

7 Conner Sorensen, "A History of Irrigation in the Arkansas River Valley in Western Kansas, 1880–1910" (master's thesis, Wichita State University, 1965), 83–84.

8 Philip Eastman, "Windmill Irrigation in Kansas," *Review of Reviews* 29 (February 1904): 183–87 and "Irrigation by Windmills," *Scientific American Supplement*, April 11, 1896, 169–81.

9 Sorensen, "A History of Irrigation," 78.

10 Henry Worral, "Irrigation in Southwestern Kansas," *Harper's Weekly*, September 29, 1894, 931, quoted in Sorensen, "A History of Irrigation," 81.

11 Sorensen, "A History of Irrigation," 85–86.

12 Quoted in Webb, *Great Plains*, 346.

13 See Andy Erhart, "Early Kansas Irrigation," *Irrigation Age*, February 1969, 20-CN2.

14 McCall, "Growth of Irrigation in Scott County," 14–15.

15 The *Yankton* (S.Dak.) *Press and Dakotan*, November 12, 1896, quoted in Donald E. Green, *Land of the Underground Rain: Irrigation on the Texas High Plains, 1910–1970* (Austin: University of Texas Press, 1973), 28.

16 Sorensen, "A History of Irrigation," 90.

17 William E. Smythe, *The Conquest of Arid America*, 2nd ed. (New York: Macmillan, 1905), 118.

18 Webb, *Great Plains*, 346.

19 Ibid., 348.

20 Johnson, "The High Plains," *Twenty-First Annual Report of the United States Geological Survey*, 681, quoted in Webb, *Great Plains*, 342.

21 Quoted in ibid., 343.

22 Quoted in ibid.

23 Paul B. Thompson, *The Spirit of the Soil: Agriculture and Environmental Ethics* (London: Routledge, 1995), 47–49.

24 Ibid., 51–58.

25 See E. W. Bennison, *Ground Water: Its Development, Uses, and Conservation* (St. Paul, Minn.: Edward E. Johnson, 1947), 197, 373–76, and B. A. Etcheverry, *Irrigation Practice and Engineering*, vol. 1 (New York: McGraw-Hill, 1915), 182.

26 Quoted in Green, *Land of the Underground Rain*, 51.

27 Ibid., 43–46.

28 Newell, *Irrigation in the United States*, 271.

29 See the discussion of other unsuccessful attempts in Green, *Land of the Underground Rain*, 47–53.

30 Quoted in ibid., 106.

31 Sorensen, "A History of Irrigation," 88.

32 Ray Palmer Teele, "Review of Ten Years of Irrigation Investigations," *Annual Report of the Office of Experiment Stations* (Washington, USDA, 1908), 386.

33 Quoted in Green, *Land of the Underground Rain*, 53.

34 For an excellent discussion see ibid., 53–60.

35 Sorensen, "A History of Irrigation," 88.

36 Ibid., 89.

37 Green, *Land of the Underground Rain*, 53.

38 Ibid, 60.

39 The Texas Land & Development Company sold a typical 160-acre irrigated farm for $18,400, with a down payment of $2,300, a first installment of $3,200, and annual payments of about $2,000. In comparison, unimproved 160-acre farms sold for $4,000. Farmers could install their own irrigation plant for another $10,500, about half the cost of turn-key irrigation farming (ibid., 116–17).

40 Ibid., 113–15.

41 Ibid., 115–16.

42 See George Soule, *Prosperity Decade, From War to Depression: 1917–1929*, vol.8 of *The Economic History of the United States* (New York: Holt, Rinehart and Winston, 1947), 229–30, and Gilbert C. Fite, "The Farmers' Dilemma, 1919–1929," in *Change and Continuity in Twentieth Century America, the 1920s*, ed. John Braeman (Columbus: Ohio State University Press, 1968), 67–102.

43 Green, *Land of the Underground Rain*, 120.

44 U.S. Department of Commerce, *The Future of the Great Plains: Report of the Great Plains Committee to the House of Representatives*, 75th Cong., 1st sess., 1937, Doc.144, 1937, 76–77.

45 Green, *Land of the Underground Rain*, 136–39.

46 Quoted in ibid., 139–40.

47 Ibid., 141–43.

48 Ibid., 125–30.

49 Quoted in Pamela Riney-Kehrberg, "From the Horse's Mouth: Dust Bowl Farmers and Their Solutions to the Problem of Aridity" (paper presented to the symposium on Agriculture and the Environment, USDA and the Agricultural History Society, Washington, June 19–22, 1991), 17.

50 Excellent details on costs and equipment are in Green, *Land of the Underground Rain*, 129.

51 Census data reported in ibid., 125.

52 See the discussion in Roy E. Huffman, *Irrigation Development and Public Water Policy* (New York: Ronald Press, 1953).

53 Hughes and Joe R. Motheral, *Irrigated Agriculture in Texas*, bulletin no.59, Texas Agricultural Experiment Station (College Station: Texas A&M University, 1950).

54 Green, *Land of the Underground Rain*, 160.

55 Leon New, *1977 High Plains Irrigation Survey* (Lubbock: Texas Agricultural Extension Service, 1978). Also see Green, *Land of the Underground Rain*, 146–48.

56 Hughes and A. C. Magee, *Water and Associated Costs in the Production of Cotton and Grain Sorghum, Texas High Plains*, bulletin no.851, Texas Agricultural Experiment Station (College Station: Texas A&M University, 1957).

57 Bureau of the Census, *United States Census of Agriculture, 1959*, (Washington, 1961), vol.1, part 37, 154–73.

58 Kansas Water Resources Fact Finding and Research Committee, *Water in Kansas, 1955: A Report to the Kansas State Legislature* (Lawrence, 1955), 53–55.

59 Donald E. Worster, *Dust Bowl: The Southern Plains in the 1930s* (New York: Oxford University Press, 1979), 228, 269.

60 Green, *Land of the Underground Rain*, 151–53.

61 C. A. Bonnen et al., *Use of Irrigation Water on the High Plains*, bulletin no.756, Texas Agricultural Experiment Station (College Station: Texas A&M University, 1952), and Green, *Land of the Underground Rain*, 153–55.

62 Green, *Land of the Underground Rain*, 153, 160.

63 Johnson, "The High Plains," quoted in Webb, *Great Plains*, 343.

64 Green, *Land of the Underground Rain*, 161. Also see Magee et al., *Production Practices for Irrigated Crops on the High Plains*, bulletin no.763, Texas Agricultural Experiment Station (College Station: Texas A&M University, 1953).

65 Green, *Land of the Underground Rain*, 159–60.

66 William E. Splinter, "Center-Pivot Irrigation," *Scientific American* (June 1976). Also see "Center Pivot Development Reviewed," *The Cross Section* 34, no.5 (May 1988): 1, 4.

67 Splinter, "Center-Pivot Irrigation," 8; see Splinter, "Modelling of Plant Growth for Yield Prediction," in *Plant Modification for More Efficient Water Use*, ed. John F. Stone (Netherlands: Elsevier Scientific Publishing, 1975).

68 This information is based on interviews by the author in May, 1988, at Gigot Irrigation, the major regional supplier of center-pivot equipment, and at Gigot Feeders, a feedlot operation with a capacity of thirty-five thousand cattle. Additional data on Gigot enterprises came from interviews with other irrigators, scs

officials, and the critical study made by the Kansas Rural Center: Mary Fund and Elise Watkins Clement, *Distribution of Land and Water Ownership in Southwest Kansas* (Whiting: Kansas Rural Center, 1982), 33–37.

69 Jim Toyayko, "Garden City: 'The Centre and Inspiration' of Irrigation," *Garden City Times*, June 29, 1979.

70 Typescript, dated January 1957, by Andrew B. Erhart, "Conservation Irrigation," for a special edition of the *Pratt (Kans.) Daily Tribune*, 3–4.

71 Soil Conservation Service and U.S. Department of Agriculture, *Finney County Soil Survey, Series 1961* (Wichita, Kans., 1965), 1–89, esp.22. Also see the discussion in Green, *Land of the Underground Rain*, 149.

72 See the chart and discussion in Fund and Clement, *Distribution of Land and Water Ownership*, 23.

73 See the articles in *Cross Section*, the newsletter of the High Plains Underground Water Conservation District No.1, Lubbock, Texas: "Income-Tax Deduction Sought for Depletion of Ground Water" 7, no.1 (June 1960); "Underground Water Depletion Suit Filed" 7, no.9 (February 1961); "Depletion Case Won," 9, no.8 (January 1963); and "Water Depletion Claim Upheld by High Court" 12, no.1 (June 1965).

74 Wayne Bossert, manager of Kansas Groundwater Management District No.4 in Colby, Kans., writes in a letter to author (January 19, 1991) that the "tax relief under the water depletion ruling is not as simple as a $2,400 deduction for a Kansas quarter of land. It depends entirely on the price paid for the land versus the base rate for dryland [hence one's 'cost in water'], the rate of depletion, the monitoring used to claim the allowance, and probably a few other items the IRS has tacked on to discourage the process."

75 See the detailed analysis in Fund and Clement, *Distribution of Land and Water Ownership*, 34–37.

76 "Dean Gigot: He Turns the Sandhills Green," *Wichita Eagle-Beacon*, May 30, 1982.

77 Quoted in "An Odyssey Through Kansas," *U & I*, no.2 [1986?]: 5.

78 Quoted in ibid., 4–5.

79 Kenny Ochs, sales manager of Gigot Irrigation Company, interview by author, May 18, 1988, Garden City, Kans.; Ron Crocker, manager of Gigot Feeders, corroborated this data in an interview, May 18, 1988, Garden City.

80 Green, *Land of the Underground Rain*, 156–57.

81 Splinter, "Center Pivot Irrigation," 5.

82 See Douglas Constance and William Heffernan, "IBP's Dominance in the Meat Packing Industry: Boxed Beef and Busted Unions" (paper presented at a conference of the Food, Agriculture, and Human Values Society, Little Rock, Ark., November 15, 1989), and John W. Helmuth, "Meat Packer Concentration" (paper presented at the annual meeting of the Dakota Resource Council, November 4, 1989).

83 "An Odyssey Through Kansas," 6–7.

84 Quoted in Constance and Heffernan, "IBP's Dominance," 13.

85 See the critical account in Fund and Clement, *Distribution of Land and Water Ownership*, 50.

86 Constance and Heffernan, "IBP's Dominance," 3.

87 In addition, water quality may be affected by chloride contamination from the IBP plant (Bossert, letter to author, January 19, 1991).

88 Tim Unruh, "Board in Limbo on Gigot Operation," *Garden City Telegram*, March 26, 1998, on-line version.

89 Steve Irsik, e-mail to the author, January 21, 1998.

90 Interview by the author, Irsik Farms, Kans., May 18, 1997.

91 Ann Scott Tyson, "Farmers' Use of Water Is High Plains Dilemma," *Christian Science Monitor*, November 28, 1994.

92 Ibid.

93 Owen J. Furuseth, "Restructuring of Hog Farming in North Carolina: Explosion and Implosion," *The Professional Geographer* 49, no.4 (November 1997): 391–403, and John Fraser Hart, "A Map of the Agricultural Implosion," *Annals of the Association of American Geographers*, 60, no.2 (June 1970): 68–71.

94 Neil Hamilton, "Agriculture Without Farmers," *Successful Farming* (April 1994): 28–29.

95 Betsy Freese and Rod Fee, "Livestock-Hungry States," *Successful Farming* (January 1994): 19–21.

96 Jim Stafford, "Family Hog Farm Doing Just Swine," *Sunday Oklahoman*, January 12, 1997, on-line version.

97 Karen McMahon, "Westward Bound! Oklahoma Building Frenzy Doubles Sow Numbers," *National Hog Farmer*, May 15, 1994, 34–42. Also see "Corporate Producers Expand in Isolated Fringe Areas," *National Hog Farmer*, 44–45.

98 See, for example, "Rural Opposition to Hog Farms Grows," *New York Times*,

September 22, 1997, and Fund, "Citizens Brace Themselves for the New Hog Invasion," *Rural Papers*, no.140 (June–July 1997): 1, 3.

99 "Corporations Begin to Turn Hog Business into an Assembly Line," *Wall Street Journal*, March 18, 1994. Also see Harold F. Breimyer, "Do Mega Hog Farms Foretell Farming of the Future?" *Economic and Policy Information for Missouri Agriculture*, 37, no.5 (September–October 1994).

100 "Corporations Begin to Turn Hog Business into an Assembly Line," *Wall Street Journal*, March 18, 1994.

101 Ibid.

102 Quoted in Humane Farming Association's unsympathetic critique, *Bringing Home the Bacon: A Look Inside the Pork Industry* (1995), broadside.

103 Mark Obmascik, "Welcome to Hog Haven," *Denver Post*, July 31, 1994. *Bringing Home the Bacon*, by the Humane Farming Association, describes the process: "After impregnation, the sow is locked in a narrow metal gestation crate. The width of the crate varies from 18 to 24 inches, and the length extends just barely beyond the sow's own body. She is restrained in this unbedded, cement-floored crate for her entire pregnancy—nearly four months. She is unable to walk or turn around. She is fed at one end of the crate and her feces collect at the other. Confinement severely frustrates the natural behaviors involved in nest seeking, nest building, and the rearing of piglets. Near the end of her pregnancy, the sow is moved from the gestation crate to the farrowing crate. Against all her natural instincts, she must give birth to piglets, nurse them, eat, sleep, defecate, drink, stand and lie in the same cramped space. The nursing period is cut drastically short by the premature separation of the piglets from their mother. The sow is immediately reimpregnated and sent back to the gestation crate. This vicious cycle is repeated over and over again until the sow's 'productivity' wanes, and she is sent to slaughter. . . . Laws in Europe are being enacted to outlaw gestation crates."

104 See Val Farmer, "Problems At Hog Hotel Heaven," *Grass & Grain*, August 2, 1994, 27.

105 Michael McNutt, "Guymon Plant's Growth Defies Skeptics—Firm Brings Pigs to Cattle Country," *Sunday Oklahoman*, May 18, 1997, on-line version.

106 "Researchers Study How Many Hogs Too Many to Live Around," *Wichita Eagle*, June 15, 1994, and see editorial, *Hutchinson News*, August 5, 1994. A Texas County, Okla., resident added that a ton of hogs produces thirty-two tons of waste, as much as four times as much waste annually as a human. Four hundred

thousand proposed new Cimarron County swine would excrete the same sewage as 1.2 million people—"more waste than the combined cities of Oklahoma City, Ein and Lawton" (Jarrod Stewart, letter, *Sunday Oklahoman*, January 11, 1998), on-line version.

107 Unruh, "Lagoon Science Still a Bit Cloudy," *The Garden City Telegram*, February 17, 1998, on-line version.

108 Angie Gaddy, "Waste Check Valve Safeguards Urged," *Sunday Oklahoman*, May 4, 1997.

109 Unruh, "Lagoon Science Still a Bit Cloudy."

110 "KSU Lagoon Study Awaits Green Light," *Rural Papers*, no.132 (September 1996): 3; "KPPC Tells Producers to Not Participate in KSU Lagoon Study," *Rural Papers*, no.138 (April 1997): 3.

111 McNutt, "Murphy Farms Touts Efforts to Be Responsible Neighbor," *Sunday Oklahoman*, May 4, 1997, on-line version.

112 Mick Hinton, "Bad Rap Undeserved, Hog Farmer Asserts," *Sunday Oklahoman*, May 4, 1997.

113 Mark Obmascik, "Welcome to Hog Haven," *The Denver Post*, July 31, 1994. Also see Rocky Mountain Farmer's Union, "Concerns Expressed over Latest Corporate Hog Proposal," *Union Farmer*, December 1994–January 1995; "Water Quality Impact of Large Hog Farms Need More Study," *Rural Papers*, no.132 (September 1996): 6, and "Review Criticizes State's Livestock Permitting Program," *Rural Papers*, no.133 (October 1996): 1, 8.

114 Jason M. Peters, letter, "Swine Effluent Beneficial," *Sunday Oklahoman*, January 11, 1998, on-line version.

115 Laura Hamod Zuckerman, "Squeals of Protest," *Topeka Capitol-Journal*, May 1, 1995.

116 Jarrod Stewart, letter, *Sunday Oklahoman*, January 11, 1998, on-line version.

117 Angie Gaddy, "Odors 'Nauseating,' Farmers Complain," *Sunday Oklahoman*, May 4, 1997, on-line version. Also see David Zizzo, "Downwind of Corporate Push," *Sunday Oklahoman*, May 9, 1993, on-line version.

118 Gaddy, "Odors 'Nauseating,' Farmers Complain."

119 Mark Parker, "SW MO Farm Folks Unhappy with New Mega-Hog Neighbors," *Farm Talk*, July 27, 1994, 1.

120 Alan Montgomery, "Seaboard Violates Its KWPC Permit," *Hutchinson News*, November 17, 1995. Also see "Instead of Money, Hogs Smell of Pollution," *U.S. Water News*, August 1994.

A May 1996 study in Renville County, Minnesota, reported that levels of hydrogen sulfide in 25 percent of the air near seventeen large-scale hog manure lagoons were greater than allowed by Minnesota air-quality standards. Two sites showed hydrogen sulfide levels of more than 100 parts per billion (ppb) up to a mile and a half away and the maximum allowed is 50 parts per billion (ppb) for a half-hour period no more than twice a year. ("Sulfide Tests Prompt Lagoon Investigation," *Rural Papers*, no.132 [September 1996]: 3.) Also see Gaddy, "Odors 'Nauseating,' Farmers Complain."

121 Quoted in Zizzo, "Hold Your Nose, but Not Your Breath—No Easy Answers for Smelly Hog Farms' Neighbors," *Daily Oklahoman*, January 12, 1998, on-line version.

122 Ibid.

123 Hinton, "Bad Rap Undeserved, Hog Farmer Asserts," *Sunday Oklahoman*, May 4, 1997.

124 *Guymon* (Okla.) *Daily Herald*, August 17, 1995. A similar report from Iowa is described by Tom Seery, "Big Hog Farms Anger Iowans," *Wichita Eagle*, June 26, 1994.

125 Hinton and Gaddy, "Ag Board Toughens Rules for Hog Farms," *Daily Oklahoman*, March 27, 1997, on-line version.

126 Ibid.

127 Ibid.

128 Stafford, "Neighbors Raising Stink over State's Swine Industry," *Sunday Oklahoman*, May 12, 1996, on-line version.

129 Danny M. Boyd, "Plant Could Remove 'Yuck' from Piggery," *Daily Oklahoman*, February 15, 1998, on-line version.

130 Paul H. Hitch, letter, "County Vote on Animal Operations a Bad Idea," *Daily Oklahoman*, December 19, 1997, on-line version.

131 Stafford, "Hitch Goes Whole Hog into Pig Business," *Daily Oklahoman*, August 17, 1995, on-line version.

132 Ibid.

133 Ibid.

134 Boyd, "Family at Center of Hog Dispute—Hitch Name Now Stirs Panhandle Controversy," *Sunday Oklahoman*, January 25, 1998, on-line version.

135 Ibid.

136 McNutt, "Feedlot to Expand into Hogs," *Daily Oklahoman*, July 29, 1993, on-line version.

137 Hinton and Paul English, "Tighter Rules Signed for State Hog Farms," *Daily Oklahoman*, May 2, 1997, on-line version.

138 McNutt, "Cattle Rancher Defends His Role in Hog Industry," *Daily Oklahoman*, July 11, 1997, on-line version.

139 Paul English, "Letters to Seek Hitch's Ouster," *Daily Oklahoman*, October 21, 1997, on-line version. Also see Hinton and Gaddy, "Ag Board Toughens Rules for Hog Farms," on-line version.

140 Chris Mayda, e-mail to the author, May 3, 1998.

141 Boyd, "Family at Center of Hog Dispute."

142 This data is based on a personal interview with Bossert in Colby, Kans., on March 5, 1996, a phone interview with Bossert on May 17, 1996, and "Groundwater Considerations and Concerns for Confined Swine Feeding Facilities" (document obtained from Bossert, n.d.).

143 Mike Berry, "Southwest Kansans Turn Down Corporate Hog Farm Proposal," *Wichita Eagle*, November 10, 1994. For Hodgeman County, see "Hodgeman County Narrowly Defeats Corporate Hogs," *Rural Papers*, no.138 (April 1997): 3; this article also notes, "The debate in Hodgeman County was heated due to a number of farmers already contracting swine production." Also see Fund, "County by County Summary of Factory Hog Activity in Kansas," *Rural Papers*, no.140 (June–July 1997): 10, and "Seward County Votes No," *Rural Papers*, no.142 (September 1997): 1, 11.

144 Alan Montgomery, "Hamilton Voters Nix Hogs," *Hutchinson News*, November 8, 1995.

145 Kansas Rural Center, *Rural Papers*, no.122 (September 1995): 7; and *Rural Papers*, no.124 (November–December 1995): 1.

146 Unruh, "Great Bend Voters Oust Hog Backers," *Garden City Telegram*, April 8, 1998, on-line version.

147 "Great Bend Narrowly Endorses Hog Plan, *Rural Papers*, no.158 (April 1999): 3.

148 Steve Painter, "Like the Smell, Hog Issue Won't Go Away," *Wichita Eagle*, January 26, 1998, on-line version.

149 Sarah Kessinger, "Senate OKS Hog Bill," *Garden City Telegram*, April 2, 1998, on-line version.

150 See Edward Walsh "Iowa Grapples with Huge Corporate Hog Farms," *Topeka Capital-Journal*, October 20, 1994.

151 "Why the Fish Are Dying," editorial, *New York Times*, September 22, 1997, and Kansas Rural Center, *Rural Papers*, no.121 (June–July 1995): 3. Also see "On the Corporate Front," *Rural Papers*, no.127 (March 1996): 3.

152 Alan Montgomery, "Seaboard Violates Its KWPC Permit," *Hutchinson News*, November 17, 1995 and "Water Pipe Damaged Seaboard Hog Lagoon," *Hutchinson News*, December 8, 1995.

153 Paul English, "Seaboard to Contest State's $157,500 Hog Farm Fine—Settlement Rejected in Alleged Violations of Carcass Disposal Rules," *Daily Oklahoman*, January 1, 1998, on-line version, and Hinton, "Seaboard Settles Hog Case—Corporation Agrees to Pay State $88,200," *Daily Oklahoman*, February 7, 1988, on-line version.

154 U.S. Environmental Protection Agency, "Draft Strategy for Addressing Environmental and Public Health Impacts from Animal Feeding Operations" (Washington, March 1998).

155 "Feedlots Face EPA Waste Rules," *Lubbock Avalanche-Journal*, March 6, 1998, on-line version.

156 See, for example, Mark Eddy, "Hog-Farm Controls Passed," *Denver Post*, March 19, 1998, and Kay Ledbetter, "Ruling Upsets Feed Operators," *Amarillo Globe-News*, November 29, 1997.

157 McMahon, "Westward Bound!" *National Hog Farmer*, May 15, 1994, 34–42.

158 McNutt, "Guymon's Economy Booming," *Sunday Oklahoman*, December 11, 1994, on-line version.

159 Stafford, "Neighbors Raising Stink."

160 Ibid.

161 Hinton, "Seaboard Seeks Approval for 8,000-Acre Hog Farm," *Daily Oklahoman*, December 10, 1997, on-line version.

162 Hinton, "Seaboard Seeks Approval" and "Hog Moratorium Bill May See Senate Changes," *Daily Oklahoman*, March 2, 1998, on-line version.

163 Boyd, "Farmers Take Sides in Battle over Hogs," *Sunday Oklahoman*, January 25, 1998, on-line version.

164 Hinton, "Seaboard Cleans up for Task Force Visit," *Sunday Oklahoman*, August 10, 1997, on-line version.

165 *Guymon* (Okla.) *Daily Herald*, November 29–30, 1994, and September 2–3, 1995, and McNutt, "Guymon's Economy Booming," *Sunday Oklahoman*, on-line version. See Impact Committee Memo on Goals, Strategic Planning Task Force, January 30, 1995, Guymon City Council, Guymon, Okla. (material re-

ceived from Bonita Hoeme, March 1996), and McNutt, "Hog Plants Smell like Money to Guymon," *Sunday Oklahoman*, May 11, 1997, on-line version.

166 Stafford, "Hitch Goes Whole Hog."

167 Nixon and Associates, *Preliminary Engineering Report: Projected Water Needs, Guymon Utility Authority* (Guymon, Okla., January 1993), file no.6219.

168 Bonita Hoeme, phone conversation with author, November 1995, and OWRB, *Permits and Pending Applications for Swine Operations in Texas, Cimmarron, or Beaver County*, July 18, 1995, Oklahoma City, Okla. Also see Randy Ellis, "Hog Outfit, Neighbors Clash on Groundwater," *Daily Oklahoman*, April 12, 1995.

169 McNutt, "Seaboard's Opening Seen as Panhandle Magnet," *Daily Oklahoman*, January 5, 1996, on-line version.

170 Bonita Hoeme, phone conversation with author, November, 1995.

171 Ibid.

172 *Guymon Daily Herald*, August 17, 1995. Also see Tom Seery, "Big Hog Farms Anger Iowans," *Wichita Eagle*, June 26, 1994.

173 Hinton, "Ag Board Drags Its Heels on Hog Farm Regulations," *Sunday Oklahoman*, April 13, 1997, on-line version, and Hinton, "Senate OKs Hog Farm Regulations," *Daily Oklahoman*, April 16, 1997, on-line version.

174 Paul English, "Keating Signs Hog Farm Bill; Plan's Backers Rejoice," *Daily Oklahoman*, June 5, 1997; Hinton, "Corporate Hog Farms Rush to Beat New Rules, *Daily Oklahoman*, June 6, 1997, on-line version; Hinton, "Keating Set to Throttle Hog Industry; Special Session Considered," *Daily Oklahoman*, December 2, 1997.

175 "Board's New Emergency Rule Lines Water Use to Ag License," *Oklahoma Water News*, July–August 1997, 1; Hinton, "Pork Industry Pushes for Rule Changes," *Daily Oklahoman*, April 3, 1997, on-line version; Hinton, "Corporate Hog Farms Rush."

176 Hinton, "Governor Signs Statewide Hold on Hog Farms," *Daily Oklahoman*, March 10, 1998, on-line version.

177 Hinton, "Don't Dilute Hog Curbs, Environment Chief Says," *Daily Oklahoman*, April 21, 1998.

178 Hinton, "Well Law Taps into Hog Farm Debate," *Sunday Oklahoman*, April 19, 1998, on-line version.

179 Kansas Legislature, Committee on Environment, Substitute for House Bill No.2950, Topeka, 1998 Session (March 11, 1998).

180 *Daily Oklahoman*, April 3, 1997, May 2, 1997, and March 10, 1998.

181 U.S. Department of Agriculture figures quoted in the *Chicago Tribune*, July 10, 1988. As fears rose about food price increases, the media paid attention to the ripple effect of the drought of 1988, as in Barbara Rudolph, "The Drought's Food-Chain Reaction," *Time*, July 11, 1988, 40.

182 Steve Frost, manager of Kansas Groundwater Management District No.3, phone interview by author, Garden City, Kansas, May 17, 1996.

183 *Hutchinson News*, January 25, 1996. Also see *Hutchinson News*, June 22, 1995.

184 Fund, "Corporate Chickens Come to Kansas to Roost," *Rural Papers*, no.132 (September 1996): 1.

185 Hinton, "Chickens Worse than Hogs, Keating Says," *Daily Oklahoman*, January 20, 1997, on-line version.

186 Ibid.

187 Heiser, *Seeds to Civilization*, 35–36, 48, 53–55.

Chapter 5

1 P. Barkley, "The Sustainability of Rural Non-Farm Economics in Water Dependent Agricultural Areas," OTA commissioned paper, 1983, excerpted in OTA, *Water-Related Technologies for Sustainable Agriculture in U.S. Arid-Semiarid Lands* (Washington, October 1983), 137.

2 Commentary by Frank J. Trelease in Ernest A. Engelbert and Ann Foley Scheuring, eds., *Water Scarcity: Impacts on Western Agriculture* (Berkeley: University of California Press, 1984), 78.

3 *Ground Water: An Overview* (Washington: General Accounting Office, June 21, 1977), 9–14; see also "West Texas and Eastern New Mexico Import Project," *Critical Water Problems Facing the Eleven Western States* (Washington: USDI, April 1975); and *Projected Economic Life of Water Resources, Subdivision Number 1, High Plains Underground Water Reservoir* (College Station: Technical Monograph 6, Texas Agricultural Experiment Station, Texas A&M University, December 1969).

4 R. Young, "Allocating the Water Resource: Market Systems and the Economic Value of Water," OTA commissioned paper, 1982, excerpted in OTA, *Water-Related Technologies for Sustainable Agriculture in U.S. Arid/Semiarid Lands*, 388ff.

5 Donald E. Green, *Land of the Underground Rain* (Austin: University of Texas Press, 1973), 165–69.

6 Quoted in ibid., 167.

7 Ibid., 168.

8 See the discussion in ibid., 169–70.

9 See the discussion by Henry P. Caulfield, Jr., in Engelbert and Scheuring, *Water Scarcity*, 462–63; see also J. David Aiken, "Development of the Appropriation Doctrine: Adapting Water Allocation Policies to Semiarid Environs," *Great Plains Quarterly* 8 (Winter 1988): 38–44.

10 This is a major thesis in Mark Sagoff, *The Economy of the Earth: Philosophy, Law, and the Environment* (New York: Cambridge University Press, 1988); see also F. Lee Brown et al., "Water Reallocation, Market Proficiency, and Conflicting Social Values," in Gary D. Weatherford et al., *Western Water Institutions in a Changing Environment* (Boulder, Colo.: Westview Press, 1980).

11 Oklahoma Supreme Court, *Canada* v. *Shawnee*, 179 Okl. 53 64 P. 2d 694 (1936, 1937).

12 This is a variant on the social goals of irrigation communities described by F. Lee Brown and Charles T. DuMars, "Water Rights and Market Transfers," in Engelbert and Scheuring, *Water Scarcity*, 411–13. See also A. Maass and R. L. Anderson, *And the Desert Shall Rejoice: Conflict, Growth and Justice in Arid Environments* (Cambridge, Mass.: MIT Press, 1978), Kenneth Boulding, *Western Water Resources: Coming Problems and the Policy Alternatives* (Boulder, Colo.: Westview Press, 1980), and Brown et al., "Water Reallocation, Market Proficiency, and Conflicting Social Values."

13 A recent example that links sustainable development with local decision making is the study by the World Commission on Environment and Development, *Our Common Future* (New York: Oxford University Press, 1987).

14 Robert A. Young, "Local and Regional Economics Impacts," in Engelbert and Scheuring, *Water Scarcity*, 244–45.

15 See, for example, the data and conclusions in Edwin D. Gutentag et al., *Geohydrology of the High Plains Aquifer in Parts of Colorado, Kansas, Nebraska, New Mexico, Oklahoma, South Dakota, Texas, and Wyoming* (Washington: U.S. Geological Survey Professional Paper 1400-B, USGPO, 1984); also based on USGS data in the personal papers of Edwin G. Gutentag, U.S. Geological Survey, Department of the Interior, Denver Federal Center.

16 Green, *Land of the Underground Rain*, 172–87.

17 All quoted in ibid., 179–83.

18 Ibid., 177.

19 Ibid., 188, 189.

20 *Rules of Texas High Plains Underground Water Conservation District No.1, 1954.*

21 See John Opie, *The Law of the Land: 200 Years of American Farmland Policy* (Lincoln: University of Nebraska Press, 1987).

22 Interview with Wayne Wyatt in Lubbock, Texas, in May 1987.

23 See also Neville P. Clarke, *Texas Agriculture in the 80's: The Critical Decade* (College Station: Texas Agricultural Experiment Station Report B-1341, Texas A&M University, 1980).

24 Abstracted in High Plains Underground Water Conservation District No.1 brochure received May 1986.

25 Chap. 52, Vernon's Civil Statues of Texas.

26 Abstracted in High Plains Underground Water Conservation District No.1 brochure received May 1986.

27 Frank A. Rayner, *Government and Groundwater Management* (Lubbock: Texas High Plains Underground Water Conservation District No.1, 1975), 2.

28 Ibid., 1, 2.

29 Ibid., 3–4. Texas water law states: "The water of the ordinary flow, under-flow, and tides of every flowing river, natural stream, and lake, and of every bay or arm of the gulf of Mexico, and the storm water, floodwater, and rainwater of every river, natural stream, canyon, ravine, depression, and watershed in the state is the property of the state." Chap. 5.021, Vernon's Texas Codes Annotated.

30 Rayner, *Government and Groundwater Management*, 10.

31 *Friendswood Development Company* v. *Smith-Southwest Industries, Inc.*, 576 S.W.2d 21 (Texas Supreme Court, 1978).

32 "The Case for Local Regulation," *The Cross Section*, 28, no.12 (December 1982): 1–4.

33 Frank L. Baird, *District Groundwater Planning and Management Policies on the Texas High Plains: The Views of the People* (Lubbock: Texas High Plains Underground Water Conservation District No.1, July 1976), 4–5.

34 *Oklahoma Water Resources Board and Mobil Oil Corporation* v. *Texas County Irrigation and Water Resources Association*, Supreme Court of the State of Oklahoma, 56,355, December 20, 1984.

35 "Chemicals of Potential Use in Surfactant/Polymer Flooding, Appendix L,"

Cumulative Production/Consumption Effects of the Crude Oil Price Incentive Rulemakings: Final Environmental Impact Statement (Washington: U.S. Department of Energy, 1978), IV-71, 76.

36 Data received from Bonita Hoeme of the Texas County Irrigation and Water Resources Association, May 1987.

37 Quoted by Esther Groves, "Area Water, Oil Interests Battle," *Liberal Daily Times*, April 8, 1985.

38 Minutes, Oklahoma Water Resources Board, December 3, 1985, 7.

39 570 p.2d 49 (Okla. 1977).

40 82 O.S. Supp. 1972, para 1020.15.

41 82 O.S. 1981, para 926.1.

42 The issues are outlined in an April 1, 1985, news release from the Texas County Irrigation and Water Resources Association in Guymon, Oklahoma.

43 Records of hearings in archives of Texas County Irrigation and Water Resources Association, Guymon, Oklahoma.

44 In a 1982 report, of the 460 billion barrels of known U.S. oil reserves, 120 billion can be obtained by primary drilling. Enhanced oil recovery can capture 18 to 50 billion, leaving 300 billion barrels to be gotten "using technology not yet discovered." This leaves 83 to 94 percent of the remaining oil still in the ground. See Gregory Seay, "Enhanced recovery gets big play," *Sunday Oklahoman*, April 4, 1982.

45 In records of TCIWRA.

46 "Finding of Fact, Conclusions of Law and Board Order on Application No.85–581," Oklahoma Water Resources Board, December 3, 1985.

47 Ibid.

48 Quoted by Esther Groves, "Panhandle Irrigators File to Save Water Resources," *Liberal Daily Times*, December 29, 1985.

49 Quoted by Esther Groves, "Irrigators Plan Appeal," *Liberal Daily Times*, December 11, 1985.

50 Copy of testimony to Oklahoma House Natural Resources Committee, May 13, 1985, from Gene Barby; interview with Barby in May 1986.

51 Typescript, dated January 1957, by Andrew B. Erhart, "Conservation Irrigation," for a special edition of the *Pratt* (Kans.) *Daily Tribune*.

52 Interviews (May 1986, September 1987) with Rick Illgner and Gary Baker, former and current managers of Southwest Kansas Groundwater Management

District No.3; see the excellent analysis of the issues of the Stone case and Kansas groundwater policies in general in Mary Fund and Elsie Watkins Clement, *Distribution of Land and Water Ownership in Southwest Kansas* (Whiting: Kansas Rural Center, 1982), 40–48, and also *Water Marker Update* 1, no.5 (May 1987): 2.

53 See Mary Fund, *Water in Kansas: A Primer* (Whiting: Kansas Rural Center, 1984), 8–11, and Robert G. Dunbar, *Forging New Rights in Western Water* (Lincoln: University of Nebraska Press, 1983), chaps. 6–10.

54 Wayne Bossert writes (January 19, 1991): "The Kansas Water Appropriate Act states that for three consecutive years of non-use *without due and sufficient cause* the state can determine the right abandoned. However, the state has provided for a series of 'due and sufficient causes' whereby non-use does not necessarily mean abandonment. This wording in Kansas is an attempt to move away from the 'use it or lose it' concept while still recognizing that one cannot sit indefinitely on a water right to the exclusion of others who may want to use the resource."

55 See Earl B. Shurtz, *Kansas Water Law* (Wichita: Kansas Water Resources Board, 1967).

56 Ibid., 20.

57 Fund, *Water in Kansas*, 32–34.

58 John Wesley Powell, *Water for the West*, quoted in *Management Programs* frontispiece.

59 Fund, *Water in Kansas*, 62.

60 *Management Programs*, 15–16.

61 According to the common United States Geological Survey location notation that provides precise identification for the Soil Conservation Service and Southwest Kansas Groundwater Management District No.3, Stapleton's well was NE1/4-31-31-33, Dufield's was SW1/4-25-31-31, and Guttridge's was NW 1/4-32-33-34. Dufield's Seward County well was at 32-32W-14BBB.

62 Data provided by the Liberal, Kansas, office of the Soil Conservation Service, USDA, May, 1987. See also "Ground-water Supply Problems," in *Revised Management Program III: Rules and Regulations, and Policies and Standards* (Garden City, Kans.: Southwest Kansas Groundwater Management District No.3, 1986), 6–7.

63 *Management Programs*, 1.

64 Fund and Clement, *Distribution of Land and Water Ownership in Southwest Kansas*, 17–19, 33–34.

65 Kansas Water Office, *Summary: Ogallala Aquifer Study in Kansas*, 11.

66 *Management Programs*, 20.

67 Fund, *Water in Kansas*, 43–44.

68 Fund and Clement, *Distribution of Land and Water Ownership*, 45–46.

69 Ibid., 46.

70 Kansas Water Office, *Agricultural Water Conservation: Irrigation Plan Guidelines* (enclosed in letter to "Fellow Kansans" from the Kansas Water Office, Topeka, dated December 18, 1986).

71 Kansas State Board of Agriculture, Division of Water Resources, "Administrative Policy No.88-3" (attached to letter dated December 12, 1988, addressed to "All County Conservation Districts").

72 Bossert, letter to the author, January 19, 1991, and interviews, Colby, Kans., March 4–5, 1996.

73 Kip Lowe, "Groundwater Future a Continuing Concern," *Colby* (Kans.) *Free Press*, June 15, 1990. Also see "Groundwater District Halts Water Rights," *Atwood* (Kans.) *Citizen-Patriot*, February 22, 1990.

74 Orlan Buller, "Potential Economic Effects of a Zero Depletion Policy in Northwest Kansas" (paper presented at the Symposium on the Effects of a Zero Depletion Policy on the Ogallala Aquifer of the Great Plains, Ft. Hays State University, Hays, Kans., April 16, 1991), 13.

75 Data provided by Northwest Kansas Groundwater Management District No.4, January 1991. Also see data on county groundwater decline levels between 1964 and 1994 reported in *Water Table* (a Northwest Kansas Groundwater Management District No.4 publication) 18, no.1 (January–February 1995): 1, *Water Table* 18, no.2 (March–April 1995): 3, and *Water Table* 18, no.3 (May–June 1995): 3.

76 Bossert, letter to the author, January 19, 1991.

77 Bossert, letter to Division of Water Resources, October 8, 1990.

78 "Status of Zero Depletion Discussions," *Water Table* 16, no.1 (January–February 1993): 1. Also see "DWR's New Policy Explained," *Water Table* 16, no.1 (January–February 1993): 2.

79 Bossert, "Approaches to Improved Irrigation Water Conservation under Consideration by Northwest Kansas Groundwater Management District No.4," (pa-

per presented during "Water Organizations in a Changing West," a conference at the Natural Resources Law Center, University of Colorado School of Law, Boulder, June 14–16, 1993), 1.

80 Bossert, interview, March 5, 1996. See "Draft Ogallala Decline Committee Recommendations to Northwest Kansas Groundwater Management District No.4" (Colby, Kans.: Northwest Kansas Groundwater Management District No.4, October 4, 1990); Bossert, letter to Division of Water Resources, October 8, 1990 (in files in office of the Northwest Kansas Groundwater Management District No.4); "Declines Committee Makes Recommendation," *Water Table* 13, no.6 (November–December 1990).

81 Mike Corn, "Groundwater District Endorses Zero Depletion Recommendations," *Hays* (Kans.) *Daily News*, October 5, 1990.

82 "Irrigation Use Efficiency Being Carefully Considered," *Water Table* 16, no.5 (September–October 1993): 1. Also see "KSBA Committee Update," *Water Table* 16, no.3 (May–June 1993): 2.

83 "Water Use Report Monitoring News," *Water Table* 18, no.5 (September–October 1995): 1.

84 "State Considers Water Banking," *Water Table* 18, no.4 (July–August 1995): 2.

85 Bossert, "Approaches to Improved Irrigation Water Conservation," 5. Also see "Northwest Kansas Use Reporting May Be High," *Water Table* 16, no.2 (March–April 1993): 3, and "Subbasin Plan Explained," *Water Table* 18, no.4 (July–August 1995): 3.

86 Lowe, "Groundwater Future a Continuing Concern."

87 Bossert, "Approaches to Improved Irrigation Water Conservation," 8.

88 Buller, "Potential Economic Effects," 13.

89 Bossert, letter to Kansas Department of Commerce, May 4, 1990.

90 Bossert and Curtis D. Smith, e-mail to the author, July 2, 1998, and Western Kansas Weather Modification Program (WKWMP) on-line newsletter, nos.98-4, May 9–15, 1998 and 98-7, May 30–June 5, 1998. All such newsletters are available from hailman@pld.com. Also see <pta6000.pld.com/hailman/>. This site also references Utah and Colorado reports.

91 WKWMP, on-line newsletter nos.98-1, April 22–24, 1998, and 98-2, April 25–May 1, 1998.

92 WKWMP, on-line newsletter nos.98-4, May 9–15, 1998.

93 WKWMP, on-line weather modification update for June 19, 1998.

94 WKWMP, on-line newsletter no.98-7, May 30–June 5, 1998.

95 Bossert, e-mail to the author, July 2, 1998.

96 WKWMP, on-line newsletter (no issue number), April 22–24, 1998. Also see 1997 on-line annual report.

97 WKWMP, on-line. This site includes details on weather-modification science, technology, and methodologies.

98 WKWMP, on-line weather modification update for June 19, 1998.

99 "New Mexico Counties Added to Precipitation Enhancement Target Area," *Cross Section* 43, no.8 (August 1997): 1–2.

100 Texas Underground Water Management District No.1. on-line precipitation enhancement fact sheet, <www.hub.ofthe.net/hpwd/rain-faq.html> (May 12, 1999).

101 John Bredehoeft, "Physical Limitations of Water Resources," in *Water Scarcity: Impacts on Western Agriculture*, ed. Ernest A. Engelbert and Ann Foley Scheuring (Berkeley: University of California Press, 1984), 43.

102 Earl O. Heady, "National and International Commodity Price Impacts," in *Water Scarcity*, ed. Engelbert and Scheuring, 277–78.

103 OTA, *Water-Related Technologies*, 39.

104 Heady, "National and International Commodity Price Impacts," 274, 277–78.

Chapter 6

1 Phil Tooms, interview with author at the Toomses' home in southwest Kansas, May 1986, 1987, and 1988. All subsequent citations come from these interviews with Phil and Linda Tooms. (These names are pseudonyms for real people who wish to protect their privacy.) The information from these interviews is not singular, but representative. It is confirmed by data on the Toomses and similar operations collected at the Garden City office of the USDA Soil Conservation Service.

2 See Mary Fund and Elise Watkins Clement, *Distribution of Land and Water Ownership in Southwest Kansas* (Whiting: Kansas Rural Center, 1982), 41–48, and Fund, *Water in Kansas: A Primer* (Whiting, Kans.: Kansas Rural Center, 1984), 56–73.

3 See Paul B. Thompson, *The Spirit of the Soil: Agriculture and Environmental Ethics* (London: Routledge, 1995), 18–19, 119. Also see John Lemons, "Structural Trends in Agriculture and Preservation of Family Farms," *Environmental Management* 10, no.1 (1986): 75–88; David M. Kendall et al., *Tomorrow's Har-*

vest: A Study Guide (Lawrence: University of Kansas Press, 1982); the essays in Michael Chibnik, ed., *Farm Work and Fieldwork: American Agriculture in Anthropological Perspective* (Ithaca: Cornell University Press, 1987); Gary Comstock, ed., *Is There a Moral Obligation to Save the Family Farm?* (Ames: Iowa State University Press, 1988); and Marty Strange, *Family Farming: A New Economic Vision* (Lincoln: University of Nebraska Press, 1988).

4 Willard C. Cochrane, *The Development of American Agriculture: A Historical Analysis* (Minneapolis: University of Minnesota Press, 1979), 355–78.

5 [Center for Rural Affairs (Walthill, Nebr.)] "Center's Dialogue on Farm Structure," *New Land Review* (Winter 1979–80): 8. Also see the discussion of absentee, corporate, and family farmland ownership in Fund and Clement, *Distribution of Land and Water Ownership*, 24–32.

6 Cornelia Butler Flora, "Values and the Agricultural Crisis: Differential Problems, Solutions, and Value Constraints," *Agriculture and Human Values* 3, no.4 (Fall 1986): 16–23.

7 Flora, "Values and the Agricultural Crisis," 19.

8 This is a major thesis in John Opie, *The Law of the Land: Two Hundred Years of American Farmland Policy* (Lincoln: University of Nebraska Press, 1994).

9 Cochrane, *Development of American Agriculture*, 150–69.

10 Ibid., 398–99.

11 USDA, *A Time to Act: A Report of the USDA National Commission on Small Farms*, miscellaneous publication 1545 (Washington, January 1998), on-line version, n.p.

12 James Gleick, *Chaos: Making of a New Science* (New York: Penguin Books, 1987), 24.

13 The literature has become voluminous. See particularly William W. Kellogg and Robert Schware, *Climate Change and Society: Consequences of Increasing Atmospheric Carbon Dioxide* (Boulder: Westview Press, 1981); Lloyd E. Slater and Susan K. Levin, eds., *Climate's Impact on Food Supplies: Strategies and Technologies for Climate-Defensive Food Production* (Boulder: AAAS and Westview Press, 1981); Rosenberg, ed., *Drought in the Great Plains: Research on Impacts and Strategies* (Littleton, Colo.: Water Resources Publications, 1980); Rosenberg, ed., *North American Droughts* (Boulder: AAAS and Westview Press, 1978); Donald A. Wilhite et al., eds., *Planning for Drought: Toward a Reduction of Societal Vulnerability* (Boulder: UNEP and Westview

Press, 1987); and *Water Scarcity: Impacts on Western Agriculture*, ed. Ernest A. Engelbert and Ann Foley Scheuring (Berkeley: University of California Press, 1984).

14 USDA, *A Time to Act*, on-line version, n.p.

15 Ibid., n.p.

16 USDA, *A Time to Choose: Summary Report on the Structure of Agriculture* (Washington, January 1981), 142.

17 USDA, *A Time to Act*, on-line version, n.p.

18 Stewart Smith, "Farming: It's Declining in the U.S.," *Choices*, first quarter, 1992.

19 USDA, *A Time to Act*, on-line version, n.p.

20 Ibid., n.p.

21 Ibid., n.p. This report utilized the study made by Willis L. Peterson, "Are Large Farms More Efficient?" Department of Applied Economics, staff paper P97-2 (St. Paul: University of Minnesota, January 1997).

22 USDA, *A Time to Act*, on-line version, n.p.

23 Ron Macher (editor of *Small Farm Today Magazine*), testimony at Memphis, Tenn., public meeting, July 28, 1997. This was one of several public meetings held by the USDA in preparation for *A Time to Act*.

24 Dean MacCannell, "Agribusiness and the Small Community" (Background paper to *Technology, Public Policy and the Changing Structure of American Agriculture*) (Washington: OTA, U.S. Congress, 1983).

25 USDA, *A Time to Act*, on-line version, n.p.

26 Ibid.

27 J. B. Penn, "The Changing Farm Sector and Future Public Policy: An Economic Perspective" in *Agricultural Food Policy Review: Perspectives for the 1980s* (Washington: USDA, 1980), ESS AFPR-4, 48ff. Also see Wesley F. Peterson, "Agricultural Structure and Economic Adjustment," *Agriculture and Human Values* 3, no.4 (Fall 1986): 7.

28 Penn, "Changing Farm Sector," 48–49.

29 Paul Johnson, "Federal Farm Policy: Anatomy of a Farm Bill," *Rural Papers*, no.131 (January 1995): 1, 4.

30 See, for example, the critical analyses by Elizabeth Ann R. Bird, *Research for Sustainability? The National Research Initiative's Social Plan for Agriculture* (Walthill, Nebr.: Center for Rural Affairs, August 1991), and *Sustainable Agri-*

culture in the National Research Initiative: Recommendations of a Panel (Walthill, Nebr.: Center for Rural Affairs, October 1991).

31 Differences between time frames cannot be ignored. Typical frontier farmers required three extremely good years to achieve stability; failures normally took three to five years. In contrast, the political planning process to aid farmers ranged from two to ten years. The ability of a society to respond to climate change takes at least ten years, but farmers needed a quicker response. In addition, climatologists today argue that a climate pattern takes a minimum of thirty years to determine, and climatological planning is accomplished on a scale of fifty to one hundred years or more.

32 See Frederick C. Luebke, *Ethnicity on the Great Plains* (Lincoln: University of Nebraska Press, 1980) and *Immigrants and Politics: The Germans of Nebraska, 1880–1900* (Lincoln: University of Nebraska Press, 1969). Irrigation communities like historic Greeley and modern Lamar in Colorado appear to have been equally long-lasting.

33 Ironically, on June 30, 1987, Russian president Mikhail S. Gorbachev called for a sharp increase in "small-scale family farming," and in February 1990 approved a local option to lease small-farm units that could also be inherited. It also approved, in principle, private ownership of farmland, not for speculative resale, but "for farmers who take proper ecological care of their land." Gorbachev spoke of letting demoralized farmers once again feel like "masters of the land" so they might be productive and reduce expensive grain imports. By late 1995 the new Russian state opened its farmland to private ownership by its citizens. ("News of the Week in Review," *New York Times*, July 1, 1987; *Newark (N.J.) Star-Ledger*, February 21, 1990; Francis X. Clines, "Gorbachev Plan for Family Farms Is Approved by Soviet Lawmakers," *New York Times*, March 1, 1990.)

34 David Hendee, "Outcome of 1995 Farm Bill Will Ripple across Midlands," *Omaha World-Herald*, February 12, 1995.

35 See, for example, the historical discussion of farm policies in light of the debate over the 1996 farm bill in Hendee, "Outcome of 1995 Farm Bill"; David C. Beeder, "Legislation Has Roots in the 1930s," *Omaha World-Herald*, February 13, 1995; and William Neikirk, "So Long Subsidies; Farmers Turned Loose on a Freer Market. New Law Has a Little Bit for Everyone," *Chicago Tribune*, April 5, 1996. Also see "The History of Soil and Water Conservation: A Sympo-

sium," *Agricultural History* 59 (April 1985): 2, and Cochrane, *Development of American Agriculture,* 122–23.

36 Peterson, "Agricultural Structure and Economic Adjustment," 7.

37 Joel Sokloff, *The Politics of Food* (San Francisco: Sierra Club Books, 1985), 32–36.

38 *Oklahoma Comprehensive Water Plan*, publication 94 (Oklahoma City, 1980), 15, 39, 150, and passim.

39 Robert Rodale, "Internal Resources and External Inputs—The Two Sources of All Production Needs," in *Regenerative Farming Systems* (Emmaus, Pa.: Rodale Institute, 1985).

40 David Stern, letter, "On Chemical Dependence," *Journal of Soil and Water Conservation* 45, no.1 (January–February 1990): 6. See the interaction between federal legislation (the Conservation Reserve Program), conservation tillage practices, soil erosion, and nonpoint source pollution discussed in Basil Gomez, "Assessing the Impact of the 1985 Farm Bill on Sediment-Related Nonpoint Source Pollution," *Journal of Soil and Water Conservation* 50, no.4 (July–August 1995): 374–77.

41 Richard Lowrance, "Research Approaches for Ecological Sustainability," *Journal of Soil and Water Conservation* 45, no.1 (January–February 1990): 52.

42 Fee Busby, "Sustainable Agriculture: Who Will Lead?" *Journal of Soil and Water Conservation* 45, no.1 (January–February 1990): 89–91.

43 Patrick Madden and Thompson, unpublished paper, "Ethical Perspectives on Changing Agricultural Technology in the United States," quoted in Peterson, "Agricultural Structure and Economic Adjustment," 13.

44 "Sustainability's Promise," *Journal of Soil and Water Conservation* 45, no.1 (January–February 1990): 4.

45 Charles W. Stenholm and Daniel B. Waggoner, "Low-Input, Sustainable Agriculture: Myth or Method?" *Journal of Soil and Water Conservation* 45, no.1 (January–February 1990), 16.

46 Tom Webb, "Senate Votes to Give Farmers the Freedom to Plant What They Choose," *Newark* (N.J.) *Star-Ledger*, February 8, 1996. Also see Tom Webb, "Congress Clears Massive Farm Legislation Eliminating Price-Based Subsidies," *Newark* (N.J.) *Star-Ledger*, March 29, 1996, and Richard Orr, "New U.S. Agriculture Policy Leaves Farmers at Odds," *Chicago Tribune*, April 8, 1996.

47 Ibid.

48 Ibid.

49 Ibid.

50 Neikirk, "So Long Subsidies."

51 Ann Toner, "A Lifetime in the Fields," *Omaha World-Herald*, February 12, 1995.

52 Dan Nagengast, "You Can Get There from Here," *Rural Papers*, no. 121 (March 1996): 2.

53 Nagengast, "An Open Letter to USDA Secretary Glockman," *Rural Papers*, no. 115 (September 1995): 2–3.

54 Quoted in David M. Smith, "Geography and Moral Philosophy: Some Common Ground," (paper presented at the annual meeting of the American Association of Geographers, Ft. Worth, Tex., April 5, 1997).

55 This can also be said about Appalachia, a region that offered serious environmental challenges to successful human habitation. Much of it was not inhabited by Native Americans and it was looked upon by Europeans as, again, mostly "empty and useless," a place to be skipped over for better territory. The colonizing of Appalachia was linked first to primitive farming that destroyed thin soil, then to the primeval forest that was logged out, and later to large seams of coal that were stripped off, with the remains left to erode and poison watersheds. In Appalachia, the rugged terrain divided a rural society into isolated pockets. The "mountaineer mentality" made inhabitants unusually defenseless against the American industrial mainstream. Recovery of either the Appalachian environment or its people into healthy stability is unlikely. Appalachia's moral geography took the form of dam-building for electric power and flood control, a project that the Tennessee Valley Authority undertook during the 1930s and 1940s to revive an entire regional society, one to which they committed hundreds of millions of dollars gathered by the federal government from the nation at large.

56 Tronto, Joan C., *Moral Boundaries: A Political Argument for an Ethic of Care* (New York: Routledge, 1993).

57 Don Paarlberg, "The Changing Policy Environment for the 1990 Farm Bill," *Journal of Soil and Water Conservation* 45, no. 1 (January–February 1990): 8.

58 John E. Ikerd, "Agriculture's Search for Sustainability and Profitability," *Journal of Soil and Water Conservation* 45, no. 1 (January–February 1990): 21.

Chapter 7

1 These figures are based on 2.5 acre-feet for corn and 1.5 acre-feet for wheat. In Seward County, in southwest Kansas, irrigated wheat might produce 45 to 60 bushels per acre, while irrigated corn offers 100 to 150 bushels per acre (SCS, Liberal, Kans., May 1986).

2 Heady and Hexem, *Water Production Functions in Irrigated Agriculture* (Ames: Iowa State University Press, 1978).

3 *Review Draft: The Second RCA Appraisal. Soil, Water, and Related Resources on Nonfederal Land in the United States* (Washington: USDA, 1987), 2–6, 7–15.

4 "Irrigators Save Water and Improve Efficiencies," *Cross Section* 32, no.2 (October 1986): 4.

5 "LISA Offers Farmers Alternatives," *Rural Papers* no.79 (November 1989): 1–2; David R. Cressman, "The Promise of Low-Input Agriculture," *Journal of Soil and Water Conservation* 44, no.2 (March–April 1989): 98.

6 Cressman, "The Promise of Low-Input Agriculture," 98.

7 David E. Kromm and Stephen E. White, *Conserving the Ogallala: What Next?* (Manhattan: Kansas State University, 1985).

8 Kenneth D. Frederick and Allen V. Kneese, "Competition for Water," in *Water Scarcity: Impacts on Western Agriculture*, ed. Ernest A. Engelbert and Ann Foley Scheuring (Berkeley: University of California Press, 1984), 81–108.

9 See, for example, James R. Ehleringer, "Photosynthesis and Photorespiration: Biochemistry, Physiology and Ecological Implications," *Hortscience* 14, no.3 (1979): 217–22; R. B. Austin et al., "Genetic Improvements in Winter Wheat Yields since 1900 and Associated Physiological Changes," *Journal of Agricultural Science* 94 (1980): 675–89; J. S. Boyer, "Plant Productivity and the Environment," *Science*, 1983, 361–405.

10 See Gary L. Laklig and J. W. Twigg, "Historical Crop Studies," in *Feasibility of Introducing New Crops: Production, Marketing, Consumption (PMS) Systems*, ed. E. G. Knox and A. A. Theison (Emmaus, Pa.: Rodale Press, 1981), 174–91, and E. D. Putt, "History and Present World Status," in *Sunflower Science and Technology*, ed. J. F. Carter (Madison, Wis.: American Society of Agronomy, 1978), 1–28.

11 See Willard C. Cochrane, *The Development of American Agriculture: A Historical Analysis* (Minneapolis: University of Minnesota Press, 1979), 156–57.

12 Earl O. Heady, "National and International Commodity Price Impacts," in *Water Scarcity*, ed. Engelbert and Scheuring, 277. Also see Dee S. H. Wittwer, "New Technology, Agricultural Productivity and Conservation," in *Soil Conservation Policies, Institutions and Incentives*, ed. Heady et al. (Ankeny, Iowa: Soil Conservation Society of America, 1982); Yoo-Chi Loo, Philip Cline, and Leroy Quance, *Prospects for Productivity Growth in U.S. Agriculture*, USDA, ESCS Agricultural Economic Report 435 (Washington, 1979); and *Soil, Water, and Related Resources in the United States: Status, Condition, and Trends, 1980 Appraisal*, part 1(Washington: USDA, 1981).

13 OTA, *Water-Related Technologies for Sustainable Agriculture in U.S. Arid-Semiarid Lands* (Washington, October 1983), 244–56.

14 N. C. Turner and P. F. Kramer, eds., *Adaptation of Plants to Water and High Temperature Stress* (New York: John Wiley, 1980), 179–85.

15 This is, of course, an oversimplification. "Growing degree days" or "heat units" are only cumulatively added while within a range of from sixty to eighty degrees Fahrenheit (Bossert, letter, January 19, 1991).

16 M. E. Jensen, "Water Consumption by Agricultural Plants," in *Water Deficits and Plant Growth, II: Plant Water Consumption and Response*, ed. T. T. Kozlowski (New York: Academic Press, 1968).

17 *Thirty Years: A Tradition of Service: 1951–1981* (Lubbock, Tex.: High Plains Underground Water Conservation District No. 1, 1952), 71.

18 See the discussion in Rosenberg, "Improving Land and Water Use Practices," in *Water Scarcity*, ed. Engelbert and Scheuring, 212–14.

19 "Scientists Listen to Noises of Plants in Drought," *New York Times*, September 4, 1988.

20 Mike Risinger and Ken Carver, "Soil Moisture Monitoring: An Overview of Monitoring Methods and Devices," *Water Management Note* (Lubbock, Tex.: High Plains Underground Water Conservation District No.1, n.d.). Also see OTA, *Water-Related Technologies*, 214.

21 Risinger and Carver, "Neutron Moisture Meters: The Scientific Approach to Monitoring Soil Moisture," *Water Management Notes* (Lubbock, Tex.: High Plains Underground Water Conservation District No.1, n. d.).

22 Risinger, A. Wayne Wyatt, and Carver, "Estimating Soil Moisture by Feel and Appearance," *Water Management Notes* (Lubbock Tex.: High Plains Underground Water Conservation District No.1, n.d.).

23 Ibid.

24 Wilford R. Gardner, "Discussion of Chapters 8 and 9," in *Water Scarcity*, ed. Engelbert and Scheuring, 241–42.

25 "District Salutes Water Savings by Area Irrigators: You've Come a Long Way, Baby!" *Cross Section* 35, no.11 (November 1989): 1–3. Also see "Irrigation Systems Upgraded through Pilot Ag Loan Program Have Cumulatively Saved 25,000 Acre-Feet of Groundwater," *Cross Section* 35, no.10 (October 1989): 4.

26 Larry J. Kuder et al., "Surge Irrigation in Southwestern Kansas," working paper, distributed by the SCS Area Target Team of Garden City, Kans. (n.d., but probably in the early 1980s). Also see "Lubbock County Producers Praise Surge Irrigation Benefits," *Cross Section* 35, no.4 (May 1989): 4.

27 C. G. Karasov, "Irrigation Efficiency in Water Delivery," *Technology* 3 (1982): 62–74.

28 Based on interviews of local USDA officials by Marvin E. Jensen, "Improving Irrigation Systems," in *Water Scarcity*, ed. Engelbert and Scheuring, 232–33.

29 Robert D. Lacewell and Glenn S. Collins, "Improving Crop Management," in *Water Scarcity*, ed. Engelbert and Scheuring, 194–95; "New Improved Irrigation Spray Nozzles," *Cross Section* 34, no.6 (June 1988): 1, 3.

30 OTA, *Water-Related Technologies*, 234–35.

31 *Dallas Morning News*, 19 August 1984.

32 U.S. Department of Irrigation, U.S. Department of Agriculture, Environmental Protection Agency, *Irrigation Water Use and Management*, Interagency Task Force Report (Washington, 1979).

33 "Drier than Normal Conditions Revealed in Soil Moisture Survey," *Cross Section* 35, no.2 (February 1989): 2.

34 Jensen, "Improving Irrigation Systems," 232–33.

35 See B. A. Stewart and J. T. Musick, "Conjunctive Use of Rainfall and Irrigation in Semi-Arid Regions," in *Advances in Irrigation Science*, vol.1, ed. Dan Hillel (New York: Academic Press, 1983). Also see *Better Federal Coordination Needed to Promote More Efficient Farm Irrigation* (Washington: General Accounting Office, June 22, 1976), 23–30.

36 "Shut Off the Water—The Root Zone Is Full" (Washington: U.S. Bureau of Reclamation, March 1973).

37 Barry Flinchbaugh et al., *Who Will Control Our Water Supply?* (Manhattan, Kans.: Kansas State University Cooperative Extension Service, 1984), 48–49.

38 Marshall J. English, "Discussion of Chapters 8 and 9," in *Water Scarcity*, ed. Engelbert and Scheuring, 237–39.

39 See Herman Bouwer, "Discussion," in *Water Scarcity*, ed. Engelbert and Scheuring, 128. Also see OTA, *Water-Related Technologies*, 216–19.

40 See the useful discussion in Fund, *Water in Kansas: A Primer* (Whiting, Kans.: Kansas Rural Center, 1984), 53–55. Also see OTA, *Water-Related Technologies*, 219–23.

41 See Robert D. Lacewell and Collins, "Improving Crop Management," in *Water Scarcity*, ed. Engelbert and Scheuring, 180–203.

42 Wayne Bossert of Kansas District Four estimates that pumpage in northwest Kansas ranges from fifteen dollars an acre-foot for natural gas to thirty dollars an acre-foot for electricity, alongside capital costs.

43 Pierre R. Crosson and Norman J. Rosenberg, "Strategies for Agriculture," *Scientific American* 261, no.3 (September 1989): 128.

44 The privatization argument is clearly established in a series of essays edited by Terry L. Andersen, *Water Rights: Scarce Resource Allocation, Bureaucracy, and the Environment* (Cambridge, Mass.: Pacific Institute for Public Policy Research/Ballinger, 1983). A stance critical of privatization is in Robert G. Dunbar, *Forging New Rights in Western Waters* (Lincoln: University of Nebraska Press, 1983).

45 New Mexico law professor Charles DuMars, quoted in *Wall Street Journal*, November 19, 1984; see also Kenneth Frederick and James C. Hanson, *Water for Western Agriculture* (Washington: Resources for the Future, 1982).

46 Lawrence Mosher, "Will the real leaders in national water policy please stand up?" *Journal of Soil and Water Conservation* 44, no.2 (March–April 1989): 135.

47 K. W. Easter, J. A. Leitch, and D. F. Scott, "Competition for Water, a Capricious Resource," in Ted L. Napier et al., eds., *Water Resources Research* (Ankeny, Ia.: Soil and Water Conservation Service, 1983), 135–53; Kenneth D. Frederick, "Water Supplies," in Paul Portney, ed., *Current Issues in Natural Resource Policy* (Washington: Resources for the Future, 1982), 216ff., and Kenneth D. Frederick and James C. Hanson, *Water for Western Agriculture* (Washington: Resources for the Future, 1982), 165–84.

48 *Six-State High Plains-Ogallala Aquifer Regional Resources Study* (Washington: Department of Commerce, 1982), 6–77; Easter, Leitch, and Scott, "Competition for Water," 135–53.

49 Heady, "National and International Commodity Price Impacts," 280. In the National Water Assessment of 1976, at the same time that water supplies declined from 86.7 acre-feet to 64.6 acre-feet per year, wheat prices rose from $3.84 to $8.82 (in 1972 dollars).

50 This is the central argument in Mark Sagoff, *The Economy of the Earth* (New York: Cambridge University Press, 1988).

51 Frederick and Kneese, "Competition for Water," 99.

52 OTA, *Water-Related Technologies*, 141; see the data in Frederick and Hanson, *Water for Western Agriculture*.

53 See the analysis in OTA, *Water-Related Technologies*, 154–59.

54 See *Investigation of Secondary Recovery of Ground Water from the Ogallala Formation, High Plains of Texas* (Lubbock: Texas High Plains Underground Water Conservation District No. 1, 1982), 2–4, 6–7, 13–20, 25–30, 55–57.

55 A copy of the address is with the XIT Ranch Papers, Panhandle-Plains Historical Museum, Canyon, Texas, 4.

56 *The Texas Water Plan* (Austin: Texas Water Development Board, 1968); see the excellent discussion of the various water-import projects in Morton W. Bittinger and Elizabeth B. Green, *You Never Miss The Water Till . . . (The Ogallala Story)* (Littleton, Colo.: Water Resources Publications, 1980), 90ff.

57 R. E. Bathen, P. R. Cunningham, and W. R. Mayben, "A New Water Resource Plan for the Great Plains," paper presented at the annual meeting of the Midwest Electric Consumers Association, Omaha, Nebraska, December 8, 1967. The authors were employees of R. W. Beck and Associates, an engineering consulting firm, which also published the plan.

58 See the discussion in Harvey O. Banks, Jean O. Williams, and Joe B. Harris, "Developing New Water Supplies," in Engelbert and Scheuring, *Water Scarcity*, 111–12.

59 Lewis Gordy Smith, "Toward a National Water Plan," *Irrigation Age* (April 1969).

60 Quoted in Bittinger and Green, *You Never Miss the Water*, 96.

61 In Engelbert and Scheuring, *Water Scarcity*, 126.

62 *A Water Policy for the American People*, 3 vols. (Washington: President's Water Resources Policy Commission, 1950, 1951).

63 *Water Resources Policy* (Washington: Presidential Advisory Committee on Water Resources Policy, 1955).

64 *Water Policies for the Future* (Washington: National Water Commission, 1973); see also Charles E. Corker, "Ground Water Law, Management, and Administration," Report prepared for the National Water Commission, 1971.

65 *Southwest Kansas Irrigator*, December 25, 1978, quoted in Bittinger and Green, *You Never Miss the Water*, 106.

66 Quoted in Bittinger and Green, *You Never Miss the Water*, 107.

67 See the discussion in John Opie, *The Law of the Land: 200 Years of American Farmland Policy* (Lincoln: University of Nebraska Press, 1987), xiii–xvi; see also n.115.

68 Bittinger and Green, *You Never Miss the Water*, 109.

69 The results of the study and its recommendations were summarized in a review draft dated April 23, 1982: *A Summary of the Results of the Ogallala Aquifer Regional Study, with Recommendations to the Secretary of Commerce and Congress: Colorado, Kansas, Nebraska, New Mexico, Oklahoma, Texas* (n.p.: High Plains Study Council, 1982). Many versions of the study appeared in short and long forms, divided according to states and topics. See, for example, *Six-State High Plains Ogallala Aquifer Regional Resources Study: Summary* (Austin, Tex.: High Plains Associates, 1982), and *A Summary of Results of the Ogallala Aquifer Regional Study, with Recommendations to the Secretary of Commerce and Congress* (Austin, Tex.: High Plains Study Council, December 13, 1982).

70 *Summary of Results*, 13–16.

71 Ibid., 1.

72 Ibid., 16.

73 John B. Weeks, "Proposed Plan of Study for the High Plains Regional Aquifer-System Analysis," working paper for February 2–3, 1978, staff meeting. Water Resources Division, Geological Survey, USDI, Denver Federal Center, 6.

74 *Summary of Results*, 5, 8.

75 Communication from Donald Worster, November 1991.

76 "Review Draft," *Summary of Results*, 4–5.

77 Ibid., 14.

78 See also the analysis in Raymond J. Supalla, Robert R. Landsford, and Noel R. Gollehon, "Is the Ogallala going dry? A review of the High Plains study and its land and water policy implications," *Journal of Soil and Water Conservation* (November–December 1982): 311–14.

433

79 "Review Draft," *Summary of Results*, 5–8.

80 Ibid., 15, 16.

81 Ibid., 8–10; *Summary of Results*, 22–23.

82 *Summary of Results*, opening abstract summary letter.

83 See K. G. Brengle, *Principles and Practices of Dryland Farming* (Boulder, Colo.: Associated University Press, 1982), and Hayden Ferguson et al., "Dryland Agriculture," OTA commissioned paper, excerpted in OTA, *Water-Related Technologies*, 21ff.; C. Robert Taylor, Duane R. Reneau, Richard Trimble, "Economics of Conservation Tillage Systems," in B. L. Harris and A. E. Colburn, eds., *Conservation Tillage in Texas* (College Station: Texas Agricultural Extension Service Bulletin B-1290, 1979); see also the discussion by Norman J. Rosenberg, "Improving Land and Water Use Practice," in Engelbert and Scheuring, *Water Scarcity*, 204–17, and the essays in Norman J. Rosenberg, ed., *Drought in the Great Plains: Research on Impacts and Strategies* (Littleton, Colo.: Water Resources Publications, 1980); J. Grace, *Plant Response to Wind* (New York: Academic Press, 1977).

84 See OTA, *Water-Related Technologies*, 300–302.

85 General Accounting Office Report to Congress, *Action Needed to Discourage Removal of Trees that Shelter Cropland on the Great Plains* (Washington: GAO publications RED-75-375, 1975).

86 Rosenberg, "Improving Land and Water Use Practices," 211–12.

87 J. R. Gilley and E. Fereres-Castiel, "Efficient Use of Water on the Farm," OTA commissioned paper, excerpted in OTA, *Water-Related Technologies*, 237.

88 See Office of Technology Assessment, *Impacts of Technology on U.S. Cropland and Rangeland Productivity* (Washington: U.S. Congress, OTA-F-166, 1982).

89 See B. W. Greb, *Reducing Drought Effects on Croplands in the West Central Great Plains* (Washington: USDA Information Bulletin 420, 1979).

90 Wes Jackson, *New Roots for Agriculture* (San Francisco: Friends of the Earth, 1980), 24–29.

91 "The Case Against Crop Chemicals," *Science* 251 (1 February 1991): 517.

92 Lacewell and Collins, "Improving Crop Management," 193.

93 See the commentary by Kenneth R. Farrell in Engelbert and Scheuring, *Water Scarcity*, 293–94.

94 See W. G. Matlock, *Realistic Planning for Arid Lands: Natural Resources Limitations to Agricultural Development* (London: Harwood Academic Publishers, 1981), 4; T. W. Box, *The Arid Lands Revisited—One Hundred Years Since John*

Wesley Powell (Logan: Utah State University, n.d.), 4–7; Carle Hodge, ed., *Aridity and Man: The Challenge of the Arid Lands in the United States* (Washington: AAAS, 1963).

95 Albert Schaffer and Ruth C. Schaffer, "Social Impacts on Rural Communities," in Engelbert and Scheuring, *Water Scarcity*, 312–15.

96 Schaffer and Schaffer, "Social Impacts on Rural Communities," 322.

97 A. A. Theisen, E. G. Knox, and F. L. Mann, eds., *Feasibility of Introducing Food Crops Better Adapted to Environmental Stress*, vol. 1 (Washington: Government Printing Office, NSF/RA/780289, 1978).

98 See the observations of Donald Worster, *Dust Bowl: The Southern Plains in the 1930s* (New York: Oxford University Press, 1979), 146 passim.

99 Interviews with Keith Allen were conducted at his farm in May 1987 and at the Pheasant Inn in Sublette, Kansas, in May 1988.

100 Interviews with Baker and Schmidt on June 27, 1989.

101 See Lacewell and Collins, "Improving Crop Management," 190–91, and Ellis G. Knox and Arthur A. Theisen, "Feasibility of Introducing New Crops: Production-Marketing-Consumption Systems," a report to the National Science Foundation by Soil and Land Use Technology, Inc., 1981, and the analysis in OTA, *Water-Related Technologies*, 256–64.

102 "Researchers Investigate Year-Round Forage System," *The Cross Section* 32, no.9 (September 1986): 3.

103 Brad Burritt, "Leymus: A Plant with a History of Human Use," *The Land Report* 28 (1986): 10–12.

104 Jon K. Piper, "The Prairie as a Model for Sustainable Agriculture: A Preliminary Study," in *The Land Report Research Supplement* 3 (1986): 1–4; see also Mark Gernes and Jon Piper, "Vegetation Patterns in Tallgrass Prairie and Their Implications for Sustainable Agriculture"; Amy Kullenberg, "Survey of Insects in Native Prairie and Agricultural Plots"; Doug Dittman, "Soil Moisture and Nutrient Patterns in Agricultural Plots and Native Prairie"; and Randolph Kempa, "Seed Systems," all in *The Land Report Research Supplement* 4 (1987).

105 *The Land Institute Research Report* 5 (1988), i and passim.

106 Quoted in *The Land Report* 32 (Spring 1988): 9.

107 Drawn from Wes Jackson's influential 1980 classic, *New Roots for Agriculture*, esp. 114–36.

108 Dennis Rinehart, "Sorghum: A Perennial Future?" *The Land Report* 28 (1986):

12–14; see also "Paul Bramel-Cox: Sorghum Breeder," *The Land Report* 34 (Fall 1988): 12–15, and Jennifer M. Delisle, "Perennial Sorghum Breeding: 1988 Progress Report," *The Land Institute Research Report* 5 (1988): 30.

109 Keith Allen and Paul Boles (local irrigators), interviews, 1986 and 1987; Jeff Schmidt (Liberal, Kans., office of the USDA Soil Conservation Service), personal discussion. Also see Edwin D. Gutentag, David H. Lobmeyer, and Steven E. Slagle, *Geohydrology of Southwestern Kansas*, Kansas Geological Survey Irrigation Series 7 (Lawrence, Kans.: University of Kansas, 1981), 59–64.

110 Wyatt, Ann E. Bell, and Shelly Morrison, *Analytical Study of the Ogallala Aquifer in Parmer County, Texas*, Texas Water Development Board Report 205 (Austin, 1976), 5–9.

111 Cochrane, *Development of American Agriculture*, 324–27.

Chapter 8

1 W. E. Riebsame, S. A. Changnon, and T. R. Karl, *Drought and Natural Resources Management in the United States: Impacts and Implications of the 1987–1989 Drought* (Boulder, Colo.: Westview Press, 1990).

2 Dennis Farney and Bruce Ingersoll, "Drought Damages Bush's Chances in Farm Belt; Rain Now Would Be Too Late for Many Victims," *Wall Street Journal*, June 27, 1988.

3 Kevin E. Trenberth, Grant W. Branstator, Philip A. Arkin, "Orgins of the 1988 North American Drought," *Science* 242 (23 December 1988): 1640–45.

4 Quoted in "The Heat is On," *Time*, October 19, 1987, 63.

5 Bruce Ingersoll, "Extensive Erosion in Great Plains Tied to Dust Storm Is at Worst Level Since 1955," *Wall Street Journal*, June 27, 1988.

6 B. Drummond Ayres, Jr., "Vast Parched Stretches of U.S. Await Hot Summer," *New York Times*, May 15, 1988.

7 Mobilizing to Help Farmers Through the Drought," *New York Times*, June 27, 1988.

8 Letter from Leland B. Taylor to *Journal of Soil and Water Conservation* 45, no. 3 (May–June 1990): 357.

9 Jonathan R. Laing, "Greenhouse Effect," *Barrons*, June 27, 1988.

10 Quoted in ibid.

11 Julia Flynn Siler, "Losses Bring Gains For Farmer in Futures," *New York Times*, August 4, 1988; see also Siler, "Drought Means Deluge in Grain Pit,"

and Keith Schneider, "World Grain Supplies Are Dropping," *New York Times*, August 4, 1988.

12 Laing, "Greenhouse Effect."

13 Scott Kilman and Richard Gibson, "Killing Drought Raises Food Prices, Portends Worsening of Inflation," *Wall Street Journal*, June 14, 1988; Barbara Rudolph, "The Drought's Food-Chain Reaction," *Time*, July 11, 1988.

14 "Worldwide effects of the drought," *Newark* (N.J.) *Star-Ledger*, June 27, 1988.

15 John F. Burns, "Drought Also Lays Waste to Canada's Farm Belt," and Edward A. Gargan, "Flash Floods and Drought Ravage China," *New York Times*, August 3, 1988.

16 Keith Schneider, "Drought Stirs Debate on Wheat Export Subsidies," *New York Times*, June 29, 1988.

17 Keith Schneider, "The Green Revolution: How Much Farther Can It Go?" *New York Times*, August 21, 1988.

18 Lester Brown et al., *State of the World 1989* (New York: W. W. Norton and Company, 1989), 3–58.

19 But it made front-page news almost daily in national newspapers. See, for example, Keith Schneider, "1988 Drought Evokes Ghost of Dust Bowl," *New York Times*, July 7, 1988.

20 William Robbins, "On the Farm, A Disaster That Wasn't," *New York Times*, October 16, 1988.

21 Ingersoll, "Extensive Erosion in Great Plains Tied to Dust Storm Is at Worst Level Since 1955."

22 William Robbins, "Dry Soil Blows Away, Carrying Hope With It," *New York Times*, August 7, 1988.

23 The efforts received front-page attention nationally; see Keith Schneider, "Scientists Trying to Give Crops An Edge Over Nature's Forces," *New York Times*, August 1, 1988.

24 Conversation with John Perkins, Evergreen State College, on his forthcoming NSF-financed study of the politics of agricultural research, November 1990.

25 Quoted in Schneider, "1988 Drought Evokes Ghost of Dust Bowl."

26 Letter from John T. Bird, Hays, Kansas, "Kansan on Kansas," *Wall Street Journal*, April 17, 1989.

27 "Bitter Harvest: A Seasoned Farm-Belt Watcher Assesses the Damage of the Drought" *Barrons*, June 27, 1988.

28 Kilman and Gibson, "Killing Drought Raises Food Prices."

29 Andrew Cassel, "As water level sinks, concerns rise," *Philadelphia Enquirer*, May 29, 1989, and telephone interview with Gary Baker on June 27, 1989; see also "Water Table Drop in Parts of Kansas," *Southwest Daily Times*, June 8, 1989.

30 Interview on June 27, 1989.

31 Quoted in Sue Shellenbarger, "U.S. Farmers Face an Easier Row to Hoe," *Wall Street Journal*, October 25, 1988.

32 Data received in May 1986 and May 1987 from the Garden City and Liberal, Kansas, offices of the Soil Conservation Service.

33 Robbins, "On the Farm, A Disaster That Wasn't"; Philip Shabecoff, "Draft Report on Global Warming Foresees Environmental Havoc in U.S.," *New York Times*, October 20, 1988; "Worldwide effects of the drought," *Newark* (N.J.) *Star-Ledger*, June 27, 1988.

34 See the sequence of articles in the *Wall Street Journal*: Bruce Ingersoll, "Drought Likely to Bring Down Acreage of Harvest to Record Low This Century," September 27, 1988; Carlee R. Scott, "Drought Lingers as Threat to Winter Wheat Crop," December 12, 1988; Sue Shellenbarger, "Unforgiving Climate of Kansas Is Punishing Winter Wheat Again," March 14, 1989; Bruce Ingersoll, "U.S. Sees Wheat Stocks at 17-Year Low Unless Rains Temper Drought's Effect," April 7, 1989; and Sue Shellenbarger and Bruce Ingersoll, "Second Drought in a Row Is Threatening 40% of Farm Belt, Some Western States," and "Wheat Futures in Kansas City Expected to Climb Following U.S. Prediction of 8% Drop in Harvest," both on May 12, 1989. The *New York Times* missed badly in its front-page story by Keith Schneider, "Serious Drought Seen as Unlikely in U.S. This Year," February 20, 1989, but it turned around by November: William Robbins, "Wheat Crop Faces Threat of Drought," November 29, 1989.

35 Telephone interview with Jeff Schmidt, district conservationist, Soil Conservation Service, Liberal, Kansas, June 21, 1989.

36 William Robbins, "Winter Wheat Farmers Fear Second Year's Crop Failure," *New York Times*, January 2, 1990.

37 Irvin Molotsky, "Drought Has Eased, U.S. Reports," *New York Times*, September 13, 1988.

38 *Scientific Assessment of Climate Change*, Intergovernmental Panel on Climate

Change, WMO, UNEP (Geneva 1990); Paul E. Waggoner, "U.S. Water Resources versus an Announced but Uncertain Climate Change," *Science*, March 1, 1991, 1002.

39 "Using Forests to Counter the 'Greenhouse Effect,'" *Science*, February 26, 1988, 973.

40 Michael Oppenheimer, "How to Cool Our Warming Planet," *New York Times*, July 23, 1988.

41 Philip Shabecoff, "The Heat Is On," *New York Times*, June 26, 1988; Shabecoff, "Global Warming: Experts Ponder Bewildering Feedback Effects," *New York Times*, January 17, 1989.

42 Stephen H. Schneider, "The Greenhouse Effect: Science and Policy," *Science*, February 10, 1989, 771–81.

43 "Is the Greenhouse Here?" *Science*, February 5, 1988, 559–61; Shabecoff, "Global Warmth in '88 Is Found to Set a Record," *New York Times*, February 4, 1989; Board on Atmospheric Sciences and Climate, National Research Council, "Do We Know Enough to Act?" in *Current Issues in Atmospheric Change* (Washington: National Academy Press, 1987), 23–27. Also see the useful summary review of the evidence, its impacts, and response strategies in Christopher Flavin, *Slowing Global Warming: A Worldwide Strategy*, Worldwatch Paper 91 (Washington: Worldwatch Institute, 1989); Ray Bradley, ed., *Global Changes of the Past* (Boulder, Colo.: University Corporation for Atmospheric Research, 1991); and Thomas J. Crowley and Gerald R. North, *Paleoclimatology* (New York: Oxford University Press, 1991); and Paul E. Waggoner, ed., *Climate Change and U.S. Water Resources* (New York: John Wiley 1990).

44 See the report by William K. Stevens, "Global Warming: Search for the Signs," *New York Times*, January 29, 1991.

45 R. F. Diffendal, Jr., "Plate Tectonics, Space, Geologic Time, and the Great Plains," *Great Plains Quarterly* 2, no.11 (Spring 1991): 93–94.

46 See Roger A. Pielke, Jr., "Rethinking the Role of Adaptation in Climate Policy," *Global Environmental Change* (July 1998): 5–6.

47 "Is the Greenhouse Here?" 561

48 Jesse H. Ausubel, "Does Climate Still Matter?" *Nature* 350 (April 25, 1991): 650; Raymond J. Supalla, Robert R. Lansford, and Noel R. Gollehon, "Is the Ogallala Going Dry?" *Journal of Soil and Water Conservation* 37, no.6 (November–December 1982): 310–14; and Glantz, Barbara G. Brown, and Maria E.

Krenz, *Societal Responses to Regional Climate Change: Forecasting by Analogy*, ESIG/EPA study (Boulder: Environmental and Societal Impacts Group, NCAR, 1988), 13. Also see Emmanuel Le Roy Ladurie, *Times of Feast, Times of Famine: A History of Climate since the Year 1000*, trans. Barbara Bray (Garden City, N.Y.: Doubleday, 1971).

49 Oppenheimer, "How to Cool Our Warming Planet."

50 Intergovernmental Committee on Climate Change, UNEP, "Will Climate Change Lead to More Extremes and Disasters," Telaine, Switzerland, 1992, revised December 1, 1993, on-line report (last accessed March 15, 1994). This report is no longer available on-line. The committee was renamed in 1995 as the Intergovernmental Panel on Climate Change (IPCC). Updated climate change reports covering the same material are available at <www.unep.ch/ipcc/>. See especially the reports from working group 2, Summary for Policymakers: Scientific-Technical Analyses of Impacts, Adaptations, and Mitigation of Climate Change; and working group 3, Summary for Policymakers: The Economic and Social Dimensions of Climate Change. Other relevant websites are <www.dir.ucar.edu/iss/lib/> and <www.ipcc.ddc.cru.uea.ac.uk>.

51 Author's research at NCAR, May 23, 1986.

52 Edward Lorenz, "The Predictability of Hydrodynamic Flow," *Transactions of the New York Academy of Sciences* 2, no.25 (1963): 4, 409–32, quoted in James Gleick, *Chaos: Making of a New Science* (New York: Penguin Books, 1987), 25.

53 Schneider, "The Greenhouse Effect: Science and Policy."

54 "The Heat is On," *Time*, October 19, 1987, 59.

55 "The Greenhouse Effect," *Newark* (N.J.) *Star-Ledger*, June 7, 1988.

56 "The Heat is On," 63.

57 V. Ramanathan, "The Greenhouse Theory of Climate Change: A Test by an Inadvertent Global Experiment," *Science*, April 15, 1988, 293–99.

58 "It's Official: First Glimmer of Greenhouse Warming Seen," *Science*, December 8, 1995, 1565–66. Also see Stevens, "Talk about Weather: U.N. Says People Do Something about It," *New York Times*, December 1, 1995.

59 "It's Official," 1566.

60 "1995 the Warmest Year? Yes and No," *Science*, January 12, 1996, 137.

61 "Global Change and Terrestrial Ecosystems," *Global Change Newsletter* no.23 (September 1995): 6–7. See Stevens, "Scientists Say Earth's Warming Could Set Off Wide Disruptions," *New York Times*, September 18, 1995.

62 "A New Dawn for Sun-Climate Links?" *Science*, March 8, 1996, 1360–61.

63 Intergovernmental Committee on Climate Change, UNEP, Telaine, Switzerland, "Climate and Food Security," 1992, revised May 1, 1993, on-line report (March 15, 1994).

64 "Is a Climate Jump in Store for Earth?" *Science*, January 15, 1988, 259.

65 John Noble Wilford, "His Bold Statement Transforms the Debate on Greenhouse Effect," *New York Times*, August 23, 1988. Also see Shabecoff, "U.S. Data since 1895 Fail to Show Warming Trend," *New York Times*, January 26, 1989; "Could the Sun Be Warming the Climate?" *Science*, November 1, 1991, 652–53; and Stevens, "Earth's Temperature Has Dropped a Little after a Warm Spell," *New York Times*, December 24, 1991.

66 Intergovernmental Committee on Climate Change, UNEP, Telaine, Switzerland, "How GCMs Work," 1992, on-line report (March 15, 1994).

67 Stephen H. Schneider, "Climate Modeling," *Scientific American* 256, no.3 (May 1987): 77, 80. Also see Glantz and Ausubel, "The Ogallala Aquifer and Carbon Dioxide: Comparison and Convergence," *Environmental Conservation* 11, no.2 (Summer 1984): 123–31; Thomas R. Karl, Richard R. Heim, Jr., and Robert G. Quayle, "The Greenhouse Effect in Central North America: If Not Now, When?" *Science*, March 1, 1991, 1058–61; and Stevens, "In a Warming World, Who Comes Out Ahead?" *New York Times*, February 5, 1991.

68 Schneider, "The Greenhouse Effect: Science and Policy," 772. Also see *Preparing for Climate Change: Proceedings, Washington, 27 to 29 October, 1988*, ed. J. I. Hanchey et al. (Rockville, Md.: Government Institutes, 1988), 394–405.

69 Intergovernmental Committee on Climate Change, UNEP, Telaine, Switzerland, "The Impact of Climate Change on Agriculture," 1992, revised May 1, 1993, on-line report (March 15, 1994).

70 Linda O. Mearns et al., "The Effect of Changes in Daily and Interannual Climatic Variability on CERES-Wheat: A Sensitivity Study," *Climatic Change* 32 (1996): 257–92. Also see Mearns et al., "Mean and Variance Change in Climate Scenarios: Methods, Agricultural Applications, and Measures of Uncertainty," *Climate Change* 35 (1997): 367–96.

71 William J. Parton, Dennis S. Ojima, David S. Schimel, "Environmental Change in Grasslands: Assessment Using Models," *Climate Change* 28 (1994): 111–41.

72 Parton et al., "Environmental Change in Grasslands," 119–22.

73 Glantz and Nicolai Orlovsky, "Desertification: A Review of the Concept," *Desertification Control Bulletin* 9 (December 1983): 15–21. Also see Donald A. Wilhite and Glantz, "Understanding the Drought Phenomenon: The Role of Definitions," *Water International* 10 (1985): 111–20; Glantz, "Politics, Forecasts and Forecasting: Forecasts Are the Answer, but What Was the Question?" in *Policy Aspects of Climate Forecasting*, ed. Richard Krasnow (Washington: Resources for the Future, 1987), 81–95; Glantz, "Drought Follows the Plow," *The World & I*, April 1988, 208–13; and Jonathan G. Taylor, Thomas R. Stewart, and Mary Downton, "Perceptions of Drought in the Ogallala Aquifer Region," *Environment and Behavior* 20, no.2 (March 1988): 150–75.

74 Glantz and Orlovsky, "Desertification," 15.

75 Observations made for OSTP/USGCRP Workshop, Climate Change Impacts on the Great Plains, Colorado State University, May 27–29, 1997.

76 See Stevens, "Great Plains or Great Desert?" *New York Times*, May 28, 1996.

77 Observations made for OSTP/USGCRP Workshop, Climate Change Impacts on the Great Plains. Colorado State University, 27–29 May 1997.

78 Pielke, "Rethinking the Role of Adaptation," 16; IUCC, Intergovernmental Committee on Climate Change, UNEP, "Climate and Food Security," on-line report.

79 Parton et al., "Environmental Change in Grasslands," 134–35.

80 Robert Lewis, "Global Warming: The Cold Facts," *Newark* (N.J.) *Star-Ledger*, February 5, 1989; Stevens, "With Cloudy Crystal Balls, Scientists Race to Assess Global Warming," *New York Times*, February 7, 1989.

81 Ric Jensen, "Are Things Warming Up? How Climate Changes Could Affect Texas," *Texas Water Resources* 15, no.1 (Spring 1989): n.p. Also see Judith Clarkson and Robert King, *Global Warming and the Future of Texas Agriculture: Impacts and Policy* (Austin: Texas Department of Agriculture, 1989); Daniel Dudek, "Economic Implications of Climate Change Impacts on Southern Agriculture" in *Proceedings of the Symposium on Climate Change in the Southern U.S.: Future Impacts and Present Policy Issues* (Washington: USEPA, 1987); and Rosenberg, "Drought and Climate Change: For Better or Worse?" *Planning for Drought: Toward a Reduction in Societal Vulnerability* (Boulder, Colo.: Westview Press, 1987).

82 Intergovernmental Committee on Climate Change, UNEP, "The Impact of Climate Change on Water Resources," on-line report.

83 Jensen, "Are Things Warming Up?" Also see Judith Clarkson, "Global Climate Change and Its Implications for Agricultural Productivity in Texas," *Grassroots* 3 (Fall 1988): 21–24.

84 Pielke, "Rethinking the Role of Adaptation," 20.

85 Parton et al., "Environmental Change in Grasslands," 136.

86 Pielke, "Rethinking the Role of Adaptation," 7–8.

87 Intergovernmental Panel on Climate Change, UNEP, "Climate and Food Security," on-line report.

Chapter 9

1 Clifford Geertz, *The Interpretation of Cultures* (New York: Basic Books, 1973); Michael Walzer, *Spheres of Justice: A Defence of Pluralism and Equality* (Oxford: Basil Blackwell, 1983); and *Thick and Thin: Moral Argument at Home and Abroad* (South Bend: University of Notre Dame Press, 1996).

2 Peirce F. Lewis, "Axioms for Reading the Landscape: Some Guides to the American Scene," in *The Interpretation of Ordinary Landscapes: Geographical Essays*, ed. D. W. Meinig (New York: Oxford University Press, 1979), 11–32.

3 Stephen S. Birdsall, "Regard, Respect, and Responsibility: Sketches for a Moral Geography of the Everyday," *Annals of the Association of American Geographers* 86, no.4 (December 1996): 619–29.

4 David M. Smith, "Geography and Moral Philosophy: Some Common Ground," (paper presented at the annual meeting of the American Association of Geographers, Ft. Worth, Tex., April 5, 1997), 19.

5 Douglas Aberley, "Mapping the Terrain of Hope," *Wild Earth* 4, no.2 (Summer 1994): 62–63.

6 Douglas Coffman, "'Buffalo Commons': An Encouraging Word," *Wild Earth* 5, no.3 (Fall 1995): 31.

7 The literature is vast and diverse. See, for example, Baruch Fischhoff, "For Those Condemned to Study the Past: Reflections on Historical Judgment," *New Directions for Methodology of Behavioral Science: Fallible Judgment in Behavioral Research*, ed. R. A. Shweder and D. W. Fiske (San Francisco: Jossey-Bass, 1980); Mary Douglas and Aaron Wildavsky, *Risk and Culture: An Essay on the Selection of Technological and Environmental Dangers* (Berkeley: University of California Press, 1982); Board on Atmospheric Sciences and Climate, National Research Council, *Current Issues in Atmospheric Change* (Washington: National Academy Press, 1987); Thomas R. Stewart and Glantz, "Expert Judgment and Climate Forecasting: A Methodological Critique of Climate

Change to the Year 2000," in *Climatic Change* 7 (1985): 159–83; Donald A. Wilhite and Glantz, "Understanding the Drought Phenomenon: The Role of Definitions," *Water International* 10 (1985): 111–20; Cochrane, "A Conceptual Model of Agricultural Development: 1950–1977," in Cochrane, *The Development of American Agriculture: A Historical Analysis* (Minneapolis: University of Minnesota Press, 1979), 355–428; Walter Firey, *Man, Mind, and Land* (Glencoe: Free Press, 1960); Jantsch, *The Self-Organizing Universe* (New York: Pergamon Press, 1980); Ervin Laszlo, *The Systems View of the World* (New York: George Braziller, 1972); Immanuel Wallerstein, *The Modern World-System* (New York: Academic Press, 1974).

8 Duane D. Williams and Leonard E. Bloomquist, "From Dust Bowl to Green Circles: A Case Study of Haskell County, Kansas," in *Thirteenth Annual Water and the Future of Kansas Conference Proceedings, Kansas State University College of Agriculture* (Manhattan: Kansas State University, 1996), 24–29.

9 See the discussion about using historical analogies and comparisons to understand future climate change in Glantz and Ausubel, "The Ogallala Aquifer and Carbon Dioxide: Comparison and Convergence," *Environmental Conservation* 11, no.2 (Summer 1984): 123–31.

10 See Carl Ortwin Sauer, "Homestead and Community on the Middle Border," "Historical Geography and the Western Frontier," and "Theme of Plant and Animal Destruction in Economic History," in *Land and Life: A Selection From the Writings of Carl Ortwin Sauer*, ed. John Leighly (Berkeley: University of California Press, 1963), 32–41, 45–52, and 145–54, respectively. In "The $5,000 Flat Tire," Jackson, of the Land Institute of Kansas, suggests that the situation has only been made worse, not better, by contemporary mechanization (*New Roots for Agriculture* [San Francisco: Friends of the Earth, 1980], 32–36).

11 James Gleick, *Chaos: Making of a New Science* (New York: Penguin Books, 1987), 67–68, 85.

12 Ibid., 105.

13 Donald E. Green, *Land of the Underground Rain: Irrigation on the Texas High Plains, 1910–1970* (Austin: University of Texas Press, 1973), 161–62. Thirty-two-year-old Keith Allen corroborated Green's perspective when I visited him in the early evening in his irrigated fields north of Sublette, Kans., in May, 1987.

14 See the discussion in Cochrane, *Development of American Agriculture*, esp. 8–9, 76–77, 85–88, 183–89.

15 See the pathbreaking study by Fite, *American Farmers: The New Minority* (Bloomington: Indiana University Press, 1981).

16 See the discussions in Cressman, "The Promise of Low-Input Agriculture," *Journal of Soil and Water Conservation* 44, no.2 (March–April 1989): 98, and Kenneth A. Cook, "The Environmental Era of U.S. Agricultural Policy," *Journal of Soil and Water Conservation* 44, no.5 (September–October 1989): 363.

17 The literature is large and growing. Water issues are debated in Marc Reisner, *Cadillac Desert: The American West and Its Disappearing Water* (New York: Viking Penguin, 1986) and Worster, *Rivers of Empire: Water, Aridity, and the Growth of the American West* (New York: Pantheon Books, 1985). Also see Paul B. Sears's 1935 classic, now in its fourth edition, *Deserts on the March* (Norman: University of Oklahoma Press, 1980), and Lawrence B. Lee's *Reclaiming the American West: A Historiography and Guide* (Santa Barbara, Calif.: ABC Clio, 1980).

18 Jeffrey A. Zinn and John E. Blodgett, "Agriculture versus the Environment: Communicating Perspectives," *Journal of Soil and Water Conservation* 44, no.3 (May–June 1990): 187.

19 Rudy Boschwitz et al., "Building a Conservation-Centered Farm Policy," *Journal of Soil and Water Conservation* 44, no.5 (September–October 1989): 451.

20 Ibid.

21 Tim T. Phipps and Katherine Reichelderfer, "Farm Support and Environmental Quality at Odds?" *Resources* 95 (Spring 1989): 14–16.

22 Maximum Economic Yield and Maximum Sustainable Yield are reviewed in another context in Arthur F. McEvoy, "Toward an Interactive Theory of Nature and Culture: Ecology, Production, and Cognition in the California Fishing Industry" in *The Ends of the Earth: Perspectives on Modern Environmental History*, ed. Worster (Cambridge: Cambridge University Press, 1988), 219–29.

23 See Pierre Crosson and Janet Ekey Ostrov, "Sorting Out the Environmental Benefits of Alternative Agriculture," *Journal of Soil and Water Conservation* 45, no.1 (January–February 1990): 34–35.

24 See Linda Schroeder, "Low-Input Agriculture: Overcoming the Impediments," *Journal of Soil and Water Conservation* 45, no.1 (January–February 1990): 40.

25 See Lester R. Brown, "Sustaining World Agriculture," *State of the World 1987* (New York: W. W. Norton, 1987), 132–36.

26 MacNeill, "Strategies for Sustainable Economic Development," *Scientific American* 261, no.3 (September 1989): 158–59, 163–64.

27 Paul B. Thompson, "The Social Goals of Agriculture," *Agriculture and Human Values* 3 (Fall 1986): 41.

28 See the discussion in Thompson, "Social Goals of Agriculture," 35–40.

29 Ibid., 32–43.

30 Keith Schneider, "Science Academy Recommends Resumption of Natural Farming," *New York Times*, September 8, 1989. Also see "Academy of Sciences Endorses Low-Input Farming," *The Sciences* no.78 (October 1989): 12.

31 The following discussion of global sustainable development is based largely on *Our Common Future* by the World Commission on Environment and Development (New York: Oxford University Press, 1987), especially 43–66, and the special issue, "Managing Planet Earth," of the *Scientific American* 261, no.3 (September 1989).

32 World Commission on Environment and Development, *Our Common Future*, 8. Also see R. Boardman, *International Organization and the Conservation of Nature* (Bloomington: Indiana University Press, 1981); Lynton K. Caldwell, *International Environmental Policy: Emergence and Dimensions* (Durham, N.C.: Duke University Press, 1984); L. W. Milbrath, *Envisioning a Sustainable Society: Learning Our Way Out* (Albany: SUNY Press, 1989); Edward Pestel, *Beyond the Limits to Growth: A Report to the Club of Rome* (New York: Universe Books, 1989); M. Redclift, *Sustainable Development: Exploring the Contradictions* (London: Metheun, 1987); and L. Stark, *Signs of Hope: Working towards Our Common Future* (Oxford: Oxford University Press, 1990). Also see the editorial in the special issue, "The Promise of Low-Input Agriculture: A Search for Sustainability and Profitability," *Journal of Soil and Water Conservation* 45, no.1 (January–February 1990): 4.

33 See Timothy O'Riordan, "The Politics of Sustainability," in *Sustainable Environmental Management*, ed. R. Kelly Turner (Boulder, Colo.: Westview Press, 1988), 29–49.

34 Neill Schaller, "Mainstreaming Low-Input Agriculture," *Journal of Soil and Water Conservation* 45, no.1 (January–February 1990): 10. Schaller is director of the Low-Input Sustainable Agriculture Research and Education Program of the USDA.

35 See Curtis E. Beus and Riley E. Dunlap, "Conventional versus Alternative Agriculture: The Paradigmatic Roots of the Debate," *Rural Sociology* 55, no.4

(1990): 590–616, and Wendell Berry et al., eds., *Meeting the Expectations: Essays in Sustainable Agriculture and Stewardship* (San Francisco: North Point Press, 1984).

36 James Nelson, "Health and Disease as 'Thick' Concepts in Ecosystemic Contexts," *Environmental Values* 4, no.4 (1995): 311.

37 USDA, *A Time to Act: A Report of the USDA National Commission on Small Farms*, miscellaneous publication 1545 (Washington, January 1998), on-line version, n.p.

38 See, for example, Collin Fallat, "What Role Land Use Planning in the Restructuring of American Agriculture?" *Journal of Soil and Water Conservation* 43, no.6 (November–December 1988): 470; National Research Council, Committee on the Role of Alternative Farming Methods in Modern Production Agriculture, *Alternative Agriculture* (Washington: National Academy Press, 1989); the combined USDI, USDA, and EPA analysis, *Better Federal Coordination Needed to Promote More Efficient Farm Irrigation* (Washington: General Accounting Office, June 22, 1976); and Stuart B. Hill, "Redesigning the Food System for Sustainability," *Alternatives* 12, no.3 (Fall 1985): 32–36.

39 Jeffrey A. Zinn and John E. Blodgett, "Agriculture versus the Environment: Communicating Perspectives," *Journal of Soil and Water Conservation* 44, no.3 (May–June 1989): 184–87.

40 Ibid., 184.

41 Boschwitz et al., "Building a Conservation-Centered Farm Policy," 451.

42 Stenholm and Daniel B. Waggoner, "Low-Input, Sustainable Agriculture: Myth or Method?" *Journal of Soil and Water Conservation* 45, no.1 (January–February 1990), 13–17. Also see the critique by Elizabeth Ann R. Bird, *Research for Sustainability? The National Research Initiative's Social Plan for Agriculture* (Walthill, Nebr.: Center for Rural Affairs, August 1991).

43 Worster, "A Sense of Soil: Agricultural Conservation and American Culture," *Agriculture and Human Values* 2, no.4 (Winter 1985): 30.

44 Lockeretz, *Issues in Sustainable Agriculture* (Washington: Rural Economic Policy Program, Aspen Institute, 1988), and Cook, "The Environmental Era of U.S. Agricultural Policy," 366. Also see Christine A. Ervin, "Implementing the Conservation Title," *Journal of Soil and Water Conservation* 44, no.5 (September–October 1989): 367, and Cressman, "The Promise of Low-Input Agriculture," 98.

45 Schaller, "Mainstreaming Low-Input Agriculture," 9.

46 Stenholm and Daniel B. Waggoner, "Low-Input Sustainable Agriculture: Myth or Method?" 13.

47 Rodale, "A Brief History of Sustainable Agriculture," *Journal of Soil and Water Conservation* 45, no. 1 (January–February 1990): 15.

48 Schaller, "Mainstreaming Low-Input Agriculture," 10.

49 *Conservogram*, newsletter of the Soil and Water Conservation Society 1, no. 7 (April 1995): 1, and Chuck Hassebrook, of the Center for Rural Affairs, interview, *Rural Papers* no. 143 (August 1995): 2.

50 Stephen O. Myers and Lorenz Sutherland, "CRP: A Baca County, Colorado Perspective," *Journal of Soil and Water Conservation* 44, no. 5 (September–October 1989): 431–36. In contrast, see Sutherland and J. A. Knapp, "The Impacts of Limited Water: A Colorado Cost Study," *Journal of Soil and Water Conservation* 43, no. 4 (July–August 1988): 294–98.

51 Charles M. Benbrook, "The Environment and the 1990 Farm Bill," *Journal of Soil and Water Conservation* 43, no. 6 (November–December 1988): 440–43.

52 Stephen R. Crutchfield, "Federal Farm Policy and Water Quality," *Journal of Soil and Water Conservation* 44, no. 5 (September–October 1989): 377.

53 Marc O. Ribaudo et al., "CRP: What Economic Benefits?" *Journal of Soil and Water Conservation* 44, no. 5 (September–October 1989): 421. Also see Ribaudo et al., *The Economic Impacts of the Conservation Reserve Program on Natural Resources* (Washington: USDA, Economic Research Service, 1989); Elbert E. Dickey et. al, "To Till or Not to Till during Drought," *Journal of Soil and Water Conservation* 44, no. 2 (March–April 1989): 117–20; Jeffrey R. Williams, Richard V. Llewelyn, and Chris L. Mikesell, "An Economic Risk Analysis of Conservation Tillage Systems for Wheat, Grain Sorghum, and Soybeans in the Great Plains," *Journal of Soil and Water Conservation* 44, no. 3 (May–June 1989): 234–39; and G. Sloggett and C. Dickason, *Groundwater Mining in the United States* (Washington: USDA, Economic Research Service, 1986), AER-555.

54 Mark Sagoff, *The Economy of the Earth: Philosophy, Law, and the Environment* (Cambridge: Cambridge University Press, 1988), 114–21. See also Cochrane, *Development of American Agriculture*, 137, 183–86, 320.

55 Newell, "Irrigation on the Great Plains," *Yearbook of the United States Department of Agriculture* (Washington, 1897), 193.

56 Ibid., 167.

57 Worster, "Doing Environmental History," in *Ends of the Earth*, ed. Worster, 290.

58 Odum, "The Emergence of Ecology as a New Integrative Discipline," *Science*, March 25, 1977, 1292. Also see Odum and J. L. Cooley, *Biological Evaluation of Environmental Impact* (Washington: Council for Environmental Quality, n.d.).

59 See the discussion in Mark Sagoff, *The Economy of the Earth*, 114–21.

60 Mary Fund, "The Promise of Sustainable Agriculture for the Ogallala Aquifer" (paper presented at a conference of Water and the Future of Kansas, Colby, Kans., March 5–6, 1996).

61 D. Scott Slocombe and Caroline Van Bers, "Seeking Substance in Sustainable Development" (paper presented at an annual conference of the North American Association for Environmental Education, San Antonio, Tex., November 4, 1990).

62 The points in this list are based on the analysis offered by Bird, *Research for Sustainability?* 2–3. Also see Wendell Berry, *The Unsettling of America: Culture and Agriculture* (New York: Avon Books, 1977); Strange, *Family Farming: A New Economic Vision* (Lincoln: University of Nebraska Press, 1988); National Research Council, Committee on the Role of Alternative Farming Methods in Modern Production Agriculture, *Alternative Agriculture*; and Comstock, ed., *Is There a Moral Obligation to Save the Family Farm?* (Ames: Iowa State University Press, 1988).

63 Riebsame, "The United States Great Plains," in *The Earth as Transformed by Human Action; Global and Regional Changes in the Biosphere over the Past 300 Years*, ed. B. L. Turner II (New York: Cambridge University Press, 1990), elaborates on the major themes in Sears's *Deserts on the March* and Andrew H. Clark's "The Impact of Exotic Invasion of the Remaining New World Mid-latitude Grasslands," in *Man's Role in Changing the Face of the Earth*, ed. William L. Thomas, Jr. (Chicago: University of Chicago Press, 1956), 737–62.

64 Smith, "Geography and Moral Philosophy," 7, 19.

65 Riebsame, "The United States Great Plains."

66 Cook, "The Environmental Era of U.S. Agricultural Policy," 366.

67 Sagoff, *Economy of the Earth*; David M. Smith "Geography and Moral Philosophy."

Appendix

1 Claude Lévi-Strauss, *The Savage Mind* (Chicago: University of Chicago Press, 1966), 245–69.

2 Paul Ricoeur, *Time and Narrative*, vol. 1, trans. Kathleen McLaughlin and David Pellauer (Chicago: University of Chicago Press, 1983), 216.

3 Max Weber, *The Methodology of the Social Sciences*, trans. and ed. Edward A. Shils and Henry A. Finch (New York: Free Press, 1949), 78–79. Also see J. Nicholas Entrikin, *The Betweenness of Place: Towards a Geography of Modernity* (Baltimore: Johns Hopkins University Press, 1991), 89.

4 See the collection of Frederick Jackson Turner's essays, *The Frontier in American History* (New York: Henry Holt, 1920). See also Ray Allen Billington, *Frederick Jackson Turner: Historian, Scholar, Teacher* (New York: Oxford University Press, 1973); Billington's *America's Frontier Heritage* (New York: Holt, Rinehart, Winston, 1966); John Wesley Powell, *Report on the Lands of the Arid Region of the United States* (Cambridge: Belknap-Harvard University Press, 1962); Wallace Stegner's biography of Powell, *Beyond the Hundredth Meridian: The Exploration of the Grand Canyon and the Second Opening of the West* (Boston: Houghton Mifflin, 1953); and William H. Goetzmann, *Exploration and Empire: The Explorer and the Scientist in the Winning of the American West* (New York: Alfred A. Knopf, 1966).

5 Frederick Jackson Turner, "The Significance of the Frontier in American History," in *Frontier in American History*, 38.

6 See, for example, Billington's still-definitive textbook of classic frontier expansion, *Westward Expansion: A History of the American Frontier*, 4th ed. (New York: Macmillan, 1974), particularly 599–629.

7 See Billington's foreword to Fite, *The Farmers' Frontier, 1865–1900* (New York: Holt, Rinehart and Winston, 1966), v–vii.

8 Walter Prescott Webb, *The Great Frontier* (Austin: University of Texas Press, 1951–52), 19n. 1.

9 Ibid., 17.

10 Robert DeCourcy Ward, *The Climates of the United States* (Boston: Ginn, 1925), 125f, quoted in ibid., 22.

11 Ward, *Climates of the United States*, 156f, quoted in ibid., 22.

12 Webb, *The Great Plains* (Boston: Ginn, 1931), 22, 23–24.

13 Ibid., 415

14 Ibid., 418.

15 Ibid., 15n. 1.

16 This is the primary thesis in the influential book by Fite, *The Farmers' Frontier*, ix and passim.

17 Ibid., 216.

18 Ibid., ix.

19 Ibid., 10.

20 See Chapter 5, "Destitution on the Frontier in the 1870s," in ibid., 55–74; also see 221.

21 The National Resources Planning Board opened its doors in 1933 as the National Planning Board. In 1934 it was named the National Resources Board; in 1935 it was renamed the National Resources Committee; and in 1939 it was renamed again as the National Resources Planning Board. For an excellent analysis of its activities, see Tim Lehman, *Public Values, Private Lands: Farmland Preservation Policy, 1933–1985* (Chapel Hill: University of North Carolina Press, 1995), 18–26.

22 Quoted in Lehman, *Public Values, Private Lands*, 20.

23 Sears, *Deserts on the March* (Norman: University of Oklahoma Press, 1980).

24 Ibid., 174–84.

25 Ibid., 10–13.

26 Ibid., 85; also see 83–91, 107–16.

27 Donald Worster's *Dust Bowl* thesis on capitalism was reinforced in "Grassland Follies: Agricultural Capitalism on the Plains," in *Under Western Skies: Nature and History in the American West* (New York: Oxford University Press, 1992), 93–105.

28 Also see Worster's discussion of the field of environmental history in "Nature as Natural History: An Essay on Theory and Method," *Pacific Historical Review* 53 (February 1984): 1–19 and his opening and closing essays in Worster, ed., *The Ends of the Earth* (New York: Cambridge University Press, 1988), 3–22, 289–308.

29 This is even more clearly expressed in Worster, "The Dirty Thirties: A Study in Agricultural Capitalism," *Great Plains Quarterly* 6 (Spring 1986): 107–14. See the critique of Worster by Harry C. McDean, "Dust Bowl Historiography," *Great Plains Quarterly* 6 (Spring 1986): 121–23.

30 Worster, *Dust Bowl: The Southern Plains in the 1930s* (New York: Oxford University Press, 1979), 4.

31 Ibid., 231.

32 Deborah Epstein Popper and Frank J. Popper, "The Great Plains: From Dust to Dust, *Planning* 53 (December 1987): 12–18. Also see the Poppers' "The Fate of the Plains," in *Reopening the Western Frontier*, ed. Ed Marston (Covelo,

Calif.: Island Press, 1989), 98–113; Frederick C. Luebke, "Back to the Future of the Great Plains," *Montana: The Magazine of Western History* 40, no.4 (Autumn 1990); and Anne Matthews, "The Poppers and the Plain," *New York Times Magazine*, June 24, 1990, 24–26, 41, 48–49, 53.

33 Frank and Deborah Popper, "The American Frontier, the Great Plains and the Buffalo Commons," *Wild Earth* 2, no.1 (Spring 1992): 17.

34 Ibid.

35 Brian W. Blouet and Merlin Lawson, eds., *Images of the Plains: The Role of Human Nature in Settlement* (Lincoln: University of Nebraska Press, 1975).

36 Blouet and Luebke, *The Great Plains: Environment and Culture* (Lincoln: University of Nebraska Press, 1979).

37 Lawson and Maurice E. Baker, eds., *The Great Plains: Perspectives and Prospects* (Lincoln: University of Nebraska Press, 1981).

38 Gutentag et al., *Geohydrology of the High Plains Aquifer in Parts of Colorado, Kansas, Nebraska, New Mexico, Oklahoma, South Dakota, Texas, and Wyoming (High Plains RASA Project)*, U.S. Geological Survey professional paper 1400-B (Washington, 1984).

39 Donald E. Green, *Land of the Underground Rain: Irrigation on the Texas High Plains, 1910–1970* (Austin: University of Texas Press, 1973).

40 Kromm and Stephen E. White, *Conserving the Ogallala: What Next?* (Manhattan: Kansas State University, 1985).

41 Stephen E. White and Kromm, "Who Should Manage the High Plains Aquifer? The Irrigators' Perspective," *Water Resources Bulletin* 31, no.4 (August 1995). Also see "Local Groundwater Management Effectiveness in the Colorado and Kansas Ogallala Region," *Natural Resources Journal* 35 (Spring 1995), 275–307.

42 Stephen E. White, "Population Change in the High Plains Ogallala Region: 1980–1990," *Great Plains Research* 2, no.2 (1995): 179. Also see "Ogallala Oases: Water Use, Population Redistribution, and Policy Implications in the High Plains of Western Kansas, 1980–1990," *Annals of the Association of American Geographers* 84, no.1 (1994): 29–45.

43 James Earl Sherow, *Watering the Valley: Development along the High Plains Arkansas River, 1870–1950* (Lawrence: University Press of Kansas, 1990).

44 Sherow, *Watering the Valley*, 5.

45 Ibid., 4.

46 See Rosenberg, ed., *North American Droughts* (Boulder, Colo.: AAAS and

Westview Press, 1978), and Rosenberg, ed., *Drought in the Great Plains: Research on Impacts and Strategies* (Littleton, Colo.: Water Resources Publications, 1980).

47 Richard A. Warrick and Martyn J. Bowden, "The Changing Impacts of Droughts in the Great Plains," in *Great Plains: Perspective and Prospects*, ed. Lawson and Maurice E. Baker, 111–37.

48 Bowden, "The Great American Desert and the American Frontier, 1800–1882: Popular Images of the Plains," in *Anonymous Americans: Explorations in Nineteenth Century Social History*, ed. T. K. Hareven (Englewood Cliffs, N.J.: Prentice-Hall, 1971), 48–79.

49 Glantz and Ausubel, "The Ogallala Aquifer and Carbon Dioxide: Comparison and Convergence," *Environmental Conservation* 2, no.2 (Summer 1984): 123–31. Also see Glantz and Nicolai Orlovsky, "Desertification: A Review of the Concept," *Desertification Control Bulletin* 9 (December 1983): 15–21; Donald A. Wilhite and Glantz, "Understanding the Drought Phenomenon: The Role of Definitions," *Water International* 10 (1985): 111–20; Glantz, "Politics, Forecasts and Forecasting: Forecasts are the Answer, but What Was the Question?" in *Policy Aspects of Climate Forecasting*, ed. Richard Krasnow (Washington: Resources for the Future, 1987), 81–95; Glantz, "Drought Follows the Plow," *The World & I*, April 1988, 208–13; and Jonathan G. Taylor, Thomas R. Stewart, and Mary Downton, "Perceptions of Drought in the Ogallala Aquifer Region," *Environment and Behavior* 20, no.2 (March 1988), 150–75.

50 Worster, *Nature's Economy* (Garden City, N.Y.: Anchor Books, 1979), 209–20.

51 Ibid., 209.

52 Quoted in ibid., 211.

53 Quoted in ibid., 216.

54 Quoted in ibid., 219.

55 Malin's primary interpretations have been gathered together in his *History and Ecology: Studies of the Grassland*, with an introduction by Robert Swierenga (Lincoln: University of Nebraska Press, 1984). Also see Worster's perceptive and critical comments in "The Dirty Thirties."

56 Malin, "Dust Storms: Part One, 1850–1860," *Kansas Historical Quarterly* 14 (May 1946): 129–44, and "Dust Storms: Part Three, 1881–1890," *Kansas Historical Quarterly* 14 (November 1946): 391–413.

57 See Swierenga's introduction to Malin, *History and Ecology*, xv.

58 Quoted in ibid., xxii.

59 See the introductory note by Leighly in *Land and Life: A Selection From the Writings of Carl Ortwin Sauer*, ed. John Leighly (Berkeley: University of California Press, 1963).

60 Sauer, "The Education of a Geographer," in *Land and Life*, 389–404.

61 Sauer, "Theme of Plant and Animal Destruction in Economic History," in *Land and Life*, 145–54.

62 Sauer, "The Morphology of Landscape," in *Land and Life*, 315–50.

63 Sauer, "Conditions of Pioneer Life in the Upper Illinois Valley" (1916), in *Land and Life*, 11–22; "The Barrens of Kentucky" (1927), in *Land and Life*, 23–31; and "Homestead and Community on the Middle Border" (1962), in *Land and Life*, 123–33.

64 Thomas, ed., *Man's Role in Changing the Face of the Earth* (Chicago: University of Chicago Press, 1956), vii.

65 B. L. Turner II et al., eds, *The Earth As Transformed by Human Action: Global and Regional Changes in the Biosphere over the Past 300 Years* (New York: Cambridge University Press, 1990).

66 Riebsame, "Sustainable Development Questioned: The Historical Debate between Adaptationism and Catastrophism in Great Plains Studies" (paper presented at a conference of the American Society for Environmental History, Pittsburgh, Pa., March 7, 1993).

67 Ibid., 133.

68 Ibid., 144.

69 Jesse H. Ausubel, "Does Climate Still Matter?" *Nature* 350 (April 25, 1991): 650.

70 Morris Berman, *The Reenchantment of the World* (Ithaca: Cornell University Press, 1981), 257.

71 Jon Piper, "Prairie Patterns and their Relevance to Sustainable Agriculture," *Land Report* 33 (Summer 1988): 23.

72 Ibid., 23.

73 Stuart Pimm, "Species Shakedown," *Land Report* 49 (Spring 1994): 11.

74 Mary Fund and Elise Watkins Clement, *Distribution of Land and Water Ownership in Southwest Kansas* (Whiting: Kansas Rural Center, 1982); Fund, *Water in Kansas: A Primer* (Whiting, Kans.: Kansas Rural Center, 1984); Vic Studer,

Groundwater in Kansas: Current Perspectives, New Initiatives (Whiting: Kansas Rural Center, 1987).

75 Quoted in *Rural Papers*, no.120 (June–July 1995): 1–2, 7. Also see "Clean Water Farming News," *Rural Papers*, no.127 (March 1996): 5–8, and *Monitoring Sustainable Agriculture with Conventional Financial Data* (White Bear Lake, Minn.: Land Stewardship Project, 1996).

76 Frederick Kirschenmann, "Fundamental Fallacies of Building Agricultural Sustainability," *Journal of Soil and Water Conservation* 46, no.3 (May–June 1991): 165–68.

77 Ibid., 167.

78 Slocombe and Alex Grzybowski, "Self-Organization Theories and Sociobiophysical Systems: The Case of South Moresby" (paper presented at the annual conference of the North American Association for Environmental Education, University of Oregon, Eugene, September 16, 1986), 21.

79 William E. Reeds, "The Ecology of Sustainable Development," *Ecologist* 41 (January–February 1990), quoted in Kirschenmann, "Fundamental Fallacies," 167.

80 Slocombe and Grzybowski, "Self-Organization Theories and Sociobiophysical Systems." Also see Slocombe, "History and Environmental Messes: A Nonequilibrium Systems View," *Environmental Review* 13, nos.3–4 (Fall–Winter 1989): 1–14.

81 Odum, "The Emergence of Ecology as a New Integrative Discipline," *Science*, March 25, 1977, 1289.

82 Fund and Clement, *Distribution of Land and Water Ownership*, 17–18.

83 See, for example, Feng Xu, Tony Prato, and Jian C. Ma, "A Farm-Level Case Study of Sustainable Agricultural Production," *Journal of Soil and Water Conservation* 50, no.1 (January–February 1995): 39–44, and Brian W. Sindelar, Clifford Montagne, and Roland R. H. Kroos, "Holistic Resource Management: An Approach to Sustainable Agriculture on Montana's Great Plains," *Journal of Soil and Water Conservation* 50, no.1 (January–February 1995): 45–49.

84 D. T. Walters, D. A. Mortensen, C. A. Francis, R. W. Elmore, and J. W. King, "Specificity: The Context of Research for Sustainability," *Journal of Soil and Water Conservation* 45, no.1 (January–February 1990): 55–57.

85 Yi-Fu Tuan, "Space and Place: Humanistic Perspective," *Progress in Geography* 6 (1974): 213.

86 Quoted in Entrikin, *Betweenness of Place*, 21.

87 Kirschenmann, "Fundamental Fallacies of Building Agricultural Sustainability," 168. Also see Benbrook, "Protecting Iowa's Common Wealth: Challenges for the Leopold Center for Sustainable Agriculture," *Journal of Soil and Water Conservation* 46, no.2 (March–April 1991): 89–95.

88 David Harvey, *The Limits to Capital* (Oxford: Basil Blackwell, 1982), 373.

89 Entrikin, *Betweenness of Place*, 48.

90 Quoted in ibid., 70.

91 For two examples of on-site decision making, see Francis, "Practical Applications of Low-Input Agriculture in the Midwest," *Journal of Soil and Water Conservation* 45, no.1 (January–February 1990): 66–67, and Douglas E. Romig et al., "How Farmers Assess Soil Health and Quality," *Journal of Soil and Water Conservation* 50, no.3 (May–June 1995): 229–36.

92 Recent discussions include Jantsch, *The Self-Organizing Universe* (New York: Pergamon Press, 1980); Nicolis and Prigogine, *Self-Organization in Non-Equilibrium Systems* (New York: John Wiley, 1977); Parkes and Thrift, *Times, Spaces, and Places: A Chronogeographic Perspective* (New York: John Wiley, 1980); Ulrich and Probst, eds, *Self-Organization and Management of Social Systems* (Berlin: Springer Verlag, 1984), as well as the broader perspectives offered in Berman, *The Reenchantment of the World* (Ithaca: Cornell University Press, 1981), and Gleick, *Chaos: Making of a New Science* (New York: Penguin Books, 1987).

93 Odum, "Input Management of Production Systems," *Science*, January 13, 1989, 177.

94 Gleick, *Chaos*, 8, 20–23.

95 John T. Curtis, "The Modification of Mid-latitude Grasslands and Forests by Man," in *Man's Role in Changing the Face of the Earth*, ed. William L. Thomas, Jr. (Chicago: University of Chicago Press, 1956), 729.

96 Odum, "Input Management of Production Systems," 177.

97 Cornelia Butler Flora, "Values and the Agricultural Crisis: Differential Problems, Solutions, and Value Constraints," *Agriculture and Human Values* 3, no.4 (Fall 1986): 17.

98 Paul B. Thompson, "The Social Goals of Agriculture," *Agriculture and Human Values* 3 (Fall 1986): 40.

99 Odum, "The Emergence of Ecology," 1292.

Index

In the Our Sustainable Future series